ECONOMICS AND THE MODERN WORLD

ECONOMICS AND THE MODERN WORLD

MAURICE LEVI
University of British Columbia

D. C. Heath and Company
Lexington, Massachusetts   Toronto

Address editorial correspondence to:

D. C. Heath and Company
125 Spring Street
Lexington, MA 02173

Developmental Editor:	Stephen Wasserstein
Production Editor:	Carolyn Ingalls
Designer:	Jan Shapiro
Photo Researcher:	Nancy Hale
Art Editor:	Diane Grossman
Production Coordinator:	Chuck Dutton
Permissions Editor:	Margaret Roll

Published simultaneously in Canada.

Printed in the United States of America.

International Standard Book Number: 0–669–21668–2

Library of Congress Catalog Number: 93–70462

10   9   8   7   6   5   4   3   2

To the new owners of Levi genes,
Adam, Naomi, and Jonathan

No profit grows where is no pleasure ta'en;
In brief, study what you most affect.

William Shakespeare
The Taming of the Shrew

A WORD TO THE INSTRUCTOR

In writing this brief introduction to economics, I have kept two important objectives in mind, namely, to produce a book that despite its brevity,

1. does not sacrifice the analytical content of the very best two-semester texts, and

2. captures the student's interest early on by showing how useful it is to learn economics and holds that interest by showing how closely connected economics is to other disciplines.

Of course, maintaining analytical content and student motivation in half the number of pages of a typical full-length text means confronting the essence of the economic problem itself, requiring very difficult choices over what subject matter to include. Fortunately, so much material has been assimilated into most longer texts that while the task of meeting the stated objectives seemed formidable at first, I feel comfortable that the completed book has, if anything, gained from making careful choices about content. These gains arise from the smoother flow between central economic principles that occurs when nonessential matter is avoided and from the quicker pace of learning that brevity allows. Furthermore, by demonstrating the close connections of economics with the other areas of inquiry from which introductory economics students are typically drawn, the chance of capturing and holding the student's interest is greatly enhanced.

The importance of capturing the student's interest, and doing this early on, can be given no stronger testimony than by the lament so many instructors have heard near the end of their introductory courses: "If I had known how interesting this course would have been, I would have studied harder." To avoid this lamentable situation, this book demonstrates in the opening chapter how economic principles can be applied usefully to a problem the student has certainly faced—that of deciding whether to enter college, and if already in college, whether to remain. This immediately brings economics within the students' experience and vividly demonstrates the value of mastering the subject.

Of course, in learning economics, students must be prepared for unrealistic-sounding assumptions and not immediately discount everything that follows before seeing how helpful the assumptions can be. Therefore, the nature and role of assumptions are described in the context of the opening example. This keeps the explanation from being abstract and allows us to show immediately that assumptions are just a step in reaching testable implications. The opening example also shows how predictions of economics can be subjected to the evidence in order to judge the validity of theories.

As the book proceeds and deals with the analytical material that is usually covered in full-length texts, Crossing Bridges sections show the interconnectedness of economics and a wide range of subject areas that students are also studying. The connections that are drawn link economics to an eclectic array of subjects from theology to physics, history, law, psychology, sociology, anthropology, mathematics, and literature. The purpose of showing the connections between economics and other disciplines is to demonstrate that economics does not exist in a vacuum, having influenced other disciplines, having been greatly influenced itself, and having interests in common with other disciplines. With so many students in introductory economics courses being majors (or intended majors) in the humanities, natural sciences, business, and other social sciences, it is particularly important to link economics to their principal areas of inquiry; no presumption can be made that such students come with a strong motivation to learn economics, as might be so for two-semester courses which may contain economics majors. Indeed, many one-semester students take economics as a program requirement, often with great reluctance. The quick demonstration of the payoffs from learning economics and the steady stream of connections explained in the Crossing Bridges sections are especially aimed at such skeptical students.

Economics instructors, whose passion by choice of discipline is economics, can easily forget that students' interests lie elsewhere. Therefore, even though some instructors may consider bridges between economics and psychology, engineering, biology, marketing, theology, physics, or literature a distraction, the student majoring or interested in one of these fields may view the matter very differently. Indeed, identification of just one or two close connections might be the spark that lights the fire of interest in economics, showing that it is not detached from the student's other subjects. The variety of bridges considered is purposely large to provide lots of sparks. This should appeal particularly to economics instructors in liberal arts colleges, but instructors should explain that the Crossing Bridges sections are not for studying or learning in the same way as the main body of the text. Rather, these sections are for reading to gain a sense of how economics connects to the student's principal interest and to the body of human knowledge. Every effort has been made to make the material accessible and include something of interest to everyone.

It should be emphasized that it is *connections,* broadly defined, that are traced in the Crossing Bridges sections. That is, these sections do not simply describe the contributions that economics has made to other disciplines. Nor do they simply describe the debts owed by economics to other fields. Indeed, the connections go beyond the busy two-way flow of traffic of ideas between economics and other areas of scholarly inquiry. Some of the connections involve no intellectual arbitrage between economics and other fields but represent, for example, a common interest in a matter, even if the matter may be viewed from a very different perspective. The idea is to show the reader that an education in just about any field is likely to touch on subjects dealt with in economics, just as an education in economics is likely to touch on subjects in other fields.

As well as being distinct in its preservation of analytical content and in its relating of economics to an eclectic array of disciplines, this book has a few other idiosyncratic features. One difference is that rather than describe concepts and methods at the beginning of the book in an abstract way as is done in many textbooks, this book defines terms and explains concepts as they are used. They therefore appear, not in a vacuum, but in the context of the initial application. This is a more natural way of learning and corresponds to what has been learned in language education. (Extensive research has shown the rote method of learning lists of vocabulary, verb conjugation, and so on is an ineffective way of learning a foreign language. Just as we grow up learning our mother tongue by using it in practical situations, so we can learn foreign languages most effectively by using them in practical situations and in context.)

This book differs from many other introductory texts by dealing with the background to the supply and demand curves before introducing the laws of supply and demand. I believe that presenting the laws of supply and demand before the background to these curves, as is so often done, is like reading a celebrated period novel without knowledge of the period or like viewing a painting without knowledge of its context; qualities are missed without the relevant background. By developing the background to the demand curve and supply curve before putting them together for the laws of supply and demand, it is possible to provide a deeper appreciation of this central economic paradigm.

Another difference of this book from many other introductory texts is that the approach to macroeconomics is one of topical orientation rather than methodological orientation. In particular, the chapters revolve around the central economic issues on the student's mind, such as inflation, unemployment, interest rates, and exchange rates, rather than revolve around the circular flow of income, goods market equilibrium, and other abstract matters. Of course, the methodology that is used is that of the circular flow of income and so on found in traditional texts. The way the treatment differs is in the organization of material to fit it around the issues. This is done so that as students read, for example, about inflation, they find the answers to the questions they already had in their minds, such as "What causes inflation?" "Who gains and loses from inflation?" and so on. The idea is to open the door on the students' existing curiosity.

Two background chapters lead into the macro section; the first describes the national income and product accounts, and the second deals with money and financial intermediation. This book puts money early in the macro chapter sequence so that references can later be made to money supply and monetary policy. The consequences of macroeconomic policies are explained in the context of the phenomena, or variables, that the policies affect rather than in a separate chapter about macroeconomic policy. The consequences of policies are dealt with after explaining how each macroeconomic variable is measured, what factors affect the variable, and what effects the variable has on ordinary people.

A further characteristic of the book involves the description of the gains from international trade, which, rather than being left to the end of the book, is covered very early on along with the gains from domestic trade. Given that the gains have the very same sources, it would seem only natural to discuss them at the same time.

If the instructor elects to skip the generally more challenging sections marked as "omittable without loss of continuity" and if some of the stand-alone examples are skipped, the pace and level are similar to other middle-level brief texts. The reason the slightly more challenging, omittable sections are included is to allow introductory students who are so turned on by economics that they want to take further courses to be able to get up to speed with students having a full-length introductory experience. The reason the stand-alone examples concerning recent news stories are included is to show students that economics can help them make sense of what they read and hear. I feel that it is better to offer too much and have the instructor elect whether to cover certain material than to offer too little. Furthermore, many students are up to the challenge of covering the entire book.

ACKNOWLEDGMENTS

The idea for this book evolved over a lengthy interval, and it is difficult to apportion credit to the many universities in which I taught or did research while working on it. I would like to thank all of them in the chronological order in which they played a role: the Hebrew University of Jerusalem, the University of California at Berkeley, MIT, the London Business School, the University of Exeter, and the University of British Columbia. My debt to the University of British Columbia cannot be repaid: it has been my home between visits to other universities, and it has treated me well since receiving my Ph.D. in economics from the University of Chicago. Moreover, the Faculty of Commerce and Business Administration of the University of British Columbia provided me with both the resources and the stimulation needed to write this book.

My colleagues and good friends, Al Dexter, Michael Goldberg, Michael Hayden, and Ernie Greenwood, offered particularly significant amounts of help. Several reviewers of early drafts helped to iron out countless wrinkles and to produce a smoother flow of ideas. I am sincerely grateful for the constructive comments and advice of the reviewers listed here:

Richard Barnes, *Southeastern College*
Arthur Benavie, *University of North Carolina, Chapel Hill*
Melvin Burke, *University of Maine*
William Davis, *Western Kentucky University*
Pauline Fox, *Southeast Missouri State University*
Darrell Glenn, *Providence College*
Kiaran Honderich, *Williams College*
Kaye Husbands, *Williams College*
Bruce Johnson, *Centre College*
Nick Kamrany, *University of Southern California*
Lori Kletzer, *Williams College*
Stephen Lile, *Western Kentucky University*
Eng Seng Loh, *Kent State University*
Alvin Marty, *Baruch College*
Drew Mattson, *Anoka–Ramsey Community College*

Robert Prasch, *University of Maine*
Charles Roberts, *Western Kentucky University*
Mark Rush, *University of Florida*
Leslie Stratton, *University of Arizona*
Robert Thomas, *Iowa State University*
Donald Wells, *University of Arizona*
Charles Wilber, *University of Notre Dame*

A very special acknowledgment goes to Mark Rush. His meticulous, detailed review identified areas of unnecessary difficulty, points of ambiguity, and topics insufficiently related to actual economic experience. None of the reviewers bears blame for any remaining errors, and all deserve credit for making this book far better than it would have been.

Prior experience has taught me the importance of working with a professional publisher and editorial team, and in the case of this book the credits due to publisher and editors are especially notable. The book has been through so many drafts that it would not be possible to thank all the typists that have helped. However, for pulling together the various pieces and preparing the final manuscript I must offer special thanks to Nancy Hill and Catherine Schittecatte.

Finally, I acknowledge a debt that I carry from previous books, that to Kate, my wife, typist, editor, proofreader, page organizer, and source of comfort. Had she not served in these roles, and at the same time taken care of the homefront, I could not have found the time or maintained the enthusiasm to write this book.

Maurice Levi
Bank of Montreal Professor
University of British Columbia

A WORD TO THE STUDENT

While most of the steps in economic arguments are not difficult to follow, the cumulative effect of the many steps it can often take to reach conclusions sometimes leaves the student dizzy. This problem can be overcome by taking a number of precautions.

In order to ensure that you recall conclusions when they are used later as a part of an argument, it helps periodically to close the textbook and to retrace the argument you have just read. This can be done by jotting it down on a writing pad, making sure to include all graphical figures, complete with labeling of the axes. This procedure of retracing arguments with the book closed is useful both for committing the material to memory and for checking whether you are ready to move ahead. You should be meticulous about rereading the parts you are unable to retrace. Even if it takes several rereadings, it is well worth doing. If you try to push ahead when you have been unable to retrace the preceding few pages, you are almost certain eventually to become stuck. Moreover, once stuck, it may not be obvious where you need to turn to find the step needed to clear up your confusion. It is difficult to overstate this need to ensure that you follow everything before moving ahead, because otherwise at some point, after a long chain of reasoning, "if A then B, if B then C" and so on, you may face the statement, "if A then D," and you won't know where it came from or even where to look in order to find out.

After you have opened and closed the book and reached the end of a chapter, you should look over the Summary that is provided to ensure that every point is completely clear. Only after you feel comfortable with the statements in the Summary should you move on to the next chapter.

The preceding warning should make it clear that economics is not the sort of subject you can read casually during the semester and expect to learn during the last couple of weeks to take the final exam. Economics is a subject you must work at. In this sense it is like mathematics. However, it doesn't take any mathematics beyond that from high school to read this book. What it takes is your own patient testing that you properly understand what you are reading before you move ahead. If you do this, you will not only move ahead with little difficulty, you will also know what you need to know when the final exam rolls around.

On the subject of exams, it might comfort you to know that I have included the Crossing Bridges sections at the end of each chapter not to be studied and learned like the main body of the text but to be read for a sense of how economics relates to other areas of enquiry. Students majoring in the sciences, history, political science, literature, and so on could be surprised at the connections between their principal interest and economics. They will almost certainly be surprised by how many connections there are between economics and a vast array of subjects. Because of their different purpose, you can read the Crossing Bridges sections more quickly than the other parts of the book. However, you are advised to read them all. They give the broadest possible perspective on economics, and like *The Wizard of Oz* connections drawn in Chapter 18, they can be fun.

Finally, please note that sections marked with an asterisk are generally more difficult than other sections and can be omitted without a loss of continuity; nothing that follows depends on these sections. Questions and summary items relating to sections marked with an asterisk are also marked with an asterisk.

M. L.

BRIEF CONTENTS

* Chapters marked with an asterisk can be omitted without a loss of continuity.

CONTENTS

* Sections and chapters marked with an asterisk can be omitted without a loss of continuity.

PART 1

INTRODUCING ECONOMICS

English economists . . . have never set much store by matters of definition, and no doubt it is true that the nature of the pudding is best discovered by eating it.

Sir Denis H. Robertson

. . . .
. . . .
. . . .
. . . .
. . . .
. . . . The Practical Value of Economics
. . . .
. . . .

The less we trouble ourselves with scholastic enquiries as to whether a certain consideration comes within the scope of economics, the better. If the matter is important, let us take account of it as far as we can.

Alfred Marshall

Key Concepts

Role of assumptions; comparison of costs and benefits; incremental costs and benefits; opportunity cost; present value; qualitative and quantitative predictions; irrelevance of sunk costs; scientific nature of the economic approach

PLUNGING IN:
AN EXAMPLE OF ECONOMIC REASONING

We can gain a rapid appreciation of the value of studying economics, and at the same time introduce many of the central principles of the subject, by considering how an important decision can be made with the help of economics. The decision concerns a problem confronted by individuals, but the approach could be applied to a vast range of problems faced by firms or governments.

A decision you have likely faced or you would not be reading this book is whether to go to college. Why don't you stop reading for a moment and jot down how you would or did tackle the question so you can see afterwards how close your approach is to that taken by economists.

Benefits Versus Costs of College

To apply some actual numbers to the problem, suppose that you have not yet entered college and have the opportunity to take a job immediately that pays $1800 per month indefinitely. Suppose that by going to college, you could expect to earn $2500 per month, also indefinitely, after graduating. (See Example 1.1 for evidence on the higher wages from extra years of schooling).

The assumption that both monthly incomes are fixed for an indefinite period is to avoid the need to build growing incomes into the problem. The assumption is not made because it is impossible to allow for growing incomes. Indeed, it is even possible to allow for a faster growing income with a college education than without a college education. However, allowing for these factors makes the solution more difficult. That is, the assumption is for simplicity, and it could be relaxed at a later stage for greater realism. Many assumptions are of this kind, allowing the economist to begin with a problem in its most elemental form and then to graft on further levels of difficulty, if and when necessary. Often the gist of the problem is clearest in its stripped-down form.

Let us suppose you are considering a 4-year college course for which tuition and books cost $6000 per year, and food and rent cost a further $10,000 per year, with the latter amount being the same as the cost of food and rent you would face if you did not attend college. Finally, assume that the additional expected income of $700 (or $2500 − $1800) per month is the only benefit from attending college and that we can ignore all taxes. As before, these assumptions can be relaxed and the problem solved without them. They are made only to leave the main outline of the problem in sharp relief and to allow a step-by-step approach.

The economist reasons that college is a good proposition if the value of benefits derived exceeds the cost of attending. But what is the value of benefits and the correct cost?

The benefit of college, by assumption, has been limited to the additional income it can provide. From the college and noncollege incomes we have given, the benefit is $700 per month. It is this extra or **incremental income** that is attributable to attending college. Consider that the amount is $8400 per year, and assume that your expected working life is 40 years. How much is $8400 per year for 40 years worth?

Many assumptions are made to simplify a problem and can later be relaxed.

Economic decisions are based on costs versus benefits.

Present Value of Future Benefits and Costs

You might think that $8400 per year for 40 years is worth simply $336,000 (or 40 × $8400). In fact, however, it is worth considerably less. The actual amount it is worth depends on the interest rate. This can be seen by reasoning as follows: If you were forced to choose between an offer of $1.00 to be received immediately and an offer of $1.00 to be received in 1 year's time, there is little doubt that you would choose the $1.00 immediately, even if the offer of $1.00 for next year was ironclad and could not be revoked. After all, even if you intended spending the $1.00 next year, you could still take it immediately and invest it for 1 year. You would then have more than $1.00 next year. If the 1-year interest rate is, for example, 5%, then by taking $1.00 immediately, you could have $1.05 next year. But what if you were offered a choice between $1.00 immediately and $1.05 next year?

Example 1.1

IT DOES PAY TO STUDY

The effect of extra years of schooling on peoples' wages has been studied in a variety of ways, but one of the most intriguing and compelling approaches involved investigating the earnings of identical twins. The information for the study, which was directed by economists Orley Ashenfelter and Alan Krueger, was gathered at the 16th Annual Twins Day Festival in Twinsburg, Ohio, in 1991.* Almost 500 separate individuals over 18 years of age took part in the study by providing answers to a variety of questions concerning factors that could conceivably affect wages earned. By focusing only on identical twins—called monozygotic twins, being from the same egg, and

*Orley Ashenfelter and Alan Krueger, "Estimates of the Economic Return to Schooling from a New Sample of Twins," National Bureau of Economic Research, Working Paper Number 4143, August 1992, Cambridge, Mass.

sometimes also called "maternal" twins—the researchers were able to control for nature and nurture; identical twins have the same heredity and have generally shared very similar experiences in early years. Particular care was also paid in the study to ensure data were accurate, with cross references being made to check years of schooling, and with questions concerning wages being asked in private to avoid misreporting by an individual twin trying to impress or avoid embarrassing his or her sibling.

Previous studies of the economic returns to schooling had faced the problem of a possible connection between peoples' innate ability and their years of schooling. For example, if those with the most innate ability spent more years attending school, it would be difficult to separate the effect of ability from the effect of more years of education; with no easy way of

measuring innate ability, higher wages might incorrectly be attributed to the schooling instead of the ability. However, by using identical twins, ability can be controlled for and differences in wages can be attributed to education received. Even fraternal (or dizygotic) twins—those from different eggs—would represent a less accurate source of data than identical twins, since fraternal twins have shared inheritances that are no different from those of ordinary brothers and sisters. This is what makes the identical twin study so intriguing and compelling.

The results were striking: each year of additional schooling was found to increase wages 16%! At a 16% wage increase per school year, 4 years of college would turn an $1800 per month wage without college into almost $3000, substantially more than the $2500 per month wage assumed in the example in the text.

Most people would have a difficult time making a choice between $1 immediately and $1.05 in 1 year if the interest rate is 5%, because they would consider the two alternatives as being of equal value.

The value *today* of $1.05 which is to be received in 1 year's time is called the **current value** or **present value** of this amount. For example, when the interest rate is 5%, the present value of $1.05 to be received next year is $1.00. This provides us with a procedure for valuing income to be received, or costs to be incurred, at some future date. Each $1.05 to be received or paid in 1 year has a present value of $1.00, so each $1.00 to be received or paid in 1 year has a present value of $0.9524 (or $1 ÷ 1.05). But what of income to be received or costs to be paid in the more distant future than next year?

If for each year money is invested you can earn 5%, then you can take $1.00 today and turn it into $1.05 next year and then take the $1.05 next year and invest

The present value of a given amount to be received in the future is the amount that would have to be invested *today* to provide the given amount in the *future*. Present value depends on the interest rate.

this for a further year at 5%, turning it into $1.1025 (or $1.05 × 1.05). Therefore, a person facing an interest rate of 5% would consider an offer of $1.1025 in 2 years' time as having a present value of $1.00. It follows that the person would consider $1.00 in 2 years' time as having a present value of $0.9070 (or $1.00 ÷ 1.1025). Similarly, that person would consider $1.1576 (or $1.05 × 1.05 × 1.05) in 3 years' time as having a present value of $1.00 and, therefore, $1.00 in 3 years' time as having a present value of $0.8638 (or $1.00 ÷ 1.1576), and so on. These values allow us to compute the present value of each $1.00 in each year, as shown in Table 1.1.

The values in Table 1.1, which are available in any of a number of published present-value tables, from hand-held calculators, or from microcomputer software packages, allow us to compute the present value of the extra $8400 per year from a college degree. However, allowance must be made for the fact that for the first $8400 you must wait the 4 years it takes to earn the degree. Therefore, it is necessary to look up the present value of $8400 per year for each of the assumed 40 years of work, with this extra income beginning after the 4 years of college. Doing this and summing the results gives a value of $124,510 when the interest

TABLE 1.1 $PV = n(1+r)^t$

The longer the period before a receipt or payment, the lower is its present value.

YEARS AHEAD BEFORE $1.00 IS RECEIVED	PRESENT VALUE (@ 5%)
0	$1.00
1	$0.9524 (= $1.00 ÷ 1.0500)
2	$0.9070 (= $1.00 ÷ 1.1025)
3	$0.8638 (= $1.00 ÷ 1.1576)
4	$0.8227 (= $1.00 ÷ 1.2155)
5	$0.7835 (= $1.00 ÷ 1.2753)
6	$0.7462 (= $1.00 ÷ 1.3401)
7	$0.7107 (= $1.00 ÷ 1.4071)
8	$0.6768 (= $1.00 ÷ 1.4775)
9	$0.6446 (= $1.00 ÷ 1.5513)
10	$0.6139 (= $1.00 ÷ 1.6289)
.	
.	
.	
20	$0.3769 (= $1.00 ÷ 2.6533)
.	
.	
.	
30	$0.2314 (= $1.00 ÷ 4.3219)
.	
.	
.	
40	$0.1420 (= $1.00 ÷ 7.0400)

rate is 5%.[1] This is the benefit of the degree. If the interest rate had been 10% instead of 5%, the present value of the extra income of $8400 per year from the degree for 40 years, starting after the 4 years of college, would have been considerably smaller and equal to $61,716. Present values are smaller at higher interest rates because it takes less money today to turn it into a given amount in the future.

> The *present* value of a given *future* amount is smaller at higher interest rates.

The cost to which the benefit of attending college must be compared might appear to be the present value of tuition and books plus the present value of the cost of food and rent. However, this is incorrect.

The True Cost of College:
Opportunity Cost and Incremental Cost

Tuition *is* a cost attributable to attending college, and when put in terms of present value, it is part of the **total cost** to be compared to the benefit. However, we have assumed that the cost of food and rent is the same at college as it is if you do not attend college. Therefore, it is not an **incremental cost** attributable to college. Only if food and rent are more expensive at college is it necessary to include this cost, and then only the extra or incremental amount is included. To keep our example simple, we ignore this factor.

While it is not necessary to include the cost of food and rent, there is a very important cost of being at college that must be included. This is the value of income that is forgone for 4 years, which is assumed to be $1800 per month. This is an **opportunity cost,** which is the cost in terms of the next best forgone opportunity: if you attend college full time, you can't work at the job you would have taken paying $1800 per month. Forgone income while at college is clearly a cost attributable to attending college, because if you did not go, you would be earning.[2] This opportunity cost is large: $12 \times \$1800 = \$21,600$ per year before calculating the present value. The annual cost of being at college is the opportunity cost plus tuition, that is, $21,600 + $6000 = $27,600 per year for 4 years. This has a present value of $102,762 (or $27,600 + $26,286 + $25,034 + $23,842) when the interest rate is 5% and $96,237 (or $27,600 + $25,091 + $22,810 + $20,736) when the interest rate is 10%.[3]

> Opportunity cost is the cost in terms of the value of the *next best* forgone opportunity.

In summary, the benefits and costs are

INTEREST RATE	BENEFIT	COST	(BENEFIT – COST)
5%	$124,510	$102,762	$21,748
10%	$ 61,716	$ 96,237	–$34,521

[1] For simplicity we assume that the income is received at the beginning of the year, starting at the beginning of the first year after finishing college.

[2] Example 1.2 explains the calculation of forgone income in a different context, that of the determination of compensation in the case of divorce.

[3] Again, for simplicity, we assume that the costs are incurred at the beginning of each of the 4 years.

Example 1.2

STUDY ECONOMICS: IT'S THE LAW

The principle of opportunity cost is not merely some abstract, academic notion batted about in dreary economics texts with little or no practical significance. Indeed, enter a court of law dealing with civil matters such as compensation for personal injury or divorce, and you might think the judge and lawyers had spent more time studying economics than law.

Consider, for example, the case of **Elliot** v. **Elliot** heard in a family court in Ontario, Canada, in 1992. The court learned that after 8 years of marriage, Deborah and Michael Elliot had split up. Mrs. Elliot told the court that by staying at home to raise her two young children, her career progress had been adversely affected. With the advice and assistance of an economist, the argument was presented that Mrs. Elliot would

have lower earnings than she would otherwise have enjoyed, constituting a substantial opportunity cost of having been a homemaker while her husband pursued his career.

Citing a precedent in the same court, **Ormerod** v. **Ormerod,** 1990, Mr. Justice David Steinberg ordered Mr. Elliot to pay Mrs. Elliot a lump sum of $59,000, in addition to child support. In reaching this lump sum, the court made a projection of what Mrs. Elliot would have been earning currently and in future years had she **not** withdrawn from the labor market for 8 years. This was then contrasted to what she was actually earning and could be expected to earn during the remainder of her career, which was assumed to extend to age 65. The difference between the two earnings series represented the

before-tax opportunity cost each year of having been the homemaker. It was assumed that the income tax rate would be 33%, so only 67% of the lost income represented an after-tax loss. The present value of the after-tax lost income from each year was calculated at the court-approved discount rate.

The present value of the opportunity cost amounted to $118,000. However, stating that the risk of breakup of a marriage partnership is shared, Mr. Justice David Steinberg made the controversial decision to award Mrs. Elliot only half the loss, specifically, $59,000.

Source: Sean Fine , "Evaluating Economics of Ending Marriage," **The Globe and Mail,** October 12, 1992, p. 1.

We see that at a 5% interest rate, college is worthwhile; the benefit exceeds the cost by more than $20,000. However, at a 10% interest rate, the cost of college outweighs the benefit. The higher interest rate has reduced the present value of benefits that accrue far into the future more than it reduces the costs that occur closer to the present time, that is, while attending college. (Take a look back at your notes on how you would have approached the problem of college entrance. How close did you come to listing the correct costs and benefits?)

The Role of Assumptions

It is instructive to examine our assumptions to see what effect they have had on the conclusion. We began by assuming that incomes with and without college are constant, year in, year out, when in fact people can generally expect faster growth of income with a college education. When using a 5% interest rate, which gives the conclusion that it is worth attending college, we can say that if the assumption of constant income is dropped and replaced with a faster growth of income after attending college, the conclusion would be unchanged. Indeed, there is even stronger reason to attend college. Therefore, when an assumption that simplifies a problem tilts the odds against reaching a particular conclusion and yet that conclusion is reached, there is no need to drop the assumption and face the extra complexity. If we had concluded, while assuming constant incomes, that college is not worthwhile, as with a 10% interest rate, we would have had to determine whether the conclusion would be different if the assumption were not made. This can be done by allowing the incremental income from attending college to rise and then taking the present values of this growing series of numbers.

Another assumption was that the cost of rent and food is the same at college as it would otherwise be. This assumption can be relaxed, and any extra cost of food and rent at college could be included along with tuition costs and the opportunity cost. If food and rent happen instead to be cheaper at college, it is possible to deduct the savings from the other costs. Alternatively, the lower cost of food and rent could be treated as a benefit of attending college. Whichever way the assumption is relaxed, it requires only some extra simple addition or subtraction.

Many assumptions in economics, like those described so far, are solely to help in exposition. You should not, therefore, reject the analysis that follows such assumptions because you think them unrealistic; eventually the assumptions are, or at least could be, relaxed.

Some assumptions are not motivated by expositional convenience but are made because it is not possible to make headway without them. For example, the assumption that the only benefit of college is extra income is made because it is difficult to attach values to other benefits, such as being more able to enjoy and appreciate what we see around us. Even here, though, when the assumptions cannot be relaxed because the problem would become unmanageable, what is learned with the assumptions can still be valuable. There are two reasons for this that can be illustrated from our example.

Many assumptions are to help in expositions of economic principles. You should not reject the associated argument before giving it a chance.

1. If you find, even without including additional benefits, that attending college is worthwhile, you know that if you could include the benefits, college would be even more worthwhile. Therefore, it is sometimes possible to make decisions based on an analysis in which assumptions are made by necessity.

2. Even without including the extra benefits, predictions can still be made. For example, we can still predict that the lower the interest rate, the more likely people are to find college worthwhile for them.

We can still learn from conclusions based on assumptions that are made by necessity, because relaxation of the assumptions may reinforce the conclusions, or because predictions can still be made.

Qualitative and Quantitative Predictions

The prediction that the lower the interest rate, the higher is the number of college applications is a **qualitative prediction** that can be checked against available data on the number of college applications to see whether in the past they have varied with interest rates in this way. There are many other predictions of the college-entry decision-framework that we have used which can be tested.

The major cost of going to college in the example is the opportunity cost of 4 years' forgone income. However, what if you are unable to find a job if you do not go to college? If you expect to be out of work for the first year only, the cost of attending college is reduced by $21,600. If unemployment is likely to last for 2 years, the cost of attending college is reduced by $42,172, at a 5% interest rate, and so on. Therefore, the higher unemployment is, especially among those leaving high school, the greater are the number of applications to college we should observe. Again, this can be checked against the data to see whether college applications and unemployment move up and down jointly in this way.[4]

You might be surprised by the prediction that more people apply to college when unemployment is high. Might high unemployment make it more difficult to save for college, so fewer can afford to attend? Looking back at the approach we have taken, however, there is no mention of being able to afford college. Indeed, as far as the comparison of costs and benefits is concerned, a student's savings, or those of his or her family, are irrelevant. But is this realistic?

Savings should not matter if people can borrow to attend college: when the benefit of college exceeds the cost, it is worthwhile going to college even if this involves borrowing. But what if students cannot borrow? In this case, the inability to save for college or earn while at college because of unemployment may have a negative effect on college applications. Consequently, unemployment could have a negative effect on college applications when the difficulty of saving for college outweighs the positive effect on applications of a reduced opportunity cost.

It is not uncommon, as in this case, for predictions to be ambiguous, and when they are, we must look at the empirical evidence to see which predictions and the theories behind them are consistent with the evidence and which must be rejected.[5] Testing of theories by comparing their predictions against available empirical evidence is an important step in economics that involves special statistical techniques developed by **econometricians.** We might find, for example, that college applications increase during periods of heavy unemployment. We can then say that the effect of the decline in opportunity cost dominates any effect unemployment has because of the difficulty of saving for college or of earning while attending college. However, because many factors affect college applications, and because these factors change simultaneously, it can be difficult to disentangle all the separate effects. The disentanglement is particularly difficult because the economist is in the unfortunate position of rarely being able to design laboratory experiments to test theories; virtually all testing involves data concerning the past, and this is the result of many forces occurring simultaneously.

Even when predictions reached with a theory are not ambiguous, it still helps to look at the data in order to judge the magnitude of qualitative predictions, that is, to make **quantitative predictions.** For example, suppose there is an increase in income earned by college graduates versus nongraduates. The benefits versus costs approach we have taken predicts unequivocally that more people will apply to colleges. But *how many* more will apply? It may be possible to determine this by looking back at applications figures and data on graduates' incomes versus nongraduates' incomes to examine the extent of the link in the past.

When qualitative predictions of an economic theory are ambiguous, they can be compared with the empirical evidence to see whether the predictions are consistent with or contradicted by the data.

[4]The connection between college applications and unemployment has been observed. See, for example, "Unemployment Boosting College Applications by 13 Percent," *Toronto Star*, June 3, 1982, p. D21; and "Jobless Swelling University Enrolment: Statscan," *The Globe and Mail*, September 2, 1983, p.10.

[5]An economic theory can never be proved to be true, because there is always a chance that new data could cause us to reject it. Therefore, all we can do is retain or reject a theory.

Considering One Factor at a Time: Ceteris Paribus

When deriving implications of a theory—for example, the effect of interest rates, unemployment, and so on, on college applications—we have seen that it is possible to proceed more readily by considering each individual factor on its own, thereby assuming that the other factors are constant. This type of assumption is called the assumption of **_ceteris paribus._** (This means "other things," _ceteris,_ like etcetera, "are equal," _paribus,_ like parity.) When we make a _ceteris paribus_ assumption, we do not for a moment believe that each individual factor is conveniently changing on its own. Such an assumption is made only to find the way each factor works on its own. This is therefore a simplifying assumption, like most others.

A prediction that can be reached by making a _ceteris paribus_ assumption which surprises many people concerns the effect of **sunk costs.** A sunk cost is a cost that is borne whatever is done, so tuition payments already made or income already forgone would be considered sunk costs.

Sunk costs are those which have already been incurred and cannot be changed.

In order to reach the surprising prediction about sunk costs, suppose that you have been at college for 3½ years when you get a chance to take the very job for which you entered college. Suppose further that it is a chance that may be gone in 6 months when you would otherwise be finishing college. In this case, the benefit of staying at college is zero; there is no incremental income from staying. Indeed, the "benefit" may even be negative if you would have to settle for a lower-paying job than is currently offered. Even if you have already paid the tuition for your fourth year and cannot obtain a refund, the cost of completing college is half a year's forgone income at the wage that you have just been offered. With a benefit of zero and a cost of half a year's forgone income, it does not pay to stay at college.

But what of the 3½ years of opportunity cost and 4 years of tuition payments? Why don't these enter the calculation? They do not count because you have paid them whether you leave college or stay. What matters is the benefit of staying on at college versus the cost of staying on, and a sunk cost such as past tuition is not a cost of staying on.

Sunk costs are irrelevant.

If you are thinking it would be silly to quit college with only 6 months to go, you may have in mind that a college degree gives you more opportunities because of added flexibility, and you would not as likely find yourself without work some day in the future. This is indeed a benefit of completing college, but we have not included it because, like many theories in traditional economics, we have considered only _expected_ costs and benefits and have not allowed for the fact that people value flexibility and do not like taking risks. Flexibility and aversion to uncertainty can be incorporated into the decision-making framework by using techniques from the business subject of finance. If this is done, it might well be smarter to finish college.[6]

---

[6]The benefits of education go well beyond those we have mentioned, especially in developing nations, where women have traditionally been denied the educational opportunities of men. Example 1.3 describes these benefits and also illustrates the application of the cost versus benefit approach in the context of public policy.

Example   1.3

FAIRER AND BETTER: THE COST AND BENEFITS OF WOMEN'S EDUCATION

The economic approach of comparing costs and benefits can be used for public as well as private decisions. Take, for example, the decision to invest in the education of women in a poor, developing nation such as Pakistan.

According to the Chief Economist of the World Bank, Lawrence Summers, the cost of educating an extra 1000 girls in Pakistan for an additional year is approximately $40,000. In return, a lengthy list of benefits would be enjoyed, so many that Summers declares "[E]ducating girls quite possibly yields a higher rate of return than any other investment available in the developing world."* Included among the benefits are the following:

- **The higher wages earned by women as a direct benefit of their training**. Estimates suggest female wages could increase by as much as 10% to 20% from every additional year of education.

- **Reduced infant and child mortality as a result of better prenatal care of**

* Lawrence Summers, Chief Economist, World Bank, "The Most Influential Investment," **Scientific American,** August 1992, p. 132.

mothers and better postnatal care of children. Research indicates that every additional year of education of 1000 Pakistani women would save as many as 60 lives of children younger than 5 years. To achieve the same saving with institutionalized health care would cost $48,000, an amount that on its own exceeds the cost of the extra schooling.

- **Educated women choosing to have smaller families**. Econometricians estimate that each additional year at school results in a 10% reduction in the number of births per woman from the current average of 6.6 in Pakistan. That is, there would be 0.66 fewer births per woman, and 660 (or 0.66 × 1000) per 1000 women receiving an extra year of education. With the cost of delivery estimated at $65 per birth, the cost saving on the 660 fewer births amounts to $43,000 (or $65 × 660). Even when considered on its own, this benefit exceeds the cost of the education. Furthermore, the benefit is multiplied at each generation; fewer births today mean fewer women bearing children in all subsequent generations.

- **Extra schooling reducing mortality of women in childbirth**. Specifically, each additional year of education for 1000 women saves 4 women's lives. A similar reduction in mortality from medical treatment would cost $10,000, yet a further benefit to set against the cost of schooling.

It is little surprise that with all these benefits, Lawrence Summers concludes that "[T]he social improvements brought about by educating women are more than sufficient to cover its costs. Given that education also yields higher wages, it seems reasonable to conclude that the return on getting more girls into school is in excess of 20%, and probably much greater. In fact, it may well be the single most influential investment that can be made in the developing world."† What is fairer, namely, providing education for women in a world that has favored men because they bring more direct financial benefits to their parents, is also better. There is just as much reason for governments to provide education as for people to demand it.

† Ibid.

OVERVIEW OF THE ECONOMIC APPROACH

As well as introducing several central economic principles used later in this book, the preceding example illustrates the basic structure of the economic approach. This basic structure is shared with other sciences and is illustrated in Figure 1.1.

If you glance back over the argument we made, you will notice that terms were defined, such as present value and opportunity cost. The need to define terms is noted at the top of Figure 1.1. It is possible to proceed without definitions, but this adds to the length of arguments. Using carefully defined terms is helpful because a relatively limited number of terms reappear in a broad range of problems. Of course, when a reader meets a definition for the first time, it is necessary to learn what it means, and it may be necessary to recheck the meaning until the term has been faced a few times. However, in the long run, the use of definitions provides considerable economy in the presentation of economic arguments. Also interspersed in the example were a number of assumptions, as shown at stage 2 of Figure 1.1. For example, we assumed that the only benefit from college is higher income and that extra or incremental income does not grow over time. We explained that these assumptions are made to make the problem more tractable and that they could be dropped at the cost of extra complexity if and when necessary.

Among the assumptions was that we could consider the effects of one factor at a time on the benefits versus costs of attending college, holding all other possibly relevant factors constant. We associated this with the expression *ceteris paribus,* or other things being equal. The *ceteris paribus* assumption is used so often in economics it has become the hallmark of the economics profession and is the source of a number of jokes. However, consideration of one matter at a time while other effects are assumed constant is a common practice in all sciences.

An assumption that was not made explicit in the example was that people *in general* view the matter of whether to apply to college in the same way. That is, we implicitly assumed that people in general compare costs and benefits, properly calculated, and apply to college when their benefits exceed their costs. This assumption is necessary to extend the inquiry from whether *you* should have applied to college—the way the example was motivated—to what affects the number of people applying to college. Economists are usually more interested in the behavior of people in general than in the behavior of particular individuals. Consequently, it is necessary to assume that people behave in predictable ways as well as to assume that this predictable behavior is **rational,** that is, based on comparing costs and benefits.

*Economists are usually more interested in the behavior of **people in general** than in the behavior of individuals.*

Economists have faced substantial criticism for assuming that they can predict how people in general behave and for assuming that people behave rationally, for example, making decisions by comparing costs and benefits. In their defense, economists usually invoke the "law of large numbers," which implies that while some may behave idiosyncratically and "irrationally," the idiosyncrasies and irrationalities average out so that people in general behave predictably and rationally. The test of assumptions, many economists claim, is whether they result in useful predictions that are consistent with observed behavior rather than the "accuracy"

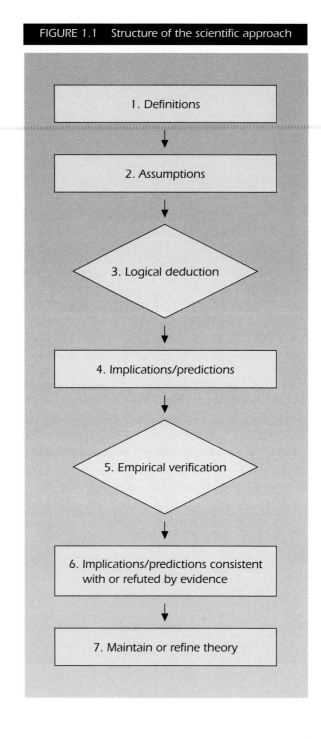

FIGURE 1.1   Structure of the scientific approach

of the assumptions per se. But where do these verifiable predictions come from? This is the next step in the economists' approach and can again be related to the example.

We used the benefit versus cost view of college applications to argue that lower interest rates and higher unemployment rates would increase the number of college applications. These implications follow from the assumption that people compare the benefits and costs of college. While only a simple verbal argument and a few specialized terms were used, the derivation of the implications follows a process of deductive logic. That is, the implications/predictions at stage 4 in Figure 1.1 come after applying logic in stage 3.

Frequently, when dealing with more complex problems, economists use mathematical symbols and procedures to derive implications from theories. The need to use mathematics is particularly great when there are a number of relevant factors in a problem and where these factors interact with each other.

Deductive logic is applied to derive the implications of the assumptions made in an economic theory.

Suppose, for example, that not only does the number of college applications depend on the extra income earned from attending college but also, at the same time, the reverse connection holds. That is, suppose also that the incremental income earned from a college degree depends on the number of people going to college; perhaps the higher the number enrolling in college, *ceteris paribus*, the smaller is the premium they earn over those without college degrees. In this more complex theory we have a two-way connection between college applications and the incremental income from college that is best described with simultaneous equations. In such a theory, economists are unlikely to be able to consider the implications without using mathematics.

If economics is to be useful, it should provide implications that correspond closely to the evidence. This comparison of implications and evidence is the next step in the economists' approach, as shown in stage 5 in Figure 1.1. The comparison requires data against which the implications can be checked, and in this regard economists are more fortunate than many other scientists. For decades, records have been kept about all sorts of economic phenomena from the sizes of global trade and capital flows down to prices of fish meal and individual stocks and bonds. These data give economists enormous scope to test their theories without resorting to laboratory experiments or the collection of relevant data themselves. The branch of economics that specializes in using statistical procedures to test theories against empirical evidence is called **econometrics.**

As with the testing of theories in other sciences, the econometrician cannot prove a theory to be true. Rather, it is possible to conclude only whether the evidence is consistent with the theory; it is impossible to prove a theory because there is always a chance that further evidence will be found that is inconsistent with the theory.

We should emphasize that economists typically test the *implications* of theories rather than the *assumptions* behind the theories. For example, they would test whether college applications increase during recessions rather than the assumption that potential applicants compare costs and benefits.

Economic theories are tested by comparing the implications of the theories with the empirical evidence.

If a theory's implications are found to disagree with the data—at stage 6 in Figure 1.1—the theory is rejected, and it is necessary to refine the assumptions—at stage 7. As with other sciences, through this process of building, testing, and

 **1.4**

THE IMPECCABLE COUNTENANCE OF ECONOMICS

The study of economics has been recommended by the church. The following grants economics the most impeccable countenance.

That Political Economy is a science having nothing to do with morals or religion, nor in any way appertaining to human welfare, except so far as relates to the production and accumulation of wealth, is a common opinion; but it may be fearlessly asserted, that no other science is so intimately connected with the destiny of the human race, in its highest and most enduring interests. Such has been the uniform testimony of those in the clerical profession who have given special attention to its teachings. Dr. Chalmers, while he held the chair of Divinity in the University of Edinburgh, gave lectures upon Political Economy. In the preface to the volume he published upon the subject, he says, "We cannot bid adieu to Political Economy without an earnest recommendation of its lessons to all who enter upon the ecclesiastical profession." Rev. Dr. Bethume, in his address before the Literary Society of Yale College, 1845, spoke of Political Economy "as that philanthropic science, which, next to the gospel, whose legitimate offspring it is, will do more than any thing else for the elevation and fraternization of our race." Bishop Whately was heard to remark, a short time before his death, that "no theological seminary should be without its chair of Political Economy." Agreeing fully with the opinions expressed by these eminent men, I have felt desirous to show how perfectly the laws of wealth accord with all those moral and social laws which appertain to the higher nature and aspirations of man.

Source: Amasa Walker, **The Science of Wealth** (Boston: Little, Brown and Co., 1866), pp. vi–vii.

refining theories, economists have moved toward a better understanding of the universe of issues they believe to have an economic component.[7]

The galvanizing connection between economics and other sciences in their sharing of the scientific approach is but one of an extremely long list of more specific connections between economics and other fields. This book deals with a number of these specific connections as it traces out the bridges between economics and a broad range of other fields of intellectual inquiry from physics to theology. This is done to demonstrate that economics does not exist in a vacuum but has shared its developments with other disciplines, as well as having moved along strikingly similar paths even when the process of discovery has been independent. The Crossing Bridges section preceding the Summary of this chapter traces out some of the parallels that exist in the way economists and biologists organize the divisions of their inquiry.[8] Even those with no background in biology should read this section because it describes the traditional units of study in economics that fill the remainder of this book and does so without requiring any prior knowledge of biology or, of course, of economics.

---

[7]The economists' universe is constantly expanding as economists march imperialistically into an ever-widening area of inquiry. As Example 1.4 shows, the cooption of the economic way of thinking has received impeccable countenance.

[8]Example 1.5 suggests that the connection between economics and biology involves more than organizational parallels. Indeed, it suggests they are both part of a broader discipline, "general economy."

Example   1.5

THE ECONOMY OF THE BODY

It has been argued that economics and biology are really two branches of the same field of inquiry, called general economy. The following excerpt from a paper presented to the American Economics Association explains why.

The process of interrelating disciplines takes many forms. In some cases there is simply an analogizing or a borrowing of jargon—perhaps a mere transfer of metaphor, as when we speak of "the body politic." In other instances one discipline provides useful "tools" for the study of others; for example, physics has given economics and biology units of measurement for the study of energy. Sometimes there is an area of overlap between two fields and a hybrid discipline arises: biochemistry and biophysics are good examples.

Finally we have cases in which two disciplines are really branches of a more general one. The obvious example is zoology and botany forming subdivisions of biology. In the present work I shall take the position that economics and biology do not merely share common interests; they have more than just a few lessons to learn from one another, or an interdisciplinary boundary at which common problems are dealt with. Rather, they constitute a single branch of knowledge.

Just as biology deals with both plant and animal life, there should be recognized a branch of knowledge that deals with economic processes irrespective of whether they are man-made or not, concerning itself with such phenomena as competition that are common to all economies. Thus I propose that we recognize a body of knowledge called *natural economy* (biology) coordinate with *political economy* (economics), together forming a branch of knowledge which we may call *general economy*.

If it be argued that biology is not wholly an economic discipline, I can only answer that it actually is. All the properties of organisms, without exception, are the result of evolution, and the mechanism of evolution, selection, is nothing more than reproductive competition between members of the same species. Competition, of course, is as fundamental an economic phenomenon as can be imagined.

Source: *"The Economy of the Body" by Michael T. Ghiselin,* **The American Economic Review; Papers and Proceedings,** May 1978, p.233. *Reprinted by permission of the American Economic Association.*

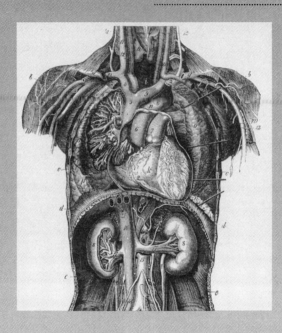

THE PARALLEL ORGANIZATIONAL STRUCTURES OF ECONOMICS AND BIOLOGY

The decision whether to enter or remain in college is in the realm of **microeconomics.** Microeconomics is one of the two major divisions of economics, the other being **macroeconomics.**

Microeconomics, like microbiology, is concerned with the smaller elements of life. Rather than describing the full economy as a whole, it looks at the behavior of consumers and firms that together make up the economy and at the way prices of individual products are determined. It asks how consumers respond to changes in the prices of what they buy and how producers respond to changes in the prices of what they sell. Microeconomics also shows how firms respond to changes in the wages and raw materials prices they must pay. The principles of microeconomics can be used even to show what economic measures can reduce environmental pollution and why some needed services would not be provided without the government.

Macroeconomics is concerned with the entire body of economic life and not the living cells of which it is made. It is concerned with the level of unemployment, the rate of inflation, the size of the total national output, the balance of payments, and other big economic issues of that kind. Of course, the level of unemployment is made up of all the separate living individuals who do not have a job, and the rate of inflation is composed of the rising prices of bread, meat, apples, gasoline, textbooks, and other individual goods and services. But macroeconomics ignores the special causes of particular people being unemployed and why bread prices went up. These are considered in the realm of the other part of economics, namely microeconomics.

The basic organizational units of study in microeconomics, the firms that produce the goods and services and the consumers who buy them, are analogous to the cells that form the basic organizational units of study in biology. Indeed, there are strong parallels between the two disciplines also at the sub-cellular and more aggregate levels of study in biology.

The cell consists of a number of components—the **nucleus** and its **nucleolus,** the **ribosomes,** and so on. In the same way, the firm consists of some finer divisions—the senior and middle managers, the quality controllers, the line workers, and so on.[9] Similarly, the family, which is the basic unit of study of consumer demand, consists of a head of household and other family members. The sub-components of firms and families perform specialized tasks just as do the subcomponents of living cells. Indeed, the **division of labor** is used to describe the specialization that occurs inside cells as well as the specialization within the firm or family.

Divisions of labor operate not only within cells, firms, and groups of consumers but also between them. Let us illustrate this by concentrating on the parallels between the structure of the cell and the firm.

Tissues such as the **epidermis** and bone in animals and the **pith** or **phloem** in plants are aggregates of cells of one type or of only a few types.[10] In a similar way, **industries,** a principle unit of study in economics, are made up of aggregates of firms of a common or similar kind. A major topic of interest in biology is how the cells that constitute tissues are organized; do they attach to each other or float freely, and when they attach, do they line up vertically or horizontally, and so on? In the same way, economists are interested in the organization of firms in an industry; to what extent are the firms **vertically** or **horizontally integrated,** do firms cooperate by forming cartels, or do they compete, and so on?[11] Indeed, there is a growing branch of economics with its own specialized courses, research journals, and textbooks known as **industrial organization.**

Several tissues grouped together constitute organs. The heart, lungs, stomach, brain, and skin are examples of organs in animals, while roots, leaves, flowers, and stems are examples of organs in plants. Organs are analogous to **sectors** of an economy. Energy, resource extraction, manufacturing, financial services, transportation, and retailing are examples of economic sectors. Just as the tissues that comprise an organ interact and are highly dependent on each other, so are an economy's sectors. We could not have a heart without the supply of oxygen and fuel from other organs any more than we could have a manufacturing sector without the supply of raw materials from mining and other extractive firms and without sectors for distributing and selling the products. Just as biologists specialize in the study of organs, so too do economists specialize in finance, energy, transportation, education, and so on.

Biologists consider larger aggregates than individual organs. The next level up from organs is **systems.** For example, the brain and nerves make up the nervous system, while the heart and blood vessels make up the circulatory system. Economists also sometimes deal with a level of aggregation above that of sectors. In moving to form the larger aggregates from sectors,

> *Divisions of labor operate not only within cells, firms, and consumers but also between them.*

---

[9]A more extensive examination of the parallels between the cell and the firm that considers the flow of internal information, the monitoring of inputs and outputs, and so on is discussed in the Crossing Bridges section in Chapter 5.

[10]The pith and phloem are components of stems, holding up the plant and carrying nutrients.

[11]Vertically integrated firms deal with many different stages of production. Horizontally integrated frims deal with different products, often concentrating on only one stage of production, such as extraction, fabrication, marketing, and so on.

economists move from microeconomics to macroeconomics. The important aggregates of consumption and investment are of particular interest to the macroeconomist.

Organs, grouped together into their larger aggregates, systems, work together to form an **organism,** just as economic sectors grouped into their larger aggregates work together to form an economy. The organism is the animal or plant that can be considered as having an independence, just as can an economy.

As we have become patently aware in recent years, all plants and animals, the organisms that are the large organizational units of study in biology, are highly dependent on each other. This growing awareness of the interdependence of organisms has resulted in increased attention to the higher-level biologic study of **ecology.** Most of the work in ecology involves showing how, without an appreciation of the fundamental interdependence between everything on this Earth, we run the risk of damaging the entire **biosystem** of which we humans are part. In a strikingly similar way, economists have become increasingly aware in recent years that different economies, for example, those of the United States, Europe, Canada, Japan, Korea, and so on, are highly dependent on each other. This is part of the **globalization** that has taken place. Globalization is manifest in the growing importance of international versus domestic trade. It also has been manifest in the way financial panics have spread around the globe and in how problems in one country, such as huge fiscal deficits or imbalances between imports and exports, have had repercussions in other countries. That is, the growing importance of the biologic field of ecology has a strong parallel in the growing importance of international economics.

SUMMARY

1. Personal decisions can be made using economic principles. For example, it is possible to decide whether to enter college by comparing the cost of going to college with the benefit, where the cost includes any opportunity cost of forgone income and the benefit includes the increase in income.

2. Future benefits and costs can be put in terms of present value by using the interest rate.

3. An increase in the interest rate reduces the likelihood that attending college is worthwhile because it reduces the present value of benefits that accrue far into the future more than it reduces costs incurred while attending college.

4. When people can borrow to attend college, the number applying is likely to increase with increases in unemployment. However, when it is difficult or expensive to borrow, higher unemployment may reduce college applications.

5. Assumptions are frequently made only to help in the exposition of economic principles and to identify the effects of individual factors. Therefore, the economists' approach should not be rejected before giving it a chance just because the assumptions seem to be unrealistic.

6. Even when assumptions are made because it is not possible to proceed without them, it may still be possible to learn from the conclusions reached, because relaxation of the assumptions may only reinforce what can be concluded with the assumptions, or because the effects of individual factors, while other things are assumed constant, may still be valid.

7. When predictions are ambiguous, they can be checked against empirical evidence that has been collected in the past.

8. Sunk costs are costs that have already been incurred and cannot be changed. Since sunk costs relate to the past and not the future, they should have no effect on rational behavior.

9. The economic approach follows the same steps as the approach taken in other sciences. All sciences start with definitions and assumptions, derive implications of the assumptions by means of logical deduction, compare the implications with the data, and reject or maintain the theory depending on the accuracy of its predictions.

QUESTIONS AND PROBLEMS

1. How much is your college program costing you? Use your own tuition fees and opportunity cost and a 5% interest rate.

2. What is your (incremental) benefit of attending college? Use the income you expect to earn versus what you might earn without college.

3. What nonmonetary benefits might be gained with a college degree, and does the existence of these benefits make the comparison of monetary costs and benefits of no use?

4. Think through the main elements of the benefit versus cost approach for deciding whether to attend college in terms of whether you should go to law school, business school, or any other higher qualification you might have in mind. Can you attach values to all the crucial magnitudes?

5. How might economics be applied to decide whether a couple should have a child?

6. If it were possible to evaluate only the financial cost of having a child and it were impossible to evaluate the other "costs" or to value the many but intangible benefits, might we still make qualitative predictions about what could influence the number of couples trying to have children? Which factors would you include in such an economic theory of child-bearing behavior?

7. Why is it not possible to prove a theory to be true?

8. Can you think of noneconomic matters in which the behavior of a group is more predictable than the behavior of the individuals within the group?

. . . .
. . . .
. . . .
. . . .
. . . . Scarcity and the Need to Choose
. . . .
. . . .

. . . cursed is the ground for thy sake; in toil shalt thou eat of it
all the days of thy life. . . . In the sweat of thy face shalt thou
eat bread.

Genesis 3,17

Key Concepts

Scarcity; choice; production possibilities curve; factors of production; opportunity cost; trade-offs; relative versus absolute prices; price system; free enterprise versus command and control economies; mixed economies

SCARCITY: THE CENTRAL ECONOMIC PROBLEM

While economics includes a vast range of topics such as supply and demand, inflation, unemployment, interest rates, national income, and so on, scarcity is common to all topics covered. This is why economics may be defined as the branch of human inquiry dealing with the scarcity of goods and services.

A good or service is considered scarce if having more of it means having less of something else. For example, from the perspective of a country in which all the arable land is under cultivation, growing more wheat means having less of some other crop, such as oats or barley. Similarly, from the perspective of an individual with a given income to spend, buying more books means buying less of something else, such as compact discs or tickets to the movies. More generally, whatever the domain over which it is considered—the world, a country or an

Economics is the branch of human inquiry dealing with the scarcity of goods and services.

23

Scarcity results in a need to choose between alternatives.

individual—the essence of scarcity is a need to choose between alternatives. The cause of scarcity and the nature of the choices scarcity necessitates depend on the perspective taken. Let us begin by considering the perspective of a nation.

SCARCITY: THE PERSPECTIVE OF THE NATION

Scarcity is ultimately the result of limits on the available supplies of factors of production.

Ultimately, scarcity is the result of limits on the availability of land, raw materials, machines, and human effort, which are the resources needed to produce what people want. Land, raw materials, machines (or **capital**) and human effort (or **labor**) are known as **factors of production.**[1] The factors of production are the **inputs** required to produce the **outputs** people want. The limitation in the availability of the factors of production is the cause of scarcity of the outputs of goods and services available to people within a nation. That is, the limited amounts of land, raw materials, capital, and labor are responsible for the need to choose between different products.

The limits on the availability of land, particularly good agricultural land, are obvious. The limits on raw materials are also quite apparent. For example, there are only so many trees that can be cut to produce houses and paper products. Trees are a renewable resource, but if they are cut too quickly, fewer remain in the future. There are also limits on the exhaustible resources, with only so much oil, copper, iron, and coal. Furthermore, it takes other inputs to extract them and transport them to where they are in demand.

The machines that constitute the capital input—the tools, farm equipment, and so on that so greatly help in production—must themselves be produced. In producing capital goods, resources are used that could otherwise have provided for people's immediate satisfaction. The items produced to help add to future output constitute **investment,** while items produced for immediate use constitute **consumption.** By reducing what is produced for consumption in order to free up inputs to build more machines and other capital goods, people are forced to forgo some of today's wants for those of tomorrow.[2] This need to sacrifice the present for the future is a further manifestation of scarcity.

There are limits on what people are prepared to sacrifice out of today's wants, and therefore, there are limits on investment. In poor countries these limits are set by today's need to eat and stay alive. In richer countries the limits are set by the patience of the people who can choose how much of their incomes they wish to **save.** The amount saved determines the amount of inputs that can be shifted from producing consumption goods and services into producing capital.

The input of labor is limited by the number of people who can work. However, there are also limits set by the number of hours per week people are willing to work and the effort they apply during those hours.

---

[1] Capital refers to machines, not to financial instruments such as stocks and bonds.

[2] As Example 2.1 explains, the use of capital adds substantially to output, even though producing capital involves an opportunity cost.

Example   2.1

THE SHORTEST DISTANCE IS NOT DIRECT

Capital makes production indirect, or "roundabout," because the capital has to be produced before one can enjoy its fruits. As the following examples explain, the harvest from relatively simple detours to produce capital can be bountiful, even when the capital is distinctly "low-tech."

A peasant requires drinking water. The spring is some distance from his house. There are various ways in which he may supply his daily wants. First, he may go to the spring each time he is thirsty, and drink out of his hollowed hand. This is the most direct way; satisfaction follows immediately on exertion. But it is an inconvenient way, for our peasant has to take his way to the well as often as he is thirsty. And it is an insufficient way, for he can never collect and store any great quantity such as he requires for various other purposes.

Second, he may take a log of wood, hollow it out into a kind of pail, and carry his day's supply from the spring to his cottage. The advantage is obvious, but it necessitates a roundabout way of considerable length. The man must spend, perhaps, a day in cutting out the pail; before doing so he must have felled a tree in the forest; to do this, again, he must have made an axe, and so on. But there is still a third way; instead of felling one tree he fells a number of trees, splits and hollows them, lays them end for end, and so constructs a runnel or rhone which brings a full head of water to his cottage. *Here, obviously, between the expenditure of the labour and the obtaining of the water we have a very roundabout way, but, then, the result is ever so much greater.* Our peasant need no longer take his weary way from house to well with the heavy pail on his shoulder, and yet he has a constant and full supply of the freshest water at his very door.

Another example. I require stone for building a house. There is a rich vein of excellent sandstone in a neighbouring hill. How is it to be got out? First, I may work the loose stones back and forward with my bare fingers, and break off what can be broken off. This is the most direct, but also the least productive way. Second, I may take a piece of iron, make a hammer and chisel out of it, and use them on the hard stone—a roundabout way, which, of course, leads to a very much better result that the former. Third method—Having a hammer and chisel I use them to drill a hole in the rock; next I turn my attention to procuring charcoal, sulphur, and nitre, and mixing them in a powder, then I pour the powder into the hole, and the explosion that follows splits the stone into convenient pieces—still more of a roundabout way, but one which, as experience shows, is as much superior to the second way in result as the second was to the first.

The lesson to be drawn from these examples is obvious. It is— that *a greater result is obtained by producing goods in roundabout ways than by producing them directly.* Where a good can be produced in either way, we have the fact that, by the indirect way, a greater product can be got with equal labour, or the same product with less labour. But, beyond this, the superiority of the indirect way manifests itself in being the only way in which certain goods can be obtained.

Source: Eugen von Böhm-Bawerk, **Positive Theory of Capital** (New York: G. E. Stechert, 1891, reprinted 1923). (Emphases in original.)

Production Possibilities with Given Technology and Factors of Production

The limited production possibilities resulting from the limited supply of land, raw materials, capital, and labor can be described graphically, as is done in Figure 2.1. The two axes in Figure 2.1 show the outputs of wheat and automobiles produced

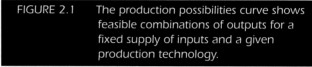

FIGURE 2.1   The production possibilities curve shows feasible combinations of outputs for a fixed supply of inputs and a given production technology.

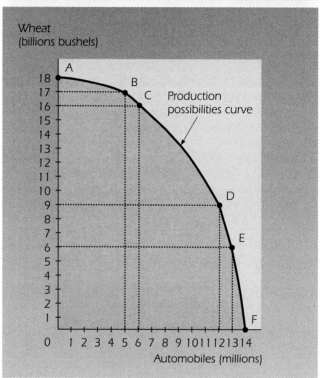

The production possibilities curve shows the combinations of production levels of different products that are possible when a nation's factors of production are fully employed. Because it slopes downward, the production possibilities curve shows that in order to produce more of one good it is necessary to reduce the output of other goods. That is, there is a trade-off between products. The extent to which the output of one good must be reduced to expand the output of another good is shown by the slope of the curve. For example, to produce 1 million more cars than at point **B**, it is necessary to reduce wheat output by 1 billion bushels, but to produce 1 million more cars than at point **D**, it is necessary to reduce wheat output by 3 billion bushels.

by an economy during a 1-year interval.[3] For simplicity, these two products are assumed to be all that the economy produces, and the technology available to producers of both products is assumed to be given.[4] Point *A* on the vertical axis shows how much wheat could be produced if all the nation's factors of production were devoted to producing wheat. At point *A* there are 18 billion bushels of wheat and no automobiles. Point *F* on the horizontal axis shows how many automobiles could be produced if all the nation's factors of production were devoted to producing automobiles. At point *F* there are 14 million automobiles but no wheat. Points on the curve between points *A* and *F* show other feasible combinations of wheat and automobile production for different allocations of the nation's factors of production to the two products when all of each factor is being used.

The curve between points *A* and *F* is called the **production possibilities curve.** It is also sometimes called the **production frontier.** As its name suggests, the production possibilities curve shows the maximum output combinations that can be produced with the available factors of production, as well as with the given, available technology. This means that the economy is using all the available factors—that is, there are no unemployed factors—and that the factors are being used in the most efficient way given available methods of production. Output combinations in the shaded region inside the production possibilities curve are also feasible. However, since it is possible to have more of both outputs by moving from a point inside the production possibilities curve to a point on the curve, it is always possible to improve on output combinations inside the curve; being inside the curve means some factors of production are idle or are being used inefficiently. Of course, combinations of outputs beyond the production possibilities curve are not attainable.

The first feature that can be noted about the production possibilities curve is that it slopes downward from left to right. This means that more of one product can be obtained only by having less of the other. For example, starting from point *A* and moving toward point *F,* the figure makes clear that to add to the output of automobiles it is necessary to accept a lower output of wheat. Alternatively, starting from point *F* and moving toward point *A,* it is clear that to produce more wheat it is necessary to accept a lower output of automobiles. That is, there is a trade-off between the products. The trade-off is the result of the limits in available supplies of factors of production; more of the factors used for one product means less available for producing the other product.

Another feature of the production possibilities curve worth noting is that the trade-off between wheat and automobiles differs according to the section of curve being considered. For example, beginning at point *B* and moving to point *C* in Figure 2.1, there is an increase in the output of automobiles of 1 million, from 5 to 6 million, and a decrease in wheat output of 1 billion bushels, from 17 to 16 billion

> The production possibilities curve shows the *maximum* output combinations of products that are attainable with the available factors of production and technology.

> The production possibilities curve slopes downward because more factors being used to produce one product means fewer factors available to produce something else.

---

[3] With the use of mathematics, it is possible to show how the production of all goods and services is restricted by the limited supply of factors of production. The assumption of two outputs is made only because it is difficult to deal with more than two outputs on two-dimensional paper.

[4] The technology consists of the available methods of production and know-how.

bushels. However, when beginning at point *D* and moving to point *E,* increasing automobile output by the same amount, 1 million (or 13−12 million), as when going from point *B* to point *C,* the decrease in the output of wheat is then 3 billion bushels, from 9 to 6 billion bushels. More generally, moving along the production possibilities curve from producing only wheat toward producing only automobiles—that is, from point *A* toward point *F*—involves forgoing more and more wheat for the same increase in output of automobiles. Alternatively, as should be clear from looking at Figure 2.1, moving from producing only automobiles toward producing only wheat—that is, from point *F* toward point *A*— involves larger and larger sacrifices of automobile production for the same-sized increase in the output of wheat.

The reason for the changing trade-offs when moving along the production possibilities curve is that as, for example, more and more of the nation's resources are moved over to producing wheat, at first the best land, capital, and labor can be employed growing wheat. For example, starting at point *F,* with all the nation's resources producing automobiles and none of them producing wheat, if wheat production is begun, the very best land, capital, and labor for producing wheat can be put to use first. The gain in wheat output from a given transfer of factors of production is therefore large. However, subsequently, less and less suitable land and other factors must be employed. For example, if we start at point *B,* where 17 billion bushels of wheat are already being produced, attempting to add yet further to wheat output means using relatively lower-quality land, capital, and labor for producing wheat. The gain in wheat output from a given transfer of factors of production is therefore small. That is, the gains in wheat production are largest at first when moving up from point *F* and diminish when moving further and further toward point *A*. This makes the curve flatter as we move from point *F* to point *A*.[5]

> The trade-offs vary along the production possibilities curve because each factor of production varies in quality.

Opportunity Cost and the Production Possibilities Curve

The need to forgo wheat to have more automobiles is the essence of scarcity. Economists describe this need to sacrifice one thing for another in terms of opportunity cost, a concept met in the example in the preceding chapter. In particular, when there is a choice between only two alternatives, such as between wheat and automobiles, the opportunity cost of an automobile is the amount of wheat forgone. Similarly, the opportunity cost of extra wheat is the number of automobiles forgone. More generally, when there are choices between more than two alternatives, opportunity cost is measured in terms of the *most preferred alternative* forgone. For example, if the economy produces wheat, oats, barley, rye, and other grains as well as automobiles, and if oats would have been produced if wheat had not been grown, the opportunity cost of wheat is the forgone output of oats.

It is the downward slope from left to right of the production possibilities curve in Figure 2.1 that reflects the opportunity cost of one product in terms of the other

> Opportunity cost is the amount of the *next-best alternative* given up in order to have more of a particular product.

---

[5] Of course, capital used in automobile production may not be suitable for use in wheat farming, so the slope of the production possibilities curve depends on the length of time over which the transition occurs. Similarly, labor may have to be retrained.

product.[6] As the production possibilities curve makes clear, as long as all the factors of production are used, more of any output means less of some other output. Building more hospitals means building fewer schools; preserving forests means having less lumber for building and making paper; creating more parks means having less land for housing; producing larger outputs of munitions mean having lower outputs of civilian goods. There is therefore a need to choose between competing objectives when a nation's factors of production are being fully used. That is, there is scarcity. Nevertheless, as obvious as this is, it is remarkable how many times the public makes demands or the government makes promises that people believe can be satisfied without having to give up something else.

Production Possibilities with Changing Technology and Factor Supplies

The production possibilities curve in Figure 2.1 was drawn for a given fixed supply of factors of production and for a given state of technological knowledge of how to use them. Improvements in technology or in the available supplies of factors of production change the position of the production possibilities curve.

The Effect of Improved Technology.   The effect of an improvement in technological know-how on the production possibilities curve is shown in Figure 2.2. The curve before the improvement in technology is labeled *AF*, while the curve after the improvement in technology is *A'F'*. Comparison of the two curves shows that if all resources are devoted to producing wheat, the advance in technology makes it possible to produce extra wheat output given by distance *AA'*. Similarly, if all resources are given over to automobile production, the advance in technology makes it possible to produce an extra *FF'* automobiles. Any combination of wheat and automobiles in which both are produced can similarly be improved on. For example, instead of the combination shown by point *C*, it is possible after the improvement in technology to produce the combination shown by point *C'*.

Advances in technology shift the production possibilities curve upward and to the right.

In drawing the new production possibilities curve, we have shifted it upward and to the right and also have changed its slope. In particular, we have moved the intersection with the horizontal axis by a proportionately greater amount than the intersection with the vertical axis. This would happen if the technological advance favored automobile production more than wheat production. Of course, were the technological progress to be greater on the farm than in the factory, the shift along the vertical axis would exceed that along the horizontal axis.

Limits on the rate of technological change restrict the speed at which the production possibilities curve shifts upward and to the right. That is, the inability to devote unlimited resources to research and development and the limitations implied by environmental and safety concerns that restrict the application of new technologies slow the speed at which the production possibilities curve moves outward.

---

[6] Our earlier discussion about the change in slope of the curve when moving between point *A* and point *F* reflects the changing sizes of opportunity costs when moving along the curve. For example, at point *B* the opportunity cost of another 1 million automobiles is 1 billion bushels of wheat, whereas at point *D* the opportunity cost of another 1 million automobiles is 3 billion bushels of wheat.

The Effect of Increasing Available Supplies of Factors of Production.   Growth in available supplies of factors of production has a similar effect on the production possibilities curve as advances in technology. For example, growth in the number of machines due to past investment would cause an upward and rightward shift in the production possibilities curve like that in Figure 2.2, from AF to $A'F'$. Similarly, larger available supplies of raw materials also mean an upward and rightward shift in the curve like that in Figure 2.2. However, as explained in Example 2.2, *if* the higher raw materials supplies mean an earlier date at which a nation runs out of these materials, the upward and rightward shifts of the curve could cease. Indeed, the production possibilities curve could shift backward if a nation began to run out of raw materials.

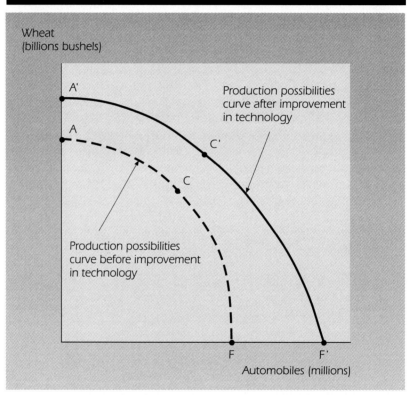

FIGURE 2.2   The production possibilities curve is shifted upward and to the right by technological progress and increased supplies of factors of production.

Improvements in technology increase the combinations of outputs that are feasible with a given, limited supply of factors of production. This means that technology shifts the production possibilities curve upward and to the right. The production possibilities curve is also shifted upward and to the right by increased supplies of factors of production. If, for example, technological progress or increased factor supplies favor automobile production more than wheat production, the shift along the horizontal axis is larger than that along the vertical axis.

Example 2.2

EXHAUSTIBLE RESOURCES AND PRODUCTION POSSIBILITIES

The rapid expansion in living standards that has accompanied the Industrial Revolution that began in Britain in the mid-eighteenth century has been associated with technological advances and capital investments, many of which depend on the use of energy in the form of fossil fuels—coal, oil, and natural gas. The importance of these fuels for the current standard of living is illustrated vividly by the following:

At present, energy conversions for which humans are responsible are being carried out, in the United States, at a rate more than 100 times greater than that at which energy could be converted by the unaided manual labor of the whole population. It is as if each one of us had 100 full-time slaves working for us. Although very few people could afford to have 100 full-time servants, most Americans can and do command the equivalent amount of energy.*

An essential question around which there is considerable disagreement is how long the inheritance of fossil fuels will last? Let us first consider the answer without allowing for the effect of prices on conservation and the search for substitute forms of energy. After this we can consider how prices might change and affect the conclusion.

At a growth rate of consumption of 7% per annum—the approximate average growth rate of fossil fuel consumption from 1900 to 1970—a doubling of consumption occurs every 10 years. The effect of this mathematical fact on the rate at which fossil fuel energy reserves are used up is illustrated in Figure 2.A. With 7% growth and the consequent doubling of consumption in each decade, there is as much energy used in each decade as was used in all history preceding that decade. For example, the series 1, 2, 4, 8, 16, 32, 64, 128, . . . , where each number is double the previous number, has the property that each number in the series is equal to the sum of all the preceding numbers plus 1. It becomes clear that were fossil fuel energy consumption to continue indefinitely along a 7% growth path, it would be necessary to find as much new fossil fuel in each decade as had been found and used in all the previous years on

FIGURE 2.A   Fossil fuel consumption at a 7% per annum growth rate doubles every decade.

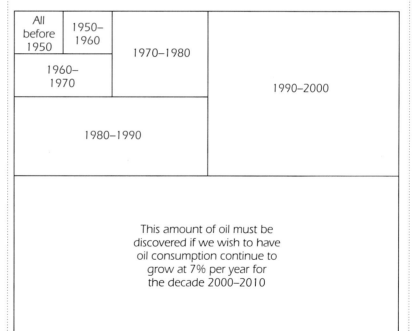

*Robert H. Romer, **Energy—An Introduction to Physics** (San Francisco: W. H. Freeman, 1976), p. 5.

Source: Mary E. Clark, **Ariadne's Thread** (New York: St. Martin's Press, 1989), and A. A. Barlett, "Forgotten Fundamentals of the Energy Crisis," **American Journal of Physics** 9:46, 1978, pp. 876–88.

Example 2.2 (continued)

the planet. Using relatively conservative figures for known and potential energy reserves and an unchanged growth rate of consumption, if such a growth rate were to continue, fossil fuel reserves would be depleted in perhaps only a matter of decades. That is, in a couple of hundred years since the Industrial Revolution, nations would collectively have used up what nature took hundreds of millions of years to produce.

The preceding discussion ignored the effect of the growing shortage of fossil fuels on their price. Economic arguments suggest that were supplies to diminish rapidly, this would drive up fossil fuel prices. As the oil crises of the 1970s have shown, the growth rate of consumption can be reduced substantially by an increase in energy prices via the incentive to conserve. This is shown clearly by the statistics in Figure 2.B. In addition, higher prices brought about by scarcity can greatly increase available supply. This is also clear in Figure 2.B. The increased supply results both from increased search for new sources of fossil fuels and from improved profitability of tapping sources of supply that were considered too costly at lower energy prices. Higher energy prices also greatly increase the incentive to look for and develop alternatives to fossil fuels. By means of these various routes of conservation, increased fossil fuel output, and search for alternatives, the problem of fossil fuel depletion is deferred. Indeed,

FIGURE 2.B   Proven oil reserves have risen and consumption has leveled off.

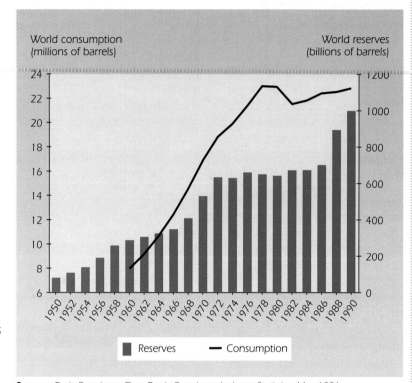

Source: Basic Petroleum Data Book, Petroleum Industry Statistics, May 1991

The oil price increases of the 1970s led to both a leveling of oil consumption and the discovery of new reserves. That is, high oil prices reduced demand and increased future

to the extent that higher fossil fuel prices increase incentives to search for and develop alternative sources of energy, the problem may be deferred indefinitely.

It must be admitted that without conservation and success in finding alternatives, economic development of the populous countries of Asia and Africa, were it to take a similar form as that in North America and Europe with extensive use of automobiles, air conditioning, home heating, electrical appliances, and energy-

intensive methods of production, would result in a major energy crisis, far worse than in the 1970s. In other words, the energy problem remains highly controversial. The controversy hinges in part on the extent to which economic forces could help to solve the problem.

Source: Mary E. Clark, **Ariadne's Thread** (New York: St. Martin's Press, 1989), and A. A. Barlett, "Forgotten Fundamentals of the Energy Crisis," **American Journal of Physics** 9:46, 1978, pp. 876–88.

An increase in the labor force also shifts the production possibilities curve upward and to the right, although the larger feasible outputs from a larger labor force do not necessarily mean more consumption per person. Only if total output expands by more than the number of people is there more for each person to consume.

It should be clear that however far the production possibilities curve moves outward, whether from technological advance or as a result of an increase in available supplies of factors of production, there is still an opportunity cost of producing more of any particular product in terms of producing some other product. That is, whatever the position of the production possibilities curve, the downward slope from left to right means there is scarcity, that is, a need to forgo some product to have more of something else.

Increases in supplies of factors of production shift the production possibilities curve upward and to the right. However, there always remains an opportunity cost of one product versus another.

SCARCITY: THE PERSPECTIVE OF AN INDIVIDUAL

The Need to Choose Between Alternatives

A need to choose between alternatives faces individuals within a nation as well as the nation as a whole. That is, individuals face scarcity and a consequent need to make choices just as do nations. In the case of individuals, scarcity means that if they buy more of one item, they can afford less of something else. This means that buying more of any item involves an opportunity cost.

Consider an individual choosing between buying compact discs (CDs) costing $10 each and books costing $40 each. Each book purchased means forgoing 4 CDs, and each CD purchased means forgoing one-quarter of a book. That is, assuming that these are the only products between which one can choose, the opportunity cost of a book is four CDs, and the opportunity cost of a CD is one-quarter of a book. More generally, the opportunity cost of any product is the amount of the next most preferred alternative product that would have been bought.

To an individual, the opportunity cost of buying any product is the amount of the next most preferred alternative that would have been bought.

Table 2.1 describes the scarcity problem involving CDs and books. The table assumes that a budget of $200 has been allocated to the two products. The top

TABLE 2.1

For an individual to have more of one product, he or she must forgo having some other product.

ATTAINABLE COMBINATIONS WITH $200 BUDGET (CDs = $10, BOOKS = $40)	
CDs	**BOOKS**
20	0
16	1
12	2
8	3
4	4
0	5

If the consumer allocates $200 to CDs and books, and CDs cost $10 and books cost $40, the consumer can buy 20 CDs and zero books if all the budget is spent on CDs. The consumer can buy 5 books and zero CDs if all the budget is spent on books. The consumer also can buy combinations of CDs and books between these extremes. For example, the $200 budget purchases 12 CDs and 2 books.

row of the table shows that if the entire budget is spent on CDs, 20 can be purchased, but of course, there is nothing left for buying books. The bottom row of the table shows that if the entire budget is spent on books, 5 can be purchased, but of course, nothing remains for buying CDs. Various intermediate combinations are also attainable, as shown in the table. By going down the table from top to bottom it is apparent that each extra book means giving up 4 CDs. That is, the opportunity cost of books is constant at 4 CDs per book. Working up the table from bottom to top shows that each extra 4 CDs involves an opportunity cost of 1 book, or one-quarter of a book per CD.

The feasible combinations in Table 2.1 are plotted graphically in Figure 2.3. The figure shows that the attainable or feasible combinations lie along a straight line. Points in the shaded region interior to the line are also attainable, but points beyond the line are not. If all the budget is allocated to the two products, one of the combinations along the line must be chosen.

The reason the attainable combinations for an individual lie along a straight line is that each individual can trade off *consumption* of one product for the other at a rate determined by the product prices; in the example, this is 4 CDs per book, whatever the number of books and CDs purchased. Recall that for a nation as a whole the trade-off between *producing* different products is along a curve, the production possibilities curve; see Figure 2.1. The curvature of the production possibilities curve is the result of different quality factors of production. This is an important difference between the nature of opportunity costs facing an individual and a nation.

The attainable combinations of products facing an individual lie along a straight line.

The Effect of Changing Prices

If CD and book prices increase in the same proportion, for example, by 25% to $12.50 per CD and $50 per book, the opportunity costs of books in terms of CDs, and of CDs in terms of books, are not changed. That is, each book still involves forgoing 4 CDs, and each CD involves forgoing one-quarter of a book. The unchanged opportunity costs mean that the slope of the line representing attainable combinations also remains unchanged. This is illustrated in Figure 2.4, which is based on Table 2.2. on page 37. The figure shows attainable combinations with a budget of $200 and prices of $12.50 per CD and $50 per book. These attainable combinations are the points along the solid black line. This line has the same slope as that of the line of feasible combinations with CD prices of $10 and book prices of $40, shown in Figure 2.4 as a dashed black line.

When CD and book prices change differently, there is a change in opportunity costs and in the slope of the line of feasible combinations. For example, if CD prices remain at $10 and book prices increase to $50, the opportunity cost of a book increases to 5 CDs, and the attainable combinations line, shown by the solid blue line in Figure 2.4, becomes steeper.

This example illustrates that opportunity costs involved in individuals' buying decisions depend on **relative prices,** that is, on one price relative to another. Opportunity costs do not depend on **absolute prices,** that is, on the dollar level of prices. When both prices increase by the same amount, there is no change in the opportunity costs.

It might seem that an individual could try to avoid having to lose some alternative opportunities by working harder and increasing the total amount available to

Opportunity costs of one product in terms of another depend on relative *prices, not* absolute *prices.*

FIGURE 2.3   Attainable combinations of purchases with a fixed
budget lie along a downward-sloping line.

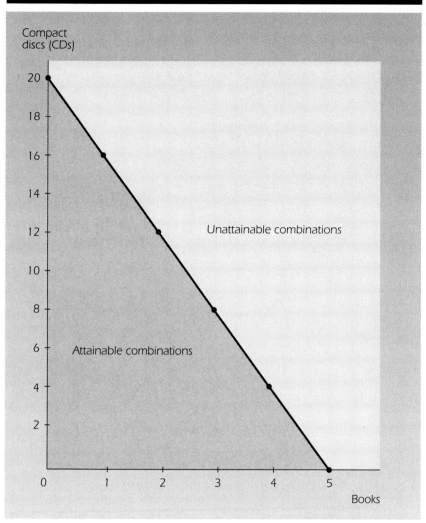

When we plot the attainable combinations of products as shown in Table 2.1, they fall
on a straight line. The slope of this line, which is the height of the line divided by its
base, is the opportunity cost of a book in terms of forgone CDs.

spend. However, even if, for example, a person buys a new car by working
harder, something is still being forgone, namely the leisure time that is lost by
spending more time and effort at work. This is still an opportunity cost.
Opportunity cost is the inevitable cost of scarcity of incomes and time. The ubiquitous nature of opportunity cost is behind the popular statement of economists,
"There is no such thing as a free lunch." This means that every decision involves
an opportunity cost in terms of what else we might have done, whether this be
with time, money, education, choice of career, or vacation.

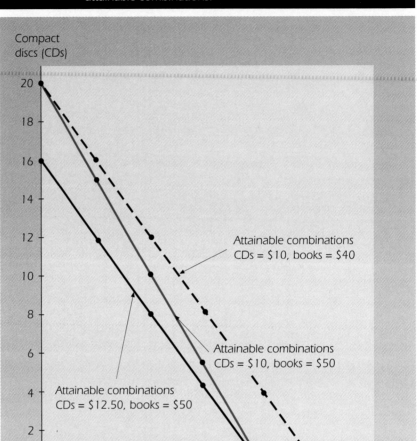

FIGURE 2.4   Only relative price changes alter the slope of the line of attainable combinations.

When prices increase in the same proportion, the slope of the line of attainable combinations is not changed, and hence opportunity costs are not changed. For example, when CD prices go from $10 to $12.50 and book prices go from $40 to $50, the line of attainable combinations shifts to the left but retains the same slope. Only different proportional changes in prices affect the slope of the line of attainable combinations. For example, if CD prices are unchanged at $10 but book prices increase from $40 to $50, the line becomes steeper. This reflects the increase in opportunity cost of books in terms of forgone CDs.

TABLE 2.2

Relative not absolute, prices determine the opportunity cost of one product in terms of another.

ATTAINABLE COMBINATIONS WITH $200 BUDGET			
CDs = $12.50, BOOKS = $50		CDs = $10, BOOKS = $50	
CDs	BOOKS	CDs	BOOKS
16	0	20	0
12	1	15	1
8	2	10	2
4	3	5	3
0	4	0	4

If prices increase in the same proportion, the amount of one good forgone to have more of the other good is not affected. For example, the combinations of CDs and books on the left of the table involve an opportunity cost of four CDs per book, just as in Table 2.1, even though in this table prices of both products are 25 percent higher than in Table 2.1. When prices change by a different amount, as on the right of this table, opportunity costs are changed. In particular, with book prices increasing but not CD prices, the opportunity cost of a book in terms of forgone CDs is increased.

PRODUCTION AND ALLOCATION DECISIONS

The Perspective of the Nation

The fact that there are limits on what can be produced in a nation means that a mechanism is required to determine how much of different products is to be produced. For example, a mechanism is required to determine how much wheat to grow and how many automobiles to manufacture. The need for such a mechanism is, of course, the result of scarcity, which for a nation as a whole can be characterized by a production possibilities curve. In terms of the production possibilities curve in Figure 2.1, the mechanism required is one that determines where along the curve the economy should operate, that is, how much wheat versus how many automobiles should be produced. More generally, we need a mechanism to determine the outputs of toothbrushes, spectacles, pencils, haircuts, houses, and all the other goods and services people purchase.

*Under the price
system, prices are
determined in markets
according to supply
and demand.*

In economies such as those of the United States, Canada, Japan, and Britain, the determination of how much of each product to produce is achieved via the **price system.** The price system involves product prices being determined by the willingness of buyers to purchase products relative to the willingness of suppliers to make products available. Buyers and sellers interact in **markets,** the domain over which the exchange of products between buyers (or demanders) and sellers (or suppliers) takes place. A market could be a specific location in which buyers and sellers meet face to face, as in a street market or on the floor of a stock exchange. However, it could be that buyers and sellers do not meet but communicate by telephone, telex, and so on, as in most wholesale commodity markets. Some markets occur within a relatively contained geographic area, such as a fresh fish or produce market in a town or city, while other markets are global, such as the oil market or the foreign exchange market. What is common to all markets is that buyers exchange with sellers, and via the strength of buyers' interests and the willingness of sellers to supply products, product prices are determined.

Those buyers who are willing and able to pay enough to induce sellers to make their products available are able to obtain what they are seeking. Sellers are willing to make products available if this is profitable. If, for example, there is an increase in people's willingness to buy a product, with this being manifest in their willingness to pay a higher price, sellers are likely to make more available; higher prices mean higher profits. In this way, buyers' desires for products, as reflected in the prices they are willing to pay, are fulfilled via the price system.

The price system can be viewed as a mechanism telling suppliers what and how much to make, with the signal being the price. The price system also can be viewed as a mechanism for sharing whatever is supplied among the many people who might want to buy it. In particular, prices adjust until they are such that buyers (demanders) are willing to buy just the amounts that sellers (suppliers) are willing to make available. The various aspects of the price system are discussed in Part II of this book.

The price system is only one way to determine how much of different products to produce and who should receive them. The few remaining socialist countries do a substantial amount of their determination of production and allocation of goods and services according to **commands and controls,** that is, according to directions issued by their governments. Producers are told how much to make, and buyers are told how much they can purchase, usually with ration tickets needed to make the purchases. However, more and more production and allocation decisions in socialist countries are being made via the price system, as is evidenced by the reforms in presocialist countries in eastern Europe and in the independent republics of the former USSR.[7] Similarly, the market-oriented economies of the United States, Canada, western Europe, Japan, and so on are not exclusively capitalistic but are also **mixed economies** in that some determination of production is according to the price system and some is according to directions or inducements of governments. For example, in the United States, the provision of elementary and secondary education, roads and highways, and so on is determined by some level of government.

*Most economies today
are mixed economies,
using both the price
system and comands
and controls.*

---

[7] As Example 2.3 explains, the price system emerges naturally and flourishes when it is unhindered by state planners.

Example   2.3

DOING WHAT COMES NATURALLY

The capitalist system has been defended on grounds of morality and justice. Among the most cited such defenses is that of Ayn Rand, who said, "The moral justification of capitalism lies in the fact that it is the only system consonant with man's rational nature, that it protects man's survival **qua** *man, and that its ruling principle is: justice."* While many disagree with such a heady claim, few question the natural tendency of humankind toward capitalism. Consider, for example, the following article from* **The Wall Street Journal**. *It explains how capitalism has survived and flourished in and around the Chinese city of Wenzhou (pronounced "one-joe").*

Communist leaders in Beijing are wringing their hands over how to revive rotting Soviet-style state factories. But while they agonize over how best to blend central planning and free markets into a "socialist commodity economy," the entrepreneurial folk of Wenzhou don't waste any time in theory. They just do it.

Isolated along the seacoast near Taiwan, and long paid little heed by the central government, Wenzhou has become one of China's thriving hubs of private enterprise. Its citizens have found their own secret to success: Act Chinese—as in work hard, innovate and try to make money. Without having left China, they pursue business ambitions in the manner of millions of Chinese who have scattered across the globe

in the past 150 years, whether to Malaysia, Peru, Paris or San Francisco.

The typical Wenzhou living room doubles as either a factory or shop. Family members and employees paid by piece-work often toil past midnight, cobbling shoes, sewing together clothes, or providing haircuts, laundry and other services. Profits get plowed into bigger stores, fancier restaurants, more-efficient factories or other businesses.

All this is done without outside investment. While the economies of China's other boom towns are fueled by foreign capital and export markets, Wenzhou's entrepreneurs use their own savings and target domestic markets. . . .

"We've always had to depend on ourselves," says Xu Shunsheng, head of the city's Private Business Management Department. He thinks the rest of China should do likewise. "A few years from now, when you look back and ask why is the Chinese economy so alive, it will be because of private enterprise," he says.

Wenzhou started taking off in the early 1980s when Chinese leader Deng Xiaoping closed communes and sanctioned small-scale private business. Unencumbered by big state factories, Wenzhou flourished fast, so fast that economists now call the process of revival through private enterprise the "Wenzhou model."

The city is so entrepreneurial that the main form of transport isn't public buses but 3,000 privately owned Polish Fiat cabs that swarm the streets day and night. Hop in and you are apt to find a driver looking to cut a deal. "You don't know where I can buy some

modern lamps from Hong Kong?" a driver asks two foreign passengers. "My brother has a factory and we need some new models to copy."

Stop at a three-table sidewalk café and you discover a family sideline. The food is dished out by Lin Xiao, who during the day works for China's airline. The site is rented from the school where his father teaches. "Mom was sitting home at night with nothing to do so we decided to open this café for her," says Mr. Lin, whose girlfriend serves the sodas.

These days Wenzhou is jubilant. Its entrepreneurs—forced to lie low after the 1989 Tiananmen massacre and hard-liner resurgence—were emboldened anew . . . by Mr. Deng. Touring south China, the aging patriarch lashed out at ideologies and declared, in essence, that it is all right to use capitalism to save socialism.

Wenzhou needs no prodding. Yang Jiaxing kneels on the floor of his office, scanning blueprints for an office tower he wants to build. In 1986 Mr. Yang founded the first private bank in China since the Communist era began—not bothering to get prior authorization. Now he is dusting off some old schemes and dreams. "We want to do stock and bond trading, property development, whatever we can get [the central bank] to approve," he says. . . .

*Ayn Rand, **Capitalism: The Unknown Ideal** *(New York: New American Library, 1966).*

Source: *James McGregor, "Born Capitalists: Free Enterprise Comes Naturally to Residents of Wenzhou, China,"* **The Wall Street Journal**, *August 13, 1992, pp. A1, A10. Reprinted by permission of The Wall Street Journal, © 1992 Dow Jones & Company, Inc. All Rights Reserved Worldwide.*

According to Winston Churchill, "The inherent vice of capitalism is the unequal sharing of blessings; the inherent virtue of socialism is the equal sharing of miseries." This is only a slightly less balanced version of the anonymous quip that "under capitalism man exploits man; under socialism it's just the opposite." The reality is that both capitalism and socialism must deal with self-interest, although they do so in different ways. Economists who favor the price system, which is also called the **free-enterprise** or **laissez-faire system,** argue that an advantage of the price system is that nobody needs to decide what should be produced and to whom the production should be allocated. Pro free-enterprise economists also argue that the price system provides better incentives for people to work hard and be efficient and therefore also provides more goods and services than would be provided by a centrally controlled allocation. (In terms of the production possibilities curve, pro free-enterprise economists argue that under the free-enterprise system the position of the curve is further out from the origin, involving the output of more goods and services from the same factors of production than with commands and controls.)

The Perspective of the Individual

The scarcity problem faced by an individual is the result of the individual's income being limited. This makes it necessary to decide how much to buy of each of the many different products competing for the individual's attention. In terms of the line of attainable combinations shown in, for example, Figure 2.3, the individual's problem is which particular combination of CDs and books to purchase, that is, where along the line to choose to be. More generally, the problem of an individual is to decide on the combination to select with a limited income: how much bread, meat, gasoline, toothpaste, and so on. As Example 2.4 explains, people do expend substantial effort in deciding what to buy.

In free-enterprise, market-oriented economies, each individual makes choices according to her or his own individual **preferences** or **tastes.** In the context of our example of CDs versus books, those who like music buy CDs, and those who enjoy reading buy books. As we have just seen, in a command and control system, products are allocated by the government. This means people receive what the government thinks they should have rather than what they individually prefer. While the government might claim that its allocation is based on people's different "needs" so as to be "fair," the possibility exists for allocation to be affected by the influence and contacts people have with those making allocation decisions. Indeed, it was the abuse of influence in many eastern European economies, with lavish lifestyles among Communist Party members while ordinary people were forced to line up for meager allocations, that played an important role in the downfall of communism between 1989 and 1991.

In free-enterprise economies people choose between products according to their own preferences.

Example   2.4

CHOOSING CAREFULLY

People have always "watched their pennies" when making choices between alternatives. As the following article from **The Wall Street Journal** *explains, "penny pinching" is a fact of life even in America.*

Judging by the cash-register receipts at many supermarkets, you would think Americans had stopped eating. . . . Grocery shoppers are still buying, of course, but they are minding what they spend on each trip to the store. They are scrimping on everything from cereal to cigarettes by switching to cheaper brands or buying private-label products. Consumers seem eager to shop around, routinely driving miles out of their way to save a few dollars by buying food at warehouse clubs or discount drugstores. . . .

"There are so many bargains around you feel like a fool if you don't get a deal," says Judith Langer, a consumer-behavior specialist in New York.

Retailers call this "value-consciousness." But the truth is that price has become the food shopper's passion. Forget about convenience, health or the environment. In a recent poll, 72% of supermarket shoppers said prices were their most important consideration, according to Mona Doyle, president of Consumer

Network Inc., a Philadelphia firm that surveys shoppers. Only 60% said they considered freshness as critical. . . .

[A] host of new competitors benefited from consumers' sharper focus on price. Warehouse stores such as Wal-Mart Stores Inc.'s Sam's Club and Price Co.'s Price Club; deep-discount drug stores like those of Drug Emporium Inc.; and mass merchandisers including the Wal-Mart chain, Kmart Corp. and Dayton Hudson Corp's Target Stores Inc. all stocked up on the foodstuffs that were once the exclusive purview of the neighborhood grocer. Even some Toys "R" Us stores now sell snacks. . . .

[S]upermarkets are scrambling to get their carts rolling again. Many stores now routinely offer to credit consumers two or three times the face value of manufacturers' coupons. Full-scale price wars have broken out in the Texas cities of Houston and Dallas and in Dayton, Ohio, and Memphis, Tenn. More are likely to follow. . . .

Uncertainty about the economy has made Dorothy Scheppelman more conscious than ever about her grocery budget. The 70-year-old retiree draws up a shopping list and then compares prices in several grocery stores. She goes to a Sam's warehouse several times a year to stock up on household staples. At a

Kroger store in Clarksville, Ind., Mrs. Scheppelman eyes a large "family" pack of meat, though she is only shopping for two. "I've always been careful, but I've gotten even more careful," she says. . . .

What really rattles industry executives, though, is that even relatively affluent shoppers now get a thrill from bargain food shopping. Once a month, Blair Brewster, an entrepreneur who lives in New York's affluent Brooklyn Heights, loads his two kids into his car and drives 45 minutes to the Price Club warehouse store in Edison, N.J. "It's a real outing," he says. "You can go shopping there with your kids and get a pretzel and a soda for $1."

Mr. Brewster has plenty of company in the colossal stores, where the decor typically features concrete floors and industrial metal shelving. Only a few years ago, nontraditional stores accounted for an insignificant percentage of total grocery sales, but their share has risen to 6.2% and could double over the next 10 years, according to a recent study commissioned by the Food Marketing Institute.

Source: Kathleen Deveny, "Stingy Shoppers Stir Up Supermarkets," **The Wall Street Journal**, September 22, 1992, p. B1. Reprinted by permission of The Wall Street Journal, © 1992 Dow Jones & Company, Inc. All Rights Reserved Worldwide.

Thomas Robert Malthus
(1766–1834)

SCARCITY: A MATTER OF CONTINUOUS INTEREST
SINCE CREATION

Scholars in theology can cite numerous references to economic matters in the Bible and in biblical commentaries, tracing the very origin of scarcity, which is at the center of the study of economics, to the first book of the Old Testament. According to the story of creation in the Book of Genesis, in the beginning there was no scarcity and, therefore, no "economic problem." Rather, the Garden of Eden contained everything its inhabitants could possibly want. The Bible tells us that scarcity, and the "economic problem" that accompanies it, resulted from what happened in the Garden of Eden. In particular, immediately after being tempted by the "fruit of the tree of knowledge of good and evil," Adam and Eve are told, "cursed is the ground for thy sake; in toil shalt thou eat of it all the days of thy life. . . . In the sweat of thy face shalt thou eat bread" (Genesis 3, 17). That is, according to the biblical account of creation, the very first act after creation was the creation of the "economic prob-

lem." Scarcity and scholarly interest in it have very early roots.

Biblical scholars and theologians have maintained an interest in the matter of scarcity through the ages. One of the most important inquiries into the matter was that of the English cleric, Thomas Malthus. In **An Essay on the Principle of Populations** (1798), Malthus attributed scarcity to the growth of the human population relative to the growth in the amount of food the planet could produce. In particular, Malthus argued that populations grow according to **geometric progression**.[8] For example, if each man and woman have four surviving children, the population doubles each generation. This is shown in Table 2.3. It is worth noting in

---

[8] In a geometric progression, each number is a constant multiple of the previous number in the series. For example, 2, 4, 8, 16, 32, 64, . . . is a geometric progression with each number twice the previous number.

Thomas Malthus thought the population would expand to the point of bare subsistence.

GENERATION NUMBER	CURRENT POPULATION	FOOD OUTPUT
1	2	2
2	4	4
3	8	6
4	16	8
5	32	10
6	64	12
7	128	14
8	256	16
9	512	18
10	1,024	20

According to Thomas Malthus, population grows according to a geometric progression, while food output grows according to an arithmetic progression. Were this to continue indefinitely, population growth would run into the limit of subsistence.

the table that the population at each stage exceeds by 2 the combined population of all previous generations. For example, in generation 10, the population of 1024 is 2 larger than the sum of all the people who have been alive before this generation.[9]

Malthus argued that while population growth follows a geometric progression, agricultural output follows an **arithmetic progression**.[10] As Table 2.3 makes clear, were population growth and agricultural output to behave indefinitely in the ways Malthus claimed, food output would eventually fall behind the number of mouths to feed, making famine an inescapable destiny. With plenty of examples in nature of animal and plant populations expanding to the limits of their environments, Malthus predicted that humankind would face a similar fate, expanding until those who survived could merely subsist; any growth in agricultural output that put people above subsistence levels would result in a population spurt that forced them back to subsistence.[11]

While agricultural development of the New World, the introduction of new seed strains, and increased use of fertilizers, pesticides, and herbicides have so far prevented the realization of the worst of Malthus' predictions, the connection between population and scarcity remains part of theological debate. For example, a central argument in debates over birth control involves the conflict between the size of the population and the scarcity due to limited production possibilities of the planet.

Scarcity also interests biologists. Not only does scarcity of resources facing a species affect the **steady-state population** of that species—how many can survive with the given, constant resource supply—but scarcity also plays a role in evolution.[12] The fact that only a few, favored variations survive is because they must compete for resources. For example, giraffes with longer necks would not have been at much of an advantage were it not for the scarcity of leaves at lower levels. The more scarcity is faced, the fewer variations can survive, and the more rapid is the rate of natural selection.

Science and engineering are directly involved with scarcity. This is true not only because science has its own scarcity law, **the law of conservation of matter,** but also because scientific and engineering endeavors involve efforts to improve efficiency. That is, science and engineering are directed at moving the production frontier outward to reduce the scarcity problem, subject, of course, to the invincible law that governs conversion. (Production is, of course, a process of conversion.) As we shall see in Chapter 16, it is largely via the development and building of newer and better means of production that living

---

[9] The consequence of doubling is also met in Example 2.2 in the context of energy consumption.

[10] In an arithmetic progression, each number is increased by a constant amount from the previous number. For example, 2, 4, 6, 8, 10, 12, . . . is an arithmetic progression with each number being the previous number plus 2.

[11] The inevitability of this awful plight prompted Thomas Carlyle to dub economics the "dismal science," a label that has stuck.

[12] This is discussed more extensively in the Crossing Bridges section concerning competition in Chapter 7.

standards have advanced. Indeed, the economist John Maynard Keynes believed science and technology would eventually bring an end to scarcity. In a highly optimistic and widely read article, "Economic Possibilities for Our Grandchildren," published in 1930, Keynes wrote

> I draw the conclusion that, assuming no important wars and no important increase in population, the **economic problem** may be solved, or be at least within sight of solution, within a hundred years. This means that the economic problem is not—if we look into the future—**the permanent problem of the human race**.[13]

With such a marvelous prospect, Keynes was led to say

> Thus for the first time since his creation man will be faced with his real, his permanent problem—how to use his freedom from pressing economic cares, how to occupy the leisure, which science and compound interest have won for him, to live wisely and agreeably and well.[14]

Keynes' optimism was based on the prospect of great advances in productivity from substantial increases in the stock of capital and on the view, widespread among economists in the first half of the twentieth century, that there were no binding constraints on the other factors of production. In particular, Keynes did not consider the constraint imposed by exhaustible resources such as fossil fuels used to drive the capital that would solve the economic problem. Finally, as he did explicitly mention, Keynes was assuming no important war or population increase, both of which turned out to be incorrect; since Keynes made his optimistic projections in 1930, the global population has almost tripled, and as recently as 1955 the population was only about one-half of what it is today.[15]

The energy crises of the 1970s led to widespread discussion among scientists, politicians, and others about the possibility that by exhausting the supply of energy, people would face an eventual decline in living standards.[16] Of course, as we explain in Example 2.2, not everybody agrees with this dire prediction. For example, many economists argue that alternative supplies of energy will be discovered and developed. Indeed, economists claim that a growing shortage of fossil fuel energy will cause higher energy prices, thereby stimulating the search for alternatives. For this reason, many economists argue that technology will continue to shift the production possibilities curve outward. Others, while accepting that the price mechanism will induce a search for alternatives, do not feel the search for alternative energy sources can be counted on and consequently believe that the production possibilities curve will cease to shift outward and may even shift backward.

The reasons given for the production possibilities curve ceasing to shift outward or even shifting backward are not limited to the possibility of running out of nonrenewable energy. It has been argued by scientists in various fields that there is further reason in the nature of the technologies that have been used in pushing out the production possibilities frontier.[17] For example, atmospheric and bioresource scientists have warned of the consequences of global warming caused by burning fossil fuels for future output. Were it to occur, global warming would cause the ocean levels to rise as the ice caps melt. This would flood coastal farmland and urban areas, reducing agricultural and industrial output. At the same time, the changes in climate would cause damage to crops from increases in temperatures and shifts in rainfall. Added to this might be infestations from insects that prosper in higher temperatures and which may take advantage of the weaker crops.

---

[13] John Maynard Keynes, **Essays in Persuasion** (London: Macmillan, 1933). (Emphases in original.)

[14] Keynes, **op. cit.** In light of the biblical account of the Garden of Eden, perhaps Keynes should have said "for the first time since [just after] his creation. . . ."

[15] **World Population Prospects, 1990** (Washington: United Nations, 1991).

---

[16] See, for example, E. Meadows et al., **The Limits to Growth: A Report for the Club of Rome's Project on the Predicament of Mankind** (New York: Universe Books, 1972).

[17] See Meadows, **op. cit.** See also, Mary E. Clark, **Ariadne's Thread** (New York: St. Martin's Press, 1989).

The interrelations between the use of raw materials, environmental degradation, and economic growth have been studied via computer simulations involving researchers from numerous fields working together. The most discussed of the simulations is that of the so-called Club of Rome.[18] This study attracted attention because whatever assumptions its authors made about resource depletion, technological advance, and population growth, the model predicted catastrophe. For example, when it was assumed that no more major resource discoveries would be made, the computer simulations predicted eventual economic collapse. Alternatively, when it was assumed that extra resources would be discovered, the simulations predicted that growth in population and environmental destruction accompanying the exploitation of these resources would result in catastrophe. On the other hand, when it was assumed that rapid improvements in technology would be made that would overcome the problems of exhaustible resources and of destroying the environment, the simulations predicted that population growth would eventually outstrip the ability of the planet to feed the population. That is, the computer projections gave frighteningly pessimistic forecasts no matter what assumptions were made.

Forecasting is, of course, a precarious business, and events do have a habit of unfolding in ways that make forecasters look foolish. For example, in the mid-nineteenth century it was forecast that by the end of the twentieth century many large cities would have been long buried under meters of horse manure, a prediction that did not foresee the arrival of the combustion engine. Predictions of the aforementioned research therefore remain controversial. So far, the dire predictions from this research have proven to be premature. Some people doubt that the predictions will be any more prophetic than those of the manure crisis and expect the production possibilities curve to continue to move outward.

> *. . . Malthus attributed scarcity to the growth of the human population relative to the growth in the amount of food the planet could produce.*

[18] Meadows et al., **op. cit.**

SUMMARY

1. Economics is concerned with the study of scarcity of goods and services. Anything for which having more of it means having less of something else is considered scarce.

2. It is scarcity of factors of production—land, raw materials, labor, and capital—that causes scarcity of outputs.

3. What is produced for immediate enjoyment constitutes consumption, while what is produced to help add to future output constitutes investment. Because of the limited availability of factors of production, it is necessary to reduce consumption in order to increase investment.

4. The feasible combinations of outputs that can be produced in an economy can be described by a production possibilities curve.

5. The production possibilities curve shows that in order for a nation to produce more of one product, it is necessary to produce less of something else. This is so because if more factors of production are engaged in making one product, there are fewer factors of production for making other products.

6. The amount of the most preferred alternative that is forgone in order to have more of a particular product is called the opportunity cost of that particular product.

7. Economic growth, which means an outward shift in the production possibilities curve, can result from technological advances or increases in supplies of the factors of production. Economic growth does not eliminate the opportunity cost of having more of any particular product.

8. Individuals also face an opportunity cost when they buy more of a product. The opportunity cost is the amount of the most preferred alternative product that would otherwise have been bought.

9. Opportunity costs are faced by individuals because of limits on what they have available to spend.

10. The opportunity cost to an individual of one product in terms of another depends on relative prices, not on absolute prices.

11. In free-enterprise economies, the choice of which goods to produce is determined by the price system. The price system involves allowing market prices to signal sellers what they should make and sell.

12. The alternative to the price system is a command and control system, where production and consumption decisions are made by government.

QUESTIONS AND PROBLEMS

1. What can you think of that is not scarce in the sense you can have it in any location, as much as you like, without having to pay or give up something else? (After air, it gets difficult, doesn't it? And what about air deep down in a mine or clean air in urban areas?)

2. What are some of the competing objectives faced by governments, and in what sense are the incomes of governments limited?

3. Is there an opportunity cost of protecting the spotted owl which lives in old-growth forests in the western United States?

4. How does the opportunity cost change as you move along the following two production possibilities curves?

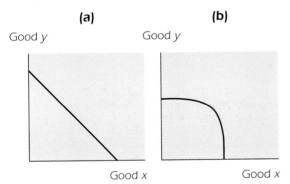

5. How is a production possibilities curve between two products using similar inputs likely to differ from a production possibilities curve between two products using completely different inputs?

6. What is the cost of your decision to study economics?

7. In what way(s) might today's growth involve an opportunity cost in terms of the future standard or quality of living?

8. What is being forgone when you go out to eat a lunch for which you do not have to pay?

9. Draw the combination of attainable purchases of food and rental accommodations for a person spending $1000 per month. Assume that food costs $2 per pound and that apartments of different size rent for $1 per square foot per month. What happens to the line of attainable combinations if the amount spent and the price of food and rent all double? What does this example tell us about what really matters for the standard of living?

10. Why does the production possibilities curve for the nation slope as it does in Figure 2.1, whereas the line of attainable combinations facing an individual in Figure 2.3 is a straight line?

CHAPTER 3

· · · · · · · · ·
· · · · · · · · ·
· · · · · · · · ·
· · · · · · · · ·
· · · · · · · Gains from Specialization and Trade
· · · · · · · · ·
· · · · · · · · ·

A professor is a person who learns more and more about less and less until he knows everything about nothing. On the other hand, a politician is a person who learns less and less about more and more until he knows nothing about everything.

Anonymous

Key Concepts

Gains from division of labor; absolute advantage versus comparative advantage; gains from free trade; terms of trade; costs of trade

THE GAINS FROM SPECIALIZATION: DOMESTIC TRADE

Perhaps one of the most remarkable features of a modern capitalistic industrial economy is how it provides for our varied desires for food, clothing, housing, entertainment, education, and so on despite a very high degree of specialization of labor. We are able to put food on our tables, clothes on our bodies, roofs over our heads, and gas in our tanks, even though most of us are engaged in only one activity, repairing cars, serving food, selling shoes, or writing economics textbooks.

Modern economies are based on a **system of exchange** in which people provide their labor and skills for money and then use this money to purchase things other people have made. Because people receive money for what they sell and

48

Example 3.1   PINNING DOWN THE SPECIALIZATION GAINS

In his great classic book, **An Inquiry into the Nature and Causes of the Wealth of Nations,** (1776), Adam Smith dealt elegantly with a vast number of economic topics that occupy us today, some 200 years later. Smith's account of the gains from specialization in a pin factory in Lanark, Scotland, is still hard to beat.

[A] workman not educated to this business . . . nor acquainted with the use of machinery employed in it . . . could scarce, perhaps, with his utmost industry, make one pin a day, and certainly could not make twenty. But in the way in which this business is now carried on, not only the whole work is a peculiar trade, but it is divided into a number of branches, of which the greater part are likewise peculiar trades. One man draws out the wire, another straightens it, a thirds cuts it, a fourth points it, a fifth grinds it to the top for receiving the head; to make the head requires two or three distinct operations; to put it on, is a peculiar business, to whiten the pins is another; it is even a trade by itself to put them into the paper; and the important business of making a pin is, in this manner, divided into about eighteen distinct operations, which, in some manufactories, are all performed by distinct hands, though in others the same man will sometimes perform two or three of them. I have seen a small manufactory of this kind where ten men only were employed, and where some of them consequently performed two or three distinct operations. . . . [T]hey could, when they exerted themselves, make among them about twelve pounds of pins in a day [or] upward of forty-eight thousand pins in a day.

Source: Adam Smith, **An Inquiry into the Nature and Causes of the Wealth of Nations** (London: W. Strahan and T. Caddel, 1776), pp. 4–5.

then use money for what they buy, money is called a **medium of exchange.** The system of exchange, using money as a medium of exchange and markets to allocate scarce goods and services, allows people to specialize in jobs they can do well. Through specialization, people enjoy a far higher standard of living than if everybody had to be self-sufficient. Specialization also means a far greater variety of goods and services available for people to buy.

The specialization of tasks with people doing different, distinct jobs is called the **division of labor.** There are a number of reasons why the division of labor has increased the standard of living. Adam Smith identified several of these in his classic work, *An Inquiry into the Nature and Causes of the Wealth of Nations* (1776), often referred to simply as *The Wealth of Nations.*[1] Smith used an example of a pin factory in Lanark, Scotland, where production was divided into 18 distinct tasks (see Example 3.1). As a result of the specialization, *average* output per worker was 4800 pins per day compared with fewer than 20 pins if each worker had to perform all the operations. Today, the specialization of tasks has been carried to such a point that in a modern automobile factory production line, for example, a worker might specialize in hanging right-hand doors or installing headlights.

One of the sources of increased productivity from specialization that Adam Smith described is learning by doing. If all of us had to spend our time being

> Money serves as a medium of exchange and allows people to specialize in what they do well. This specialization of labor has substantially improved the standard of living and the variety of goods and services people can buy.

> Specialization of tasks is called the division of labor. The division of labor has substantially increased output.

---

[1] Adam Smith, *An Inquiry into the Nature and Causes of the Wealth of Nations* (London: W. Strahan and T. Caddel, 1776).

self-sufficient—growing wheat, tending cattle, repairing automobiles, baking bread, making clothes, and so on—we would not have an opportunity to learn how to do any of them well. Each of us would be a "jack-of-all-trades and master of none." However, by specializing in automobile repair or brain surgery, for example, we acquire particular skills.

Another source of gain from specialization comes from a reduction in lost time when switching between tasks. For example, if we had to change from overalls into operating room clothes and clean up when changing from automobile repair to brain surgery, we would lose valuable time.

A further gain from specialization comes from investment in better machines and education that specialization makes worthwhile by expanding the **scale of production.** For example, if brain surgeons had to spend time repairing their own automobiles, they would have less time for brain surgery. It might not pay them to invest in learning new techniques or in buying expensive brain-scanning equipment. Similarly, if automobile mechanics were repairing fewer automobiles, it might not pay them to invest in computer-assisted diagnostic equipment or in learning how to use such equipment. However, by specializing and expanding utilization of equipment and knowledge, such investments may well be worth making.[2]

> There are gains from division of labor as a result of learning by doing, reduced time lost switching between tasks, and investments made possible by larger-scale production.

Even when there are no advantages from learning by doing, reduced lost time switching between tasks, or investment made possible by an increased scale of production, there is still a gain from specialization from people having different *relative* abilities. We can illustrate this gain by taking an example.

An Example of Specialization Gains

Consider an economy consisting of two people, Albert and Henry.[3] Assume that they can both perform automobile repair and brain surgery equally well, but that Henry is quicker at both. The time taken by each of them to tune a four-cylinder engine and perform a brain operation are shown in Table 3.1. For example, we assume that it takes Albert 8 hours and Henry 2 hours to do a brain operation. We can see from the top two rows of the table that while Henry is faster at both activities, he is a lot faster at brain surgery and only a little faster doing tune-ups. We assume that initially both Albert and Henry divide their working time equally between the two activities.

Despite the fact that Henry is quicker than Albert at tuning automobile engines, he is better off if he reduces the time he spends doing this and spends more time in the operating room doing brain surgery. Similarly, Albert is better off if he spends less time doing brain surgery and more time tuning cars. In order to show this, let us consider what they both earn when not specializing and then ask what

---

[2] The gain from investment in education is a different result of specialization than is learning by doing. Learning by doing results from increased *time* spent at a task when specialization occurs, whereas investment in education is made worthwhile by the increased *scale* of production when specialization occurs.

[3] The gains from specialization in nature and the home have similar origins to those in an economy. See Examples 3.2 and 3.3.

....
TABLE 3.1

Without specialization, both individuals divide their time between different jobs.

	WITHOUT SPECIALIZATION	
	ALBERT	**HENRY**
Hours/brain operation	8	2
Hours/tune-up	2	1.6
Surgery hours/month	80	80
Garage hours/month	80	80
Brain operations	10	40
Tune-ups	40	50
Price/operation	$200	$200
Price/tune-up	$60	$60
Surgery income	$ 2,000	$ 8,000
Garage income	$ 2,400	$ 3,000
Total income	$ 4,400	$11,000

Henry is quicker than Albert at brain surgery and tune-ups but is substantially quicker at brain surgery and only slightly quicker at tune-ups. When not specializing, both work 80 hours at each activity, with Albert doing 10 operations and 40 tune-ups, while Henry does 40 operations and 50 tune-ups. At the assumed amounts paid for these services, Albert earns $2000 from brain surgery and $2400 from tune-ups, a total of $4400 per month. Henry earns $8000 from surgery and $3000 from tune-ups, a total of $11,000 per month.

they could earn if they specialized. Assume that the payments for a brain operation and a tune-up are, respectively, $200 and $60. The relevant numbers are shown in Table 3.1.

Before specializing and with Albert spending 80 hours per month in the operating room and each operation taking 8 hours, Albert is able to perform 10 operations. With Albert spending an additional 80 hours in the garage at 2 hours per tune-up, he can tune 40 cars. On the other hand, with 80 hours spent at each activity, Henry, who takes only 2 hours per brain operation and 1.6 hours per tune-up, can perform 40 operations and tune 50 cars. When these output levels are valued at the assumed payments, we obtain the bottom rows of Table 3.1. We see that Albert receives $2000 for his 10 operations at $200 each and $2400 for his 40 tune-ups at $60 each. This gives Albert a monthly income of $4400. Henry, on the other hand, earns $8000 for the 40 operations he performs and $3000 for the 50 tune-ups, resulting in an income of $11,000 per month.

TABLE 3.2

Both individuals' incomes and the outputs of both products are increased by specialization.

	WITH SPECIALIZATION	
	ALBERT	HENRY
Hours/brain operation	8	2
Hours/tune-up	2	1.6
Surgery hours/month	0	120
Garage hours/month	160	40
Brain operations	0	60
Tune-ups	80	25
Price/operation	$200	$200
Price/tune-up	$60	$60
Surgery income	0	$ 12,000
Garage income	$ 4,800	$ 1,500
Total income	$ 4,800	$13,500

With specialization, Albert spends all his 160 hours tuning engines, while Henry spends 120 hours doing surgery and 40 hours tuning engines. With the same hours per task as without specialization and the same payments per job, both Albert and Henry enjoy higher incomes than without specialization. In particular, Albert earns $4800 compared with the $4400 he earned without specialization, while Henry earns $13,500 compared with the $11,000 he earned without specialization; compare the bottom row of Table 3.2 with the bottom row of Table 3.1. Furthermore, the total output of brain operations increases from 50 to 60 per month, and the total output of tune-ups increases from 90 to 105 per month.

As shown in Table 3.2, after specialization, we assume that Albert devotes all his time to tuning cars, while Henry spends 40 fewer hours tuning cars and spends them instead in the operating room. That is, they both continue working 160 hours per month, but Albert specializes (completely) in automobile tune-ups and Henry specializes (partially) in brain surgery.

After specializing, the number of brain operations performed by Albert is zero—he spends no time at this at all—while the number of tune-ups he does becomes 80; 160 hours is spent doing tune-ups at 2 hours per tune-up. The number of brain operations performed by Henry increases to 60, while the number of tune-ups declines to 25. If we calculate their incomes with these new outputs after specialization, we find Albert's income has increased from $4400 to $4800 per month and Henry's income has increased from $11,000 to $13,500 per month. These incomes

Example   3.2   **A HIVE OF ACTIVITY**

In a laissez-faire economy, individuals select their specializations for their own benefit, not for the benefit of society at large, and yet society as a whole is better off from the specialization that occurs. As the following excerpt explains, the principles governing the choice of specialization, and benefits that derive from it, are little different in nature than they are in an economy.

In the economics of the bumblebee colony, and particularly their organization of foraging, one can perceive the operation of individual motivation, as each individual bee tries to optimize its foraging success. And this success results in the good of the whole colony, as if the individuals were led by an "invisible hand." In this sense a bumblebee hive bears some interesting resemblances to the economic model outlined by Adam Smith in *Wealth of Nations*. Smith proposed that "the uniform, constant, and uninterrupted effort of every man to better his condition, the condition from which public and national, as well as private opulence is originally derived, is generally powerful enough to maintain natural progress of things toward improvement." Smith observed further that "It is not

out of benevolence of the butcher, the brewer, or the baker that we expect their services but out of the care for their own interests." He felt that individual initiative was the most potent force for public good. In the bumblebee society, other things being equal, those colonies whose foragers exercise the most individual initiative in finding and skillfully exploiting the most rewarding flowers will be the ones producing the most new queens and drones.

The allocation of foraging specialties in bumblebees, resulting in the specialization of individuals and consequent advantage to the colony, is also analogous to Smith's concept of specialization in human societies. Smith argued that individuals would specialize only where their labors would generate profits, and these profits would be exchanged (by money or other capital) to the benefit of others in society with other skills. Specialization, in turn, greatly improves productivity, since no one individual then need master all the skills to provide all of life's needs. Everyone benefits as the goods and services are exchanged throughout society. Individuals, with their own advantage in view, are employed in positions (or at flowers, in the case of bees) most advantageous to society. Eventually, a division of

labor results that fits society's requirements (or wants). Among bumblebees, unspecialized individuals do not reap potential rewards as rapidly as specialists, and no bees specialize on flowers with low rewards if they can find better ones.

Smith also proposed that, in a society, specialization necessarily results in interdependence. And the interdependence (and specialization) can be achieved only through an exchange of accumulated capital (representing labor). This is also true for bumblebees, except that the resources collected are immediately accessible to the whole community, rather than going first to individual pots before feeding back to society. For example, those individuals that collect only pollen feed on honey collected by others, and foraging specialists leave the hive duties and reproduction to others. In social bees, of course, the capital exchanged among different specialists in the colony is honey and pollen.

Source: Reprinted by permission of the publishers from **Bumblebee Economics** by Bernd Heinrich, pp. 144–145, Cambridge, Mass.: Harvard University Press, Copyright © 1979 by the President and Fellows of Harvard College.

are shown on the bottom row of Table 3.2. Comparing the incomes in Table 3.2 with those in Table 3.1 shows that both Albert and Henry are better off by specializing.

A comparison of Table 3.1 and Table 3.2 also shows that specialization increases the total outputs of both tune-ups and brain operations. Without specialization Albert and Henry together performed 50 operations and 90 tune-ups (see Table 3.1), whereas with specialization the combined outputs are 60 operations

Example 3.3

HOME ADVANTAGE

The theory of comparative advantage has a host of applications. The following example shows it has relevance even for the matter of which parent should work outside the home and which should be the homemaker.

Barbara and Ken, who have just had their first child, have decided that one of them should stay at home. Barbara has been earning $30,000 per year and Ken $25,000 per year. Somehow or other it has been determined that the value of Barbara's services in the house is $40,000 per year, while Ken's services are worth $32,000. This means that Barbara has an absolute advantage in going to work **and** in staying home. However, this does not mean that Barbara should do both. Rather, economic theory suggests that Barbara and Ken should exploit their comparative advantages. But where are the advantages?

The opportunity cost of Barbara continuing to work is $40,000, that is, the value of her services if

she had instead stayed at home. This can be compared with the $30,000 she earns by working, an opportunity cost ratio of working versus staying home of 1.33 (or $40,000 ÷ $30,000). In Ken's case, the opportunity cost of working is $32,000 versus the $25,000 he earns, an opportunity cost ratio of working versus staying home of 1.28 (or $32,000 ÷ $25,000). Therefore, Ken has a lower opportunity cost of working versus staying home than Barbara does. This means that Ken has a comparative advantage at working. Similarly, the opportunity cost of Barbara staying at home is the $30,000 she would have earned versus the $40,000 she contributes at home, an opportunity cost ratio of staying home versus working of 0.75 (or $30,000 ÷ $40,000). In Ken's case, the opportunity cost of staying home is the $25,000 he would have earned at work versus the $32,000 of services at home, an opportunity cost ratio of staying home versus working of 0.78 (or $25,000 ÷ $32,000). Barbara has

the comparative advantage at staying home; her opportunity cost is lower.

Basing the decision on comparative advantages, Ken should continue to work and Barbara should work in the home. In this way, Barbara specializes in her comparative advantage and Ken in his. This is so even though Barbara has an absolute advantage in both activities. We can check this outcome by computing the total value of the couple's services if they pursue their comparative advantages versus if they do not. With Ken working and Barbara at home in accordance with their comparative advantages, their combined value is $65,000 (or $25,000 + $40,000) per year. If they did the reverse, ignoring their comparative advantages, the combined value from Barbara's work and Ken's homemaking is only $62,000 (or $30,000 + $32,000) per year. Specialization according to comparative advantages is indeed the better alternative.

Incomes and outputs are increased by people specializing in doing what they can do relatively well.

and 105 tune-ups (see Table 3.2). These gains in outputs occur even though neither Albert nor Henry is working any harder or is any "smarter." Their hours worked and productivity levels—hours per task—are unchanged. All that has happened is an increase in specialization.

The only source of the gain from specialization in this example is that Albert and Henry have different relative abilities. In particular, there are no assumed benefits from learning by doing, time saved in moving between tasks, investing in specialized equipment and education, or any other advantage of specialization other than the assumed differences in relative abilities. That is, the increases in incomes and outputs result only from Henry specializing in what he does a lot better than Albert, namely brain surgery, and Albert specializing in what he does only a little worse than Henry, namely tuning cars. Were there also to be other benefits of specialization, they would make the gains in outputs and incomes even greater than in this example.

The source of the gain from specialization when abilities differ is known as a gain from **comparative advantage.** We can most easily explain the meaning of comparative advantage by considering another example, one that involves specialization by countries engaged in international trade.[4] In the case of countries, the gain from "being different" can come from more than just differences in abilities of workers. It can come from anything that makes the countries differ, such as different types of land for growing crops, different climates, different minerals, different sources of energy, and so on.

When there are benefits from learning by doing, time saved in moving between tasks, and so on, there are further gains from specialization in addition to those from people doing what they do relatively well.

THE GAINS FROM SPECIALIZATION: INTERNATIONAL TRADE

Records of trade are as old as recorded history. The earliest written accounts tell of journeys across land and sea in search of rare spices, exotic woods, furs, and fragrances. The quest to trade is attested by the dangers and expenses faced in these early explorations to find what peoples in other lands could provide. Indeed, the great voyages of discovery were motivated by an intense interest in finding opportunities for trade.

International trade continues to grow in importance. For example, during just the last 25 years, the fraction of all trade that is international trade has doubled, reaching approximately 20% by 1993.[5] The potential to gain from trade has been the powerful force that has, for example, driven the establishment and expansion of the European Community (EC). In conjunction with the European Free Trade Association (EFTA), the European free trading arrangement now consists of 19 countries from Iceland to Greece and has a total market of 380 million people. Yet further countries have applied for membership. The U.S.–Canada Free Trade Agreement of 1989 and the Australia–New Zealand Trade Agreement of 1983 provide more testimony for the gains from international trade. So too does the U.S. effort to expand free trade, first in North America via free trade with Canada and Mexico and then via free trade with the nations of South America. The basis of all this interest in international trade is the economic well-being it provides.

In order to see the source of the gain from international trade, let us consider an example of trade in wheat and automobiles between the United States and Japan. The top two rows of Table 3.3 show the assumed labor inputs required for wheat and automobile production in both countries. We see that it takes more workers to produce automobiles and wheat in Japan than in the United States. Therefore, the United States has an **absolute advantage**—it is absolutely more

[4] It was in this context that the concept of comparative advantage was first introduced by David Ricardo in his *On the Principles of Political Economy and Taxation* (London: J. Murray, 1817).

[5] This is calculated from the ratio of combined exports of all market-oriented economies to the total value of all goods and services these nations produced.

TABLE 3.3

Comparative advantages exist in producing outputs for which opportunity costs are lower.

	WITHOUT TRADE	
	JAPAN	UNITED STATES
Worker-months/automobile	2.2	2.1
Worker-months/ thousand bushels of wheat	2.0	0.5
Opportunity cost, thousand bushels/car	1.1	4.2
Opportunity cost, cars/ thousand bushels of wheat	0.91	0.24
Automobile worker-months	8.8 million	10.5 million
Wheat worker-months	4.4 million	8.0 million
Automobiles produced	4.0 million	5.0 million
Wheat produced (bushels)	2.2 billion	16.0 billion
Automobiles consumed	4.0 million	5.0 million
Wheat consumed (bushels)	2.2 billion	16.0 billion

The United States has an absolute advantage producing both wheat and automobiles. However, in Japan the opportunity cost of an automobile in terms of forgone wheat output is 1.1 (or 2.2 ÷ 2) thousand bushels, while in the United States the opportunity cost of an automobile in terms of wheat is 4.2 (or 2.1 ÷ 0.5) thousand bushels. Therefore, Japan has a comparative advantage in automobiles. In Japan the opportunity cost of a thousand bushels of wheat is 0.91 (or 2 ÷ 2.2) automobiles, whereas in the United States the opportunity cost of a thousand bushels of wheat is 0.24 (or 0.5 ÷ 2.1) automobiles. Therefore, the United States has a comparative advantage in wheat. Production is calculated by dividing the numbers of worker-months available in each industry by the worker-months needed to produce each product. Without trade, consumption equals production.

efficient—making both products.[6] It might seem that the United States would have nothing to gain from trade with Japan and that Japan would lose out in trade with a more efficient partner. However, there are gains from trade for both Japan and the United States, because Japan has a *comparative* advantage in producing automobiles, while the United States has a *comparative* advantage in producing wheat. What do we mean, however, by comparative advantage?

---

[6] In the same way, Henry had an absolute advantage in both tasks in the preceding example.

Comparative Advantage Defined

A country has a comparative advantage in producing goods or services for which its opportunity cost is lower than in other countries. From Table 3.3, the opportunity cost of an automobile in Japan is 1.1 (or $2.2 \div 2$) thousand bushels of wheat. This follows because the 2.2 worker-months required to produce an automobile in Japan could alternatively produce 1.1 thousand bushels of wheat. The opportunity cost of an automobile in the United States is 4.2 (or $2.1 \div 0.5$) thousand bushels of wheat. With Japan's opportunity cost of an automobile being 1.1 thousand bushels of wheat and the U.S. opportunity cost being 4.2 thousand bushels of wheat, Japan has a comparative advantage producing automobiles; that is, Japan's opportunity cost is lower.

While Japan has a comparative advantage producing automobiles, the United States has a comparative advantage producing wheat. This occurs because in Japan each thousand bushels of wheat requires forgoing 0.91 (or $2 \div 2.2$) automobiles, whereas in the United States each thousand bushels of wheat costs only 0.24 (or $0.5 \div 2.1$) automobiles. Therefore, the opportunity cost of wheat is lower in the United States than in Japan. That is, the United States has a comparative advantage in producing wheat. We find that Japan has a comparative advantage in producing automobiles, while the United States has a comparative advantage in producing wheat.[7]

A producer enjoys a comparative advantage in producing a good or service for which the opportunity cost is lower than for some other producer.

The Gain from Exploiting Comparative Advantage

Table 3.3 shows that *when there is no trade,* 8.8 million worker-months are employed producing automobiles in Japan. Therefore, with 2.2 worker-months required per automobile, Japanese automobile output is 4 million (or 8.8 million $\div 2.2$) per year. Similarly, when there is no trade, 8 million worker-months are employed producing wheat in the United States. With 0.5 worker-month required to produce a thousand bushels, wheat output is 16 billion [or (8.0 million $\div 0.5$) $\times 1000$] bushels per year.[8] Without international trade, consumption of automobiles and wheat in both countries would be the same as production, as shown in Table 3.3. Let us compare these output and consumption amounts without international trade with those when there is trade.

International trade allows countries to consume a different combination of goods and services than they produce. Therefore, international trade allows countries to specialize without restricting consumption to what the country produces.

Table 3.4 shows the effect of specialization of production made possible by international trade. The worker-months per unit of output figures in the top two rows of the table are the same with trade as they are without trade; compare Table

International trade allows countries to specialize by allowing them to consume a different bundle of goods and services than they produce.

---

[7] While a country may have no absolute advantages, as with Japan in this example, every country has a comparative advantage. This must be so because the opportunity cost of, for example, wheat in terms of automobiles is merely the inverse of the opportunity cost of automobiles in terms of wheat. Therefore, if the United States has a higher value for one of these opportunity costs, Japan must have a higher value for the other.

[8] The output of wheat is in billions of bushels because each of the 8 *million* worker-months results in 2 *thousand* bushels; each 0.5 worker-month produces 1 thousand bushels.

TABLE 3.4

Both countries gain from international trade even if one country is more efficient at producing both products.

	WITH TRADE	
	JAPAN	**UNITED STATES**
Worker-months/automobile	2.2	2.1
Worker-months/ thousand bushels of wheat	2.0	0.5
Opportunity cost, thousand bushels/car	1.1	4.2
Opportunity cost, cars/ thousand bushels	0.91	0.24
Automobile worker-months	13.2 million	8.4 million
Wheat worker-months	0	10.1 million
Automobiles produced	6.0 million	4.0 million
Wheat produced (bushels)	0	20.2 billion
Automobiles consumed	4.5 million	5.5 million
Wheat consumed (bushels)	2.8 billion	17.4 billion

Trade allows countries to consume different bundles of goods than they produce. Therefore, international trade allows specialization of production without consumption being restricted in the same way. This table shows the consequence of specialization of production, where Japan has all workers producing automobiles and the United States has moved 2.1 million worker-months from automobiles to wheat. With the same total numbers of worker-months and the same outputs per worker-month as in the situation without trade in Table 3.3, the total outputs of both products have been increased. This is the result of both countries exploiting their comparative advantages. Despite the fact that one country is more efficient at producing both products, consumption of both products is higher in both counties with trade than without trade; compare this table with Table 3.3.

3.4 with Table 3.3. However, in Table 3.4, workers have been shifted between the industries. In Japan, all workers have been moved into the automobile industry—where Japan enjoys a comparative advantage—and in the United States, 2.1 million workers have been moved from the automobile industry into wheat production.[9] Note that the total number of worker-months in each country is the same with trade as without; only the allocation between industries is different.

The outputs in both countries for both industries are calculated with the rearranged work forces by again dividing the number of worker-months employed in each industry and country by the required labor inputs. For example, with 13.2 million worker-months producing automobiles in Japan and 2.2 worker-months

---

[9] We talk of workers being moved as if it is the result of an edict. In fact, it is market forces that move workers between industries.

needed per automobile, Japanese automobile production is 6 million (or 13.2 million ÷ 2.2) per year.

Table 3.3 shows that total automobile output of the two countries without trade is 9 million. Table 3.4 shows that with trade, total automobile output is 10 million. At the same time, the output of wheat is increased from 18.2 billion bushels without trade to 20.2 billion bushels with trade; compare Table 3.3 with Table 3.4. The outputs of both products have increased as a result of each country specializing in producing the item in which it enjoys a comparative advantage. This specialization is an indirect benefit of trade because it is by means of trade that each country is able to produce a different bundle of goods than its people consume.

The distribution of the extra outputs between the countries depends on their **terms of trade.** A country's terms of trade are the amount of exports that must be sold to pay for one unit of imports.[10] The more exports that must be sold for a unit of imports, the more unfavorable are the export country's terms of trade.

Table 3.4 shows the division of outputs from specialization for a particular, assumed terms of trade. Japan is shown selling 1.5 million of its automobiles for 2.8 billion bushels of wheat, implying terms of trade of 1867 (or 2.8 billion ÷ 1.5 million) bushels of wheat per automobile. Other divisions of the gains from trade would occur with different terms of trade. However, both countries can enjoy more of both products when they trade than when they do not, for other terms of trade. Moreover, this is the result only of the countries pursuing their comparative advantages.

The gains from specialization may seem surprising when, as in Tables 3.3 and 3.4, one country, in this case the United States, has an absolute advantage producing both products. In particular, it might be thought better for the United States to produce all the automobiles and wheat it needs for itself because it is more efficient than Japan in producing both. The example shows that this is not so. The reason it pays to trade is that by buying automobiles from Japan, more people in the United States can be employed growing wheat. Its comparative advantage in growing wheat allows the United States to trade wheat for more automobiles than Americans would have if they produced all their automobiles themselves.

The gain from exploiting each country's comparative advantage is no different from the gain we enjoy within a country from exploiting our individual comparative advantages. For example, as we saw earlier, even though Henry is a better mechanic *and* a better brain surgeon than Albert, it is still better for Henry to spend most of his time repairing brains and for Albert to repair automobiles than for Henry to share his time equally between both. This is so because Henry can work only a limited number of hours in a day, and time spent fixing automobiles might be spent more usefully in the operating room. Even Albert is better off if Henry specializes in fixing brains.

As with the example of Albert and Henry, the gains from specialization in our international trade example are not from learning by doing, from investments in human or physical capital made possible from larger-scale production, or from anything else. The gains result only from differences in abilities. If there are *also* gains from learning by doing, from investments made possible by larger-scale

The terms of trade are the number of units of the exported product that must be sold to pay for one unit of the imported product.

When countries specialize in producing those items in which they have a comparative advantage, *all* countries are better off. This specialization is made possible by trade.

---

[10] When, as in reality, numerous items are exported and imported, the terms of trade can be defined only by using indices of export and import prices.

The gains from international trade may exceed those resulting only from comparative advantage. Gains also may be enjoyed as a result of learning by doing, capital investments made possible by larger-scale production, and increased product variety.

production, and so on, these will add to the gains from trade attributable to comparative advantage. That is, if at the same time as workers are switched between industries in our international trade example we also improve the productivity figures—using lower required inputs of worker-hours in the specialized production with trade than without trade—the gains from trade will be larger than those shown. There are even further gains from increases in the variety of products available to consumers as a result of international trade. This fact is evident to anybody visiting a department store and seeing how many of the items in the store are imported.[11]

There is a potential additional gain from international trade as a result of increased competition. For example, an individual country's demand might support only one or two automobile or steel producers who charge high prices, whereas with international trade, the local firms may have to compete with numerous foreign manufacturers and charge lower prices. However, it is also possible for domestic firms to be forced out of business by a foreign monopoly supplier who then exploits the country's market. When this happens, there may be grounds for restricting international trade. In an industry such as automobiles, where there are many producers in Japan, Germany, France, Italy, Great Britain, and so on, and where the existing firms in the United States have survived competition, the concern that the market would become less competitive with international trade than without is not valid. However, in the case of aircraft manufacturing, in which context the possibility was first discussed, the problem might occur.[12]

International trade also brings gains as a result of increased competition, provided it does not open an economy to exploitation by a foreign monopoly.

Reasons for Restricting International Trade

We have just seen a possible reason for restricting international trade in situations where a powerful foreign producer might drive out domestic competitors and then exploit consumers. There are other possible grounds for restricting trade.

Protection of domestic firms by placing import tariffs or other restrictions on foreign firms can be supported economically where there is a *potential* to develop a profitable industry but help is needed while the industry becomes established.[13] In particular, if there is a potential for substantially lower production costs after workers have learned skills or after large-scale production has been achieved, temporary protection of local markets can be in a country's interest. This is known as the **infant industry argument.** Trade restrictions also can be in a country's best interest if it would be cut off from strategic supplies during war; by keeping a domestic industry the country may be better able to survive during conflict. In such a case, the military advantages can be considered to more than offset the economic costs of trade protection.[14]

---

[11] Example 3.4 summarizes the many sources of gain from free international trade in the context of the 1989 U.S.–Canadian Free Trade Agreement.

[12] See James Brander and Barbara Spencer, "Export Subsidies and International Market Share Rivalry," *Journal of International Economics* 18, February 1985, pp. 83–100.

[13] Example 3.5 explains the nature of import tariffs as well as other forms of trade protection.

[14] However, as Example 3.6 makes abundantly clear, the costs of trade protection can be extremely high.

Example 3.4

PERVASIVE GAINS FROM TRADE

The multiple sources of the gains from free trade have been described by the Canadian Department of Finance in their assessment of the benefits to Canada of the 1989 U.S.– Canadian Free Trade Agreement. The following excerpt mentions the gains described in this chapter, as well as some other gains.

The potential impacts of freer trade are pervasive in a modern industrial economy. As barriers or threats of barriers to import- and export-oriented activity are reduced, the positive impacts on the economy work through several channels:

Comparative Advantage Specialization: Trade barriers distort production decisions. Trade liberalization, in contrast, ensures that countries specialize in producing goods in which they have a comparative advantage. They are encouraged to produce and export goods that are relatively less costly to produce domestically, and to import those that are relatively expensive to produce at home. Thus, each country acquires goods less expensively than it would otherwise. Realizing one's comparative advantage in this way makes the best use of existing resources and results in higher overall productivity and an improved standard of living.

Lower Prices for Consumers: Trade barriers distort prices and hence consumption decisions. Trade liberalization means lower prices for both imported goods and the domestically produced goods that compete with them. Trade liberalization also means lower costs for imported intermediate products which in turn will lead to further reductions in consumer prices. . . .

Economies of Scale: Both foreign and domestic trade barriers impose costs. This is particularly the case for smaller economies. They prevent domestic firms from becoming large enough to capitalize on economies of scale available in markets of larger size. The removal of the trade barriers permits domestic firms to operate larger and more specialized plants, which lead to lower unit costs of production. The capacity to specialize and to exploit the economies of large-scale production are the main potential sources of gain from free trade for a small country such as Canada which, unlike other industrialized countries, does not have secure access to a large consumer market.

Increased Flexibility and Dynamism: Free trade implies greater exposure . . . to international opportunities and competition, both at home and in foreign markets. This exposure can be expected to create incentives for greater price flexibility and faster responses to changes in market conditions.

More secure access to the foreign markets, combined with the pressure of a more competitive environment, will increase both the rewards for innovation and the costs of being technologically obsolete. This will stimulate R&D investment in new products and new technologies, and will encourage . . . firms to participate in newly emerging industries.

Reduced Uncertainty: Although tariff rates throughout the world have declined over time, there has unfortunately been an increase in non-tariff barriers (NTBs). In addition to restricting the flow of trade, these measures have created uncertainty for producers with respect to investment in new facilities. Firms must have reasonably secure access to a market before they will undertake large investment projects dedicated to that market. The Canada–U.S. Free Trade Agreement, with its new rules and procedures for the application of trade remedy laws and the resolution of trade disputes, will reduce uncertainty with respect to market access and will thereby encourage investment and risk taking.

Source: The Canada–U.S. Free Trade Agreement: An Economic Assessment (Ottawa, Canada: Department of Finance, undated).

Example 3.5

FORMS OF PROTECTIONISM

Protectionism can take many forms, all of which improve the position of domestic producers vis-à-vis foreign producers. The following from the **Review** of the Federal Reserve Bank of St. Louis describes four of the most common forms of protectionism.

TARIFFS

Tariffs, which are simply taxes imposed on goods entering a country from abroad, result in higher prices and have been the most common form of protection for domestic producers. Tariffs have been popular with governments because it appears that the tax is being paid by the foreigner who wishes to sell his goods in the home economy and because the tariff revenue can be used to finance government services or reduce other taxes.

QUOTAS

A quota seems like a sensible alternative to a tariff when the intention is to restrict foreign producers' access to the domestic market. Importers typically are limited to a maximum number of products that they can sell in the home market over specific periods. A quota, similar to a tariff, causes prices to increase in the home market. This induces domestic producers to increase production and consumers to reduce consumption. One difference between a tariff and a quota is that the tariff generates revenue for the government, while the quota generates a revenue gain to the owner of import licenses. Consequently, foreign producers

might capture some of this revenue.

In recent years, a slightly different version of quotas, called either orderly marketing agreements or voluntary export restraints, has been used. In an orderly marketing agreement, the domestic government asks the foreign government to restrict the quantity of exports of a good to the domestic country. The request can be viewed as a demand, like the U.S.–Japan automobile agreement in the 1980s, because the domestic country makes it clear that more restrictive actions are likely unless the foreign government "voluntarily" complies. In effect, the orderly marketing agreement is a mutually agreed-upon quota.

REGULATORY BARRIERS

There are many other ways of restricting foreigner's access to domestic markets. The 1983 *Tariff Schedules of the United States Annotated* consists of 792 pages, plus a 78-page appendix. Over 200 tariff rates pertain to watches and clocks. Simply ascertaining the appropriate tariff classification, which requires legal assistance and can be subject to differences of opinion, is a deterrent.

Product standards are another common regulatory barrier. These standards appear in various forms and are used for many purposes. The standards can be used to serve the public interest by ensuring that imported food products are processed according to acceptable sanitary standards and that drugs have been screened before their introduction in the United States. In other cases, the standards,

sometimes intentionally, protect domestic producers. An example of unintended restrictions may be the imposition of safety or pollution standards that were not previously being met by foreign cars.

SUBSIDIES

An alternative to restricting the terms under which foreigners can compete in the home market is to subsidize domestic producers. Subsidies may be focused upon an industry in general or upon the export activities of the industry. An example of the former is the combination of credit programs, special tax incentives and direct subsidy payments that benefit the U.S. shipbuilding industry. An example of the latter is the financial assistance to increase exports provided by the U.S. Export-Import Bank through direct loans, loan guarantees and insurance, and discount loans. In either case, production will expand.

An important difference between subsidies and tariffs involves the revenue implications for government. The former involves the government in paying out money, whereas tariffs generate income for the government. The effect on domestic production and welfare, however, can be the same under subsidies as under tariffs and quotas. In all cases, the protected industry is being subsidized by the rest of the economy.

Source: Kletus C. Coughlin, K. Alec Chrystal, and Geoffrey E. Wood, "Protectionist Trade Policies: A Survey of Theory, Evidence and Rationale," **Review,** Federal Reserve Bank of St. Louis, January–February 1988, pp. 16–17.

Example 3.6

THE ABSURDITIES OF PROTECTIONISM

The cost of protectionism can be extremely high. The following excerpt describes how a tariff designed to reduce imports of foreign manufactured goods and provide revenue to government failed to stem imports, **reduced** government revenue, encouraged and rewarded organized crime, resulted in high enforcement costs, and hurt consumers.

The Austrian government, like several other Continental governments, still adheres to the system of high duties, amounting to prohibition, on foreign manufactured goods. This is done with the intention of *favouring home manufactures*. Now mark the consequences! In 1817, an order came from Vienna, assimilating the custom-houses of Lombardy to those of the rest of the empire, and subjecting foreign manufactures to a duty of 60 per cent on the value, equal, in short, to prohibition in most cases. Large buildings were soon after erected into manufactories, a few clever workmen engaged for a time, some pieces of calicoes, muslins, &c. woven and pompously exhibited, after which the *manufacturer* supplied himself with English, Swiss, and French cloths, by means of smuggling, which was carried on to an immense extent all along the vast line of frontiers, the delivery being insured by companies established in the neighbouring states, and the pieces, marked with the imperial stamp, came out of the manufactories as home productions; the shops were full of foreign goods. Meantime, the custom-house receipts fell off one-half, custom-house officers and gendarmes were multiplied and maintained at a vast expense, whilst all along the frontier districts, there sprung up a proportionate array of smugglers, men who, by their perilous vocation, become familiar with violence and bloodshed, and by whom the peace of the country is continually endangered. The mock-manufacturers, if prosecuted, can show that they are able to make such and such pieces of the goods, and unless taken in the act of smuggling, there are no means of convicting them. The smuggling is carried on chiefly through the frontiers of Piedmont and Switzerland, countries which have had the good sense to reject the *protecting* system. A great proportion of the population of the Canton Ticino lives entirely by smuggling foreign goods into Austrian Lombardy. The lakes Maggiore and Lugano, the waters of which are considered neutral, afford the smugglers great facilities. The *efficiency* of the protection afforded to home manufactures by prohibitory duties may be estimated by the fact that an insurance may be readily effected upon smuggled goods at a rate varying from 10 to 15 per cent. This fact is notorious in Austrian Lombardy. The *results* of the system are, loss to the government, which might derive a moderate duty on importation,—loss to the consumer who pays high for goods, which, after all, he must use,—and loss to the country at large, which has to support a useless host of custom-house officers, and whose exports are limited by the trammels thus imposed on importation. Besides these evils, habits of fraud and contempt for the laws are fostered among the trading classes, and among the rural population of the border districts.

Source: The Penny Magazine (April 14, 1832), p. 23. (Emphases in original.)

Emile Durkheim (1858–1917)

DIVISION OF LABOR IN OTHER AREAS OF INQUIRY

Division of labor plays an important role in biology. Not only are there specialized cells—long, very thin nerve cells to carry electrical impulses; short, round white blood cells to swallow bacteria; and so on—but there is also specialization of tasks within cells. Similarly, tissues, organs, and organisms, like their economic counterparts, industries, sectors, and economies, are highly specialized. That is, divisions of labor are found in **natural economy**, as biology has been called, just as they are found in **political economy**.[15] A particularly fascinating example of division of labor in biology, one that occurs at the level of the organism, is that occurring among the so-called **social insects**.[16]

Ants and termites have divided the labor in their colonies into very specialized tasks, and the individuals performing these tasks have developed their own specialized physiologies. For example, in a typical colony of ants, genus **Atta**, there are foragers who collect leaves, weavers who bend leaves into nests, masticaters who chew leaves into pulp, gluers who use the pulp to make building materials, herders who round up aphids and mealybugs for food, soldiers who protect the colony, groomers who keep it clean, fungus gardeners who grow food for larvae, queens who specialize in laying eggs, nurses who care for them, and so on. Each specialization has its own physiology, with specially adapted

---

[15] Biology has been referred to as "natural economy" by Michael Ghiselin in **The Economy of Nature and the Evolution of Sex** (Berkeley, University of California Press, 1974). See also Example 1.5.

[16] For a detailed account of division of labor in the social insects, see Edward Wilson, **Sociobiology** (Cambridge, Mass.:

Harvard University Press, 1980), or Henry Hermann, **Social Insects** (New York: Academic Press, 1979). A specific account of division-of-labor arrangements of different types of bees can be found in Bernd Heinrich, **Bumblebee Economics** (Cambridge, Mass.: Harvard University Press, 1979).

legs, pincers, mouths, pelvices, and so on. A colony might work most efficiently with about 2 million members all doing their special-ized jobs for the benefit of the community.[17]

Bees also have developed a high degree of division of labor, with hive members specializing in gathering pollen, building combs, producing eggs, fertilizing eggs, nursing larvae, and so on. The hive is far better off from the division of labor, and indeed, this is why this form of organization evolved at the expense of alternative systems involving less specialization.

Sociologists and social anthropologists have studied the division of labor at various levels of society, and it is useful to consider how the sociologic and anthropologic views of specialization compare with those of economists. As we shall see, the sociologist and anthropologist look at the human dimensions of the division of labor in terms of the effect increased specialization has on social order, people's self-respect, and so on.

Perhaps one of the most distinctive markers of a person's social class, income, education, and social circle is what they "do for a living," that is, their specialization within the division of labor. Indeed, if this is not the first question asked when people meet for the first time, the second is almost certainty, "And what do you do?"

In hunter-gatherer societies studied by anthropologists, the division of labor is very limited. What divisions there are tend to be based on age and sex. Apart from these divisions, people generally have similar roles within society. Agricultural societies, whether they be pastoral, horticultural, or both, also have a limited division of labor, although in wealthier communities, where a sur-plus can be produced, there may be some specialists, for example, artists, storytellers, and so on.[18]

It is in industrial societies that the division of labor has been carried to a very high degree. For example, the United States Department of Labor classifies over 20,000 occupations, including such specializations as sheep shearer, fish scaler, bagel baker, cookie cutter, book binder, and business professor. Sociologists view this high degree of specialization not in terms of its effect on increasing efficiency but in terms of the strains it places on the social fabric.

A particularly influential view of the division of labor is that of French sociologist Emile Durkheim. In his **The Division of Labor in Society** (1893), Durkheim argued that as people's tasks become more differentiated, so do their values and norms.[19] An overriding theme of Durkheim's writings is that social solidarity requires that values and norms be very sim ilar so that a community develops a "collective consciousness," that is, common values and behavioral standards. This is achieved by the similarity of the lives of different individuals in traditional societies that have what Durkheim called a **mechanical solidarity**, a solidarity based on their similar experiences and common values. However, in modern industrial societies with their highly developed divisions of labor, individuals have very different experiences and hence fewer common values. This damages the collective consciousness and results in people viewing themselves as individuals rather than as part of society. Instead of the mechanical solidarity that galvanizes members of a traditional society, the highly specialized industrial society is held

---

[17] Just as cities tend to work more efficiently at a particular size, becoming congested and subject to problems when they are too large and forgoing economies of proximity of firms and factors of production when they are too small, so it would appear that social insects' "cities" function most efficiently at a particular size. Of course, technology, policing, and other human innovations are constantly changing the optimal city size, whereas the ants, termites, and bees have had about 100 million years of relatively unchanged technology and institutions from which to select their optimal-sized colonies.

[18] In hunter-gatherer societies in which surpluses were common, such as among the relatively opulent Haida Indians of the Pacific North West of North America, some specialization developed. However, the majority of the community still fished, gathered, and had similar roles.

[19] Emile Durkheim, **The Division of Labor in Society**, trans. from the French by George Simpson (Glencoe, Ill.: Free Press, 1949).

together by the weaker bond of **organic solidarity**, a solidarity based only on people's mutual dependence. This dependence is, of course, the very result of specialized roles. However, while being dependent on each other, individuals lose their loyalty to the community and pursue their own selfish interests. This situation Durkheim called **anomie**, which he feared would lead to social disorder and perhaps to the disintegration of society.

Another consequence of the division of labor that has concerned sociologists as well as psychologists is the effect highly specialized tasks have on an individual's sense of self-worth and the potential this has for generating feelings of alienation. The target of concern has been the production line, in which people are viewed as standing day after day, year after year, in the mind-numbing hollow activity of turning a screw or pulling a lever. The popular image of the production line, captured on so many silent movies running faster than life as a gigantic industrial nightmare, led some sociologists, psychologists, and economists to argue that the division of labor could lead to empty, inactive minds, shut off to keep out the emptiness of existence. The fear of alienation was reinforced by a belief that workers would become detached from the purpose of their tasks, lacking a sense of the contribution of their own narrow involvement. Fortunately, many manual repetitive tasks have been mechanized; the more repetitive tasks are, the easier in general it is to replicate the tasks mechanically. Furthermore, alienation and detachment in the workplace were found to damage productivity. That is, the psychological consequences of the division of labor fed back negatively to the economic effects. This spurred the mechanization of repetitive tasks and encouraged management to institute changes designed to make work more meaningful.

> *[A] consequence of the division of labor . . . is the effect highly specialized tasks have on an individual's sense of self-worth and the potential this has for generating feelings of alienation.*

Sociologists also have considered the effect of division of labor on the family.[20] While changing with customs and the increasingly important role of women in the modern economy, a division of labor has always existed in the family. For physiologic reasons, women have specialized in the care of children, especially newborns, while men have generally been involved with providing. The division of labor from which the family is likely to benefit presumably explains why specialization evolved. Of course, there have been changes in the division of labor in the family, and this may well be because the previous divisions no longer serve us so well. Indeed, it is instructive to consider why these changes are occurring because this helps identify another factor limiting the degree of specialization, namely, uncertainty.

With increased mobility, extended families in which several generations of family members as well as aunts, uncles, and cousins are all nearby are increasingly rare. The "modern" family is typically a nuclear unit, perhaps hundreds or even thousands of miles from other relatives. This means that if, for example, a mother becomes ill, it is not possible for a grandmother, sister, or other family member to come and help. In such a case, the father has to cook, shop, care for the children, clean, and so on. It has been argued that because of this, in families away from a complex network of outside support, a husband and wife have less specialized tasks, tending to share

---

[20] Of course, the alienation and destruction of self-esteem described above can have indirect effects on the family in terms of breakdown, violence, and so on. These effects are studied by psychologists.

their roles and thereby providing an ability to take over the role of the other when necessary.[21]

The family example shows that uncertainty may be an additional factor limiting the division of labor; it is uncertainty about the health of the spouse that reduces specialization. This view on the effect of uncertainty is reinforced by considering the division of labor among social insects. For example, wasps and bumblebees that face particularly frequent crises from attacking bears, severe weather conditions, and so on tend to maintain the ability to perform a variety of tasks. More stable communities like some types of termites, in which uncertainties are not as important, have developed greater specialization.

[21] See Elizabeth Bott, **Family and Social Networks: Roles, Norms and External Relationships in Ordinary Urban Families** (London: Tavistock, 1957).

SUMMARY

1. Specialization has substantially increased the standard of living.

2. Modern economies use a system of exchange based on markets and the use of money as a medium of exchange. This allows people to specialize in what they do well, to sell the results of their efforts for money, and then to use the money to buy goods and services from others who specialize at what they do well.

3. The gains from specialization include learning by doing, reduction in time lost switching between tasks, increased efficiency from investing in knowledge and machines made worthwhile by larger-scale production, and exploitation of comparative advantages.

4. A country has a comparative advantage in producing items for which the opportunity cost in terms of other products is lower than it is elsewhere. Gains are made by all countries when each exploits its comparative advantage, just as individuals gain within a nation by working at what they do well vis-à-vis other people.

5. The gains from international trade come from the same sources as the gains from domestic trade. International trade also may bring benefits from increased competition.

6. Countries gain from international trade even if they have an absolute advantage or disadvantage at everything.

7. There are grounds for restricting international trade when consumers might be exploited by a powerful foreign monopoly and when an industry has the potential to develop comparative advantages if given the opportunity. Military considerations also may rationalize restrictions on trade.

QUESTIONS AND PROBLEMS

1. Calculate the opportunity costs facing Albert and Henry in their choices between tune-ups and brain surgery in Tables 3.1 and 3.2. What are their comparative advantages?

2. Change the number of worker-months per automobile in the top rows of Tables 3.3 and 3.4 from 2.1 to 0.55. That is, where the number 2.1 appears in the top rows of Tables 3.3 and 3.4, write 0.55. Keep all other productivity numbers in the top two rows of the tables unchanged. Now calculate the opportunity costs. Note that they are the same in both countries. Finally, calculate the outputs of automobiles and wheat using the numbers of worker-months in the two tables. That is, calculate the outputs for the "without trade" and "with trade" scenarios. How do the combined outputs compare?

3. Why is the gain from trade via exploiting comparative advantage only part of the gain from specialization of production?

4. In trade between the United States and Mexico, in what industries do you think the United States has a comparative advantage?

5. Why can no country have a comparative advantage at everything?

6. Why do you think so many Western governments that support free enterprise at home have tariffs (import taxes) on imports?

7. Why is the division of labor dependent on there being a system of exchange?

8. How do learning by doing and investment affect the position of the production possibilities curve?

9. How does time saved when switching between tasks affect the production possibilities curve?

10. How does size limit the division of labor in the army, a school, a family business, and a hospital?

PART II

SUPPLY AND DEMAND

Long before Einstein, economists have been aware that Earthly matter has four dimensions: Length, breadth, thickness, and price.

Evan Esar

. . . .
. . . .
. . . .
. . . .
. . . .

Consumer Decisions and Demand

The theory of consumer behavior is a thing of great aesthetic beauty, a jewel set in a glass case.

Kevin Lancaster

Key Concepts

Total and marginal utility; law of diminishing marginal utility; utility-maximizing budget allocation; equating marginal utilities per dollar; individual consumer and market demand curves; substitutes and complements; consumer preferences; normal goods and inferior goods; elasticity of demand; elastic, inelastic

As we explained in Chapter 2, it is necessary to choose among the many goods and services competing for our attention because there are lots of things we would like to have but for which our incomes cannot stretch to buy. The need to choose is the inevitable result of scarcity, and we face this choice when we decide what to buy at the supermarket, how much to spend on rent versus clothes, on entertainment versus food, on a car versus a vacation, and so on. In all spending decisions a trade-off must be made between the enjoyment or satisfaction alternative purchases could provide. Whether aware of them or not, we make these trade-offs all the time in our effort to make the best use of what we have to spend.

This chapter describes the economists' way of thinking about spending decisions facing an individual consumer and how all individuals' decisions when taken together translate into the amounts of different products demanded. The purpose is to explain how the quantities of products people buy depend on their tastes as well as on product prices and the incomes people have available to spend.

UTILITY AND CONSUMER DEMAND

The Consumers' Objective

In their capacity as buyers, people are referred to as **consumers.** The consumers' choice about which goods and services to buy and in what quantities is referred to as the problem of **budget allocation.** Economists assume that consumers allocate budgets to maximize the total satisfaction they enjoy. The term **utility** is used to describe satisfaction, and the expression **total utility** is used to describe the total satisfaction enjoyed by a consumer from his or her budget.

Because actual satisfaction or utility from some products may not be known until after they have been consumed, it is the *expected* total utility that consumers attempt to maximize in allocating their budgets. That is, consumers are assumed to choose between alternative ways of spending their budgets so as to maximize the total satisfaction they expect to enjoy.

The Law of Diminishing Marginal Utility

Simply assuming that consumers make choices between alternatives in order to maximize expected total utility is not sufficient on its own to explain the quantities of different products consumers buy or how quantities bought depend on prices, incomes, and other factors. In order to explain the quantities purchased and the responses of quantities purchased to product prices and consumers' incomes, it is necessary to make a further assumption about how utilities of products vary with quantities consumed.

The way utilities vary with quantities consumed is described by the **law of diminishing marginal utility.** The term **marginal utility** refers to the amount of *extra* utility—satisfaction or pleasure—a person enjoys from one more unit of a product.

The law of diminishing marginal utility states that as more of a product is consumed during a given time interval, eventually the marginal utility of that product declines relative to the marginal utility of other products. For example, the law argues that as more compact discs (CDs) are bought per month, the marginal utility from an additional CD declines relative to that of books or other products. The meaning of the law of diminishing marginal utility and the connection between total utility and marginal utility can be explained by an example.

Table 4.1 shows the total and marginal utility a consumer enjoys from CDs as the consumer buys from 0 to 10 CDs per year. One CD per year is shown to give a total utility of 110 utils, 2 CDs per year give a total utility of 170 utils, and so on. The marginal utilities from each extra CD per year implied by these total utilities are shown in the right-hand column of the table. The first CD per year gives 110 utils of total utility, and all this is marginal utility, since it involves going from no CDs to 1 CD. The second CD adds 60 (or 170 − 110) utils of utility over buying only 1 CD per year. That is, the second CD has a marginal utility of 60 utils. The table shows that the marginal utility of each level of consumption of CDs per month is the total utility with that consumption level minus the total utility with consumption of 1 less CD per month. For example, the total utility of 7 CDs per month is 288 utils, while the total utility of 6 CDs is 274 utils. Therefore, the seventh CD has a marginal utility of 14 (or 288 − 274) utils.

Total utility is the total satisfaction a consumer enjoys from what he or she purchases with a given budget.

Consumers are assumed to allocate their budgets to different goods and services to maximize expected total utility.

Marginal utility is the *extra* utility obtained from one more unit of a product.

The law of diminishing marginal utility states that the marginal utility of a product declines as more of it is consumed during a given time interval.

....
TABLE 4.1

Marginal utility declines as more of a product is consumed.

NUMBER OF CDs PER YEAR	TOTAL UTILITY (utils)	MARGINAL UTILITY (utils)
0	—	—
1	110	110
2	170	60
3	210	40
4	236	26
5	256	20
6	274	18
7	288	14
8	300	12
9	310	10
10	318	8

Marginal utility is the extra total utility enjoyed by consuming one more unit of a product during a given interval of time. For example, the marginal utility of the fourth CD is 26 utils. This is the total utility from 4 CDs, namely 236 utils, minus the total utility from 3 CDs, which is 210 utils. Each marginal utility is calculated in the same way. The law of diminishing marginal utility states that marginal utilities are smaller as consumption increases in a given period of time.

The relationship between total utility and marginal utility is illustrated graphically in Figure 4.1. This figure is based on the values in Table 4.1. The top of the figure shows total utility increasing as the number of CDs bought per year increases. It also shows that the rate of increase, given by the slope of the line, steadily declines. The bottom part of the figure shows the marginal utility steadily decreasing. This is the law of diminishing marginal utility at work. It is worth noting that marginal utility remains positive throughout, since having an extra CD is unlikely to make somebody feel worse off.[1]

Maximizing Utility

The law of diminishing marginal utility, together with the assumption that consumers allocate budgets to maximize expected total utility, makes it possible to determine how much of different products consumers buy and how these amounts depend on prices and other factors. We can do this in the context of an example.

Table 4.2 shows marginal utilities of CDs and books at different numbers consumed per year. The combinations in the table are those considered in Table 2.1 (page 33) that can be bought for $200 when CDs cost $10 and books $40. For example, the top row, which involves 20 CDs and no books, costs $200 (or 20×$10).

[1] If it is costly to store or dispose of a product, then it is possible for it to have negative marginal utility. This is not likely to happen with CDs, however.

This figure plots the total utility and marginal utility values in Table 4.1. It shows graphically the law of diminishing marginal utility, with decreasing marginal utilities as consumption increases. The figure makes clear that decreasing marginal utilities mean that total utility increases less as more is consumed. Note, however, that marginal utility remains positive at all rates of consumption.

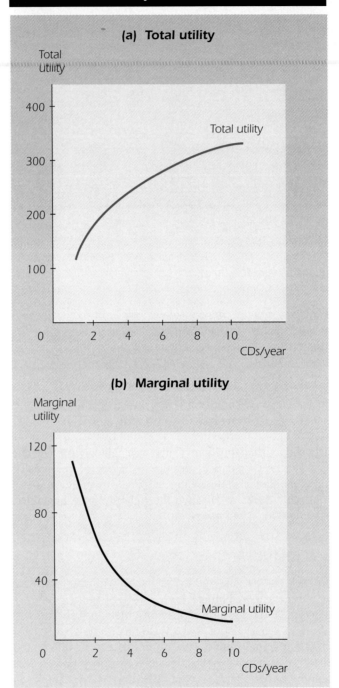

FIGURE 4.1   Declining marginal utility is reflected in a total utility curve that becomes flatter.

(a) Total utility

(b) Marginal utility

TABLE 4.2

Maximum total utility is enjoyed when the marginal utilities per dollar of different items are equal.

CDs PER YEAR	MU (CDs) (utils)	PRICE (CDs)	MU (CDs) / PRICE (CDs) (utils/$)	BOOKS PER YEAR	MU (books) (utils)	PRICE (books)	MU (books) / PRICE (books) (utils/$)
20	1	$10	0.10	0	—	$40	—
16	3	10	0.30	1	70	40	1.75
12	5	10	0.50	2	20	40	0.50
8	12	10	1.2	3	12	40	0.30
4	26	10	2.6	4	10	40	0.25
0	—	10	—	5	8	40	0.20

When the marginal utility per dollar spent on one product exceeds that of another product, the consumer's total utility can be increased by buying more of the product with the higher marginal utility per dollar and less of the other product. For example, at the combination 16 CDs and 1 book, a dollar moved from CDs to books adds 1.45 (or 1.75 − 0.30) utils. Similarly, at the combination 8 CDs and 3 books, a dollar moved from books to CDs adds 0.9 (or 1.2 − 0.30) utils. Only when the marginal utilities per dollar of different products are equal is the consumer's total utility maximized. This occurs at the combination 12 CDs and 2 books, where marginal utilities per dollar are both 0.50.

Table 4.2 shows the marginal utilities of both products declining as more of the products are consumed, in accordance with the law of diminishing marginal utility. (In the case of CDs, consumption decreases as you read down the table, whereas for books it is the reverse. The reason the numbers move in opposite directions is that each row of the table represents the same total expenditure on the goods.)

Marginal utilities per dollar can be calculated by dividing the marginal utilities by the prices of the products. For example, the marginal utility per dollar of the twelfth CD per year is 0.50 utils per dollar (or 5 utils ÷ $10). Similarly, the marginal utility per dollar of the first book is 1.75 utils per dollar (or 70 utils ÷ $40).

The marginal utilities per dollar in Table 4.2 can be used to show which combination would be selected by a utility-maximizing consumer allocating $200 to the two products. In order to do this, let us suppose that the consumer buys 16 CDs and 1 book and ask if the consumer can do better than this. At the combination 16 CDs and 1 book, the marginal utility per dollar spent on books is 1.75 utils per dollar, whereas on CDs it is only 0.30 utils per dollar. This means that moving a dollar from CDs to books provides a gain in total utility of 1.45 (or 1.75 − 0.30) utils; the book gives 1.75 utils from the dollar, and only 0.30 utils are lost on the CD. Because total utility is increased by moving from 16 CDs and 1 book toward fewer CDs and more books, the combination 16 CDs and 1 book cannot maximize total utility. But how far in the direction of fewer CDs and more books should the consumer go?

Suppose the consumer moves as far as buying 8 CDs and 3 books. With this combination, the marginal utility per dollar from CDs is 1.2 utils per dollar, whereas from books it is only 0.30 utils per dollar. Therefore, a dollar moved from buying books to buying CDs causes a gain in total utility of 0.90 (or 1.2 − 0.30) utils. That is, total utility can be increased by moving from the combination 8 CDs and 3 books toward more CDs and fewer books.

With the consumer gaining by moving from 16 CDs and 1 book toward fewer CDs and more books and also gaining by moving from 8 CDs and 3 books toward more CDs and fewer books, there is only one combination that suggests itself, namely, 12 CDs and 2 books. At this combination, the marginal utilities per dollar of books and CDs are equal, and it is not possible to increase total utility by reallocating expenditure between the products.

The preceding discussion is illustrated graphically in Figure 4.2. The combinations of CDs and books in Table 4.2 are given along the horizontal axis. The marginal utilities per dollar of each product for each combination in Table 4.2 are plotted above the appropriate points on the horizontal axis. For example, the combination 16 CDs and 1 book is associated with a marginal utility of CDs of 0.30 utils per dollar, as shown by point A. Point B shows the marginal utility per dollar of books at this same combination, 16 CDs and 1 book. The other marginal utilities per dollar of CDs and books from Table 4.2 are plotted in the same way on Figure 4.2. For example, when 8 CDs and 3 books are purchased, the marginal utility of CDs is 1.2 utils per dollar, as shown by point C, and the marginal utility of books is 0.30 utils per dollar, as shown by point D.

Joining together points such as A and C, which show the marginal utilities per dollar of CDs, gives the curve labeled MU(CDs)/$. Similarly, joining points such as B and D, which show the marginal utilities per dollar of books, gives the curve labeled MU(books)/$. These two curves can be used to reach the same conclusion we did with the help of Table 4.2—that maximum possible total utility is enjoyed when marginal utilities per dollar are equal. In order to do this, let us begin by assuming that the consumer buys 16 CDs and 1 book and ask if total utility can be increased by selecting a different combination.

With the combination 16 CDs and 1 book, the consumer enjoys a marginal utility of CDs of 0.30 utils per dollar, point A, and a marginal utility per dollar of books of 1.75 utils per dollar, point B. Figure 4.2 makes it clear that the marginal utility per dollar from books exceeds that from CDs; point B is above point A. Therefore, total utility can be increased by buying more books (and consequently fewer CDs). Indeed, as long as the curve MU(books)/$ is above MU(CDs)/$, total utility is increased by moving to the right in the figure, that is, by buying more books and fewer CDs. Only when point E is reached is curve MU(books)/$ no longer above MU(CDs)/$ so that further increases in total utility cannot be achieved by selecting a combination further to the right along the horizontal axis.

Let us next assume that the consumer buys 8 CDs and 3 books. With this combination, the curve MU(CDs)/$ is above MU(books)/$. This means that buying more CDs (and consequently fewer books) increases total utility. Buying more CDs and fewer books takes the consumer to the left along the horizontal axis. As long as the curve MU(CDs)/$ is above MU(books)/$, the consumer can increase total utility by moving expenditure from books to CDs. Only at point E, where the two curves intersect, are there no further gains from shifting expenditure from books to CDs.

We have found that total utility can be increased by shifting expenditure toward the combination at point E whenever the consumer buys a combination to the left or to the right of point E. Therefore, point E, where the curves MU(CDs)/$ and MU(books)/$ intersect, is the point of maximum possible total utility. This corresponds to 12 CDs and 2 books. With the two curves at the same height at point E,

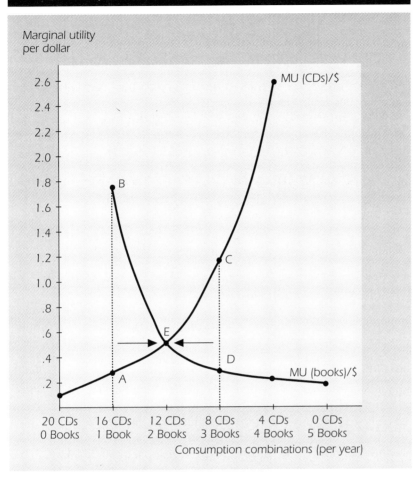

FIGURE 4.2   Total utility is maximized when the marginal utilities per dollar of different products are equal.

The curve labeled **MU(CDs)/$** shows marginal utilities per dollar of CDs at the different numbers of CDs per year shown along the horizontal axis. The curve labeled **MU(books)/$** shows marginal utilities per dollar for books. At points to the left of point **E**, **MU(books)/$** exceeds **MU(CDs)/$.** This means that by buying more books, and consequently fewer CDs, total utility is increased. At points to the right of **E**, **MU(CDs)/$** exceeds **MU(books)/$,** so total utility is increased by buying more CDs. That is, utility is increased by moving toward the combination at point **E** from both sides of **E**. Only at point **E** is it impossible to increase total utility by changing the combination. That is, point **E** is the combination with maximum total utility.

marginal utilities per dollar of CDs and books are equal. That is, at point *E*, the point of maximum total utility,

$$MU(\text{CDs})/\$ \ = \ MU(\text{books})/\$. \qquad (4.1)$$

This is the same conclusion reached earlier.

The conclusion that for maximum total utility, marginal utilities per dollar must be equal also can be written as

$$\frac{MU\,(\text{CDs})}{Price\,(\text{CDs})} = \frac{MU\,(\text{books})}{Price\,(\text{books})} \tag{4.2}$$

Equation 4.2 just makes use of the fact that marginal utility per dollar is a product's marginal utility divided by its price.

The conclusion for two commodities extends to the consumption of numerous items. A consumer's budget is "optimally" allocated, that is, total utility is being maximized over N items, when

> A consumer's total utility is maximized when marginal utilities per dollar of all items purchased are equal.

$$\frac{MU\,(1)}{P\,(1)} = \frac{MU\,(2)}{P\,(2)} = \cdots = \frac{MU\,(N)}{P\,(N)} \tag{4.3}$$

where the numbers in parentheses refer to all the different commodities a consumer buys.

The framework we have described, in which the consumer is viewed as allocating his or her budget to achieve equal satisfaction from the last dollar spent on everything, provides a useful way of thinking about the objective of marketing, which involves packaging, advertising, and so on. As we shall explain in the Crossing Bridges section, the role of marketing is to push the MU/P on the advertised product higher so that it exceeds the MU/P on other products. Reestablishing the total utility–maximizing allocation of the consumer's budget involves buying more of the product with the increased MU/P until the extra consumption of that product relative to other products has reequalized the MU/Ps. This occurs with a higher quantity of the promoted product in the consumer's budget. Viewed this way, marketing is seen as a method of influencing the satisfaction people expect to receive from products, and this is why so much of our advertising shows people enjoying themselves with the advertised items.

> Marketing is designed to increase consumers' expected utility per dollar.

Product Prices and Quantity Demanded

The condition for utility maximization in Equation 4.2 can be used to reach the well-known conclusion that the quantity of a product demanded declines as the price of that product increases, and vice versa. To do this, suppose a consumer is maximizing total utility so that the marginal utilities per dollar of CDs and books are equal. Suppose the price of CDs then rises. Clearly, if before the price increase

$$\frac{MU\,(\text{CDs})}{Price\,(\text{CDs})} = \frac{MU\,(\text{books})}{Price\,(\text{books})}$$

then after the price of CDs has increased,

$$\frac{MU\,(\text{CDs})}{Price\,(\text{CDs})} < \frac{MU\,(\text{books})}{Price\,(\text{books})} \tag{4.4}$$

where $<$ is simply shorthand for "less than." The situation that is shown in Equation 4.4 means that the consumer can increase total utility by reallocating expenditures toward books and away from CDs. That is, at higher CD prices, a smaller quantity of CDs is purchased. More generally, at higher prices, a smaller quantity is demanded.

Suppose again that a consumer is maximizing total utility, but CD prices decline rather than increase. With

$$\frac{MU\,(\text{CDs})}{Price\,(\text{CDs})} = \frac{MU\,(\text{books})}{Price\,(\text{books})}$$

before the decline in the price of CDs, then after the decline,

$$\frac{MU\,(\text{CDs})}{Price\,(\text{CDs})} > \frac{MU\,(\text{books})}{Price\,(\text{books})} \tag{4.5}$$

where $>$ is shorthand for "greater than." The situation in Equation 4.5 means total utility can be increased by buying more CDs. That is, the decline in CD prices causes an increase in the quantity demanded. More generally, at lower prices, a larger quantity is demanded. (This conclusion, and several other conclusions reached in this chapter, are derived by an alternative approach that involves indifference curves in an appendix at the end of the book.)

In the example, the only price that is assumed to change is the price of CDs. In particular, the price of books is unchanged. Because book prices are assumed unchanged, changes in CD prices mean a change in the **relative price** of CDs versus books. Therefore, the effects of prices described above are **relative price effects.**

The conclusions concerning the effects of relative prices on quantity demanded can be illustrated by considering Figure 4.3, where the curves labeled $MU_1(\text{CDs})/\$$ and $MU_1(\text{books})/\$$ are the curves *before* prices change. Suppose the price of CDs increases, but that the price of books remains unchanged. At each level of consumption of CDs, the marginal utility per dollar is reduced in proportion to the price increase. That is, below each of the points on the curve $MU_1(\text{CDs})/\$$ is a new point, lower than the original point by the percentage increase in the CD price. When joined, these points give the new marginal utility per dollar of CDs curve, labeled $MU_2(\text{CDs})/\$$. Since the consumer maximizes total utility by choosing the combination where the marginal utilities per dollar are equal, that is, where the relevant curves intersect, the new total utility-maximizing combination is point E_2. This is where the new marginal utility curve for CDs, $MU_2(\text{CDs})/\$$, intersects $MU_1(\text{books})/\$$, which is still the relevant curve for books; we have assumed that book prices are unchanged and that the consumer's budget is adjusted so that the same combination as before can be purchased. Figure 4.3 shows that the increase in the price of CDs has shifted the utility-maximizing combination from point E_1 to point E_2. The new combination involves a smaller quantity of CDs in response to the increase in CD prices.

An *increase* in the price of a product causes a decrease in the quantity of that product demanded, while a *decrease* in price causes an increase in quantity demanded.

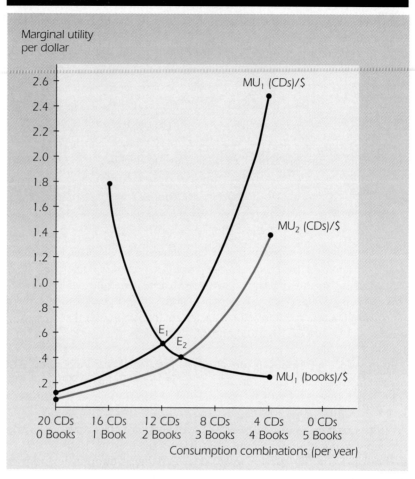

FIGURE 4.3   Increases in relative prices reduce the quantity of a product demanded.

When the price of CDs increases, the curve showing marginal utilities per dollar of CDs shifts down by the same percentage as the increase in price. If the shift is from **MU₁(CDs)/$** to **MU₂(CDs)/$,** the utility-maximizing combination shifts from point **E₁** to point **E₂**. This involves a decrease in the quantity of CDs demanded and is the result of higher CD prices. That is, increases in price reduce quantity demanded.

DEMAND CURVES

The individual consumer's demand curve is downward-sloping, showing an increase in quantity demanded as the price declines.

The effect of relative prices on quantities demanded can be drawn directly as in Figure 4.4. The vertical axis shows the price of CDs, and the horizontal axis shows the quantities of CDs demanded at each price, *on the assumption that book prices and everything else that might affect the quantity of CDs demanded are unchanged.* Point *A* shows that at a CD price of $10, the consumer buys 12 per year. Point *B* shows that at the higher price of $14, the consumer buys a smaller quantity, 8 per year, while point *C* shows that at the lower price of $6, the con-

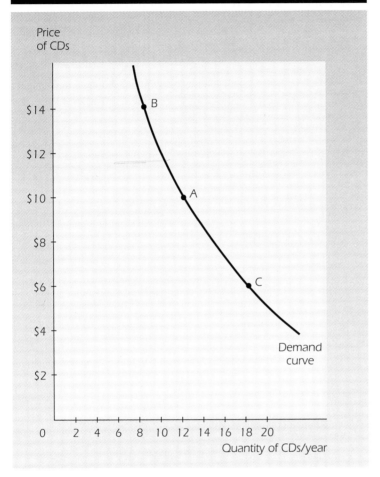

FIGURE 4.4   The relation between the price of a product and the quantity a consumer demands can be plotted as the individual consumer's demand curve.

Point **A** shows the original price of CDs, $10 each, and the original quantity demanded, 12 CDs per year. Point **B** shows a higher price of CDs, $14 each, associated with the reduced quantity demanded, 8 CDs per year. Point **C** shows what happens at lower CD prices. The curve joining these points is the consumer's demand curve. It is downward-sloping, showing an increase in quantity demanded as the price declines. The demand curve assumes that all prices other than that of the product in question are constant.

sumer buys 18 per year. Joining points such as *A*, *B*, and *C* gives a downward-sloping relation, the **individual consumer's demand curve.**

If a typical consumer increases the quantity of a product demanded as the price of that product declines, then consumers in general exhibit the same behavior. That is, when the price of a product declines, the quantity demanded by the aggregate of all consumers increases. The relation between a product's price and the quantity demanded by all consumers collectively is called the **market**

The market demand curve shows the quantity demanded by *all* consumers collectively at each price.

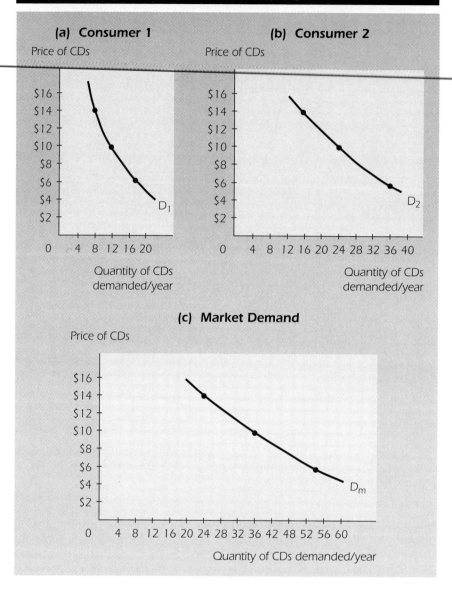

FIGURE 4.5   The market demand curve shows the aggregate of quantities demanded by all consumers at different prices.

(a) Consumer 1

Price of CDs

(b) Consumer 2

Price of CDs

(c) Market Demand

Price of CDs

Consumer 1 buys 12 CDs per year at $10 per CD, while Consumer 2 buys 24 CDs at this price. The sum of the quantities demanded by the two consumers together is therefore 36 (or 12 + 24) CDs per year. If the market consists of only these two consumers, the market quantity demanded at $10 is 36 CDs per year, as plotted in part (c). Similarly, at each other price the quantities demanded by the two consumers, as given on the horizontal axes, are added to give market quantities demanded. The collection of points giving market quantities demanded at each price is the market demand curve.

demand curve. The term **market** is used to distinguish this curve from the demand curve of an individual. The derivation of the market demand curve when the market consists of only two individuals is illustrated in Figure 4.5. Consumer 1 has the same demand curve as the individual in Figure 4.4. Consumer 2 has a different demand curve, buying twice as much as Consumer 1 at each price.

The market demand curve shows the total amount bought by all consumers at each given price. For example, at $14 per CD, Consumer 1 buys 8 CDs, Consumer 2 buys 16 CDs, and so the market quantity demanded is 24 CDs. This is shown in part (c) of Figure 4.5, where at $14 per CD the quantity demanded is 24 per year. Similarly, at a CD price of $10, Consumer 1 buys 12 CDs, Consumer 2 buys 24 CDs, and the market quantity demanded is 36 CDs.

Inspection of Figure 4.5 shows that at each possible price the market quantity demanded is the sum of the quantities demanded on the individuals' demand curves. This allows us to think of the market demand curve as the sum of individuals' demand curves, where the summation is of quantities along the horizontal axes. With all individuals' demand curves sloping downward, the market demand curve also must slope downward. That is, at lower prices, the market quantity demanded is higher, and vice versa.[2]

> *The market demand curve is obtained from the horizontal summation of quantities demanded by* all *consumers at* different *possible prices. Because each consumer's demand curve slopes downward, so does the market demand curve.*

Effects of Prices of Substitutes and Complements

When deriving the effect of CD prices on the quantity of CDs demanded, we assumed that book prices and everything else affecting the demand for CDs were constant. Let us relax this simplifying assumption and consider what happens to the demand for CDs when book prices change, but where CD prices are constant.

Consumers maximize total utility from CDs and books when they allocate their budgets such that

$$\frac{MU\,(\text{CDs})}{Price\,(\text{CDs})} = \frac{MU\,(\text{books})}{Price\,(\text{books})} \qquad (4.6)$$

If, after allocating expenditures so that Equation 4.6 holds, the price of books then increases, before expenditures have been reallocated,

$$\frac{MU\,(\text{CDs})}{Price\,(\text{CDs})} > \frac{MU\,(\text{books})}{Price\,(\text{books})}$$

With the marginal utility per dollar of CDs exceeding that of books, total utility is no longer at its maximum. Achieving maximum total utility requires buying more CDs, and consequently fewer books, until Equation 4.6 holds, this time with the higher book price. [The buying of more CDs and fewer books reduces MU (CDs) and increases MU (books) until this is achieved.] We find that an increase in book prices causes an increase in the demand for CDs. This is true for each individual consumer and hence also for the market.

---

[2] Example 4.1 considers firms' awareness of downward-sloping demand in two major industries, automobiles and airlines.

Example 4.1

THE PRICE OF HIGHER SALES

Price cutting in order to boost quantity demanded comes in a variety of forms. For example, automobile manufacturers may offer rebates, options without charge, below-market interest rates, free gas for a period of time, and so on. Rent cutting may take the form of the first month rent-free, free parking, an advance toward moving expenses, free power and cable vision, and so on. Here are two examples of direct, explicit price reductions to increase the quantity demanded described in **The Wall Street Journal.** Television advertisements and local newspapers provide many more examples on a daily basis.

AUTOMOBILE DEMAND

Detroit's making a stunning discovery: Price cuts work.

Ford Motor Co. yesterday said it will slash by about $4,000 the prices of well-equipped versions of its slow-selling Thunderbird and Cougar midsized coupes. The move comes after similar price cuts boosted sales of the Thunderbird in California by 50% since the beginning of 1992.

Earlier this year, Ford expanded a one-price strategy for certain 1993

Escort models, pricing four versions of the car at $10,899. Now, Ford is betting even more chips on a no-haggle, "value" pricing strategy, along with a growing cadre of car dealers and a few manufacturers, notably General Motors Corp.'s Saturn unit and Chrysler Corp., which has spurred sales of its minivan with a family-value package that allows buyers to get a moderately equipped minivan for $14,273.

AIR TRAVEL

Even with losses continuing to mount as a result of cut-rate summer air fares, airlines are already waging another fare war. . . .

Northwest Airlines raised the ante in the fall and winter showdown by cutting prices for its European flights by as much as 45%. Less than one week ago, Northwest and other major airlines followed the lead of Delta Air Lines, which slashed its European fares up to 40%. . . . Northwest's willingness to undercut the levels set by Delta indicates that major airlines expect weak trans-Atlantic trends to continue and it may lead to yet another bloodletting as they compete for customers in the region. . . .

"The European cuts are going to escalate until there's a huge upswing in traffic," said Robert

Cross of Aeronomics Inc., an Atlanta-based airline consulting firm. The dilemma that airlines face, he says, is that they must cut fares enough to stimulate traffic but avoid cutting them so much that it dilutes profits. . . .

Even with their continuing losses, other airlines don't seem reluctant to slash fares in other areas. Late last week, United initiated fare cuts of about 30% for fall travel to Hawaii from the contiguous 48 states. Delta quickly followed the move and added cuts for flights to Alaska from the contiguous states.

Kevin Murphy, an industry analyst at Morgan Stanley & Co., said he doesn't expect the fall and winter initiatives to fall to the unprofitable levels that this summer's fares did. "I don't view this round of cuts as a destructive move, but more of a move that reflects the weakness of demand," he said.

Sources: "Ford to Slash Prices by About $4,000 On Some Thunderbirds and Cougars," **The Wall Street Journal,** September 10, 1992, p. B3; and Brett Pulley, "Air-Fare Wars in Fall, Winter Target Europe," **The Wall Street Journal,** August 11, 1992, p. B1. Reprinted by permission of The Wall Street Journal, © 1992 Dow Jones & Company, Inc. All Rights Reserved Worldwide.

The conclusion that an increase in book prices causes an increase in demand for CDs follows at each possible price of CDs. That is, given the price of CDs, an increase in book prices causes an increase in the demand for CDs, whatever the price of CDs.

The effect of book prices on the demand for CDs is illustrated in Figure 4.6. Before the increase in the price of books, the demand curve for CDs is D_1. After

FIGURE 4.6   An increase in the price of books, a substitute for CDs, causes an increase in the demand for CDs.

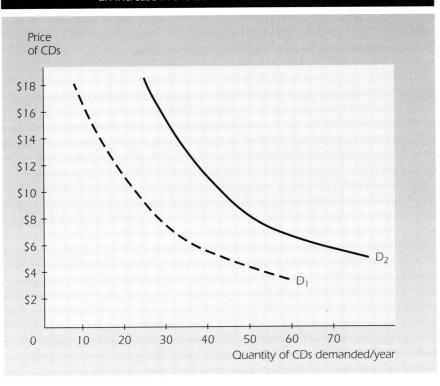

The demand curve for CDs at the original price of books is **D**₁. After book prices have increased, the demand curve for CDs is **D**₂. The new demand curve is to the right of the original demand curve. This means that at every price there is an increase in the number of CDs demanded. Such a shift of the demand curve is called an increase in demand and occurs here as a result of an increase in the price of a substitute.

the increase in the price of books, the demand curve for CDs is D_2. Demand curve D_2 is to the right of D_1. This means that at each price of CDs, more CDs are demanded after the increase in the price of books.

When the demand curve shifts to the right as in Figure 4.6, we say that there has been "an increase in demand." This is to distinguish such a *shift* in the demand curve from a movement *along* the demand curve. When there is a movement along the demand curve, as there is when the price of CDs declines and more CDs are purchased, we say there has been "an increase in quantity demanded." That is, an increase in demand means more demand at every possible price—as in the case of CD demand when book prices increase—while an increase in quantity demanded means more of a product is demanded because that product's own price is lower. A similar distinction applies to a decrease in demand, meaning a leftward shift of the demand curve, versus a decrease in quantity demanded, meaning a movement up and along a given demand curve.

An increase in *demand* means a rightward shift of the demand curve. An increase in *quantity demanded* means a movement down and along a given demand curve.

Products for which an increase in the price of one causes an increase in demand for the other are known as **substitutes.**[3] Substitutes are products that fill a similar want, such as Coke versus Pepsi, Brand X beer versus Brand Y beer, whole-wheat bread versus rye bread, butter versus margarine, beef versus chicken, or CDs versus books. We can think of what happens along the following lines: as the price, for example, of chicken goes up, people reduce the quantity of chicken they buy—this is the effect of the product's own price—and this causes people to want to buy more substitutes for chicken that have become relatively cheaper, such as beef, turkey, and so on.

There are products for which an increase in the price of one product causes a *decrease* in the demand for another, the opposite to what happens for substitutes. For example, an increase in the price of CD players can be expected to reduce the quantity of CD players bought and, consequently, reduce the demand for CDs. That is, a higher price of CD players reduces the demand for CDs. Similarly, a lower price of CD players increases the demand for CDs. This happens because a lower price of CD players means more CD players bought, and this means a greater demand for CDs.

Products for which an increase in the price of one causes a *decrease* in the demand for the other are called **complements.**[4] Complements are products that are enjoyed together, such as golf clubs and golf balls, bread and butter, ice cream and ice cream toppings, computer hardware and computer software, and CDs and CD players.[5] Complements are opposite to substitutes in that an increase in the price of one substitute causes an increase in the demand for the other, whereas with complements it is the other way around. For example, an increase in the price of computer hardware would cause a decrease in the demand for software. This would occur because an increase in the price of computer hardware would reduce the quantity of hardware demanded—the usual effect of a product's price on the quantity of that product demanded—and because the reduced quantity of hardware demanded would reduce the demand for software.

The effect of prices on the demand for complements is shown in Figure 4.7. The demand curve D_1 shows the demand for CDs before a change in the price of CD players. The demand curve D_2 shows the demand curve for CDs after an increase in the price of CD players and consequent reduction in the number of CD players purchased. Comparing curve D_2 with curve D_1 shows a reduced demand for CDs at each price after the increase in CD player prices. More generally, there is a downward or leftward shift of demand curves from an increase in the price of a complement and an upward or rightward shift of demand curves from a decrease in the price of a complement.

Substitutes are products that fill a similar want. An increase *in the price of a product causes an* increase *in the demand for its substitutes, and vice versa.*

Complements are products that are enjoyed together. An increase *in the price of a product causes a* decrease *in demand for its complements, and vice versa.*

---

[3] Alternatively, we can think of substitutes as products for which an increase in the quantity of one product reduces the marginal utility of the other. Strictly speaking, unless we control for the effects of price increases on the purchasing ability of a consumer, products for which an increase in the price of one causes an increase in demand for the other are **gross substitutes.**

[4] Alternatively, we can think of complements as products for which an increase in the quantity of one causes an increase in the marginal utility of the other. This is the opposite to a substitute, where an increase in the quantity of one reduces the marginal utility of the other.

[5] Example 4.2 suggests that CDs are also a complement of jukeboxes and possibly even of fast food.

FIGURE 4.7   An increase in the price of CD players, a complement of CDs, causes a decrease in demand for CDs.

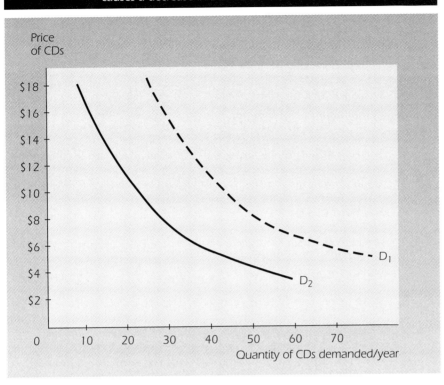

The demand curve for CDs at the original price of CD players is **D**₁. After CD player prices increase, the demand curve for CDs is **D**₂. This curve is below and to the left of **D**₁. This means that at every price of CDs there is a decrease in the number of CDs demanded. Such a downward or leftward shift of the demand curve results from an increase in the price of a complement.

Effects of Consumer Preferences

Demand curves also shift as a result of changes in the **preferences** or **tastes** of consumers for different goods and services. For example, if it becomes fashionable to own a pedigree dog, ride a 21-speed mountain bike, use a graphite tennis racket, wear running shoes, or eat at a particular chic restaurant, demand will be higher at all prices of these goods or services. That is, a shift in tastes or preferences toward particular goods or services causes a rightward shift in demand curves. Similarly, reduced interest in eating high-fat meat, using high-phosphate detergent, or wearing polyester clothing and formal Oxford shoes means reduced demand for these items at all prices. That is, a shift in tastes away from particular goods or services causes a leftward shift in demand curves.[6]

Demand curves shift to the right and left with changes in taste.

─────────────────────

[6] Example 4.3 explains how substantially and rapidly tastes can change in the music business.

Example 4.2

BETTER TOGETHER: THE CD JUKEBOX AND PIZZA

It's not only personal CD players which are complementary to CDs. Jukeboxes, which almost disappeared in the 1970s and 1980s, have faced rising demand with the advent of CDs. Furthermore, as the following explains, the CD jukebox may well be a complement of pizza and hamburgers in family and fast food outlets. Consumers appear to like to consume food and music at the same time.

Jukeboxes, those beacons of the 1950s popular culture with their glowing, gumball-colored bubble lights, faded away in the ensuing decades as surely as dance crazes like the twist.

But, today the beat goes on: The jukebox is back, thanks largely to the compact disk and aggressive promotional efforts. Makers have found that a sales slump can be reversed—even if it has lasted a quarter of a century.

Rowe International, Whippany, N.J., says its jukebox sales have jumped 30% or 40% since 1988, when it introduced its first CD jukebox. . . . Like its main U.S. competitors, Wurlitzer Co. and Rock-Ola Manufacturing Inc., Rowe is touting the versatility of the CD jukeboxes. Because the new players hold up to 1,400 selections, compared with just 160 for the old-fashioned varieties, their manufacturers are advertising them as nifty additions to almost any enclosed space, from suburban basements and trendy clothing stores to the dressing rooms and gymnasiums of physical-fitness centers. . . .

While CD jukeboxes are making new inroads, they are also making a comeback at their old bastions: family restaurants, soda shops, and bars. At Margaritaville, a Mexican restaurant in Pittsburgh, manager Max Hinkle says the CD jukebox is so popular that "songs are still playing at 5 a.m.—hours after we

close." Across town, at Chief's, a popular bar for college students, the CD jukebox is "the primary source of entertainment when the sun goes down," says bartender Jeff Dugan. . . .

One potentially huge but so-far largely untapped market is the fast-food industry. Jukeboxes have been a mainstay in many of the 7,000 Pizza Hut locations around the U.S., but other restaurant chains have resisted. One reason: they thrive on fast turnover and don't want to be hangouts for music-loving teens.

That is changing, says Jack Kapella, general manager of Chicago's Seeburg International Inc., a jukebox maker. After many attempts by jukebox companies in the past, Seeburg says it was given permission in July to test one of its new CD jukeboxes in a McDonald's location in the Chicago area. . . .

Source: Kevin E. Cullinane, "Jukebox Sales are Booming to Beat of CDs," **The Wall Street Journal,** September 2, 1992, p. B2.

As the Crossing Bridges section explains, tastes, or more generally the matters behind consumers' preferences, are in the domain of psychology. However, tastes are also influenced by advertising and marketing, which, as we mentioned earlier, are aimed at affecting the marginal utility people expect to receive from products at given levels of consumption. Economists typically assume that tastes are exogenous, that is, something to be taken as a given. This implies that the "consumer is king," telling producers what to make, not the other way around. This is the very opposite perspective to that of marketing executives, who believe that tastes can be managed, even manipulated.[7] Furthermore, economists assume that given their preferences, consumers make rational decisions to maximize utility. Psychologists, on the other hand, do not take rationality as given. Indeed, as the Crossing Bridges section points out, psychiatry is concerned with the "irrational."

Economists assume that tastes are given and that consumers behave rationally.

[7] As Example 4.4 explains, marketing consists of more than advertising. It also involves packaging, promotion, design, display, and distribution, all of which are intended to shift the demand curve.

Example   **4.3**   **BLUES FOR THE ROCK INDUSTRY**

The importance of taste as a cause of shifts in demand varies greatly among industries. One industry where taste takes rapid turns is popular music. As the following excerpt explains, several factors are behind the swings in demand. For example, demographics and technology can play a role.

Two 13-year-old rappers who wear their clothes backwards are currently selling more records than Bruce Springsteen, while an opera recording by three famous tenors has outsold the last two Rolling Stones albums combined.

The Grammy Award for best song of 1991 went to "Unforgettable," which was written 40 years ago. One in four radio stations in the U.S. now plays country music, but only one in 15 plays Top 40 hits.

Whatever happened to rock 'n' roll? . . .

Rock has demographic problems. Teenagers still drive the record business, and rock is what their parents listened to, so they buy rap and anything else that connotes independence.

And rock has technological problems. The electronics revolution gave baby boomers Stratocaster guitars and record players, unifying their musical culture. But it gave the next generation multi-channel cable TV, isolationist Walkman technology, and recordings of

popular music from all over the world, thus encouraging musical eclecticism. Grammy awards are now bestowed in 78 musical categories, up from 28 when the awards began in 1958. Rock got a reprieve with the invention of the compact disk, which caused baby boomers to buy digitized re-issues of their youthful anthems, but that sales surge has peaked.

Source: Meg Cox, "Rhythm and Blues: Rock Is Slowly Fading as Tastes in Music Go Off in Many Directions," **The Wall Street Journal,** August 26, 1992, p. A1.

Effects of Income on Demand

Normal Goods and Services.   In considering how an individual achieves the maximum total utility, the budget allocated to CDs and books was assumed constant. It is time to consider what happens when the consumer's available budget is not constant but instead is increasing as a result, for example, of an increase in the consumer's income.

For any given set of prices facing a consumer, the higher the consumer's income, the greater is the consumer's demand for most goods and services. This means that for most goods and services, individual consumers' demand curves shift to the right, showing increased quantities demanded at each possible price. With each consumer's demand curve shifting to the right, market demand curves also shift to the right. Similarly, after decreases in incomes, individuals' demand curves and market demand curves for most goods and services shift to the left. This is the situation for **normal goods and services,** where by **normal** we mean that demand changes in the same direction as consumers' incomes.

Inferior Goods and Services.   While most goods and services are normal, experiencing increased demand after increases in incomes, this association between demand and income is not universal. For some goods and services, the demand

Increases in incomes cause individual consumers' demand curves for normal goods and services to shift to the right. Decreases in incomes cause individuals' demand curves for normal goods and services to shift to the left.

Example 4.4

MARBLES: ON A ROLL

When considering the factors affecting demand, economists focus on a product's own price, prices of substitutes and complements, and consumers' incomes. However, in the business discipline of marketing, other factors such as design, packaging, promotion, and distribution are emphasized. The following excerpt explains how the factors emphasized in marketing can play a role in shifting the demand curve even after several decades of decline.

Marble makers and sellers say they're seeing a welcome bounce in sales after three decades of slump.

Marbles were all the rage during the Depression because they were cheap and plentiful. In the 1930s, the late Berry Pink, "the Marble King," boasted that his company made enough marbles to give every American boy 50 of them. And 20 years later, marbles were still going strong. Peltier Glass Co., Ottawa, Ill., was churning out 160 million each year, says the company's president, Joseph Jankowski.

But by the late 1950s, marbles had begun rolling toward toy oblivion. Television was in. Later, toys that beeped, blinked and talked were musts. Some U.S. marble makers, fearful about liability suits over kids choking and beset by competition from imports, stopped production. By the late 1960s, some cities were canceling local marble competitions for lack of interest.

But today, marbles are rebounding in popularity, proof that smart marketing can revive even a seemingly moribund product. Marble manufacturers and sellers are racking up growing sales. Instead of spending lavishly on advertising, they are making a greater variety of marbles. Some sport Batman and Disney characters, for example. They also offer eye-grabbing packaging and keep the toys affordable. Kids can buy two fistfuls of regular marbles for around $1. More retailers, meanwhile, are displaying their marbles prominently during promotions that harken back to bygone times and prices. . . .

Responding to the growing demand, Strombecker Corp., one of the country's oldest toy companies, resumed sales two years ago after a 30-year hiatus, says Daniel Shure, the company's president, whose great-grandfather Nathan Shure founded Strombecker.

Mr. Shure and his father, Myron, the company's chairman, made the decision after noticing consumers snapping up imports from Mexico, Taiwan, South Korea, China and Brazil not just for play, but for collecting and for use in floral arrangements and crafts. "It made us sit back and think about marbles and what a marvelous basic toy they are," says Mr. Shure.

But marbles "weren't being marketed well," Mr. Shure adds. "They were in unattractive packaging—so we've provided better packaging, which on the shelf gives them more interest, and we've expanded the distribution of them by getting them into stores that haven't carried them for a while."

Today, there are all kinds of marbles in addition to the classic cat's eyes, a clear marble with a swirl of color resembling an eye; clearies, made of clear glass; and aggies, produced from stone agate. Now, there are fancy opaques, as well as irridescent and textured marbles. The new marbles have names like sparkle, glitter, meteor and diamond.

Source: Dorothy J. Gaiter, "Makers of Marbles Get Kids to Shoot Clearies Again: Savvy Marketers Succeed with Depression-Era Toy in the Video Age," **The Wall Street Journal,** August 14, 1992, p. B2. Reprinted by permission of The Wall Street Journal, © 1992 Dow Jones & Company, Inc. All Rights Reserved Worldwide.

decreases when incomes increase. These are called **inferior goods and services,** and for these, demand curves shift to the left from increases in incomes, and vice versa.

Inferior goods and services include such items as

1. **Bus rides in richer nations.** Rising incomes result in increased ownership of cars and consequent reductions in the demand for bus services.

2. **Donkeys and bicycles in poorer nations.** In nations where donkeys and bicycles are the principal means of transportation, increases in income can lead to increased demand for motorcycles and bus travel, reducing the demand for donkeys and bicycles.

3. **Potatoes and rice.** As incomes increase, people can afford more meat, fish, cheese, green vegetables, and so on, and they may therefore reduce their consumption of such staples as potatoes and rice.

4. **Chicory and beer.** Rising incomes allow people to enjoy more expensive coffees and teas, lowering the demand for drinks based on chicory. Similarly, as people become more affluent, they tend to drink more wine relative to beer.

5. **Food for cooking at home.** As the standard of living has advanced, people have patronized restaurants, hamburger chains, and so on. This reduces the demand for meals at home and the food that goes into them.[8]

ELASTICITY OF DEMAND

Quantity Demanded versus Amount Spent: The Relevance of Elasticity

While we can be confident that an individual consumer's demand curve and the market demand curve reveal increased *quantity* demanded at lower prices, we cannot be so confident about the effect of lower prices on the *amount* consumers spend. The amount consumers spend on a product is given by the quantity purchased multiplied by the price paid, and as Table 4.3 shows, this could increase, decrease, or remain unchanged as a product's price declines. In particular, Table 4.3 shows that Consumer 1 spends more on books the higher the price of books. At $20 per book, Consumer 1 spends $320 per year; at $40 per book, Consumer 1 spends $400 per year; and so on. However, Consumer 2, spends less on books as book prices increase. Consumer 3 spends the same on books as book prices change. Clearly, the effect of prices on the amount of money spent could be in any direction.

---

[8] Example 4.4, which describes the surge in marble sales during the deep recession in 1990–1992, suggests that a relatively cheap toy such as marbles may also be an inferior good.

TABLE 4.3

As the price of a product increases, the amount spent on it could increase, decrease, or remain unchanged.

	CONSUMER 1			CONSUMER 2			CONSUMER 3	
PRICE	QUANTITY PER YEAR	AMOUNT SPENT PER YEAR	PRICE	QUANTITY PER YEAR	AMOUNT SPENT PER YEAR	PRICE	QUANTITY PER YEAR	AMOUNT SPENT PER YEAR
$80	7	$560	$80	4	$320	$80	6	$480
60	8	480	60	7	420	60	8	480
40	10	400	40	12	480	40	12	480
20	16	320	20	30	600	20	24	480

Consumer 1 spends more on books the higher the price of books. Consumer 2 spends less on books the higher the price. Consumer 3 spends the same on books whatever the price. Therefore, the amount spent on a product can increase, decrease, or stay the same as the product's price changes.

Whether a consumer spends more, less, or the same on a product as its price changes depends on the **elasticity of demand.** By definition,

The elasticity of demand is the percentage change in quantity divided by the percentage change in price.

$$\text{Elasticity of demand} = \frac{\text{percent change in quantity}}{\text{percent change in price}} \qquad (4.7)$$

The elasticity of demand is a measure of how strongly people respond to changes in the price of a product. The more the quantity demanded changes when the price changes, the larger is the elasticity of demand. Because the quantity demanded changes in the opposite direction to the price, the elasticity of demand is negative. However, we generally drop the sign on the percentage changes and consider only the absolute values. This method allows us to write elasticity as

$$\eta = \frac{|\text{percent change in quantity}|}{|\text{percent change in price}|} = \frac{|\%\Delta q|}{|\%\Delta p|} \qquad (4.8)$$

where η stands for elasticity of demand and the vertical bars mean that we consider the percentage changes, designated by $\%\Delta$, always to be positive numbers, whether the changes are increases or decreases in price or quantity.

Firms clearly have a keen interest in elasticity of demand because this influences the extent to which quantity sold increases from price reductions or decreases from price hikes. For example, a fast food outlet is interested in whether a 10% increase in the price of a hamburger would cause a 15%, 20%, or even greater drop in sales. Governments and government agencies also have a keen interest in elasticity of demand. For example, in considering the consequences of the Clinton administration's hotly debated gasoline tax, the U.S. government would have to use estimates of the elasticity of demand for gasoline to determine by how much gas sales would decline. In turn, the elasticity of demand for gasoline will affect how much revenue is collected from a gasoline tax; the larger the reduction in quantity of gasoline sold, the smaller is the revenue from the tax. Similarly, a municipal bus company needs to know the elasticity of passenger demand when it considers changing fares.

The Terminology of Elasticity

When the quantity demanded changes more than the price, that is, when $|\%\Delta q|$ exceeds $|\%\Delta p|$, we say that demand is **elastic.** In this case, with $|\%\Delta q| > |\%\Delta p|$, in Equation 4.8 the value of η exceeds 1. When the quantity demanded changes less than the price, that is, when $|\%\Delta q| < |\%\Delta p|$, we say that demand is **inelastic.** In this case η is less than 1. In the special case where quantity demanded and price change by exactly the same amount, that is, $|\%\Delta q| = |\%\Delta p|$, we say that demand is **unit elastic,** because, in this case, $\eta = 1$.

The terms **elastic, inelastic,** and **unit elastic** are only part of the terminology of elasticity. Other terms used include **perfectly inelastic,** where $\eta = 0$, and **perfectly elastic,** where $\eta = \infty$. Perfectly inelastic demand requires that there is no change in quantity, that is, $|\%\Delta q| = 0$, as the price changes, while perfectly elastic demand requires that the quantity changes by an infinite amount, that is, $|\%\Delta q| = \infty$, as the price changes. Perfectly inelastic and perfectly elastic demands are the extremes of inelastic and elastic demand. Figure 4.8 shows how perfectly inelastic and perfectly elastic demand curves appear graphically, and Table 4.4 summarizes the terminology concerning elasticity. Example 4.5 explains the relevance of elasticity by means of a specific example.

When a consumer spends a larger amount on a product as the price of the product increases, as does Consumer 1 in Table 4.3, this must be because the price increase is not fully offset by a reduction in quantity purchased. From our definitions of elastic, inelastic, and unit elastic, we see that this occurs with inelastic demand, for which the reduction in quantity is smaller than the increase in price. Figure 4.9 on page 96 shows graphically what happens in this case. The figure shows the amount spent on books by Consumer 1 when book prices change. The amount spent on a product is the price paid multiplied by the quantity purchased. Since the price is measured on the vertical axis and the quantity purchased is measured on the horizontal axis, the amount spent at any price is given by the area of a rectangle. For example, the amount per year spent on books at a price of $20 is the area of the rectangle *OABC*, which is $320 (or $20 per book × 16 books). The amount spent at the higher price of $60 per book is area *ODEF*, which is $480 (or $60 per book × 8 books).

By inspecting the shaded areas of rectangles *OABC* and *ODEF*, we see that the amount spent by Consumer 1 at the price of $60 per book is larger than what is spent at $20 per book. (If it is not clear from comparing the entire shaded areas of the rectangles, it should be clear when we recognize that the darkly shaded area is common to both *OABC* and *ODEF* so that we need compare only the lightly shaded areas.)

When a consumer spends a smaller amount on a product as the product's price increases, the demand for the product must be elastic because, for this to occur, we need a larger percentage reduction in quantity demanded than the percentage increase in the product's price. Consumer 2's demand for books is elastic; as Table

Demand is *inelastic* when $\eta < 1$. This occurs when the percentage change in quantity demanded is smaller than the percentage change in price. Demand is *elastic* when $\eta > 1$. This occurs when the percentage change in quantity demanded exceeds the percentage change in price.

Perfectly inelastic demand means an *elasticity of zero* and occurs when quantity demanded does not change with changes in price. Perfectly elastic demand means an *elasticity of infinity* and occurs when quantity demanded changes an infinite amount with changes in price.

When demand is inelastic, more is spent on the product the higher the price. When demand is elastic, less is spent on the product the higher the price.

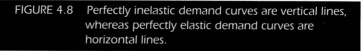

FIGURE 4.8   Perfectly inelastic demand curves are vertical lines, whereas perfectly elastic demand curves are horizontal lines.

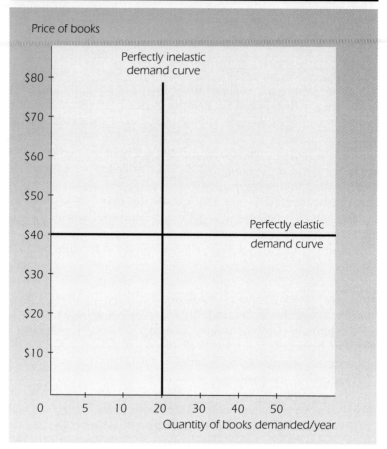

When demand is perfectly inelastic, the same quantity is demanded whatever the price. Here, this is 20 books per year at all prices. The perfectly inelastic demand curve is vertical. When demand is perfectly elastic, a tiny decrease in price causes the quantity demanded to become infinite, while a tiny increase in price causes the quantity demanded to become zero. Here, at prices above $40 per book the quantity demanded is zero, and at a price below $40 per book the quantity demanded is infinite. The perfectly elastic demand curve is flat.

4.3 shows, the amount spent decreases as the price increases. At $20 per book, spending is $600 per year; at $40 per book, spending is $480 per year; and so on. Figure 4.10 on page 97 describes the situation graphically. The amount spent on books at a price of $20 per book is given by area *OABC,* which is $600 (or $20 per book ✕ 30 books). The amount spent at the higher price, $60 per book, is area *ODEF,* which is $420 (or $60 per book ✕ 7 books). The amount spent is lower at higher prices.

....
TABLE 4.4

Elasticity of demand is described differently according to its value.

VALUE OF ELASTICITY, η	CONVENTIONAL TERMINOLOGY
$\eta = 0$	Perfectly inelastic
$0 \leq \eta < 1$	Inelastic
$\eta = 1$	Unit elastic
$1 < \eta \leq \infty$	Elastic
$\eta = \infty$	Perfectly elastic

When the elasticity of demand is smaller than 1, it is called inelastic, even if it is equal to zero. However, when it is equal to zero, it has a special name, perfectly inelastic. When the elasticity is greater than 1, it is called elastic even if it is infinite. However, when it is infinite, it has a special name, perfectly elastic.

Factors Affecting Elasticity of Demand

The principal factor affecting the elasticity of demand is the availability of substitutes. For example, the scope for substituting for gasoline is very limited, at least in the short run, so the demand for gasoline is inelastic. That is, the quantity of gasoline demanded declines by a smaller percentage than the price of gasoline increases. However, there are very close substitutes for any individual brand of gasoline, so the demand for (say) Shell gasoline is elastic. That is, the quantity of Shell gasoline demanded declines by a larger percentage than the price of Shell gasoline increases, assuming that the prices of other brands of gasoline are constant. More generally, because different brands of the same product are closer substitutes than are different products, the demand for any individual brand of a product is more elastic than is the entire market demand for the product. Furthermore, the demand facing an individual supplier of a specific brand of a product, for example, Shell gasoline from Harvey's Service Station, is more elastic than the demand collectively facing all suppliers of the brand.

Another factor affecting the elasticity of demand is the time frame over which it is measured. For example, the demand for gasoline is more elastic in the long run than in the short run. In the long run, higher gasoline prices cause people to buy more fuel-efficient cars, to buy diesel- instead of gasoline-powered cars, to have engines converted from gasoline to propane or natural gas, to form car pools, and so on. All these ways of reducing the need for gasoline take time.

The elasticity of demand is also affected by how important an item is within a consumer's total budget. For example, the demand for salt is not sensitive to price; that is, the demand is inelastic, because consumers are not likely to worry if the price of a carton of salt increases from 85 to 90 cents. However, the demand for automobiles or major appliances is price-sensitive because a jump in the prices of these expensive products makes consumers think carefully about whether to change their car or update their out-of-date appliances.

Demand is more elastic the closer are substitutes, the longer the time frame over which elasticity is measured, and the more important an item is in consumers' budgets.

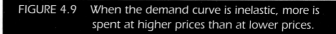

FIGURE 4.9   When the demand curve is inelastic, more is spent at higher prices than at lower prices.

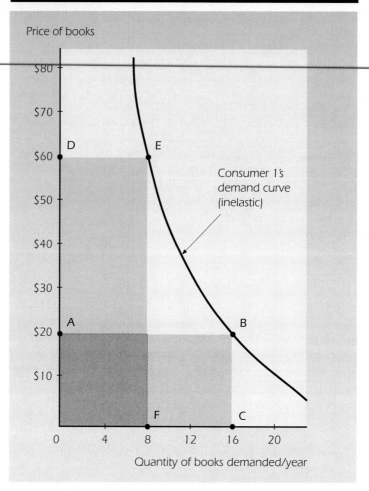

The amount spent on a product is the price paid times the quantity purchased. Therefore, it is equal to the area of the rectangle drawn with height given by the price and length given by the quantity purchased. For example, at a price of $20 per book, the amount spent is equal to the area of rectangle **OABC**, and at a price of $60 per book, it is the area of rectangle **ODEF**. Since the darkly shaded area is common to both rectangles, we can tell whether area **ODEF** exceeds area **OABC** by comparing the lightly shaded areas. There is an increase in amount spent as price increases when the demand curve is inelastic.

FIGURE 4.10   When the demand curve is elastic, less is spent at higher prices than at lower prices.

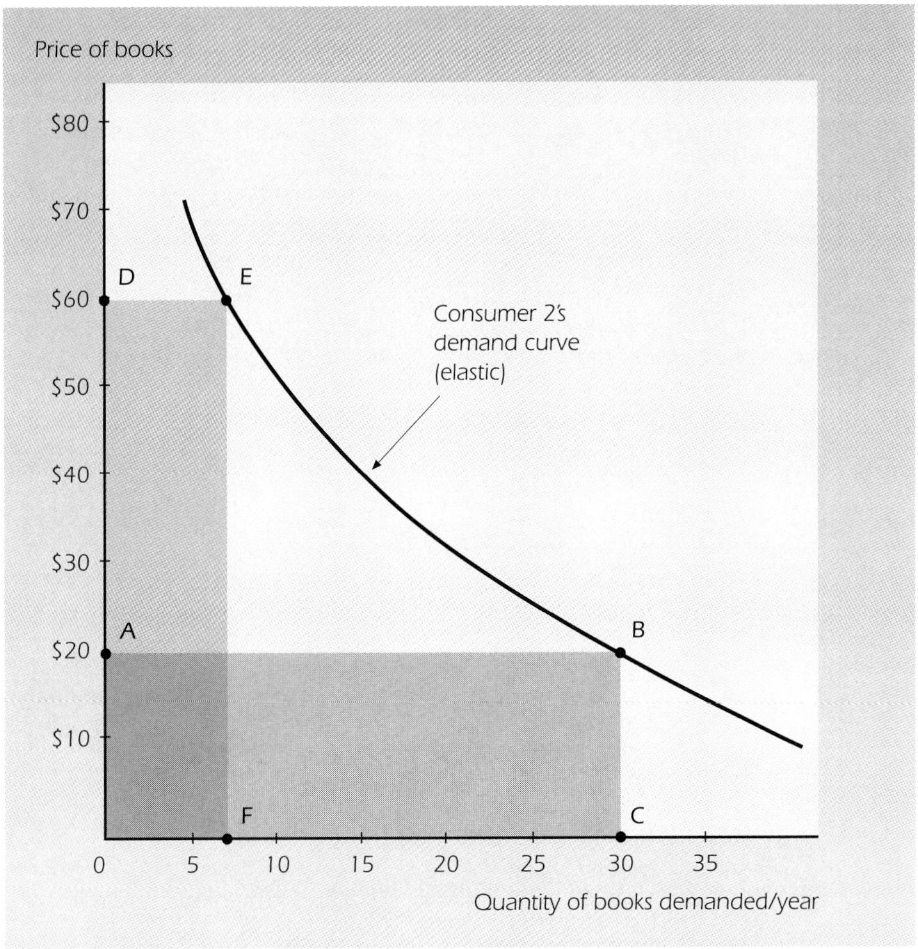

The amount spent on books per year at a price of $20 per book is $600 (or $20 per book × 30 books). At a price of $60 per book, the amount spent is $420 (or $60 per book × 7 books). The area of rectangle **OABC** is therefore larger than the area of rectangle **ODEF**. There is a decline in amount spent as the price increases when the demand curve is elastic.

Example 4.5

CREATIVE DESTRUCTION

While it may be apocryphal, the following story concerning a stamp collector vividly illustrates the relevance of elasticity of demand.

After years of quietly accumulating copies of a particular rare stamp, a collector finally realizes he has all existing specimens; advertisements have been run in all major philatelic magazines, and nobody has come forward with any extra specimens, even when the offered price has been set very high. The collector knows rare stamps face an inelastic market demand curve. What should the collector do?

The answer: the collector should destroy some of the stamps he has painstakingly and expensively acquired because the value of the remaining stamps will increase by more than the quantity declines. This is the consequence of inelastic demand, where price increases by a greater percentage than quantity declines. Indeed, if demand remains inelastic right down to one specimen, it pays to destroy all but one stamp; as each stamp before the last one is destroyed, the price of the remaining stamps increases

more than the number of stamps decreases, making the collector richer.

If the specimens of the rare stamp in our story were owned by different individuals rather than by a single collector, purposely destroying some of the stamps would probably not be profitable for any individual owner. This is true even though the **market** demand for the stamp is inelastic. For example, suppose there are 10 copies owned by 5 people, each with 2 stamps. Suppose also that if any owner were to sell one of his or her specimens, the market price would increase 25%, from $1 million to $1.25 million per specimen. This implies an inelastic market demand because the price increases 25% from a 10% decline in quantity, from 10 to 9 stamps. Indeed, the implied elasticity is

$$\text{Elasticity} = \frac{|\text{percent change in quantity}|}{|\text{percent change in price}|}$$

$$= \frac{10}{25} = 0.4$$

If one owner destroyed a stamp, the group of owners would collectively be better off;

the nine remaining stamps at $1.25 million each would be worth $11.25 million (or $9 \times \$1.25$ million) compared with the previous value of $10 million (or $10 \times \$1$ million). However, from the perspective of the individual owner who destroyed one of his two specimens, the quantity decline is 50%. The price increase for the individual collector of 25% from $1 million to $1.25 million leaves only $1.25 million compared with the original $2 million (or $2 \times \$1$ million). Therefore, the demand curve facing the individual collector is elastic. Specifically, for an individual collector,

$$\text{Elasticity} = \frac{|\text{percent change in quantity}|}{|\text{percent change in price}|}$$

$$= \frac{50}{25} = 2$$

That is, while the market demand curve is inelastic, with an elasticity of 0.4, the individual collector's demand curve is elastic, with an elasticity of 2.0. Therefore, the example illustrates the general point that individual sellers face more elastic demand than the market demand.

Sigmund Freud
(1856–1939)

THE PSYCHOLOGY OF CONSUMER BEHAVIOR

Not surprisingly, consumer behavior has attracted the attention of psychologists and sociologists as well as that of people interested in the business discipline of marketing. In many ways, the psychologists, sociologists, and marketers complement the theory developed by economists.

The economist considers marginal utilities as being determined by tastes, which are taken as exogenous, or given. As we have seen, the principal economic insight is that consumers maximize total utility subject to their limited incomes by equalizing marginal utilities per dollar of all the goods and services they buy. The intuition behind this conclusion is that if more utility could be achieved by spending a dollar on one product

rather than on another product, the utility-maximizing consumer would buy more of the product with higher marginal utility and less of the other product. This would add to total utility. It also would reduce the marginal utility of the product being bought in a larger amount—the more consumed, the lower the marginal utility of another unit—and raise the marginal utility of the product being bought in smaller amount. Only when the marginal utilities per dollar on all products have become equal is the consumer enjoying maximum possible total utility from his or her income.

While the economist takes marginal utilities as given and assumes that consumers behave "rationally" in the sense of maximizing utility, the psychologist takes marginal utilities as variables and considers why consumers may or may not behave rationally. Indeed, the psychologist considers how **expected** marginal utilities vary

1. With factors relating to commodities

2. With factors relating to consumers[9]

One factor relating to a commodity that may influence a consumer's expected marginal utility is **prestige**. For example, a Mercedes or a BMW gives some of its marginal utility in terms of the prestige it gives to its owner. Another factor relating to the expected marginal utility of a commodity is **status**. Status differs from prestige in that prestige products connote leadership, whereas status products connote membership. For example, "big name" products such as well-known brands of gasoline or breakfast cereal are said to give some of their utility in terms of status.[10]

A further factor behind the expected utility a product may offer a consumer is the reduction in **anxiety** it provides. This might be a factor influencing the marginal utility of deodorant, toothpaste, soap, dandruff shampoo, and so on. Another factor is a product's **style.** This would be relevant with clothes, automobiles, furniture, jewelry, and so on. Last but not least, we can mention the product's **function**. Clearly, the usefulness of a product is important for the marginal utility it offers. Function is likely to be a major factor with building materials, home heating oil, student note paper, fresh vegetables, and so on.

Those factors relating to the consumer, that is, those factors affecting marginal utilities and varying between individuals, include the consumer's personal characteristics. Age, lifestyle, occupation, personality, and economic circumstances can affect the marginal utilities different consumers gain from the same product. Another relevant consumer characteristic is cultural background. A consumer's race or religion is likely to affect the exposure the consumer has to a product as well as the way the consumer views the product. Yet a further characteristic of the consumer affecting his or her expected marginal utility from a given product is the consumer's **social reference group**. What friends and family believe a person should buy is the essential aspect of the reference group. Finally, personal psychological factors—those relating to the consumer's personality—will be at play, and it is these factors that have been given the most attention by psychologists.

Any account of personality and its influence on the marginal utility a consumer expects to receive from a product must begin with the views of Sigmund Freud, even though there are numerous other schools of thought. Freud divided the personality into three components, the **id**, the **ego**, and the **superego**.[11] In an emotionally healthy individual, these personality subsystems are in balance, allowing the individual to function effectively and purposefully. Each of the subsystems plays a different role in determining anticipated marginal utilities and the way the consumer behaves vis-à-vis what the economist considers rational. Imbalance in the subsystems that produces "odd" behavior is what is of particular interest in the subdiscipline of psychology called **psychiatry.**

The id is behind what Freud called the *pleasure principle.* Actions that respond to the id are aimed at releasing tension and are not restrained by rationality, logic, or ethics. The id is driven by impulse and can be satisfied by overt actions such as making purchases, as well as by

[9] Psychologists make a distinction between the utility a consumer **expects** to enjoy from consuming a product—in the jargon of the economist, the expected marginal utility—and the utility the consumer **actually** enjoys—the actual marginal utility. When actual enjoyment is less than expected enjoyment, the consumer is said to suffer from a dissatisfaction or disappointment called **cognitive dissonance**.

[10] The distinction between prestige and status products, as well as the other factors behind marginal utilities, are discussed by Walter A. Woods, "Psychological Dimensions of Consumer Decisions," **Journal of Marketing** (January 1960), pp. 15–19.

[11] For an excellent account of Freudian views of the effects of personality on buying decisions, see Ron J. Markin, **The Psychology of Consumer Behavior** (Englewood Cliffs, N.J.: Prentice-Hall, 1969).

dreams and fantasies. If a consumer were to respond only to the id subsystem, he or she could hardly be expected to equalize marginal utilities per dollar over the full range of alternatives as economists assume.

The component of the personality that works toward rational behavior as understood by the economist is the ego. Helping the healthy individual strike a balance between impulse and common sense, the ego is governed by what Freud called the **reality principle**. Through the ego, an individual gains patience and makes rational, logical choices consistent with the individual's well-being. It is to the ego that the economist must look for the utility-maximizing behavior that is assumed, and hence for equalization of marginal utilities per dollar over the full range of alternative products.

The final component of personality, the superego, seeks perfection and imposes morality on behavior. Even after the ego has imposed reality over the petulance of the id, the superego seeks to structure behavior that is not harmful to others. The reward the superego gives is a feeling of pride, while the punishment for ignoring the superego is guilt or shame. Although economists rarely relate consumer behavior to personality characteristics, it would be to the superego that they would look for explanations of contributions to charity, or the purchases of environmentally friendly products, or why consumers may pay more to buy products that will not hurt others, or other decisions involving volunteer work.

Freudian principles suggest that the marginal utility of a product depends on the way it motivates the subconscious part of the personality. Furthermore, the subconscious is believed to be heavily influenced by sexual symbolism. However, Freudians argue that consumers are unaware of what is behind their motivation, that is, behind the marginal utilities they expect to receive from different products. Indeed, Freudians maintain

Age, lifestyle, occupation, personality, and economic circumstances can affect the marginal utilities different consumers gain from the same product.

that consumers' cognitive processes play a very limited role in what is bought. For them, marginal utility depends heavily on symbolic characteristics such as shape and color, whereby the closer the shapes and colors are to appropriate sexual characteristics—what Freud called **libidinous**—the higher their marginal utility. Although not all psychologists accept the Freudian view, there is little doubt that it plays an important role in marketing and product design.[12]

A central theme of most psychological theories of consumer behavior is that people respond to tension and that buying decisions are directed toward reducing tension. Consumers try to move from a state of disequilibrium to one of harmony or equilibrium, which relates to the economist's view of achieving equilibrium by equating marginal utilities.

Abraham Maslow, the influential psychologist, has ordered the causes of tension in a hierarchy.[13] Maslow's hierarchy runs from the most basic **biogenic**, or physiologic, needs up to the higher-order **psychogenic**, or psychological, needs, and whatever their position in the hierarchy, the needs can be considered as the bases of marginal utilities.

At the bottom and most fundamental level of Maslow's hierarchy are needs such as hunger, thirst, warmth, and sex. When a person is hungry or thirsty, the marginal utility of food or drink is high. Only after the person is fed or has satisfied his or her thirst are the marginal utilities of food and drink brought down toward those of alternative products the consumer might buy. Items to

[12] See Ernest Dichter, **Handbook of Consumer Motivation** (New York: McGraw-Hill, 1964).

[13] Abraham H. Maslow, **Motivation and Personality** (New York: Harper and Row, 1954).

which the consumer turns next are those offering security and protection. For example, housing has a high marginal utility to the person who has food and drink but no place to live.

Once essential physiological and security needs have been satisfied, the consumer is likely to gain relatively high marginal utility from items satisfying social needs, including those expected to offer a sense of belonging and love. After these items come those satisfying ego-bolstering needs involving recognition and status.[14] Next are those involving self-actualization. The top of the hierarchy includes ego-defense needs, involving products that defend the ego from loss of prestige.

The vast majority of needs in the richer industrial societies of today are the higher-order needs, which are perhaps more aptly described as "wants." Of course, these wants are transformed into "demands" only when backed up by a willingness to buy at a given price, and it is the distinct view of those in the subject area of marketing that the willingness to buy can be influenced by packaging, advertising, exposure, and access to the product. That is, in the language of the economist, marketing raises the expected marginal utility at each quantity of the product that might be consumed. This means a higher quantity demanded at each price, with the demand reaching the point where the expected marginal utility per dollar spent on the product has been brought down to that of the other products the consumer buys. Stated differently, marketing people believe the marginal utilities are not just given, but can be manipulated so that demand curves can be shifted to the right.

Marketers argue that the marginal utility of, and hence demand for, a product depends on the **instrumental acts** required to utilize it.[15]

For example, the need to peel oranges may reduce their marginal utility, whereas the prepackaging and preparation of prepared food increases its marginal utility.[16] It is also argued by marketers that marginal utility can be affected by exposure to a product, either by actual experience with the product or vicariously by observing the experience of others. These two means of exposure can coexist and be reinforcing. One of the principal goals of marketing is to find the best way to create exposure—via advertising or personal experience—in order to affect memory of the object in a favorable manner. The hope is that, eventually, experience with the object will be so frequent and favorable that it will be bought without cognitive effort, that is, out of habit in a programmed manner. Of course, this depends heavily on learning, as indeed does much of effective marketing. Indeed, marketing of new products can be thought of as trying to achieve learning from a zero base, with that part of marketing called **consumer research** being concerned with finding what consumers might "learn to want." That is, marketing is in a sense at the other end of the spectrum to economics in taking marginal utilities as things to be managed or even created rather than simply given in an autonomous manner and set by fixed, inexorable tastes.

Sociologists and social anthropologists also have much to say about the determinants of marginal utilities and hence of demands. They tend to emphasize symbols, not the predominantly sexual symbols emphasized by Freudian psychologists, but those symbols involving social pressures. Sociologists and anthropologists emphasize the group dynamics by which wants emerge and spread, especially through the influence of reference groups. They would argue that the expected marginal utility from owning a car or taking a Caribbean vacation stems at least in part from social forces, something we have already said has also been recognized by psychologists.

[14] The higher-order psychogenic needs listed here are cited in James A. Bayton, "Motivation, Cognition, Learning—Basic Factors in Consumer Behavior," **Journal of Marketing** (January 1958), pp. 282–289, and in Philip Kotler, **Marketing Management**, 6th ed. (Englewood Cliffs, N.J.: Prentice-Hall, 1989).

[15] James A. Bayton, **op. cit.**

[16] For an account of how positive and negative factors can influence buying decisions, see Frederick Herzberg, **Work and the Nature of Man** (Cleveland: William Collins, 1966).

SUMMARY

1. Consumers are assumed to allocate their budgets among different goods and services so as to maximize their expected total utility.

2. Marginal utility is the utility from one more unit of a product. The law of diminishing marginal utility states that the marginal utility of a product declines as more of the product is consumed in a given interval of time.

3. Total utility is maximized when the marginal utilities per dollar of different products are equal. This follows because whenever the marginal utility per dollar of one product differs from that of another product, total utility can be increased by reallocating spending from the lower to the higher marginal utility product.

4. The reallocation of expenditures from products with lower marginal utilities per dollar to those with higher marginal utilities per dollar moves the marginal utilities per dollar toward each other. This follows from the law of diminishing marginal utility.

5. If a consumer is maximizing expected total utility and then a product's price increases, this reduces that product's marginal utility per dollar below that of other products. This causes consumers to reduce the quantity of the higher-priced product they buy. That is, at higher prices, the quantity demanded is less, and vice versa.

6. Quantities demanded are affected by relative price changes, meaning price changes of different products by different amounts.

7. A consumer's demand curve shows the quantities of a product demanded by an individual consumer at different prices. Demand curves are drawn assuming that other prices are not changing.

8. The change in quantities of a product demanded by all consumers collectively as its price changes is shown by the market demand curve. This slopes downward, like individuals' demand curves.

9. The market demand curve is the horizontal summation of individuals' demand curves.

10. The entire demand curve for a product shifts to the right when there is an increase in the price of a product's substitutes, and vice versa. Substitutes are products that satisfy a similar want.

11. The entire demand curve for a product shifts to the left when there is an increase in the price of a product's complement, and vice versa. Complements are products that are enjoyed together.

12. For normal goods and services, increases in incomes cause a rightward shift in their demand curves, and vice versa.

13. Inferior goods and services are those for which increases in incomes cause leftward shifts in their demand curves, and vice versa.

14. Demand curves can shift as a result of changes in preferences or tastes.

15. The elasticity of demand is measured from the ratio of the percentage change in the quantity demanded to the percentage change in price, with both measured as absolute values (as if they are positive numbers).

16. When the demand for a product in inelastic, the amount spent on the product increases as its price increases, and when demand is elastic, the amount spent decreases as the price increases. When demand is unit elastic, the amount spent is the same at all prices.

17. Perfectly inelastic demand occurs when the change in quantity demanded is zero as a product's price changes. Perfectly elastic demand occurs when a tiny reduction in price causes an infinite increase in demand, and vice versa.

18. The elasticity of demand for a product is higher the closer are substitutes, the longer the time frame of measurement of demand, and the more important the product is in consumers' budgets.

QUESTIONS AND PROBLEMS

1. Could marginal utility of a product become negative at extremely high rates of consumption, where the amount consumed is beyond the satiation level?

2. Why is it *expected* and not *actual* marginal utilities per dollar that are equated in maximizing a consumer's total utility? How might the frequency with which a product is purchased affect the difference between expected and actual marginal utilities?

3. What does Equation 4.2 imply about the effect on quantity demanded of equal percentage increases in CD and book prices?

4. Use Figure 4.3 to show what happens when CD and book prices increase by the same percentage, say 50%. Does the utility-maximizing combination change in this case, and if not, why not? Compare your answer with that in the preceding question.

5. How might a reduction in price of CD players and a consequent increase in their ownership affect the situation described in Figure 4.2? (Use the fact that for complements, a greater quantity of one product increases the marginal utility of the other at each level of consumption.)

6. Airfare price wars adversely affect demand for long-distance train and bus travel. Why?

7. Why does a movement up or down the vertical axis in a demand curve represent a change in relative but not absolute prices?

8. How might some books be substitutes while others are complements?

9. Name five pairs of athletic goods that are complements.

10. How might habit affect elasticity of demand?

11. Rank the following in terms of their elasticity of demand.
    a. Wheat
    b. U.S. wheat
    c. Kansas wheat
    d. Wheat from a Kansas farm

12. Why is it difficult to deduce elasticity of demand for a product from historical data on price and quantity sold?

CHAPTER 5

. . . .
. . . .
. . . .
. . . .
. . . .
. . . . . . Costs of Production and Supply
. . . .
. . . .

Nothing is enough for the man for whom enough is too little.

Epicurus

Key Concepts

Profit maximization; total revenue; total cost; marginal revenue; marginal cost; law of diminishing marginal product; fixed input versus variable input; fixed cost versus variable cost; long run versus short run; optimal output; average cost; relationships between cost curves; fixed costs and output; variable costs and output; firm's supply curve; market supply curve; elasticity of supply

PROFIT AND QUANTITY SUPPLIED

The Firm's Objective

In Chapter 4 we assumed that consumers maximize the total utility they can attain with their available budgets. We showed that utility maximization implies that the quantity of a product demanded is higher the lower the product's price. We also showed that demand depends on prices of substitutes and complements and on consumers' incomes. These conclusions concerning demand are used in Chapter 6 to explain the factors that affect prices. However, first it is necessary to look at the forces that influence the quantity of a product supplied.

In order to make headway explaining supply as we have with demand, assumptions must be made about what firms set out to achieve. Unlike the consumer, whom we can think of as an individual, perhaps acting as the head of a family, in the case of a firm there is frequently no single individual who can be identified as setting objectives.[1] In the case of public companies, there may be thousands of shareholders who own the company and numerous managers who run the company on the shareholders' behalf. Even in private companies, several individuals may own the company in a partnership, and there may be managers hired by the owners to run the company for them. Therefore, it is necessary to first decide *whose* objective is likely to be relevant before deciding *what* that objective might be.

Economists assume that owners of a firm share the common objective to maximize the firm's profits and that it is this objective, rather than any objectives of appointed managers, that managers pursue. The first part of this assumption, that owners have the common objective to maximize profits, is pragmatically motivated, while the second part, that managers pursue this objective, is motivated by the view that managers can be replaced if they do not do as the owners want. However, shareholders may not know whether managers are really taking care of shareholders' interests when there is imperfect information on the size of the profit it is feasible for managers to achieve. This has given rise to suggestions that managers may pursue their own objectives—enjoying perks, high salaries, an easy life, and so on—rather than the interests of shareholders. Indeed, there are some celebrated examples, such as that graphically illustrated in Example 5.1, of managers treating themselves so royally that it would stretch credibility to believe that the comforts and salaries could possibly pay for themselves in improved managerial loyalty and effectiveness. Nevertheless, it is generally believed to be a reasonable, although imperfect, approximation to assume that managers pursue the shareholders' objective on their behalf, namely the **maximization of profits.**[2]

> Managers are assumed to maximize profits.

The Implications of Profit Maximization

> Total revenue is the amount a firm receives from sales. Total cost is the cost of producing what is sold. Profit is total revenue minus total cost.

Profit equals a firm's **total revenue**—the amount the firm receives in revenue for all the goods and services it sells—minus its **total cost**—the amount the firm "pays" for raw materials, wages, rent, and interest on debt. That is,

$$Profit \equiv total\ revenue - total\ cost \qquad (5.1)$$

In this definition of profit, total cost consists not only of outlays for wages, raw materials, and so on but also includes the opportunity cost of firm-owned inputs or any inputs contributed by the owners of the firm. For example, if a farmer owns

---

[1] While large in number, small owner-managed businesses headed by one individual are relatively unimportant in terms of the total supply of all goods and services.

[2] In the economics subdiscipline of information economics and in the business subject areas of accounting and finance, considerable attention has been directed at the possible differences between managerial and shareholder objectives. The cost of information on the actual and potential performance of a company is central to discussions of this problem, because with perfect information, no conflict of interest could remain; errant managers would be fired.

Example 5.1

PROFIT MAXIMIZATION IS ONLY AN APPROXIMATE OBJECTIVE

It might well be that the perks that accompany executive success can motivate corporate decision makers to make more profit, thereby justifying the perks. However, the following excerpt, which describes the rewards enjoyed by F. Ross Johnson, president and chief executive of RJR Nabisco, suggests that there may be a tendency for success to lead to excess.

It was no lie. RJR executives lived like kings. The top thirty-one executives were paid a total of $14.2 million, or an average of $458,000. Some of them became legends at the Waverly for dispensing $100 tips to the shoeshine girl. Johnson's two maids were on the company payroll, and Johnson's lieutenants single-handedly perked up the upper end of Atlanta's housing market.

No expense was spared in decorating the new headquarters, highlighted by the top-floor digs of the top executives. The reception area's backdrop was an eighteenth-century $100,000 lacquered Chinese screen, complemented by a $16,000 pair of powder blue Chinese vases from a slightly later dynasty. Visitors could settle into a set of French Empire mahogany chairs ($30,000) and ogle the two matching *bibliothèque* cabinets ($30,000) from the same period. In each was an English porcelain dessert service in a tobacco-leaf pattern ($20,000). The visitor might be ushered in to see Bob Carbonell and pad across his camel-colored $50,000 Persian rug. Or, if the visitor was lucky enough to see Ross Johnson, they could jointly admire the $30,000 worth of blue-and-white eighteenth-century porcelain china scattered throughout his office.

It was, literally, the sweet life. A candy cart came around twice a day, dropping off bowls of bonbons at each floor's reception areas. Not Baby Ruths but fine French confections. The minimum perks for even lowly middle managers was one club membership and one company car, worth up to $28,000. (For serious luxury cars, executives had to kick in some of their own money.) The maximum, as nearly as anyone could tell, was Johnson's two-dozen club memberships and John Martin's $75,000 Mercedes.

POSTSCRIPT

In 1989, RJR Nabisco was purchased by Kohlberg Kravis Roberts and Company, and F. Ross Johnson and many of his fellow managers were replaced. As for Mr. Johnson:

Johnson decided not to get a new job. He played golf, travelled to London, Istanbul and Vail, and seemed happy to be unemployed. Six months after the sale closed, he had lost thirty pounds, bought several pieces of real estate . . . and sworn off ever working nine to five again.

———

Sources: Bryan Burrough and John Helyar, **Barbarians at the Gate: The Fall of RJR Nabisco** (New York: Harper Perennial, 1990), pp. 91–92; and Hope Lampert, **True Greed: What Really Happened in the Battle for RJR Nabisco** (New York: New American Library, 1990), p. 253.

---

his or her land, then the income this land could have earned if the farmer had made it available to somebody else is part of the total cost. Even if the land could not have been rented to somebody else but could have been sold, the interest income on the money the farmer would have received on the land is an opportunity cost and therefore part of total cost. Similar arguments apply to the use of company-owned raw materials and machines, as well as an entrepreneur's labor and money used in running a firm. For example, an owner of a corner store who works in the store should include what he or she could otherwise have earned if not working in the store as part of the total cost. The opportunity cost also includes any lost interest on entrepreneurs' own money used in businesses. That is, total cost includes amounts actually paid out for raw materials, labor, land, capital equipment, and interest on borrowed funds, as well as the opportunity cost of

Total cost includes amounts actually paid out for raw materials, labor, land, capital, and interest, as well as the opportunity cost of the firm's and entrepreneurs' own raw materials, labor, land, capital, and funds used in a business.

the firm's and entrepreneurs' own raw materials, labor, land, capital equipment, and funds used in a business.

Because total cost in Equation 5.1 includes the opportunity costs of company-owned and entrepreneur-owned inputs, the profit calculated with Equation 5.1 differs from the profit that appears in accounting statements. That is, the economists' concept of profit is different from **accounting profit.** In particular, because the total cost used in the economists' concept of profit includes opportunity costs in addition to actual outlays, the economists' profit is smaller than accounting profit.[3] In what follows, the interpretation of the word **profit** is **economic profit** unless otherwise stated. Economic profit is that calculated from Equation 5.1, where the total cost includes all opportunity costs.

> Economic profit is the difference between total revenue and total cost, where the total cost includes all opportunity costs of the firm's and entrepreneurs' own time, capital, and other resources.

Let us assume that a firm is considering whether a change in output would increase profit. Equation 5.1 implies that the change in profit caused by a change in output can be written as

$$\Delta Profit \equiv \Delta total\ revenue - \Delta total\ cost \qquad (5.2)$$

where Δ is the Greek capital "delta," for difference, or change. Equation 5.2 says that the change in profit is the change in total revenue minus the change in total cost. In the context of producing wheat, if total revenue is increased by $5 from selling another bushel and total cost is increased by $4 from producing the extra bushel, profit is increased by $1 (or $5−$4). This provides the conclusion that production should be increased as long as this increases total revenue more than it increases total cost.

> Marginal revenue is the increase in total revenue from selling one more unit of an item. Marginal cost is the increase in total cost from producing one more unit of an item.

The change in total revenue from the sale of an extra unit is called the **marginal revenue** MR, while the change in total cost from producing that item is called the **marginal cost** MC.[4] This means we can write the change in profit as

$$\Delta Profit \equiv MR - MC \qquad (5.3)$$

Equation 5.3 shows that production should be increased as long as MR exceeds MC.

> Production should be increased as long as this increases total revenue more than it increases total cost. Therefore, production should be increased when marginal revenue exceeds marginal cost.

If the increase in total revenue from extra production always exceeded the increase in total cost, that is, if MR always exceeded MC, there would be no limit to how much a profit-maximizing firm would want to produce. However, no firm produces an infinite amount. This must therefore be either because MR eventually falls or because MC eventually increases to a point where MR equals MC; after reaching such a point, profits cannot be increased by further production. Determination of how much to produce therefore involves studying what makes MR decline, or what makes MC increase, as production expands. As we shall see, a decline in MR can be attributed to limitations of the market, and an increase in MC can be attributed to limitations on the productivity of inputs.

[3] Some of the procedures used by accountants have the effect of overstating costs. For example, research expenses and capital costs are sometimes generously interpreted for accounting purposes. Where accounting costs are overstated, accounting profit is made smaller and could, in principle, be smaller than economic profit. However, normally, economic profit is smaller than accounting profit.

[4] The cost of producing an extra unit of an item, that is, the MC, depends on the combination of inputs used to produce the extra unit. We generally assume that the best possible combination of inputs is used so that MC is the lowest possible MC for a given output.

COSTS, REVENUES, AND PROFIT-MAXIMIZING OUTPUT

Marginal Revenue Facing an Individual Producer

The simplest way to explain the determination of profit-maximizing output is to use an example. Let us consider the profit-maximizing decision of a wheat farmer. Rather than introduce any unessential complexity at the beginning of the discussion, let us assume that our wheat farmer is one of many wheat farmers and can therefore sell various amounts without having an impact on the market price of wheat. This means that the increase in revenue from an extra bushel of wheat is the price of that bushel, or in other words,

$$MR = price \qquad (5.4)$$

It is not always the case that $MR = price$. However, this is not the best place to deal with the more general connection between MR and price.[5] Therefore, let us stick with the case where more can be sold at the going market price, so that MR is the same as the price, and see what then limits output. With MR constant and equal to the product's price, the limit on output must be the result of increasing MC as output expands; the increasing MC would eventually exceed the (constant) $MR = price$.

For an individual producer who can sell more without reducing the market price, marginal revenue equals price.

The Law of Diminishing Marginal Product

An increase in MC as output expands is attributable to the **law of diminishing marginal product.** The law of diminishing marginal product says that after some level of output, the extra output from using successively more of an input declines *if there is a fixed amount of some other input.* For example, the law says that if a wheat farmer uses more and more workers on a farm that is fixed in size, then eventually there will be diminishing extra outputs from each extra worker hired. This is so because extra workers cannot keep on squeezing more wheat from a given wheat farm. It is not that adding more workers to the farm of fixed size reduces output, but only that the extra output from each extra worker eventually declines. Viewed alternatively, the law of diminishing marginal product implies that after some level of output, it takes more added workers to produce an extra bushel of wheat on a given farm. When viewed in this way, the law of diminishing marginal product means an eventual increase in the marginal cost of adding to production; if it eventually takes more workers to produce an extra bushel of wheat, the cost of the extra bushel must increase.[6]

The law of diminishing marginal product states that the extra output from using more of an input eventually diminishes when some other input is fixed in amount. This means that marginal cost eventually increases.

Fixed Cost versus Variable Cost

An input that can be varied in amount is called a **variable input,** and the cost of production consisting of payments to variable inputs is called the **variable cost.**

---

[5] The connection between marginal revenue and price is discussed in Chapter 8.

[6] The law of diminishing marginal product is discussed in more detail in Chapter 10.

Inputs that *can* be varied in amount are variable inputs, and their cost is a variable cost of production. Inputs that *cannot be* varied in amount are fixed inputs, and their cost is a fixed cost of production.

An input that cannot be varied in amount, at least in the time available, is a **fixed input,** and the cost of fixed inputs is called the **fixed cost.**

In terms of the example, land is a fixed input, and the cost of the land is a fixed cost. On the other hand, labor is a variable input, and the cost of labor is a variable cost. Similarly, in a factory, the factory building itself is a fixed input. So too is specialized equipment used in the factory. On the other hand, raw materials being processed into final product and the labor employed in the factory are variable inputs, and their costs are variable costs.

In the long run, a firm's input of land or of plant and equipment is not fixed, and indeed, all input amounts can be changed given a sufficient period of adjustment. What is considered as a fixed input versus a variable input, and therefore a fixed cost versus a variable cost, depends on the time frame being considered. In order to be explicit about the time frame, it is necessary to distinguish between the **long run,** which is the period of time over which the quantity of all inputs can be changed, and the **short run,** which is the period of time over which the quantity *of at least one input* cannot be changed. For the remainder of this chapter, we will concentrate on the short run.

The long run is the period of time over which the quantity of *all* inputs can be varied. The short run is the period over which the quantity of *at least one* input cannot be varied.

Suppose that a farmer is using 45 acres of land. Suppose this costs the farmer $150 per acre per year. This would be the cost of renting the land if the farmer does not own it. Alternatively, it would be the opportunity cost of the land if the farmer owns it, where the opportunity cost is what the land, or money invested in it, would otherwise have earned. Let us assume that once the decision has been made to farm the 45 acres, nothing else can be done with the land. Therefore, land is a fixed input, and its cost is a fixed cost. If this is the only fixed cost, the farmer's **total fixed cost** *TFC,* which is the sum of actual and opportunity costs of all fixed inputs, is $6750 (or $45 \times \$150$). This is shown under the heading *TFC* in Table 5.1.

Total fixed cost is the sum of actual and opportunity costs of all *fixed inputs*. This does not vary with output. Total variable cost is the sum of actual and opportunity costs of all *variable inputs*. This increases with output. Total cost is the sum of total fixed cost *and* total variable cost.

The **total variable cost** *TVC* of each possible level of output is the sum of actual and opportunity costs of all variable inputs used to produce that output. For example, the *TVC* includes the cost of seed, fertilizer, fuel, and the value of the farmer's own time if he or she had been employed elsewhere. Total cost *TC* is equal to total fixed cost plus total variable cost. The *TVC*s and *TC*s for different outputs are shown in Table 5.1. We have assumed the total variable cost of 500 bushels is $1800, that 1000 bushels has a *TVC* of $3000, and so on. Therefore, the total cost of 500 bushels is $8550 (or $6750 + $1800), the total cost of 1000 bushels is $9750 (or $6750 + $3000), and so on.

The values of *TC,* along with its components, *TFC* and *TVC,* are plotted in Figure 5.1. Figure 5.1 shows *TFC* as a horizontal line, reflecting the fact that it does not change as output is changed. *TVC* at first increases slowly, but as output is expanded with the farm size fixed, the law of diminishing marginal product means that eventually the costs of further increases in output increase more quickly. After an output of about 5000 bushels per year, the increases in costs from adding further to output become extremely large, reflecting the difficulty of squeezing a greater output from the farm of fixed size. *TC* is the sum of *TFC* and *TVC*. Since *TFC* is constant, *TC* is a constant distance above *TVC* at all production levels. (If it appears that *TVC* is closer to *TC* at higher outputs, this is the result of looking at the figure incorrectly. *TC* is a constant distance *above TVC;* cost graphs are to be read vertically, not horizontally.)

....
TABLE 5.1

Marginal costs may decline initially as output expands, but eventually, with a fixed factor of production, marginal costs will increase.

OUTPUT (bushels per year)	TFC	TVC	TC	MC PER 500 BUSHELS	MC PER BUSHEL
0	$6,750	$0	$6,750	n/d	n/d
500	6,750	1,800	8,550	$1,800	$3.60
1,000	6,750	3,000	9,750	1,200	2.40
1,500	6,750	3,900	10,650	900	1.80
2,000	6,750	4,700	11,450	800	1.60
2,500	6,750	5,500	12,250	800	1.60
3,000	6,750	6,400	13,150	900	1.80
3,500	6,750	7,450	14,200	1,050	2.10
4,000	6,750	8,750	15,500	1,300	2.60
4,500	6,750	10,450	17,200	1,700	3.40
5,000	6,750	12,700	19,450	2,250	4.50
5,500	6,750	15,800	22,550	3,100	6.20
6,000	6,750	20,800	27,550	5,000	10.00
6,500	6,750	28,800	35,550	8,000	16.00

TFC is total fixed cost, **TVC** is total variable cost, **TC** is total cost, **MC** is marginal cost, and n/d means "not defined." **TC** is the sum of **TFC** and **TVC**. **MC** per 500 bushels is obtained from the difference between **TC** for each rate of production and **TC** for the next lowest rate of production in steps of 500 bushels. For example, **MC** per 500 bushels at the production rate of 4000 bushels is the **TC** for 4000 bushels minus the **TC** for 3500 bushels, that is, $1300 (or $15,500 − $14,200). The last column is the **MC** per 500 bushels divided by 500, providing the **MC** per bushel.

Marginal Cost at Different Outputs

Recall that the marginal cost of wheat is the increase in total cost from producing one extra bushel. Precise values of *MC per bushel* cannot be obtained from Table 5.1 because the steps in the measurement of output are for 500 bushels, not for individual extra bushels. To obtain an approximate value of *MC* per bushel, we begin by computing the additional costs of each extra 500 bushels, which are given in the column headed "*MC* per 500 bushels." We see that this is not defined for zero bushels, since there cannot be an extra 500 bushels at an output of zero. The *MC* of the first 500 bushels is the *TC* for 500 bushels, that is, $8550, minus the *TC* for zero bushels, that is, $6750, giving an *MC* per 500 bushels of $1800 (or $8550 − $6750) for the first 500 bushels. This is shown at the 500 bushel rate of wheat output. The *MC* of the second 500 bushels, that is, the increase in *TC* in going from 500 to 1000 bushels per year, is $1200 (or $9750 − $8550). This is shown at the 1000 bushel rate of wheat output.

The reduction in *MC* when increasing output from 500 to 1000 bushels may be due to an ability to use inputs more fully when output is expanded from very low

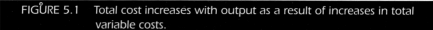

FIGURE 5.1   Total cost increases with output as a result of increases in total variable costs.

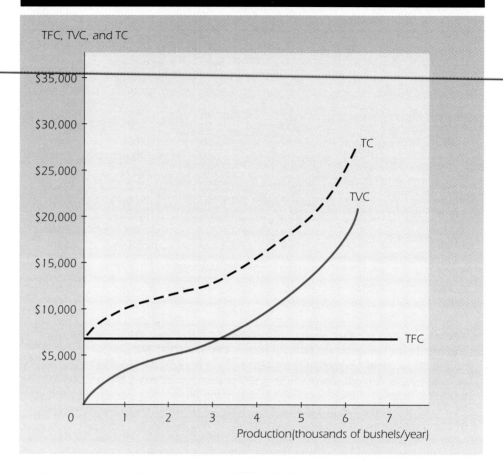

This figure shows graphically the values of **TFC**, **TVC**, and **TC** in Table 5.1. Total fixed costs are constant, so the line labeled **TFC** is horizontal. **TVC** slopes upward and becomes steeper at increasing outputs as a result of the law of diminishing marginal product. **TC** is the sum of **TFC** and **TVC**. This means that **TC** is vertically above **TVC** by the (constant) amount equal to **TFC**.

As output is expanded, marginal costs typically decline, then increase rather slowly, and then increase rapidly.

rates of production. By looking down the column for *MC* per 500 bushels, we see further reductions in marginal costs from adding to production. For example, when going from 1000 to 1500 bushels, the *MC* of the 500 bushels is $900. The next 500 bushels comes even cheaper, at $800. *MC* per 500 bushels remains at this level for the production increase from 2000 to 2500 bushels but then begins to increase. At first the increase is slow. However, eventually, the costs of further expansions of output become more substantial.

It is important to recognize in all the foregoing that we are talking about different *potential* outputs during a particular year. The *TC*s and the consequent *MC*s are the costs of taking alternative actions. That is, the farmer is not hiring each worker after the preceding worker and watching what happens to output. Rather, the farmer is considering *ex ante,* before actually changing the number of workers, what the costs would be for different outputs.

We can obtain the approximate *MC* per bushel by dividing the *MC* per 500 bushels at each **rate** of production by 500.[7] That is, we attribute one five-hundredth of the cost of 500 bushels to each separate bushel. These approximate *MC*s per bushel are given in the last column of Table 5.1. As we have explained, they dip initially, then increase rather slowly, and then increase rapidly. Examples 5.2, 5.3, and 5.4 describe why marginal costs increase in some nonfarming situations, each example revealing the importance of there being a fixed factor of production.

Finding the Optimal Output

Armed with the *MC* and the assumption that the farm can sell whatever it produces at the going price so that *MR = price,* it is possible to determine the farm's profit-maximizing output. This is perhaps most easily found by examining Figure 5.2, which plots the *MC*s from Table 5.1.

We have already seen that, by definition, profits increase by adding to output, provided

$$MR > MC$$

Since we are assuming that *MR = price,* profits increase as long as

$$Price > MC$$

In other words, it pays to expand production provided the extra output can be sold for more than it costs to produce the extra output. Therefore, output should be expanded until *MC* has risen to the point where

$$Price = MC$$

This is the **profit-maximizing output,** which is also called the **optimal output.** Let us see what this profit-maximizing, or optimal, output is in our example by assuming a specific price of wheat, say $4.50 per bushel.

If wheat production were set at, for example, 3000 bushels, Table 5.1 shows that an additional bushel could be produced for $1.80. Since this bushel can be sold for $4.50, profits are increased by $2.70 (or $4.50 − $1.80) from producing an extra bushel. This also can be seen from Figure 5.2 by the vertical distance between the *MC* curve at the output of 3000 bushels and the height of the horizontal line at $4.50. This gap is $2.70. With price greater than *MC* at 3000 bushels per annum, profits cannot be at their maximum possible level at this output.

If production is set at 4000 bushels per year, Table 5.1 and Figure 5.2 show that price still exceeds *MC,* so profits are increased by continuing to add to production. The same is true at 4500 bushels per year. However, the situation changes at 5000 bushels. This is the rate of production at which *MC* is $4.50, the same as the price

The profit-maximizing output is also called the optimal output.

---

[7] We use the term **rate** of production because output is measured as the number of bushels *per period of time,* for example, per year.

FIGURE 5.2 The profit-maximizing ouput is that rate of production where the price equals *MC*, provided the firm can sell all it produces at that price, and provided *MC* is increasing.

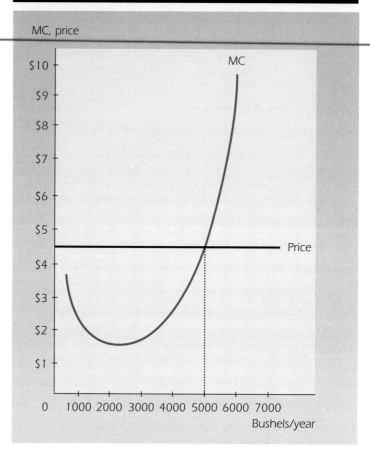

Profits increase from increased production if extra output increases total revenue more than total cost, that is, if marginal revenue exceeds marginal cost. If more can be sold without affecting price, then **MR** = **price**. Thus a firm should always add to production whenever **price** exceeds **MC**. For example, if the price of wheat is $4.50 per bushel, output should be expanded when the cost of production of an extra unit, the **MC**, is below $4.50. Maximum profits occur when **price** = **MC**, because going beyond this output means **price** is less than **MC**, so adding to production increases costs more than revenue. The output at which **price** = **MC** with a price of $4.50 is 5000 bushels. (Note that the **price** also may equal **MC** at a lower output, but this would not maximize profits. For maximum profits, it is necessary for **MC** to be increasing as well as to have **price** = **MC**.)

Example 5.2

THE COST OF PUMPING GAS

There are various reasons why marginal costs increase with expanding output in the short run. While all result from there being a fixed factor of production, the factor that is fixed depends on the firm being considered. Typically, as in this chapter, increasing marginal cost is illustrated by reference to farming, where the fixed factor is land. However, with the relative decline in farming vis-à-vis services and manufacturing, land is not the relevant fixed factor in an increasing number of cases. In this example we consider the cause of increasing marginal cost in a service-oriented firm, a gas station. Examples 5.3 and 5.4 examine the situation in fishing and in a lumber mill.

Henry's is a small, independent gas station generating most of its revenue from selling gas. In the short-run, in order to increase "output" in terms of the number of gallons pumped, the only options are to extend the hours of operation or to add attendants so there is never a line at the pumps; customers often do not stop if there is a line-up.

Opening extra hours beyond the normal business day of 6 A.M. to 11 P.M. means serving relatively few extra customers; the flow of traffic during nighttime hours is far below that during the daytime. The cost of nighttime operation cannot be reduced as much as is the flow of customers; it is still necessary to pay a cashier; and there are added costs of lighting, security and so on. This means that extending operating hours to increase output involves increased marginal cost per gallon of gas.

The alternative of adding attendants during the normal daytime hours also results in increasing marginal cost. The problem with this route of expansion is that in order to avoid line-ups at any time, it is necessary to have a sufficient number of attendants to deal with peak periods—around 8 A.M. and 5 P.M. Other than at these peak periods, the extra attendants, who earn the same hourly rate as others, are not busy. This means that the marginal cost per additional gallon of gas pumped increases as Henry's gas throughput expands.

In the long run, Henry's could expand not by extending hours or adding attendants, but by adding gas stations. This involves expanding the entire scale of operations. Costs of the new stations would be little different from the old. However, in the short run, with fixed inputs, this route of expansion is precluded; it takes time to find and develop new sites. Therefore, in the short run it is not possible to pump more gas without increasing marginal costs.

---

of wheat. Therefore, the five-thousandth bushel adds the same to total cost as to total revenue, implying a zero profit from producing and selling the five-thousandth bushel.[8] As output is pushed above 5000 bushels, *MC* moves above $4.50, so expansion of output adds more to total cost than to total revenue. That is, profit is reduced as output is expanded beyond 5000 bushels. Therefore, we find that producing less than 5000 bushels results in less than maximum profit and producing more than 5000 bushels results in less than maximum profit. It follows that the maximum profit occurs by setting annual production equal to 5000 bushels, the output at which *price = MC*.

---

[8] Because total cost includes the opportunity cost of all inputs owned by the firm, a zero economic profit means a positive accounting profit.

Example 5.3

FISH SCALES AND TALES

The increasing marginal cost of output in the short run is evident to fishermen. Consider the case of the following commercial salmon fisherman in the Pacific Northwest.

Fred fishes for salmon from his 30-foot boat, using the trolling method. This consists of pulling a number of fishing lines slowly through the water, with lures and hooks attached to the end of each line. Fred's boat needs a crew of three, one to steer, one to operate the trolling equipment, and one to work at the stern unhooking fish and keeping the lines clear. Having a larger crew would not add to the number of fish they could catch, which depends on how long and during what part of the day they fish. Fred

is licensed to operate a fixed number of lines.

The easiest time to catch salmon is during the period around sunrise and sunset, although there are also more active times during "slack tides," which occur when the tide shifts from coming in to going out, or vice versa. Salmon may be caught at other times, but the frequency of catch is much lower; the fish go deeper and do not feed.

In the short run, for Fred and his crew to catch more salmon, their only option is to extend the number of hours spent fishing; adding more crew does not help, and the commercial fishing license limits the number of lines to those already in place. By fishing the

most productive hours of the day first, then the next most productive, and so on, each extra hour spent fishing produces fewer and fewer fish. However, the cost per hour of fishing is the same all day long. With fewer fish each hour as the output is expanded and the same cost per hour, the marginal cost per fish increases with the daily number of fish caught.

In the long run, Fred can add an extra boat plus crew, and he can then fish both of the boats during the best times of the day. However, in the short run with a fixed factor, the number of boats and lines, increasing output is subject to increasing marginal cost.

> Profit is maximized by selecting the output at which *price = MC*, provided *MC* is increasing at that output.

Figure 5.2 shows graphically that profit is maximized by setting output at the level where a horizontal line drawn at the market price cuts the *MC* curve; this is the output at which *price = MC*. However, it should be pointed out that for profit to be maximized, it is also necessary for the *MC* curve to be upward-sloping at the chosen output. This warning is necessary because there may be another output at which *price = MC* but where the *MC* curve slopes downward. For example, rather than the left-hand end of the *MC* curve ending as in Figure 5.2, it might continue and cut the price line. Such an intersection of the *MC* curve and the price line where the *MC* curve is sloping downward does not provide an output at which profit is maximized; going beyond that output increases total revenue more than total cost. Therefore, profit-maximization requires both that *price = MC* and that the *MC* curve be upward-sloping.

Determining Profits

Knowing that profits are maximized by selecting the rate of production where *MC = price* and *MC* is increasing does not tell us what is the maximum level of profits or whether profits can be made at all; perhaps the "optimal" or profit-maximizing rate of production merely minimizes losses.

Example 5.4

THE GROWING COST OF LUMBER

A firm facing higher overtime wage rates and machines that break down more frequently when run at capacity knows why marginal cost increases with increased output. Consider the situation facing the following western U.S. lumber mill, which can expand output in the short run either by adding shifts or by increasing the throughput rate of logs.

During the two weekday daytime shifts, 6 A.M. to 2 P.M. and 2 P.M. to 10 P.M., the hourly wages for the unionized workforce are fixed. However, for the weekday night shift, wages are 50% higher, as they are for the Saturday daytime shift. With the output per worker at the mill the same for all shifts, expanding output beyond that possible during the weekday daytime shifts means a higher cost of lumber. Further expansion of output by running the mill on Saturday evenings means facing double-time overtime rates and on Sunday triple-time. This means that the marginal cost of lumber requiring Sunday operation is higher than that requiring Saturday evening operation, which is again higher than that requiring weekday evening work, and this again is above the cost of lumber produced during the usual two daytime weekday shifts.

The throughput of lumber on the so-called green chain, which runs the logs past the rapidly spinning cutting blades, can be increased during any shift, but breakdowns become more frequent as the throughput rate expands. Each minute that the green chain is down increases the cost per unit of lumber produced; the wage bills do not stop mounting while the mill is idle. This means that expanding output by running the mill faster rather than by adding shifts also increases marginal costs.

In the long run, the mill owners can build a new mill or expand the old one and increase output, not by adding shifts or the throughput rate, but by adding new capacity. However, in the short run with the fixed factor of the given-sized mill, increasing marginal costs cannot be avoided.

In order to calculate what profits or losses are at the optimal output, it is necessary to consider the **average cost** AC. The average cost is the total cost divided by the number of units of output over which it is spread.

Just as we can think of total cost as consisting of two components, a fixed and variable cost, so we can think of average cost as consisting of these same components. In particular, we can divide total fixed cost TFC by the number of bushels produced to find the **average fixed cost** AFC. That is, the AFC numbers in Table 5.2 are obtained from TFC in Table 5.1 divided by the number of bushels produced. Similarly, we can divide the total variable cost TVC by the number of bushels produced to get the **average variable cost** AVC. The AFC numbers corresponding to TVC in Table 5.1 are also shown in Table 5.2. Finally, we can divide the total cost by the number of bushels to find the **average (total) cost** or, more simply, **average cost** AC. Since total cost equals total fixed cost plus total variable cost, the average cost must equal average fixed cost plus average variable cost. That is, $AC = AFC + AVC$. This is readily seen in Table 5.2. The values of AFC, AVC, and AC in Table 5.2 are plotted along with MC from Table 5.1 in Figure 5.3.

As fixed cost is spread over a larger output, the average fixed cost declines, as shown by reading down the AFC column in Table 5.2 and from the downward slope of AFC in Figure 5.3. Average variable cost AVC declines until reaching a

Average cost is total cost divided by output.

Average fixed cost is total fixed cost divided by output. Average variable cost is total variable cost divided by output. Average total cost at any output is the sum of average fixed cost and average variable cost.

TABLE 5.2

All forms of average cost are merely the relevant total cost divided by output.

OUTPUT (bushels per year)	$AFC = \dfrac{TFC}{OUTPUT}$	$AVC = \dfrac{TVC}{OUTPUT}$	$AC = \dfrac{TC}{OUTPUT}$
0	∞	n/d	∞
500	$13.50	$3.60	$17.10
1,000	6.75	3.00	9.75
1,500	4.50	2.60	7.10
2,000	3.38	2.35	5.73
2,500	2.70	2.20	4.90
3,000	2.25	2.13	4.38
3,500	1.93	2.13	4.06
4,000	1.69	2.19	3.88
4,500	1.50	2.32	3.82
5,000	1.35	2.54	3.89
5,500	· 1.23	2.87	4.10
6,000	1.13	3.47	4.60
6,500	1.04	4.43	5.47

All average costs are obtained by taking the associated total costs in Table 5.1 and dividing by the output.

minimum at an output somewhere in the region of 3000 or 3500 bushels per annum, but after this point, *AVC* increases. The plot of *AVC* is hence U-shaped, as is shown in Figure 5.3.

AC is the sum of *AFC* and *AVC*. Table 5.2 shows *AC* declining until an output of about 4500 bushels, from which point it increases. What happens is that while *AFC* continues to decline with expanding output, the other component of *AC,* that is, *AVC,* begins to dominate so that *AC* increases. Figure 5.3 shows the nature of *AC* with its minimum at a slightly higher output than the minimum of *AVC.* Figure 5.3 also shows *MC* from Table 5.1.

Examination of Figure 5.3 reveals that the *MC* curve cuts the *AVC* and *AC* curves at their respective minimums. This is not by chance but is due to the nature of the relationship between marginal and average costs.

Any average of a list of numbers is decreased if an additional number is added to that list that is lower than the previous average. [Think of your grade point average (GPA); if the grade from another course is less than your GPA, your GPA falls.] The average is unaffected if the new number is the same as the average of numbers already in the list, and the average is increased if a number is added that is larger than the average of preexisting numbers. (Again, think of your GPA.) This is what explains the relation between *MC, AVC,* and *AC.* For example, at low outputs, the cost of producing another bushel, that is, the *MC,* is lower than the average cost at these outputs. This is clear in both Table 5.2 and Figure 5.3. Consequently, if another unit is produced, *AC* is reduced. At the point that *MC* is equal to *AC,* producing another unit leaves *AC* unchanged; its production cost is

The MC curve cuts the AVC and AC curves at their respective minimums.

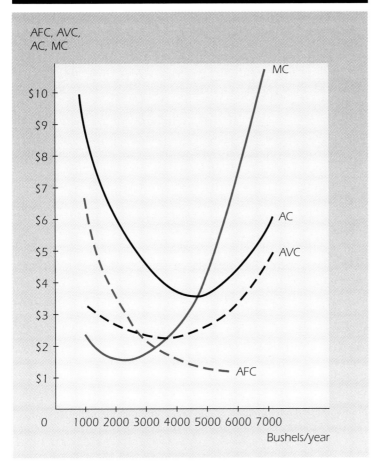

FIGURE 5.3   Average fixed cost declines continuously as ouput is expanded, while average variable cost and average (total) cost curves are U-shaped with minimums where they are intersected by the marginal cost curve MC.

Average fixed cost decreases as output expands, since this cost is spread over a larger output. Average variable cost and average (total) cost decrease before increasing with output and have their minimums at the rates of production at which their curves are intersected by the **MC** curve.

the same as the average cost. After the output where $MC=AC$, that is, beyond the output at which these curves intersect in Figure 5.3, then $MC>AC$ so that producing more increases AC. Hence, as in Figure 5.3, AC is declining at outputs where the MC curve is below the AC curve, AC is flat where the MC curve intersects the AC curve, and AC is increasing at outputs where the MC curve is above the AC curve. Therefore, it must be that MC intersects the AC curve at the point that AC turns from decreasing to increasing, that is, at the minimum on the AC curve.

The *MC* and *AC* curves can be used to show graphically both the output at which profits are maximized and the profits (or losses) at different outputs. This is done in Figure 5.4, which gives *AC, MC,* and the price line in the upper part and profits in the lower part.[9] In interpreting Figure 5.4, we can note that, by definition, total revenue *TR* is given by

$$TR = price \times output \tag{5.5}$$

For example, with a price of wheat of $4.50, at the profit-maximizing output of 5000 bushels, total revenue is $22,500 (or $4.50 × 5000). We also can note that, by definition, total cost *TC* is given by

$$TC = AC \times output \tag{5.6}$$

For example, with the average cost *AC* at the profit-maximizing output of 5000 bushels at $3.89 per bushel, the total cost of the 5000 bushels is $19,450 (or $3.89 × 5000). Therefore, in Figure 5.4 at 5000 bushels, profit is given by

$$Profit = TR - TC = \$22,500 - \$19,450 = \$3050$$

The definitions of total revenue *TR* and total cost *TC* in Equations 5.5 and 5.6 can be used to express profit in terms of price and average cost. Specifically, since

$$Profit = TR - TC$$

using Equations 5.5 and 5.6, profit can be written as

$$Profit = price \times output - AC \times output$$

that is,

$$Profit = (price - AC) \times output \tag{5.7}$$

Profits are made when price exceeds average cost.

Equation 5.7 means that when *price = AC,* as at Q_L and Q_U in Figure 5.3, profits are zero. At outputs below Q_L and above Q_U, profits are negative; that is, there are losses, because in these regions (*price − AC*) in Equation (5.7) is negative. Between Q_L and Q_U, profits are positive because (*price − AC*) is positive. Profits are at their maximum at output Q^* in Figure 5.4, where *price = MC.* The profit-maximizing output Q^* is 5000 bushels, as shown earlier. We can note that Q^* is not the output at which the difference between *AC* and the price is at its maximum; (*price − AC*) is only the *average profit per item sold,* and this must be multiplied by the amount sold to obtain total profit from all the items sold.

---

[9]We also plot the *AVC* curve in the upper part.

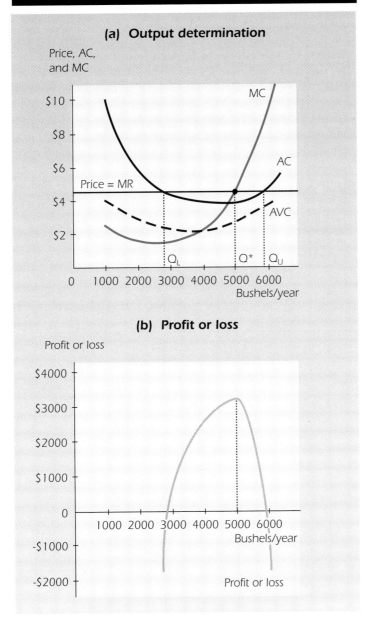

FIGURE 5.4   Production where price equals *AC* results in a zero profit and where price is less than *AC* results in losses. Profits are positive only where price exceeds *AC*, with a maximum where price equals *MC*.

(a) Output determination

(b) Profit or loss

Where **price** = **AC**, as at **Q**$_L$ and **Q**$_U$, profits are zero, since **profit** = (**price** − **AC**) × **output**. These zero profits are shown in the lower part of the figure, along with the positive profits made by producing between **Q**$_L$ and **Q**$_U$ and the losses made by producing less than **Q**$_L$ or more than **Q**$_U$.

LOSS MINIMIZATION VERSUS PROFIT MAXIMIZATION

The Effect of Fixed Costs

It should be clear from Figure 5.4 that if the *AC* curve is above the price at all rates of production, producing where *MC*=*price* cannot provide profits. The firm *must* lose money. What, then, does the rate of production where *MC*=*price* achieve? Producing where *MC*=*price* when *AC* is always higher than the price allows a producer to minimize losses. This can be seen from Figure 5.5, which is based on Table 5.3. The numbers in Table 5.3 are obtained from Tables 5.1 and 5.2, with the change being in total fixed cost *TFC*, which is increased by $3250, from the previous $6750 to $10,000.

From comparing the *AVC* and *MC* curves in the top part of Figure 5.5 with the *AVC* and *MC* curves in Figure 5.4, we see that the change in *TFC* has left the *AVC* and *MC* curves unchanged. (This must be so because changing fixed cost, which, by definition, does not vary with output, cannot affect the cost of *extra* output.) With the *MC* curve in the upper part of Figure 5.5 the same as that in Figure 5.4, the output at which *MC*=*price* is still 5000 bushels. However, this is the best, or optimal, output in the sense of providing the smallest loss. This is clear from examining the lower part of Figure 5.5. The smallest loss is $200, which is no

TABLE 5.3

Increasing **TFC** by the same amount at each output leaves **MC** and **AVC** unchanged.

OUTPUT (bushels per year)	TFC	TVC	TC	AFC	AVC	AC	MC
0	$10,000	$0	$10,000	∞	n/d	∞	n/d
500	10,000	1,800	11,800	$20.00	$3.60	$23.60	$3.60
1,000	10,000	3,000	13,000	10.00	3.00	13.00	2.40
1,500	10,000	3,900	13,900	6.67	2.60	9.27	1.80
2,000	10,000	4,700	14,700	5.00	2.35	7.35	1.60
2,500	10,000	5,500	15,500	4.00	2.20	6.20	1.60
3,000	10,000	6,400	16,400	3.33	2.13	5.46	1.80
3,500	10,000	7,450	17,450	2.86	2.13	4.99	2.10
4,000	10,000	8,750	18,750	2.50	2.19	4.69	2.60
4,500	10,000	10,450	20,450	2.22	2.32	4.54	3.40
5,000	10,000	12,700	22,700	2.00	2.54	4.54	4.50
5,500	10,000	15,800	25,800	1.82	2.87	4.69	6.20
6,000	10,000	20,800	30,800	1.67	3.47	5.14	10.00
6,500	10,000	28,800	38,800	1.54	4.43	5.97	16.00

The values in this table are obtained from Tables 5.1 and 5.2 by adding $3250 to **TFC** at all outputs. Since **MC** is the change in **TC**, it is unaffected by **TFC**. Similarly, **TFC** and **AVC** are unaffected because variable costs have not changed. With **MC** unchanged, there is no change in the profit-maximizing output.

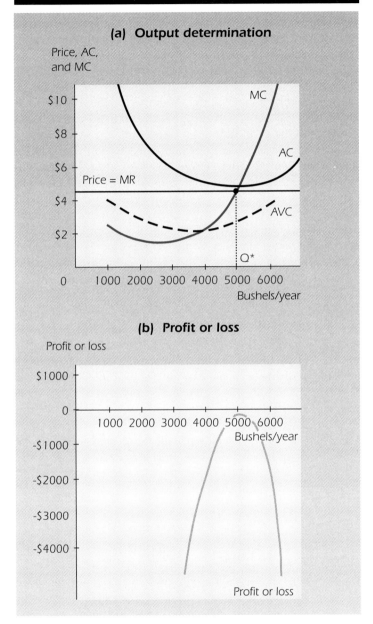

FIGURE 5.5 If *AC* is everywhere above the price of the product, selecting the output at which *MC* equals the price means minimizing losses.

(a) Output determination

(b) Profit or loss

If there is no output at which the price exceeds the average cost, selecting the output at which **MC = price** minimizes losses. It is hence still the best the firm can do.

surprise, since the increase in fixed costs is $3250 and the profit at the output of 5000 bushels was $3050 before the increase in fixed costs occurred.

It might at first be thought reasonable for a farm to stop operating, that is, to cease planting wheat, if $200 is being lost even when it is doing the best that it can. However, since the farm must pay $10,000 in fixed costs even if it ceases to operate—either in rent or in opportunity cost—it is better to keep farming, even at a loss of $200. If it shut down, the loss would be $10,000, the fixed and unavoidable cost. Operating and losing $200 is clearly better than shutting down and losing $10,000.

If *TFC* had increased by some amount other than $3250, it would have made no difference to the conclusion. Whatever the change in fixed costs, the best output is unchanged, at least in the short run.

Let us put our conclusion in terms of land used by the wheat farmer. Suppose that after agreeing to rent land for the next year or after deciding to use owned land for wheat farming, the local authorities increase property taxes. Suppose that these property taxes must be paid whether the land is farmed or not. Nothing is gained by closing down the farm or by changing planned wheat output. If the taxes must be paid, the best that can be done is to produce where *MC = price*, even if this results in losses. Similarly, if interest rates increased on borrowed funds or on funds the farmer has committed, the higher debt cost or opportunity cost of funds does not affect the optimal output, at least in the short run.

In the short run, a firm should operate at a loss if the loss would be even larger if the firm shut down.

The size of fixed costs has no effect on the optimal output of a firm in the short run.

The Effect of Variable Costs

Unlike fixed costs, which are irrelevant for profit-maximizing output, at least in the short run, changes in variable costs do influence the optimal production. We can show this by letting variable costs increase by, for example, 20%.[10]

Table 5.4 shows the result of the increase in *TVC*s from those in Table 5.1 by 20%. The result is a 20% increase in *AVC* and *MC*. Because *MC* is increased at every rate of production, this reduces the output at which *price = MC*. This is seen in Figure 5.6, which shows the situation after the 20% increase in *MC*. The new optimal production is approximately 4600 bushels per annum compared with the optimal production of 5000 bushels before the increase in *MC*.

The new profit at the optimal rate of production is

An increase in variable costs increases MC and reduces the rate of output at which price=MC. That is, an increase in variable costs reduces the profit-maximizing output.

$$Profit = total\ revenue - total\ cost$$
$$= (price \times output) - (AC \times output) = (price - AC) \times output$$
$$= \$(4.50 - 4.28) \times 4600 = \$1012$$

Before the increase in variable costs, profits were $3050, so there has been a reduction in profits.

If variable costs had increased somewhat more than 20%, there would have remained no output at which profits could be made. As with an increase in fixed

---

[10] In the example, the only variable cost is the cost of labor, so we consider an increase of 20% in monthly wages. Increases in raw materials prices, energy costs, and prices of other variable inputs have the same effect.

TABLE 5.4

Changes in variable costs influence marginal costs and average costs and thereby the profit-maximizing output and profit.

OUTPUT (bushels per year)	TFC	TVC	TC	AFC	AVC	AC	MC
0	$6,750	$0	$6,750	∞	n/d	∞	n/d
500	6,750	2,160	8,910	$13.50	$4.32	$17.82	$4.32
1,000	6,750	3,600	10,350	6.75	3.60	10.35	2.88
1,500	6,750	4,680	11,430	4.50	3.12	7.62	2.16
2,000	6,750	5,640	12,390	3.38	2.82	6.20	1.92
2,500	6,750	6,600	13,350	2.70	2.64	5.34	1.92
3,000	6,750	7,680	14,430	2.25	2.56	4.81	2.16
3,500	6,750	8,940	15,690	1.93	2.55	4.48	2.52
4,000	6,750	10,500	17,250	1.69	2.63	4.31	3.12
4,500	6,750	12,540	19,290	1.50	2.79	4.29	4.08
5,000	6,750	15,240	21,990	1.35	3.05	4.40	5.40
5,500	6,750	18,960	25,710	1.23	2.45	4.67	7.44
6,000	6,750	24,960	31,710	1.13	4.16	5.29	12.00
6,500	6,750	34,560	41,310	1.04	5.32	6.36	19.20

Table 5.4 is based on Table 5.1 with **TFC** unchanged but with **TVC** increased by 20%. **AVC** and **MC** are 20% higher than before, while **AC** is increased less than 20%.

costs, it may have still been better to continue producing at the output at which *price=MC* rather than to shut down. However, this is not always the case for increases in variable costs. Unlike the effect of increases in fixed costs, increases in variable costs can make it better to shut down rather than to continue, even in the short run. In order to explain why, we can use the definition of profit in Equation 5.7, which is

$$Profit = (price - AC) \times output$$

As explained, total cost *TC* is the sum of total fixed cost *TFC* and total variable cost *TVC*. Therefore, average cost *AC* is the sum of average fixed cost *AFC* and average variable cost *AVC*. That is:

$$AC = AFC + AVC \tag{5.8}$$

Substituting Equation 5.8 into Equation 5.7 gives

$$Profit = (price - AFC - AVC) \times output \tag{5.9}$$

Rearranging Equation 5.9 by taking *AFC* out of the parentheses gives

$$Profit = (price - AVC) \times output - AFC \times output \tag{5.10}$$

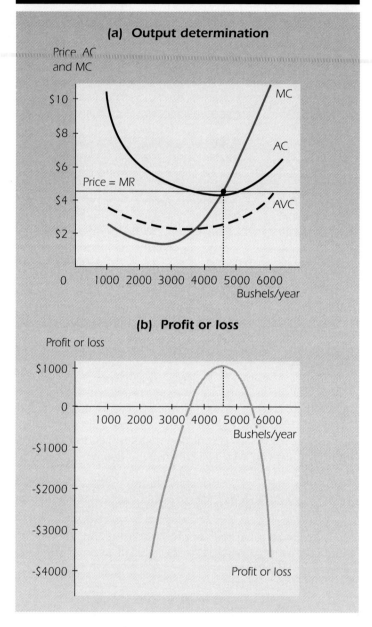

FIGURE 5.6 An increase in variable costs reduces the optimal output and the profits made at this and other outputs.

(a) Output determination

(b) Profit or loss

Optimal output, where **price** = **MC**, occurs at a lower rate of output after **MC** is increased. This is seen by comparing this figure with Figure 5.4. This comparison also shows that profits have been reduced.

The last term, *AFC × output*, is total fixed cost *TFC*, and therefore,

$$Profit = (price - AVC) \times output - TFC \qquad (5.11)$$

By setting output at zero, profits are $-TFC$. That is, the producer has losses equal to fixed costs. Losses are larger than this when production occurs and the price is less than *AVC*, because there is an extra negative component of profits. That is, if price is less than *AVC*, it is better for the firm to cease operations, even in the short run. However, when there is an output at which the price exceeds *AVC*, it pays to produce in the short run even though losses may be made; the losses are smaller than with zero output.

Production ceases in the short run when the price is less than average variable cost at every output. However, if the price exceeds average variable cost at any output, production continues in the short run even though losses might be made.

PRODUCT PRICE AND QUANTITY SUPPLIED

The Individual Firm's Supply Curve

Since the profit-maximizing output is where *price* = *MC*, it should come as no surprise that changes in price change the profit-maximizing output. This is seen in Figure 5.7, which repeats the *MC*, *AC*, and *AVC* curves from Figure 5.3. We see that when the price of wheat is $3 per bushel, the profit-maximizing output, that output at which *price* = *MC*, is approximately 4300 bushels. At a wheat price of $4, the profit-maximizing output is approximately 4800 bushels. Similarly, at a wheat price of $5, the profit-maximizing output is approximately 5150 bushels; at $6, it is 5450 bushels; and so on. More generally, the higher a product's price, the larger is the profit-maximizing quantity supplied.

The quantity supplied is larger, the higher the price.

If the price of wheat were to fall to as low as $2 per bushel, Figure 5.7 shows that there is no output at which this price is above *AVC*. This is confirmed by looking at *AVC* in Table 5.2; *AVC* is never below $2. We have seen that if the price is less than *AVC* at every output, it is better for the firm to cease operating, even in the short run. This is so because if total revenue does not cover the variable costs at any output, it is better not to produce at all. That is, the quantity supplied is zero at a price of $2 per bushel.

The lowest price of wheat at which it is worthwhile to produce in the short run is the minimum *AVC*. This is a price of $2.13, as is seen in Table 5.2. At prices just above $2.13 and hence just above the minimum *AVC*, losses are reduced by producing rather than closing down. At prices just below $2.13, it is better to shut down and face short-run losses equal to the fixed costs. Let us consider what this means for quantity supplied at different prices.

Production is zero equal to prices below the minimum *AVC* and equal to the rate of output where *price*=*MC* at prices above the minimum *AVC*.

Table 5.5 on page 129 and Figure 5.8 on page 130 show the optimal outputs at different prices. The table and figure show that it is optimal in the short run to operate only at prices above the minimum *AVC* and at those prices above *AVC* to pick outputs where *price* = *MC*.

The curve *MC* = *S* in Figure 5.8 shows the optimal output at each price. This is the **supply curve** of the farmer, linking the quantity supplied to the price. A comparison of the farmer's supply curve with the *MC* curve in Figure 5.7 reveals that the supply curve for an individual producer is the producer's *MC* curve for that segment of the *MC* curve above the minimum *AVC*. This curve is valid in the short run while the amount of land is fixed.

The short-run supply curve of an individual producer is the producer's *MC* curve along that segment of *MC* above the minimum *AVC*.

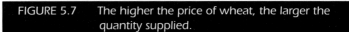

FIGURE 5.7   The higher the price of wheat, the larger the quantity supplied.

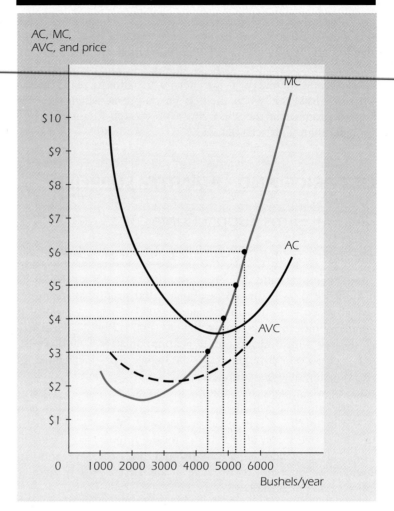

At a price of $3 per bushel, **price = MC** at an output of approximately 4300 bushels. This is therefore the profit-maximizing rate of production at this price. As the price of wheat increases, the profit-maximizing rate of production, where **price = MC**, occurs at larger outputs. For example, at $4 per bushel, **price = MC** at an output of 4800 bushels; at $5 per bushel, **price = MC** at an output of 5150 bushels; and so on. That is, the higher the price, the larger is the quantity supplied.

TABLE 5.5

Quantity supplied in the short run is zero at prices below the minimum **AVC** and equal to the output at which **price** = **MC** at prices above the minimum **AVC**.

WHEAT PRICE (bushels per year)	WHEAT OUTPUT
$0.00	0
0.50	0
1.00	0
1.50	0
2.00	0
2.50	3,900
3.00	4,300
3.50	4,575
4.00	4,800
4.50	5,000
5.00	5,175
5.50	5,325
6.00	5,450
6.50	5,560
7.00	5,660
7.50	5,750
8.00	5,825
8.50	5,880
9.00	5,930
9.50	5,975
10.00	6,000

If the price is below the **AVC** at every possible output, it pays to shut down operations in the short run. The short-run startup point is where the price moves above the minimum **AVC**. At prices above this, output is set where **price** = **MC**.

Market Supply

The individual producers' supply curves, when considered collectively, provide the **market supply curve,** which is the supply curve of all producers taken together. In order to obtain the market supply curve, it is necessary to add individual producers' quantities supplied at each possible price.

Figure 5.9 shows the construction of the market supply curve for the case of two producers with the same *MC* curves, and hence the same short-run supply curves, as those in our example. The market quantity supplied at each price is obtained by adding the outputs of the two producers at each price and plotting the resulting total output against price. We see that at $2.00 per bushel nothing is produced by either producer. Therefore, market supply is zero at a price of $2.00.

The market supply curve shows the quantity supplied by all *producers taken together at each possible price.*

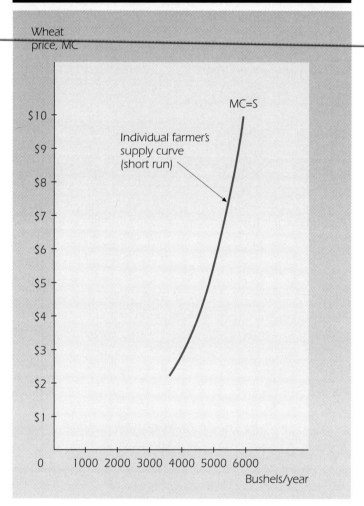

FIGURE 5.8   The individual producer's short-run supply curve is the producer's *MC* curve for the part of the *MC* curve above the minimum point on the producer's *AVC* curve.

The individual producer's short-run supply curve is identical with the **MC** curve, but only for prices above the minimum **AVC**. At prices below the minimum **AVC**, there is zero supply in the short run.

At $2.50 per bushel each farmer produces 3900 bushels, so the market quantity supplied is 7800 bushels. Similarly, at $4.00 per bushel, each farmer produces 4800 bushels, so the market quantity supplied is 9600 bushels, and so on.[11]

---

[11] We are assuming that there is a plentiful supply of labor and other variable inputs from farms that do not grow wheat and from outside of farming so that all wheat farms can expand simultaneously without increasing variable costs. This means that each firm's *MC* curve is the same whether it expands on its own or all wheat farms expand at the same time.

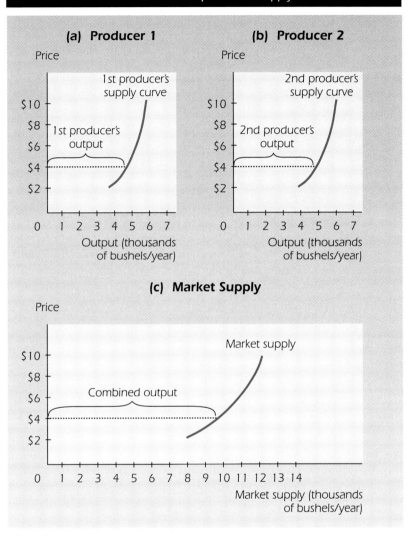

FIGURE 5.9   The market supply curve is the horizontal summation of the individual producers' supply curves.

The market supply is obtained by taking each price and adding the quantities supplied by all producers at that price. For example, at $4 per bushel, Producer 1's output is 4800 bushels and Producer 2's output is also 4800 bushels, so total output is 9600 bushels.

Inspection of the way the market supply curve is obtained from the individual producers' supply curves shows that it involves adding the individual supply curves horizontally, just as with market demand. Since the individual supply curves are the firms' MC curves above the minimum AVC, the market supply curve is the horizontal sum of MC curves above the minimum AVC. If there were 2000 producers instead of 2, the procedure would be the same. Even if the producers had different supply curves because they had different MC curves, the procedure would be unchanged, involving the addition of quantities supplied at each price.

The market supply curve is the horizontal summation of individual firms' MC curves above the minimum AVC.

How the resulting market supply curve looks relative to the individual curves depends on the scale used on the horizontal axis. The market supply curve will involve far larger amounts than those shown on individual producers' curves.

Factors Shifting the Short-Run Supply Curve

Changes in Productivities of Variable Inputs.   With the market supply curve being derived from the MC curves of individual firms, shifts in the market supply curve result from the same factors that shift individual firms' MC curves. One factor that can shift MC curves is a change in the quantities of variable inputs required to produce an extra unit of output.

The quantities of inputs required to produce an extra unit of output depend on the productivities of the variable inputs. For example, an improvement in the productivity of a variable input reduces the quantity of that input required to produce another unit of output. This means that the marginal cost is smaller. Such reductions in marginal cost may result from the use of more or better equipment or better trained workers. Marginal cost reductions also can result from better management. For example, the use of better cost or quality control could reduce marginal costs by reducing waste. Similarly, the use of better methods of motivating workers could improve efficiency and thereby reduce marginal costs.

Figure 5.10 shows the effect of a reduction in marginal cost. The figure shows downward shifts in the MC curves of two firms. The MC curves of the two firms are labeled MC_1 and MC_2 before the improvement in productivity and MC_1' and MC_2' afterwards. The resulting market supply curves are also shown, where these are the horizontal summations of the individual firms' MC curves. The market supply curve is labeled S before the improvement in productivity and S' afterwards. We see that the market supply curve shifts downward and to the right in the same way as the individual firm's MC curves shift as a result of the improvement in productivity.

Changes in Prices of Variable Inputs.   The effect on the supply curve of a decline in the price of a variable input, such as the wage paid on a wheat farm, is similar to the effect of an improvement in the productivity of a variable input. This is so because the cost of producing another unit of output, that is, MC, is the number of units of variable inputs required multiplied by the prices of these inputs. Consequently, a decline in the number of units of input required—an increase in productivity—is equivalent to a fall in the price of that input. A decline in the prices of variable inputs reduces MC and hence shifts the supply curve downward and to the right, just as in Figure 5.10. Similarly, an increase in the prices of variable inputs shifts the supply curve upward and to the left.

Changes in Taxes on Variable Inputs.   Another factor that can shift the market supply curve is a tax paid on variable inputs. In order to see this, suppose that a tax equal to 25% of variable costs is applied when previously there had been no tax.[12]

From the perspective of the firm, the effect of the tax is to increase TVC and MC by 25%. The effect is therefore to shift the MC curves of producers upward by 25% and hence also to shift the supply curve upward by 25%, as shown in Figure 5.11.

An improvement in the productivity of variable inputs reduces marginal costs and shifts the supply curve downward and to the right.

Decreases in the prices of variable inputs shift the MC curves and hence the market supply curve downward and to the right, and vice versa.

A tax on variable inputs shifts the supply curve upward by the amount of the tax.

---

[12] The "tax" assumed for our supply curve shift might take the form of contributions by firms toward Social Security or health insurance for company employees.

FIGURE 5.10 When firms' marginal costs decline, the market supply curve shifts downward and to the right.

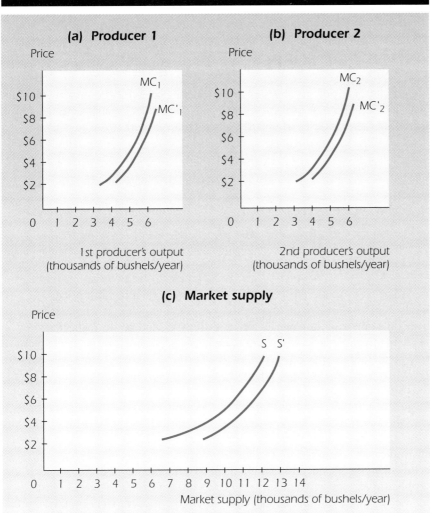

(a) Producer 1

Price

MC₁

MC'₁

1st producer's output
(thousands of bushels/year)

(b) Producer 2

Price

MC₂

MC'₂

2nd producer's output
(thousands of bushels/year)

(c) Market supply

Price

S   S'

Market supply (thousands of bushels/year)

The curves **MC**₁ and **MC**₂ give the outputs of two producers at each market price before a reduction in **MC**s, and **MC'**₁ and **MC'**₂ give the outputs of the first two firms afterwards. The market supply curve is the horizontal sum of the marginal cost curves of the individual producers. Therefore, the market supply curve is **S** before the reduction in marginal costs and **S'** afterwards. The supply curve is seen to shift downward and to the right from an improvement in productivity of a variable input.

The market supply
curve for agricultural
goods is shifted to the
left by bad weather,
and vice versa.

Bad Weather for Agricultural Production. An obvious factor affecting the supply of an agricultural commodity is the weather. The poorer the weather for growing, the further to the left is the supply curve, and vice versa.[13]

ELASTICITY OF SUPPLY

The sensitivity of supply to changes in a product's price can be measured in a similar way to measurement of the sensitivity of demand. The sensitivity of supply is measured by the **elasticity of supply** ϵ, which is defined as

$$\text{Elasticity of supply} = \frac{\text{percent change in quantity supplied}}{\text{percent change in price}}$$

Using symbols, the elasticity of supply can be written as

$$\epsilon = \frac{\%\Delta q}{\%\Delta p} \tag{5.12}$$

Elasticity of supply is the
percentage change
in quantity supplied
divided by the percent-
age change in price.

where $\%\Delta q$ and $\%\Delta p$ are the percentage changes in quantity and price.

The larger the elasticity of supply, the greater is the change in quantity supplied for a given percentage change in price. Supply is said to be inelastic when $\epsilon < 1$, just as demand is inelastic when $\eta < 1$. An inelastic supply means a relatively small change in quantity supplied as the product's price changes. Supply is said to be elastic when $\epsilon > 1$, meaning a relatively large change in quantity supplied as the product's price changes.

Inelastic supply, which
is where the supply
elasticity is less than 1,
occurs when the MC
curve is relatively steep.
This occurs when the
firms' production is
inflexible. Elastic supply,
which is where the
supply elasticity exceeds
1, occurs when the
MC curve is relatively
flat. This occurs when
production is flexible.

Because the market supply curve is the horizontal summation of firms' MC curves, the elasticity of supply depends on the elasticity of firms' MC curves. Inelastic MC curves mean that higher production can be achieved only at relatively rapidly increasing costs per unit of added output, whereas elastic MC curves mean extra units can be produced at similar cost to previous units. It follows that inelastic supply curves occur when firms' outputs are inflexible, whereas elastic supply curves occur when outputs are flexible. Inelastic supply occurs with agricultural outputs in the short run, when the only way to increase output is by expensive added care of an existing crop. Elastic supply occurs with manufactured goods when firms have substantial unused capacity.

---

[13] We have previously spoken of the supply curve moving up and down, not to the right or left. When we consider changes in productivity, prices of inputs, and so on, consideration of the vertical shift is more useful because we know the magnitude of movement in this direction, but when we consider factors such as weather, the known magnitude is more likely to be changes in output, which is measured along the horizontal axis.

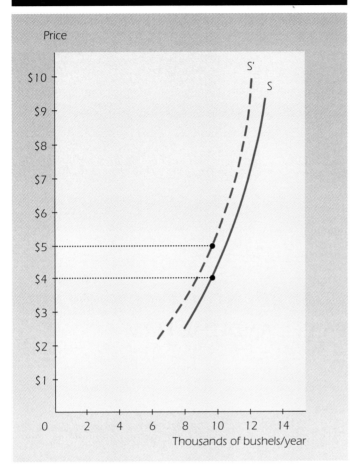

FIGURE 5.11   A tax that increases marginal cost shifts the supply curve upward by the amount of tax.

A 25% tax on variable inputs increases marginal costs by 25%. If the **MC** curves shift upward by 25%, so too does the market supply curve.

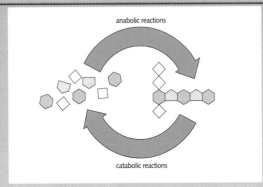

Anabolic and catabolic reactions exist within the chemical activity of the cell's metabolism.

Charles Darwin (1809–1882)

THE CELL AND THE FIRM

The Crossing Bridges section in Chapter 1 suggests a close organizational parallel between the different levels at which economists view production and biologists view life. At every level at which the analogy is made, firm versus cell, industry versus tissue, organ versus sector, and country versus organism, we find a remarkable correspondence in the ways economists and biologists have developed their ideas. The correspondence is striking even though most economists and most biologists have developed their ideas independently. Firms, as we know, engage in the production of outputs, which may, in turn, be inputs to other firms, and use inputs, including energy, to produce their outputs. Cells are producing units too, taking in inputs, including energy, which may be outputs of other cells and turning these inputs into outputs.

The chemical production process within a cell or living organism is called **metabolism.** By employing energy, which the cell may manufacture itself, but which it more likely obtains from other cells in the form of glucose, either the cell breaks substances down, a process called **catabolism,** or builds substances up, **anabolism.** In a similar fashion, some firms use energy to break materials down—ores into metals, crude oil into gasoline, trees into lumber and paper, wheat into flour, and cattle into meat products. Other firms take in energy to build products up, specifically those engaged in manufacturing automobiles, aircraft, clothing, footwear, and so on. Without energy and exchange between different cells and firms, cells and firms would cease to function.

The organization of activity inside a cell is governed by instructions from the **nucleus,** which itself takes its cues from the **nucleolus.** The nucleolus, where the DNA resides, can be viewed as the cell's command center. To remain in control in a variable environment, the management center of the cell, the nucleus, and the managing director itself, the nucleolus, must be able to gather, store, process, and dispense vast amounts of information to reduce waste of crucial inputs and to ensure that the cell's many chemical processes remain in balance. Firms must similarly maintain management information systems to run efficiently, keeping track of inputs, sales, and so on.

Outside the nucleus, in the main body of the cell, the work is performed by **proteins.** The proteins are like the labor input in production; just as the activities of labor on the shop floor are watched over and directed by foremen and middle managers, so in the cell the activities of the proteins are supervised by the **nucleic acids,** which tell the proteins what to do. Of course, messages must be correctly interpreted so that errors are avoided, a job done by **ribosomes.** But when cells are under great stress, the divisions of labor break down, with the nucleic acids working alongside the proteins, just as managers may work shoulder to shoulder on the shop floor when the firm is facing unusual demands. The channels of information between workers in the cell, that is, the proteins, their supervisors, the nucleic acids, the managers in the nucleus, and the "boss" in the nucleolus, must be kept open for efficient operation. Cell biologists believe that this information transfer is assisted by the **mitochondria,** which play a similar role to the management information systems of firms, which keep track of financial flows, inventory, shipments of raw materials, output, and sales records.

Just as a firm must use its inputs economically, combining them in the "optimal" mix to minimize costs, so the cell must manage its affairs economically or else face being put out of action. Competition among organisms ensures efficient organization both within cells and among cells.

Firms . . . engage in the production of outputs, which may, in turn, be inputs to other firms. . . . Cells are producing units too, taking in inputs, including energy . . . and turning these inputs into outputs.

Indeed, competition ensures that what cells do themselves, versus what they "contract" with other cells to do, is the most efficient possible arrangement.

Similarly, competition in the marketplace ensures that the organization of industry is efficient in terms of the stages of production performed within the firm—the extent of vertical integration—and the range of products produced by the firm—the extent of horizontal integration. The terminology used in economics and biology differs, with economists referring to "optimization" and biologists to "adaptation," but the meanings of these terms, that firms and cells must do the best that they can or else no longer exist, are very similar.

As well as being involved in metabolism, that is, in taking in inputs and generating outputs, cells are also engaged in **replication.** Replication involves the production of copies of parent cells. The process of replication has its parallel in the firm in the activity of branching, where copies of, for example, fast food establishments, ice cream parlors, hotels, or convenience stores are based on successful blueprints operating elsewhere. Furthermore, just as cell replication involves copies that are close to the original but yet have their own unique characteristics via **mutation,** so branches too may be close but imperfect copies of the original model. Thus mutations to the biologist and **innovations** to the economist are parts of the biologic view of **evolution** and the economic view of **progress.** Again, the mechanism by which the favored mutations and innovations are selected is competition. It is little wonder that Charles Darwin in his **Origin of Species** (1859) found himself drawing extensively on the economic classic of Adam Smith's, **The Wealth of Nations** (1776), written almost 100 years earlier.

SUMMARY

1. Firms are assumed to maximize profits. ~~Because firms are often run by managers~~ who serve as agents of shareholders, profit maximization assumes that there is no conflict between the objectives of owners and managers.

2. Profit is total revenue minus total cost. Total cost includes the opportunity cost of time and other resources of owners of the firm.

3. Marginal revenue is the increase in total revenue from selling one more unit of output. When a firm can sell more output without having to lower the price, marginal revenue equals the product's price.

4. Marginal cost is the increase in total cost from producing one more unit.

5. Total cost can be divided into total fixed cost—which is the same whatever quantity is produced—and total variable cost—which is higher for larger quantities produced.

6. The law of diminishing marginal product ensures that after some output, marginal costs increase.

7. When the individual firm cannot affect the price it receives for its product, profit maximization occurs at the output at which $price = MC$, provided MC is increasing.

8. Average cost is total cost divided by the number of units produced. Average fixed cost and average variable cost equal total fixed cost and total variable cost divided by the number of units produced.

9. For profits to be made, it is necessary that $price > AC$.

10. Changes in fixed costs have no effect on quantity supplied in the short run.

11. An increase in variable costs reduces the profit-maximizing quantity supplied.

12. Production will cease in the short run only when $price < AVC$. In this case, losses equal the total fixed cost.

13. The short-run supply curve of an individual producer is that producer's MC curve above the minimum of the AVC curve. The firm's supply curve gives the output at each price.

14. The short-run market supply curve is the horizontal sum of supply curves of individual producers. Since the individual producers' supply curves are their MC curves, the short-run market supply curve is the horizontal sum of MC curves.

15. The supply curve is shifted downward and to the right by
   a. An increase in the productivity of variable inputs
   b. A decrease in the cost of variable inputs
   c. A decrease in taxes on variable inputs
   d. Good weather for agricultural commodities

16. The price elasticity of supply measures the sensitivity of quantity supplied to changes in price. It is given by the ratio of the percentage change in the quantity supplied divided by the percentage change in the product's price.

17. Inelastic supply, which means an elasticity of supply of less than 1, occurs when MC increases rapidly, and this occurs when production is inflexible. Elastic supply, meaning an elasticity of supply of greater than 1, occurs when the MC curve is relatively flat, and this occurs when production is flexible.

QUESTIONS AND PROBLEMS

1. Why is it reasonable to assume that for an individual wheat farmer, $MR = price$?

2. Why doesn't a firm maximize profit by producing where $price = MC$ with MC *decreasing?* Is it that the condition $price = MC$ provides either a maximum or minimum, while the increasing or decreasing nature of MC tells us which of these it is?

3. Do you face the law of diminishing marginal product when studying?

4. From the fixed cost and total cost values in the following table, calculate the total variable cost, the average cost, and marginal cost. Calculate the average cost and marginal cost "per bicycle."

BICYCLE OUTPUT	FIXED COST	TOTAL COST
0	$5,000	$5,000
10	5,000	10,000
20	5,000	10,800
30	5,000	11,400
40	5,000	12,200
50	5,000	13,200
60	5,000	14,800
70	5,000	17,000
80	5,000	20,500

5. a. Using the costs in Question 4, what is the profit-maximizing rate of output if the firm can sell as many bicycles as it produces at $160 each?

   b. Using the price of $160 per bicycle, what is the profit or loss at each output?

6. If the opportunity cost of investment in an industry increases because of improved returns elsewhere, what happens to AC curves in the industry, and how can this eventually affect industry output?

7. Why are traditional accounting data of little use for locating the profit-maximizing output?

8. Why is the supply curve consisting of the sum of individual firm's MC curves only a short-run supply curve?

9. Calculate the elasticities of supply of wheat from the individual farmer whose output at different prices is shown in Table 5.5. Does the elasticity change as the output changes, and if so, why?

10. Assume that there are two wheat farmers in an industry like the farmer in Table 5.5. Calculate market quantity supplied at each output and the elasticity of supply at each output. How do the market supply elasticities compare with the individual producers' supply elasticities?

. . . .
. . . .
. . . .
. . . .

CHAPTER 6

Supply and Demand

If buyers won't fall for prices, then prices must fall for buyers.

Evan Esar

Key Concepts

Equilibrium price and quantity; effects of excess supply and demand; comparative statics; effects of changes in incomes; effects of substitute and complement prices; input prices and product prices; taxes and equilibrium prices; shifts of curves versus movements along curves; effects of price ceilings and floors

While of considerable interest in and of themselves, the supply curve and the demand curve come to the fore when combined into the most essential principle of economics, the **law of supply and demand.** Before revealing the nature of this fundamental economic paradigm, it would be useful to review the background to the supply curve and the demand curve.

A REVIEW

Chapter 4 explained why the demand curve shows a reduced quantity demanded as a product's price increases. The basis of the effect of a product's price on the quantity demanded is the need for the marginal utility per dollar of different products to be equal for a consumer to be maximizing utility; if the marginal utilities per dollar are not equal, the consumer can increase total utility by buying smaller

140

quantities of items with lower marginal utilities and greater quantities of items with higher marginal utilities. If the consumer is maximizing utility and then there is an increase in the price of a product, its per-dollar marginal utility falls below that of other products. This causes a reduction in the quantity of the product demanded; the consumer reallocates spending toward products offering higher utility per dollar. The new utility-maximizing allocation of the consumer's budget is that for which the marginal utility of the last unit of the more expensive item has been increased by its reduced consumption and equals the marginal utility per dollar on other products. With all consumers behaving this way, reducing the quantity purchased as a product's price increases, market quantity demanded is reduced.

Chapter 5 explained why the supply curve shows quantity produced increasing as a product's price increases. This occurs as a result of firms maximizing profits while subject to increasing marginal cost. The basis of the increasing marginal cost is the law of diminishing marginal product that applies in the short run when there is a fixed input, such as the amount of land available for farming. Chapter 5 showed that with each price-taking firm maximizing profits by producing the output at which $price = MC$, the individual firm's supply curve is its MC curve.[1] Furthermore, in the short run, during which time all producers are subject to fixed inputs and there is a fixed number of producers, the market supply curve becomes the horizontal summation of the marginal cost curves of firms. With all firms' MC curves sloping upward, so does the market supply curve.

EQUILIBRIUM OF SUPPLY AND DEMAND

The supply and demand curves considered individually cannot tell us what price we can expect to see. They tell us what quantity producers supply or consumers demand at any *given* price. In order to determine the price we can expect to observe, we must employ both the supply and the demand relationships to see at what price the quantity supplied is equal to the quantity demanded. This price at which the quantity supplied equals the quantity demanded is called the **equilibrium price.** The term **equilibrium** is used because the quantity buyers are willing to purchase is in the balance with the quantity sellers are willing to provide at this price.

The actual price we observe in the market, the **market price,** is not necessarily the equilibrium price. However, there are forces at work pushing market prices toward equilibrium prices, and these are the appropriately often-cited and highly acclaimed forces of supply and demand.

The equilibrium price is the price at which the quantity demanded equals the quantity supplied.

The Forces of Supply and Demand

We can illustrate the forces of supply and demand by extending the example of wheat developed in the preceding chapter. The relevant information is listed in Table 6.1 and is plotted graphically in Figure 6.1.

[1] More precisely, Chapter 5 showed that the firm's supply curve is its MC curve above the minimum average variable cost. This is so because the firm is shut down when price is less than AVC.

....
TABLE 6.1

The equilibrium price is the price at which the quantity supplied and quantity demanded are equal.

WHEAT PRICE	QUANTITY SUPPLIED (bushels per year)	QUANTITY DEMANDED (bushels per year)	EXCESS SUPPLY (+) AND EXCESS DEMAND (−)
$0.00	0	∞	−∞
0.50	0	100,000	−100,000
1.00	0	65,000	−65,000
1.50	0	44,000	−44,000
2.00	0	30,000	−30,000
2.50	7,800	20,000	−12,200
3.00	8,600	15,000	−6,400
3.50	9,150	12,000	−2,850
4.00	9,600	9,600	0
4.50	10,000	7,800	+2,200
5.00	10,350	6,400	+3,950
5.50	10,650	5,300	+5,350
6.00	10,900	4,400	+6,500
6.50	11,120	3,600	+7,520
7.00	11,320	3,100	+8,220
7.50	11,500	2,600	+8,900
8.00	11,650	2,200	+9,450
8.50	11,760	1,800	+9,960
9.00	11,860	1,500	+10,360
9.50	11,950	1,300	+10,650
10.00	12,000	1,000	+11,000

At prices below $4.00 per bushel, there is an excess of demand over supply. This puts upward pressure on prices as buyers find themselves unable to secure their desired quantities at these prices and therefore offer higher prices in order to induce suppliers to sell to them. At prices above $4.00 per bushel, there is an excess supply. This puts downward pressure on prices as producers are unable to find buyers and therefore reduce prices. Only at a price of $4.00 is the quantity supplied equal to the quantity demanded, so there is no reason for the price to change. That is, the equilibrium price is $4.00 per bushel.

Table 6.1 shows the market supply of wheat associated with different prices. We see that there is zero supply at $2.00 per bushel and lower prices because these prices are below the firms' minimum *AVC*. At prices of $2.50 per bushel and higher, wheat is supplied, and the higher the price, the greater is the quantity supplied. The data points in Table 6.1 are plotted in Figure 6.1, and the resulting curve, the market supply curve for wheat, is labeled *S*. This curve is seen to be upward-sloping, as we would expect.

FIGURE 6.1   At above equilibrium prices the quantity supplied
exceeds the quantity demanded, causing
downward pressure on prices, and at below
equilibrium prices the quantity demanded exceeds
the quantity supplied, causing upward pressure
on prices.

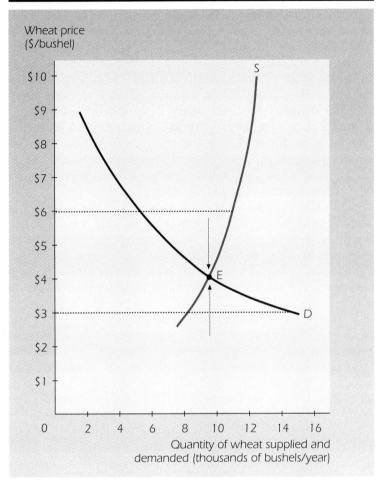

At prices above $4.00 per bushel, there is an excess of quantity supplied over quantity
demanded: the supply curve **S** is to the right of the demand curve **D**. Some or all
producers are therefore unable to find buyers for all their output. They will offer lower
prices than competitors in order to find buyers, and only when this has brought the
market price down to $4.00 per bushel can all producers find buyers for their output.
At prices below $4.00 per bushel, there is an excess of quantity demanded over quantity
supplied: the demand curve **D** is to the right of the supply curve **S**. Some or all
demanders are therefore unable to get suppliers to sell to them. Demanders will offer
higher prices, and only when this has brought the market price up to $4.00 per bushel
can all demanders get a quantity that satisfies them. Only at the price of $4.00 per
bushel is there no reason for the price to change.

Table 6.1 also shows the demand for wheat associated with different prices. The quantity demanded is shown to decline as wheat prices increase, being infinite at a zero price and dropping to 1000 bushels per year at $10.00 per bushel. The data points in Table 6.1 are plotted in Figure 6.1, and the resulting curve, the demand curve for wheat, is labeled *D*. This is downward-sloping, as expected.

The equilibrium price is the price at which the market supply curve for a product intersects the market demand curve.

The final column in Table 6.1 shows the **excess supply** of or **excess demand** for wheat at different wheat prices. When the quantity supplied exceeds the quantity demanded, there is excess supply, which is identified with a +. When the quantity demanded exceeds the quantity supplied, there is excess demand, which is identified with a −. The table shows that above $4.00 per bushel there is an excess of quantity supplied over quantity demanded and below $4.00 per bushel there is an excess of quantity demanded over quantity supplied. Only at $4.00 does the quantity supplied equal the quantity demanded. This is also clear from Figure 6.1, which shows graphically that quantities supplied and demanded are equal only at $4.00 per bushel. This is the price at which the supply and demand curves intersect in Figure 6.1. This price, where the supply and demand curves intersect, is the equilibrium price, which is, by definition, the price at which market quantities supplied and demanded are equal.

It is difficult to determine whether the price observed in the market, the market price, is also the equilibrium price. However, if the market price is not equal to the equilibrium price, the market price should be moving toward the equilibrium price. We can see why by asking what happens when the market price differs from the equilibrium price. Let us begin by considering what would happen if for some reason the market price is $6.00 per bushel when, as we know, the equilibrium price is $4.00 per bushel.

At a price of $6.00 per bushel, the quantity of wheat supplied exceeds the quantity demanded. This means that while some suppliers find buyers willing to pay this price, other suppliers find themselves with wheat they cannot sell. Those holding the unsold wheat realize they can find buyers if they reduce the price below that being asked by other suppliers; buyers will be happy to purchase at a lower price. Suppose the price fell to $5.00. There is still excess supply, so some sellers again cut prices. Only when the incentive for each supplier to reduce the price has brought the market price down to the equilibrium price of $4.00 per bushel is the excess supply eliminated, both via increased quantity demanded and decreased quantity supplied. We indicate the downward pressure on market price when it is above the equilibrium price by the downward-pointing arrow in Figure 6.1.

At market prices above *the equilibrium price, there is downward pressure on price from suppliers unable to sell all they have produced. At market prices* below *the equilibrium price, there is upward pressure on price from demanders unable to obtain their desired quantity.*

If the market price is below the equilibrium price, the pressure on the market price is also to return it to equilibrium. For example, as Figure 6.1 shows, at a market price of $3.00 per bushel, the quantity of wheat demanded exceeds the quantity supplied. Some demanders must therefore be unable to acquire the quantity of wheat they want. However, by paying a little above what others are paying, an individual demander can induce suppliers to sell to him or her. Only when the market price has reached the equilibrium price can all demanders acquire the amounts they want, ending the incentive to offer higher prices. Therefore, we have upward pressure on the market price when it is below the equilibrium price, as is shown by the upward-pointing arrow in Figure 6.1. We can see that the pressure to reduce prices when they are above the equilibrium is among suppliers, whereas the pressure to increase prices when they are below the equilibrium is among demanders.

Comparative Statics

The paradigm of supply and demand plays an essential role in economics by providing an easy-to-use, yet powerful framework for explaining how product prices and quantities bought and sold respond to conditions that affect markets. For example, it provides a way of determining how a tax on gasoline will affect gas prices and the quantities of gas bought and sold or how lower prices of compact disc players will affect prices of compact discs and the quantity bought and sold.

The approach taken in applying supply and demand is to assume that the market price and quantity are initially in equilibrium. Then, some event is assumed to occur, such as the introduction of a new tax or a change in consumers' incomes. This event is called **exogenous** because it is assumed to have an external source; the gas tax is a government decision, the change in prices of compact disc *players* happens outside the compact *disc* market, and so on. The impact of an exogenous event is viewed in terms of how it affects the supply or demand curve. The market reaction to the exogenous event is examined by finding the new equilibrium price and quantity from the new supply and demand curves. The new equilibrium price and quantity are then compared with the original equilibrium price and quantity. The changes in equilibrium price and quantity that occur are attributed to the assumed event. In viewing the resulting predictions of supply and demand, economists are frequently as concerned with the directions of changes in prices and quantities as with precise measurement of these changes.

The procedure of comparing one equilibrium with another equilibrium where the change in equilibrium is due to some assumed exogenous event is called the **principle of comparative statics.** When we apply comparative statics, it is helpful to hold one of the curves constant while the other is shifted. That is, it helps to assume *ceteris paribus* with the other curve.

> Comparative statics involves the comparison of one equilibrium with another in order to determine the effect of some exogenous event.

SHIFTS IN SUPPLY AND DEMAND

Let us begin by holding the supply curve constant to determine the effects of factors that influence demand.

Factors Shifting the Demand Curve

Changes in Consumers' Incomes.　In Chapter 4 we saw that for normal goods a general increase in consumers' incomes increases demand, and vice versa. Table 6.2 gives the quantities of wheat demanded at each price for two income levels of wheat consumers. The first column, labeled "Quantity demanded, income Y_1," shows the same quantities demanded as in Table 6.1. These quantities therefore correspond to the same demand curve as in Figure 6.1, which is redrawn in Figure 6.2 as $D(Y_1)$ to identify it as the relevant demand curve when income is Y_1. The second column of quantities demanded in Table 6.2 is for a higher income, Y_2. When these quantities are plotted against price, we obtain demand curve $D(Y_2)$. We see from both the table and the figure that at each price more is demanded at the higher income; the demand curve has shifted upward and to the right. As

TABLE 6.2

For normal goods, an increase in income causes an increase in demand at each price.

WHEAT PRICE	QUANTITY DEMANDED AT INCOME Y₁ (Bushels per year)	QUANTITY DEMANDED AT INCOME Y₂ (Bushels per year)	QUANTITY SUPPLIED (Bushels per year)
$0.00	∞	∞	0
0.50	100,000	135,000	0
1.00	65,000	87,750	0
1.50	44,000	59,400	0
2.00	30,000	40,500	0
2.50	20,000	27,000	7,800
3.00	15,000	20,250	8,600
3.50	12,000	16,200	9,150
4.00	9,600	12,960	9,600
4.50	7,800	10,530	10,000
5.00	6,400	8,640	10,350
5.50	5,300	7,155	10,650
6.00	4,400	5,940	10,900
6.50	3,600	4,860	11,120
7.00	3,100	4,185	11,320
7.50	2,600	3,510	11,500
8.00	2,200	2,970	11,650
8.50	1,850	2,430	11,760
9.00	1,500	2,025	11,860
9.50	1,300	1,755	11,950
10.00	1,000	1,350	12,000

For normal goods, market demand is higher at each price the higher is income. At any given income, the quantity demanded is higher the lower is the price. These characteristics of demand are seen from the two columns giving quantity demanded at different prices. Demand with higher income **Y₂** is higher than with income **Y₁**. However, with both income levels, a greater quantity is demanded the lower is the price.

explained in Chapter 4, this is the way demand curves shift from increases in income in the case of normal goods.

In order to determine the effects of the assumed change in income on the equilibrium price and quantity, we also need the supply curve, which has not shifted and is the same as in Figure 6.1. This is added to Figure 6.2, along with the original and new demand curves $D(Y_1)$ and $D(Y_2)$. Figure 6.2 shows immediately the effect of the increased income on equilibrium price and quantity. The equilibrium is changed from E_1 to E_2. The new equilibrium is at a higher price, approximately $4.60 versus $4.00 per bushel, and a higher quantity, approximately 10,100 bushels

For normal goods, an increase in income causes an increase in equilibrium price and quantity.

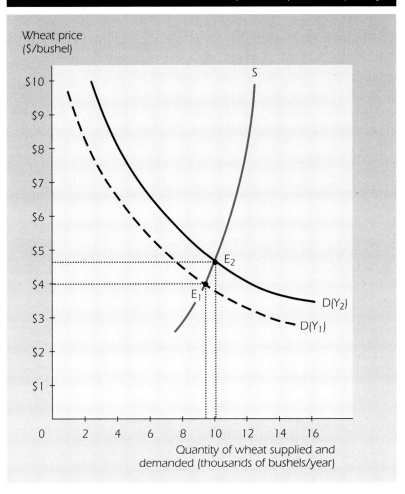

FIGURE 6.2 For normal goods, an increase in consumers' incomes causes an increase in the equilibrium price and quantity.

The original equilibrium price and quantity bought and sold are at point **E**₁, with the wheat price of $4.00 per bushel and 9600 bushels bought and sold. When income increases, the demand curve shifts to the right, resulting in a new equilibrium at point **E**₂ with a higher price, approximately $4.60 per bushel, and higher quantity bought and sold, approximately 10,100 bushels per year.

versus 9600 bushels. That is, in the case of normal goods, an increase in income increases the equilibrium price and quantity.

We can think of the move from point E_1 to point E_2 in Figure 6.2 as follows: When income increases from Y_1 to Y_2, the resulting shift in the demand curve causes an excess demand at the original price of $4.00 per bushel. Table 6.2 tells us this excess demand equals $(12{,}960 - 9600) = 3360$ bushels per year. The shortage puts upward pressure on prices as buyers bid for the (insufficient) supply.

Only when the price has risen to approximately $4.60 per bushel is the quantity demanded sufficiently reduced, and the quantity supplied sufficiently expanded, for equilibrium to be restored.

Changes in Prices of Substitutes.   We saw in Chapter 4 that an increase in the price of a substitute has the same qualitative effect on the demand curve as a general increase in consumers' incomes with normal goods: the demand curve shifts to the right. For example, an increase in the price of rye bread increases the demand for whole-wheat bread at every given price of whole-wheat bread; consumers move to the relatively cheaper bread. That is, the entire demand curve for whole-wheat bread shifts to the right as the price of rye bread increases. Similarly, the entire demand curve for chicken shifts to the right as the price of beef increases.

The effect of an increase in the price of a substitute on the equilibrium is qualitatively the same as the effect of an increase in income for normal goods. In Figure 6.3,

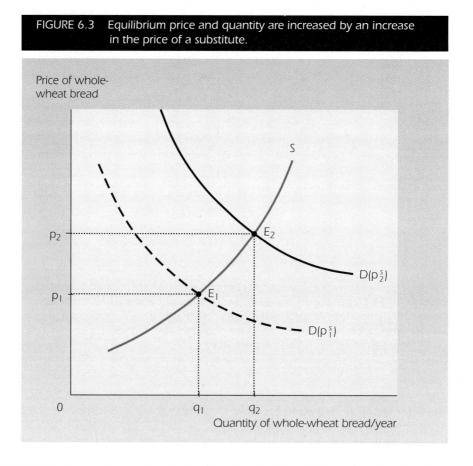

FIGURE 6.3   Equilibrium price and quantity are increased by an increase in the price of a substitute.

$D(p_1^s)$ is the demand curve for whole-wheat bread at the original price of rye bread, a substitute for whole-wheat bread. $D(p_2^s)$ is the demand curve for whole-wheat bread after an increase in the price of rye bread. The increase in demand for whole-wheat bread increases the equilibrium price and quantity. That is, price and quantity increase as a result of an increase in the price of a substitute.

$D(p_1^s)$ is the demand curve for whole-wheat bread before an increase in the price of rye bread. (The p_1^s in parentheses shows that demand is drawn for a particular price of a substitute.) $D(p_2^s)$ is the demand curve for whole-wheat bread after an increase in the price of rye bread. The equilibrium shifts from point E_1 to point E_2 in Figure 6.3. That is, the effect of the higher price of rye bread is an increase in the price and quantity of whole-wheat bread bought and sold. Similarly, a decrease in the price of rye bread would cause a decrease in demand for whole-wheat bread and a consequent decrease in its equilibrium price and quantity bought and sold.

Changes in Prices of Complements.   As we saw in Chapter 4, an increase in a product's price reduces the demand for its complement, the opposite to what occurs with substitutes. For example, an increase in the price of computer hardware reduces the quantity of software demanded at any given price of software. This occurs because the increase in the price of hardware reduces the quantity of hardware purchased and hence the need for software to use with the hardware. In terms of the demand curve, an increase in the price of a product shifts the demand curve for its complements downward and to the left.

Figure 6.4 shows the effect of an increase in the price of a complement. Curve $D(p_1^c)$ is the demand curve at the complement's price of p_1^c, and curve $D(p_2^c)$ is the demand curve at a higher price, p_2^c, of the complement. We see that the demand curve shifts to the left as the price of the complement increases. As a result, the equilibrium price and quantity are reduced, the opposite to what occurs with an increase in the price of a substitute. (Compare Figure 6.4 with Figure 6.3.)

Changes in Tastes Toward Products.   Any supply and demand figure such as Figure 6.2 tells us that taste changes that favor a product and shift the demand curve to the right increase equilibrium price and quantity. Taste changes against a product reduce the price and quantity.

Figures 6.2, 6.3, and 6.4 show that shifts in demand curves change equilibrium price and quantity in the same direction. Let us compare this situation to what happens from shifts in the supply curve.

Factors Shifting the Supply Curve

Changes in Productivities of Variable Inputs.   In Chapter 5 we saw that the market supply curve, which is the horizontal sum of the MC curves of firms, shifts downward and to the right as a result of an improvement in the productivity of a variable input.[2] The effect of such a shift in the supply curve on equilibrium price and quantity is described in Figure 6.5. The demand curve and original supply curve are labeled D and S_1, and the new supply curve is labeled S_2. The original equilibrium is at point E_1, and the new equilibrium is at point E_2. We see that the shift in the supply curve has reduced the equilibrium price and increased the quantity bought and sold. Productivity improvements therefore translate into lower prices for consumers and more product being produced and consumed.

It should be noted that shifts in the supply curve cause price and quantity to move in opposite directions. This differs from the effect of shifting demand curves, where price and quantity move in the same direction.

If two goods are substitutes, an increase in the price of one causes an increase in the equilibrium price and quantity of the other.

If two goods are complements, an increase in the price of one causes a decrease in the equilibrium price and quantity of the other.

Shifts in demand curves change price and quantity in the same direction.

Shifts in the supply curves change equilibrium price and quantity in opposite directions.

[2] Such shifts could result from improved machines, better training, or increased managerial efficiency.

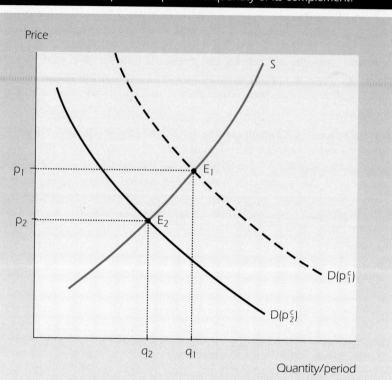

FIGURE 6.4 An increase in the price of a good reduces the equilibrium price and quantity of its complement.

$D(p_1^c)$ is the demand curve before an increase in the price of a complement. For example, $D(p_1^c)$ is the demand curve for computer software before an increase in the price of computer hardware. $D(p_2^c)$ is the demand curve after an increase in the price of the complement. It shows a lower quantity demanded at each price, that is, a leftward shift in the demand curve. The effect of an increase in the price of the complement is a lower equilibrium price and quantity, the opposite to the effect for substitutes.

Decreases in the prices of variable inputs shift the supply curve downward and to the right. This results in a lower equilibrium price and an increase in the equilibrium quantity bought and sold.

Changes in Prices of Variable Inputs. As we saw in Chapter 5, a decrease in the price of a variable input, such as the wage rate paid on a wheat farm, has the same effect on the supply curve as an increase in productivity of the input. This is so because the cost of another unit of output, the *MC*, is the number of units of inputs required multiplied by their prices. Consequently, a decline in the price of a variable input shifts individual firms' *MC* curves downward and hence shifts the market supply curve downward and to the right as in Figure 6.5. Therefore, a reduction in the price of an input lowers the equilibrium price and increases the equilibrium quantity bought and sold.

Taxes on Variable Inputs. Supply curves are shifted by taxes on variable inputs just as they are by changes in the prices and productivities of these inputs. Indeed, as we saw in Figure 5.11 and the accompanying discussion in Chapter 5, a change in taxes on all variable inputs shifts the supply curve upward by the same percentage as the change in tax. (In Chapter 5 we considered a 25% tax on

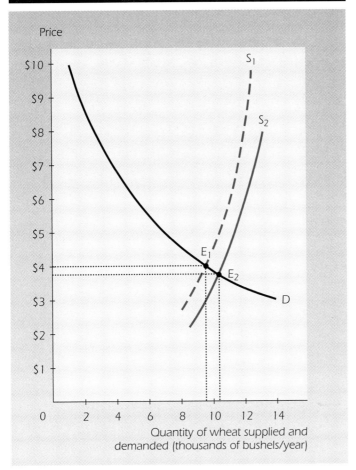

FIGURE 6.5   A rightward shift in the supply curve causes a reduction in equilibrium price and an increase in the quantity bought and sold.

When the supply curve shifts to the right from an improvement in the productivity of a variable input, the new equilibrium is at a lower price and higher quantity. Note that the price and quantity move in opposite directions.

variable inputs. We showed that firms' *MC* curves, and hence the market supply curve, shift up 25% as a result of such a tax.)

Suppose that a tax is placed on the cost of labor facing a firm, where this "tax" results from, for example, firms being required to pay 25% of wages as a Social Security contribution for their workers. Assume that before-tax wages are not affected by the tax and that wages are the only variable cost. This means that wages and hence marginal costs inclusive of the tax increase by 25% at each output. In turn, this causes the supply curve to shift upward by 25%, as it did in Figure 5.11. Such an upward shift of the supply curve is shown in Figure 6.6, where at each output, S_2 is 25% higher than S_1. For example, point *A* on the supply curve S_2 is 25% higher than point *B* on supply curve S_1.

FIGURE 6.6 An increase in tax on a variable input causes an increase in equilibrium price by less than the increase in the tax.

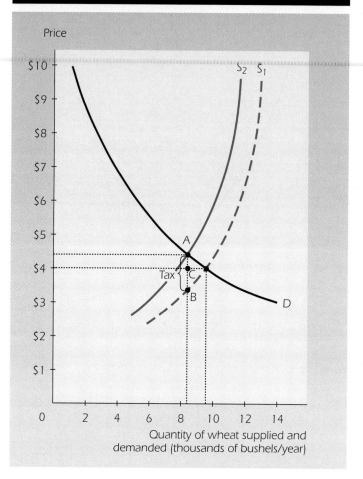

The imposition of a tax on variable inputs increases **MC** and shifts the market supply curve upward. The new equilibrium price is higher and the quantity bought and sold is lower, but the increase in price is less than the increase in tax.

A tax on variable inputs increases equilibrium price and reduces equilibrium quantity. The tax is in general *shared* by the consumer and the producer, but the more inelastic the demand, the higher is the proportion paid by the consumer.

   With the supply curve shifting upward as in Figure 6.6, the equilibrium price is higher and the equilibrium quantity lower than before the tax. That is, the intersection of S_2 with D is at a higher price and lower quantity than the intersection of S_1 with D. However, we can say more than this. As we have noted, the supply curve has shifted upward by the amount of the tax, shifting the distance AB at the new equilibrium output, specifically, by 25% of variable costs. The figure shows that the price increase, which is distance AC, is less than the vertical shift in the supply curve. That is, the price of the output increases less than the tax. For example, in Figure 6.6 the 25% tax on variable inputs has increased the equilibrium price by about 10%, from $4.00 to $4.40 per bushel. Since the consumer pays only part of the 25% tax, the producer must absorb the rest.

The extent to which the consumer or producer bears a tax involves the question of **tax incidence**. Figure 6.7 shows that a major determinant of tax incidence is the elasticity of the demand curve. When demand is perfectly inelastic, as in part (a) of Figure 6.7, all the tax is borne by the consumer; the price increases by 25% from $4.00 to $5.00, the same as the tax. This is no surprise, since a vertical demand curve means consumers buy the same amount whatever the price. In the opposite situation of a perfectly elastic demand curve, as in part (b) of Figure 6.7, all the tax is born by producers, at least in the short run for which the supply curves are drawn; consumers pay the same, so producers must absorb the tax. This occurs because consumers are not willing to buy anything at a higher price when demand is perfectly elastic. In general, the more inelastic the demand, the greater is the share of a tax on variable inputs that is paid by the consumer. The more elastic the demand curve, the greater is the share of a tax borne by the producer.

The conclusion for the incidence of a tax carries over to the effect of an increase in the cost of a variable input. An increase in the cost of a variable input shifts the supply curve upward in the same way as a tax on variable inputs. It follows that in the short run, an increase in the cost of a variable input is paid for partly by the consumer and partly by the producer. As with a tax, the consumer pays a larger share the more inelastic is the demand curve. (In the long run, the incidence of a higher cost of inputs depends on whether they force firms out of the industry. If firms are forced out of the industry, reducing market supply and increasing market price, consumers pay more toward the higher input costs in the long run.)

Increases in the cost of inputs are borne partly by consumers and partly by producers. The consumer bears more, the more inelastic is demand.

Supply Disruptions from Weather and Wars.   Poor weather for growing crops and infestations of insects shift supply curves for agricultural crops to the left.[3] This increases the equilibrium price and reduces the quantity demanded, keeping this in line with the reduced quantity supplied. The shopper sees such consequences of poor growing conditions in the supermarket with, for example, jumps in lettuce prices after unusually cold weather in California or more expensive oranges after frosts in Florida. Disruptions in supplies of other basic commodities such as oil, as occur when shipping is affected by military conflicts, also show up quickly in prices. Labor disputes in principal sources of supply of, for example, copper from Peru or nickel from Canada also translate quickly into higher commodity prices.

Supply disruptions force prices higher.

Surprisingly perhaps, events such as bad harvests can increase total revenue and profits of producers. The condition under which this occurs is illustrated in Figure 6.8. In part (a) of Figure 6.8, demand is assumed to be inelastic. A movement up an inelastic demand curve from right to left is associated with a percentage increase in price that is larger than the percentage reduction in quantity demanded; recall that with inelastic demand, $|\%\Delta p| > |\%\Delta q|$. It follows that the amount spent increases. That is, in part (a) of Figure 6.8 the percentage increase in price from p_1 to p_2 is larger than the percentage decrease in quantity from q_1 to q_2.

Poor harvests increase total revenue and profit if demand is inelastic and reduce total revenue and profit if demand is elastic.

---

[3] As explained in Chapter 5, when we consider changes in productivity, prices of inputs, and so on, consideration of the vertical shift of the supply curve is more useful because we know the magnitude of movement in this direction. However, when we consider such factors as weather, the known magnitude is more likely to be the change in output, which is measured on the horizontal axis.

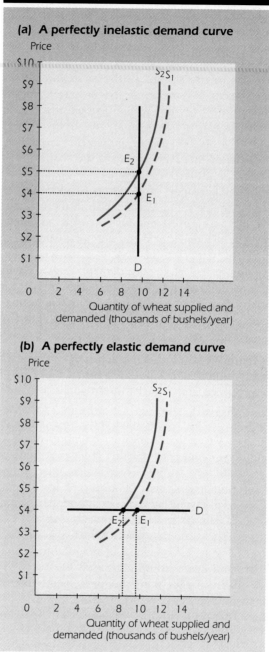

FIGURE 6.7   The more elastic the demand curve, the greater is the extent to which a tax falls on the producer.

(a) A perfectly inelastic demand curve

(b) A perfectly elastic demand curve

When the demand curve is perfectly inelastic as in (a), all the burden of a tax on variable inputs falls on consumers. This results from the consumers' insensitivity to price. When the demand curve is perfectly elastic as in (b), all the burden of a tax falls on the producer, at least in the short run for which the given supply curves are relevant. The producer must absorb all the tax because none could be sold at a higher price. In general, the more elastic the demand curve, the more the tax falls on the producer.

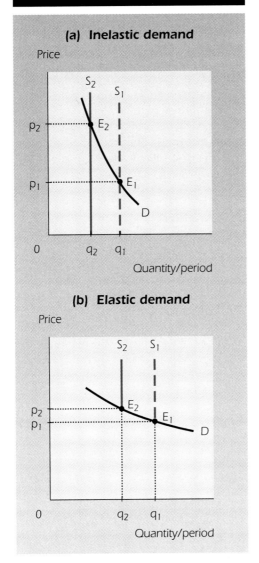

FIGURE 6.8 Supply disruptions increase total revenue and profit if demand is inelastic.

(a) Inelastic demand

(b) Elastic demand

In part (a), where demand is assumed to be inelastic, a reduction in supply forces the price up by a larger percentage than the reduction in supply, thereby increasing total revenue. For given costs, the increase in total revenue means higher profit. In part (b), where demand is assumed to be elastic, a reduction in supply forces the price up by a smaller percentage than the reduction in quantity, reducing total revenue. For given costs, this means smaller profit.

This means that a poor harvest increases the total revenue of farmers. If total costs are not increased, the higher total revenue also means a higher profit.

Part (b) of Figure 6.8 shows the situation where demand is elastic. By definition, with elastic demand, the percentage increase in price is less than the percentage reduction in quantity. That is, total revenue of a product with elastic demand is decreased by a poor harvest. For given costs, this means lower profits for suppliers.

While it is true that a reduction in *market* supply increases firms' revenues and profits if demand is inelastic, it does not pay an *individual firm* to destroy crops or plan on a lower output because this one firm would have a negligible effect on the market price when other firms continue to produce. The firm withholding supply would therefore lose by such an action. Only if all firms could combine to reduce supply and prevent cheating could they increase profit by reducing supply when demand is elastic. This possibility is taken up later when we discuss **cartels.**

AVOIDING CONFUSION

Shifts of Curves versus Movements Along Curves

The effects of shifting supply and demand curves on equilibrium price and quantity are quite straightforward. These effects are summarized in Table 6.3, but we need not memorize them, because it takes no more than a quickly drawn figure on a scrap of paper or in one's mind's eye to generate the outcomes.

In view of the straightforward nature of the workings of supply and demand, it is remarkable how often people reach incorrect conclusions. For example, consider the following answer—heard by many economics instructors—to the question, "What happens after an increase in demand?"

> *When demand increases, this increases the price. The higher price causes an increase in supply. The higher supply reduces the price. The lower price increases demand, which raises the price, increasing supply, which lowers the price . . . , and so on.*

Such an answer can continue *ad nauseam,* but is incorrect. Can you spot where the answer begins to go astray?

The problem is that the answer confuses *shifts* of supply and demand curves with movements *along* the curves. The question refers to an upward and rightward shift of the demand curve. This does indeed cause a higher price, as the answer states. This higher price, in turn, does mean a greater *quantity* supplied, but this is due to a movement along the supply curve, not to a shift in the supply curve. We can see this by referring to, for example, Figure 6.3. The rightward shift in the demand curve causes a higher price, and this causes producers to increase the quantity supplied as they move from point E_1 to point E_2 along the supply curve. We therefore end up with a higher price and an increase in quantity supplied. That's it. The process ends at this point. It is incorrect to continue beyond this point to consider the effects of a higher supply, because there has been no shift in the supply curve.

....
TABLE 6.3

Equilibrium price and quantity move in the same direction after a shift in demand but in opposite directions after a shift in supply.

| | DIRECTION OF SHIFT IN DEMAND | | DIRECTION OF SHIFT IN SUPPLY | |
	INCREASE	DECREASE	INCREASE	DECREASE
Price	Higher	Lower	Lower	Higher
Quantity	Higher	Lower	Higher	Lower

The direction of price and quantity changes after shifts in supply or demand are quickly confirmed by drawing a diagram. However, it does not take a diagram to conclude that price and quantity move in the same direction as a shift in demand, whereas only quantity moves in the same direction as a shift in supply.

Confusion cannot occur if we draw supply and demand figures. Alternatively, errors can be avoided by distinguishing between "changes in demand" or "changes in supply" on the one hand and "changes in the *quantity* demanded" or "changes in the *quantity* supplied" on the other. The former refer to shifts in demand and supply curves, and the latter refer to movements along curves. This book uses this distinction where there is a chance of confusion. You need not be so particular if you draw figures to reach conclusions.

Equilibrium Prices and Quantities versus Supply and Demand Curves

Another common mistake concerns inferences about supply and demand curves from price and quantity observations. For example, you might hear it said that because the price of oil and the quantity consumed have both fallen in recent years, the demand curve cannot slope downward; otherwise, the lower price would have meant more being consumed. In reality, the observation of simultaneously lower prices and quantities may be the result of a demand curve that has shifted downward, as in part (a) of Figure 6.9. Alternatively, you might hear it said that because copper output has expanded while copper prices have fallen, the supply curve cannot slope upward; otherwise, the lower price would have meant less being produced. In reality, the observation of lower prices and higher production could have resulted from a rightward shift of the supply curve as in part (b) of Figure 6.9.

In general, data on prices and quantities cannot be used to prove anything about the slopes of supply or demand curves unless it is known which curve was shifting; was demand shifting, was supply shifting, or both. For example, if it were known that the demand curve for oil had been shifting to the left, as shown in part (a) of Figure 6.9, we could have deduced that the lower prices and quantities

The slopes of supply and demand curves cannot simply be inferred from observations of prices and quantities.

FIGURE 6.9 Observations on prices and quantities do not provide evidence about the slopes of supply or demand curves.

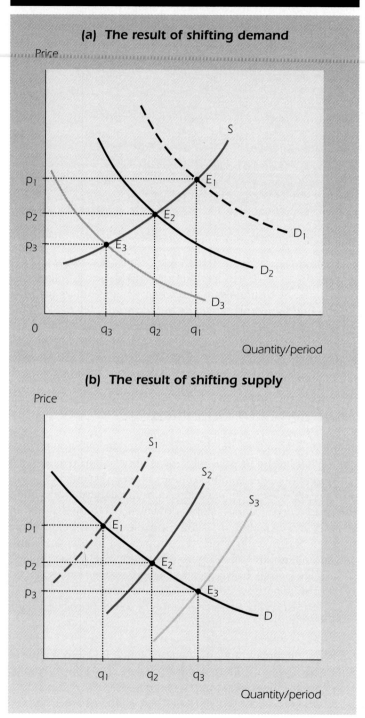

(a) The result of shifting demand

(b) The result of shifting supply

Observations on prices and quantities cannot be used to draw inferences about slopes of supply or demand curves unless it is known which curve is shifting. In general, price and quantity observations tell us nothing more than the history of prices and quantities.

were evidence of an upward-sloping supply curve. Similarly, if it were known that the supply curve for copper had been shifting to the right, as in part (b) of Figure 6.9, we could have deduced that lower prices and higher quantities were evidence of a downward-sloping demand curve. However, because the supply and demand curves have probably *both* been shifting, it is necessary to know which curve has been shifting at which time. Without this information, all that observations on prices and quantities tell us is about the history of prices and quantities and nothing more than that.

INTERFERING WITH SUPPLY AND DEMAND

The Price Mechanism at Work

As explained in Chapter 2, the free movement of prices in response to changes in supply and demand is a means for rationing scarce goods and services. If we did not have market prices able to vary until they are such that consumers want to buy only just those quantities producers are supplying, it would be necessary to find some alternative mechanism to allocate production between demanders.

Prices serve as more than a rationing mechanism. They also serve as signals for producers to know how much to produce and even what to produce. For example, we have seen that an increase in demand—a shift of the demand curve—increases price and that producers respond by moving up their supply curves, making additional amounts available. It is the increase in market price that tells the supplier to produce more and makes it worthwhile to expand production.[4]

The price-signaling mechanism is also responsible for the types of goods and services that surround us. For example, it explains why the selection of more environmentally friendly, or "green," products has expanded; a willingness of some consumers to pay a premium for biodegradable packages, phosphate-free detergents, unbleached paper, reusable containers, and so on has translated into a willingness of producers to provide such products.[5] In general, it was not that producers on their own initiative made the altruistic decision to produce such products to help the environment. Rather, the decision to make "green" products was typically a response to a shift in consumers' tastes toward such products. This shift in demand translated into higher prices. In turn, these higher prices made the "green" products more profitable than less environmentally friendly products that could have been produced.[6]

The same price-signaling role of supply and demand explains the broader choices of healthy cereals, cholesterol-free cooking oil, low-fat dairy products and

Market prices tell producers **what** *to produce and* **what** *quantities* *to produce.*

Consumers signal producers what to supply via the price mechanism.

---

[4] Example 6.1 suggests that even the supply of begging might respond to market forces.

[5] Example 6.2 shows that the market for environmentally friendly products has worked its way to the production of inputs as well as outputs.

[6] Nevertheless, as Example 6.3 explains, while demand may bring forth a supply, the reverse does not necessarily occur. That is, supply does not bring forth a demand.

Example **6.1**

THE MARKET FOR BENEVOLENCE

We do not typically think of supply and demand for "services" such as begging, but as the following excerpt shows, we can indeed think in such terms.

Let us first take up the familiar case of a beggar. A gentleman is implored for relief by a repulsive piece of humanity, enshrouded in rags and covered with dirt. Moved by pity, he gives him a dime and passes on. What is the economical nature of this transaction? We reply that the transaction is one of supply and demand, belonging to the same class as the supply of and demand for personal services. The combined willingness and ability of a number of persons in the community to give dimes to beggars constitutes a demand for beggary, just as much as if an advertisement, "Beggars wanted; liberal alms guaranteed," were conspicuously inserted in the columns of a newspaper. If there is any difficulty in seeing the truth of this statement, it should disappear when the reader reflects that nothing is necessary to constitute an economic demand except readiness to make payments on certain conditions. Among a crowd of children fond of music, an ability and a willingness to give pennies to organ grinders constitute a demand for their services. . . .

. . . So in a community where there is a demand for beggars a certain number are sure to become beggars, and to study the professional accomplishments which will be most likely to draw money from the pockets of the benevolent. Hence, in the case supposed, mendicity will exist according to the same laws that govern the existence of other trades and occupations.

Source: Simon Newcomb, **Principles of Political Economy** (New York: Harper & Bros., 1886).

Example **6.2**

GROWING DEMAND FOR "GREEN" PRODUCTS

*The market is a rigorous testing ground for new products, so for a product to be successful, people must be willing to pay a high enough price to leave a profit. As the following excerpt from **The Wall Street Journal** shows, people are increasingly willing to pay enough to support more environmentally friendly production methods.*

Americans in recent years have displayed a growing appetite for organically grown food, which costs a bit more because it is grown without the help of chemicals.

Now, a New Jersey start-up is touting organically grown cotton— and getting an enthusiastic response.

Daniel and Marylou Marsh Sanders started Ecosport Inc. in December 1990 to sell clothes made from cotton that is cultivated without toxic pesticides, herbicides or defoliants and is processed without bleach. They say their sales this year will exceed $4 million. . . .

It wasn't easy to find "environmentally responsible" cotton growers. The few the company found—in Texas, California, Tennessee and Arizona—had to be signed to long-term contracts to assure a steady supply, and their fiber costs as much as 10% more.

Mr. Sanders says he got Ecosport's first order by asking Greenpeace why it marketed T-shirts and other items that weren't totally "green." Today, Ecosport also sells through catalogs, department stores and environmental stores.

Source: "Some 'Green' Clothes for 'Green' Consumers," **The Wall Street Journal,** September 29, 1992, p. B1. Reprinted by permission of The Wall Street Journal, © 1992 Dow Jones & Company, Inc. All Rights Reserved Worldwide.

Example   6.3

IS RECYCLING JUST A WASTE?

For a market to function, there must be both supply and demand. As the following article explains, problems occur when an attempt is made to create a market by creating a supply. Hopefully, in this case involving the market for recycled waste, the demand will eventually appear.

The recycling business is down in the dumps.

In Seattle, one of America's most zealous recycling communities, Donald Kneass looks out his office window at the crest of a 25-foot mound of crushed glass in the distance. It contains 6,000 tons of the stuff, collected at curbside from 170,000 homes. The company Mr. Kneass works for, Waste Management Inc., owns the glass and can't get rid of it. No one around Seattle wants to buy it, and shipping it elsewhere is too costly.

Collection centers in many other cities and towns, particularly in the Northeast and Midwest, are buried in old newspapers, green wine and beer bottles and plastic milk jugs that nobody wants. Aluminum cans bring only a pittance, victims of the former Soviet Union's desperate effort to raise hard currency last year by dumping bauxite ingot on the market. And rising labor and shipping costs have combined with the recession to squeeze waste haulers, materials brokers and processors.

Some haulers in the Minneapolis–St. Paul area, having run out of indoor storage space, are dumping or burning recyclable materials, says Timothy Nolan of Minnesota's Office of Waste Management. "Nobody wants the negative PR," he says, "but with so many things hitting all at once, it's tough to make ends meet. Some processors are going out of business."

Many experts say this crunch was bound to happen. The supply side of America's recycling revolution has been growing at an explosive rate, but the demand side is still barely under way. Manufacturers simply aren't geared up to absorb the huge volumes suddenly available. Mr. Kneass fears the country's entire recycling infrastructure could collapse if efforts to expand markets don't take hold soon.

In parts of the Northeast and Midwest, where strong after-markets haven't developed, the oversupply is so great that state officials report instances of separated trash being mixed together again and hauled to dumps and incinerators at taxpayer expense.

Recycling critics are gloating. For years, they have viewed recycling as a craze driven by panic about vanishing landfills. Many also believe recycling initiatives are based on faulty economic assumptions and that such efforts ultimately cost more in time, labor, energy and transportation than they're worth.

"Recycling programs are efficient when they are able to turn a profit," says Jerry Taylor, director of natural resource studies at the Cato Institute, a libertarian think tank in Washington. "But most of these mandatory curbside programs aren't profitable. They're simply subsidizing the collection and processing of materials that probably should be buried or burned."

An exception, say Mr. Taylor and other critics, is aluminum cans, now being recycled at a 65% rate. These efforts, which preceded government mandates, always have been efficient because they require less energy, and therefore cost less than producing cans from bauxite ore.

"The best way to tell if something should be recycled," says Mr. Taylor, "is whether it's already being recycled because of market forces. If you need government intervention to achieve recycling, then it probably will distort the markets."

Source: Frank Edward Allen, "Piling Up: As Recycling Surges, Market for Materials Slow to Develop," **The Wall Street Journal,** January 17, 1992, p. 1. Reprinted by permission of The Wall Street Journal, © 1992 Dow Jones & Company, Inc. All Rights Reserved Worldwide.

meat, and so on that today line supermarket shelves. The shifts in demand toward these products pushed their prices up, thereby increasing the quantities supplied. Typically, it was not that producers wanted the people buying their products to be healthier; rather, it was simply a matter of response to market forces.[7] Consumers have "told" producers what to provide via their market demand and the impact of this demand on prices. Similarly, declines in demand, and consequent declines in market prices, signaled suppliers to reduce production of high-fat hamburgers, low-fiber bread, and so on. These changes were the result of business decisions made via the forces of supply and demand, not the result of social concerns of management.

Despite the signaling and rationing provided by supply and demand, few societies leave the pricing of everything to the unregulated marketplace. As explained in Chapter 2, most economies are mixed economies, with some prices set freely and others determined by the authorities.[8] Even in free-enterprise or *laissez-faire* economies like those of the United States, Japan, Canada, and the countries of western Europe, some prices are determined by the government or an agency of the government. There are numerous examples of rent controls, interest-rate ceilings, agricultural price supports, minimum wages, officially determined utility prices, and so on in generally free market economies. (At the other extreme, in socialist countries we find numerous examples of free markets in fresh produce, repair services, and so on.) It is useful to consider the effects of price regulations, because perhaps more than anything else it is the consequences of price regulations that provide the clearest appreciation of the supply and demand mechanism.

Price Ceilings

Rent Controls. It is very difficult to quickly expand the housing stock. Consequently, if there is an unusually rapid growth in housing demand, there is likely to be a sharp increase in rents while housing supply lags demand.

The problem with housing that can result in rent "overshooting" is illustrated in Figure 6.10. Initially, the rental housing market is assumed to be in equilibrium with rent p_1 and quantity q_1. Then demand is assumed to increase from D_1 to D_2. A jump in demand cannot instantaneously increase the quantity of rental housing supplied. Therefore, the price, or rent, increases until the quantity demanded is reduced to the currently fixed available quantity.[9] This is shown in Figure 6.10,

---

[7] There are exceptions where producers have responded to government regulations rather than to the market. For example, the production of less polluting and more efficient automobiles and the switch to lead-free gasoline were, at least initially, responses to government regulations. So too was the shift away from chlorofluorocarbons (CFCs) in aerosol cans, refrigerators, and air conditioners.

[8] The decision as to whether prices should be determined freely by the forces of supply and demand or regulated by the government has at times been at the center of political debate. For example, Example 6.4 explains how the means of delivery of health care to Americans led to a showdown between Democrats and Republicans.

[9] In fact, even in the short run, more existing rental space may be made available as rents increase as, for example, home owners rent their basements or unused space. The possibility of some limited increase in supply in the short run can be incorporated by making S(short run) less than perfectly inelastic, although this does not affect the qualitative conclusions.

Example 6.4

ECONOMICS AND POLITICS OF HEALTH

Health care, the cost of which constitutes almost one-sixth of the U.S. gross domestic product (GDP), became one of the central political issues in the 1992 U.S. presidential campaign. As the following article makes clear, the focus of the political debate was whether health care should be provided by the government, left to the market, or be a mixture of market and government.

. . . Can the market for health care work like the market for autos or tomatoes? Or is health care an exception, like defense and highways, that is unsuited to market mechanisms and must be provided by the government? . . .

[M]any conservative economists believe they can use the tax code to fix the system by making people more sensitive to the cost of their health care, and by forcing insurers, doctors, hospitals, nursing homes and all others to compete on price and quality for patients' business. But critics say there isn't enough information made available for people to shop intelligently. . . .

By using tax credits or vouchers, rather than providing government insurance outright, the administration hopes to force people to shop for the best quality coverage at the lowest price. Under the free-market approach, tax credits or vouchers might even eventually replace Medicaid and Medicare, further reducing the government's role. . . .

Democrats have introduced dozens of health-care reform bills over the past year, all based on the premise that private markets can't be expected to address such a fundamental human need as health. "No one can distribute Gucci loafers better than the market," says Uwe Reinhardt, a Princeton economist who specializes in health care. "But a pure market cannot distribute health care." . . .

Many experts argue that a comprehensive health-care overhaul will only be achieved incrementally. The U.S. political process, they say, is too cumbersome for radical change. But even those who favor a cautious approach say it is critical that the nation decide on which general direction it is heading: toward more competition or toward more regulation.

Source: Hilary Stout, "Health Care Choices: A Bigger Federal Role or a Market Approach?" **The Wall Street Journal,** January 15, 1992, pp. A1, A4. Reprinted by permission of The Wall Street Journal, © 1992 Dow Jones & Company, Inc. All Rights Reserved Worldwide.

where we have drawn a short-run supply curve S(short term) of rental housing that is perfectly inelastic. The figure shows an increase in demand from D_1 to D_2 causing rent to increase in the short run from p_1 to p_2^s per month.

If allowed to operate, the price mechanism would signal via the higher rent that more housing is wanted and can be provided profitably. That is, in the long run the supply curve of housing is more elastic than in the short run, like S(long run) versus S(short run). The additional supply that would occur in the long run would eventually bring rents down to p_2^L and increase the quantity of rental housing to q_2. However, at the controlled rent, p_1, the supply of rental housing does not increase in the long run but remains at S(short run) with quantity q_1. This means a short-run and long-run excess demand of the distance between D_2 and S(short run) at the controlled rent, p_1. Those who are able to obtain housing are those already with housing or those paying bribes in the form of favors or "key money," which is a lump-sum payment to a property owner for offering the key to a particular renter. For those who cannot pay the necessary bribes, the policy of keeping rents low means that they may not have a place to live.

Rent controls cause a short-run and long-run housing shortage.

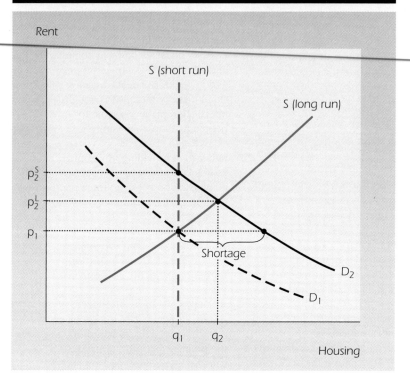

FIGURE 6.10   Because it takes time to increase the stock of housing, rents can increase in the short run to above their new long run equilibrium.

With the supply of housing fixed in the short run, an increase in demand from **D**$_1$ to **D**$_2$ causes a substantial increase in rents from **p**$_1$ to **p**$_2^s$ per month if there are no rent controls. Over time, the higher rents will make it profitable to provide more rental accommodations. If the long-run supply curve of rental accommodations is **S (long run)**, rents will end up at **p**$_2^l$ where this supply curve intersects the new demand curve. However, with rent controls keeping rents at **p**$_1$, the supply of housing remains fixed at **q**$_1$; there is then no incentive to provide more housing, and there is permanent excess demand.

Usury Laws.   Limitations on interest rates have a history that goes back to biblical times. In the modern era they have come in the form of maximum rates payable on deposits or chargeable on mortgages.[10]

Figure 6.11 shows what happens if interest rates are held below equilibrium. The interest rate, which is the price of credit, is on the vertical axis, and the amount saved and borrowed is on the horizontal axis. Curve *D* shows that the higher the interest rate, the lower is the quantity of funds demanded by borrowers. Curve *S* shows that the higher the interest rate, the higher is the quantity of funds

[10] In 1991 there was also a move in the United States to cap credit card interest rates. However, Congress decided to stop short of regulation after extended debate.

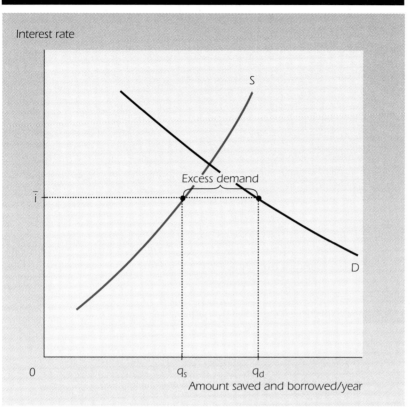

FIGURE 6.11   Usury laws cause rationing of funds to those offering the best security.

The lower the interest rate, the higher the quantity of funds demanded by borrowers. This is shown by the downward-sloping demand curve. The higher the interest rate, the higher the quantity of funds made available by savers. This is shown by the upward-sloping supply curve. If the interest rate is held at $\bar{i}$, there is an excess demand. The funds made available by borrowers, in amount q_s, must be rationed between those demanding funds, in amount q_d. Those who are able to borrow are likely to be those who can offer the best security.

made available by savers. If the interest rate is held at $\bar{i}$ by a usury law, there is excess demand for funds. To deal with the excess demand, there must be an allocation of funds that is not based on price, that is, the interest rate. This is likely to take the form of loans being made only to the safest borrowers. The safest borrowers are generally those who already have assets to put up as security, such as fully paid-for homes. Those without assets, such as young couples wanting to buy their first home, may not be able to borrow at the below-equilibrium interest rate.[11]

Usury laws cause funds to be loaned to borrowers offering the best security.

[11] A further example of a price being kept below the market clearing level is water used by California farmers. Example 6.5 explains the consequences of this price distortion and the several benefits of establishing a market for water.

Example 6.5

WATER: FINDING THE RIGHT LEVEL

Water shortages have put a damper on housing and industrial development in some of the more arid areas of California. Is the problem that there is simply insufficient water supply to meet the demand? Alternatively, is the problem too low a price for water? Economics teaches us that these alternatives amount to the same thing: at too low a price the quantity demanded exceeds the quantity supplied. Indeed, whenever price is below the equilibrium, demand exceeds supply. This has most definitely been the case for water in California, with market prices often a mere fraction of their equilibrium level.

It might seem that in the case of water, price affects only the quantity demanded, because the amount of rain falling during any period—the supply—is for Mother Nature to decide. However, is the supply curve of water perfectly inelastic, being unaffected by the market price? The answer is that while nature alone determines how much rain falls on the Golden State, the amount collected and available for use depends on decisions which are affected very much by price: at higher water prices it pays to build more reservoirs, save more of the billions of gallons that drain to the sea, and reduce the loss from evaporation.

The quantity of water demanded is even more sensitive to market price than is the quantity supplied. Currently, about 85% of the state's water is used for agriculture. Some of this is used to grow crops requiring vast amounts of irrigation such as alfalfa, cotton, and even rice! Why shouldn't farmers use the water in this way when it is available for only a few cents for thousands of gallons, even though prices to urban users are hundreds of times higher? If the price of water were to rise, farmers would surely reduce the quantity they demand. However, since they would give up historical rights to water supplies, they have no reason to conserve, at least as long as they can obtain water at subsidized prices and they are prohibited from selling water to others at market prices. This is why California is moving toward a statewide water market, one that would allow farmers with ample water to sell it to cities, businesses, and other farmers desperate for new sources of supply.

The benefits of California's burgeoning water market flow to just about everybody in the state. Consider, for example, the following account of the beneficiaries in a **Business Week** article:

. . .[A]lmost everyone would benefit from a water market. Farmers who sold water would have to fallow land or pump groundwater, but they'd be paid by cities for that water—at least as much as they'd get from growing crops. . . . Moreover, while they might have to pay higher prices for Central Valley Project water, their remaining supplies would be more certain. Cities could assure supplies without building new projects, and even the environment might gain because large-scale new construction might not be needed. During shortages, rising prices would encourage local water districts to build reservoirs to catch the higher-value water. And farmers might put extra money earned from water sales into conservation equipment that would free up more water. . . .

California's water problem, which reached new depths during the severe drought of 1985–1992, shows how dangerous it can be to tamper with the price mechanism. The maintenance of artificially low prices that failed to reflect the opportunity cost of water dampened activity in other parts of the economy. Fortunately, the solution has been found. It involves nothing more than letting the price of water find its own level.

Source: Robert D. Hof, "California's Next Cash Crop May Soon Be . . . Water?" **Business Week,** March 2, 1992, pp. 76–78.

Price Floors

Agricultural Price Supports.   Because of the obvious importance of farming to the welfare of a society, and because farmers have frequently developed effective lobbies, **floor prices,** or minimum prices, have been imposed on many commodities. At some time or other and in some country or other, we have seen floor prices on wheat, butter, eggs, milk, and cheese.

The effect of minimum agricultural prices is illustrated in Figure 6.12. If the price is set at $\bar{p}$, which is above the equilibrium level p_e, farmers will want to produce more than consumers want to buy. In order for the government to prevent the excess supply from forcing prices below the support level, the government must be willing to be the **residual buyer,** purchasing $(q_s - q_d)$ in each period. Over time, the government purchases result in larger and larger stockpiles unless the floor price is equal to or below the average equilibrium price. There are many

Floor prices for agricultural commodities usually result in government stockpiles.

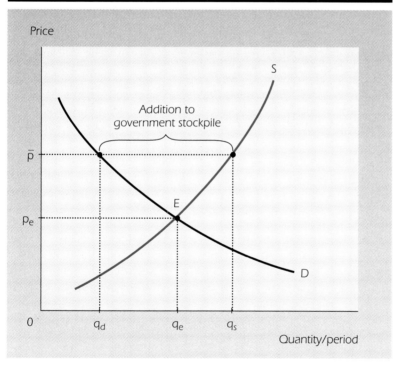

FIGURE 6.12   For agricultural prices to be held above equilibrium, the government must buy the excess supply at the support price.

If the price of an agricultural commodity is held above the equilibrium price **p**ₑ at, for example, **p̄**, it is necessary for the government to buy the excess supply at the support price, that is, to buy (**q**ₛ−**q**ₔ) each period. This is true because farmers will otherwise reduce prices below the support level. With many individual farmers, enforcement of the minimum price requires government intervention at the support level to buy up residual supply. Over time, if the price is kept above equilibrium, the government will accumulate large stockpiles.

examples of growing stockpiles, such as grain stocks in the United States and "butter mountains" and "wine lakes" in the European Community (EC).

Minimum wage laws cause unemployment of the young and unskilled.

Minimum Wages. In the case of minimum wages, the government does not purchase the excess supply to keep wages from falling below the legal minimum; the government is not a residual hirer of labor. Rather, the government depends on fines against employers who break the law. The supply and demand for labor are shown in Figure 6.13.[12] The equilibrium wage is w_e. If the legal minimum wage is set above this level, there will be more people willing to work than there are jobs available. Therefore, there is unemployment equal to the distance between the supply and demand curves for labor at the minimum wage. Minimum wage laws are just one of the causes of **wage rigidity** that can be responsible for unemployment. Those who are unable to find work are those with a value to employers that is below the legal minimum wage, and these are generally young and unskilled workers, the very workers the wage law is designed to help.

Import Quotas*

An import quota is a restriction on the quantity of a good that can be imported.

Governments sometimes influence prices indirectly by limiting the quantities available to consumers rather than by regulating prices directly. One way that quantities available are limited is by setting ceilings on the amounts that can be imported.

A product that faces a ceiling on the amount that can be imported is subject to an **import quota.** The motivation for import quotas is usually to reduce job losses in a particular industry. The United States has imposed quotas on automobiles, steel, televisions, sugar, clothing, and footwear. Generally, the quotas are managed by the importing country's government, although in the case of automobiles and clothing entering the United States, the restrictions are part of **voluntary export restraint programs;** voluntary export restraints are managed by the exporting countries' governments. While voluntary restraint has some legal and political advantages, from a purely economic point of view, the consequences are the same as for quotas managed by the importing country's government.[13]

Figure 6.14 describes the effect of an import quota. The curve labeled D in part (a) shows the total quantity of a product demanded in a country at each price, while S_L shows the quantity supplied by local producers. In the figure, the quantity demanded exceeds the quantity local producers are willing to supply. If there are no restrictions on imports, the excess of the quantity demanded over the quantity supplied locally will be imported. For example, from part (a), at price p_1 the total quantity demanded is Q_2, while only Q_1 is supplied by local producers. The quantity of imports demanded is therefore (Q_2-Q_1). This is shown in part (b), where at p_1 the quantity of imports demanded is $q_1=(Q_2-Q_1)$. This is a point on the

---

[12] The market demand for labor assumes many employers. We consider the background to the supply and demand curve for labor in Chapter 15 in our discussion of unemployment.

*Sections or numbered items marked with an asterisk can be omitted without loss of continuity. They contain material usually found in two-semester courses.

[13] The legal and political advantages occur because with voluntary export restraint, foreign governments decide how quotas are to be divided among their own countries' producers. Therefore, the importing country's government does not have to interfere in other countries' internal affairs.

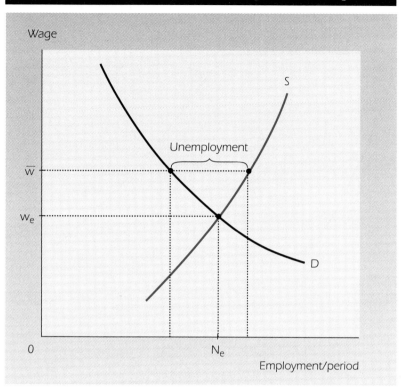

FIGURE 6.13   Minimum wage laws, while aimed at improving workers' living standards, leave some workers unable to find employment at the legal minimum wage.

If the minimum wage is set at $\overline{w}$, which is above the equilibrium level w_e, more people will seek employment than there are jobs available. Those unable to find work are generally the young and unskilled.

demand curve for imports, D_1. Similarly, at p_2 in part (a) of Figure 6.14 the quantity of clothing demanded is Q_4, the quantity supplied locally is Q_3, and therefore the quantity of imports demanded is $q_2 = (Q_4 - Q_3)$. This gives another point on the demand curve for imports in part (b), namely at price p_2 and quantity q_2. More generally, the demand curve for imports is constructed by calculating the excess of the quantity demanded over the quantity supplied locally at each price.

If a country is only one of many countries which buy a product and therefore represents a small part of the global demand for the product, it will be able to buy different quantities without affecting the price. In this case, the supply curve of imports facing the country is a horizontal line. This is shown in part (b) of Figure 6.14 as S_w. With the demand curve for imports of D_1 and the supply curve of imports of S_w, the quantity of imports is q_1, and consumers pay the world price p_1. This presumes that there is no import quota.

Suppose that the government imposes an import quota of quantity q_2 in part (b) of Figure 6.14. The supply curve of imports is now the vertical line S_Q at the quantity q_2. With import demand D_1, the price of the product becomes p_2; at this price, the quantity of imports demanded, given off D_1, equals the quantity

Import quotas increase prices paid by consumers above those paid in other countries and reduce quantities purchased. The higher prices are enjoyed by foreign as well as domestic producers.

FIGURE 6.14 An import quota increases the prices consumers pay foreign producers.

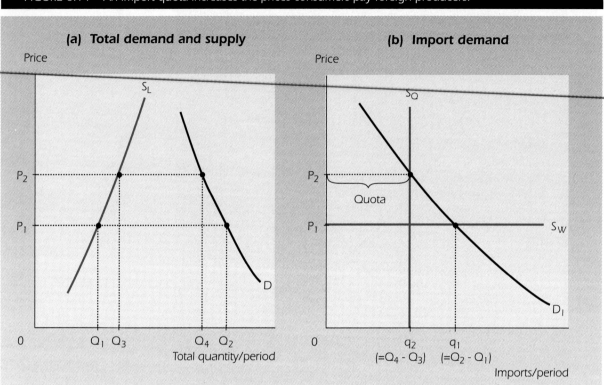

(a) Total demand and supply

Price

S_L

P_2

P_1

D

0 Q_1 Q_3 Q_4 Q_2

Total quantity/period

(b) Import demand

Price

S_Q

P_2

Quota

P_1 S_W

D_I

0 q_2 q_1

$(=Q_4 - Q_3)$ $(=Q_2 - Q_1)$

Imports/period

Curve **D** in part (a) shows the total quantity of the product demanded at each price, and curve **S**$_L$ in part (a) shows the quantity supplied locally. Part (b) shows the demand curve for imports **D**$_I$. The import demand curve **D**$_I$ is calculated from the difference between the total quantity demanded and the quantity supplied locally at each price. If the country can import different quantities without affecting the price, the supply of imports is the horizontal line **S**$_w$ in part (b). With import demand of **D**$_I$ and supply **S**$_w$, **q**$_1$ is imported at the world price **p**$_1$; local consumers pay the world price. If an import quota of **q**$_2$ is imposed, the supply curve of imports becomes the vertical line **S**$_Q$. In this case, local consumers pay **p**$_2$, which is higher than the world price **p**$_1$. Local producers increase production from **Q**$_1$ to **Q**$_3$, but consumers end up consuming less; **Q**$_4$ is consumed with the quota versus **Q**$_2$ without the quota. The effect of the quota is therefore that consumers pay higher prices to foreign producers and consume less.

available. At p_2, domestic producers will increase their production to Q_3 in part (a), while domestic consumers will reduce the quantity demanded to Q_4, and where q_2, the import quota quantity, equals $(Q_4 - Q_3)$.

The main effect of the quota is that consumers pay more than the world price for the product; the local price is p_2 versus the world price of p_1. At the same time, consumers enjoy less of the product; total quantity demanded is reduced from Q_2 to Q_4. The quota increases the prices received by the foreign producers as well as by local producers. Local production is increased by the quota, from Q_1 to Q_3, but the gains of local producers come at the expense of local consumers.[14]

[14] Because foreign producers also enjoy a higher price, the cost of a quota borne by consumers exceeds the gain by local producers.

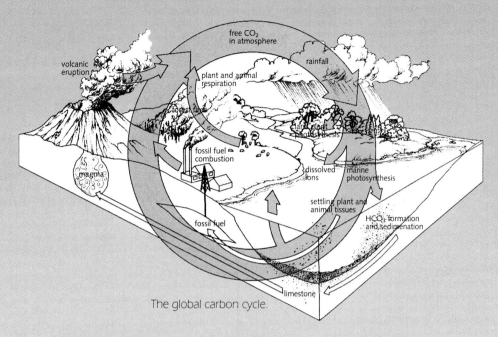

The global carbon cycle.

ACHIEVING BALANCE: A COMMON SCIENTIFIC PRINCIPLE

The laws of supply and demand in economics have distinct counterparts in the natural and social sciences, in which mechanisms for reaching "balance," or "equilibrium," often play a central role.

Principles of equilibrium are met frequently in physics. For example, in classical mechanics, an object is in equilibrium at a point where there is no **force** acting on it. This situation occurs when the object is at a maximum or minimum of its **potential energy**. For example, a marble at the bottom of a bowl is at the minimum of its potential energy and therefore has no force acting upon it. This means that the marble is in equilibrium. Movement away from the bottom of the bowl creates potential energy by means of the force of gravity, which pushes the marble back to equilibrium. That is, the equilibrium is **stable**. The situation is analogous to that of a market in

which equilibrium is disturbed by the price becoming too high. The "potential energy" created by the force of market price helps restore equilibrium, provided an excess demand causes a lower price, and this lower price reduces the force toward further price reductions.

A marble at the zenith of an inverted bowl is also in equilibrium with no force acting on it. However, in this case the marble is at a maximum of its potential energy. The tiniest disturbance of equilibrium caused by pushing the marble away from the top of the bowl allows the force of gravity to come into play to move the marble lower. As the marble drops, its decline accelerates. This would be analogous to a lower price causing greater rather than less excess supply and hence increasing the force for further price reductions and consequently even greater excess supply, and so on.

In astronomy, the concept of equilibrium is invoked to explain the orbits of planets around the Sun, of moons around planets, of stars around stars, of stars around galactic centers, and of galaxies around galaxies. The common principle here is that orbiting bodies have two forces acting on them, one pulling the bodies toward each other via mutual attraction, called **centripetal force**, and the other forcing them apart via acceleration caused by the curvature of orbits, called **centrifugal force**. Stable orbits, such as those of the Earth around the Sun or of the Moon around the Earth, are based on the achievement of the exact distances which maintain equilibrium or balance between the centripetal and centrifugal forces.

Equilibrium is also a central concept in biology. The **carbon cycle** is one of the fundamental balances of nature on which life depends, involving the mechanism for striking a balance between carbon production and carbon consumption and for maintaining this balance. Carbon is emitted into the atmosphere in the form of carbon dioxide via **respiration**, the decay of plants and animals, and combustion. At the same time, carbon is removed from the atmosphere via the **photosynthesis** of plants. If the amount of carbon dioxide emitted by plants and animals by means of respiration, decay, and combustion equals the amount of carbon dioxide consumed by plants by means of photosynthesis, then the amount of carbon dioxide in the atmosphere remains steady. That is, equilibrium prevails. However, if, for example, more carbon dioxide is removed than emitted, the growing shortage of carbon dioxide and increase in atmospheric oxygen slows the growth of plants and favors the growth of animals. This helps restore equilibrium because less photosynthesis of plants means less carbon dioxide removed and

more respiration of animals means more carbon dioxide emitted. Similar concepts of equilibrium and stability apply to the **nitrogen cycle**, in which nitrates are added to the soil by nitrifying bacteria and nitrogen-fixing bacteria and removed from the soil by plants and denitrifying bacteria.

In the area of ecology, the concept of equilibrium is absolutely central. Ecology studies such matters as how nature maintains the balance between predators and prey. If, for example, the balance is disturbed by relative growth in the population of predators, there is a shortage of prey. With the demand for prey exceeding the supply, the "price" of prey increases in terms of the effort and energy needed to obtain it. This forces the weakest predators out of the "market," thereby helping to restore equilibrium.

Equilibrium is also a central concept in political science. A **balance of power** is said to exist when countries view themselves as having equal military strength. In such a case, neither country wishes to provoke confrontation. If increasing strength of one country causes the other to take action to increase its own strength, the balance of power can occur at higher and higher levels of the potential to destroy. However, if each country sees the futility of escalating the scale of destructiveness, an equilibrium may be found by means of mutual arms reductions.

Not surprisingly, wherever the concept of equilibrium is used, the mathematics that has been employed to describe and study it takes on a very similar form. Indeed, economists often feel quite at home with research papers in, for example, ecology journals, just as the ecologist, physicist, and others can feel comfortable with economics, a clear testimony to the similarity of principles employed.

The "potential energy" created by the force of market price helps restore equilibrium. . . .

SUMMARY

1. Supply and demand curves determine the equilibrium price and quantity. The equilibrium price is that at which the quantity demanded equals the quantity supplied.

2. Forces exist to restore equilibrium when it has been disturbed. When prices are below equilibrium, there is excess demand, and pressure among buyers forces prices up. When prices are above equilibrium, there is excess supply, and pressure among sellers forces prices down.

3. Supply and demand analysis is used to consider what effect exogenous, or outside, changes affecting market conditions have on equilibrium prices and quantities. The comparison of equilibria is called comparative statics.

4. Demand is increased by
   a. An increase in incomes when goods are "normal."
   b. An increase in the price of a substitute.
   c. A decrease in the price of a complement.
   d. A favorable shift in tastes.

5. An increase in demand—a rightward and upward shift of the demand curve—increases equilibrium price and quantity. The price increase occurs because, after the increase in demand, the quantity demanded exceeds the quantity supplied at the original price.

6. Supply is increased by
   a. An increase in the productivity of variable inputs.
   b. A decrease in the cost of variable inputs.
   c. A decrease in taxes which affect variable costs of production.
   d. Good weather for agricultural commodities.

7. An increase in supply—a rightward or downward shift of the supply curve—causes a lower equilibrium price and a higher equilibrium quantity.

8. In the short run, increases in variable costs due to taxes, input price increases, and so on are borne by both producers and consumers. The more elastic the demand curve, the higher the share borne by producers.

9. Industry-wide supply disruptions increase revenue when market demand is inelastic.

10. When considering the effects of changes in supply and demand, a shift in a curve must be distinguished from a movement along a curve. Confusion can be avoided by always using diagrams.

11. Data on observed prices and quantities cannot generally be used to check the slopes of supply or demand curves.

12. Price variation in response to supply and demand constitutes a mechanism for rationing scarce goods and services. Movements in market prices also signal producers as to what and how much to produce.

13. Examples of situations where prices are controlled to keep them below equilibrium are rent controls and interest-rate ceilings. Rent controls cause a shortage of housing that is rationed by bribery or queuing, while interest-rate controls cause rationing of loans according to which borrowers offer the best security.

14. Examples of situations where prices are kept above equilibrium are agricultural price supports and minimum wage laws. Agricultural price supports result in stockpiles of unsold goods, while minimum wage laws cause unemployment, especially among the young and unskilled.

15. Import quotas increase prices paid to foreign and domestic producers and reduce quantities demanded.

QUESTIONS AND PROBLEMS

1. In words, explain what happens to equilibrium price and quantity after an increase in supply.

2. Use supply and demand curves to illustrate the phenomenon of college applications greatly exceeding college admissions. When might this occur?

3. What signals might a socialist country watch in order to know how to shift national resources?

4. Show the effects of rent controls over time when they result in housing being allowed to deteriorate so that new, uncontrolled housing can be built in its stead. (Think in terms of shifts in both the supply and demand curves.)

5. Use diagrams to show why a bad harvest can help all farmers considered collectively but can hurt an individual farmer who alone suffers a poor harvest.

6. Might an agricultural price stabilization policy work if the support price were set equal to the average equilibrium price?

7. Assume that the quantity demanded of a good at each price is given from the equation

$$q^d = 100 - 0.5p$$

where q^d is quantity demanded and p is the price in dollars. Assume that the quantity supplied of the good at each price is given from

$$q^s = 20 + 0.3p$$

What is the equilibrium price and quantity supplied and demanded?

8. Assume in Question 7 above that demand increases to

$$q^{d} = 180 - 0.5p$$

   and that the supply equation is unchanged; demand is higher at every output than in Question 7 because the constant term is larger. Calculate the new equilibrium price and quantity, and compare these with the answer to Question 7.

9. Calculate the elasticities of demand at the equilibrium prices and quantities in Questions 7 and 8. In each case, is demand elastic, inelastic, or unit elastic? (*Hint:* You can change p by $1 to calculate the change in q, Δq, when $\Delta p = 1$ and then use the equilibrium p and q.)

10. What is the elasticity of supply at the equilibrium price and quantity for the supply equation in Question 7?

11. Use a supply and demand diagram to show the effect of a sales tax paid by consumers on the market price including and excluding the tax. (Such a sales tax shifts the demand curve vertically downward by the percentage of the tax.)

12. What determines the extent to which the incidence of a consumer-paid sales tax falls on the buyer, and how does your conclusion agree with your intuition?

13. Would a 10% tax on the price of gasoline increase gasoline prices by 10%, and if not, why not?

14. Use a supply and demand diagram to show the effect of higher gas prices on the equilibrium price of automobiles. Might large automobile prices fall more than small automobile prices?

PART III

THE THEORY OF FIRMS AND MARKETS

Without competition there are no winners.

Kate Levi

. . . .
. . . .
. . . .
. . . .
. . . .
. . . . . . Competitive Markets
. . . .
. . . .

There is no resting place for an enterprise in a competitive economy.

Alfred P. Sloan

Key Concepts

Long run versus short run; free entry and exit; perfect competition; increasing, decreasing, and constant returns to scale; long-run equilibrium output of a firm; economic profit and accounting profit; normal profit; long-run equilibrium output of an industry; the long-run market supply curve

People are often proclaiming the virtues of competition. This chapter describes why it is that competition has achieved such high and frequent commendation.

THE LONG RUN AND FREE ENTRY

The Long Run versus the Short Run

The supply and demand analysis in the preceding chapter gives only short-run market equilibria. This is so because the supply curves are constructed assuming a fixed input and do not allow for the entry of firms into or exit of firms from an industry.

The long run differs from the short run because in the long run existing firms can expand or contract all inputs and because new firms can enter and old firms can leave an industry.

By definition, in the long run the quantities of all inputs can be changed. More land can be acquired and prepared, or leases can be allowed to expire without being renewed. New machinery can be installed, or existing machinery can be allowed to wear out. Therefore, long-run supply curves cannot be based on short-run marginal cost curves that are derived with the assumption of at least one fixed input. Furthermore, in the long run in industries without restrictions on entry or exit, the number of firms also can change. As with the expansion or contraction of existing firms, the establishment of new firms and the departure of old firms take time. Where unrestricted entry and exit exist, changes in the number of firms can be an even more important influence on market supply than changes in the sizes of firms already in the industry.

Free Entry and Perfect Competition

A perfectly competitive industry has free entry and exit and so many firms with small outputs relative to market supply that each firm can take market price as a given.

Industries with free entry and exit and a market of sufficient size to support a vast number of firms are called **perfectly competitive** industries. Because there are a very large number of firms in a perfectly competitive industry, each individual firm supplies only a small part of the total market supply. Consequently, an individual firm can vary its output by substantial amounts from its own point of view without changing the market supply by a sufficient amount to affect the market price. This means that in a perfectly competitive industry each individual firm can take the market price as given.[1]

Free entry of new firms into an industry is not always possible, nor even is free exit always possible. Sometimes it is necessary to obtain a license to operate a business—as is the case in banking and broadcasting. Sometimes free entry is restricted by the large size of the investment in plant and equipment necessary to compete effectively. For example, the automobile industry has only a limited number of firms because it takes considerable capital to build an automobile plant. In the case of free exit, firms may be prohibited from leaving an industry by law. For example, an electric utility or telephone company cannot decide to stop providing service to its customers because it has become unprofitable.

Perfect competition also requires that each firm produces a good or service that is indistinguishable from the outputs of other producers and that consumers know each supplier's price.

Having numerous firms and free entry and exit does not mean firms can take the market price as given if different firms produce slightly different (branded) products or if buyers do not know the prices of all suppliers. In these situations, firms can continue having sales even if they are charging more than others. Consequently, we must add the need for all firms in an industry to produce indistinguishable (homogeneous) products and for buyers to be fully informed about prices of different firms to the other prerequisites for perfect competition.

Wheat farming is an example of a perfectly competitive industry. There is no limit on the entry of new farms growing wheat, perhaps on land previously used for other products, and unprofitable farms can be shifted to growing other crops. No farmer is sufficiently large to influence the market, especially when it is recognized that prices are determined in a vast international marketplace. Furthermore,

[1] We used this assumption in Chapter 5, where in order to find the profit-maximizing output, we assumed that a firm could sell different amounts without affecting the market price. Therefore, we were implicitly assuming that the firm operated in a perfectly competitive industry.

it is not possible for buyers to distinguish between wheat grown by different farmers. Finally, prices of different suppliers can quickly be observed by buyers.

To derive the long-run supply curve of the product of a perfectly competitive industry, we first must consider the effect of allowing an individual firm to vary its use of *all* inputs. We then must describe the implications of free entry into and exit from an industry. Before beginning, we need some background on long-run costs. This background is relevant for all firms, whether perfectly competitive or not.

LONG-RUN COSTS

Returns to Scale versus the Law of Diminishing Marginal Product

When all inputs can be varied in amount, as they can in the long run, a firm is not subject to the law of diminishing marginal product. Recall from Chapter 5 that this law applies only when there is at least one fixed input, such as the amount of land a farmer can use. In the long run, there is no compelling reason to expect average costs of production to increase as output is increased. When a firm can change the quantity of all its inputs, holding the proportions of one to the other constant, it changes its **scale** of production and may face one of the following possible conditions.

Constant Returns to Scale.   The curve labeled *SAC*(200) in Figure 7.1 shows the average cost of different outputs of a farm that has 200 acres to plant. The prefix *S* on *SAC* signifies that it is a short-run average cost curve, and the 200 in parentheses indicates that the amount of land is limited to 200 acres. *SAC*(200) shows that while constrained to use 200 acres, the minimum average cost occurs at 4000 bushels per year. Expansion of output from 4000 to 5000 bushels while using 200 acres increases average cost from approximately $3.00 per bushel to approximately $3.50 per bushel. This increase in short-run average cost occurs because of the law of diminishing marginal product.

In the long run, when more land can be used along with more of all other inputs, the expansion of output from 4000 to 5000 bushels may not increase average cost. For example, average cost is unchanged if a 25% increase in output from 4000 to 5000 bushels is achieved with 25% more land, 25% more labor, and 25% more of all other inputs. That is, average cost is constant as output is increased if 25% more of all inputs produces 25% more output. This must be so because 25% more inputs means a 25% increase in total cost, and by definition,[2]

$$Average\ cost = \frac{total\ cost}{output}$$

If all inputs increase by the same percentage as output, both the numerator and denominator increase by the same percentage, and average cost remains unchanged.

---

[2] We assume that input prices remain constant as the scale of the firm expands. Later we drop this assumption.

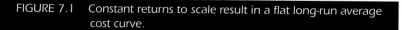

FIGURE 7.1   Constant returns to scale result in a flat long-run average cost curve.

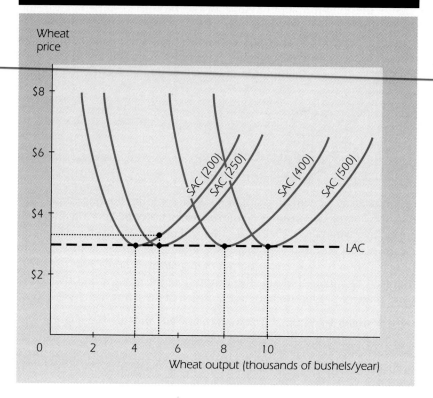

While constrained by a fixed amount of land, the farm is subject to increasing average cost as it expands output because of the law of diminishing marginal product. For example, with the 200 acres of land assumed for the curve **SAC(200)**, an expansion of output from 4000 to 5000 bushels increases average cost from $3.00 per bushel to almost $3.50 per bushel. However, in the long run, when all inputs can be varied, a 25% increase in all inputs causes a 25% increase in output. Therefore, average cost remains constant in the long run. Such a situation is called constant returns to scale.

Figure 7.1 shows the short-run average cost curve with 25% more land, that is, with 250 acres vis-à-vis the original 200 acres. This is the curve $SAC(250)$. This is U-shaped because once the amount of land is fixed at 250 acres, the farm is again subject to the law of diminishing marginal product. Curve $SAC(250)$ shows the same average cost at 5000 bushels as $SAC(200)$ shows at 4000 bushels; the height of $SAC(200)$ at 4000 bushels equals the height of $SAC(250)$ at 5000 bushels. That is, as the amount of land and all other factors are increased by 25% so that total cost increases 25%, output increases by 25%.

The average cost when all inputs can be varied is called the **long-run average cost** (LAC). The LAC curve is constructed by finding the lowest possible average cost of each output and drawing a line through these particular average costs. Figure 7.1 shows the SAC curves for 200, 250, 400, and 500 acres and the resulting LAC curve. In the case where a given-sized expansion of all inputs causes an equal

The average cost when *all* inputs can be varied is the long-run average cost.

expansion of output, long-run average cost is constant. A firm with constant long-run average cost is said to have **constant returns to scale.** The case of constant returns to scale is illustrated in Figure 7.1, with the horizontal line *LAC* showing the same average cost at different scales of production.

In the case of constant returns to scale, an x% increase in the quantity of all inputs causes an x% increase in output. Constant returns is a special case that divides two other possibilities, increasing returns and decreasing returns.

Increasing Returns to Scale.   When an x% increase in the quantity of all inputs causes more than an x% increase in output, a firm has **increasing returns to scale**, often referred to simply as **economies of scale**. With output increasing by more than inputs, average cost decreases as the firm expands output.

Increasing returns to scale occur when a larger scale of production allows better use of land, labor, and capital. For example, planting and harvesting on a larger farm involve less land lost at the edges of fields relative to the total amount planted and involve relatively less time spent turning back and forth when planting and harvesting. Larger farms also may make better use of farming equipment. The situation of increasing returns to scale is illustrated in part (a) of Figure 7.2. We can see that long-run average cost, given by the *LAC* curve, is lower as output increases. That is, average cost decreases as output expands when all inputs can be varied. However, note that the farm is still subject to the law of diminishing marginal product if it expands output with any fixed amount of land, as evidenced by the U-shaped *SAC* curves for each amount of land.[3]

As an aside, we can note that as well as economies of scale, firms' operations may be subject to **economies of scope.** An economy of scope exists when there are cost advantages to producing or handling a variety of different products rather than producing or handling a large amount of a single product.

An example of an industry with economies of scope is college textbook publishing. The same sales representative of, for example, D. C. Heath or another college textbook publisher, can introduce instructors throughout a college campus to a publisher's offerings in every subject from astronomy to zoology. It would be more expensive for a publisher selling books in only one subject area to reach a typical instructor; sales representatives would spend almost all of their time traveling from college to college. Economies of scope can coexist with economies of scale. For example, when Delta Airlines purchased Pan American's European routes in 1991, Delta expected to enjoy economies of scale by reducing empty seats and hence costs per passenger-mile from integration of Pan Am's and Delta's European traffic. At the same time, Delta expected to enjoy economies of scope by offering a larger variety of destinations to both Pan Am and Delta passengers; connections between smaller U.S. cities and Europe can be improved by integrating flight schedules.

When an x% increase in the quantity of *all* inputs causes an x% increase in output, a firm is subject to constant returns to scale, and long-run average cost is *constant*.

When an x% increase in the quantity of *all* inputs causes more than an x% increase in output, a firm is subject to increasing returns to scale. In this case, long-run average costs *decline* as output expands.

DIVERSIFY

Economies of scope occur when there are cost savings from producing a variety of different products. Economies of scope may coexist with economies of scale.

---

[3] The *LAC* curves shown in Figure 7.2 are not constructed from the *minimums* of the *SAC* curves but rather by finding the *best SAC* curves, and hence the best amounts of land, for each output. It may be that expansion of all inputs in the same proportion is more expensive than allowing proportions of inputs to vary. The *LAC* curves shown in Figure 7.2 allow for such changes in proportions. This is the reason why the *LAC* curves are below the minimums on *SAC* curves; the *LAC* curve uses a better combination of inputs for each output than does the *SAC* curve whose minimum is directly above that output.

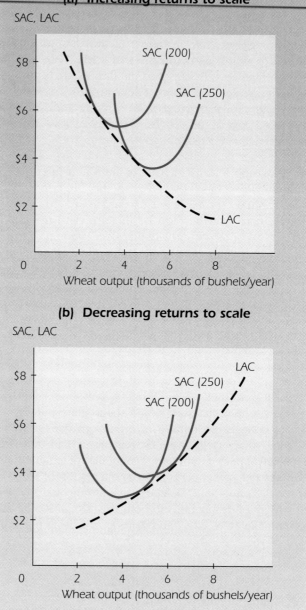

FIGURE 7.2 Increasing returns to scale involve a downward-sloping *LAC* curve, while decreasing returns to scale involve an upward-sloping *LAC* curve.

In part (a), the long-run average cost declines as production increases, even though with any given amount of land, short-run average costs are increasing. Therefore, in part (a) there are increasing returns to scale. In part (b), there are increasing long-run average costs and decreasing returns to scale. Note that the **LAC** curve is never higher than the **SAC** curves. This is so because it is never worse to have flexibility in amounts of all inputs than to have a fixed input.

Decreasing Returns to Scale. When an x% increase in the quantity of all inputs causes less than an x% increase in output, a firm is subject to **decreasing returns to scale**. In this case, long-run average costs increase with output, as shown by the *LAC* curve in part (b) of Figure 7.2.

While it is commonly thought that firms have increasing returns to scale, there are reasons for expecting increasing long-run average costs to occur eventually. That is, there are reasons for expecting a firm to eventually face decreasing returns.

One reason for expecting eventual decreasing returns is managerial inefficiency which can set in as the scale of operations expands. A small firm might be managed effectively by one or only a few managers who can see directly how their efforts translate into the profitability of the firm. As the firm expands and more managers are hired, each manager's efforts become less directly connected to the goals of the firm. Indeed, managers have different interests from those of shareholders who own the firm. For example, managers may be interested in maximizing their salaries or their sphere of influence rather than the profitability of the company, provided the profits are large enough to keep shareholders from complaining. The shareholders may not be able to tell that managers are not maximizing profits, because it is difficult to tell from accounting statements whether optimal performance is being achieved. As pointed out in Chapter 5, when there is a difference between the objectives of managers and owners, we say there is an agency problem.

Even if there is not an agency problem, as a firm expands, it may be necessary to employ numerous managers to supervise different and specialized parts of the operation. The firm may need a financial manager, a personnel manager, or so on. These divisional managers need to be coordinated. Further expansion results in extra tiers of managers and therefore a further need for coordinators. In addition, compartmentalization and bureaucratization can give rise to inefficiencies due to poor coordination or communication. Small errors may not be spotted. Large changes, when warranted, may take an inordinate amount of time to be approved.[4] The managerial diseconomies may dominate any technical efficiencies that may be derived from increasing scale.

> When an x% increase in *all* inputs causes less than an x% increase in output, a firm is subject to decreasing returns to scale, and long-run average costs *increase* with output.

> Increasing managerial inefficiencies at larger-scale production may eventually result in decreasing returns to scale.

The Long-Run Marginal Cost Curve

The **long-run marginal cost curve** gives the increase in total cost of producing one more unit of output when all inputs can be varied. The long-run marginal cost curve can be drawn by recalling what we said in Chapter 5 concerning average versus marginal costs.

As was noted in Chapter 5, in order for your grade point average (GPA) to increase, the grades in new courses must exceed your average grade in previous

> The long-run marginal cost curve gives the cost of producing one more unit of output when *all* inputs can be varied.

---

[4] Recognizing the problem of managerial inefficiency in large and expanding organizations, some giant corporations have preserved the autonomy of the units they have acquired. For example, General Motors has kept a number of different divisions for marketing purposes, where quick response is important, but can still enjoy economies of scale in such functions as financing and research and development, which are coordinated centrally.

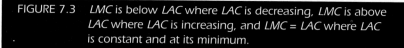

FIGURE 7.3 *LMC* is below *LAC* where *LAC* is decreasing, *LMC* is above *LAC* where *LAC* is increasing, and *LMC* = *LAC* where *LAC* is constant and at its minimum.

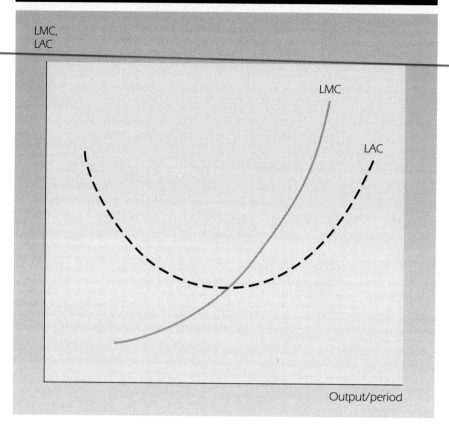

The **LAC** curve is decreasing when the **LMC** curve is below the **LAC** curve. The **LAC** curve is increasing when the **LMC** curve is above the **LAC** curve. The **LAC** curve is flat at the output where the **LMC** curve intersects the **LAC** curve. This means that the **LMC** curve intersects the **LAC** curve at the minimum point on the **LAC** curve.

courses. In the context of cost curves, for average cost to be increasing, the marginal cost must exceed the average cost, whether these be long-run or short-run costs. For example, the long-run average cost curve *LAC* is upward-sloping when the long-run marginal cost curve *LMC* is above the *LAC* curve. This is shown in Figure 7.3, where *LMC* is above *LAC* where *LAC* is increasing. Similarly, just as your GPA is reduced by receiving grades below your grade average, so average cost declines if marginal cost is lower than average cost. In Figure 7.3 the *LAC* curve is downward-sloping when the *LMC* curve is below the *LAC* curve. Your GPA remains constant if your grades on new courses are the same as your grade average. This means that *LAC* is constant as output increases if *LMC=LAC*. At this point, where *LAC* is constant, *LAC* switches from declining to increasing and is therefore the minimum point of the *LAC* curve. That is, *LMC* intersects *LAC* at the minimum of the *LAC* curve.

As with short-run costs, the long-run marginal cost curve intersects the long-run average cost curve at the minimum on the LAC curve.

FIRM AND INDUSTRY IN THE LONG RUN

With the help of the long-run marginal and average cost curves, we can describe the long-run equilibrium of a perfectly competitive firm and of a perfectly competitive industry. We begin by considering an individual perfectly competitive firm.

The Firm's Long-Run Profit-Maximizing Output

We have seen that an individual firm in a perfectly competitive industry can take the market price as given. Therefore, the increase in total revenue from producing and selling another unit—the marginal revenue—is the price received.

This means that the demand curve facing an individual firm in a perfectly competitive industry is perfectly elastic at the market price. At a price above the market price, the firm sells nothing as buyers purchase from other firms, and at a price below the market price, the firm could sell unlimited amounts. In the long run, when a farmer or some other producer has the opportunity to vary all inputs—land, workers, seed, fertilizer, and so on—the relevant cost curves are *LAC* and *LMC*. This means that in the long run, profits are increased by increasing output whenever *price* > *LMC;* in such a case, total revenue is increased more than total cost. Profits are reduced by increasing output to a level where *price* < *LMC* because this involves increasing total revenue less than total cost. In the long run, maximum profits occur at the output where *price* = *LMC*, just as in the short run, maximum profits occur where the price equals short-run marginal cost.

> For an individual firm in a perfectly competitive industry, the demand curve is perfectly elastic at the market price. Therefore, the firm's marginal revenue equals the market price.

Since the long-run profit-maximizing output of a firm in a perfectly competitive industry is where *price* = *LMC*, the firm's output at any price can be found by drawing a horizontal line at each price and finding the output on the *LMC* curve. This is shown in Figure 7.4. At a price of $4.50, long-run profit-maximizing output is approximately 10,500 bushels; at $6.00, long-run profit-maximizing output is approximately 14,000 bushels; and so on.

> For firms in a perfectly competitive industry, long-run profit maximization occurs at that output where *price* = *LMC*.

With the firm producing where *price* = *LMC*, the firm's long-run supply curve is the *LMC* curve, just as the short-run supply curve is the short-run marginal cost curve. That is, as Figure 7.4 shows, the quantity supplied is determined by drawing a horizontal line at any given price and reading the long-run profit-maximizing output off the firm's *LMC* curve. However, recall from Chapter 5 that the short-run supply curve is that segment of the firm's marginal cost curve *MC* above the minimum average *variable* cost *AVC*. A similar restriction applies to the long-run supply curve, but in the long run, it is not the *AVC* that matters. Rather, it is the average *total* cost *AC*. Let us consider why.

With all costs avoidable in the long run, firms will not produce if this involves making economic losses.[5] Economic losses are made whenever the price is less than the average (total) cost. We can see this by recalling that

> The perfectly competitive firm's long-run supply curve is its *LMC* curve above the minimum *LAC*.

$$Profit = total\ revenue - total\ cost \qquad (7.1)$$

$$= price \times output - AC \times output$$

$$= (price - AC) \times output \qquad (7.2)$$

---

[5] Economic losses occur when profit, given by *profit* = (*total revenue* − *total cost*), is negative.

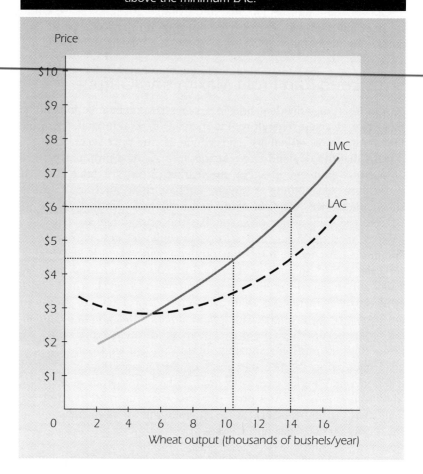

FIGURE 7.4   The firm's long-run supply curve is its *LMC* curve above the minimum *LAC*.

The relevant cost curves in the long run when all inputs can be varied are the long-run marginal and average cost curves, **LMC** and **LAC.** In a perfectly competitive industry where marginal revenue equals price, profits are maximized in the long run by producing the output at which **price=LMC**. At a price of $4.50 per bushel, this is approximately 10,500 bushels per year, while at $6.00 per bushel, this is 14,000 bushels per year. Production would be zero in the long run if the price is below the minimum **LAC**, since there would be no new investment when profits cannot be made. Therefore, the long-run supply curve of the perfectly competitive firm is its **LMC** curve above the minimum **LAC**.

Therefore, losses occur when *price < AC* and where the relevant average cost in the long run is the long-run average cost. Firms facing such a situation will cease investing and consequently cease production in the long run, although, as we saw in Chapter 5, they will continue producing in the short run as long as price exceeds average *variable* cost.

The ability of firms to vary all inputs in the long run means that *LMC* curves are more elastic than short-run marginal cost (*SMC*) curves.[6] This is so because *SMC* curves are drawn for at least one fixed factor of production. When a farmer, for example, can use more land, farm equipment, workers, seed, fertilizer, and so on, marginal costs increase more gradually with increasing output than when the farmer is constrained to use only a given, fixed amount of land. More generally, the flexibility of varying all inputs in the long run means less steeply increasing marginal costs than in the short run, when firms are subject to the law of diminishing marginal product. With the *SMC* curve being the firm's short-run supply curve and *LMC* being the firm's long-run supply curve, it follows that the firm's long-run supply curve is more elastic than the firm's short-run supply curve.

The individual firm's long-run supply curve is more elastic than its short-run supply curve.

The Industry in the Long Run

Recall from Chapter 5 that the short-run market supply curve is the horizontal sum of the short-run marginal cost curves of individual firms. If there were no change in the number of firms, the long-run market supply curve would similarly be the horizontal sum of the firms' *LMC* curves. Since the *LMC* curves are more elastic than *SMC* curves, the sum of *LMC* curves also would be more elastic than the sum of *SMC* curves. Hence, even if no new firms were to enter an industry as the market price increased, the long-run market supply curve would be more elastic than the short-run market supply curve. Put differently, even without free entry, the long-run market supply curve is more elastic than the short-run supply curve.

When we allow for the fact that new firms can enter and old firms can leave a perfectly competitive industry, the greater elasticity of the long-run supply curve is even more pronounced than indicated by the slope of the sum of exiting firms' *LMC* curves. This occurs because as the product's price increases, there is an expansion of market supply not only from the expansion of existing firms but also from new firms entering the industry. Similarly, as a product's price decreases, there is a contraction of market supply not only from the reduced output of some firms but also from the exit of other firms.

The long-run perfectly competitive industry supply curve is more *elastic than the short-run supply curve because firms have more elastic long-run LMC curves, and because new firms can enter and existing firms can leave an industry in the long run.*

Accounting Profit versus Economic Profit

Firms enter an industry when profits are sufficiently high to reward entrepreneurs for setting up new firms. In order to be sufficiently high, a firm's expected accounting profits must at least compensate for the opportunity cost of the entrepreneurs' capital, labor, and other resources drawn into the firm. In Chapter 5 we included the opportunity cost of entrepreneurs' capital, labor, and other resources in the total cost. We then defined economic profit as the difference between total revenue and total cost, where total cost included the entrepreneurs' opportunity cost. That is, the profit in Equation (7.1) is *economic* profit.

When a firm's economic profit is zero, the firm earns just enough to compensate for the opportunity cost of capital, labor, and other entrepreneur-provided resources drawn into the firm. That is, when economic profit is zero, the firm's

The accounting profit at which economic profit is zero is called the normal profit. The normal profit just, and only just, *compensates for the opportunity cost of resources drawn into the firm.*

---

[6] The *SMC* curve is what we labeled as *MC* in Chapter 5.

accounting profit equals the opportunity cost of what entrepreneurs contribute to the firm. This particular level of accounting profit at which the economic profit is zero is called the **normal profit.** It is called **normal** because it just compensates for the opportunity cost of entrepreneurs' capital, labor, and other resources.

Figure 7.5 illustrates the connection between economic profit, accounting profit, and normal profit. The figure shows that total cost consists of the outlays for raw materials, labor, and capital, referred to as **operating costs,** and the opportunity cost of entrepreneurs' capital, labor, and other resources used by the firm. The figure also shows that economic profit is the difference between total revenue and total cost. Finally, the figure shows that when economic profit is zero, the accounting profit is the normal profit. More generally, we can see from Figure 7.5 that economic profit is accounting profit minus normal profit.

Entry into a perfectly competitive industry occurs as entrepreneurs, who are always seeking high returns on their investments, seek out economic profits. Exit occurs when economic profits are negative, even though this might still involve positive accounting profits; when economic profits are negative, the entrepreneur does not cover her or his opportunity cost and looks for other investments.[7]

> Economic profit equals accounting profit minus normal profit.
>
> Entry into a perfectly competitive industry occurs when entrepreneurs expect to make *economic* profits. Exit occurs when entrepreneurs do not expect *economic* profits.

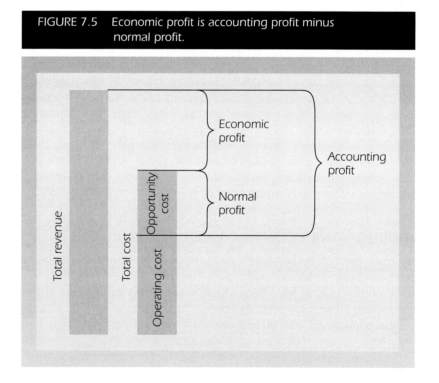

FIGURE 7.5   Economic profit is accounting profit minus normal profit.

Total cost consists of the outlays for raw materials, labor, and capital, which are the operating costs, as well as the opportunity cost of entrepreneurs' own capital, labor, and other resources used in the business. Economic profit is the difference between total revenue and total cost. Normal profit equals the opportunity cost. Accounting profit is the sum of economic and normal profits.

[7] See Example 7.1 for the implication of free entry and exit in the stock market.

Example 7.1

A MODEL OF PERFECT COMPETITION

There is an economists' in-joke that succinctly captures the implications of perfect competition for financial markets such as the stock and bond markets. It goes like this: A professor of finance and a student are engrossed in conversation as they walk across campus. "Look!" the student says, "There's a $20 dollar bill down by your feet!" "Don't be silly!" says the professor. "There can't be. If there were, it would have been picked up!"

The background to this joke concerns what in finance is called market efficiency and which follows from the fact that financial markets such as the stock and bond markets are perfectly competitive. So why are these markets perfectly competitive, and what is meant by market efficiency?

There are a large number of buyers and sellers of each stock traded in the stock market. For example, there are many thousands of people who during a particular period may sell their IBM stock and thousands who may buy it. That is, the requirement of perfect competition that there be many buyers and sellers is met by the stock market. Next, anybody who holds a stock can enter the market to sell, so there is free entry. Further, each potential buyer and seller of a stock knows the going price, and therefore, all market participants are informed about prices. With one IBM share like another, the "product" is homogeneous, meeting yet a further requirement of perfect competition. Indeed, the stock market is as perfectly competitive a market as there is.

Market efficiency means that all the relevant publicly available information about the true value of a stock is reflected in its market price. For example, if a company is doing well with increasing sales and consequent good prospects for making profit, this will be reflected in the price; the stock price will be appropriately high. Similarly, if a company is doing badly, this also will be reflected in the company's stock price; the price will be appropriately low. The stock market is "efficient" because there is free entry, common information about the price, and so on. That is, market efficiency is the direct consequence of perfect competition.

Another way of viewing the comment of the finance professor, that if a $20 bill had been dropped, somebody would have picked it up, involves the fact that in a perfectly competitive market like the stock market, economic profit cannot persist. If a stock offers an improved prospect, the price immediately goes up to reflect this fact, and the economic profit is gone. As in any perfectly competitive market, free entry ensures this, with free entry in the finance professor joke being the chance for any passer-by to pick up the $20. Of course, as with other perfectly competitive situations, this does not mean economic profits never occur. They do, just as people sometimes find money. What free entry and free stooping to pick up money ensure is that economic profits do not persist, as is testified to by a less-often heard sequel to the finance professor joke: The next day the same professor and student were walking past the spot where the student had said there was $20. The professor said: "See! I told you there was no $20 here!"

Economic Profit: An Example.   Figure 7.6 shows the *LMC* and *LAC* curves for a wheat farmer. The *LMC* curve is such that at an assumed market price of $4.50 per bushel, the profit-maximizing output is approximately 10,500 bushels per year. Total revenue *TR* at this output is given by the product of price and output, that is,

$$TR = price \times output = \$4.50 \times 10,500 = \$47,250$$

Total cost *TC* is given by the product of average cost and output, that is,

$$TC = LAC \times output \tag{7.3}$$

Figure 7.6 shows that at the profit-maximizing output of 10,500 bushels, *LAC* is $3.00. Therefore, using Equation 7.3,

$$TC = \$3 \times 10,500 = \$31,500$$

It follows that economic profit, which from Equation 7.1 is total revenue minus total cost, is

$$Profit = TR - TC = \$47,250 - \$31,500 = \$15,750$$

We find that the farmer earns $15,750 per year above the normal profit included in the total cost.

Total Revenue, Total Cost, and Profit as Areas of Rectangles.   Total revenue, total cost, and economic profit all can be measured by areas of rectangles. This is a useful way to measure them because it helps in deriving the long-run market supply curve.

The area of a rectangle is the length of its base multiplied by its height. In terms of Figure 7.6, total revenue is measured by the area of the rectangle 0*pAq*; this rectangle has a base of length 0*q*, the output, and a height 0*p*, the market price of wheat. The area of rectangle 0*pAq* is therefore the product of the price and output, which is the total revenue. Total cost is measured by the area of rectangle 0*CBq*; this rectangle has a base with length 0*q*, the output, and a height *Bq*, which is the long-run average cost at the selected output *q*.

Economic profit, which is the difference between total revenue and total cost, is

$$Economic\ profit = area\ 0pAq - area\ 0CBq$$

Since rectangle 0*pAq* includes rectangle 0*CBq*, the difference between the areas of the two rectangles is that part of 0*pAq* which excludes area 0*CBq*, that is, rectangle *CpAB*. This is the shaded area in Figure 7.6. We can think of this area as being the output, 0*q*, multiplied by the excess of the price over the average cost of production, *AB*. An economic profit can be made as long as the market price is above the *LAC* curve at some output. Only when *price* = *LAC* is economic profit zero. Of course, even when economic profit is zero, an accounting profit is still being made, but it is equal only to the normal profit included in *LAC*.

An economic profit can be made when the market price is above the *LAC*. When *price* = *LAC*, economic profit is zero.

FIGURE 7.6   Economic profit is earned when the price exceeds the *LAC*.

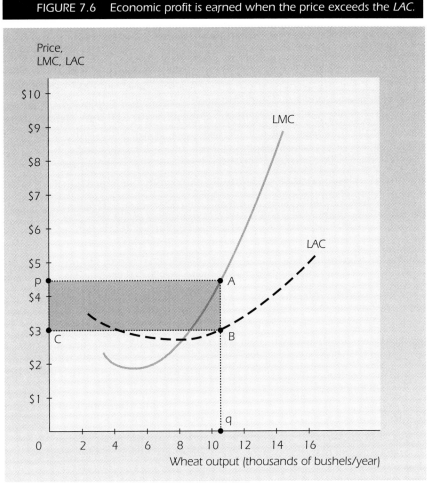

With an assumed market price of $4.50 per bushel, the profit-maximizing output, where **price=LMC**, occurs at 10,500 bushels per year. Total revenue is therefore $47,250 (or $4.50×10,500), which is the area of rectangle **0pAq**. Total cost at 10,500 bushels is the height of the **LAC** curve at this output, $3.00 per bushel, times the output, 10,500 bushels, that is, $31,500 (or $3.00×10,500). This is the area of rectangle **0CBq**. Economic profit is given by the difference between total revenue and total cost, that is, $15,750 (or $47,250−$31,500). This is equal to the area of rectangle **CpAB**, which is the difference between the rectangle giving total revenue, **0pAq**, and the rectangle giving total cost, **0CBq**.

Long-Run Supply Curve with Constant Input Costs

Derivation of the long-run perfectly competitive market supply curve takes several steps. Let us first derive a point on the curve using the simplifying assumption, which we later drop, that input costs are constant.

A Point on the Long-Run Supply Curve.   Part (a) of Figure 7.7 shows the *LMC* and *LAC* curves for an individual wheat farm, although we can think in terms of a firm in any industry. We assume that all farms have the same minimum long-run average cost. This is not as strong an assumption as you might believe. It is true that different farms have land of different fertility, different levels of irrigation, and so on and that these differences could contribute to different operating costs. It is also true that some farms could be better managed, be nearer to shipping terminals, and so on, which also might contribute to different operating costs. However, recall that the long-run average cost consists of both operating costs *and* the opportunity cost of capital, labor, and other resources. Wheat farmers who have, for example, better land and therefore lower operating costs may have correspondingly higher opportunity costs. Specifically, farmers with better land have higher opportunity costs if their land is also better at growing other crops. Therefore, total costs, consisting of operating costs plus opportunity costs, may be the same even when operating costs differ.[8] If total costs of given output levels are the same, so are average costs.

Part (b) of Figure 7.7 shows the market demand curve *D* and the horizontal sum of *SMC* and *LMC* curves of existing firms, labeled ΣSMC and ΣLMC. (Σ is the Greek letter "sigma," which is conventionally used to signify summation.) Before the entry of new firms or expansion of existing firms, the market price of wheat is approximately $7.50 per bushel, which is where the short-run market supply curve, given by ΣSMC in part (b), intersects the market demand curve *D*. This short-run equilibrium price of $7.50 per bushel provides economic profits.

When the existing firms expand all inputs, their cost curves become *LMC* and *LAC*. The existing firms' supply curves, given by their *LMC* curves, provide an industry supply curve of ΣLMC, where ΣLMC is the horizontal sum of existing firms' *LMC* curves. Therefore, before the entry of new firms but after the expansion of existing firms, the price of wheat is $4.50 per bushel, which is where the curve ΣLMC meets the demand curve *D*. Part (a) shows that at $4.50 per bushel each firm produces a little more than 10,000 bushels and earns an economic profit given by the shaded area. These profits will draw new firms into the industry.[9]

The entry of new firms shifts the ΣLMC curve to the right because the new firms' *LMC* curves must be added to those of existing firms. As the ΣLMC curve shifts to the right, the market price declines below $4.50; the added supply forces the price lower. The entry of new firms continues until the price has declined to a point where economic profits can no longer be made. This situation occurs only after a sufficient number of firms has entered to shift the ΣLMC curve to the point where the market price is approximately $2.75 per bushel, which is the minimum (common) *LAC*. At this price each firm produces approximately 8000 bushels, and industry supply is approximately 43 million bushels. With this market output and price, for each firm *price = LAC*. With price equal to *LAC*, only normal profits can be made; economic profits are zero. Furthermore, because *LAC* is at its minimum, no better

---

Total and average costs of different producers are equal if opportunity costs reflect differences in the quality of owner-supplied inputs.

A perfectly competitive industry is in *long-run* equilibrium when price equals the minimum *LAC*.

---

[8] In terms of Figure 7.5, this means that the height of the bar representing total costs does not depend on operating costs. Differences in operating costs merely affect the division of total cost between operating cost and opportunity cost.

[9] In reality, new firms enter while existing firms expand so that the two causes of expansion of industry output occur simultaneously.

FIGURE 7.7   The market is in long-run equilibrium when the price equals the minimum long-run average cost.

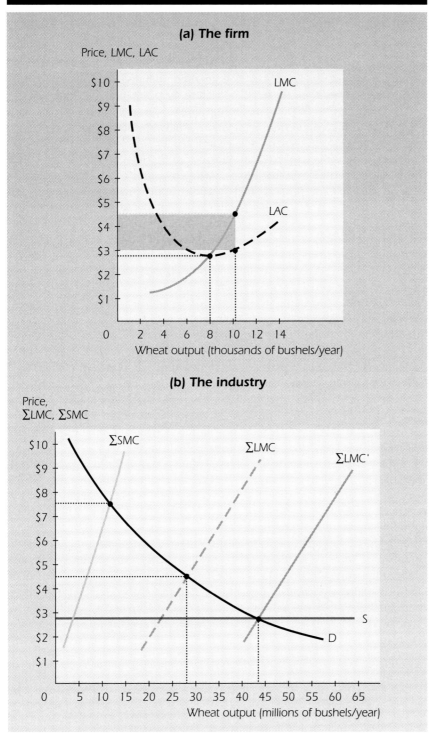

(a) The firm

(b) The industry

The short-run supply curve is the horizontal sum of existing firms' **SMC** curves, ΣSMC in part (b). With market demand curve **D** and supply curve ΣSMC, the market price is $7.50, which provides economic profit. As existing firms expand, their relevant marginal cost curves become **LMC** and the market supply curve becomes ΣLMC. This supply curve, in conjunction with the demand curve, gives the reduced equilibrium price, $4.50, with the drop in price from $7.50 to $4.50 being due to the expansion of existing firms. At $4.50, part (a) shows each firm producing a little more than 10,000 bushels and making economic profits equal to the shaded area. The economic profit attracts new firms, which continue entering until there are no longer economic profits. If all firms have the same minimum long-run average cost, economic profits are eliminated when the market price has been reduced to $2.75, which requires sufficient new entrants to shift the sum of the **LMC** curves to ΣLMC'. Note that $2.75 per bushel equals the (common) minimum long-run average cost.

output exists. This means that with no economic profit being possible, no more firms enter the industry. When no firms are entering (or leaving) a perfectly competitive industry and when economic profits are zero, the industry is in **long-run equilibrium.** We see that this occurs when price equals the minimum *LAC*.

Other Points on the Long-Run Supply Curve.   The price $2.75 per bushel, equal to the minimum *LAC,* and the market quantity supplied at that price, approximately 43 million bushels, constitute a point on the long-run supply curve. To determine another point on the long-run supply curve, let us consider what happens to the equilibrium price and quantity supplied if there is an increase in demand from *D* to *D'*, as shown in Figure 7.8.

If only existing firms expanded in response to the increase in demand, industry output would expand along the curve ΣLMC—the sum of *LMC* curves of existing firms—and the market price would become approximately $4.00 per bushel, where ΣLMC intersects *D'*. At this price, each firm would produce approximately 9500 bushels, which is where the price equals each firm's *LMC*. With this price and output, the total revenue of each firm is $38,000 (or 4.00×9500). The *LAC* at 9500 bushels is approximately $2.85 per bushel. Therefore, total cost at 9500 bushels, which is average cost multiplied by output, is $27,075 (or 2.85×9500). Economic profit is equal to total revenue minus total cost, that is, $10,925 (or $38,000 - $27,075).

The existence of economic profit attracts new firms. As the new firms enter the industry, there are more *LMC* curves to sum, so ΣLMC in part (b) of Figure 7.8 shifts to the right. This reduces the market price, which is where *D'* and the ΣLMC curve intersect. Industry expansion continues until economic profits have been eliminated. Assuming expansion does not affect input prices and hence the long-run average cost, economic profits cease when the increased market supply from existing and newly entering firms brings the price down to where it equals the minimum *LAC*. At this price there is no output at which economic profits can be earned.[10] Each firm produces approximately 8000 bushels and has a total revenue and total cost of approximately $22,000 (or 2.75×8000). For the price to be $2.75 per bushel with the demand curve *D'*, a sufficient number of firms must enter the industry so that the sum of their *LMC* curves is $\Sigma LMC'$; with demand curve *D'* and output given off $\Sigma LMC'$, market price is $2.75. Part (b) of Figure 7.8 shows a market quantity supplied of approximately 64 million bushels.

Let us suppose next that demand declines from *D* to *D"*, as in Figure 7.9. While the number of firms is at the original level, industry output varies with market price along the curve ΣLMC, which is the horizontal sum of the *LMC* curves of the original firms. The reduction in demand from *D* to *D"* therefore reduces the price to approximately $1.75 per bushel. At this price, below-normal profits are made. The inability to make normal profits reduces the number of firms in the industry. This may occur as firms decide not to reinvest as capital wears out, or it may

---

[10] This means that if a firm selects the wrong output or has higher costs than its competitors, it makes losses and eventually goes out of business. It is therefore little wonder, as Example 7.2 explains, that where competition has not previously existed but has been encouraged, as in the former Soviet Union, it has been fiercely resisted by the competitors themselves.

FIGURE 7.8 Increases in demand leave price unchanged in the long run when input prices are constant and all firms have the same minimum *LAC*.

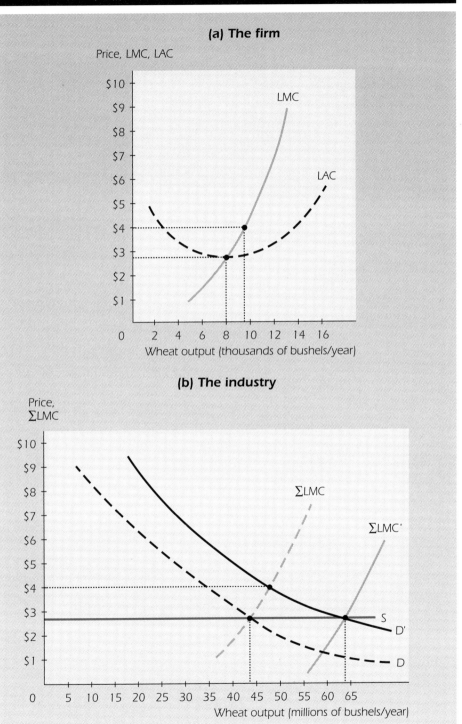

With the demand curve **D** and the number of firms in the industry such that the horizontal sum of their **LMC** curves is Σ**LMC,** the long-run equilibrium price is approximately $2.75 per bushel. This is the equilibrium price because only a normal profit can be made. Suppose that the market demand curve shifts from **D** to **D'**. With the original number of firms, the price increases to approximately $4.00 per bushel, where **D'** intersects Σ**LMC**. At $4.00 per bushel, each firm produces approximately 9500 bushels. This output allows an economic profit. Firms will therefore enter the industry, which will shift Σ**LMC** to the right; there are more **LMC** curves to add. Only when the increased quantity supplied has reduced the price to the minimum value of **LAC** will the entry of firms cease. Hence there is a new point on the long-run supply curve at the original price, but with a higher output.

FIGURE 7.9   If industry expansion and contraction do not affect input costs, the long-run market supply curve is perfectly elastic at the minimum *LAC*.

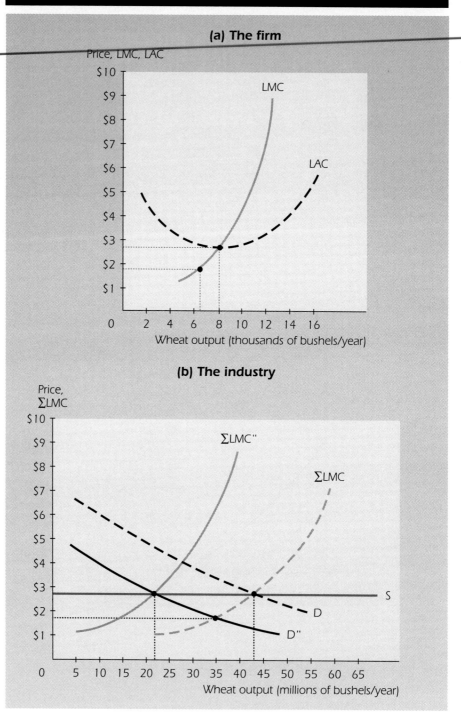

(a) The firm

Price, LMC, LAC

Wheat output (thousands of bushels/year)

(b) The industry

Price, ΣLMC

Wheat output (millions of bushels/year)

If demand declines to **D"**, before any firms have left the industry the market quantity supplied varies along ΣLMC, the horizontal sum of the firms' **LMC** curves. The market price therefore declines to approximately $1.75 per bushel. Each firm continues to produce if this price exceeds its **AVC** but makes less than normal profit. The inability to make normal profits causes firms to leave the industry. As firms leave, there are fewer **LMC** curves to add horizontally so ΣLMC shifts to the left to ΣLMC". Firms leave until the reduced supply has forced the market price back to $2.75. We see that in the long run the market supply curve is perfectly elastic at the minimum **LAC**.

Example 7.2

FREE MARKET AND COMPETITION BAFFLE BAKERS

The pressure of perfect competition to eliminate pure profits means that the best that firms can do, even if everybody works hard, is make a normal profit. Any firm that does not keep costs at a minimum makes less than a normal profit. It is perhaps little wonder, then, that where producers have been able to enjoy a market that lacked price competition, moves to make the market competitive have been fiercely resisted. The following article from **The Wall Street Journal** explains the panic among Moscow bread producers after moves to increase competition in their market.

Late last month, on the eve of Russia's historic plunge into a market economy, Vladimir Grechanik, the top financial planner of Moscow's Bread Factory No. 14, went into a panic.

After 70 years of government control of everything from the cost of raw materials to salaries, the factory suddenly would be able to set its own prices. He and his fellow producers anxiously tried to calculate how much flour would cost, how much transportation might rise and what consumers would be willing to pay.

Just before prices were freed Jan. 2 [1992], Mr. Grechanik and executives from Moscow's other bread factories were called to a meeting at the Moscow Consortium, the *de facto* ministry of bread. They eyed one another nervously, suspicious that, after years of mandated equality, the system might make rivals of former comrades. The bread consortium suggested raising the free-market bread price to 3½ times the old price, but not a kopeck more. The factory men were confused. In the old days, such a "suggestion" carried the full weight of a decree. But there were no certainties any

more. The new freedom was unbearable.

Left to his own devices, Mr. Grechanik returned to his office and got on the phone. For the next two days he and the other factory directors discussed their fears. Finally, they came to a decision: If the state was no longer to set prices, the factories themselves would jointly fix them—to ensure their mutual survival.

"We all agreed on a single price," says Mr. Grechanik, as he walks past huge vats of flour on the factory floor. Lowering his voice, he confides, "I've heard that Bread Factory No. 26 is charging a little less, but I hope it's just a rumor. . . ."

Source: Laurie Hays and Adi Ignatius, "Moscow's 'Capitalists' Decide the Best Price is a Firmly Fixed One," **The Wall Street Journal,** January 21, 1992, p. 1. Reprinted by permission of The Wall Street Journal, © 1992 Dow Jones & Company, Inc. All Rights Reserved Worldwide.

---

involve immediate exit. Which form it takes depends on whether $1.75 is above or below the firms' average variable cost AVC.[11] The decline in the number of firms shifts the ΣLMC curve to the left. Firms continue leaving until the shift in the ΣLMC curve has forced the market price back to $2.75 per bushel. This occurs when the ΣLMC curve has become $\Sigma LMC''$. We then have a new equilibrium market quantity supplied of approximately 22 million bushels and the same price as before the decline in demand, namely, $2.75 per bushel, the minimum LAC.

The price $2.75 and quantity 22 million bushels constitute another point on the long-run supply curve. This point is in addition to that at $2.75 and quantity 43 million when demand is at D and $2.75 and quantity 64 million bushels when demand is at D' as in Figure 7.8. We see that the long-run market supply curve which joins these points is perfectly elastic at the price of $2.75 per bushel. This

When industry expansion does not affect input costs, the long-run market supply curve is perfectly elastic at the minimum (common) LAC.

---

[11] As we saw in Chapter 5, if a firm can more than cover its variable costs by continuing to produce, it will continue producing and thereby reduce losses, but it will not reinvest. If the price is less than the average variable cost, the firm will immediately cease production.

price equals the minimum *LAC*. That is, the long-run market supply curve is a perfectly elastic curve at the height of the minimum (common) *LAC*. This curve is labeled *S*.

Long-Run Supply with Changing Input Costs*

The perfectly elastic supply curve *S* in Figure 7.9 assumes that firms' production costs do not increase as the industry expands. This requires that input prices facing firms do not increase as the demand for inputs increases along with industry expansion. When the supply of inputs is perfectly elastic within the range of demand variations of an individual industry, this is a reasonable assumption; shifts in demand for inputs with perfectly elastic supply leave the input prices unchanged. However, the assumption of constant input prices as demand for these inputs changes is not valid when the supply of inputs is not perfectly elastic. For example, suppose that for more land to grow wheat it is necessary to pay higher and higher prices to attract land from higher-value uses; land may have to be bid away from market gardening or even from property development. In this case, the more the wheat industry expands, the higher are the prices all wheat producers must pay for land.[12]

Figure 7.10 shows the effect of increased input prices as an industry expands. In part (b), the original demand curve is *D*, the equilibrium price is $2.75 per bushel, and industry output is 43 million bushels. Part (a) assumes that this output is produced by *n* farms whose cost curves are LMC_n and LAC_n. At the price $2.75, each farm produces the output at which $price = LMC_n$, approximately 8000 bushels per year. Furthermore, at this profit-maximizing output, the price equals the minimum long-run average cost, so only a normal profit is made. This is the best that can be done; at every other output, $price < LAC_n$, so below-normal profits are made.

Suppose that demand increases to *D'* and this increases the price of wheat. New firms enter the industry until the increased supply of wheat has pushed the price of wheat down to the new minimum *LAC*. However, the new minimum *LAC* is higher than before because the expansion of the industry pushes input costs higher. In Figure 7.10, firms enter until the price of wheat is $3.50 per bushel, and there are *N* firms—more than the original *n* firms—and the cost curves are LMC_N and LAC_N. Part (a) shows that these costs are higher than before. For example, at the profit maximizing output, which is 8000 bushels, the LAC_N is $3.50 per bushel. The *N* firms just make a normal profit. Part (b) shows the industry output, given by the summation of the outputs of all *N* firms from the *LMC* curves. The industry is again in equilibrium at price $3.50 per bushel and output of 53 million bushels because there is no reason for firms to enter or leave the industry.

The long-run market supply curve is found by drawing a line showing the market quantities supplied at each price, which is *S* in Figure 7.10. The reason the long-run market supply curve is upward-sloping is that when the industry expands, the long-run average costs of all firms increase because of higher input prices.

When input prices increase as an industry expands, the long-run market supply curve is upward-sloping.

---

*Sections and numbered items marked by an asterisk can be omitted without loss of continuity.

[12] Even if inputs are owned by entrepreneurs, provided they can be sold, their opportunity cost increases as input prices are bid up.

FIGURE 7.10   When an industry expansion causes higher input prices, the long-run industry supply curve is upward-sloping.

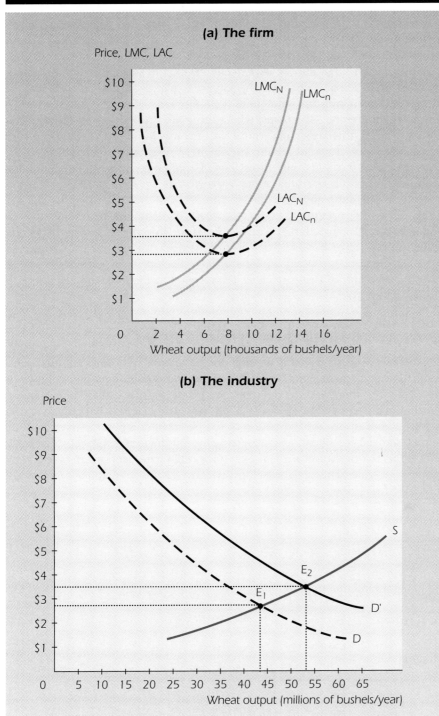

(a) The firm

(b) The industry

The initial equilibrium price with demand curve **D** is $2.75 per bushel, and the market quantity supplied and demanded is 43 million bushels. This quantity is produced by **n** firms which just make a normal profit because the **LAC** facing **n** firms, labeled **LAC$_n$**, is $2.75 per bushel at the output where **price** = **LMC$_n$**. If demand increases to **D'**, the price of wheat increases, and this attracts new firms. New firms enter until the minimum **LAC** is equal to the new equilibrium price. The new price is assumed to be $3.50 per bushel, with **N** firms all having long-run average cost curves **LAC$_N$** which have a minimum at $3.50 per bushel. By drawing a line showing market supply at different prices, we find that the long-run market supply curve is upward-sloping.

The elasticity of the long-run market supply curve depends on the extent to which input costs increase as an industry expands. When there are higher-value alternative uses of inputs, attracting additional inputs requires greater increases in prices than when there are large amounts of inputs available with similar values in alternative uses. That is, the more elastic the supply of inputs, the more elastic is the long-run market supply curve of the good. Indeed, as we have seen earlier in this chapter, when input supply is perfectly elastic, meaning that input prices are constant as their demand changes, the long-run market supply curve is also perfectly elastic. This marks one extreme of the spectrum.

If firms had different *LAC* curves, where these are properly measured to include opportunity costs, this also could cause an upward-sloping market supply curve. This occurs because it would require ever higher prices to draw extra firms into an industry to cover the additional firms' higher minimum long-run average costs.[13] Firms do differ in their operating costs. However, as we have noted, to the extent differences in operating costs are due to differences in qualities of inputs that manifest themselves in opportunity costs, total costs, consisting of operating costs plus opportunity costs, might still be constant. Therefore, in order for an upward-sloping long-run supply curve to arise from cost differences among firms, it is necessary that quality differences among inputs are not reflected in opportunity costs. This requires that the inputs' better qualities are relevant to the industry in question but not to other industries.

A Downward-Sloping Long-Run Supply Curve?*

Under special circumstances it is possible that industry expansion can reduce input prices. This can happen when there are increasing returns to scale in producing inputs. Then, as more inputs are demanded and supplied, their prices decline. While this might appear to be an unlikely possibility, it has happened in some industries. For example, the expansion of the personal computer market caused an increased demand for silicon chips. Silicon chip production is subject to increasing returns, so as the demand for them expanded, chip producers were able to enjoy economies of scale. This reduced chip prices to computer manufacturers and, in turn, helped bring down computer prices.

The more elastic the supply of inputs, the more elastic is the long-run market supply curve of a product.

When firms have different-quality inputs and the differences in quality do not translate into higher opportunity costs, the market supply curve is upward-sloping.

When inputs are produced subject to increasing returns to scale so that input prices decline as the industry using the inputs expands, the long-run market supply curve may slope downward.

[13] Example 7.3 illustrates this in the context of coal production.

Example   7.3

THE SUPPLY CURVE OF COAL

While there are different grades of coal, especially with regard to sulfur content, the international market for coal meets the criteria for perfect competition. Specifically, coal is produced in hundreds of different mines, appearing as it does in many locations in North and South America, Russia, Great Britain, Germany, China, and so on. There are also many buyers who can observe the prices of different producers. Firms are free to enter the industry by developing any of the numerous as yet undeveloped reserves in the western United States, Australia, Canada, and parts of Asia. Mines also can be closed when the price does not cover the average variable cost of production.

Consider an increase in the price of coal brought about by increased demand. In the short run, each mining company can add extra workers and workshifts and thereby increase output at existing mines, but only at an increasing marginal cost. After a point, extra workers add smaller marginal products than previously hired workers because they must share the same equipment and work the same coal faces. However, in the long run, each firm can add equipment as well as workers, allowing output to expand without such rapidly increasing marginal cost. Indeed, new coal faces can be mined, although if these are less accessible than those already in production, marginal costs will be higher than for existing faces. Therefore, for each mining company, the long-run supply curve is more elastic than the short-run supply curve, but the long-run supply curve is still likely to slope upward.

The global supply curve of coal, that is, the supply curve for the industry as a whole, is even more elastic than that for an individual firm. This is so because new mines with the necessary equipment can be opened in a large number of different places. Indeed, if there are many sources of coal which can be mined at a similar cost, the long-run industry supply curve is perfectly elastic because new mines can be opened with the same operating costs as old mines. However, if more and more expensive sources must be tapped as the industry expands, the industry supply curve will slope upward.

Adam Smith (1723–1790)

THE MANY FACES OF COMPETITION

Economists hold no monopoly on the concept of competition. While, as we have seen, competition is an important matter in economics, it also plays a role in biology, political science, history, ethics, and theology.

Beginning with the life sciences, it is worth noting that in formulating his views on evolution, Charles Darwin was influenced by Adam Smith's **The Wealth of Nations** (1776). Indeed, Darwin's **Origin of Species** (1859) used many of Smith's ideas, especially his ideas on competition.

As is well know, Darwin and the generations of biologists who have followed him explained how, in the process of meiosis and mutation of genes that takes place with reproduction and replication, random variations appear. The varia-

tions in the **genotypes**—the gene combinations themselves—manifest in a variety of **phenotypes**—the organisms reflecting the genotypes. Some variations prove to be useful to the phenotypes manifesting these variations, and they pass them on to future generations; the variations are favored by the environment. Other variations, indeed the vast majority of them, are not passed on because the phenotypes which result from them are not favored.

The selection between the favored and unfavored variations depends on competition. Through the struggle of phenotypes to survive in competition with each other and with other organisms, the process of natural selection occurs. In turn, competition is the result of scarcity of sources of energy from food and sunlight. Indeed, if scarcity did not exist, more variations would be transmitted to future generations, and the lack of selection would slow or even halt evolution.

The paradigm of Darwinian evolution has implications for the forces shaping economic progress. For example, firms innovate in methods of production and in the development of new products. For innovations in production methodology to survive the competition among firms, they must improve efficiency. Otherwise, with profits reduced by free entry to the point of being only just sufficient to keep firms in an industry, if the innovators' costs are not the same as or lower than those of their competitors, they are forced out of business. Similarly, for new product innovations to survive, they must meet the test of the market or face termination.

What is more, the fiercer the competition, the quicker the selection of favored variations/innovations occurs. That is, the **pace** of evolution and of economic change depends on the level of competition. In turn, the level of competition depends on the scarcity of resources in the biologic arena or the market. This so-called **teleological** role of scarcity and competition for the pace of evolution or economic change is essentially dynamic. It is not the role typically emphasized in economics, where competition, as in this chapter, is viewed in more static terms as keeping prices equal to minimum long-run average cost. Nevertheless, the parallels confirm what Alfred Marshall, the great developer of economic theory, said: "[Economics] is a branch of biology broadly interpreted."

Competition among members of a given species—**intraspecies competition**—is typically more intense than competition among members of different species—**interspecies competition**—because the resources over which different species' members compete are usually more alike than the resources exploited by different species. Analogously, firms in the same industry compete more fiercely than firms in different industries; firms in the same industry compete for the same "resource," or market, whereas different industries compete in different markets. Furthermore, the intensity of biologic competition typically increases with resource scarcity. In the same way, economic competition is frequently more intense during times of weak demand.

The emphasis that competition places on the right of individuals to pursue their own satisfaction or profit, in contrast to the emphasis most religions place on societal values, has parallels with language development. The "ancient" languages of liturgical writings did not extensively use separate pronouns and instead modified the verb or noun to distinguish possession or association. For example, Hebrew, Aramaic, and Latin use verb and noun modification. Modern languages such as English, French, German, and Spanish heavily employ possessive pronouns such as **mine**, **yours**, **ours**, **hers**, and **his**. It has been suggested that this shift in language reflects changing attitudes toward property rights of individuals versus society, with the shift toward individual property rights being a necessary ingredient for the acceptance of competitive forces in the marketplace.

The fact that competition places a focus on the individual and involves a "hands off" survival of the fittest has troubled a number of theologians. In particular, the instruction in Leviticus, Chapter 19, to "love thy neighbor as thyself,"

> " . . .a person who intends only his own gain . . . is . . . led by an invisible hand to promote an end which was not part of his intentions. . . . [and] by pursuing his interests he frequently promotes that of society more effectively than when he really intends to promote it."

which became the central tenet of Paul's teachings, does not seem consistent with the view that competition should be allowed to weed out the weak and inefficient. Indeed, it has been argued by some theologians and writers in the field of ethics that economic theories about competition have been used by those who have gained from competition to legitimize and preserve the system that has rewarded them. For example, in his 1967 encyclical, Pope Paul VI made it clear that he believes that "Individual initiative alone and the free play of competition could never assure successful development. . . . It pertains to the public authorities to . . . choose, even to lay down, the objectives to be pursued, the ends to be achieved and the means of attaining these." Pro–free-market economists might answer not only that the record of competition makes it clearly superior to the alternatives in terms of economic outcomes and human freedoms but also that there is good reason for this. They might cite Adam Smith, who said "a person who intends only his own gain . . . is . . . led by an invisible hand to promote an end which was not part of his intentions . . . [and] by pursuing his interests he frequently promotes that of society more effectively than when he really intends to promote it." However, it should be added that Smith did recognize limits imposed by generally accepted moral laws. This, and the persuasive way Smith made his case, may well explain why **The Wealth of Nations**, unlike Darwin's **Origin of Species**, did not provoke any outcry from the Church.

SUMMARY

1. The short run is the period of time during which at least one input and the number of firms in an industry are fixed. The long run is the amount of time necessary for existing firms to change their use of all inputs and for new firms to enter or old firms to leave an industry.

2. A perfectly competitive industry has free entry and exit, a very large number of firms selling an indistinguishable product, and a large number of customers who know the prices of all suppliers. Each firm in a perfectly competitive industry takes the market price as given.

3. The long-run supply curve of a perfectly competitive industry is more elastic than the short-run supply curve because firms can change all inputs and because the number of firms can change.

4. When all inputs are variable, long-run average cost does not necessarily increase with increasing output. When a firm's LAC declines as output expands, the firm has increasing returns to scale; when LAC increases as output expands, the firm has decreasing returns to scale; and when LAC is constant, the firm has constant returns to scale.

5. Increasing, decreasing, and constant returns to scale are defined in terms of the percentage change in output relative to the percentage change in all inputs. Increasing returns occur when an x% increase in all inputs causes a more than x% increase in output; decreasing returns occur when an x% increase in all inputs causes a less than x% increase in output; and constant returns occur when an x% increase in all inputs causes an x% increase in output.

6. Economies of scope occur when costs are reduced by increasing the variety of items produced. Economies of scope may coexist with economies of scale.

7. The perfectly competitive firm's long-run supply curve is its long-run marginal cost curve above the minimum *LAC*. The firm maximizes profit by finding the output at which *price = LMC*.

8. Existing firms' *LMC* curves cannot be summed horizontally to obtain the long-run perfectly competitive market supply curve because of free entry and exit.

9. When total revenue equals total cost, economic profit is zero and accounting profit equals normal profit. Normal profit equals the opportunity cost of entrepreneur-provided capital, labor, and other resources used in a firm.

10. Economic profit equals accounting profit minus normal profit.

11. When there are economic profits, new firms enter a perfectly competitive industry until the last entrant expects to make only a normal profit. When there are below-normal profits, firms leave the industry until a normal profit is expected by the remaining firms.

12. When input prices are constant as an industry expands and all firms face the same minimum *LAC*, the long-run market supply curve is perfectly elastic at the minimum *LAC*. Only when the price is at this level are all firms making normal profits with no firms entering or leaving the industry.

13. When all firms face the same minimum *LAC* and there is free entry and exit, all firms produce the output at which the *LAC* is at its minimum. This is so because any other output would result in below-normal profits.

14.* When industry expansion causes higher input prices, the long-run perfectly competitive market supply curve is upward-sloping. The long-run market supply curve also slopes upward when different firms have different average costs.

15.* The long-run competitive market supply curve can slope downward if input prices fall as the industry expands. This can happen when input production is subject to increasing returns.

QUESTIONS AND PROBLEMS

1. What characteristics of perfectly competitive markets are present or absent in the following "industries"?

   a. Apple growing

   b. Furniture manufacturing

   c. Passenger airlines between Los Angeles and New York

   d. Banking

   e. Postsecondary education

2. Does international trade increase the number of markets that are perfectly competitive?

3. How do you think the time for new firms to become established would differ from the time that it takes for existing firms to expand?

4. Why might there be a difference between the time it takes for an industry to expand and the time it takes for an industry to contract?

5. Draw the *LMC* curves corresponding to the *LAC* curves in Figure 7.2.

6. Why must an *MC* curve cut the associated *AC* curve at the minimum of the *AC* curve?

7. Why are the *LAC* curves in Figure 7.2 lower than the minimums on the *SAC* curves?

8. What might be the form or nature of economies of scale and of economies of scope in the following industries?

   a. Computer software

   b. Financial services

   c. Publishing

   d. Forest products

9. From the output levels in parts (a) and (b) of Figure 7.7, can you say how many firms there are in the industry when it is in long-run equilibrium?

10. Do you think profits are normal or above-normal in the following industries?

    a. Major league baseball franchises

    b. Network television

    c. Hairdressing

    d. Local newspapers

11. How does the sale of a license to operate a concession, such as ice cream sales on a public beach, affect the economic profit that can be earned?

12.* Why is an industry supply curve likely to be perfectly elastic if the industry is only a small user of each of its inputs vis-à-vis the total use of inputs by all users?

Monopoly

A man is known by the company he keeps, and a company is known by the men it keeps.

Evan Esar

Key Concepts

Causes of monopoly; natural monopoly; marginal revenue versus price; profit maximization for a monopolist; monopolistic versus competitive equilibria; monopolistic versus competitive costs; monopolistic versus competitive incentives to innovate; fixed costs and monopoly pricing; price regulation of monopolies; price-discriminating monopoly

While the perfectly competitive model is a good approximation of the situation in, for example, the stock market and in commodity markets like those for wheat, corn, zinc, and coal, the model is not valid in many other settings. One reason the perfectly competitive model may be invalid is that there may not be a very large number of firms. This chapter considers the other extreme to perfect competition, where instead of many firms there is only one. The following chapter considers situations of more than one firm but where there is not perfect competition. Later, in Chapter 11, we show that when there is monopoly or *any* other form of imperfect competition, consumers and the economy in general are, *ceteris paribus,* worse off than with perfect competition.

THE NATURE OF MONOPOLISTIC MARKETS

The Causes of Monopoly

A **monopoly** is an industry with only one supplier.[1] There are several reasons why monopolies occur.

An industry with *one* supplier is a monopoly

Natural Monopoly.   When there are economies of scale over a range of output that is large relative to market demand, the industry tends over time to become a monopoly. This occurs because the producer that becomes the largest has the lowest costs and therefore can charge prices at which small producers would not find the industry profitable. The situation of scale economies over a range of output that is large relative to market demand is shown in Figure 8.1. Such situations of

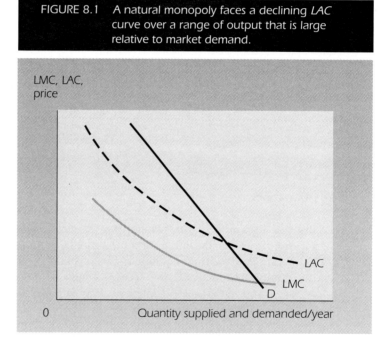

FIGURE 8.1   A natural monopoly faces a declining *LAC* curve over a range of output that is large relative to market demand.

When the **LAC** curve slopes downward over a range of output that is greater than market demand, the firm that is largest has the lowest **LAC**. Therefore, the largest firm may be in a position to charge a price that makes other firms leave the industry or prevents new firms from entering. This is the situation for many public utilities such as electric power and water supply companies. Governments often allow monopolies in such cases but subject them to price regulations to give consumers the benefit of lower costs without the drawbacks of monopoly.

---

[1] The board game with the same name therefore involves monopoly in that the objective is to eliminate the competition. Furthermore, houses can be built and high rents enjoyed only after players have exclusive control of a set.

declining *LAC* give rise to **natural monopolies.** Examples of natural monopolies are local telephone companies, electric and gas utilities, and water supply. In these industries, fixed costs of, for example, the telephone exchange, power-generating station, or reservoir are large relative to the costs of serving additional customers. That is, marginal costs are small relative to fixed costs. The spreading of the fixed costs over larger outputs as output expands causes the decline in *LAC.*

When *LAC* declines over a large range, a monopoly faces a lower *LAC* for a given output than would be faced by a number of producers each supplying a small part of that output. In terms of Figure 8.1, with many producers, each would supply a relatively small output and therefore have a higher *LAC* than a monopolist. However, while a monopoly's production costs may be lower, there are numerous drawbacks to monopolization, which we shall describe. Therefore, when there are declining *LAC* curves, as with local telephone companies, electricity and gas utilities, and water supply, governments often try to capture the benefit of lower costs enjoyed by having only one producer without the drawbacks of monopoly. Governments do this either by providing the products themselves or by issuing licenses to private firms and subjecting them to price regulations.

Licenses. Licenses are themselves a reason for some monopolized markets. Sometimes the licenses are purchased, perhaps via competitive bidding, to gain monopoly power. This happens with duty-free shops in international airports, newspaper and candy concessions in public buildings, ice cream concessions in parks, limousine services to some airports, garbage collection, and so on.[2] Sometimes governments grant licenses without a payment but with the stipulation that the monopoly provides subsidized services to some buyers. For example, bus companies sometimes have to serve unprofitable routes to obtain a license to operate profitable routes.

Unique Resources. A monopoly can result from control over a unique resource. This is the case for diamonds, where marketing from the principal known sources is controlled by one company, de Beers. Market control also may result from owning a patent, as with many pharmaceutical products and computer software (see Example 8.2). Even when a product itself has not been patented, a monopoly may result from a patent on part of the production process. This may make a company's production so much cheaper than that of other firms that other firms cannot compete successfully.

Despite the rather impressive list of causes of monopoly, few firms face no competition at all. This situation occurs because even in the case in which a firm controls a narrowly defined market, there is competition from related products in other markets. In other words, firms face competition from other firms producing substitutes. For example, local telephone service might be controlled by one telephone company, but letters, telegrams, messages via couriers, CB radios, and so on offer alternative means of communication. In a similar way, railways compete with airlines, electric utilities compete in the home heating market with oil and natural gas, and so on. Even when a firm has a monopoly at home and does not face competition from different but related products, there may be stiff competition

Natural monopolies are the result of economies of scale. They occur when fixed costs are high relative to marginal costs.

Monopolies result from economies of scale, licenses, patents, and control over a unique resource of production process.

Few, if any, firms face no competition at all.

---

[2] Example 8.1 describes how licensing has given monopoly power to local cable television franchises in the United States. Example 8.2 summarizes the history of U.S. monopoly legislation.

Example 8.1

PRYING OPEN THE CABLE TELEVISION MONOPOLIES

When monopolies are granted by governments, there is a danger that the process can become corrupt. This and some other aspects of monopoly are discussed in the following account of the cable television business from **The Wall Street Journal**.

. . . With a handful of exceptions, the roughly 9000 cable franchises in the U.S. are monopolies, granted by local governments to a favored company, one usually partly owned by politically well-connected people. Governments pass out such monopolies and fiercely defend them, yet don't regulate prices charged to customers. The "franchise fees" that local governments charge cable operators rise with the revenues, and total hundreds of millions of dollars annually.

But the winds of competition are rustling in the cable business. Two or three dozen communities now allow second cable companies to compete, estimates John Mansell, a senior analyst with Paul Kagan Associates, a media research firm. Public unhappiness over service and rising prices is fueling the push for competition. . . .

Nationally, the status quo is a recipe for bad government and bad cable service, critics contend. "It is one of the most corrupt processes imaginable," says Sol Schildhause, former chief of the cable-TV branch of the Federal Communications Commission and now a private attorney. . . .

Defenders argue that cable television is one of those businesses, like a utility, that works best as a monopoly. Given the expense and street disruption required to lay cable to every home in an area, putting in more than one system is simply a waste of resources and an annoyance for residents in the area, they say.

Operators argue that in some places competition was tried, but it failed, leaving a monopoly anyway. "It's simply not viable to have two franchises in one area," says Marc Nathanson, chairman of Los Angeles-based Falcon Cable TV, which operates cable franchises nationwide.

Source: John R. Emshwiller, "Prying Open the Cable-T.V. Monopolies," **The Wall Street Journal,** August 10, 1989, p. B1. Reprinted by permission of The Wall Street Journal, © 1989 Dow Jones & Company, Inc. All Rights Reserved Worldwide.

Example 8.2

MONOPOLIZING MARIO

Ultimately it is the courts which must decide if a company has the right to the exclusive production and sale of a product. As the following article shows, the courts have a difficult time reaching decisions concerning monopolies.

A federal appeals court has ruled that Nintendo of America Inc. may sue retailers who buy unauthorized Nintendo video games from its competitors, strengthening Nintendo's dominant position in the industry.

The decision goes to the heart of Nintendo's strategy of tightly controlling the quality of its video games as well as the supply. Nintendo game cartridges, which sell for $23 to $45 each, are some of the best-selling items in the toy business. Such leading retailers as Toys "R" Us and Wal-Mart Stores Inc. once carried unsanctioned games for Nintendo, but the company's lawyers successfully persuaded them to withdraw the products before filing a lawsuit.

Nintendo, based in Redmond, Wash., had more than 80 percent of the $3.4 billion video-game business last year.

The United States Court of Appeals for the Federal Circuit in Washington . . . voided a preliminary injunction stopping Nintendo from suing retailers for patent infringement when they carried unsanctioned games.

The injunction stems from a lawsuit charging Nintendo with monopolistic practices. It was filed in December 1988 by the Atari Games Corporation, an arcade-game developer in Milpitas, Calif. In February 1989, Atari Games persuaded a federal court in San Francisco to grant the injunction.

Nintendo had developed a security system consisting of a "master" computer chip in the Nintendo game deck and a "slave" chip in the game cartridge inserted into the deck. Without both, the game cannot be played. But Atari Games developed a way to circumvent the Nintendo system, making possible the development of unsanctioned games.

In its decision, the appeals court said that patents, like Nintendo's on its video games, were presumed to be valid and that the San Francisco court had erred in granting the injunction to Atari Games.

The U.S. justice system has never had an easy time dealing with monopoly, or more generally, with matters relating to restriction of competition. Numerous legislative efforts have been made to foster competition, but the U.S. Congress has been rather vague about what constitutes "restraint of trade," or even "monopoly."

The first major attempt to provide a legislative framework to deal with the restriction of competition was the Sherman Antitrust Act of 1890. The two most important provisions of this Act are the following:

Section 1: Every contract, combination in the form of trust or otherwise, or conspiracy, in restraint of trade or commerce . . . is hereby declared to be illegal.

Section 2: Every person who shall monopolize, or attempt to monopolize, or combine or conspire with any other person or persons to monopolize . . . trade or commerce . . . shall be guilty of a misdemeanor.

Despite the lack of a definition of the key terms in the Sherman Act—"restraint of trade" and "monopolize"—in 1906 the justice system was able to use the Act successfully to prosecute the oil giant, Standard Oil of New Jersey, which before being broken in several parts controlled over 80% of U.S. oil refining capacity. Standard Oil was accused of using unreasonably low prices to drive out competition—called predatory price-cutting—and of using its power to gain preferential treatment in transporting oil. These practices, and not the extent of market control, were responsible for the finding against the company by the district and the Supreme Court.

The antitrust provisions of the Sherman Act have been extended and sharpened by a variety of further enactments. Most important among these are the Clayton Act of 1914, which describes specific types of behavior as being "unreasonable" restraints on trade—specifically, discriminatory pricing, and refusal to supply firms buying from competitors—and the Robinson–Patman Act of 1936, which explicitly prohibits predatory pricing. However, despite these and further efforts to restrict the ability to limit competition, as the back-and-forth rulings on Nintendo clearly show, enforcement has been difficult. Nevertheless, perhaps the main achievement of the more than a century of efforts to control monopolies should be measured not in the courts themselves but in the recognition that restraint of competition is very likely to be investigated. Indeed, today the U.S. Justice Department rules on every proposed major merger or takeover.

Source: Anthony Ramirez, "Court Backs Nintendo on Video-Game Suits," **The New York Times**, March 15, 1990, p. D5. Copyright © 1990 by The New York Times Company. Reprinted by permission.

from foreign companies. For example, while several countries have only one car manufacturer, the international market for automobiles is very competitive indeed.

Monopolistic Equilibrium

Marginal Revenue versus Price. A monopoly faces a downward-sloping demand curve, the same as that facing the industry, since the firm *is* the industry. A downward-sloping demand curve means that unlike a competitive firm, the monopolist is not a price-taker. The need to reduce price in order to sell a larger quantity means the lower price received on all other units offsets the increase in revenue from selling an extra unit.[3] The marginal revenue—the increase in revenue from selling another unit—is therefore smaller than the price charged for the last unit sold by the amount of revenue lost on all other units. This is illustrated in Table 8.1 and Figure 8.2, which show the demand for cable television service in a small town.

Reading down Table 8.1 shows that the quantity of subscriptions demanded increases as the price of a subscription declines. For example, a price decrease from $19 to $18 per month results in an increase in the quantity of subscriptions from 6 to 7 households. The need to reduce the subscription price to sell another subscription means the increase in total revenue from selling the extra subscription is less than the $18 received. Specifically, the total revenue from 6 subscriptions at $19 is $114 (or 6 × $19), while the total revenue from 7 subscriptions at $18 is $126 (or 7 × $18), resulting in a marginal revenue of $12 (or $126 − $114) from the seventh subscription. This marginal revenue of $12 is $6 smaller than the $18 charged when selling 7 subscriptions. That is, *MR* is less than price. The difference between *MR* and price is the $6 lost on the 6 subscriptions previously sold at $19 each. Reading down the table shows that the *MR* at each quantity sold is lower than the price.

Figure 8.2 plots the demand curve and the associated marginal revenue curve. The height of the demand curve at every quantity sold is, of course, the price at which that unit is just sold, and the height of the marginal revenue curve is the marginal revenue of that unit. The figure shows that the marginal revenue curve is below the demand curve. This is true whenever a firm must reduce price in order to increase the quantity demanded, whether or not this is a monopoly.

Profit Maximization. Profit maximization requires supplying the quantity at which $MC = MR$. This is so because if $MR > MC$, more is added to total revenue than to total cost from producing and selling another unit. That is, profit is increased by increasing the quantity supplied when $MR > MC$. However, to go

> When a firm must reduce its price to sell another unit of output, the marginal revenue—the increase in total revenue from selling another unit—is smaller than the price of that unit. Therefore, the *MR* curve is *below* the demand curve facing the firm.

---

[3] This assumes that the firm must charge the same price on all units and cannot "discriminate" by charging new buyers lower prices while maintaining prices paid by others. A monopolist that is able to charge different prices to different buyers of the same product is called a **discriminating monopolist** and is discussed later in this chapter.

TABLE 8.1

When a firm must reduce price to increase the quantity demanded, the marginal revenue is smaller than the price.

PRICE PER MONTH (p)	NUMBER OF CABLE SUBSCRIPTIONS (q)	TOTAL REVENUE PER MONTH (p × q)	MARGINAL REVENUE
$20	5	$100	N/d*
19	6	114	$14
18	7	126	12
17	8	136	10
16	9	144	8
15	10	150	6
14	11	154	4
13	12	156	2
12	13	156	0
11	14	154	−2
10	15	150	−4

By definition, the marginal revenue is the increase in total revenue from selling one more unit of output. When the sale of an extra unit requires a reduction in price, the marginal revenue is smaller than the price. This occurs because revenue is lost on all other units sold. For example, in going from 6 to 7 cable subscriptions by reducing the price of subscription by $1, against the $18 received on the seventh unit must be netted the $6 (or $1 × 6) lost on the 6 units previously sold, giving a marginal revenue on the seventh unit of $12 (or $18 − $6). Alternatively, the marginal revenue can be calculated directly from the difference between the total revenue for successive quantities sold.

*N/d=not defined.

beyond the output where $MR = MC$ so that, with MR decreasing and MC increasing, $MC > MR$ means adding more to total cost than to total revenue, thereby reducing profit by increasing the quantity supplied. Only when output has been set such that $MR = MC$ is profit being maximized. This is the same as with perfect competition, although with perfect competition $MR = price$ so that, as we explained in Chapter 5, profit maximization occurs when $price = MC$.

Figure 8.3 shows the market price and output that maximize a monopolist's profit. The profit-maximizing output is found by determining where $MC = MR$. This output, labeled q_m, commands a price of p_m. This price can be determined from the demand curve above the point q_m. The price is higher than the marginal cost at q_m. This is always the case for a monopoly, since $price > MR$, so if $MR = MC$, then $price > MC$.

Monopoly price exceeds the marginal cost of production.

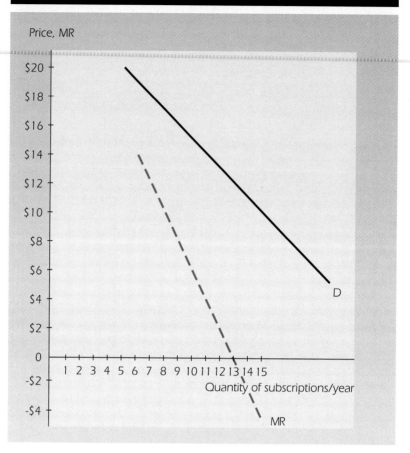

FIGURE 8.2   The marginal revenue curve is below the demand curve when the price must be reduced to increase the quantity sold.

For a firm such as a monopolist, which must reduce its price to increase the quantity sold, the marginal revenue on each unit is smaller than the price needed to sell that unit. Therefore, the marginal revenue curve **MR** is always below the corresponding demand curve **D**.

MONOPOLISTIC VERSUS COMPETITIVE EQUILIBRIA

Comparing Equilibria Assuming Common Costs

If costs of production and demand are the same for a monopolist as for a group of perfectly competitive firms, the price of the product with monopoly would be higher and the output lower than with perfect competition.

If we assume that costs and demand are unaffected by whether an industry is competitive or not, we can use Figure 8.3 to compare the equilibrium price and output of a monopolist with the price and output if the industry were perfectly competitive. As we know, when an industry is perfectly competitive, the industry supply curve is the horizontal sum of all firms' *MC* curves. Hence, if instead of being monopolized the industry in Figure 8.3 were perfectly competitive, the equilibrium price would be where the demand curve *D* intersects the perfectly competitive supply curve, which would be *MC*. That is, the perfectly competitive

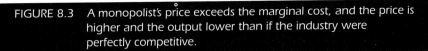

FIGURE 8.3   A monopolist's price exceeds the marginal cost, and the price is higher and the output lower than if the industry were perfectly competitive.

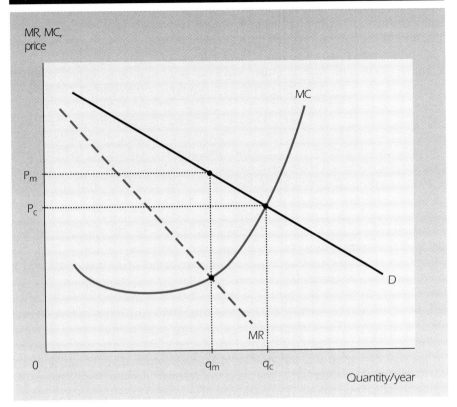

Profits are maximized at the output where **MR** = **MC**, that is the output **q**$_m$. The price this output will command is given by the height of the demand curve at the chosen output, that is, **p**$_m$. Since the **MR** curve is always below the demand curve, and since **MC** = **MR** at the chosen output, it follows that the price exceeds the **MC**. This must be so because **price** > **MR** while **MR** = **MC**, so **price** > **MC**. If the industry were perfectly competitive rather than a monopoly and costs were unaffected by whether the industry was competitive or not so that **MC** represents the horizontal sum of **MC** curves for all competitive firms, the **MC** curve would be the supply curve. Then, with the demand curve **D** being the same as with monopoly, the perfectly competitive price would be **p**$_c$—which is lower than **p**$_m$—and the output would be **q**$_c$—which is higher than **q**$_m$.

price is p_c, and the output is q_c. We see that the perfectly competitive price p_c is lower than the monopolist's price p_m and the perfectly competitive output q_c is larger than the monopolist's output q_m.

The comparison of perfect competition and monopoly in Figure 8.3 shows that for a monopolist the *MC* curve is not the supply curve. Indeed, because the monopolist determines the profit-maximizing output only in conjunction with the demand curve, there is no supply curve for a monopolist; we do not know how

There is no supply curve for a monopolist.

much is produced at different prices. Only after the demand curve is drawn can the monopolist's profit-maximizing output be determined. This is why in Chapter 6 we referred to the supply and demand analysis as applying to perfectly competitive markets. Of course, there is supply of products when there is monopoly; it is the supply *curve,* and not product supply itself, that is missing.

Because of the absence of free entry, a monopolist's economic profits persist in the long run. Indeed, because in the long run costs can be reduced by finding the best input combination with all inputs variable, long-run monopoly profits generally exceed short-run monopoly profits, the opposite situation to perfect competition.

In order to show graphically the size of the profits of a monopolist, we need to include the average cost curve. Whether we need the short-run or the long-run average cost curve depends on the length of time we are considering. Figure 8.4 shows long-run profits by including the *LMC* and *LAC* curves. At the profit-maximizing output where $MR = LMC$, labeled q_m, the *LAC* per unit is $0A$ so that the total cost is $0ABq_m$; this is the product of the average cost $0A$ and the quantity produced q_m. Similarly, the total revenue is $0p_mCq_m$, which is the product of the price p_m and the quantity sold q_m. Economic profit is the difference between total revenue $0p_mCq_m$ and total cost $0ABq_m$, that is, the shaded area Ap_mCB. Furthermore, in the absence of free entry, this profit can persist in the long run.

Figure 8.5 illustrates another important difference between monopoly and perfect competition. In particular, we saw that in perfect competition, free entry ensures that firms select the output at which *LAC* is a minimum; since the price equals the minimum (common) *LAC* in the long run, at any other output economic profits are negative. This conclusion does not carry over to monopoly. For example, if the long-run average cost curve is increasing at the profit-maximizing output as in part (a) of Figure 8.5, the profit-maximizing output q_m is above that where *LAC* is a minimum. However, if the long-run average cost curve is decreasing at the profit-maximizing output as in part (b) of Figure 8.5, the profit-maximizing output q_m is less than where *LAC* is a minimum. (This is the situation that prevails in a natural monopoly, where *LAC* declines over a large range of output relative to demand.) Only if by coincidence does the *MR* curve intersect the *LMC* curve at the minimum *LAC* is monopoly output where the long-run average cost is minimized. Unlike the case of competition, where free entry changes the market price until this happens, monopolists continue producing outputs that do not minimize long-run average cost.

Monopolistic versus Competitive Costs: The Short Run

In our comparison of monopolistic versus competitive equilibria summarized in Figure 8.3, we assumed that production costs are not affected by whether an industry is served by one firm or a number of competing firms. Therefore, we interpreted the *MC* curve as that of a monopolist and as that of a number of perfectly competitive firms. However, in reality, costs of production may be affected by whether an industry is perfectly competitive or controlled by a monopoly. Different factors may be responsible for cost differences in the short run than in the long run.

It is unclear whether a monopolist's costs would be higher or lower than those of an industry consisting of perfectly competitive firms. Working toward a lower cost for a monopoly than for a perfectly competitive industry is the possibility of

> Unlike the case of perfect competition, a monopolist's economic profit *can* persist in the long run.

> Monopolists do not in general select outputs where long-run average cost is lowest.

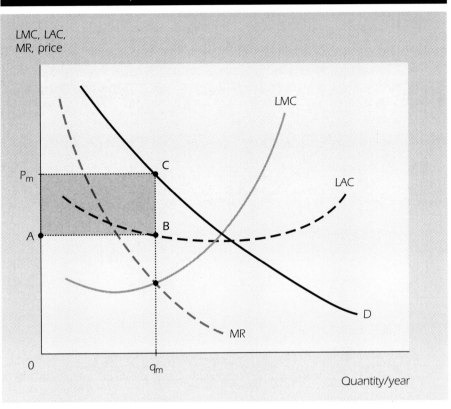

FIGURE 8.4   A monopolist can earn economic profit even in the long run.

At the monopolist's long-run profit-maximizing output **q_m**, at which **price = LMC**, the long-run average cost is distance **0A**. Therefore, total cost is **0A** $\times$ **$0q_m$** = area **0ABq$_m$**. Total revenue at **q_m** is the price times quantity sold, that is, **$0p_m$** $\times$ **$0q_m$** = **$0p_m$Cq_m**. Therefore, profit is area **$0p_m$Cq_m** $-$ area **0ABq_m** = area **Ap_mCB**. Because the **LAC** curve includes opportunity cost, all the profit is economic profit. The absence of free entry means that this economic profit can persist.

economies of scale, which, as we have mentioned, may be the cause of a monopoly. The economies of scale may be the result of a large indivisible input which an individual perfectly competitive firm cannot afford or share with other firms. This could occur, for example, with a large piece of integrated farm equipment such as a combine harvester.[4] Working toward a higher cost for a monopoly is the lack of market pressure ensuring that the most cost-effective method of production is employed; while all firms have an incentive to minimize costs for a given output or they are not maximizing profits, this is a matter of survival for perfectly competitive firms but not essential for a profitable monopoly.

A monopoly may have lower costs than a perfect competitor if there are scale economies. However, a monopolist may have higher costs as a result of less pressure to be efficient.

[4] When the equipment can be rented, shared, or leased, the indivisibility problem often can be overcome.

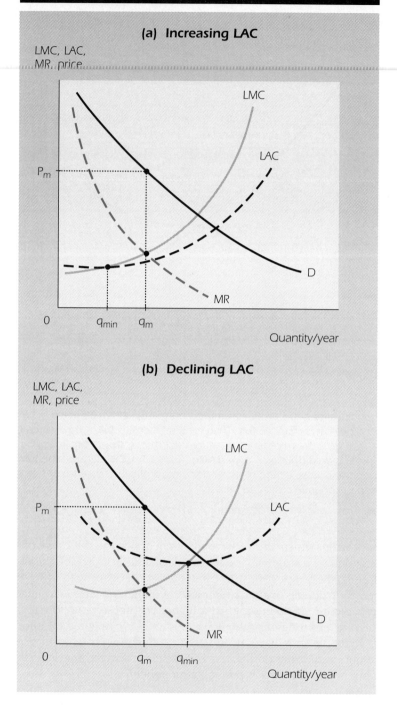

FIGURE 8.5   The monopolist does not in general produce the output at which *LAC* is at its minimum.

The profit-maximizing output of a monopolist may be above or below where **LAC** is at its minimum. In the case of the **LAC** curve in part (a), the profit-maximizing output is above the output at which **LAC** is at its minimum. However, in the case of the **LAC** curve in part (b), the profit maximizing output is below the output at which **LAC** is a minimum. With perfect competition and equal minimum **LAC**s, all firms produce at the minimum **LAC** because any firm producing where **LAC** is not at its minimum would make economic losses and eventually leave the industry.

If the result of the forces affecting costs in different directions is that the monopoly faces lower costs, the consequence could be a lower price and higher output with monopoly than would occur with perfect competition. This is shown in Figure 8.6.

If the industry were competitive, the market supply curve would be given by ΣMC_c, the horizontal sum of individual firms' MC curves. The equilibrium price

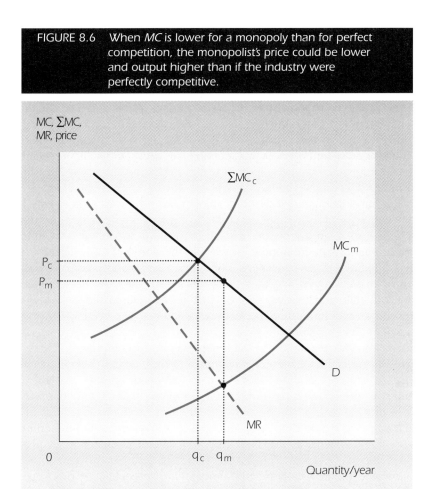

FIGURE 8.6   When *MC* is lower for a monopoly than for perfect competition, the monopolist's price could be lower and output higher than if the industry were perfectly competitive.

If the industry is perfectly competitive, the supply curve is Σ**MC**$_c$. The equilibrium price is where the supply curve intersects the demand curve, that is, **p**$_c$, and the equilibrium quantity bought and sold is **q**$_c$. If the industry is controlled by a monopolist and the marginal cost curve is **MC**$_m$, the profit-maximizing output is where this intercepts the **MR** curve, that is, **q**$_m$. This output commands a price **p**$_m$, given off the demand curve. Therefore, if a monopoly would enjoy substantially lower costs than would perfectly competitive firms, the monopoly price could be lower and the output higher than with perfect competition.

would thus be p_c, where ΣMC_c, the competitive industry market supply curve, intersects the demand curve, and the equilibrium quantity would be q_c.[5]

Let us suppose that because of savings on indivisible inputs, the monopolist's marginal cost curve would be MC_m. The monopolist would maximize profits by producing q_m, at which output the MC_m curve intersects the MR curve. When put on the market, an output of q_m would sell at price p_m. The figure shows that in the case of substantially lower costs facing a monopoly vis-à-vis perfect competition, the monopoly *could* have a lower price and higher output.

Monopolistic versus Competitive Costs: The Long Run

The factors we have already mentioned that can cause a difference between costs facing a monopoly and costs facing perfectly competitive firms in the short run, namely, the problems of indivisible inputs and a lack of incentive to use the most cost-effective method of production, also could cause differences in costs in the long run. However, in the long run there is a further reason for cost differences between monopoly and perfect competition resulting from differences in the incentive to innovate. Arguments point in both directions as to whether a monopoly or a perfectly competitive environment provides greater encouragement to discover better production methods or develop new products. Monopolies have a greater incentive to innovate than do perfectly competitive firms because monopolies can benefit for a longer period from an innovation. Indeed, it is by innovating that a firm might gain monopoly power in the form of an exclusive patent. Perfectly competitive firms can enjoy economic profits made possible by an innovation only in the short run. Other firms will adopt the new development, and new firms will enter until economic profits have been eliminated via a lower price of the product. The innovating perfectly competitive firm therefore enjoys economic profits only temporarily.

Companies in, for example, the pharmaceutical and computer software development businesses which have exclusive rights to their products claim, not surprisingly, that it is because they hope to earn economic profits that they make investments in research and development. They argue that to deny them the right to profit from their innovations by allowing others to produce their drugs or reproduce their software would drastically reduce future investment. On the other hand, customers would benefit in the short run from added competition in producing already-developed products. This is the trade-off that exists if monopolies do indeed innovate more than perfectly competitive firms; cheaper products in the short run from competition versus more new products in the long run from monopoly.[6]

A further reason why monopolies may innovate more than competitive firms stems from their ability to finance research and development. It has been claimed that when a firm has high profits, it can devote more funds to research and development. For this argument to be valid, internally generated funds must be cheaper

---

[5] Because we are considering the short-run equilibrium, we do not need the *LAC* curve. However, we do need to assume that p_c exceeds the average variable cost for the firms to want to produce.

[6] Example 8.3, which reinforces what we have said, explains why exclusive rights to innovations amount to monopoly rights to "intellectual property."

than borrowed funds. However, because internally generated funds involve an opportunity cost—they could be invested outside of the firm—profitable monopolies enjoy a financing advantage only to the extent that perfectly competitive firms are unable to borrow at a cost as low as the opportunity cost of a monopolist's internally generated funds.

While the duration of economic profits from innovating and the better availability of funds both indicate more innovation by monopolistic than by competitive industries, there are arguments pointing in the other direction. It has been argued that perfectly competitive firms may have to innovate to survive. If other firms are systematically taking the lead with cheaper production technologies, the noninnovators' economic profits will never be positive and may often be negative. All perfectly competitive firms must therefore constantly be attuned to new ideas, whereas monopolies do not feel such a need. In addition, it has been argued that the potential benefit to a perfectly competitive firm from innovating, while of short duration, may be substantial because of the vast number of customers that could be drawn from other firms, albeit temporarily. After all, in a perfectly competitive market there are numerous firms and well-informed buyers, so even the most minuscule reduction in price allowed by the discovery of a cost-saving technology could draw in many new customers.

Perfectly competitive firms may have to innovate to survive and may have a strong incentive to innovate to enjoy large gains by attracting customers from their many competitors.

Fixed Costs and Monopoly Pricing

In the case of perfect competition, we noted that changes in fixed costs have no effect on short-run equilibrium output or prices. We also noted that in the long run, prices change with fixed costs because firms enter and leave the industry and, for example, higher fixed costs cause firms to exit until the market price has been forced up sufficiently to return economic profits to zero.

In the case of monopoly, fixed costs do not affect prices or outputs in the short run and generally also have no effect in the long run. The conclusion of no effect in the short run follows from the same reasoning as in the case of perfect competition, namely, that output is determined by the equality of *marginal* cost and *marginal* revenue, and neither of these is affected by fixed costs. In the long run, changes in fixed costs do not affect prices or outputs of monopolies, provided that economic profits are made. This differs from perfect competition, because with perfect competition, entry and exit depend on the size of profits. With monopoly, it is only if the increase in fixed costs is sufficient to leave no output with an economic profit that fixed costs have an effect, and in this case the monopoly ceases to produce—a dramatic effect indeed.

Fixed costs do not affect output or prices of monopolies in the short run and do not affect them in the long run either, provided costs do not increase sufficiently to leave no output with an economic profit.

REGULATION OF NATURAL MONOPOLY*

Where there are economies of scale and a consequent tendency toward natural monopoly, a monopoly enjoys lower costs than would a number of small firms each producing part of the market supply. For this reason, monopolies are sometimes permitted to exist, although governments generally regulate their prices.

Governments often permit natural monopolies to occur so that they can take advantage of economies of scale but regulate prices so that consumers are not exploited.

* Sections and numbered items marked by an asterisk can be omitted without loss of continuity.

Example   8.3   **THE ECONOMICS OF INNOVATION**

The economics of innovation sharply reveals a trade-off between competition and monopoly. On the one hand, the promise of exclusive rights to profit from new ideas motivates the discovery of new processes and products. On the other hand, after discoveries have been made, the benefits enjoyed are greatest if unconstrained competition is permitted, reducing or even eliminating the economic profit of the innovator. Yet, without the expectation of profit, firms may not embark on the path of discovery, especially given the costs and uncertainties involved. This tension and other aspects of innovation come through clearly in the following excerpt from an article in the **Review** of the Federal Reserve Bank of St. Louis.

There are essentially two types of technological innovations: *process* innovations, which are new production processes or improvements on existing technology, and *product* innovations, which are the creation of new products or improvements on existing products. Both types of innovation are patentable. Because the economics of these two are essentially the same, the discussion focuses on production innovation for simplicity.

Intellectual property has the unusual (although not unique) property that the knowledge it contains is not depleted with use. For example, no matter how many times the formula for aspirin is used, the formula itself (that is, the knowledge contained in the patent) remains unchanged. As a result, the marginal cost of using this knowledge (e.g., the formula for aspirin) is zero. For economic

efficiency, this knowledge should be made available to anyone interested, because doing so does not diminish the stock of knowledge (or reduce the number of times aspirin can be made). Over time, however, such a policy would have some unfortunate consequences.

Generally, innovation is the result of investment expenditures on research and development (R&D). Because expenditures on R&D occur before a new product is created, the firm's decision to incur these costs involves considerable uncertainty. The expected rate of return on R&D . . . has to be at least as great as the opportunity cost of resources devoted to R&D—that is, the expected rate of return that would have been earned if the same resources allocated to R&D were invested elsewhere.

While the opportunity cost of capital is easy to determine (it is

Examples of monopolies whose prices are regulated include electric and gas utilities, local telephone companies, public transportation in many communities, water supply, and garbage collection. A central question facing a monopoly-regulating body such as a utility commission, a city council, a public transport commission, and so on is what prices to allow monopolies to charge.

Two aspects of prices in perfectly competitive markets have been considered in the setting of monopoly prices, namely, that

1. Prices equal long-run marginal costs.

2. Prices are such that economic profits are zero.

Let us examine the consequences of imposing these outcomes of perfectly competitive markets on monopolies as a means of giving consumers the benefits of economies of scale monopolies enjoy without the exploitation that occurs without price regulation.

simply the interest rate), the rate of return on R&D is more difficult to ascertain. It depends on how much R&D must be spent before a new product is discovered and developed, how much demand there will be for the new product, and how much production costs will be. The return on R&D also depends on the time the firm can produce the product exclusively and therefore earn economic profits. . . .

In the absence of government intervention, maintaining exclusive rights to an innovation for any period of time is often difficult. Given that the marginal cost of using the knowledge created by the innovation is zero, one could conclude that governments have no reason to award these rights. Without assigning exclusive rights to produce the innovation, however, the amount of time the innovating firm can produce the product is both

less certain and likely shorter; any other firm that can figure out how to make the product could also produce it without changing the knowledge associated with the innovation. For example, a firm that did not discover the formula for aspirin but, instead, was able to produce it would reduce the return earned by the innovating firm. This is true even though entry by the non-innovating firm in this market does not diminish the innovating firm's ability to produce aspirin. This reduced return on the investment in R&D appears to increase efficiency by promoting competition; however, it also reduces the number of R&D projects that will be undertaken. If, however, the government assigns property rights to innovations (and enforces them), then the amount of time the product can be produced exclusively will increase, raising the rate of return on R&D, which in turn

has a positive effect on the amount of innovation.

Of course, the world is not certain. There is no way of knowing in advance whether the R&D expenditures will produce an economically viable product. Intellectual property rights are a way of rewarding firms for incurring the risk associated with R&D by increasing the expected rate of return on R&D, thereby making more projects possible.

As long as innovation is considered desirable, assigning property rights to intellectual property is one way to encourage firms to innovate.

Source: Alison Butler, "The Trade Related Aspects of Intellectual Property: What Is at Stake?," **Review**, Federal Reserve Bank of St. Louis (November/December 1990), pp. 39–40.

The Policy of Marginal Cost Pricing*

A policy of requiring a monopoly to set price equal to long-run marginal cost does allow a natural monopoly to enjoy economies of scale but results in nothing being produced at all unless its operations are subsidized. This is illustrated in Figure 8.7.

Marginal cost pricing involves setting a price equal to marginal cost at the point the LMC curve intersects the demand curve.[7] This regulated price is labeled p_r in Figure 8.7. The marginal revenue of the regulated monopolist is p_r. That is, with the regulation to sell all units at p_r, total revenue is increased by p_r for each unit sold. With $MR = p_r$, a profit-maximizing monopoly will produce q_r, the output where $p_r = LMC$. At price p_r, quantity q_r is also the quantity demanded; the quantities produced and demanded are equal. The figure shows that some of the economies of scale are enjoyed, something that would not occur if many perfectly competitive firms were operating.

[7] We show in Chapter 11 that when *price = MC* on all products, a nation's resources are used in an efficient manner.

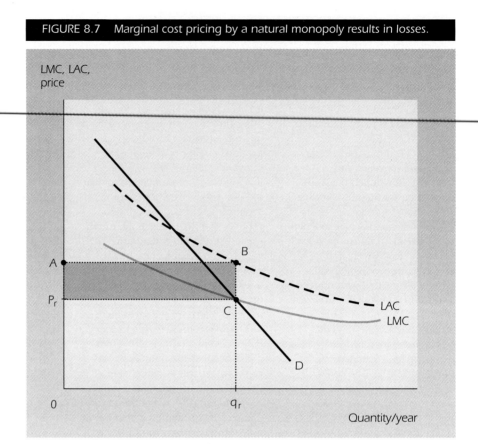

FIGURE 8.7   *Marginal cost pricing by a natural monopoly results in losses.*

Marginal cost pricing involves setting the price at the level where the long-run marginal cost curve intersects the demand curve. At this price, which is **p**ᵣ, the profit-maximizing output is **q**ᵣ. This is so because when all units are sold at price **p**ᵣ, the monopolist's marginal revenue is constant at **p**ᵣ, that is, **MR** = **p**ᵣ, and **MR** = **LMC** at **q**ᵣ. Allowing a regulated natural monopoly to exist avoids having many firms each producing small amounts and facing high **LAC**s. However, the natural monopolist sustains losses equal to the shaded area unless subsidized.

It could appear that the policy of regulating a monopoly to set price equal to long-run marginal cost achieves the best of both worlds, allowing the firm and ultimately the consumer to enjoy the benefit of lower-cost production while preventing the firm from exploiting the consumer. However, a marginal cost pricing policy leaves the monopoly with an economic loss, so only a subsidized monopoly would operate. This is seen in Figure 8.7. The figure shows that at the natural monopoly's selected output q_r, the *LAC* curve is above the price. This is an inevitable consequence of marginal cost pricing with natural monopoly because with *LAC* declining, *LMC* is below *LAC*; average cost can decline only if marginal cost is below average cost. If $p_r = LMC$ as at the monopolist's output and $LAC > LMC$, then $LAC > p_r$. Therefore, profits are below normal; total cost is area $0ABq_r$, while total revenue is the smaller area $0p_rCq_r$, so profit is below normal by the shaded area p_rABC. We see that in the case of a natural monopoly there is no incentive for a privately owned, regulated firm to produce when price is set equal to marginal cost. Consequently, the policy of marginal cost pricing, which is intended to allow scale economies to be enjoyed without an accompanying exploitation of the consumer, results in no output at all unless the monopoly is granted a per-unit subsidy with a total value given by the shaded area.

*A policy of marginal cost pricing of natural monopolies results in economic losses and therefore **no** output unless the monopoly is subsidized.*

The Policy of Average-Cost Pricing.*

The idea of average-cost pricing stems from the view that a monopoly should make a zero economic profit, just like perfectly competitive firms; as we saw in Chapter 7, if *price=LAC,* economic profit is zero.[8] The effects of the policy are illustrated in Figure 8.8.

The policy of average-cost pricing requires a monopoly to charge a price equal to the *LAC* at the point where the *LAC* curve intersects the demand curve, that is, the price p_r. At this price, the quantity demand is q_r. Furthermore, economic profit is zero because, by design, total revenue and total cost are equal, at area $0p_rAq_r$. However, while the regulatory policy ensures a zero economic profit, it leaves the price above *LMC*. This is inevitable with a natural monopoly because with *LAC* declining, *LMC < LAC,* and so if $p_r = LAC$, then $LMC < p_r$.[9]

Average-cost pricing of monopolies results in price being greater than the marginal cost.

DISCRIMINATING MONOPOLY*

When explaining the connection between price and marginal revenue earlier in this chapter, we assumed that firms charge the same price for all units sold. However, there are situations in which firms can charge different prices for different units of the same product. A monopoly that can do this is called a **discriminating monopoly.** The term **discriminating** is used only to signify that the firm charges some consumers more than others.[10]

An examination of the ticket prices paid by different passengers on an aircraft indicates that prices can differ for the same product, in this case a service (see Example 8.4). Of course, the different ticket prices are for first class, coach, advanced purchase, or charter, but these distinctions are designed at least in part to separate passengers into different categories according to what they are willing to pay. Well-known professors of economics also price discriminate, charging more to talk to the board of directors of a major corporation than to an audience

*A discriminating monopoly charges a different price for **different** units of the same good or service.*

---

[8] Regulating the price to ensure a zero economic profit requires that regulators know the size of the producer's opportunity cost, which is included in the total cost. The determination of opportunity cost must allow for the risk shareholders or other owners of the monopoly must bear. The explicit and opportunity costs are assessed at "rate hearings," where the monopoly supplier, consumer groups and other interested parties give evidence.

[9] This, as we shall show in Chapter 11, means that a nation's resources are not efficiently allocated to producing different goods and services.

[10] When an industry is supplied by several firms instead of one firm, any one of these several firms may charge different prices for different units. Such a situation involves **discriminating oligopoly.** What we say here applies to discriminating oligopoly as well as to discriminating monopoly.

FIGURE 8.8   An average-cost pricing policy for a natural monopoly results in price exceeding marginal cost.

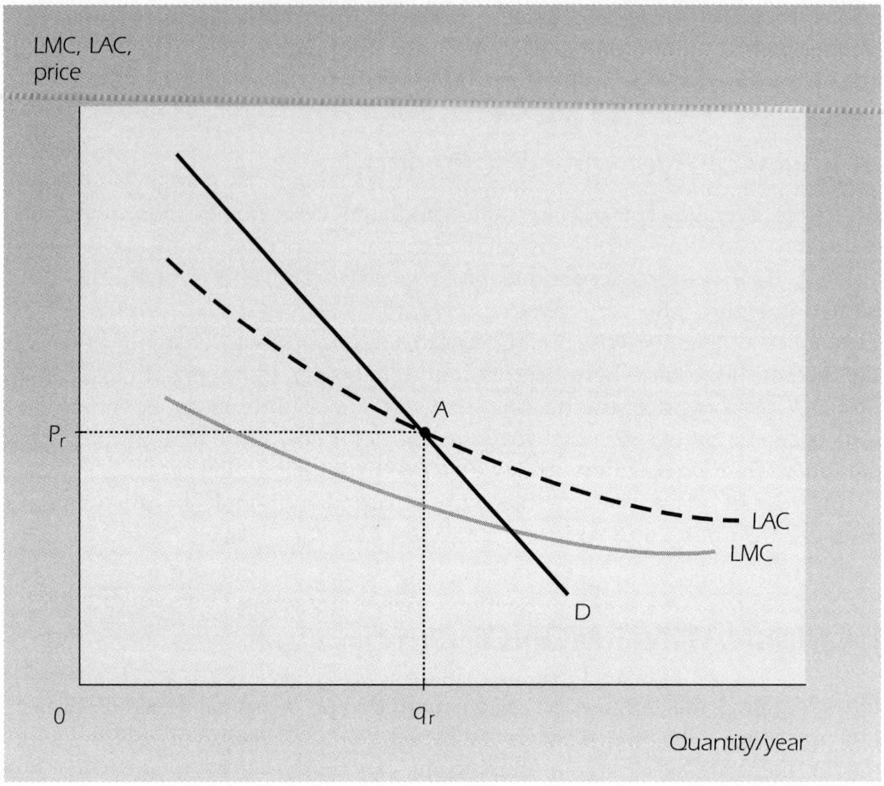

A policy of average-cost pricing involves setting the price at the level where the **LAC** curve intersects the demand curve, which is at price **p**$_r$. At this price, total revenue and total cost are both **0p**$_r$**Aq**$_r$, so economic profit is zero. However, at the quantity demanded **q**$_r$, the price exceeds **LMC**. This is an inevitable consequence of natural monopoly because with **LAC** declining, **LMC** < **LAC**.

of scholars at an academic conference. Doctors in small towns are also known to charge wealthier patients more than poorer patients for the same treatment. Department stores sometimes price discriminate by offering the same good at a lower price for customers who are sufficiently price sensitive that they will wait and suffer the crowds at a big annual sale or who are willing to hunt around the bargain basement. Price discrimination is also found at the movies, with discounts for the elderly, the young, or those willing to see movies in the afternoon. Families may be given discounts at restaurants, in motels and hotels, at museums and galleries, in amusement parks, and so on. Students may enjoy lower ticket prices than are faced by alumni at college football games, and nonstudents and non-alumni may pay even more than alumni. Bars offer cheaper drinks before 5:00 P.M. or on otherwise quiet days, car rental companies offer cheaper rates on weekends, long-distance telephone companies offer cheaper calls during nonbusiness hours, electric

Example 8.4

THE COST OF PRICE DISCRIMINATION

The extent to which a firm can charge different prices is limited by the administration costs of such a pricing policy and by the cheating that occurs. As the following article from **The New York Times** *explains, administration costs and cheating were behind a move by American Airlines in 1992 to reduce the number of different fares charged on its routes by 86%.*

American Airlines, the nation's largest carrier, said yesterday that it would scrap the convoluted system of airline fares that has evolved over the last decade. It announced a simplified system that includes only four kinds of fares instead of 16, and will mean lower prices for most business and leisure travelers. . . .

Under the new system, American will offer only a first-class fare, a coach fare that can be bought until flight time, and two discount fares, one requiring purchase 21 days in advance of travel and another requiring purchase seven days in advance.

In simplifying its fare system, American is eliminating all but 70,000 of the 500,000 fares in its computerized reservation system—an 86% drop. The resulting reduction in administrative burden will be so large that the carrier expects to save $25 million annually by reassigning about 600 employees to other tasks.

"The whole fares system has become chaotic, inflexible, illogical and unfair," Robert L. Crandall, American's chairman and president, said in announcing the new fares in a news conference in New York. "The system just has not been working. . . ."

The new system cuts a wide swath through the thicket of air fares by eliminating many discounts—some discreetly offered to companies with many employees—and other special fares, including those for Government employees, passengers bound for conventions and members of the armed forces. This way, Mr. Crandall said, "Every customer can get the best price available."

The new system should also deter cheating by crafty travelers who beat the old system through tricks like buying two steeply discounted tickets that together amount to less than an unrestricted fare and using half of each ticket. . . .

Mr. Crandall said American had been spurred by a litany of complaints from business travelers, who disliked the high fares, and leisure travelers, who were frustrated by the many restrictions. He cited a difference of $1166 in the highest and lowest current round-trip transcontinental fare. . . .

Don Carty, American's executive vice president and chief financial officer, said that 10% of American's excursion travel "is probably people gaming us"—that is, circumventing the rules applicable to discount tickets. But the fault, he said, "is simply because of how aberrant the system is. . . ."

While he did not rule out the possibility that the industry could again begin offering an array of special fares, he said that now, having learned that lesson, "hopefully we won't repeat it."

POSTSCRIPT
Six months after introducing its new, simplified fare structure, American Airlines was forced to admit the program had not been successful, and the airline resorted to a larger variety of fares than it had planned. This suggests that the use of price discrimination is beneficial to firms; experiments with alternatives that fail and lead back to previously tried methods provide a test of what works.

Sources: Edwin McDowell, "American Air Cuts Most Fares in Simplification of Rate System," **The New York Times**, April 10, 1992, pp. A1, C3. Copyright © 1992 by The New York Times Company. Reprinted by permission. Julie Schmit, "American Says Fare Structure Failed," **USA Today**, October 12, 1992, p. 1.

power companies charge lower rates to price-sensitive industrial users, and railways charge different firms different freight charges for the same distance.

In order for a monopoly to use price discrimination effectively, it is necessary to be able to identify how much satisfaction different consumers, or at least different classifiable groups of consumers, obtain from a product. Price discrimination also requires that consumers cannot cheat by pretending to attach a lower value to the product than they do. Even when consumers can be identified as to the price they would pay, there is an incentive for buyers to ask others who are charged a lower price to do their shopping. Hence price discrimination cannot be practiced with items that can be exchanged. This explains why the conditions for successful price discrimination are most likely to be found in the case of services, such as medical services, sports events, theaters, motels, restaurants, air travel, and railway freight.

When a discriminating monopolist can sell every unit at the maximum price somebody is prepared to pay for that unit, the firm is a **perfectly discriminating monopolist.** The situation of a perfectly discriminating monopolist selling freight services on a railway is shown in Figure 8.9.

Suppose that by knowing the needs of all the companies that have freight to be moved, the railway knows the maximum amount each would pay per ton of freight moved per 100 miles. Suppose no company would pay more than $100. Therefore, above $100, the quantity demanded is zero. Suppose that one company would be willing to pay $100 for 1 ton of freight. This is illustrated by point A in Figure 8.9, which shows 1 ton at the price $100. Therefore, the price and marginal revenue for the first ton are $100.

Suppose that another company would be willing to pay $90, but not more, for moving 1 ton of freight. This is illustrated by point B, which shows a second ton being shipped at $90. We assume that the first company is still paying $100, even though the second pays $90; otherwise, the situation is the same for a regular monopoly, not a perfectly discriminating monopoly. With the first company still paying $100, the marginal revenue from the second ton is the price paid, $90; unlike the case of a nondiscriminating firm, no revenue is lost from the previous ton. Point C shows a third company willing to pay $80, point D a fourth company willing to pay $70, and so on. The entire demand curve can be constructed this way.[11] Because selling another unit does not require a reduction in the price of previously sold units, the marginal revenue of each ton equals the price paid. Since the price paid for each ton carried is given from the demand curve, the marginal revenue curve is the same as the demand curve.

Profits are always maximized by producing the output at which $MC=MR$. In Figure 8.10, which shows the demand curve and long-run cost curves of a discriminating monopolist, this means producing output q_{dm}. This is the same output as would be produced if instead of being supplied by the perfectly discriminating monopolist the industry had been perfectly competitive. This is so because in a perfectly competitive industry the supply curve is the sum of the LMC curves, and if this sum is the curve LMC in Figure 8.10, it is intersected by the demand curve at output q_{dm}. In the case of perfect competition, the market price is p_c, which is where the supply curve for perfect competition LMC intersects the demand curve.

Price discrimination is most common in the sale of services.

A perfectly discriminating monopolist charges a different price for each unit of the same good or service sold.

The demand curve facing a perfectly discriminating monopolist is also the MR curve.

---

[11] The curve joining points A, B, C, and D in Figure 8.9 is really an approximation of the steps that exist if freight is moved in 1-ton minimum amounts. See Question 11.

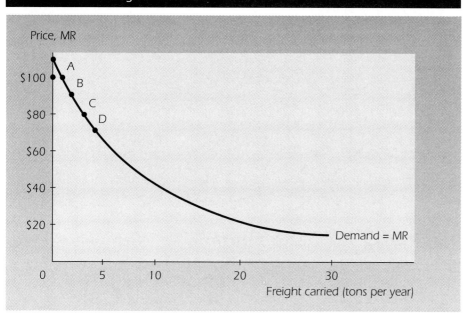

FIGURE 8.9   The perfectly discriminating monopolist's demand curve is also the marginal revenue curve.

No company is willing to pay more than $100 for 1 ton of freight to be moved. Therefore, the quantity demanded above $100 per ton is zero. One company is willing to pay $100. Therefore, the quantity of freight carried at $100 per ton is 1 ton, as shown by point **A**. A second company is willing to pay $90, so 2 tons are shipped at $90, with the first company still paying $100. Similarly, a third company pays $80, while the first two still pay $100 and $90, and so on. The marginal revenue from the first ton is $100, the price paid. The marginal revenue from the second ton is $90, since no revenue is lost on the first ton. That is, the marginal revenue of the second ton is also the price paid. The same goes for all freight carried. Because nothing is lost on previous freight when an additional ton is moved by lowering the price, the demand curve is also the marginal revenue curve.

The price p_c is paid by all customers of a perfectly competitive industry but only by the last customer of the perfectly discriminating monopolist; all other customers pay higher prices than the last customer to the discriminating monopolist. That is, consumers collectively pay more to a discriminating monopolist than they would to perfectly competitive firms for the same amount of output, assuming that costs and demands are the same.

The total revenue collected by charging the maximum that would be paid for each unit is given by the area under the demand curve up to the amount sold. This is the sum of the amounts that are collected on each unit. For example, in Figure 8.9 the total revenue from carrying 4 tons of freight for 100 miles is $340 (or $100 + $90 + $80 + $70), which in the area under the demand curve up to 4 on the horizontal axis. Similarly, at output q_{dm} in Figure 8.10, the discriminating monopolist's total revenue is area $0ABq_{dm}$. This is larger than the total revenue of a

A perfectly discriminating monopolist produces the *same* output as would be produced if an industry were perfectly competitive. Consumers collectively pay more to a discriminating monopolist than they would to perfectly competitive firms for this output.

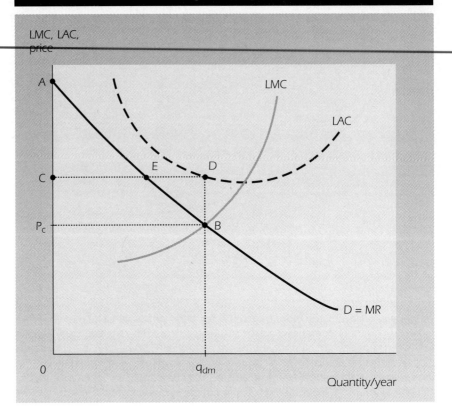

FIGURE 8.10   A discriminating monopolist may provide a good or service that would not be provided in a perfectly competitive or a nondiscriminating monopoly situation.

A perfectly discriminating monopolist can charge the maximum amount a buyer would pay for each unit. Therefore, a perfectly discriminating monopolist enjoys a total revenue equal to the area beneath the demand curve. Marginal revenue for each unit is the price charged for that unit, since there is no need to reduce prices on other units. Therefore, the **MR** curve is the same as the demand curve. The profit-maximizing output, which is where marginal cost equals marginal revenue, is therefore where the **LMC** curve intersects the demand curve. This output, q_{dm}, is the same as would result from perfect competition, since it is the output at which the demand curve intersects the perfectly competitive supply curve **LMC**. When the **LAC** curve is everywhere above the demand curve, there is no output for a perfectly competitive industry or a nondiscriminating monopolist which avoids losses. Therefore, the good or service would not be provided. However, if the discriminating monopolist's total revenue, given by area **0ABq**$_{dm}$, exceeds total cost, given by area **0CDq**$_{dm}$, the discriminating monopolist will provide the good or service.

nondiscriminating firm which must lower the price on all units to sell one more unit; a nondiscriminating firm selling q_{dm} at p_c has a total revenue of area $0p_cBq_{dm}$.

In Figure 8.10, the *LAC* curve is everywhere above the demand curve. Therefore, at no output can profits be made by a firm that charges the same price on all units. For example, as we have just seen, at output q_{dm}, the total revenue is area $0p_cBq_{dm}$; this is the price p_c times the quantity sold q_{dm}. The total cost of q_{dm} is the larger area $0CDq_{dm}$; this is the *LAC* times the quantity produced q_{dm}. Inspection of Figure 8.10 shows that there is no output at which a nondiscriminating firm can avoid losses; *LAC* is everywhere above the demand curve. Therefore, the product would not be supplied by a nondiscriminating firm.

While a nondiscriminating firm would not produce the product in the conditions described by Figure 8.10, a perfectly discriminating monopolist would. For the perfectly discriminating monopolist, total revenue at the profit-maximizing output of q_{dm} is the area under the demand curve up to q_{dm}, that is, area $0ABq_{dm}$. In Figure 8.10, this exceeds the total cost at output q_{dm}, which is area $0CDq_{dm}$. (We know that area $0ABq_{dm}$ exceeds $0CDq_{dm}$ because area $0CEBq_{dm}$ is common to both areas and area *CAE* exceeds area *EDB*.) Therefore, the perfectly discriminating monopolist makes a profit. Consequently, in this example it pays for a perfectly discriminating monopolist to provide the product, but it would not pay a nondiscriminating firm to provide it. When the good or service produced is deemed to be something that *should* be provided, such as medical services in a rural area, rail or air service to remote places, college theater, college sports, and so on, it may be viewed as preferable to allow discriminating monopoly than to insist on competition and have no product provided.[12]

A perfectly discriminating monopolist may provide a good or service that would not be provided by a firm that could not charge different prices on different units.

Perfectly discriminating monopoly where *everybody* pays a different price is not found in practice, but rather we do frequently find a limited number of different prices, as on an airline, at a college football game, in museums, hotels, movie theaters, and so on. Even when a monopoly can charge only a limited number of prices rather than perfectly price discriminate, it may still be feasible for the discriminating monopolist to function where nondiscriminating firms would not, and this may make the situation acceptable when it is deemed worthwhile to provide the good or service.

[12] Whether a product "should" be provided is a normative question of public choice.

THE NATURAL OBJECTIVE OF MONOPOLY

Milton Friedman has written, "The business-man is in favor of free enterprise for everyone else, but not for himself. . . ."[13] Indeed, the pursuit of monopolistic advantage is the purpose of a large part of business and nature. Business-people in particular promote the ideal of competition while at the same time trying hard to restrict it in the area of their own enterprise. Similarly, in politics, science, marketing, and organized religion, the objective is to secure and exploit a monopoly of ideas even though the politicians, scientists, and others would readily espouse the virtues of free thought and choice.

As we have seen, with free entry in perfectly competitive markets, economic profits are zero in

---

[13] Milton Friedman, **An Economist's Protest: Columns in Political Economy** (Glen Ridge, N.J.: Thomas Horton and Co., 1972), p. 203.

the long run. The main goal of business is, however, to make economic profit and to maintain such profit. One way to achieve this is to gain a monopoly from the development or discovery of a new product, one that no other firm can offer. This is the principal pursuit of pharmaceutical companies, computer software developers, and others in areas where monopolistic advantage can be achieved by means of successful research and development. Although it is commonly believed that discovery is an accident, in reality it is very often the pursuit of profit that is the engine of scientific breakthroughs. So many comforts and medical miracles that have enriched and lengthened our lives have come from the efforts of firms to achieve a monopoly that it can be said that the supply of new ideas depends positively on the profits that may be enjoyed. Even university-based research is frequently based on a pursuit of monopoly profit, with most leading universities having specialized departments to register, protect, and exploit discoveries.

Even in the area of basic research, where there is no obvious profit to new discovery, it could be claimed that the passion of researchers is to claim a monopoly to the discovery of new ideas. The most noble scientist is usually at least in part driven by a desire to associate his or her name with a monopoly claim to a new discovery, whether this be a new supernova in the heavens, a comet, a new form of microorganism, or a new interpretation of history or human behavior.

Where technological monopoly is not achievable, business activity is still often directed by an attempt to create the perception in consumers' minds that a product is different and to profit from this perception. This is the goal of marketing, where through advertising, packaging, and the association of a desirable lifestyle with the consumption of a particular product, firms try to create a downward-sloping demand curve and to maintain this demand by building customer loyalty or a habit of buying the product.

Monopoly is associated with geography. This is true because geography is the study of all aspects of space, and one effect of space is to create **local monopolies** or, at least, **overlapping monopolies**; with it being costly to travel to another source of supply of a product, and with the availability of information on price and quality diminishing with distance, firms such as local grocery stores and gas stations frequently enjoy economic profits.

Historically, monopolies have had political origins. For example, during the age of exploitation, royal charters were granted for the exclusive right to pursue profit abroad. A substantial amount of European discovery, including that of the Americas, India, the South Seas, and China, involved the pursuit of profit from monopolies granted by the British and French crowns or other political authorities. The French, Dutch, and British East India companies, the Hudson Bay Company, and the South Sea Company are examples.

A substantial amount of European discovery, including that of the Americas, India, the South Seas, and China, involved the pursuit of profit from monopolies granted by the British and French crowns or other political authorities.

Even today, some monopolies have political origins. Utilities with exclusive rights to deliver local telephone services, electricity, water, and gas are granted by political bodies, and the process of granting and regulating these monopolies is studied in political science and in the business fields of finance and accounting. In Great Britain, **royal warrants** are still granted or sold, although today they give their holders the right to declare that they are the suppliers to a member of the Royal Family rather than an exclusive monopoly on a product. Nevertheless, they are an attempt to obtain some monopoly power via an endorsement and therefore are little different from endorsements by sports figures and other celebrities, which are also attempts to gain monopoly power by giving products unique attributes.

Political parties may be viewed as striving to achieve monopoly in the sense that in the political systems in most Western democracies, the party with the most seats in Parliament or the Electoral College achieves a monopoly in the running of the country. However, this may well be tempered, as in the United States, by important checks and balances.

In the sphere of international relations, we may view the objective of the superpowers as attempting to achieve a monopoly of influence. With there being one main player in the field, some political scientists have in fact applied arguments developed in the context of monopoly to the area of international relations.

Biologic models of territoriality, which have been built to explain the sizes of territories claimed by certain species and the methods used to protect these territories, can in principle be thought of as monopoly models. What a territorial animal is trying to do is achieve monopoly control in a particular location in order to exploit the food resources or supply of mates the area provides. Of course, there is often fierce fighting associated with the protection of territory, as there usually is in economic monopolies; other firms are always trying to penetrate a market, imitate a product, and so on, with the courts often busy trying to decide when legal monopoly rights have been violated. That is, even the law has connections to monopoly. Indeed, the vast legal and legislative apparatus associated with **cartels** is designed to consider cases involving the granting and violation of monopoly rights.

There is a paradigm in ecology that is directly related to the issue of monopoly. **Gause's exclusion principle** states that within ecologic systems where species fill the same niche, eventually only one of the species survives. This is parallel to the conclusion in economics about the eventual equilibrium where there is a natural monopoly. Indeed, with the use of the term **natural** in economics, the biologic and economic principles may well be referred to by the same name. Both are **natural** monopolies.

SUMMARY

1. A monopoly is an industry with only one supplier.

2. Natural monopolies emerge where long-run average cost declines over a range of output that is large relative to market demand. This allows the largest firm to enjoy the lowest cost and thereby to squeeze out smaller firms.

3. Natural monopolies offer the advantage of lower costs of production than would be faced by a number of competing firms. However, this advantage must be set against the drawback of a monopoly using its market power to earn higher profits from consumers.

4. Monopolies can result from economies of scale, licenses and patents, control over a unique resource, and control over a cheap production technology. However, few firms face no competition at all.

5. The demand curve facing a monopolist is the market demand curve and is hence downward-sloping. This means that $MR < price$, and therefore, at the profit-maximizing output where $MR = MC$, for monopolies $MC < price$.

6. If costs of production and demand are the same for a monopolist as for a group of competitive firms, the price is lower and the output higher with perfect competition than with monopoly.

7. There is no supply curve for the product of a monopolist because output can be determined only in conjunction with the demand curve.

8. Monopolists do not produce the output at which long-run average cost is at a minimum.

9. Short-run costs for a monopoly might be lower than for a group of competitive firms when there are indivisible inputs that smaller firms cannot use efficiently. Monopoly costs can exceed those facing a collection of perfectly competitive firms because there is less pressure for a monopoly to keep costs down.

10. Long-run costs may differ between monopoly and perfect competition because of differences in the incentive and ability to innovate.

11. Whereas fixed costs affect output and price in perfect competition in the long run but not the short run, with monopoly fixed costs have no effect in either the short run or the long run unless they cause losses.

12.* Requiring natural monopolies to set prices equal to the marginal cost allows consumers to benefit from scale economies, but marginal cost pricing causes losses unless operations are subsidized. The policy of regulating monopolies to set prices equal to average cost ensures a zero economic profit but results in $price > LMC$.

13.* A discriminating monopolist can charge more than one price for the same item, and a perfectly discriminating monopolist can charge a different price for every unit sold. For the perfectly discriminating monopolist, the MR curve is the demand curve.

14.* For a monopoly to price discriminate, different customers or groups of customers must be identified as to how much they are prepared to pay. They also must be unable to resell the product among themselves.

15.* A discriminating monopolist may provide a good or service that would not be provided by a nondiscriminating firm.

QUESTIONS AND PROBLEMS

1. Why doesn't the telephone company have an absolute monopoly?

2. The following table gives sales projections of a store selling bikes in a small town for different prices it might charge.

PRICE	BIKES SOLD PER MONTH
$250	18
245	19
240	20
235	21
230	22
225	23
220	24

a. Calculate MR at each output.

b. Assuming that the cost to the store of each bike from the supplier—the MC of the store—is $145, what price should the store charge?

3. Draw the MR "curve" for perfectly elastic demand.

4. By controlling the free movement of labor into an industry or profession, can a trade union or professional association behave as a monopoly?

5. Why can we talk of supply curves of products of perfectly competitive industries but not of the products of monopolies?

6. When there are positive economic profits from unregulated monopoly, could a policy of allowing competitive bidding for the right to run the monopoly return profits to zero?

7. What are the pros and cons of patents?

8. What considerations do you think are relevant in "rate hearings" for public utilities? (Rate hearings occur when public utilities apply to increase their charges for telephone service, electric power, and so on.)

9. Could "dumping," which means selling in a foreign market at a price below the price charged at home, be used by a firm to maintain or obtain a monopoly in a foreign country? Could a similar practice of selling periodically at a very low price be used to maintain a monopoly in a domestic setting?

10. What are the ethical implications of a single pharmaceutical company, such as the supplier of the AIDS drug AZT, behaving as a monopoly?

11.* The demand curve in Figure 8.9 which results from joining points A, B, C, and D is a smooth version of the actual demand curve, which involves steps. Can you draw the stepped curve?

12.* Is it likely to make a major difference to whether a good or service is provided that a price-discriminating monopolist can charge only several different prices rather than a different price to every buyer?

13.* Can discount coupons on laundry detergent, shampoo, and so on be considered a form of price discrimination because they mean lower prices for price-sensitive customers?

14.* Why is it typically easier to price discriminate in the sale of services than in the sale of goods?

15.* Could scholarships and stipends be used to price discriminate in setting college tuition charges?

. . . .
. . . .
. . . .
. . . .
. . . .
. . . . . . Imperfect Competition
. . . .
. . . .

Nothing is illegal if a hundred businessmen decide to do it.

Andrew Young

Key Concepts

Oligopoly; natural oligopoly; cartel formation and instability; rivals' reactions to price and output; Cournot equilibrium; Bertrand equilibrium; price wars; monopolistic competition; agency problem; sales maximization versus profit maximization; profit maximization and alternative ownership; "as if" principle; organizational theory of the firm; asymmetric information and the market for "lemons"; moral hazard

Perfect competition and monopoly are two ends of a spectrum, with a vast number of actual market situations in between. This chapter discusses two intermediate forms of market structure, **oligopoly** and **monopolistic competition.** Both are referred to as **imperfect competition** because they exhibit some aspects of competitive markets but at the same time violate some of the assumptions of perfect competition. After considering the effect of the market imperfections present in oligopoly and monopolistic competition, the chapter examines imperfections related to information. As we shall see, the behavior of firms and markets may be influenced significantly by the availability of information on revenues, costs, and product quality.

OLIGOPOLY

The Nature and Causes of Oligopoly

An oligopoly occurs
when a market is
supplied by sufficiently
few firms that each firm
must consider the
reactions of other firms
to changes in its
behavior.

An **oligopoly** is a market in which there are sufficiently few firms that each firm must consider how the others will react to changes in its own output, price, or other strategic variables.[1] The need to take other firms' reactions into account makes oligopoly different from monopoly, where there are no other firms to worry about, and perfect competition, where there are so many firms that an individual firm's behavior does not elicit a response from the others.

A large number of markets can be characterized as oligopolies, with relatively few firms each having to consider how the others would respond if, for example, it was to reduce prices. U.S. meat packing is an oligopoly, with three firms, IBP, Inc., Excel, Inc., and Conagra, supplying between them nearly three-quarters of the meat-packing market. The U.S. airline market has become oligopolistic with the three largest carriers, United, American, and Delta, controlling nearly half the market. The same trend to oligopoly also has occurred in U.S. railroads, with seven companies moving almost all the freight. Another oligopoly is the U.S. retail coffee market, where three giant firms, General Foods (selling Maxwell House and Sanka), Procter and Gamble (selling Folgers), and Nestlé (selling Nescafé and Hills Brothers), are responsible for more than 80% of retail sales. Passenger aircraft manufacturing is also an oligopoly, with Boeing, Lockheed, and McDonnell-Douglas supplying a dominant share of the market. Other industries in the United States that are oligopolies include long-distance telephone communications, television networks, steel, cigarettes, automobile and trunk rentals, breakfast cereals, courier services, and automobile manufacturing. In all these cases each of the relatively few firms pays close attention to the possible response of the other firms to a change in price, output, and other strategic variables.

Many oligopolies have arisen from **takeovers** and **mergers** occurring in what originally were markets with a large number of firms. For example, the U.S. and Canadian airline markets became more **concentrated**—meaning being controlled by fewer firms—as the result of large companies buying smaller ones, that is, from takeovers, as well as from mergers of different carriers.

Oligopolies are caused by the same factors as are monopolies. In particular, they may result from the granting of a limited number of licenses, as with banking and broadcasting in many countries. Oligopolies also result from high costs of entering a market, as with passenger aircraft manufacturing, automobile production, and so on. When oligopolies result naturally as a result of economies of scale, they are known, not surprisingly, as **natural oligopolies.**

The situation supporting the emergence of natural oligopolies from economies of scale is illustrated in part (b) of Figure 9.1. This situation is compared to that supporting natural monopoly, part (a), and to that supporting perfect competition, part (c). The type of market that will emerge naturally is seen to depend on the output at which the minimum *LAC* occurs relative to market demand. When the minimum *LAC* occurs at a very small output relative to market demand, as in part

---

[1] As we explain in the Crossing Bridges section, oligopolistic firms may need to judge other firms' reactions to a broad range of strategic variables, including changes in design, market focus, quality, and product warranty.

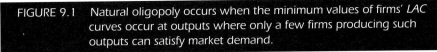

FIGURE 9.1   Natural oligopoly occurs when the minimum values of firms' *LAC* curves occur at outputs where only a few firms producing such outputs can satisfy market demand.

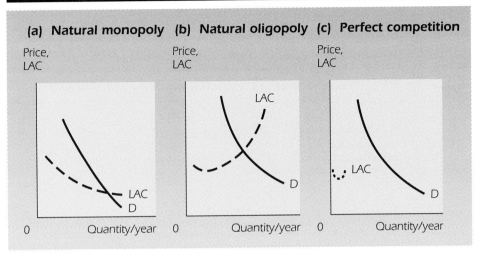

(a) Natural monopoly   (b) Natural oligopoly   (c) Perfect competition

Natural oligopoly occurs when the minimum long-run average cost occurs at an output where only a few firms, each producing at or about this output, would be able to supply the market. The minimum **LAC** therefore occurs somewhere between that which causes natural monopoly and that which would allow perfect competition.

(c) of Figure 9.1, the market is likely to be perfectly competitive. When the minimum *LAC* occurs at an output where only a few firms producing this output can satisfy market demand, as in part (b) of Figure 9.1, oligopoly is more likely to be observed than either monopoly or perfect competition. This is so because an individual firm is unlikely to supply the entire market at a price at which no other firm will want to enter, but a few firms could.

Cartels, Legislation, and Member Motivations

When there are a limited number of suppliers, there is an incentive to form a **cartel.** A cartel is an arrangement among firms to reduce competition among themselves and behave like a monopoly, sharing the greater profits a monopoly would enjoy. As Example 9.1 explains, cartels have been formed in the markets for oil, tin, nickel, coffee, cocoa, natural rubber, potash and even nutmeg. For a cartel to achieve the profit a monopoly would enjoy, it is necessary to determine the quantity a monopoly would produce and divide this quantity between cartel members by giving each a **production quota.** While there is a strong incentive to do this so as to increase members' profits, cartels are intrinsically unstable because at the production level a monopolist would choose and with this divided between members, each member of the cartel would like to produce more than it is allocated. That is, there is an incentive to reach agreement to reduce production but also an incentive for each cartel member to take advantage of the situation and produce more than its production quota.

A cartel is an arrangement of firms to reduce competition among themselves and to behave like a monopoly. Cartels are intrinsically unstable because individual members want to produce more than their production quotas.

Example 9.1

CARTELS: FROM OIL TO NUTMEG

The profit from cartels has resulted in many attempts by producers to try to restrict competition, but as the following article from **The New York Times** *explains, cartels have rarely been successful.*

One of the basic tenets of economics, related to supply and demand, is that producers will always try to control the prices of their products. A second tenet holds that they will almost always fail.

Even before the Organization of Petroleum Exporting Countries in the last decade forced a 15-fold increase in the price of oil, suppliers of tin, nickel, coffee, cocoa and natural rubber were flexing market muscle, trying to control prices.

Prodded by OPEC's successes, these and other producers—of such commodities as potash, bauxite and even nutmeg—formed alliances to control supplies to influence prices. There was even talk of a "banana OPEC," based in Central America.

Encouragement came from the United Nations Conference on Trade and Development, a body chiefly representing poor countries, which are the source of most commodities. The conference's leaders saw higher prices as a way to improve the incomes of third world countries and to achieve what they said was the urgent need for global redistribution of wealth.

In the case of tin, cocoa, natural rubber and coffee, some industrialized countries actually joined the producing countries in pacts aimed as assuring adequate supplies at remunerative prices for producers. Japan, Western Europe and even free market–oriented American administrations . . . still participate in some of the pacts, arguing that consumers as well as producers may be hurt by volatility. But most of the market alliances have encountered difficult times.

The London-based International Tin Agreement collapsed in 1985. Coffee exporters have tried to curb production to prop up prices, but neither China, a new producer, nor Brazil, an old producer, will cooperate. Instead, they are expanding both coffee production and exports.

The International Bauxite Association, founded by Jamaica, achieved limited results for a few years in the last decade, but because other producers, notably Brazil, demurred, the group foundered. It has continued as a research group.

Efforts to fix prices for many other commodities—potash, lead, zinc, copper, nickel, sugar, cotton, timber, jute—have also failed. The principal reason for such failures is the adequacy of supplies and availability of substitutes.

Even the 13 members of OPEC have had to try to cope with market reverses and struggle to continue as a power in the world oil market. They have just taken the unusual step of trying to win agreements on production limits from seven oil-exporting nations that are not members. . . .

"Cartels sow the seeds of their own destruction by driving prices to levels that cause new increases of output from new sources," said C. Fred Bergsten, director of the

---

The forces encouraging firms to attempt to form a cartel, but also tending to pull it apart, are illustrated in Figure 9.2. In part (a) we show the price p_c and the output q_c for a market if it were perfectly competitive. This price and output are those where the demand curve intersects the supply curve and where the supply curve is the horizontal sum of the firms' MC curves. In part (b) we show that at the perfectly competitive price p_c, individual firms will maximize profits by producing q_1, where $p_c = MC$. With price equal to average cost AC at this output, firms make normal profits and so the market is in equilibrium.

If the firms are successful in forming a cartel and in keeping their aggregate output at the monopoly level, they will set output to maximize their collective profit, that is, at the output where $MR = \Sigma MC$. This is so because by acting as a monopoly, the cartel will view its marginal cost curve as ΣMC and will know that its MR curve is below the demand curve. That is, the cartel will restrict aggregate output to q_m. This output will fetch a price p_m. Each firm's share of the cartel's output is assumed to be q_2. At this output, the profit per unit produced is distance TS,

Institute for International Economics. "Over the shorter periods cartels in some products can work, and even have done so spectacularly. But over the long term they fail."

The one big exception is the successful de Beers diamond cartel, which has operated through this century as the single major buyer of most of the world's diamonds. De Beers, based in South Africa, seems to have worked relatively smoothly over the years. Even the Soviet Union, the second largest diamond exporter in the world after South Africa, is apparently pleased. For the last quarter century, Moscow has sold all of its diamonds through the de Beers cartel.

De Beers, which buys diamonds from mines in South Africa, Namibia and most other regions of the world, is technically a monopsonist, or the single buyer for a commodity. Then it turns around with almost absolute market control to become the single principal source of supply.

"It works extraordinarily well," said Phillip K. Verleger, a former Yale professor who is now a

consultant on international cartel economics. "As new mines come on, de Beers manages to find them sufficient market share so that they elect to continue selling their production to de Beers and accepting the de Beers production control system rather than go it alone."

Dr. Verleger recalled that several years ago Tanzania decided to go its own way on diamonds, but paid dearly. De Beers reacted by depressing prices for the quality of stones sold by Tanzania. Soon afterward, a duly chastened Tanzania returned to the syndicate. . . .

While diamonds are the world's greatest cartel, producers of a few other commodities have also achieved successes.

One success is in natural rubber, which is more heat-and-tear-resistant than synthetic rubber and which is used for the condoms and rubber gloves now in special demand because of the AIDS epidemic. The International Natural Rubber Organization, based in Malaysia, operates with a buffer stock of

rubber that it either sells from or adds to in efforts to smooth out market prices.

For successful price intervention, obviously, the fewer the producers of a commodity the better. Indonesia and Grenada, the tiniest country of the Western Hemisphere, produce 98 percent of the world's nutmeg. Now the Indonesian Nutmeg Association and the Grenada Cooperative Nutmeg Association have formally entered into price and production agreements to form a nutmeg cartel. Eggnog drinkers need not fret, however. The Cartel has no plans to force prices higher. What they want, they say, is "no price cutting."

Source: Clyde H. Farnsworth, "OPEC Isn't the Only Cartel that Couldn't," **The New York Times,** April 24, 1988, p. E3. Copyright © 1988 by The New York Times Company. Reprinted by permission.

the difference between the price received p_m and the average cost. With TS profit per unit and q_2 units produced and sold, the individual firms' profits are given by area $p_m TSR$.

Even though each individual firm's profit with a cartel is area $p_m TSR$ versus no economic profit under perfect competition, an individual firm can do better than earn area $p_m TSR$ if it **defects** from the cartel, that is, if it cheats. At the cartel price of p_m, the individual firm would maximize its profits by producing q_3, the output at which $p_m = MC$. The per-unit profit the firm enjoys at this output is VW, which is the difference between the price received and the average cost. The firm's profit is the per-unit profit VW multiplied by the number of units sold q_3. This profit is equal to the area $p_m VWZ$, which is larger than the profit earned as part of the cartel; area $p_m VWZ$ is larger than area $p_m TSR$.

While an individual firm can do better by defecting from the cartel, this is not feasible for all firms collectively. If a large number of firms violate their production quotas, the market price declines and so do profits. That is, there is a **paradox of**

While an *individual* firm can make even larger profits by defecting from a cartel, if *many* firms defect, all make smaller profits than with a cartel. This is the common tension in cartels.

The competitive equilibrium market price and quantity are p_c and q_c, where $D = S$. At p_c, individual firms produce q_1 and have zero economic profits. An effective cartel can maximize profits for its members as a whole by restricting output to q_m, and charging p_m, that is, by producing where $MR = \Sigma MC$. (Recall that the sum of MC curves is the cartel's MC curve.) With each firm producing its quota of q_2, profits for each cartel member are area $p_m TSR$. However, at the cartel price p_m, individual firms would rather produce q_3, where $p_m = MC$. Profits are then area $p_m VWZ$. If a number of firms violate the cartel, the market price will decline toward that of the perfectly competitive equilibrium, and profits will fall.

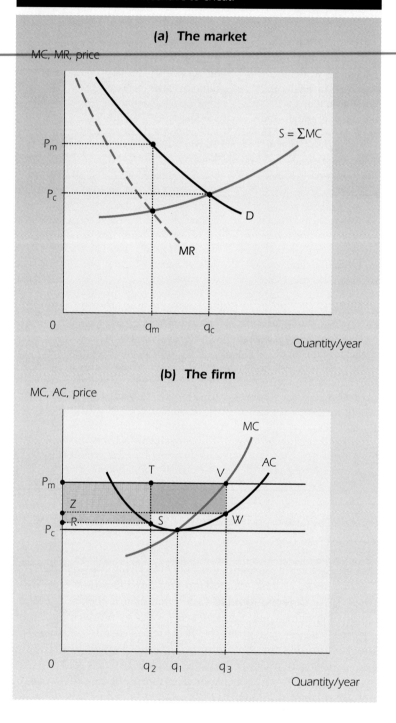

FIGURE 9.2   While there is an incentive for oligopolistic firms to form a cartel to increase profits, each cartel member has an incentive to cheat.

composition; what increases profits for each individual firm reduces profits for firms as a whole. This is the common tension that is always present in cartels; each member wants the *other* members to restrict output.

The instability of cartels resulting from the mutual incentive to comply but individual incentive not to comply has been vividly revealed in the experience of the **Organization of Petroleum Exporting Countries (OPEC).** As indicated in Figure 9.3, by restricting production during 1978–1979, OPEC managed to force prices up, helped partly by strong markets and political ties among its most important members.[2] However, as more and more oil was supplied by nonmembers at the high cartel prices, and as oil demand was restrained by alternative sources of energy and conservation, the cartel began to crack. Specifically, after 1980, several members exceeded their quota ceilings, damaging the mutual interest of the cartel members out of their separate self-interest. The experience of OPEC makes it supremely clear that for a cartel to work, it must have a means of enforcing member compliance on quota allocation and control all or most of market supply. As Example 9.1 explains, the same internal tension that has weakened OPEC has brought an end to the International Tin Agreement and the International Bauxite Agreement.

International cartels such as OPEC and the Tin and Bauxite Agreements are supranational bodies that can avoid the legislation aimed at colluding companies that exists in the United States (see Example 8.2 on page 212) and many other nations. The legislation goes variously under the names of **antimonopoly, antitrust, anticollusion, anticombine,** and **anticartel laws.** These laws are needed because, despite the inner tensions, there remains a strong incentive for oligopolists to form cartels to earn monopoly-type profits. The enforcement of anticartel legislation can be made very difficult by the informal and hidden procedures for colluding. These procedures make it hard to prove collusion has taken place. Rarely, if ever, is there a paper trail to follow, showing agreements to fix prices or reduce output. Firms having equal prices may, for example, claim that this is the result of competitive pressures; in perfectly competitive markets, firms charge the same price, just as they might in a cartel. Even different prices of different producers may hide the presence of a cartel; firms may take turns offering the lowest cartel price in, for example, bidding for government contracts. Collusion may involve no more than a tacit convention not to cut prices or increase output; each member appreciates the mutual gain from maintaining prices and restricting supply and knows that if it were to try to take advantage of other producers, this would trigger higher output and lower prices.

International cartels are difficult to control because they are supranational bodies. Laws against cartels within a country are difficult to enforce.

Equilibrium Oligopoly Prices and Outputs*

As we have already indicated, in monopolistic and perfectly competitive markets, a firm does not have to consider how other firms will respond to changes in, for example, its output. In the case of monopoly there are no other firms to worry

---

[2] The cartel also was helped substantially by the dominance of Saudi Arabia, which acted as a residual supplier, cutting output when there was excess supply and periodically flooding the market to punish countries that exceeded their quota.

*Sections and numbered items marked by an asterisk can be omitted without loss of continuity.

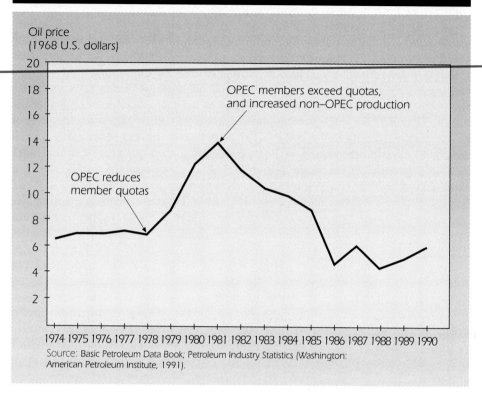

FIGURE 9.3 The relative price of oil increased in the early days of OPEC but subsequently declined.

Source: Basic Petroleum Data Book; Petroleum Industry Statistics (Washington: American Petroleum Institute, 1991).

This figure plots the "real" price of oil, which is the U.S. dollar price of crude oil divided by the U.S. consumer price index. We see that real oil prices moved higher after OPEC restricted production in 1978–1979. However, the higher price of oil caused some OPEC members to overproduce vis-à-vis their production quota and also led to exploration and development outside OPEC. This increased oil supply and eventually forced prices down.

about, and in the case of perfect competition each firm is too small to influence the market.

Oligopolistic firms must consider what their rivals will do. In particular, each firm must try to gauge how rival firms will respond to its own actions as well as what the rival firms are planning themselves. The predictions made by economic theory are highly dependent on what assumptions are made about how firms expect other firms to react to their own pricing and output decisions and how they do, in fact, react. This makes it difficult to reach definitive conclusions on how oligopolistic prices and outputs *compare* with those of monopoly and perfect competition. It also makes it difficult to predict how oligopolistic prices and outputs will *change* in response to demand and cost conditions. That is, the economic analysis of oligopoly is dependent on specific assumptions about what each firm expects other firms will do in response to what it does and on what other firms actually do.

Progress in understanding oligopoly by making a specific assumption about how firms expect competitors to react to their own output and pricing decisions was made by nineteenth-century French economist Augustine Cournot. Cournot simplified the problem by considering an oligopoly of two firms, called a **duopoly,** where the two firms produce identical products. He assumed that each firm sets its output to maximize its own profits *on the expectation that the other firm will hold its output constant.* Cournot showed that in this situation an equilibrium exists. This equilibrium consists of outputs at which each firm is indeed maximizing profits and where neither firm wants to change its output or its expectation of the other's output because actual outputs equal those each expects the other to produce. With no reason for the firms to change their outputs, this situation is an equilibrium, a **Cournot equilibrium.**

One of the reasons Cournot's duopoly model retains considerable interest is that it predicts that price and output will be in between those in a perfectly competitive versus a monopolistic market. Furthermore, as Cournot's theory is extended to more than two firms, prices and output move toward those predicted for a perfectly competitive market, and if there is only one firm, Cournot's model reduces to a monopoly with the traditional predictions for monopoly price and output.

The equilibrium described by Cournot has been shown to be part of a class of equilibria in which each "player" in a "game" is doing his or her best given the way he or she believes others are playing the game, and where the players' expectations on the way others are playing is borne out by the way they actually do play. This type of equilibrium has become known as a **Nash equilibrium** after the American mathematician John Nash, who made an important contribution to **game theory** during the middle part of this century.

Almost 50 years after Cournot's equilibrium was described, another French economist, Joseph Bertrand, posited an alternative assumption about each firm's expectation of what its rival would do in a duopoly situation. Rather than assume that the rival would keep *output* unchanged, Bertrand assumed it would keep *price* unchanged. The equilibrium Bertrand reached, the **Bertrand equilibrium**, is the perfectly competitive equilibrium where price equals *MC;* recall that in perfect competition each firm produces where *price* = *MC.* This equilibrium occurs because if either firm believed its rival would charge a price higher than *MC*, it would pay to lower its own price below that of the other firm as long as this price was not lower than the *MC;* as long as *price>MC* and the rival's price is unchanged, as in the Bertrand model, profits are increased by undercutting the rival's price and thereby increasing sales. That is, if either firm thought that the other would keep its price unchanged and above *MC,* it would take action— reduce price—which would force its rival to change its behavior— also reducing its price—making its expectation incorrect. Only if each firm sets its price equal to *MC* and expects the other firm to do the same does each firm maximize profits and at the same time find the other behaving as expected. That is, the equilibrium at which profits are maximized given the (correct) expectation about the rival's behavior is where each firm charges a price equal to *MC.* This is also what happens with perfect competition.

The assumptions for the Cournot and the Bertrand equilibria—that each firm expects its rival's output or price to remain unchanged—may not be met in many market situations. Rather, firms may expect rivals to vary their outputs and prices in response to their own actions. For example, instead of assuming that a firm expects its rival(s) to hold prices constant when it reduces its own price—as assumed by Bertrand—a firm may assume that rivals will match its own price

In a Cournot equilibrium, each firm is producing the output that maximizes its profits given its (correct) expectation about the other firm's *output*. Therefore, neither firm has an incentive to change its output or its expectations.

In a Bertrand equilibrium, each firm assumes that its rival's *price* is given. The equilibrium involves *price*=*MC*, just as with perfect competition.

---

reductions. For example, Ford might assume that price cuts or rebates would be matched by similar incentives from GM, Chrysler, and foreign producers. Similarly, American Airlines might assume that lower fares would cause United Airlines and Delta to lower their fares.

Other conjectures are also possible. For example, rather than assume that price reductions would be matched by rivals, a firm might believe that rivals would exceed its price reductions to punish it for being a "price breaker." Models in which different assumptions are made about one firm's response to the actions of other firms are called **conjectural variations models.** These models suggest that oligopolistic firms can compete fiercely. That is, the small number of firms in an oligopoly does not necessarily mean an uncompetitive market.

A problem with understanding oligopoly is that rivals can compete on dimensions other than price, such as quality, service, packaging, warranty period, and so on. While some progress has been made in developing theories that incorporate these other aspects of competition, such progress has been rather limited. In order to make headway in understanding the very important market structure of oligopoly, it may be better to take an empirical perspective, studying how oligopolists actually behave and seeing what this suggests about how firms think. However, with so much variation from one oligopoly to another, generalization may not be possible, and it may be necessary to study particular oligopolies as "cases."[3]

> Even though there are only a few firms in an oligopolistic market, these firms may compete fiercely.

Oligopoly and Infrequent Price Changes*

Prices of products in oligopolistic markets appear to change infrequently vis-à-vis prices in competitive and monopolistic markets. For example, processed-meat prices vary less than livestock prices, and air fares vary less than fuel and other costs. Several theories have been advanced to explain this. Most have to do with the assumed reaction of other firms.

Perfectly competitive firms do not have to decide on a price. They just take the price as given by the market, and the market price varies with all the factors affecting supply and demand. A monopolist *does* have to select a price—or an output which, in turn, implies a particular price—but the price selected does not have to involve consideration of the response by other firms. Therefore, if variable costs or demand happens to change, so will the monopolist's price. However, as we have seen, in the case of an oligopoly, not only must a price be set, but a firm also must judge whether other firms will follow when its price is changed. For example, if a firm assumes that other firms will *exceed* its own price decrease, an oligopolist may fear that it could set off a **price war**—a leap-frogging of price cuts that hurts all producers. Using this line of reasoning, it has been suggested that an oligopolist would leave its price unchanged until it is confident that a similar-sized price change would be made by other firms. This means waiting to see if cost or demand changes are in fact industry-wide and not idiosyncratic to the firm itself.

> Fear of setting off a price war could reduce the volatility of prices in an oligopoly.

---

[3] The case approach to probΔlem solving is practiced in many business schools. Harvard is perhaps best known for the case approach.

MONOPOLISTIC COMPETITION

The term **monopolistic competition** may appear to be an oxymoron but in fact is used to describe a market that has elements of both monopoly and perfect competition. Specifically, monopolistic competition occurs in markets with free entry and exit and many competing firms, but where firms sell slightly differentiated products. The firms may, for example, have their own individual brand labels or packaging. The monopolistic element of the market is the result of the unique aspects of each firm's product.[4] The competitive elements are free entry and exit and competition from firms producing close substitutes.

Because each firm's product is differentiated from the products of other firms, each firm faces a downward-sloping demand curve rather than the perfectly elastic demand curve facing a perfectly competitive firm. (Recall that in a perfectly competitive market firms sell a homogeneous and indistinguishable product and therefore all charge the same price. To charge more than others means selling nothing, and to charge less is unnecessary because each firm can sell all it produces at the market price.) However, while the monopolistically competitive firm's demand curve is downward-sloping, it is extremely elastic because of the presence of many close substitutes.

Equilibrium in a monopolistically competitive market occurs when there is no further entry or exit of firms. This requires that firms make only normal profits.

Figure 9.4 describes the equilibrium for a monopolistically competitive firm. The demand curve facing the firm is D_e, and the associated marginal revenue curve is MR_e. Profit is maximized by producing the output at which the marginal revenue and marginal cost are equal.[5] This is output q_{mc}. The price at which output q_{mc} can be sold is given by the height of the demand curve at q_{mc}. This price is p_{mc}.

Output q_{mc} and price p_{mc} represent an equilibrium if they result in zero economic profit. Economic profit is zero if total revenue equals total cost because, as explained in Chapter 7, total cost includes the opportunity cost of capital, land, and any other factors drawn into the firm. Total revenue is price multiplied by output. In Figure 9.4, total revenue is represented by the area $0p_{mc}Eq_{mc}$. Total cost is average cost multiplied by output. The average cost at output q_{mc} is given by the height of *LAC*, which is equal to p_{mc}, so total cost is area $0p_{mc}Eq_{mc}$, the same as total revenue. Therefore, economic profit is zero.

The equilibrium in Figure 9.4 is characterized by the firm's demand curve just touching, or being tangential to, the firm's average cost curve. If the demand curve were above the *LAC* curve instead of being tangential to it, the price would exceed average cost, and an economic profit would be earned; with price above average cost, total revenue exceeds total cost. This would attract new firms, and the competition from these firms would push the demand curve facing the firm in Figure 9.4 down and to the left until it is tangential to *LAC;* there would be more firms dividing up the market demand.[6] Similarly, if the demand curve were below the

> Monopolistic competition occurs when there is free entry and exit and a large number of competing firms, but where each firm produces a product that is *differentiated* from the products of other firms.

> A monopolistically competitive market is in equilibrium when there is no further entry or exit. This occurs when economic profits are zero, which in turn requires that firms' demand curves be tangential to their average cost curves.

---

[4] As Example 9.2 suggests, the unique aspects are often aimed at a specific market segment, or niche.

[5] We use long-run cost curves for the long-run equilibrium.

[6] The firm's demand curve also would become more elastic as more firms enter an industry because there would be more substitutes.

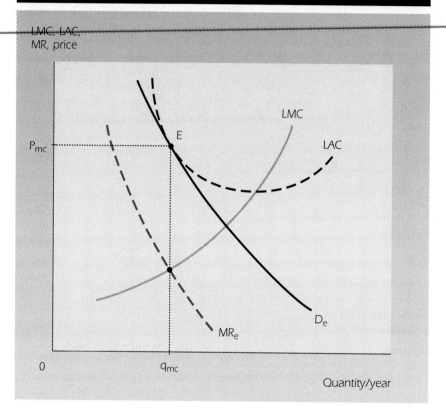

FIGURE 9.4   A monopolistically competitive market is in equilibrium when the economic profit of all firms is zero. This occurs when the demand curve facing each firm is tangential to the firm's average cost curve.

Free entry into a monopolistically competitive industry means that if there are economic profits, new firms will enter the market and produce their own brand or otherwise differentiated version of the product. This will shift the demand curves for preexisting firms downward and to the left. Entry of new firms will stop only when there are no longer economic profits to be made. This occurs when the demand curve has shifted to **D**$_e$, where it just touches the **LAC** curve. Then, by producing the corresponding output, **q**$_{mc}$, the best that the firm can do is to make a zero economic profit; at **q**$_{mc}$ total revenue and total cost are both area **0p**$_{mc}$**Eq**$_{mc}$. The equilibrium occurs when the demand curve for each firm is tangential to the firm's average cost curve.

Monopolistically competitive firms produce outputs lower than where long-run average costs are at their minimum.

LAC curve at every output, economic profits would be negative. That is, accounting profit would be less than normal. Therefore, firms would cease replacing worn-out capital or leave the industry entirely until the demand curve facing the remaining firms had shifted up and to the right until it was again just tangential to *LAC*.

Figure 9.4 shows that each monopolistically competitive firm has a long-run equilibrium output smaller than that for which *LAC* is a minimum. This must be so because there is a downward-sloping demand curve and because in the long run this must be tangential to the *LAC* curve.

Example 9.2

FAMILY FARE

In oligopolies as well as in monopolistic competition, firms distinguish their products. These distinctions are usually aimed at "market niches," that is, potential customers who are not well served by other firms in the industry and who might be induced to purchase the "right" product. Indeed, a strategic dimension of what oligopolistic and monopolistically competitive firms do is search for market niches where they can earn economic profits. Of course, whether economic profits persist depends on the nature of the market; when there is free entry, initial economic profits are eventually whittled away by increased competition. The following excerpt describes the search for a market niche in one industry, U.S. passenger airlines. It shows that even when an industry is well established, and when it takes government approval and a lot of capital to enter the industry, there are still entrepreneurs who believe there is an unexploited niche to make an economic profit.

Braniff. Eastern. Pan Am. Midway. Many people can name one of the major airlines that have failed. . . .

But what about Reno, Kiwi, Baltia, Trans-Africa, and Family? They're among the slew of start-up airlines bucking the conventional wisdom that the skyways soon will be reserved for global, megasized carriers.

The latest entry is Family Airlines, a Las Vegas–based company that . . . filed with the U.S. Transportation Department to operate as a scheduled airline. The name itself evokes what many budget-conscious consumers are in search of in this age of fiercely competitive carriers: a quaint, affordable means of travel.

"We believe there is a significant family travel market in this country that feels priced out of the marketplace by the traditional full-service airlines," said Barry Michaels, Family's chairman and chief executive officer.

Among other fledgling flyers, there's Trans-Africa Air to South Africa and Baltia to Russia and Kiwi Airlines from the Northeast to Chicago and Florida. The Transportation Department and the Federal Aviation Administration are considering the requests of nearly two dozen applicants that want to take to the skies.

If Family receives federal approval, its passengers' experience may be anything but quaint. Like flying cattle carriers, huge Boeing 747 aircraft that hold 550 passengers will be used to fly passengers on heavily traveled routes such as New York to Los Angeles, New York to Miami, and Los Angeles to Las Vegas. Amenities on board Family will include free soft drinks and a limited fast-food menu for an extra cost. No alcoholic beverages will be served, the airline said. . . .

Source: Brett Pulley and Bridget O'Brian, "New Airlines, Bucking Trend, Hunt for Niches," **The Wall Street Journal,** September 29, 1992, pp. B9–10. Reprinted by permission of The Wall Street Journal, © 1992 Dow Jones & Company, Inc. All Rights Reserved Worldwide.

It might seem that monopolistic competition is extremely common. A glance along the shelves of breakfast cereals, coffees, cigarettes, or detergents at the supermarket would give this impression, with an overwhelming array of brands and packages. However, it turns out that monopolistic competition is not as common as might appear. The apparent variety of firms suggested by the vast number of brands is misleading and is due to product differentiation within each firm, not to there being a large number of different firms. In fact, many of the industries we might think are monopolistically competitive are really oligopolistic, with firms trying to appeal to more customers and to obtain more shelf space in the supermarket by offering different varieties of their products. For example, as we have mentioned, despite the large number of brands of coffee on supermarket shelves, approximately 80% of sales are from three firms, General Foods, Procter and

Gamble, and Nestlé. Similarly, despite the many cigarette labels, six U.S. firms, the largest being R. J. Reynolds and Phillip Morris, supply virtually all the market. However, as Example 9.3 explains, there are situations that fit the monopolistically competitive model reasonably well.

AGENCY PROBLEMS: CONFLICTS BETWEEN OWNERS AND MANAGERS

Oligopolistic firms, which, as we have claimed, are more the norm than the exception, tend to be large and are often managed by people other than their owners. Indeed, the owners may at most cast a vote at the annual general meeting when the companies are public and owned by a large number of shareholders.[7] Monopolies also tend to be large and managed by people who are not principally owners or shareholders of the company. When there are managers who are not owners of firms but rather agents of the owners, the assumption of profit maximization may be inappropriate. It may well be the case, for example, that the managers are more interested in maximizing sales or the number of employees than in earning the maximum profit for the owners. Managers may believe that their salaries will be higher if they can show company owners steep upward-sloping sales charts or statistics on the large number of people they must manage rather than by earning maximum possible profits. Owners may not perceive the conflict between the managers' objectives and profits—what we referred to as **agency costs** in Chapter 5—and therefore may reward managers for growth in sales or the number of people employed. It should be clear that hiring more people may not increase owners' profits, and a little more thought suggests that increasing sales also may not produce increased profit.[8]

Sales Maximization as an Objective

Clearly, sales can be increased without limit by charging a sufficiently low price. However, even when managers' salaries or bonuses depend on sales, they will want to show reasonable profits as well as strong sales volumes. What managers may do, therefore, is shown in Figure 9.5. The upper part of the figure shows the curves needed to determine the profit-maximizing output and the profits made at this and other outputs. The bottom part of the figure shows the profits or, more precisely, the above-normal profits at each level of output and sales.

Profit is maximized at output q_p, since, as shown in the upper part of the figure, this is the output at which $MR = MC$. Because output q_p maximizes profit, the curve in the lower part of the figure, which plots profits at each output, has its maximum at this output.

---

[7] Many shareholders do not even vote, but allow the managers to vote on their behalf by granting them a proxy. Furthermore, even when shareholders do vote, important day-to-day decisions are made by managers.

[8] As we will explain later, this conflict between the interests of managers and owners cannot exist in perfectly competitive and monopolistically competitive markets, where the best that can be achieved is a normal profit and where this requires producing the profit-maximizing output.

Example 9.3

You don't have to look far for examples of situations in which the profits of the first firm offering a new product have drawn in so many competitors that prices have been driven down and economic profits reduced or eliminated. Take, for example, the consumer electronics industry.

The history of consumer electronics is one of innovative firms offering clever new products, making initially healthy profits, and then finding other producers selling "knock offs" that push down prices and profit margins. For example, the Sony Walkman, after selling well and generating profits, was followed by similar personal stereo devices from Sanyo, Panasonic, General Electric, and so on, which pushed prices lower. This is a market in which there is free entry and in which each producer's product is a little different, making it monopolistically competitive. The free entry has reduced economic profits in the long run, although the first entrant has often maintained an edge, enjoying special status and profits. A similar pattern occurred in the market for VCRs, with Sony and JVC entering first, with their alternative technologies, and

with high prices and good profit margins drawing in a host of other producers, resulting in lower prices and shrinking profits.

Burger restaurants show a similar history of an early, innovative entrant enjoying healthy profits and growth, with this drawing in competitors offering differentiated but similar products. The first major entrant was, of course, MacDonald's, with Burger King, Wendy's, and the many other local and national chains being the competitors that eventually put pressure on prices and profits.

There are many other examples of monopolistically competitive industries in which profits for initial entrants have attracted competition, forcing down prices and profits. Just look around at the number of producers of jeans who were drawn into the market by the healthy profits of Levi's, Lee, and GWG. Or consider today's extremely broad choice of running shoes which followed on the early profitability of Adidas and then Nike, Reebok, Brooks, and New Balance. In the sports drink market, Gatorade's hold has been challenged by a spate of recent entries, including challenges from the giants of soft beverages, Coca-

Cola promoting PowerAde and Pepsi-Cola selling All Sport. Nestea's hold over the iced-tea market has prompted numerous challenges to compete away the economic profit, with Snapple and Lipton's Original being two of the larger challengers drawn by profit. Body Shops, the chain selling natural soaps and cosmetics, found that early profits drew many to the market, including Bath and Body Works, Crabtree and Evelyn, and H2O Plus. Similar histories can be sketched for personal computers, where IBM clones were drawn in by the success of IBM's early PCs, and for in-line skates, where imitations followed the success of Roller Blades. These and many other examples graphically illustrate the pattern of profit and competition that is characteristic of monopolistically competitive industries.

Sources: Richard Gibson, "Coca-Cola and PepsiCo Are Preparing to Give Gatorade a Run for Its Money, " **The Wall Street Journal**, September 29, 1992, pp. B1, B6; Valerie Reitman, "Success of Body Shop Natural Cosmetics Attracts Imitators to the Scent of Profits, " **The Wall Street Journal**, September 4, 1992, pp. B1, B5; Laurie M. Grossman, "Iced-Tea Products Get Off to a Slow Start," **The Wall Street Journal**, September 28, 1992, pp. B1, B8.

FIGURE 9.5   Maximization of sales subject to making a satisfactory profit results in producing beyond the output at which profits are maximized.

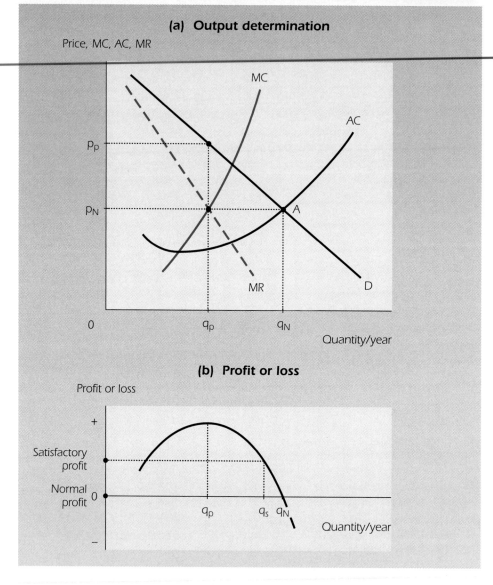

(a) Output determination

Price, MC, AC, MR

(b) Profit or loss

Profit or loss

Part (a) shows that profits are maximized at output q_p, where **MR = MC**. The economic profits made at each possible output are shown in part (b), with a maximum at q_p. If the firm produces q_N, economic profits are zero, since at this output, price p_N is equal to average cost, so total revenue equals total cost—both equal to area $0p_NAq_N$. The zero economic profit at q_N is shown in part (b). If managers think they will earn larger salaries by showing good sales but also satisfactory positive economic profit, they might produce q_S. Whether they choose this strategy or a normal profit strategy, managers produce more output than is in the interest of owners.

If managers set out to maximize sales subject to making a normal profit, they will produce q_N. As shown in the upper part of Figure 9.5, q_N is where the AC curve intersects the demand curve, so at this output total cost and total revenue are equal to area $0p_N Aq_N$.[9] The lower part of the figure shows that economic profit is zero at output q_N. If managers think their own interest is best served by high sales and also a positive economic profit—this might rationalize higher personal salaries or perks—they may produce output q_S. We see that whether managers opt for the highest sales subject to a normal profit or for the highest sales subject to a satisfactory profit, they will produce more output than if they were out to maximize profits for owners. The lower than possible profit constitutes an agency cost that results from the separation of ownership and management of the firm.[10]

> When managers are not owners and maximize sales subject to making a normal profit or a satisfactory profit, production exceeds the output that is in the interest of profit-maximizing owners.

Free Entry, Alternative Ownership, and the Managerial Objective

The ability to choose between the maximization of profit and the maximization of sales subject to a normal profit or a satisfactory profit is enjoyed by managers of firms in monopolistic or oligopolistic industries that offer above-zero economic profits. However, in perfectly competitive and monopolistically competitive markets, managers have no choice but to produce the outputs that maximize profits. This is so because the best that can be done in the long run is to make a normal profit, that is, a zero economic profit. This is ensured by free entry, because when positive economic profits are earned, new firms enter until economic profits are zero (that is, accounting profits are normal); above-zero economic profits occur only in the short run. If managers produced anything other than the profit-maximizing output, they would make below-zero economic profits in the long run and the owners would cease to provide capital to replace what wears out. This suggests that for managers not to maximize profits means ultimately losing their jobs.

> Managers of perfectly competitive or monopolistically competitive firms *must* produce the output that maximizes profits. At any other output, managers will eventually lose their jobs.

Managers of monopolistic and oligopolistic firms do have some incentive to pursue profit maximization because firms not earning maximum potential profits may be targets for takeovers. Alternative owners who, unlike the existing owners, realize that higher profits could be made by using better management may be able to acquire the firm cheaply, based on the lower than possible profits. The existing managers can be fired and be replaced. Of course, the new owners must try to prevent their managers from pursuing a non-profit-oriented goal. This can be extremely difficult. Incentives can be built in to maximize profits or, more precisely, to maximize the value of the company to the shareholders by giving the managers shares or share **options.**[11] These incentive schemes only partly

---

[9] Total revenue is price multiplied by sales, or p_N multiplied by q_N, and the total cost is average cost multiplied by sales. At q_N, average cost, given off the AC curve, equals the price, so total revenue equals total cost.

[10] As Example 9.4 points out, agency costs also can explain the failure of communism.

[11] Options give their owners the right to buy (or sell) shares at a particular price up to a particuar date. Giving managers options to buy the company's shares may encourage managers to maximize profits because such options increase in value very sharply as share prices increase.

 **E**xample   **9.4**

COMMUNISM AS ONE GIGANTIC FIRM

Agency costs, which arise when managers pursue their own interests rather than the interests of the shareholders, can be quite substantial. In case you question the potential importance of agency costs and think that we might have made too big a deal about them, consider the following, which involves agency costs when the entire economy consists of one giant "firm," a centrally managed state enterprise.

Among the principal claims of the supporters of communism is that capitalism results in wasteful duplication and the loss of economies of scale. For example, in the Peoples' Republic of China, officials frequently proclaim that having many different small firms all doing more or less the same thing means duplication of tasks and wasteful overlaps. While this argument may sound persuasive, it overlooks the distinction between **technical economies of scale,** which are due to efficiencies of bigger machines and which may well mean lower average costs for larger producers, and **organizational diseconomies of scale,** which counter the technical economies.

There may well be technical economies of scale in a number of activities. Indeed, such economies are the cause of natural monopolies. If technical economies of scale were common, we would expect countries typically to consist of a small number of giant producers, with each producer making one of the goods or services that people buy. Indeed, if there were economies of scope as well as economies of scale—the former involving economies of producing different products and the latter involving economies of producing more of an individual product—we would expect countries to have only one firm that makes everything; the firm producing the biggest variety of products and the largest outputs would have the lowest costs and would force smaller firms out of business. Consequently, those favoring communism say, "why not set the economy up as one giant firm that can enjoy all the economies of scale and scope and thereby make citizens better off?"

Well, as just about everybody knows, the record of communism in providing a good standard of living is hardly anything to brag about. Indeed, the failure of communism to "deliver the goods" led to the collapse of that economic system in the former U.S.S.R. and in eastern Europe

The better the information that exists on both the actual and the potential performance of managers, the more likely the managers are to pursue profit maximization.

overcome the problem because they are often designed by managers themselves subject to approval by shareholders. Clearly, the key problem is for shareholders to have correct information on the job being done by their agents, the managers. It is only when the information is poor that there is a need to build in an appropriate type of incentive. Since information on profits is recorded by accountants, and since the incentives offered to agents to maximize profits usually involve stocks and options, the agency problem of owners versus managers is an important research topic in accounting and finance.

during the late 1980s and early 1990s. So where did the communist system go wrong? The problem is not in the absence of technical economies of scale and scope but is in the presence of organizational diseconomies or, more specifically, agency costs.

At the risk of a little over-simplification, we can think of communism as involving the management of production under the umbrella of one gigantic centrally managed firm, the state enterprise. Bureaucratic direction of this enterprise is organized via a long chain of command. The possibilities for abuse of authority in this vast centrally focused managerial apparatus are virtually open-ended. Indeed, as investigations of officials in Poland, East Germany, and other former communist states disclosed after their regimes collapsed, the privileges that managers of state enterprise granted themselves were scandalous. These privileges included limousines, vacation homes, domestic servants, crates of champagne, cartons of caviar, and numerous expensive Western luxuries. These appropriations of benefits under communism are the distinct parallels of the agency costs in large corporations under capitalism, in each case being the result of managers running enterprises for their own benefit.

The existence of agency costs, whether we are referring to those in the communist hierarchy or those in a corporation, depend on abuses of position and power going unseen or unchallenged. In the case of a typical corporation, abuses should be at least as visible as in the much vaster state enterprises of communist states. Similarly, in a typical corporation, abuses should be kept in check by the possibility that inefficiently managed firms can be taken over and managers replaced. In the case of agency costs of communistic management, the only check is the overthrow of the entire system when the costs become so excessive the system grinds to a virtual halt. This situation occurs when the organizational diseconomies of scale and scope that are the manifestations of agency costs swamp any technical economies that may exist and the system therefore breaks down.

INCOMPLETE INFORMATION AND THE THEORY OF THE FIRM

The Ability to Maximize Profits

The availability of information necessary for owners of firms to evaluate their managers is a relatively minor matter compared with the availability of information on marginal cost and marginal revenue that managers need in order to maximize profits. Do managers know the *MC* and *MR* curves with sufficient accuracy to make the **theory of the firm** in this and the previous chapters of practical value? Furthermore, does any lack of necessary information make the theory invalid even as a qualitative description of the behavior of firms? What can be said in response to these fundamental questions?

In the case of perfect competition, two lines of defense are possible:

1. For perfectly competitive firms, marginal revenue is no more than the market price, which is easily observed, so the determination of profit-maximizing output requires knowing only the *MC* curve. Cost accountants may be able to calculate *MC* at a number of different outputs sufficiently well to construct a usable *MC* curve.

2. For perfectly competitive firms, consistent errors in selecting the output that maximizes profits results in below-zero economic profits and therefore threatens the very survival of the firm. Consequently, those firms which have survived in a competitive market must be producing the profit-maximizing output.

The second line of defense applies to both perfect competition and monopolistic competition (since both offer only zero economic profit) and is sometimes referred to as the **"as if" principle** because it says that only firms that behave "as if" they are maximizing profits by equating *MC* and *MR* will survive. Therefore, the survivors must be doing what the theory says they should do, even if the managers are not conscious of it.

Theories of monopoly and oligopoly are more difficult to defend with the "as if" principle than the theories of perfect competition and monopolistic competition, because without free entry and exit, the competitive pressure to maximize profit or be forced out of business is absent. However, even if output and prices can differ from profit-maximizing levels, predictions of the theories of monopoly and oligopoly are still *qualitatively* useful. For example, the theories still offer useful implications concerning the ways monopolies and oligopolies react to changes in fixed costs, productivity of inputs, taxes, changes in variable input prices, and so on. That is, despite incomplete information on costs and a lack of pressure to ensure profit maximization, the theories of monopoly and oligopoly offer qualitatively, if not quantitatively, useful predictions.

Organizational Theories of the Firm

Nobel Prize winner Herbert Simon has argued that rather than respond to each small change in variable costs or demand, managers change what they do only when they find that their current behavior is not producing a satisfactory result. According to this view, if a firm has a profit or market share it considers will satisfy its shareholders, managers behave conservatively, doing little until profit or market share worsen noticeably. The reason for the conservative or, in Simon's words, **satisficing behavior** is that decisions are made via long chains of approval. This causes inertia, with larger firms showing slower response than smaller firms and with bigger firms weeding out a larger proportion of new ideas. **Organizational theories** such as Simon's theory of satisficing do not rule out the effects of changes in costs and demand that are implied by the theory of the firm advanced in this and previous chapters. However, they suggest that the effects take time to occur. They also suggest that big changes in costs or demand are likely to show up in prices and output more quickly than small changes and that changes are likely to show up more quickly in smaller firms.

*In perfectly competitive and monopolistically competitive markets, firms **must** maximize profits or be forced out of business because free entry ensures that the maximum profit is a zero economic profit.*

Qualitative predictions of monopoly and oligopoly theories can still be useful even if firms do not maximize profits.

Organizational theories of the firm predict that firms take time to respond to changes in costs and demand and that larger firms take longer than smaller firms.

Organizational theories of the firm have been extended to allow for the presence in large organizations of bureaucratic procedures that have been developed over the years and handed down from generation to generation of managers. The presence of bureaucratic procedures slows down the introduction of new ideas and suggests that the age of firms as well as their size affects their speed of response to cost and demand changes. However, the ability to survive in the presence of such inertia depends on imperfect information about the profits that managers could achieve were they to respond quickly to market conditions. This is so because were shareholders to realize what is feasible with quick, responsive management, they would replace managers who did not respond quickly. Otherwise, shareholders risk their companies being taken over by shareholders who *would* change management. That is, to the extent that bureaucratic management reduces profits, replacement of management should occur in the long run unless actual and potential shareholders lack information about what could have been done.

When information exists on potential profits, managers must maximize profits or risk being fired by current or new shareholders.

Asymmetric Information*

Just as managers may know more about the market in which they are operating than do shareholders, sellers may know more about the products they are selling than do buyers. The presence of **asymmetric information** about products, specifically about their quality, has been shown to have a profound impact on the working of markets.[12]

Consider the used-car market. Suppose some fraction of vehicles of a given model and year are known to be "lemons." Each seller knows whether his or her car is a lemon but has no incentive to admit this to a prospective buyer. Buyers cannot identify lemons and recognize that sellers of lemons will misrepresent their vehicles. That is, there is an information asymmetry; sellers have information on quality, but buyers do not. Buyers can do no better than assume that what they buy has a particular probability of being a lemon. But what is that probability?[13]

With all prospective buyers recognizing that the car they are thinking of buying could be a lemon, market prices of used cars will reflect the probability that any given car being brought to market is a lemon. It might seem that this probability would be the fraction of all the cars in existence of given model and year that are lemons, but this is not correct. To see why, suppose that half of all vehicles of a given model and year that were made happen to be lemons. Suppose that these lemons are worth $1000, whereas good cars are worth $2000. If the market price reflected the fact that half of *all* cars are lemons and was, say, halfway between what a good car and a lemon are worth, that is, $1500, those owners who know their cars are good cars would be reluctant to sell. They know their cars are worth $2000, not the going $1500. However, they are unable credibly to convey this to buyers because all sellers say the same, that *their* cars are good. It follows that lemon owners, but not good car owners, would be selling. Therefore, the probability would not be one-half that a used car was a lemon; it would be much higher. In fact, the equilibrium *if sellers have discretion over whether to sell* is with

---

[12] The seminal work is by George Akerlof, "The Market for 'Lemons': Quality Uncertainty and the Market Mechanism," *Quarterly Journal of Economics* (August 1970), pp. 488–500.

[13] Probabilities lie between 0 and 1. A 0 probability means an event will definitely not occur, whereas probability of 1 means it will definitely occur.

only lemons being sold and with buyers knowing this and offering only what lemons are worth. That is, the probability that a car being sold *on the used-car market* is a lemon is 1. Therefore, the equilibrium price is $1000, the value of a lemon.

At the equilibrium price, being that for lemons, owners of lemons are willing to sell because they know buyers realize that only lemons are brought to market at this price. Furthermore, buyers are willing to pay this price because they are paying the price of a lemon, and this is what they are sure they are buying. All expectations about the nature of the equilibrium are borne out. That is, buyers expect to find lemons with probability 1, and sellers bring only lemons to market so that the buyers' assumed probability is correct. The good cars do not come to market. That is, bad specimens drive out good specimens. The good specimens do not come to market because they do not fetch an appropriate premium if buyers cannot find out they are good specimens.

The preceding has assumed that sellers who know their cars are not lemons do not have to sell. If this assumption is dropped, the equilibrium is changed a little. Nevertheless, the presence of asymmetry of information still has interesting implications for market outcomes. For one thing, asymmetric information causes sellers to look for credible ways to indicate to buyers that they are selling good-quality products. For example, when the information asymmetry about quality concerns that of a new product, those with good-quality products may offer guarantees. Indeed, used cars may be sold by dealers who can offer guarantees rather than privately, where guarantees are not enforceable.[14] Asymmetric information also implies an incentive for dealers to develop good reputations when there are repeat purchases or when buyers can communicate their dissatisfaction to other prospective customers. The theory of asymmetric information has been used to explain the growth of chains of hotels, fast food outlets, and so on. These have a stronger incentive not to misrepresent their quality than do independently managed operations because an entire chain's reputation is at stake if any one member is substandard. These are the kinds of ideas being pursued in the economics area of **industrial organization** as efforts are made to explain more and more of the structure and organization of actual markets.

Moral Hazard*

In the case of the used-car market, there is asymmetry of information in that sellers know more than do prospective buyers. However, the quality of a used car, specifically whether or not it is a lemon, is a given. The insurance market shares the "lemons" problem with the used-car market because within any risk-premium category, those who at a particularly high risk are more likely to purchase insurance. For example, travelers at high risk of being unable to go on vacation due to illness are more likely to buy trip-cancellation insurance against illness than people at low risk. Insurance companies know this but are unable to distinguish high-risk from low-risk travelers. Therefore, insurance premiums are set sufficiently high to reflect the high chance of claims being made. Furthermore, because those at low risk of not traveling find the premiums high when compared with their chance of making a claim, they are discouraged from buying insurance. Therefore, the out-

The presence of bad-quality products that buyers cannot distinguish from good-quality products drives the good-quality products out of the market.

Asymmetric information implies that guarantees are offered, that used goods are sold by dealerships, and that chains of outlets will develop.

---

[14] There are other reasons for used goods to be sold by dealerships. For example, dealerships may reduce the costs of sellers locating buyers.

come is like that in the used-car market; the people who happen to be at higher risk—the "lemons" among those who might buy insurance—are the ones who purchase it, lower-risk people do not, and the price of insurance reflects the fact that the people buying insurance are at high risk.

The problem that at the low market price of used cars only "lemons" come to market or that at the high trip-cancellation insurance premiums only those at higher risk purchase it is known as the **adverse-selection problem.** This problem, as we have seen, depends on asymmetric information. There is a further problem with insurance that is also related to the absence of complete information. In the case of insurance, the chance that an event occurs cannot be taken as given. Specifically, the probability of an insured event occurring *is increased by the purchase of insurance.* For example, after buying insurance against theft, people are typically less careful to protect their possessions. Therefore, the chance of theft is increased by buying insurance. It is not that there are high-risk and low-risk customers and only the high-risk customers buy insurance, which is the adverse-selection problem. Rather, the risk itself changes as insurance is purchased. However, as with the "lemons" problem, insurance companies know that risk increases when insurance is purchased and therefore set prices of insurance coverage accordingly.

The problem of events being more likely to occur when there is insurance against them is an example of the **moral-hazard problem.** An extreme form of the moral-hazard problem occurs when an insured party is not just less careful about preventing an insured event, such as a fire, but where the insured partly takes steps to *cause* the event; perhaps a business is burned down to collect the insurance. If the insurance company had complete information, it could prove this. Indeed, with complete information an insurance company could prove negligence when an insured party failed to take steps to protect insured property. If responsibility or negligence could be proved, insurance coverage could be revoked and insurance premiums would then be lower. However, information is not so readily available. This is how moral hazard is related to information.

If the chance of events occurring is increased when there is insurance against them, there is moral hazard.

Adverse selection and moral hazard may be at work at the same time. Consider, for example, extended warranties available to new car buyers.[15] Buyers are offered a warranty at a given price, irrespective of the care they are likely to take of their vehicles. Those drivers who inflict abuse on their vehicles are more likely to buy coverage than those who provide meticulous maintenance. The price of extended warranties is high to reflect this, and therefore, careful car owners find the coverage expensive from their perspective. This is adverse selection; those who do not take care of their cars purchase the extended warranties.

Moral hazard and adverse selection may be at work at the same time.

After a driver has purchased an extended warranty, the incentive to provide maintenance is diminished; repairs are at the cost of the insurance company rather than the driver. Therefore, the purchase of a warranty increases the likelihood of a claim being made to pay for repairs. This is moral hazard. As with adverse selection, insurance companies offering extended warranties know that this happens and set warranty prices high enough to reflect the "hazard" they face. Indeed, warranty prices reflect both moral hazard and adverse selection.

---

[15] Extended warranties are offered by insurance companies in cooperation with car dealers. They provide coverage for parts or parts plus labor beyond the normal period of warranty offered on a new car.

STRATEGIC BEHAVIOR: A PERVASIVE
SCIENTIFIC PRINCIPLE

We have seen how oligopolistic firms make judgments about their competitors' actions and plot strategies to deal with them. Even when there are a large number of competitive firms, as in monopolistically competitive markets, producers may try to distinguish themselves by strategically differentiating particular characteristics of their products. Strategic behavior is not a dimension unique to economics. In numerous disciplines "players" are viewed as selecting strategies to gain competitive advantage.

A strategic dimension of oligopolistic decision making is the variable or variables over which to compete, with price being only one of many choices. Oligopolistic firms can vary product quality, service, extras offered, credit terms, and so on. For example, automobile manufacturers can leave model prices unchanged but change the warranty coverage, the extras offered as stan-

dard, the interest rate charged, and so on. Producers also can offer customers greater convenience by having more outlets or service areas. For example, banks can compete through the availability of automatic teller machines, the number of full-service branches, hours of operation, and so on.

Just as oligopolistic firms can select from among alternative strategic variables, perhaps choosing something other than price to avoid setting off price wars, so too can competing biologic species select different strategies for dealing with rivals. By means of the process of natural selection, organisms "choose" among speed, strength, concealment capability, ability to exploit different sources of energy, and so on as competitive strategies. Similarly, just as oligopolistic firms in one industry sometimes form strategic alliances with firms in a different industry—for example, tire and auto-parts producers with automobile manufacturers and computer hardware with computer software producers—so different biologic species form strategic alliances. For example, pilot and cleaner fish associate with particular sharks, and fleas associate with particular mammals. The factors causing the symbiosis are very similar in economics and biology, involving technical complementarities and other advantages for exploiting particular niches.

Pack behavior among wolves and foxes, "social" behavior among termites and ants, flocking among birds, and schooling among fish also can be thought of as strategic alliances, this time among members of the same species. The factors favoring this strategic behavior are very similar to those prompting firms in the same industry to form strategic alliances. For example, U.S. automobile manufacturers work with Japanese automobile manufacturers and U.S. airlines work with "feeder" and foreign airlines to exchange information on rapidly changing business environments and to coordinate activities. The exchange of information on the whereabouts of threats to schooling fish in rapidly changing aquatic environments and the coordination of the hunt among wolves are parallel motivations for intra-species alliances in the biologic sphere; each member of the school or pack helps other members deal with threats, find food sources, and so on.

In addition to the parallels between economics and biology that arise from the similarity of the motivation for forming interspecies/interindustry and intraspecies/intraindustry alliances, there are parallels between the two disciplines that arise from the motivations for the adoption of **generalist strategies**. For example, firms may produce a variety of product lines because this provides diversification in unpredictable markets;

> *Pack behavior among wolves and foxes, "social" behavior among termites and ants, flocking among birds, and schooling among fish . . . can be thought of as strategic alliances. . . .*

if large luxury vehicles are not selling well, small economy vans and pickups may help maintain overall production. This can be characterized as an economy of scope, arising because of the scope, or variety, of activities. In a similar way, organisms may exploit economies of scope when they adopt generalist strategies for the exploitation of energy sources. By being able to obtain and eat a variety of plants or insects, an organism may be able to cope with vagaries in supplies of any one of them, again an economy of scope. The more volatile market demand conditions for firms or the availability of individual energy resources for organisms, the more useful are generalist strategies and the more likely they are to be manifest in the economic or biologic domains.

In characterizing competition, biologists have distinguished between actions taken to slow down rivals, known as **interference competition**, and actions taken to beat out rivals in the fight for resources, known as **scramble competition**. Consideration of advertising campaigns of oligopolistic firms shows that a similar distinction can be applied to the economic environment. A firm can point out weaknesses in its rivals' products or concentrate on the strong points of its own product. Political parties, which because they are typically few in number can be thought of as oligopolies, also use at different times interference and scramble strategies, criticizing their rivals or promoting their own performances or platforms.

The economics of oligopoly has connections to politics not only because political parties are few in number and strategically interact like oligopolistic firms but also because economic oligopolies may be the **result** of political processes. For example, in Great Britain, Canada, Australia, and New Zealand, banking is oligopolistic because only a handful of bank charters have been awarded by their respective governments. Furthermore, because oligopolistic firms have an incentive to collude, there is also a close connection between politics and economics concerning the laws restricting cartels. The courts have played a role in defining what constitutes illegal cartel behavior, tying a further connection between economics and law.

Turning from the imperfectly competitive market form of oligopoly to that of monopolistic competition, we can again find numerous parallels between economics and other areas of scholastic enquiry. Recall that in a monopolistically competitive industry there is free entry and exit as in perfect competition, but firms have some degree of market power by differentiating their products from each other. Product differentiation occurs to take advantage of market niches. This may be the result of technical differences between products or of marketing, where marketing looks at the niches that exist—**market research**—and how best to exploit these through advertising, packaging, and so on.

There is a parallel area of biology to that of **product differentiation** in economics. This is the biologic study of **speciation**. Organisms, like firms, try to find and exploit their own special advantages, whether these be in choices of energy sources, nest locations, defenses against predators, means of catching prey, and so on. The variety of birds, dogs, fish, or arthropods (insects, spiders, and so on) can be viewed as being based on the variety of environmental niches, just as we can view the variety of products in a monopolistically competitive industry as being due to the variety of market niches. There is competition between similar but different organisms just as there is among firms, with the intensity of competition depending on how close the products/organisms are along the **differentiation spectrum**.

The forces of nature have resulted in a **separation distance** between species along the spectrum of biologic speciation just as the market has resulted in a parallel **product differentiation**. We can be just as sure that every profitable opportunity in the spectrum of product differentiation is exploited as we can that every possible biologic niche is exploited. This is so because in the biologic arena there is free entry and exit just as in monopolistic competition; when new opportunities arise, organisms and firms move in rapidly, just as they leave when opportunities disappear. Of course, the time frames differ, as does the consciousness of the choice to exploit or abandon a niche; firms' decisions are made consciously by management who may apply aspects of the field of **business strategy** to identify and exploit niches, whereas organisms' "decisions" are made by the forces of nature. Nevertheless, the principles of niche selection and abandonment are very similar.

Sociologists who specialize in contemporary culture also can characterize some of their domain in ways that overlap with the economics of monopolistic competition. For example, contemporary music can be viewed as niche seeking by an immense number of bands competing for the ears of the consuming public. There is free entry into and exit from the contemporary music scene, with the pace of changeover of bands and variety of sounds and styles clear testimony to the monopolistically competitive nature of the music business. Fashion too fits well into this market structure, drawing yet another bridge between the domains of the sociologist and the economist, a bridge with a heavy two-way flow of intellectual traffic.

SUMMARY

1. An oligopoly is an industry in which there are sufficiently few firms that each firm must make judgments about how other firms will respond to its price and output decisions. Oligopoly can result from the granting of licenses and from economies of scale.

2. There is an incentive for oligopolistic firms to form a cartel to reduce competition, but each cartel member has an incentive to produce more than its quota. This conflict of incentives makes cartels intrinsically unstable.

3.* The level of price and output in an oligopolistic industry depends crucially on how each firm expects other firms to react to its own pricing and output decisions and on how they do, in fact, react. The effect of changes in costs and demand on price and output also depends on expected reactions and actions of other members of the oligopoly.

4.* Two specific assumptions about rivals' responses have been made by the French economists Augustin Cournot and Joseph Bertrand. Cournot assumed that rivals in a duopoly—an oligopoly of two firms—expect each other to hold output constant, while Bertrand assumed that each expected the other to hold price constant.

5.* An oligopoly is in equilibrium if firms are maximizing profits given their expectations about the behavior of rivals and if rivals behave as expected. This is an equilibrium because there is no incentive for any firm to change what it is doing or what it expects.

6.* The fact that there are numerous ways rivals can be expected to react, as well as

numerous dimensions in which to compete, makes it difficult to make generalized statements about oligopoly. This is unfortunate because oligopoly is a very common market structure.

7.* Price changes in oligopolistic industries are relatively infrequent. This could result from the fear that price reductions will trigger price wars.

8. Monopolistic competition occurs when there is free entry into and exit from an industry but where each firm's product is slightly different from that of others. Free entry and exit ensure zero economic profit in the long run, but product differentiation causes downward-sloping demand and an output less than where LAC is at its minimum.

9. In monopolistic and oligopolistic companies where managers are not owners but are agents of owners, sales or the number of employees may be increased at the expense of profits.

10. In perfectly competitive and monopolistically competitive markets, managers have no choice but to maximize profits, since the best long-run profit is merely a zero economic profit, that is, a normal profit.

11. Among leading alternatives to the profit-maximizing theory of the firm based on equating marginal cost and marginal revenue are organizational theories. Organizational theories predict that firms will behave conservatively, making changes only when results are unsatisfactory. This situation follows from the need for numerous levels of approval.

12. Organizational theories predict that smaller firms are more responsive and innovative than larger firms. Extensions of the organizational theories incorporate the effects of making decisions by rules which are likely to prevail in larger and longer-established firms.

13.* When sellers are better informed about quality than are buyers, that is, when there is asymmetric information, the presence of bad-quality products can drive good-quality products out of the market. Good-quality products cannot enjoy an appropriate premium if it is not possible for buyers to distinguish them from bad-quality products.

14.* Asymmetric information about quality implies that guarantees will exist, that used goods will be sold by dealerships, and that chains of outlets will develop.

15.* Moral hazard exists when the purchase of insurance increases the chance that an insured event occurs.

QUESTIONS AND PROBLEMS

1. What difficulties might be faced in determining whether a group of firms in an oligopoly have formed a clandestine cartel?

2. Can you think of any industries in the United States that appear oligopolistic but in fact have to be competitive to compete with firms from overseas?

3. Might you have concerns about oligopoly other than those about price fixing? For example, how about an oligopoly in the news media?

4. Why does industrial espionage—spying on other companies—occur in an oligopoly? Would it occur in a perfectly competitive industry?

5. Can you think of any industry that is monopolistically competitive?

6. Redraw Figure 9.4 with a positive economic profit, and explain how free entry drives the demand curve back to D_e.

7. Might marketing and advertising be designed to turn a firm that is monopolistically competitive into a monopoly?

8. Why might share options help overcome the agency problem?

9. If managers focus on market share, are they taking care of the interests of their shareholders?

10. Do you think the agency problem could exist in public institutions such as schools and hospitals and in the running of government?

11.* Why might you volunteer to pay for an independent, professional evaluation of the condition of your car if you were selling it?

12.* Why do some used-car advertisements say such things as "Must sell. Leaving country"?

13.* Why do life insurance companies require medical examinations before offering coverage?

14.* If travelers can persuade doctors that they are sick when they want to delay or cancel a journey, would trip-cancellation insurance be subject to both adverse selection *and* moral hazard?

CHAPTER 10

. . . .
. . . .
. . . .
. . . .
. . . . Markets for Factors of Production
. . . .
. . . .

Buy land young man, I hear they're not making it any more.

Mark Twain

Key Concepts

Functional distribution of income; derived demand; marginal
physical product; value of the marginal product; factor demand;
factor demand and factor productivity; factor demand and product price; the supply of labor; equilibrium wages; opportunity
cost and factor prices; product prices versus factor prices;
opportunity cost and factor supply; interest rates and the
demand for capital; economic rent; quasi-rent; factor allocation

In previous chapters our discussions of perfect competition, monopoly, oligopoly,
and monopolistic competition focused on the markets for final goods and services.
This chapter considers the markets for the inputs going into making final goods
and services.

Some inputs must themselves be produced. For example, cement, steel, glass,
copper piping, and electrical wiring are inputs going into construction which must
themselves be produced and which are sold in markets that may be perfectly competitive, monopolistic, and so on, as with markets for final goods and services. We
need not consider separately the markets for these so-called **intermediate inputs,**
because the need to produce and sell them means their markets behave like other
markets which are perfectly competitive, monopolistic, or whatever. However, if
we trace back through the intermediate inputs to the **primary inputs** going into

The primary inputs are
land, labor, and capital.

267

production, we invariably find that production is based on the inputs of labor, land, and capital, where capital consists of machines and other aids to production.[1] These primary inputs—land, labor, and capital—are the factors of production referred to in our discussion of scarcity in Chapter 2.[2]

WHY SEPARATELY CONSIDER FACTOR MARKETS?

The price of a factor of production multiplied by the amount of the factor gives the factor's income. For example, the average wage rate per hour, which is the way we measure the price of labor, times the total number of hours worked gives the income of labor. Therefore, when we know the prices of factors and the amounts of factors, we can calculate the **functional distribution of income.** The functional distribution of income describes the shares of the total income of a country going to owners of land, capital, and labor, where, of course, labor is owned by the people performing the work.

Economists have always been interested in the functional distribution of income. For example, Marxists have argued that a larger and larger share of income would accrue to the capital-owning class, the **bourgeoisie,** as they accumulated wealth via reinvestment. Other economists have been interested in the functional distribution because they are interested in how it is affected by such matters as technological change, income tax, and so on. Yet others have been interested in how the functional distribution of income varies over the business cycle or how it varies between countries.

The prices of factors of production are determined by supply and demand, as are prices of final goods and services. What makes it worthwhile studying factor prices separately are the special characteristics of factor supplies and demands. In particular, unlike final goods and services, where supply depends on marginal cost and marginal revenue, in the case of a factor of production, supply depends on the factor's opportunity cost. Similarly, whereas demands for final goods and services depend on their marginal utilities to consumers, in the case of a factor of production, demand depends on the factor's contribution to the profitability of what the factor helps produce. This makes factor demand a **derived demand,** that is, derived from the demand for the final goods or services that give rise to the factor's employment.

Similar principles apply to all factors of production, although each has its peculiarities on the supply side, demand side, or both. We can begin to explain the common principles as well as the idiosyncrasies of the different factors by considering first the market for labor.

*The functional distribution of income describes the **shares** of a country's total income going to labor and to owners of land and capital.*

*Factor supplies depend on opportunity costs. Factor demands are **derived** from the demands for what the factors produce.*

---

[1] Machines, and other items of capital, must first be produced and in this sense are like intermediate inputs. However, capital is usefully distinguished from intermediate inputs because capital contributes to production over a long period of time, unlike intermediate inputs such as cement, fabric, and so on, which are just a "stage" of production and are used up almost immediately.

[2] When discussing scarcity, we included raw materials among the factors of production. However, it has become traditional in discussions of factor markets to emphasize land, labor, and capital.

THE MARKET FOR LABOR

As with demand for final goods and services, in order to derive the market demand curve for labor, we first consider an individual demander and then add individual demands to obtain the market demand.

The Demand for Labor by an Individual Firm

Let us consider the demand for labor on a wheat farm. For simplicity, let us assume that the amount of land and capital are fixed, as they are in the short run, and that labor is the only variable input.

Table 10.1 shows the total production of the wheat farm as more workers are employed. The table shows that as the number of workers is increased from one to two, production increases by 500 (or $950 - 450$) bushels. As employment is increased from two to three workers, output increases by 850 (or $1800 - 950$) bushels, and so on. The extra output from an extra worker with other factors fixed is called the **marginal physical product of labor,** or the ***MPP* of labor** for short.

Table 10.1 shows the marginal physical product of labor *MPP* increasing until the fourth worker is employed before beginning to decrease. The range of increasing *MPP*s might result from the fact that there are a number of different tasks to be done. Then, with very few workers, each worker loses time going from one task to another, but as more workers are employed, each worker can focus on a single task. The range of decreasing *MPP*s is the result of there being a fixed amount of land, machines, and so on, which after some level of employment is reached constrains the productivity of extra workers; there is a limit on how much extra food can be grown on a given area of land merely by adding extra workers. We met this phenomenon in Chapter 5 under the heading of the law of diminishing marginal product.[3]

Let us assume that farmers maximize profit, where profit, as we know, is the difference between total revenue and total cost. If profit is being maximized, it is worthwhile hiring an additional worker provided the worker increases total revenue more than total cost. The increase in total revenue from hiring an extra worker is the **value of the marginal product of labor (*VMP*),** which when all of a firm's output can be sold without affecting the market price of the product is the marginal physical product multiplied by the product's price. In symbols, we can write the value of the marginal product *VMP* as

$$VMP \equiv MPP \times price \qquad (10.1)$$

where *MPP* is the marginal physical product of labor, and *price* is the price of the output.

> The marginal physical product of labor is the increase in output from the employment of one more unit of labor when other factors of production are fixed in amount.

> When more output can be sold without affecting the market price, the value of the marginal product of labor is the *MPP* of labor multiplied by the market price of the product labor produces.

---

[3] In Chapter 5 we stated the law of diminishing marginal product in terms of marginal cost rather than marginal physical product. That is, we spoke in terms of the marginal cost of additional output increasing after some level of output. The *MPP* perspective here and the *MC* perspective taken earlier are alternative ways of viewing the same phenomenon. That is, if *MPP*s are decreasing as employment and output expand, then *MC* must be increasing; with inputs adding less output, it becomes more costly to produce one more unit of output.

TABLE 10.1

The marginal physical product of labor may initially increase as employment is expanded, but after some level of employment, the marginal physical product diminishes.

NUMBER WORKING	TOTAL PRODUCT	MPP OF LABOR
0	0	—
1	450	450
2	950	500
3	1,800	850
4	2,800	1,000
5	3,650	850
6	4,270	620
7	4,790	520
8	5,230	440
9	5,590	360
10	5,880	290
11	6,110	230
12	6,260	150
13	6,340	80
14	6,380	40
15	6,400	20

The marginal physical product of labor **MPP** is the change in output from employing one more worker with other inputs constant. It is calculated by subtracting from the total output with any given number of workers the output with one fewer worker. For example the **MPP** of the fifth worker is obtained by taking the total production with five workers, and subtracting the total production with four workers, that is, 850 (or 3650 − 2800) bushels per year. In the table, the **MPP** of labor increases until the fourth worker is employed and then diminishes as the limitation of the farm size begins to restrict additional workers' contributions to output. However, the **MPP** of labor remains positive even after it has begun to decline.

The increase in total cost from hiring an extra worker is the wage. Therefore, employment should be expanded as long as

$$VMP > wage$$

Similarly, employment should be contracted when

$$VMP < wage$$

because by reducing employment in such a situation, total cost is reduced more than total revenue, so profit is increased. These rules for increasing or decreasing employment and their implications for the demand of labor can be illustrated by an example.[4]

Table 10.2 shows the *VMP*s for different levels of employment when the market price of wheat is $5 per bushel. The *VMP*s are simply the *MPP*s repeated from Table 10.1 multiplied by the price of wheat. If monthly wages are $2000, the farm would continue increasing profits by expanding employment until eight workers have been employed. For example, in hiring the seventh worker, total revenue is increased by $2600 per month and total cost by $2000, so profit is increased by $600 per month by hiring that worker. Hiring an eighth worker increases total revenue by $2200 and total cost by $2000, so profit is increased by $200 per month by hiring the eighth worker. However, if a ninth worker is employed, total revenue is increased by $1800 per month and total cost by $2000, so profit declines by $200 per month. The farm should therefore settle for eight workers when wages are $2000 per month.

The conclusion that eight workers should be employed at $2000 per month is depicted graphically in Figure 10.1. The vertical axis measures wages, and the horizontal axis measures the number of workers hired. At the wage of $2000, we plot the number of workers that maximizes profit, namely, eight workers. This gives point *A*.

Returning to Table 10.2, we see that if wages were to increase to $2500, it would no longer be profitable to hire the eighth worker, whose *VMP* is only $2200. It would, however, pay to hire the seventh worker, whose contribution to total revenue of $2600 covers the wage. This gives point *B* in Figure 10.1, which shows seven workers employed at $2500 per month. If wages increased to $3000 per month, Table 10.2 shows that the farm would hire only six workers. This gives point *C*. Finally, if wages were only $1500, it would pay to expand employment to nine workers, as indicated by point *D*.

The individual farmer's **demand curve for labor** is found by joining points like *A*, *B*, *C,* and *D*. Note that the demand curve slopes downward from left to right, as do demand curves for final goods and services.

The Effect of Changes in Marginal Physical Product.   The demand curve for labor in Figure 10.1 has been drawn for a given schedule of marginal physical products. We can use our example to show that an improvement in *MPP*s at each level of employment will shift the demand curve for labor upward.

Table 10.3 on page 274 shows marginal physical products before and after an increase in labor productivity of 20%. If we assume an unchanged price of the final product, the increase in *MPP*s increases the *VMP*s by the same amount.

Before the increase in *MPP*s and consequent increase in *VMP*s, the farm employs eight workers at $2000 per month, point *A*, seven workers at $2500 per month, point *B*, and so on, as shown by the curve *D(MPP₁)* in Figure 10.2 on page

Profits are increased by hiring *more* workers when the value of the marginal product of labor exceeds the wage. Profits are increased by hiring *fewer* workers when the value of the marginal product of labor is less than the wage.

The individual firm's demand curve for labor shows the number of workers hired at each possible wage. It shows that more workers are hired at lower wages, and vice versa.

[4] The rules stated here for when to expand or contract employment take the wage as a given and equal for all workers hired. In many situations, such as with managerial personnel, different people earn different wages. As Example 10.1 on page 276 explains, there are special problems in such "labor" markets. These problems are particularly severe when managers decide how much to pay themselves.

TABLE 10.2

Employment should be expanded as long as the **VMP** exceeds the wage.

NUMBER WORKING	MARGINAL PHYSICAL PRODUCT, MPP (bushels per month)	VALUE OF MARGINAL PRODUCT (MPP × $5)	MONTHLY WAGE ($ per month)
0	—	—	—
1	450	$2,250	$2,000
2	500	2,500	2,000
3	850	4,250	2,000
4	1,000	5,000	2,000
5	850	4,250	2,000
6	620	3,100	2,000
7	520	2,600	2,000
8	440	2,200	2,000
9	360	1,800	2,000
10	290	1,450	2,000
11	230	1,150	2,000
12	150	700	2,000
13	80	400	2,000
14	40	200	2,000
15	20	100	2,000

The first worker hired produces 450 bushels of wheat worth $2250 and is paid $2000. This leaves $250 of profit. A second worker adds $2500 to revenue and $2000 to cost, thereby increasing profits by $500. It is worthwhile hiring up to an eighth worker, who adds $2200 to total revenue and $2000 to total cost and who therefore adds $200 to profits. However, a ninth worker adds $1800 to total revenue and $2000 to total cost and therefore reduces profits by $200. The farm should thus stop hiring after eight workers have been employed.

275; the MPP_1 in parentheses signifies that it is the demand curve for labor before the increase in $MPPs$ and $VMPs$. This is, of course, the same demand curve as in Figure 10.1.

After the increase in $MPPs$ and $VMPs$, each point on the demand curve for labor is shifted upward in proportion to the increase in $MPPs$. For example, after the increase in $MPPs$, if the wage was also to increase by 20% from $2000 to $2400 per month, it would still pay to employ eight workers; the eighth worker adds $2640 to total revenue versus $2400 to total cost, whereas a ninth worker adds $2160 to total revenue versus $2400 to total cost. That is, there is a point on a new demand curve for labor showing eight workers demanded at $2400 per month.

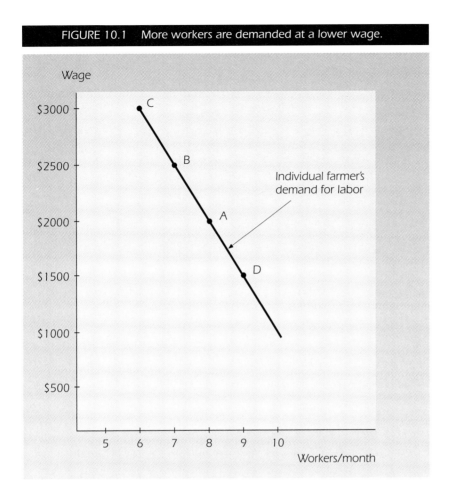

FIGURE 10.1   More workers are demanded at a lower wage.

The demand curve for labor by an individual employer shows the number of workers the employer will hire at each possible wage. The curve shows that at $2000 per month, the employer will hire eight workers, point **A**; at $2500 per month, the employer will hire seven workers, point **B**; and so on. The demand curve for labor slopes downward from left to right. That is, more workers are hired at lower wages, and vice versa.

This is described by point A' in Figure 10.2. Similarly, at $3000 per month, it pays to employ seven workers after the increase in *MPP*s, with this described by point B' in Figure 10.2. The same is true at other levels of labor demand. Therefore, an increase in *MPP*s shifts the entire demand curve for labor upward in proportion to the increase in *MPP*s. The new demand curve for labor is $D(MPP_2)$; the MPP_2 signifies the demand curve is after the increase in *MPP*s.

The Effect of Product Price.   As well as being drawn for a given schedule of marginal physical products, the demand curve for labor has been drawn for a given price of the final product. Changes in the price of the product affect the demand for labor in the same way as the *MPP*. This can be seen from Table 10.4 on page 277, which gives the *VMP*s for different prices of wheat using the original *MPP* schedule.

The individual firm's demand curve for labor shifts upward in proportion to the increase in the marginal physical product of labor.

TABLE 10.3

After an increase in the **MPP** of labor, the same number of workers are hired as before if wages are increased in proportion to the increase in **MPP**.

NUMBER WORKING	MPP BEFORE PRODUCTIVITY INCREASE	MPP AFTER PRODUCTIVITY INCREASE	VMP BEFORE PRODUCTIVITY INCREASE ($5 per bushel)	VMP AFTER PRODUCTIVITY INCREASE ($5 per bushel)
0	—	—	—	—
1	450	540	2,250	2,700
2	500	600	2,500	3,000
3	850	920	4,250	4,600
4	1,000	1,200	5,000	6,000
5	850	920	4,250	4,600
6	620	744	3,100	3,720
7	520	624	2,600	3,120
8	440	528	2,200	2,640
9	360	432	1,800	2,160
10	290	348	1,450	1,740
11	230	276	1,150	1,380
12	150	180	700	840
13	80	96	400	480
14	40	48	200	240
15	20	24	100	120

The **MPP**s at each level of employment are assumed to increase 20%. With the product's price unchanged, the **VMP**s also increase 20%. This means that the same level of demand for labor will occur after the productivity increase at wages which are 20% higher. This translates into an upward shift in the demand curve for labor by the same percentage as the increase in **MPP**s.

If the price of wheat were to increase by 20% from $5 to $6 per bushel, the *VMP*s would also increase by 20% at each level of employment. With the higher *VMP*s, Table 10.4 shows that at $2400 per month it pays to employ eight workers because an eighth worker adds $240 (or $2640 − $2400) to profit, while further hiring reduces profit.

The employment of eight workers at $2400 per month is shown in Figure 10.3 on page 278 by the point *A'*. This is the same point *A'* as occurs when the *MPP* is increased by 20%. (It is no accident that we obtain the same point on the demand curve for labor after a 20% increase in the product's price as after a 20% increase in *MPP*s; by definition, *VMP = MPP × price*, so changes in the *MPP* and the price have the same effect on the *VMP*.) Table 10.4 shows that with a wheat price of $6 per bushel, at $3000 per month it would be worthwhile to hire seven workers, point *B'* in Figure 10.3. Before, at $5 per bushel, seven workers were hired at $2500 per month. Therefore, as with the increase in *MPP*, there is a new demand curve for labor that is 20% higher than was the original curve. This is shown as *D*($6/bushel) in Figure 10.3, which is 20% above the original demand curve, *D*($5/bushel).

The individual firm's demand for labor shifts upward in proportion to the price of the product labor produces.

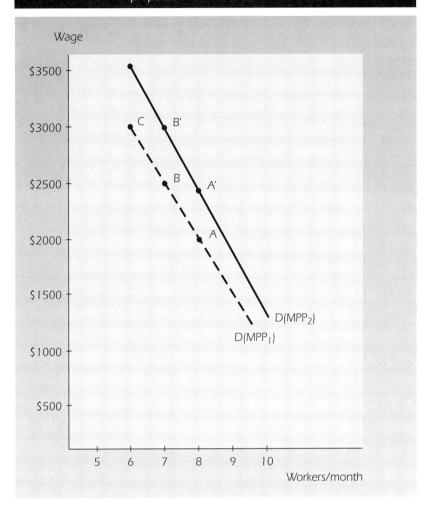

FIGURE 10.2 An increase in the marginal physical product of labor shifts the demand curve for labor upward in proportion to the increase in the *MPP.*

An increase in the **MPP** of labor increases the wage at which each level of labor demand occurs and in proportion to the increase in the **MPP.** That is, the demand curve for labor shifts upward in proportion to the increase in **MPP**.

The Market Demand for Labor

Adding the quantities of labor demanded by all firms in an industry gives the **market demand curve for labor** by that industry. For example, the market demand curve for labor by wheat farms is obtained by adding up the number of workers demanded by all wheat farms at each possible wage. With each farm demanding more workers at a lower wage, the market demand curve for wheat farm labor slopes downward from left to right, just as does an individual farm's demand for labor. The difference between individual and market demand curves is the larger number of workers represented on the market demand curve for labor.

The market demand curve for labor slopes downward.

Example 10.1

BEING BOSS: THE ULTIMATE CONFLICT OF INTEREST

In the early 1990s, as the recession deepened, a storm of protest blew up over what U.S. corporate executives were paying themselves. Newspaper stories revealed multimillion dollar salaries for corporate heads whose companies were making vast losses. The salaries often included stocks and options to buy more stocks in the companies the executives managed, as well as perks and comforts that some journalists thought were obscene. When the average was taken of chief executive officers of large U.S. corporations, the value of salaries and other benefits came to over $700,000 per year. This was almost twice the average earnings of a comparable group of Japanese executives, even when the Japanese practice of "paying" with expensive golf club memberships, housing, and other costly luxuries was counted in. With many of the Japanese firms making healthy profits and the U.S. firms covered in red ink, the obvious question people began to ask was whether the U.S.

executive labor market had gone out of control.

It is one thing to say that employees should be paid an amount that is not in excess of the value of their marginal product and quite another to know what that value is. When the work that is being done is relatively routine and being performed by many people handling a very similar task, shop-floor foremen often have a good idea of how output varies as another worker is hired. This marginal physical product, along with the product price, gives an indication, and perhaps a good indication, of what value an extra worker brings to the firm. However, the situation is very different when it comes to calculating the boss's value to a firm. Not only is there no easily measurable marginal physical product, but the assessment is usually made by the boss himself or herself, along with other executives whose own salaries the boss determines.

A new trend is emerging in the United States to try to control the

potential abuse resulting from the clear conflict of interest when top executives decide how much to pay themselves. Executive compensation review panels operated by independent personnel are popping up all over the country to check whether top-level salaries are in line with performance. While some have questioned the independence of such review panel members and others question the ability to judge "value added" on the top managerial rungs of a firm, compensation review offers the only choice. There is no other way to make judgments of value when each manager's situation is unique and where what would have happened without the manager's effort is never known. However, the panels are receiving heat from the corporate elite.

Sources: Joann S. Lublin, "Compensation Panels Get More Assertive Hiring Consultants and Sparking Clashes," **The Wall Street Journal,** July 15, 1992, pp. B1, B4; Amanda Bennett, "Managers' Incomes Aren't Worlds Apart," **The Wall Street Journal,** October 12, 1992, pp. B1, B6.

The market demand curve for labor shifts up and down in proportion to the change in the MPP of labor and price of the final product.

As with an individual employer's curve, the market demand curve for labor moves up and down with changes in the *MPP* of labor and the price of final output. Indeed, as with individual firms' curves, the market demand curve for labor shifts up and down *in proportion* to changes in the *MPP* and final output price. Figure 10.4 on page 279 illustrates these effects. The demand curve for wheat farm labor before an increase in *MPP* or the price of wheat is D_1, while the demand curve after an increase in *MPP* or the price of wheat is D_2. Curve D_2 is higher than curve D_1 by the percentage increase in the *MPP* or product price.

TABLE 10.4

The higher the price of the final product, the higher is the wage at which a given number of workers are hired.

NUMBER WORKING	MPP (bushels per month)	VMP ($5 per bushel)	VMP ($6 per bushel)
0	—	—	—
1	450	2,250	2,700
2	500	2,500	3,000
3	850	4,250	5,100
4	1,000	5,000	6,000
5	850	4,250	5,100
6	620	3100	3,720
7	520	2,600	3,120
8	440	2,200	2,640
9	360	1,800	2,160
10	290	1,450	1,740
11	230	1,150	1,380
12	150	700	900
13	80	400	480
14	40	200	240
15	20	100	120

If wheat prices increase from $5 per bushel to $6 per bushel, the number of workers demanded is the same if wages are 20% higher than before.

The Market Supply of Labor

The market supply curve of labor to wheat farming shows the number of people willing to work on wheat farms at different wages. More generally, the market supply curve of labor to an industry shows the number of people willing to work in that industry at different wages.

To explain the factors affecting the supply curve of labor, let us assume that people select where they work solely according to the wages they can earn. Suppose further that were they not to work in wheat farming, the best wage that 10,000 workers could otherwise have earned is $500 per month. Therefore, the opportunity cost of these 10,000 workers is $500 per month, and by paying this opportunity cost, or a tiny bit more, these people will be willing to work in wheat farming. That is, at $500 per month, the quantity of people willing to work on wheat farms is 10,000. We show this by point *A* on the supply curve of labor *S* in Figure 10.5 on page 280.

Suppose that there are another 8000 people who could earn $1000 per month outside wheat farming. That is, for 8000 workers the opportunity cost of wheat farming is $1000 per month. This means that at a wage of $1000 per month the number of people willing to work in wheat farming is 18,000, consisting of the 10,000 who would have worked for $500 and the 8000 requiring $1000. We show

The supply curve of labor slopes upward with respect to the wage rate.

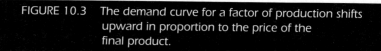

FIGURE 10.3   The demand curve for a factor of production shifts upward in proportion to the price of the final product.

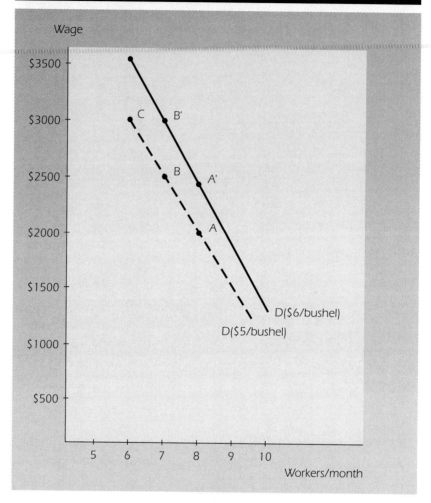

If wages increase in proportion to the price of the final product, the number employed is not changed. This can be seen by drawing a vertical line at any level of employment and reading off the wage at which this number is hired, noting the price of the final product for which the demand curve is drawn.

The height of the supply curve of labor to an industry at each quantity of labor equals the opportunity cost of the *last* person supplying his or her labor to that industry.

this by point B in Figure 10.5. As the wage is increased further, more and more people would find that they could earn more in wheat farming than in their next best alternative. That is, at higher wages in wheat farming, more and more people will find the wages to exceed their opportunity costs. This is shown by the remainder of the upward-sloping supply curve of labor to wheat farming S in Figure 10.5.

The height of the supply curve of labor to wheat farming at each number of workers is what the last worker could have earned in her or his next best alterna-

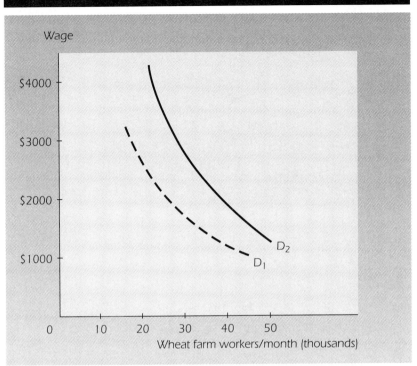

FIGURE 10.4   At a higher *MPP* or price of the final product, the market demand curve for labor is at a higher level.

At every level of employment the wage which would result in that level of employment increases in proportion to the **MPP** of labor and price of the final product. Hence the market demand curve for labor moves vertically in proportion to the **MPP** of labor and product prices.

tive employment, that is, the last worker's opportunity cost. For example, in Figure 10.5 the opportunity cost of the 10,000th worker is $500 per month, that of the 18,000th worker is $1000 per month, and so on.

With the height of the supply curve of labor being the opportunity cost, shifts in labor supply curves result from changes in opportunity costs. For example, if the wages wheat farm workers could earn in their next best employment opportunities were all to increase 20%, the supply curve of labor to wheat farms would shift upward by 20%. That is, if 10,000 workers could earn $600 rather than $500 per month in other occupations, wages on wheat farms would have to be $600 per month for the supply of labor to be 10,000 workers. The effect of an increase in wages in other industries is shown diagrammatically in Figure 10.6. S_1 is the supply curve before an increase in wages in other industries, and S_2 is the supply curve after alternative wages have increased. S_2 is above S_1 at each quantity of labor supplied by the percentage increase in the opportunity cost of wheat farm labor, that is, by 20%.

The supply curve of labor shifts up and down in proportion to the opportunity cost of labor.

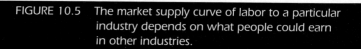

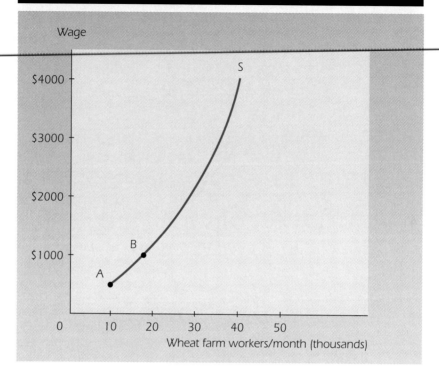

FIGURE 10.5 The market supply curve of labor to a particular industry depends on what people could earn in other industries.

The labor supply curve **S** assumes that 10,000 people could earn up to $500 per month outside wheat farming. Therefore, the quantity of labor supplied to wheat farming at $500 per month is 10,000 workers. An additional 8000 workers could earn $1000 per month in their next best opportunity. Therefore, the quantity of labor supplied to wheat farming at $1000 is 18,000 workers, and so on. The height of the supply curve of labor at each number of workers is seen to be the opportunity cost of the last person employed.

Factors Changing Equilibrium Wages

Equilibrium Wages and the *MPP* of Labor. The equilibrium wage is the wage that equates the quantity of labor demanded and the quantity supplied. That is, the equilibrium wage is where the supply and demand curves for labor intersect, just as with other prices.

An increase in the MPP of labor increases the equilibrium wage and number of workers employed.

Figure 10.7 shows the supply curve of labor to wheat farming *S* for given wages in other industries. The figure also shows demand curves for labor for two different *MPP*s of labor. The lower demand curve, D_1, is drawn for an original *MPP* of labor, while the higher curve, D_2, is drawn after the *MPP* of labor has increased. It is worth recalling that the upward shift is proportional to the increase in the *MPP* of labor.

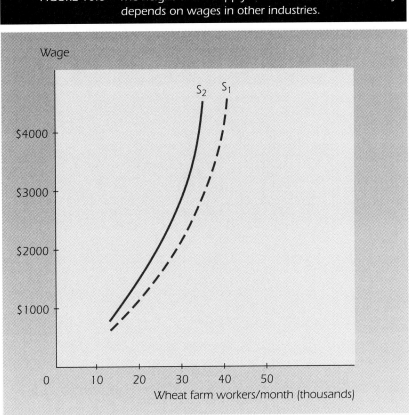

FIGURE 10.6   The height of the supply curve of labor to an industry depends on wages in other industries.

Each quantity of labor supplied is unchanged if wages increase by the same amount as the opportunity cost. For example, if 18,000 people are willing to work at a wage of $1000 per month and the wages elsewhere increase by 20%, the same number will be willing to work at $1200 per month after the increase in wages elsewhere. Therefore, the supply curve of labor shifts upward in proportion to wages in other industries.

The equilibrium wage before the increase in the *MPP* of labor is w_1, and employment is N_1. Figure 10.7 shows that an increase in the *MPP* of labor increases wages from w_1 to w_2 and increases employment from N_1 to N_2.

It is worth noting in Figure 10.7 that the increase in the equilibrium wage is smaller than the upward shift in the demand curve for labor. That is, the increase in the equilibrium wage from w_1 to w_2 is smaller than the upward shift in the demand curve for labor, which at the original level of employment is the distance *AB*. Therefore, with the upward shift in the demand curve for labor being proportional to the increase in the *MPP* of labor, it follows that the equilibrium wage increases less than the improvement in labor productivity. This occurs whenever the supply curve of labor is less than perfectly inelastic. It follows that when labor supply to an industry is less than perfectly inelastic, some of the benefit of higher productivity of labor is enjoyed by labor itself via higher wages, and some of the benefit is enjoyed by firms.

Wages increase less than the increase in productivity when the supply of labor is less than perfectly inelastic.

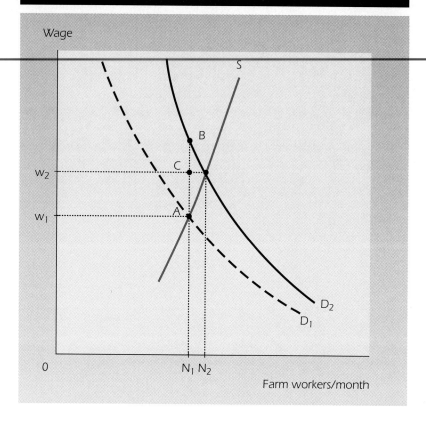

FIGURE 10.7   The equilibrium wage and number employed increase with the marginal physical product of labor and with product prices.

The two demand curves differ according to the **MPP** of labor. The lower demand curve, **D**₁, is drawn for the original **MPP** of labor, and the higher demand curve, **D**₂, is drawn for a higher **MPP** of labor. The equilibrium wage and equilibrium employment are both increased by the increase in the **MPP** of labor. Since the vertical shift in the demand curve for labor is proportional to the increase in **MPP**, the increase in wages from **w**₁ to **w**₂, which is **AC**, is smaller than the increase in **MPP**, which is **AB**. The figure also applies to the effect of an increase in the price of the product. That is, wages increase with product prices, but by less than product prices increase.

Increases in product prices increase equilibrium wages and the number employed. However, wages increase less than product prices if labor supply is less than perfectly inelastic.

By drawing a perfectly inelastic (that is, vertical) supply curve of labor instead of S in Figure 10.7, you can verify that wages increase the same extent as the *MPP* of labor; the wage increase equals the upward shift of the demand curve. The reason for this is that when labor supply is perfectly inelastic, firms compete for the fixed quantity of labor until they have forced wages up by the increase in the *MPP* of labor.

Equilibrium Wages and Product Prices.   We explained earlier that an increase in the price of the product labor produces shifts the demand curve for labor upward in the same way as an increase in the *MPP* of labor. It follows that Figure

10.7 applies to an increase in the price of the final product. That is, the demand curve for labor shifts upward in proportion to an increase in the product's price. The figure shows that wages and employment both increase with final product prices, but if the supply curve of labor is less than perfectly inelastic, wages increase less than product prices. Workers and firms share the benefit of higher prices of what they produce, just as they share the benefit of higher productivity.

Effect of Increased Wages in Other Industries. As shown earlier in this chapter, the height of the supply curve of labor at each quantity of labor supplied is the wage the last worker could have earned in his or her next best alternative employment opportunity. Therefore, if wages in other industries increase, the height of the supply curve of labor to a given industry increases by the same amount; if workers could earn more in other industries, they require comparably higher wages to supply their labor to a given industry. Figure 10.8 shows the effect of an upward shift in the supply curve of labor from such an increase in wages in other industries. The supply curve is S_1 before other industries' wages increase and S_2 afterwards. The extent of the upward shift in S equals the increase in wages each worker could earn elsewhere. For example, if the N_1th worker's alternative wage increases by \$100 per month, distance AB equals \$100. Figure 10.8 shows that the effect of higher wages in other industries is an increase in wages and a reduction in employment in the industry under study; wages are w_2 versus w_1, and employment is N_2 versus N_1. However, the increase in wages by $w_2 - w_1 = AC$ is less than the increase in wages in other industries, which for the N_1th worker is AB. That is, if labor supply is less than perfectly inelastic, an increase in wages in other industries forces wages up in a given industry, but by a smaller amount.

Increases in wages in other industries force wages up in a given industry, but by a smaller amount.

THE MARKET FOR LAND

The Demand Curve for Land

As with all factors of production, the demand for land is derived from the demand for the product the land helps produce. Furthermore, more land is demanded until the value of the marginal product from using an extra acre equals the cost of that acre. Assuming that land is used for farming and that the product price is given, the value of the marginal product of using an extra acre is, as in Equation 10.1,

$$VMP = MPP \times price$$

where MPP is the marginal physical product of an extra acre of land, and *price* is the price of the product grown. For example, if the MPP of an extra acre of wheat land is 50 bushels and wheat is \$4 per bushel, the VMP of an extra acre is \$200 (or $50 \times \$4$).

Figure 10.9 plots the VMP of land to an individual farmer. The curve slopes downward because the MPP of land declines as more land is used. This is due to the law of diminishing marginal product; more land with the same amount of labor and capital eventually faces a diminishing MPP. As with any input, land is employed if its VMP per acre exceeds its price. If land is rented, the relevant price is the rent, and if land is owned, it is the opportunity cost. For example, at price

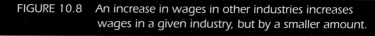

FIGURE 10.8   An increase in wages in other industries increases wages in a given industry, but by a smaller amount.

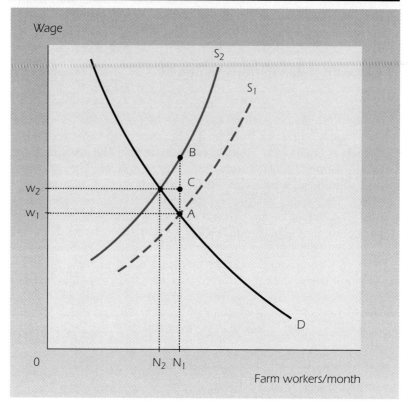

An increase in wages in other industries increases workers' opportunity costs and shifts the supply curve of labor upward. The extent of the upward shift is equal to the extent wages increase elsewhere. For example, for the **N**$_1$th worker, the alternative wage increases by **AB**. The figure shows that the effect of higher wages in other industries is to increase wages in a given industry. However, wages increase by less than they do elsewhere; $\mathbf{w_2} - \mathbf{w_1} = \mathbf{AC}$ and this is less than **AB**, where **AB** is the increase in wages elsewhere.

r_1, the quantity demanded is L_1 acres; at L_1 acres, the *VMP* is r_1 (dollars). At the lower price r_2, demand is L_2 acres; at L_2 acres, the *VMP* is r_2 (dollars).

If we sum the quantities of land demanded by all farmers of a particular product at each possible price of land, we obtain the market demand curve for land for growing that product. This is downward-sloping with respect to the price of land.

The *VMP* of land increases with the *MPP* of land and the price of the product grown on the land. That is, as with labor, the demand curve for land moves upward in proportion to the *MPP* of land and the price of the final product. Figure 10.10 shows the market demand curve for wheat land before and after an increase in the *MPP* of land or the price of wheat. Demand curve D_1 is the demand curve for wheat land before an increase in the *MPP* or the price of wheat. Demand curve

The demand curve for land is downward sloping and shifts in proportion to the MPP of land and the price of the final product grown on the land.

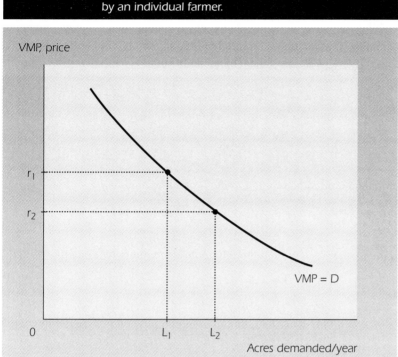

FIGURE 10.9 The lower the price of land, the more land is demanded by an individual farmer.

The contribution to total revenue from using another acre of land is the land's **VMP**, which is its **MPP** times the price of the product that is grown. A greater quantity of land is demanded whenever the **VMP** of the land exceeds its price. The relevant price is the rent or opportunity cost. Because the **MPP** of land diminishes as more is used with other factors fixed, the demand curve for land slopes downward. For example, at r_1 per acre, L_1 acres are demanded; the **VMP** at L_1 acres is r_1. At r_2 per acre, L_2 acres are demanded; the **VMP** at L_2 acres is r_2.

D_2 is the demand curve afterwards. D_2 is above D_1 in proportion to the increase in the *MPP* of land or the price of wheat.

Supply Curve of Land and Input versus Output Prices*

Other than a limited ability to reclaim land from swamps and the sea, the quantity of land is fixed. However, while this may be so for land in the aggregate, at least while we remain earthbound, there is no earthly constraint on the supply of land for wheat farming. Land can be used for growing different crops, for housing, and so on. Therefore, the amount of land made available for growing wheat at different prices of wheat land is not fixed. We can expect that given the prices paid for

The quantity of land supplied to any use increases with the price paid for land in that use.

* Sections or numbered items marked by an asterisk can be omitted without loss of continuity.

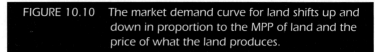

FIGURE 10.10   The market demand curve for land shifts up and down in proportion to the MPP of land and the price of what the land produces.

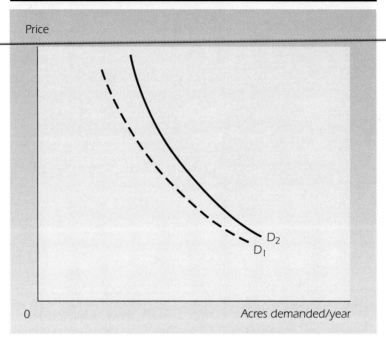

Price

D_2

D_1

0   Acres demanded/year

The height of the demand curve for land is the land's **VMP** at each quantity employed. Since **VMP = MPP × price,** the demand curve shifts up and down in proportion to the **MPP** and the **price.**

other uses of land, the higher the price paid by wheat farmers, the more land will be made available to them.

The extent to which the quantity of land supplied to wheat farmers varies with the amount paid depends on the alternative possible uses of land. Let us first consider what happens if wheat-growing land is of no use for growing anything else or even for housing. The effect of this extreme situation is shown in part (a) of Figure 10.11. The amount of land that can grow wheat is L_1. Because the land is of no use for anything else, it will be supplied to wheat farmers whatever amount they pay. Therefore, we show a perfectly inelastic supply curve of land at the fixed available quantity L_1. Let us consider the implications of such a perfectly inelastic supply for the effect of wheat prices on land prices, and vice versa.

Figure 10.11 shows two demand curves for wheat land at two different prices of wheat, p_1^w and p_2^w, where $p_2^w > p_1^w$. When the price of wheat is p_1^w, the demand curve is $D(p_1^w)$ and the equilibrium price of wheat land is r_1.[5] This is where $D(p_1^w)$ intersects the supply curve of land. At the higher price of wheat, p_2^w, the

[5] This is the price per year. We can think of this as the annual rent or the annual opportunity cost of an acre.

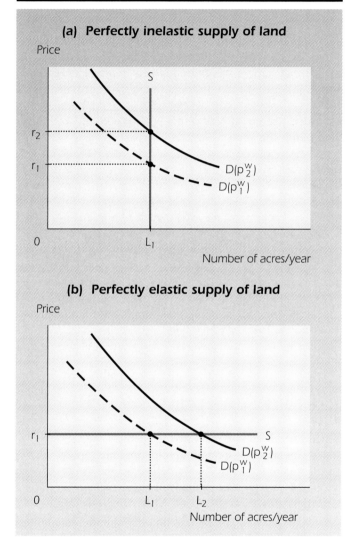

FIGURE 10.11 When input supply is perfectly inelastic, the price of outputs affects the price of inputs, but not vice versa. However, when input supply is perfectly elastic, input prices can affect output prices, but not vice versa.

(a) Perfectly inelastic supply of land

(b) Perfectly elastic supply of land

If the supply of wheat land is perfectly inelastic, as in part (a), an increase in the price of wheat, which causes an upward shift in the demand curve for wheat land, causes an increase in the price of wheat land. However, when the supply of wheat land is perfectly elastic, as in part (b), increases in the price of wheat have no effect on the price of wheat land.

price of land increases to r_2. Furthermore, because $D(p_2^w)$ is vertically above $D(p_1^w)$ by the percentage that p_2^w exceeds p_1^w, the price of wheat land is higher by the same percentage. We find that an increase in wheat prices causes an increase in the price of wheat land by an equal percentage. On the other hand, since, by assumption, the supply curve of wheat land is fixed at the amount that can be used for wheat, changes in prices of other crops have no effect on the supply of wheat land. Therefore, when the supply of land to wheat farming is perfectly inelastic, changes in wheat prices cause proportionate changes in wheat land prices, but changes in prices of other crops do not affect wheat land prices.

Let us next assume that the supply of land to wheat farming is perfectly elastic. This would occur if land for growing oats, barley, soy beans, and so on was completely interchangeable with land for growing wheat. Then wheat farmers would have to pay the going price to secure land, the price paid by farmers of other crops. Part (b) of Figure 10.11 shows a perfectly elastic supply curve of land to wheat farming S. The figure shows that when the demand curve for wheat land shifts from $D(p_1^w)$ to $D(p_2^w)$, there is no change in the price of wheat land, which remains at r_1 per acre. Therefore, there is no impact of wheat prices on the price of wheat land. All that happens is that as wheat prices increase and the demand curve shifts from $D(p_1^w)$ to $D(p_2^w)$, the amount of land in wheat farming increases from L_1 to L_2.

> When the supply curve of a factor is perfectly inelastic, changes in product prices change factor prices, but not vice versa. When the supply curve of a factor is perfectly elastic, changes in product prices do not affect factor prices, but factor prices *can* affect product prices, at least in the long run.

While wheat prices do not affect the price of wheat land with a perfectly elastic supply of wheat land, the reverse impact is possible; that is, the price of wheat land can affect wheat prices, at least in the long run, when the cost of land is not a fixed cost. To see this, suppose that there is an increase in land prices brought about by an increase in other crop prices or from urban development. While this would have no short-run effect on wheat prices—land is a fixed input, and we have seen that fixed costs have no effect in the short run—the increase in land prices would cause marginal farmers to leave wheat growing. This is so because their economic profits would fall below zero. Only when the exit of wheat farmers and the consequent increase in wheat prices fully offset the higher land price would the exit of farmers end and the price of wheat cease to increase.

What we have said about land is also true of the other primary factors of production, that is, labor and capital. When factor supplies are perfectly inelastic, the direction of causation is from product prices to factor prices, whereas when factor supplies are perfectly elastic, the direction of causation is reversed, at least in the long run.

THE MARKET FOR CAPITAL

No society operates without capital. Even the earliest societies of which we have knowledge used capital such as hunting implements, grinding stones, cooking pots, and fish and animal traps. Today, capital in the form of computers, transportation equipment, factory and office buildings, communications satellites, and so on trades in global markets. Much of what can be said about the market for capital is the same as what we have learned about labor and land. For example, the height of the demand curve for capital shifts up and down in proportion to the *MPP* of capital and in proportion to the price of the final products capital produces. However, there are special features of capital. These relate to the fact that capital enhances *future* output and profits and that capital must itself be produced.

The Demand for Capital

As with the other primary factors, the demand for capital is derived from what it produces, but in the case of capital, this production occurs over a period of time after the capital has been produced. Therefore, we need to be able to value the contributions made over time, where these contributions are the extra profits capital makes possible.

Suppose that a farmer is considering buying a combine harvester which she or he expects to increase profits by $10,000 per year over the 10-year life of the machine, after accounting for operating and maintenance costs. The question is, "How much would the farmer pay for the harvester given the machine's expected contribution to profits?"

Recall that we met a situation in Chapter 1 where benefits accrued over a period of time when we considered whether college is a worthwhile investment. Because the farmer's decision on buying a harvester and the student's decision about college are both investments, it is no surprise that what we said in Chapter 1 applies here.

Recall that in the case of college, a relevant factor is the interest rate. This affects what we called the present value of the extra income earned with a college degree. We pointed out that college is a worthwhile investment if the present value of extra income exceeds the cost of attending college. In the case of the combine harvester, the investment is worthwhile if the present value of the extra profits generated by the harvester exceeds the cost of the machine.

An investment is worthwhile if the present value of the profits it generates exceeds the cost of the investment.

The present values of each of the $10,000 of extra profit for 10 years at different interest rates are given in Table 10.5.[6] Let us review how we calculate these present values. For simplicity, we assume that the farmer already has cash that, if not spent on the combine harvester, could be left in the bank. Let us begin by assuming that the money in the bank would be earning 10% per year. We also assume that the extra profits from using the harvester are as certain in amount as the interest earned on the bank deposit. That is, the two investments are of the same risk. (The calculation of present value can still be made if we instead assume that the harvester is riskier than a bank deposit, but with some increased difficulty.)

At 10%, the present value of $10,000 in 1 year is $9091. (See the column in Table 10.5 headed "Present Value at 10%.") This follows because, if given the choice between $9091 immediately or $10,000 in 1 year, the farmer would be indifferent; $9091 invested for 1 year at 10% becomes $10,000. Similarly, $10,000 in 2 years has a present value of $8264, because $8264 invested today for 2 years at 10% per year with interest compounded becomes $10,000. The entries for present values for other years are calculated in the same way. Table 10.5 shows that the further in the future the extra profit from the investment is received, the smaller is the present value. For example, $10,000 to be received in 10 years has a present value of only $3855 at a 10% interest rate.

The present value of a given amount is smaller the longer the time before it is received

Table 10.5 also calculates present values at 5% and 15% interest rates. By reading across the table, we see that the present value of a given amount in a given year is smaller as the interest rate increases. For example, $10,000 in 1 year at a 5% interest rate has a present value of $9524; this amount invested at 5% would become $10,000 after 1 year. On the other hand, $10,000 in 1 year at a 15% interest rate has a present value of only $8696. For the time being, let us assume that the interest rate is 10% and begin to construct the demand curve for capital.

[6] For simplicity, we assume that there is no scrap or resale value at the end of 10 years.

TABLE 10.5

The present values of future incomes from capital investments are smaller at higher interest rates.

YEAR	EXTRA PROFIT	PRESENT VALUE @ 5%	PRESENT VALUE @ 10%	PRESENT VALUE @ 15%
1	$10,000	$9,524	$9,091	$8,696
2	10,000	9,070	8,264	7,561
3	10,000	8,638	7,513	6,575
4	10,000	8,227	6,830	5,718
5	10,000	7,835	6,209	4,972
6	10,000	7,462	5,645	4,323
7	10,000	7,107	5,132	3,759
8	10,000	6,768	4,665	3,269
9	10,000	6,446	4,241	2,843
10	10,000	6,139	3,855	2,472
TOTAL	$100,000	$77,216	$61,445	$50,188

The present value of a given sum to be received at a later date is the amount, which if invested today, would provide that sum at the future date. For example, the present value of $10,000 to be received in 1 year when the interest rate is 10% is $9091, because investing $9091 today at 10% would provide $10,000 in 1 year. More generally, each entry in the table is

$$PV_t = \frac{\$10,000}{(1+i)^t}$$

where PV_t is the present value of $10,000 in t years, and i is the interest rate expressed in decimal form. For example, with 10%, $i = 0.10$; with 5%, $i = 0.05$; and so on.

The present value of future income from a capital investment is smaller as the interest rate increases.

The demand curve for capital goods slopes downward with respect to the price of capital.

The present value of the extra $10,000 of profits from a combine harvester at 10% is shown in Table 10.5 to be $61,445. Therefore, if the market interest rate is 10%, the farmer expecting $10,000 extra profits per year for 10 years from the machine would be willing to buy it only if the machine costs $61,445 or less. This means that if the price of the machine is $61,445, this farmer is just willing to buy it, as are other farmers for whom the extra profits generated by the machine are above $10,000 per year, thereby making the present value greater than $61,445. If the price of a harvester were above $61,445, the farmer in our example would not buy one. However, other farmers for whom the present value is higher might buy one, because the value of a harvester to different farmers is different, even when computing present values at the same interest rate. For example, there might be farmers for whom a harvester adds $12,000 of profit per year, or even $15,000 of profit per year, for 10 years.

This example suggests that the higher the price of a harvester, the fewer farmers will buy one. That is, the demand curve for harvesters slopes downward with respect to harvester prices, as seen in Figure 10.12.

Our example also suggests that the lower the interest rate, the higher are the present values of profits from harvesters for all farmers considering a purchase. Therefore, the lower the interest rate, the larger is the demand for harvesters at each price of harvesters. That is, the demand curve shifts upward and to the right with reductions in interest rates. This is shown in Figure 10.12, with $D(i_2)$ being above and to the right of $D(i_1)$, where i_2 is less than i_1.

Demand curves for capital goods such as combine harvesters also shift up and down with changes in prices of what the capital goods help produce and with the *MPP* of capital. In this sense, the demand curve for capital behaves like the demand curves for labor and land.[7] *Ceteris paribus,* the higher the price of wheat or the higher the *MPP* of harvesters, the higher is the demand curve for harvesters. Therefore, the two demand curves for harvesters in Figure 10.12 can be thought of as being for two different wheat prices or for two different *MPP*s rather than for two interest rates, where the higher curve is for the higher wheat price or the higher *MPP* of capital.

> The demand curve shifts upward and to the right with reductions in interest rates, and vice versa.

The Supply of Capital

As with final goods and services, the supply curve of capital goods such as combine harvesters slopes upward with respect to the price of the capital goods. However, many items of capital are designed for specific tasks, and such items take time to produce.[8] This situation means that if the price were to increase, it would take time for the quantity of such capital to increase. However, given sufficient time, extra capital can be made. This means that the supply curve of capital is more elastic in the long run than it is in the short run.[9] The effects of this on the consequences of changes in interest rates for prices of capital goods are shown in Figure 10.13.

Figure 10.13 assumes that in the short run the supply of capital is fixed at S_s. Therefore, a decrease in interest rates from i_1 to i_2, which shifts the demand curve from $D(i_1)$ to $D(i_2)$, increases the price of existing capital from p_1 to p_s. However, this is only a short-run effect. In the long run it might be, for example, that the supply of capital is perfectly elastic at the original price p_1. This would occur if the capital could be produced by different firms at the same minimum long-run

> Supply curves of capital goods slope upward with respect to the price of capital goods. The supply curve is more elastic in the long run than in the short run.

> When the supply curve of capital is more elastic in the long run than in the short run, the price of capital increases more in the short run than in the long run after an increase in demand.

[7] Because land produces products over a long time and, indeed, may be thought of as being infinite in life, the demand curve for land for purchase shifts up and down with the interest rate, as does the demand curve for capital. This means that if our concern is about land *prices,* interest rates must be considered.

[8] This is not true of all capital. For example, computers can be used for different tasks, making the supply to any particular task or industry potentially elastic even though it takes time to produce new computers.

[9] What we say about capital applies to labor and land. For example, the supply of a particular type of skilled labor or of fruit trees ready to bear fruit is more elastic in the long run than in the short run.

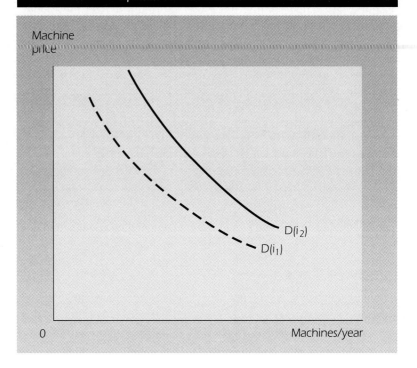

FIGURE 10.12   The demand curve for capital goods is downward-sloping vis–à–vis the price of capital goods and shifts upward with decreases in interest rates.

At any given interest rate, different potential buyers of a capital good expect it to contribute different amounts to profits. The higher the price of the capital good, the fewer buyers will find that the present value of it to them exceeds the price, so the lower will be the quantity demanded. This means that the demand curve slopes downward. In addition, the lower the interest rate, the higher is the present value to all potential buyers, so the higher is demand at each price. That is, the demand curve shifts upward and to the right with reductions in interest rates. The demand curve for capital also shifts upward and to the right with increases in final product prices and with increases in the **MPP** of capital.

average cost. A price above p_1 would then provide economic profit, which would induce new firms to enter until the price of capital goods had moved back to p_1. If the long-run supply curve of capital is perfectly elastic, the price returns to p_1 in the long run, and the quantity produced increases to q_L. For capital goods that are flexible in application, such as most computers, office equipment, trucks, lathes, and so on, the supply curve to any one use may be elastic even in the short run. The price of such capital will respond less to shifts in demand for capital in any particular use.

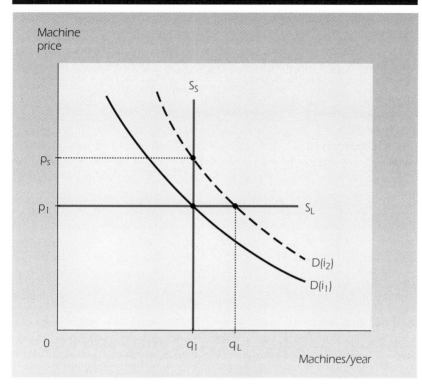

FIGURE 10.13   The supply of capital is more inelastic in the short run than in the long run, and therefore price increases are larger in the short run.

In the short run, the supply of capital is assumed to be fixed at S_s. Therefore, an increase in demand for capital from $D(i_1)$ to $D(i_2)$ increases the price of existing capital from p_1 to p_s. However, in the long run, the supply of capital is assumed to be perfectly elastic. This means that the price of capital will eventually return to p_1.

FACTOR SUPPLY AND FACTOR INCOME

Aggregate Factor Supplies versus Supplies to Individual Industries and Firms

The elasticity of supply of a factor of production to a particular use depends on how narrowly or broadly that use is defined. For example, as we have just indicated, the elasticity of supply of computers and trucks to an individual industry is more elastic than is the supply to the economy as a whole. Similarly, the supply of land to wheat farming is more elastic than the supply of land to the economy. This follows because the opportunity cost of land used for wheat farming is what the land could earn in its highest paying alternative use, whereas the opportunity cost of land as a whole is zero.[10] Furthermore, the elasticity of supply to an individual wheat farmer is more elastic than the elasticity of supply to all wheat farmers. Indeed, if all wheat farmers can derive the same *VMP* from an extra acre, the supply of land to an individual wheat farmer is perfectly elastic. The height of that perfectly elastic supply curve is the price paid for land by other farmers.

The supply of a factor of production to a particular use is more elastic the more narrowly that use is defined.

----

[10] If land is not used for wheat farming, it is used for something else, but if land in general is not used, it is, by definition, not used for something else and therefore has an opportunity cost of zero.

Economic Rent*

When the supply curve of a factor of production has an upward slope, the market price of the factor exceeds the opportunity cost of most units of that factor. This can be seen from Figure 10.14. The figure shows that the first acre of land drawn into wheat farming has an opportunity cost of approximately $85 but receives the market price, $180. It therefore earns $95 in excess of its opportunity cost. The one-millionth acre has an opportunity cost of $100 but also earns $180. It therefore earns $80 in excess of its opportunity cost. Only the last unit of land employed growing wheat, which is the three-millionth acre, earns its opportunity cost; the land has an opportunity cost of $180 and receives $180.

The payment to a factor of production over and above its opportunity cost is called its **economic rent.** That is, economic rent is the amount paid to the factor in a particular activity minus the amount necessary to draw the factor into that activity.

The economic rent for each acre in Figure 10.14 equals the distance between the supply curve at that acre and the price line. For example, the first acre has an opportunity cost of $85 and earns $180, so its economic rent is $95. This equals the distance between the supply curve and the price line. Similarly, the economic rent on the one-millionth acre is the distance between the supply curve and the price line, namely, $80 (or $180 − $100). If these amounts are added for all acres used, the sum of these distances is equal to the shaded area in Figure 10.14. The figure shows that the total economic rent of all the factor equals the area between the supply curve and a line drawn at the market price of the factor.

Use of the term **rent** may be a little confusing until we realize the context in which the concept was first applied. People used to think land had no opportunity cost, since it comes in a fixed supply. Hence economists used to draw the supply curve of land as a vertical line, as in Figure 10.15. As the figure shows, in such a case, all the payment is economic rent, and therefore, all the payment to land, its rent, was considered as *economic* rent. Subsequently, economists have realized that even land has an opportunity cost in a particular use. Hence only part of its payment is economic rent.[11]

The proportion of the total payment to a factor of production that is economic rent versus the required payment to draw the factor into an activity clearly depends on the **schedule of opportunity costs.** That is, it depends on the elasticity of the supply curve. We have already noted that when this schedule is perfectly inelastic as in Figure 10.15, all the payment is economic rent. At the other extreme, Figure 10.16 shows that when the supply curve is perfectly elastic, none of its payment is an economic rent. In general, the more elastic the supply curve, the smaller is the economic rent.

Because factor supply curves are more elastic the narrower we define the use of the factor, economic rent depends on the narrowness of focus of a factor's use. For example, the economic rent on land in general exceeds the economic rent on wheat land. Furthermore, the economic rent on wheat land exceeds the economic rent on land used by an individual wheat farmer. Indeed, if the supply curve of wheat land to an individual farmer is perfectly elastic, the economic rent is zero, as in Figure 10.16. Examples 10.2 and 10.3 give two examples of economic rents.

---

[11] However, it is still true for the aggregate of land that all its rent is economic rent.

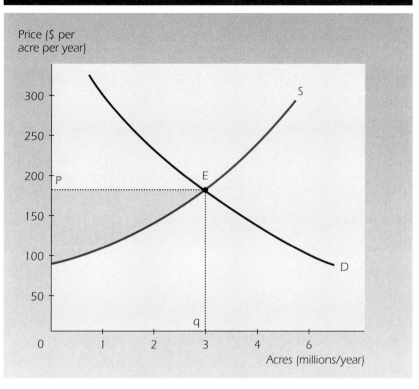

FIGURE 10.14 Economic rent is the area between the supply curve of a factor of production and the factor's market price.

The opportunity cost of the first acre is $85, but it earns the market price, $180. Therefore, the first acre earns $95 (or $180−$85) more than is necessary to draw that acre into the given use. That is, the first acre enjoys an economic rent of $95, which is the distance between the supply curve and the price line at the first acre. The one-millionth acre has an opportunity cost of $100 but earns $180. It has an economic rent of $80 (or $180−$100), which is the distance between the supply curve and price line at the one-millionth acre. Adding up the economic rents of all the land means adding the distances between the supply curve and price line for all acres. This gives the shaded area in the figure.

Quasi-Rent*

In discussing the supply curve of capital, we noted that the curve is more elastic in the long run than in the short run. For example, while the supply of combine harvesters is more or less perfectly inelastic in the short run, in the long run, the quantity of harvesters is larger as their price increases.[12] Indeed, if entry into and

---

[12] If the relevant supply is the total hours during which combine harvesters are working, and these hours of operation increase with the price—perhaps "down-time" can be reduced—supply may not be perfectly inelastic. However, avenues of flexibility are limited when the equipment is already working full time.

The supply of land in general is fixed. That is, the supply of land is perfectly inelastic. This means that even at zero payment the land would be available for somebody's use. Consequently, all the payment for land is economic rent. This is confirmed by drawing the area between the supply curve and the horizontal line at the market price. (The supply curve can be thought of as the horizontal axis up to the given quantity and then as a vertical line at that quantity).

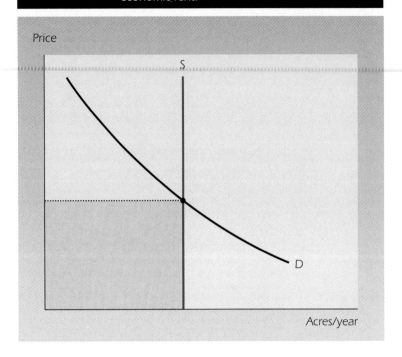

FIGURE 10.15   The payment for land in general is all economic rent.

If factor supply is perfectly elastic, as the supply of wheat land is to an individual wheat farmer who must pay the market price or have no land at all, each unit of the factor is paid its opportunity cost. This means that **all** the payment is required to attract the factor into a particular user's employment, so the land earns zero economic rent. This can be confirmed by considering economic rent as the area between the supply curve and a line at the market price. Since the supply curve **is** that line, the area representing economic rent is zero.

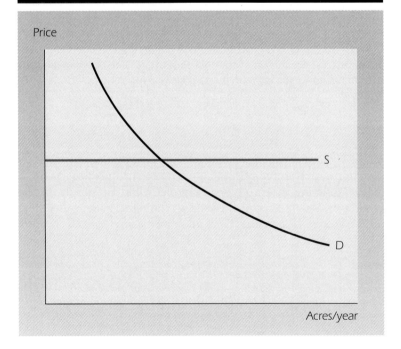

FIGURE 10.16   When the factor supply curve is perfectly elastic, economic rent is zero.

Example 10.2

MAJOR RENTS IN THE MAJORS

When Danny Tartabull signed with the New York Yankees for $5.3 million for the 1992 season, people were amazed. When Bobbie Bonilla made a deal with the New York Mets for $6.1 million, people were shocked. And when the Chicago Cubs reputedly made a 5-year deal with Ryan Sandberg for $35 million, people gasped in disbelief. These and other major league players earning fabulous amounts for playing a game that thousands play for fun must be enjoying major amounts of "rent"; many might have to settle for $20,000 or so as electricians, carpenters, or whatever if they were not able to play baseball. So why do some baseball players earn such fabulous rents?

Major league baseball players earn economic rents because there are different teams competing for them. Each team wants the players who can bring in the crowds and command the attention of the television networks. If the Mets did not pay $6 million or so for Bobbie Bonilla, then the Dodgers, Blue Jays, Yankees, or Red Sox might have done. It does not matter that Bonilla might have stayed in the game for $20,000 per year because that is what he might have earned in some other profession. From the perspective of an individual team, this is not the opportunity cost the player faces. The opportunity cost facing a player considering an individual team is what the player could earn with another team. In the case of baseball, teams have tried to reduce competition among themselves by using a draft. However, free agents have freedom to collect economic rents.

Film stars are in a similar situation to free agent baseball players in that they can enjoy economic rents. In their case, it is the fact that different studios and producers bid for their services that guarantees this.

---

exit from the combine harvester industry are free, and if harvester producers have the same minimum long-run average cost, then the long-run supply curve of harvesters is perfectly elastic. That is, while the supply curve of combine harvesters is inelastic or even perfectly inelastic in the short run, in the long run the supply curve may be perfectly elastic.

When a factor's supply curve is upward-sloping in the short run and perfectly elastic in the long run, economic rents are temporary. Such rents, which occur in the short run and disappear in the long run, are called **quasi-rents.**

> When a factor enjoys economic rents in the short run but not in the long run, the economic rents are called *quasi-rents.*

Where Factors Are Employed

Factors of production are employed by the highest bidders. These are the buyers for whom the factors are most valuable. For example, people with particular skills are hired by employers for whom these skills are most valuable, and land of a particular kind is rented or bought by users who can add the most value. This is beneficial as far as the economy's total output is concerned; factors are employed where they can do the most good in terms of the value of goods and services they produce. However, if there are consequences of a factor's employment which the buyer does not consider, such as the loss of an attractive farm to urban or industrial development, the economy might not be viewed as being better off by factors going to the highest bidder. We consider such a possibility in the next chapter, which examines the efficiency of the allocation of factors among different products.

Example 10.3

ECONOMIC RENT: NOT SO ACADEMIC

Salaries earned by many university professors exceed $50,000 per year. There might be some whose opportunity cost outside academia is so low that they would "profess" for only $25,000 per year. These individuals enjoy at least $25,000 per year of economic rent. Others may work as professors for $30,000 per year and therefore enjoy at least $20,000 of economic rent, and so on. That is, there is an upward-sloping supply curve of professors, and professors as a whole enjoy economic rent.

There would be no economic rents if their employers, the universities, could identify those who would do the job for $25,000 and if they could pay them only this amount. Other than for the obvious difficulty of identifying each individual's opportunity cost, why don't we observe universities trying to avoid paying professors economic rent?

Even if a university could identify those who have such a low opportunity cost or who love their work so much they would do it for only $25,000 per year, they would not be able to pay $25,000 if other universities were competing for these individuals in the market for professors. If professors are valued by universities in general at $50,000 per year, other universities will offer this amount to attract their faculty. Hence it is competition among universities that prevents any of them from getting away with paying the opportunity cost a person has as a professor. Stated differently, if all that professors consider is salary, the supply curve of professors to any given university is perfectly elastic at the going market salary. If a university will not pay this amount, then it will not get any professors. Only if all universities could conspire and agree to pay only the minimum required amount to each individual professor could they avoid paying economic rents.

Max Weber (1864–1920)

DIVERSE PERSPECTIVES ON FACTOR MARKETS

Our economic well-being is based on our ability to produce the various goods and services we want, but as we have seen, this ability is limited by the availability of factors of production. With well-being a matter of very general interest, it is little surprise that issues concerning factors of production have attracted the attention of scholars in numerous areas of enquiry. For example, a facet of society that sociologists explore and which concerns factors of production is the measurement of, and the consequence of, **class**. Because class is related to the distribution of income and wealth, and because income and wealth distributions depend on the distribution of ownership of factors of production, factor markets bring together the study of economics and sociology.

Who has legal rights over labor, land, and capital, and what is the extent of these **property rights**? Since the end of slavery, the issue of own-

ership of the factor of production labor has been resolved, with individuals owning their own labor and having the right to sell it. However, there is still no consensus on the property rights that should be afforded to capital and land. While economic efficiency considerations are central to the matter, debates over who should own capital and land and what limitations should apply to the owners' rights have raged among political and legal theorists. These debates revolve around conflicts between the efficient use of factors of production and the justice associated with the outcomes of different ownership arrangements.

Economists typically argue that private ownership, whereby owners can exclusively choose the use, enjoy the income, and voluntarily sell factors, gives rise to the most efficient use of factors of production. This is so because private owners have an incentive to protect factors as well as to choose the most productive use; when bidding for factors, the bidder with the highest value use would succeed in acquiring the factor. Furthermore, private owners have an incentive to invest in the factor, for example, preparing land or maintaining a machine, if they can be confident of indefinite ownership. In order to have exclusive and indefinite private rights of ownership and to the voluntary exchange of factors, it is necessary to have laws to protect owners and laws to permit the transfer of ownership. Therefore, there is a strong link between economics and law in the context of factor markets. Further, because capitalism and communism differ essentially in whether capital and land are owned privately or by the state, there is a strong link between economics and political science revolving around factor markets.

Economists as well as legal and political theorists recognize situations in which private ownership does not necessarily result in efficient outcomes from a societal perspective, and this has given rise to discussions about **eminent domain**. Under rules of eminent domain, the state has the right to purchase private property, with compensation, irrespective of the wishes of private owners. An example of a situation in which the law of eminent domain may be invoked is the construction of a highway passing through private land. An individual property owner may try to hold out until all others have sold their land and then demand the entire projected benefit of the project. Under the laws of eminent domain, public authorities have the right to compulsory purchase of the property, although under the Fifth Amendment of the United States Constitution, "just compensation" must be paid. Economic and legal debate typically rages around the conditions under which the laws of eminent domain are applicable and about what constitutes fair compensation.

Because the compensation that is considered fair is typically the present value of the income lost on the purchased property, and because this is essentially an economic matter, legal discussions of eminent domain have a major economic dimension.

The economics of the labor market has connections to psychology, particularly concerning the role of wages in motivating workers. Indeed, economic principles have recently been revised to account for the effect wages have on the **MPP** of labor. For example, higher wages can increase loyalty and reduce shirking. In part, the revision of economic principles is the consequence of economists learning from research performed in other social sciences. Psychologists have for years recognized that rats work or a reward, pushing levers for food, and have observed that, up to a point, deprivation makes rats work harder. Psychologists and sociologists also have written extensively on how, for example, parents use rewards to motivate children, offering ice cream for eating vegetables and television time for doing homework, and on how teachers offer students stickers, checkmarks, and words of praise for doing good work.

It is difficult to perform laboratory tests involving the supply of labor by humans, but laboratory experiments have been performed on rats and bees. As we have mentioned, up to a point, rats increase effort with deprivation. In the case of bees, it has been shown that increasing their "pay," in terms of pollen availability per flight, from a lower to higher level increases the number of flights. However, it also has been shown that as the "wage rate" is increased, there comes a point at which bees **reduce** effort. Economists have considered this phenomenon in the market for labor in general and have called it the **backward bending supply curve of labor**; at high wages, workers' incomes are high, causing them to demand more of the luxury

Weber argued that the acceptance of the Protestant ethic . . . triggered the engine of economic development.

"good" leisure, thereby reducing the time spent at work.

On the side of the demand for labor, we have seen in this chapter that economists have shown that profit-maximizing firms hire labor until the value of the marginal product of labor equals the wage rate. It has been argued by biologists that a parallel "marginal condition" applies to foraging; foraging animals exploit a food source until the marginal energy intake declines to equal the energy employed in the foraging activity.

Another bridge between economics and biology concerns the law of diminishing marginal product. There is a parallel principle used in biology, that of **density dependence** of an organism. Biologists argue that when a resource is limited, it becomes more and more difficult to sustain an organism as the population expands. Both the law of diminishing marginal product and the principle of density dependence relate to diminishing opportunities as the supply of a factor/organism is increased, and both depend crucially on there being a fixed factor/resource.

The factors that led to acceptance of the desire by businesspeople to make profit which is behind the demand for labor, and of the desire to have income for consumption which is behind the supply of labor, are hotly debated among economists, historians, sociologists, moral philosophers, and theologians. The name most frequently associated with this debate is the great German sociologist Max Weber, who argued in **The Protestant Ethic and Spirit of Capitalism** (1904) that profit and utility maximization are inconsistent with the other-wordly values pursued by the Catholic church. Weber argued that the acceptance of the **Protestant ethic**, central to the theory of John Calvin, triggered the engine of economic development. The fact that capitalist development occurred in non-Protestant countries (such as seventeenth-century Japan) has been used to counter Weber's claim. Nevertheless, the role of theology in changing attitudes toward money making and hard work suggests that the very foundations of the demand and supply of labor link the study of economics to other disciplines.

Turning from labor to capital, we can note that the marginal physical product of capital is ultimately the result of the technology it embodies and the labor that operates it. These are, in turn, respectively related to research and development (R&D) and education. Therefore, economics is linked to engineering and education. Similarly, the marginal product of land also depends on advances in engineering and education, especially those branches of these subjects dealt with in agricultural science. Furthermore, because the productivity of all factors depends on how well they are managed, the factor markets are one of many areas tying economics to the business subdiscipline of **management**.

SUMMARY

1. The primary factors of production are labor, land, and capital. The prices of these factors influence the functional distribution of income.

2. As with final products, the prices of factors of production are determined by supply and demand. However, in the case of factors of production, supply is principally affected by a factor's opportunity cost, while demand is derived from the demand for the product the factor helps to produce.

3. The marginal physical product *MPP* of a factor is the increase in output from employing one more unit of that factor while the amounts of other factors are fixed. The law of diminishing marginal product states that the *MPP* eventually decreases with increases in the amount of the factor employed.

4. The value of the marginal product of a factor is the marginal revenue from hiring one more unit of that factor. When a firm can sell all it produces at the market price without affecting that price, the value of the marginal product is the *MPP* multiplied by the price of the product the factor produces.

5. If profits are being maximized, it is worthwhile hiring additional units of a factor as long as the value of the marginal product of the last unit hired exceeds the price paid.

6. The higher the wage, the higher must be the value of the marginal product of a factor for it to be employed. For a given product price, this requires a higher *MPP* of the factor. This, in turn, occurs only at a lower level of employment. That is, the higher a factor's price, the smaller is the quantity demanded.

7. Improvements in the *MPP* of a factor or in the price of the final product shift a factor's demand curve upward in proportion to the factor's *MPP* or the product's price.

8. The quantity of a factor of production supplied depends on the factor's opportunity cost, which is the amount the factor could earn in its next highest paying use. The higher the price paid in any given use, the greater is the quantity of the factor supplied to that use.

9. The supply curve of a factor shifts up and down in proportion to the opportunity cost of that factor.

10. Increases in wages in other industries increase wages in a given industry, but by a smaller amount.

11.* If factor supply is perfectly inelastic, changes in product prices cause changes in factor prices, but not vice versa. When factor supply is perfectly elastic, product prices do not affect prices, but factor prices can affect product prices, at least in the long run.

12. The demand curve for capital slopes downward with respect to the price of capital and shifts up and down with the *MPP* of capital and the price of the product the capital produces. The demand curve for capital also shifts up and down with the interest rate, the demand curve being higher as the interest rate falls.

13. The supply curve of a factor to a particular use is more elastic the narrower we define that use.

14.* Economic rent is the payment to a factor of production over and above that necessary to attract that factor into a given use. The total economic rent earned by a factor is given by the area above the supply curve of the factor and below a line drawn at the market price of the factor.

15.* The supply of factors is more elastic in the long run than in the short run. Factors that enjoy economic rent in the short run but not in the long run earn quasi-rents.

QUESTIONS AND PROBLEMS

1. You are managing a small diner serving breakfast and lunch, and where the average customer's bill is $7. You have assessed the number of customers your diner can serve each day with different numbers of servers, and the results are shown in this table:

SERVERS HIRED	DAILY NUMBER OF CUSTOMERS
1	40
2	70
3	90
4	100
5	105
6	107

a. Calculate the servers' marginal physical products.

b. Assuming that the cost of food and other nonlabor costs is $2 per customer, what are the servers' values of marginal products?

c. Assuming a server's wage is $50 per day, how many servers should you employ?

d. If wages increased to $60 per day, would you reduce the number of servers?

e. What assumptions are you making about demand and nonlabor costs in the preceding answers?

2. If firms hire additional workers until the value of the marginal product *VMP* of the *last* worker equals the wage and the *MPP*s of previous workers are higher than that of the last worker, how do previous workers' wages compare with their *VMP*s?

3. Why can we think of the height of the demand curve above a particular quantity of a factor as the approximate value of the marginal product of the last unit of that factor?

4. Does your answer to Question 3 explain why increases in the *MPP* of a factor and increases in the price of what the factor produces have the same effect in shifting the demand curve for the factor upward?

5. When the supply of labor to an industry is perfectly elastic, do firms or workers gain from increases in product prices?

6. Why does the price of land depend on interest rates?

7. Under what conditions might an increase in the *MPP* of wheat land leave wheat land prices unchanged?

8. How does the impact of an increase in the *MPP* of labor depend on whether the increased *MPP* is enjoyed by all labor or just labor employed in a particular industry?

9. You are considering borrowing to buy an espresso/cappuccino machine for the diner you manage. The machine costs $4000, and you expect to sell 500 extra cups of coffee per month compared with what you have been selling. The machine is expected to last 4 years and to have little value at the end. After the cost of coffee beans and other operating costs, your profit on each cup of coffee served is 20 cents.

   a. Should you buy the machine if your borrowing interest rate is 10%?

   b. If your borrowing cost were only 5%, would this make a difference to your decision?

List any assumptions you have made in reaching your conclusions.

10.* Do you think the price of cars increases after automobile workers' wages increase, or do automobile workers' wages increase after car prices increase, or do you think it's a bit of both?

11.* Do dentists enjoy quasi-rents?

12.* Might professional organizations which determine and restrict conditions of membership use their power to extend the period of quasi-rents of their members?

. . . .
. . . .
. . . . Achievements and Failures
. . . . of Markets*
. . . .
. . . .
. . . .
. . . .

A verbal contract isn't worth the paper it's printed on.

Sam Goldwyn

Key Concepts

Allocational efficiency of perfect competition; allocational inefficiency of imperfect competition; externalities; private
cost versus social cost; private benefit versus social benefit;
internalizing externalities; Coase theorem; property rights; public
goods; free riders; economics of the global environment; tragedy
of the commons

THE ADVANTAGES OF PERFECT COMPETITION

In Chapter 7 we saw that in a perfectly competitive market, the equilibrium price
is equal to the minimum long-run average cost. This occurs because if a product's
price were higher than this, firms would make positive economic profits, thereby
attracting new firms into the industry until the extra supply had pushed the price
lower and economic profits back to zero. That is, free entry, which is a condition
of perfect competition, causes the equilibrium price to equal the lowest possible
average cost of production. Furthermore, all firms must select the level of output at
which long-run average cost is at its minimum or they will make economic losses;

---

*This entire chapter may be omitted without loss of continuity.

at any other level of output, average cost exceeds the price, so losses are made. In contrast, when discussing monopoly and other imperfectly competitive markets, we saw that firms select outputs at which average costs are not at their minimums.

This chapter shows that not only does perfect competition result in minimum long-run average costs of production, with prices equal to these minimum costs, but also that perfect competition is **allocationally efficient,** resulting in the "correct" amounts of toothpaste versus table lamps, of turkey versus telephones, and so on.[1] The conclusion that perfect competition achieves the lowest possible long-run average costs of production, with prices equaling these lowest possible costs, and also that it is allocationally efficient appears to suggest that governments should adopt policies to keep markets perfectly competitive. Unfortunately, however, a conclusion that governments should *always* leave markets alone and let them function without interference is not warranted. While perfect competition does achieve some admirable results, there are situations in which perfectly competitive markets do not achieve ideal outcomes. Such situations occur when there are costs and benefits faced by people or firms not directly engaged in the activities from which such costs and benefits arise, and these are examples of "market failures." This chapter considers these "failures," as well as the substantial achievements of perfectly competitive markets.

THE EFFICIENCY OF PERFECT COMPETITION

Optimal Allocation of Factors of Production

We saw in Chapter 5 that in a perfectly competitive market, firms select the output at which

$$Price = MC \tag{11.1}$$

This follows because each profit-maximizing firm produces until the last unit adds the same to total revenue as to total cost and each firm is so small it can take the price as given.

In Chapters 8 and 9 we saw that in imperfectly competitive markets, firms produce until the last unit adds the same to total revenue as to total cost. However, in imperfectly competitive markets, the addition to total revenue, the marginal revenue, is less than the price because selling an extra unit means losing revenue on previous units.[2] That is, for a firm that is not perfectly competitive, at the profit-maximizing output,

$$MR = MC \tag{11.2}$$

but
$$Price > MR \tag{11.3}$$

---

[1] Allocational efficiency is given more precise meaning later in this chapter.

[2] This assumes that firms must charge the same price on all units. As we showed in Chapter 8, for firms that can be perfectly price discriminate, price still equals marginal revenue.

It follows from Equations 11.2 and 11.3 that in markets that are not perfectly competitive,

$$Price > MC \tag{11.4}$$

This is in contrast to perfectly competitive markets, where

$$Price = MC$$

as explained in Equation 11.1.

We saw in Chapter 4 that a utility-maximizing consumer allocates a budget between, for example, CDs and cable television subscriptions, such that

$$\frac{MU(CDs)}{Price(CDs)} = \frac{MU(cable\ TV)}{Price(cable\ TV)} \tag{11.5}$$

Now let us suppose that the cable television market is run by a monopoly or some other imperfectly competitive firm, whereas the CD market is perfectly competitive.

In the perfectly competitive CD market, where Equation 11.1 holds,

$$Price(CDs) = MC(CDs) \tag{11.6}$$

However, in the imperfectly competitive cable television market, where Equation 11.4 holds,

$$Price(cable\ TV) > MC(cable\ TV) \tag{11.7}$$

It follows by using Equations 11.6 and 11.7 in Equation 11.5, replacing each product's price by its marginal cost, that at the combination of products utility-maximizing consumers buy,

$$\frac{MU(CDs)}{MC(CDs)} < \frac{MU(cable\ TV)}{MC(cable\ TV)} \tag{11.8}$$

The inequality in Equation 11.8 follows because the left-hand sides of Equations 11.5 and 11.8 are equal, since $price(CDs) = MC(CDs)$ from Equation 11.6. However, the right-hand sides of Equations 11.5 and 11.8 are not equal, since $price(cable\ TV) > MC(cable\ TV)$ from Equation 11.7. Indeed, with the denominator on the right-hand side of Equation 11.8 smaller than the denominator of Equation 11.5, the right-hand side of Equation 11.8 is larger than the right-hand side of Equation 11.5.

Equation 11.8 tells us that the marginal utility *per dollar of marginal cost* of providing cable television exceeds the marginal utility *per dollar of marginal cost* of providing CDs. Marginal utility per dollar of marginal cost is simply marginal utility per unit divided by marginal cost. For example, if a good gives 10 utils of marginal utility and has a marginal cost of $2, it has marginal utility of 5 utils per dollar of marginal cost. Therefore, if inputs were switched from producing CDs to providing cable television service, there would be a gain in total utility; the marginal utility of

In perfectly competitive markets, price equals marginal cost, whereas in imperfectly competitive markets, price exceeds marginal cost.

There is a gain in total utility from shifting inputs from producing goods and services sold in markets that are perfectly competitive to producing goods and services sold in markets that are not perfectly competitive.

cable television per dollar of marginal cost of providing it exceeds the marginal utility of CDs per dollar of marginal cost of providing them. With cable television being the imperfectly competitive market and CDs the perfectly competitive market, the gain in total utility is achieved by moving inputs from the perfectly competitive market to the imperfectly competitive market.

If the CD and cable television markets were both perfectly competitive, then from Equation 11.1,

$$Price\,(\text{CDs}) = MC\,(\text{CDs}),\tag{11.9}$$

and

$$Price\,(\text{cable TV}) = MC\,(\text{cable TV})\tag{11.10}$$

Then, using these in Equation 11.5,

$$\frac{MU\,(\text{CDs})}{MC\,(\text{CDs})} = \frac{MU\,(\text{cable TV})}{MC\,(\text{cable TV})}\tag{11.11}$$

There is no gain in total utility from shifting inputs between different perfectly competitive markets.

Equation 11.11 shows there is no gain from moving inputs from producing one product to producing the other; the marginal utility per dollar of marginal cost of providing more of one of the products equals the marginal utility per dollar of marginal cost forgone on the other product.

To put these ideas in a more concrete form, let us use some numbers. Suppose that the price of CDs is $10 and the marginal cost is also $10 because the CD market is perfectly competitive; with perfect competition, *price = MC*. However, suppose that the price of a cable television subscription is $20, but the marginal cost of another cable subscription is $10; with imperfect competition, *price > MC*. Let us suppose that $10 of primary inputs—labor, land, and capital—are shifted from making one CD to providing 1 more month of cable television service.

We can think of the prices of CDs and cable television as measures of the expected marginal utilities they give their purchasers. This follows because people buy more of a product when the expected marginal utility exceeds the price, and they continue to buy until the expected marginal utility on the last unit equals the price.[3] Therefore, if $10 of inputs are shifted from CD production to cable television, the reduction in CD production means $10 of lost expected marginal utility, but the increase in cable television service means $20 of increased expected marginal utility; the shifted $10 of inputs makes 1 more month of cable television service worth $20 to its subscriber. This is a gain of $10 (or $20 − $10) in total utility simply by producing a different combination of outputs. The gain results from the fact that in the case of cable television, the price exceeds marginal cost, whereas with CDs, price equals marginal cost.

When it is possible to increase total utility from producing a different combination of goods, factors of production are not allocated efficiently.

When it is possible to increase total utility from producing a different combination of goods and services, an economy's factors of production are allocated inefficiently. They are inefficiently allocated in the sense that if more of some products

---

[3] As mentioned in Chapter 4, formally, marginal utility should be measured on a relative scale—of one product versus another. However, it is sometimes easier to think of marginal utility in dollar terms, as here, or in util terms, as in Chapter 4.

were made by moving primary inputs over from other products, there would be a gain in total utility.

If there is perfect competition everywhere so that prices equal marginal costs, gains cannot be made by reallocating factors of production. For example, if CD prices are $10 and have a marginal cost of $10 and cable television subscription prices are $20 and have a marginal cost of $20, shifting $20 of resources from providing cable television to making CDs means losing $20 of expected marginal utility from cable television and gaining $20 of expected marginal utility from two extra CDs. There is no possible increase in utility from a reallocation of resources.

A Word of Caution

It is not possible to add up different people's utilities and speak of their combined utility. In the vernacular of the economist, different people's utilities are "not additive." Therefore, when any individual is made worse off by a reallocation of factors of production, it is not possible to decide whether society as a whole is better off. In order to decide unequivocally that there is a gain from a reallocation of factors of production, it is necessary for some people to be better off while nobody is worse off. For our purpose here, we assume that when there is an increase in total utility, nobody feels worse off.

The Geometry of Allocational Efficiency

The conclusion we have just reached can be illustrated geometrically. In order to do this, consider first the demand curve for cable television service in Figure 11.1. The figure shows that at a subscription price above $20 per month, zero subscriptions are sold, but that at $20 per month, one subscription is sold. It follows that the person buying the first subscription expects to enjoy $20 of utility from it.

Figure 11.1 shows that a second subscription would be sold at $19 per month, implying that the expected marginal utility to the buyer of this second subscription is $19. Similarly, a third person enjoys $18 per month of expected marginal utility, and so on. We can see that the expected marginal utility is given by the height of the demand curve above each unit sold; this is the amount somebody is just willing to pay for that unit. We can add the expected marginal utilities from all the subscriptions sold to obtain the total expected utility. For example, if four subscriptions are sold, the total expected utility from Figure 11.1 is $74 (or $20 + $19 + $18 + $17). More generally, we can calculate the expected total utility given by a product from the area under the demand curve; the area under the demand curve is the sum of the expected marginal utilities from each unit of the product. For example, in Figure 11.1, the expected total utility is the sum of the areas in each of the vertical bars, which is a close approximation of the area under the curve. (The bars have a base equal to 1 and height given by the price paid, so the area of each bar equals the price paid.)

Figure 11.2 shows the marginal cost of cable television. The figure shows that the marginal cost of the first subscription is $10. Similarly, the second subscription has a marginal cost of $11, the third subscription a marginal cost of $12, and so on. The total cost of subscriptions is the sum of the marginal costs. For example, the total cost of four subscriptions is $46 (or $10 + $11 + $12 + $13). As with

An economy is allocationally inefficient if its factors of production are allocated to producing various outputs in such a way that by using the factors to produce a different range of products, there is an *increase* in total utility, with nobody being worse off. Imperfect competition is allocationally *inefficient*, while perfect competition is allocationally *efficient*.

The expected total utility of a product is given by the area under the product's *demand* curve.

The total cost of providing a product is given by the area under the *marginal cost* curve.

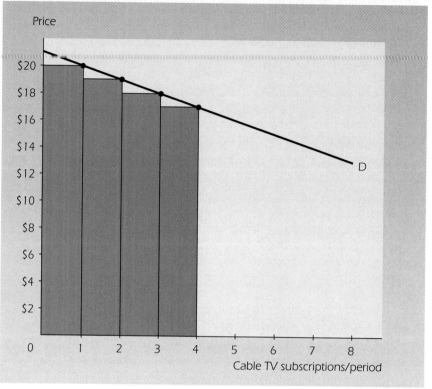

FIGURE 11.1 Total expected utility can be measured from the area under the demand curve.

At prices above $20 per cable television subscription, none are sold. Therefore, there is no buyer for whom the expected marginal utility is higher than $20. At $20, one subscription is sold. Therefore, the expected marginal utility to the buyer of that subscription is $20. Similarly, the figure shows that the second subscription sold offers its buyer an expected marginal utility of $19, the third subscription an expected marginal utility of $18, and so on. The total expected utility is the sum of the expected marginal utilities. This is given by the area under the demand curve.

demand, we can measure the total cost by the area under the curve, in this case by the area under the marginal cost curve.

Knowing that the total utility from a product is given by the area under the demand curve and the total cost of providing the product is the area under the marginal cost curve provides a way of measuring the **net benefit** from the product. In particular, the net benefit is the area between the demand and marginal cost curves. Indeed, we can measure the net benefit of each unit produced from the distance between the curves. For example, in Figure 11.3, the marginal utility from the first cable television subscription is $20, while the cost of providing it is $10, so the net benefit is $10 (or $20 − $10). Similarly, the second subscription provides a marginal utility of $19, costs $11, and therefore provides a net benefit of $8

The net benefit of producing more of a particular product is given by the area between *the demand curve and the marginal cost curve.*

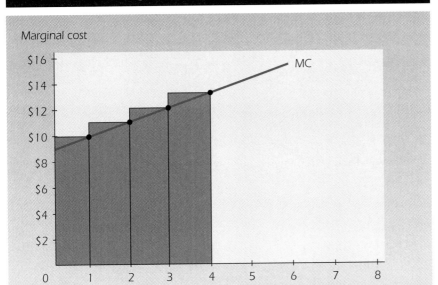

FIGURE 11.2   Total cost of providing a given amount of a product can be measured from the area under the marginal cost curve up to that given amount of the product.

The marginal cost of the first unit is $10, the marginal cost of the second unit is $11, and so on. Adding up all the marginal costs gives the total cost of providing any given output.

(or $19 − $11), and so on. If we add up all the net benefits from the different units, we obtain the area between the demand curve and the marginal cost curve.

Figure 11.4 shows the demand and marginal cost curves along with the marginal revenue curve *MR* associated with the demand curve. This figure can be used to compare the consequences of perfect competition versus imperfect competition.

As we saw in Chapter 5, the supply curve of a perfectly competitive industry is the horizontal sum of the firms' *MC* curves. The perfectly competitive market equilibrium is where this supply curve intersects the demand curve. That is, if the market described by Figure 11.4 is perfectly competitive, the price will be p_c and the output q_c. Inspection of Figure 11.4 shows that at the perfectly competitive output q_c, the area between the demand curve and the marginal cost curve is at its maximum. Let us compare this situation to what would occur if the market were imperfectly competitive.

An imperfectly competitive firm produces the output at which $MC = MR$. This is output q_m, which can be sold for price p_m. At the firm's output, the demand curve is above the marginal cost curve. That is, there is a net benefit from increasing output beyond this level. In particular, if output were increased from q_m to q_c in Figure 11.4, the increase in total utility, given by the area under the demand curve, would exceed the cost by the shaded area. This shaded area is the **deadweight**

Deadweight loss is the extent to which the additional utility from producing more of a product exceeds the cost of providing the product. There is a deadweight loss from a market not being perfectly competitive.

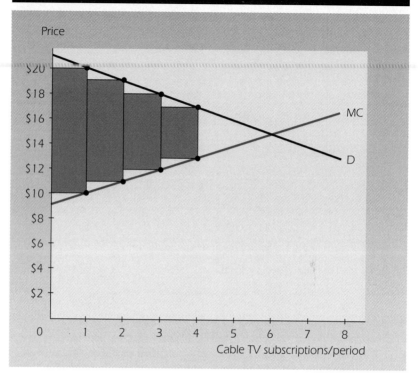

FIGURE 11.3   The net benefit from a product is the area between the demand and marginal cost curves.

The first unit gives marginal utility of $20 but has a marginal cost of $10. Therefore, the net benefit of the first unit is $10 (or $20 − $10). Similarly, the net benefit from each unit is the distance between the demand curve **D** and marginal cost curve **MC** for that unit of output. It follows that the area between the **D** and **MC** curves up to any output is the benefit of producing that product versus some other product.

loss from a market being imperfectly competitive rather than perfectly competitive.[4] The deadweight loss is the extent to which additional total utility in excess of the cost would be enjoyed from producing more of a product with perfect competition than occurs with imperfect competition.

The conclusion that perfect competition achieves allocational efficiency, avoiding the deadweight loss associated with imperfect competition, does not necessarily follow when there are costs and benefits of actions felt by people other than those taking the actions. Indeed, as we show below, perfect competition may well be allocationally inefficient in such circumstances.

MARKET FAILURES FROM EXTERNALITIES

Externalities are costs or benefits of actions that are paid or received by others who are not themselves directly engaged in the actions.

People may be hurt or may benefit from what others do. When there are costs or benefits of actions that are external to the people or firms taking those actions, these costs or benefits are called **externalities** or, sometimes, **spillovers**.

Externalities may be associated with both production and consumption. Furthermore, as indicated earlier, externalities can involve costs as well as benefits.

---

[4] The calculation of deadweight loss assumes that other markets are perfectly competitive.

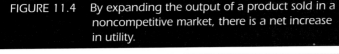

FIGURE 11.4   By expanding the output of a product sold in a noncompetitive market, there is a net increase in utility.

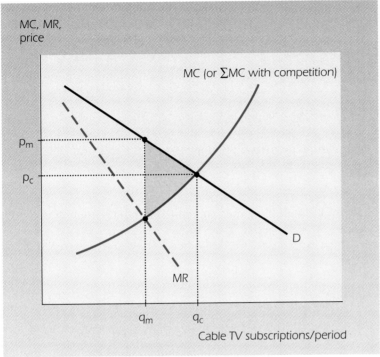

If the market is perfectly competitive, output is q_c which is where the supply curve, given from the sum of **MC** curves, intersects the demand curve. However, if the market is imperfectly competitive, output is q_m, where the **MR** curve intersects the **MC** curve. Each unit between q_m and q_c provides expected marginal utility in excess of the cost of providing it. Indeed, the perfectly competitive output q_c is the best in terms of maximizing the total utility of the product vis-à-vis the cost of providing it. The shaded area is the deadweight loss of the market being imperfectly competitive rather than perfectly competitive.

Indeed, with production and consumption both involving externalities, and with these externalities involving costs as well as benefits, logically, there are four possibilities:

1. Situations where a firm's production imposes costs on others

2. Situations where a person's consumption imposes costs on others

3. Situations where a firm's production imposes benefits on others

4. Situations where a person's consumption imposes benefits on others

Let us consider four examples that illustrate these four possibilities.

Industrial Pollution: An External Cost of Production

The private cost of production is the cost incurred by a firm itself.

The cost of production incurred by a firm itself is its **private cost.** This is the cost of inputs behind the MC and AC curves we have been drawing.

When production results in pollution of the air or water, there are additional **external costs.** These costs are not borne by the firm causing the pollution, but rather by others in society without their consent.

External costs of production are those borne not by a firm itself, but by *others* in society without their consent.

Social cost consists of private cost plus external costs. That is,

$$Social\ cost = private\ cost + external\ costs$$

For example, in the case of pollution that results from manufacturing, the private cost is the cost of production faced by the firm, and the external costs are those borne by others in society from pollution caused by the firm. The external costs could include the added expenses of health care or of obtaining safe drinking water.

The social cost of production is the total cost consisting of the private production cost incurred by the firm plus the external costs faced by others in society without their consent.

The **marginal private cost** of production is the cost incurred by the firm when producing one more unit of output. The cost borne by society of the extra unit is called the **marginal social cost.** The marginal social cost consists of the marginal private costs plus any cost incurred by other members of society from production of the extra unit. That is,

$$Marginal\ social\ cost = marginal\ private\ cost + marginal\ external\ costs$$

When there are external costs from producing an extra unit, such as added pollution,

$$Marginal\ social\ cost > marginal\ private\ cost \qquad (11.12)$$

Marginal *private* cost is the cost of producing another unit of output borne by the firm. Marginal *social* cost is the marginal private cost plus any marginal external costs, where the latter costs are borne by others without their consent.

We showed in Chapter 7 that in perfectly competitive markets, each firm chooses an output level at which

$$MC = price$$

While we did not say so explicitly, by MC we mean marginal *private* cost, so in perfectly competitive markets,

$$Marginal\ private\ cost = price \qquad (11.13)$$

By combining Equations 11.12 and 11.13, we find that in perfectly competitive markets where production causes pollution, at firms' chosen output levels,

$$Marginal\ social\ cost > price \qquad (11.14)$$

As we have explained, a product's price is a measure of the expected marginal utility from the last unit purchased. This must be so because consumers buy a product as long as the expected marginal utility exceeds the price. Indeed, they continue buying more of the product until the last unit bought has an expected marginal utility equal to the price. Therefore, on the last unit bought,

$$Price = expected\ marginal\ utility \qquad (11.15)$$

Combining Equations 11.14 and 11.15 shows that when production causes pollution,

$$Marginal\ social\ cost > expected\ marginal\ utility \qquad (11.16)$$

With production as in Equation 11.16, a nation's resources are not allocated efficiently. In particular, by producing less of an item resulting in pollution, the savings in social cost exceeds the lost expected utility of the item to the consumer. Therefore, if firms equate marginal private cost with prices, as they do in perfect competition, this is not efficient when marginal social cost exceeds marginal private cost. This occurs when there are marginal external costs. Less of such items which impose marginal external costs should be produced for a socially efficient allocation of a nation's factors of production.

*Perfect competition is not allocationally efficient when there are marginal **external** costs of production.*

The Geometry of External Costs

Allocational Inefficiency from External Costs. Figure 11.5 graphically illustrates the conclusion we have just reached. The curve ΣMPC represents the sum of marginal private costs, those which in previous chapters we have labeled MC. In a perfectly competitive market, the market supply curve is ΣMPC, the horizontal sum of private MC curves. With the demand curve D and supply curve ΣMPC, the competitive equilibrium output is q_c and the price is p_c. Suppose, however, that there are costs of production such as air pollution, noise, and so on that are external to the firm. That is, assume that the marginal social cost MSC exceeds the marginal private cost by the extent that there are marginal external costs. Suppose that the marginal external costs are $\$t$ for each unit of output produced. For example, the external costs of refining gasoline suffered by people living near the refinery might be 10 cents per gallon of refined gasoline, or the cost of electricity production for those near the power plant might be 10 cents per kilowatt generated. The sum of marginal social cost curves is the curve ΣMSC, where at each output ΣMSC is above ΣMPC by the marginal external cost $\$t$. For example, if the marginal external cost is 10 cents per unit of output, ΣMSC is above ΣMPC by 10 cents at all outputs.

The optimal output from society's point of view is q_s, where the last unit produced provides expected marginal utility to its buyer, given by the height of the demand curve, equal to the marginal social cost of producing that unit; at q_s, the demand curve has the same height as ΣMSC, so the expected marginal utility, given by the height of the demand curve, equals the marginal social cost of the last unit produced. At lower outputs than q_s, marginal utility exceeds marginal social cost, so more should be produced. At higher outputs than q_s, expected marginal utility is less than the marginal social cost, so less should be produced. That is, q_s is the optimal output from the point of view of society.

The optimal output from society's point of view is where the expected marginal utility equals the marginal social cost.

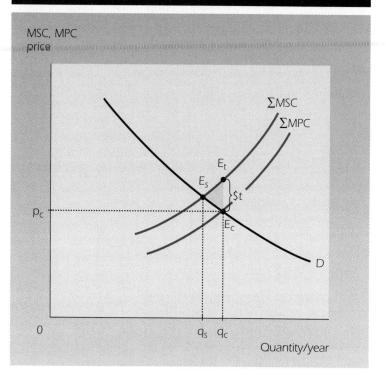

FIGURE 11.5   When there are external costs of production, perfect competition results in overproduction unless the externalities are internalized.

The supply curve in perfect competition is Σ**MPC**, where Σ**MPC** is the horizontal sum of firms' private marginal cost curves. With demand curve **D**, market equilibrium with perfect competition is output q_c and price p_c. If the marginal social cost **MSC** of each unit exceeds the marginal private cost by $\$t$, the marginal social cost of the last unit produced at q_c exceeds the price by $\$t$. Therefore, by producing one less unit than results from perfect competition, the savings in social cost, given by the height of Σ**MSC**, exceeds the price paid—which equals the expected utility of the unit to the buyer—by $\$t$. Indeed, by reducing output from q_c to q_s, the savings in cost to society—given by the area under Σ**MSC**—exceeds the expected utility the product gives buyers—given by the area under **D**—by the area of the shaded triangle. A tax of $\$t$ per unit of output paid by those imposing the externality would make Σ**MSC** the supply curve and eliminate the social loss.

There is a deadweight loss from an inefficient allocation of resources when there are *external* costs of production.

By allowing perfect competition to result in the profit-maximizing output q_c rather than the socially optimal output q_s, the increase in total utility enjoyed by consumers is the area below the demand curve between q_c and q_s in Figure 11.5, that is, area $q_s E_s E_c q_c$. The additional social cost of producing q_c rather than q_s is given from the area below the ΣMSC curve between q_c and q_s, that is, area $q_s E_s E_t q_c$. Figure 11.5 shows that the social cost of producing q_c rather than q_s exceeds the expected utility these units give consumers; the marginal social cost curve is above the demand curve. The excess of social cost over the expected utility is the difference between the areas below the two curves. This is the shaded area in Figure 11.5, and it gives the deadweight loss from the inefficient allocation of resources when there are external costs of production.

Achieving Efficiency with a Tax.   An efficient allocation of resources would occur if external costs of production were incurred by firms imposing them. One way of achieving this is to tax polluters. Such a tax would be set equal to the value of external costs, that is, $\$t$ per unit of output produced in Figure 11.5. This tax would **internalize** the externality by making the polluting firms pay for the harm they do to others. The tax would make ΣMSC the industry supply curve because each firm would consider the cost of producing an extra unit to be the marginal social cost, partly made up of the private cost and partly made up of the tax paid on each unit produced. With ΣMSC the supply curve, firms would produce q_s rather than q_c, eliminating the deadweight loss. That is, a tax equal to the external costs can achieve an efficient allocation of resources. Ideally, the revenue collected from the tax would be paid to those suffering from pollution.

Achieving Efficiency via Property Rights: The Coase Theorem.   The same outcome that can be achieved with a tax can be achieved if there are **property rights** and if compensation agreements can be negotiated and enforced inexpensively. We can clarify the meaning of **property rights** and illustrate how they overcome the problem of externalities by considering an example.

Suppose that a fertilizer manufacturer imposes an external cost by releasing effluent into a river, killing fish on a fish farm, and that fertilizer production is impossible without the external cost. Suppose that the value of lost fish or the higher cost of fish production from each pound of fertilizer manufactured is 10 cents—the marginal external cost—and that the fish farmer owns the property rights to the river. By "property rights to the river," we mean that the fish farmer can decide whether to allow the fertilizer manufacturer to discharge the effluent.

Let us consider what would happen if the fish farmer insisted on being compensated 10 cents per pound of fertilizer in order to permit the fertilizer manufacturer to discharge effluent. Would the fertilizer manufacturer agree to pay?

If the price of fertilizer exceeds the private average variable cost of production by 10 cents or more, the fertilizer manufacturer would agree to compensate the fish farmer 10 cents per pound of fertilizer manufactured. (Recall that it is better to produce in the short run than to shut down if price exceeds average variable cost, where in the example the average variable cost is the average private variable cost plus 10 cents of compensation.) Such an agreement fully compensates the fish farmer for damage and would therefore be acceptable. Similarly, the compensation is an unavoidable cost of production to the fertilizer manufacturer that is worth paying in the short run. Indeed, the damage compensation is worth paying in the long run if an economic profit remains, that is, if the price of fertilizer equals or exceeds the average total cost, including the 10 cents compensation payment.

The effect of the compensation payment on the output of fertilizer is the same as from a pollution tax collected by the government. In either case, the fertilizer manufacturer pays the marginal social cost, consisting of the marginal private cost plus the marginal external cost suffered by the fish farmer. As with a tax, when the fertilizer manufacturer faces the marginal social cost by having to pay compensation, the output of fertilizer is the socially optimal amount. Furthermore, without compensation, the fish farmer's marginal private cost exceeds the marginal social cost, and therefore, too few fish are produced from a social perspective; the price

When there are external costs of production, a socially efficient allocation of resources can be achieved by a tax on producers equal to the value of externalities from each unit produced. The tax internalizes the externalities by making the producer pay the marginal social cost of production.

Property rights give owners the authority to decide who can use their property, including the right to damage it. When property rights exist, compensation payments for damages will be negotiated.

When there are property rights, a compensation agreement will be reached between the private parties if it is not too expensive to arrange or enforce. This agreement leads to an efficient allocation of resources.

and expected marginal utility of fish exceed the marginal social cost. The receipt of compensation by the fish farmer reduces the marginal private cost to the marginal social cost, making fish production as well as fertilizer production the socially optimal amount.

If there is a dispute over who owns the property rights, or if the enforcement of property rights is very expensive, property rights may not result in a socially efficient use of resources: resources would be used in resolving the dispute or in enforcing property rights. Costs of enforcement could be a problem if there were many affected parties or many polluters fighting over the division of responsibility or over the division of compensation.

The Coase theorem states that the economic consequences of externalities are the same *irrespective of the ownership* of property rights, provided that property rights exist and compensation agreements can be negotiated and enforced inexpensively.

If property rights to the river are held by the fertilizer manufacturer rather than the fish farmer, the economic consequences for resource allocation are just the same. In this case, and again assuming that compensation agreements can be negotiated and enforced inexpensively, the fish farmer will agree to pay the fertilizer manufacturer 10 cents for each pound of fertilizer the manufacturer does *not* produce in order to reduce the associated effluent; each pound of fertilizer not produced saves the fish farmer 10 cents in reduced loss of fish or lower costs of fish production.[5] Furthermore, because the fertilizer manufacturer forgoes 10 cents of compensation for each pound of fertilizer he or she *does* produce, the marginal private cost of fertilizer production equals the marginal social cost; each pound of fertilizer costs the manufacturer the marginal private cost of inputs employed plus the 10 cents forgone from the fish farmer's payments. With the fertilizer manufacturer facing the marginal social cost, the amount of fertilizer produced is again socially optimal; resources are efficiently allocated.

We find that when property rights to the river are held by the fertilizer manufacturer rather than by the fish farmer, there is the same incentive to reach agreement, and furthermore, resource allocation is efficient. That is, the same economic consequences follow whether property rights to the river are held by those suffering from the pollution or by those causing the pollution.[6] This very important and surprising conclusion is called the **Coase theorem,** after the Nobel Laureate in economics, Ronald Coase, of the University of Chicago Law School. The Coase theorem does not provide guidance about justice, but it does tell us that as far as economic consequences are concerned, it does not matter who must be compensated by whom. What matters is that property rights exist and compensation agreements can be negotiated and enforced inexpensively.[7]

Personal Driving: An External Cost of Consumption

Because of increased pollution and traffic congestion, the marginal *social* cost of driving exceeds the marginal *private* cost.

The marginal private cost of driving an automobile another mile is the cost of gasoline, wear and tear on the tires and engine, plus the value of the driver's time at the wheel. However, these private costs are not the only costs faced by society.

---

[5] This presumes that the fish farmer knows how much fertilizer would otherwise have been produced.

[6] Clearly, the profitability of the fertilizer manufacturer and the fish farmer are affected by who owns the property rights. In particular, if the rights are owned by the fish farmer, the fish farmer is better off, being the recipient of compensation, and vice versa.

[7] The Coase theorem in the context of the favorite application of its developer, Ronald Coase, is explained in Example 11.1.

Example   11.1

PROPERTY RIGHTS AND THE LAW

*There are few conclusions in economics which are more counterintuitive than the conclusion of the Coase theorem, that from an economic efficiency standpoint, it does not matter who has property rights as long as property rights exist and agreements can be negotiated and enforced inexpensively. The following excerpt from an article in **The Economist** explains this important theorem in the context of the original problem discussed by Ronald Coase.*

. . . Mr. Coase argued that, as a rule, no form of government action is required to deal with externalities or public goods. There is no need for taxes, subsidies and public provision; and so long as property rights already exist, there is no need for energetic policies aimed at shifting them around. . . .

Mr. Coase's favorite case of externality was an American icon, the wood-burning locomotive—whose sparks, regrettably, were prone to set fire to farmers' fields. According to the conventional thinking, what matters in such a case is the allocation of property rights.

Suppose farmers have a right in law to enjoin the railway company not to set fire to their fields: the result is that the company will fit spark-suppressing equipment to their trains, and there will be less damage to the farmers' fields. Alternatively, if the company has an unfettered right to spray as many sparks as it likes, there will be plenty of damage to fields.

Mr. Coase asked if this analysis was good economics, and showed that it was not. His main point was simply that legal entitlements— property rights—can be bought and sold. They are commodities whose exchange can be analyzed like that of any other. If farmers can legally insist that locomotives are spark-free, they can sell this right to the railway. If the railway is free to spark as much as it likes, farmers can pay them to reduce the sparks that locomotives emit.

Not only that, but the outcome will be the same in either case. Suppose farmers have a right to stop the sparks. If this right to emit sparks is worth more to the railway than stopping the sparks is to the farmers (because suppressing sparks is costly, say), then the railway will buy the right to emit sparks from the farmers, and the damage will continue. Suppose instead that the railway is entitled to emit sparks—but that this right is still worth more to the railway than to the farmers. In that case, the right will not be sold, and the damage will continue.

There is one difference. The initial allocation of property rights affects the distribution of income; in other words, if you own something, you are better off than if you do not. But the allocation makes no difference at all to the amount of resources devoted to suppressing sparks. Economic forces ensure that the same efficient allocation will happen in either case. This idea is known as the "Coase Theorem.". . .

Source: *Schools Brief*, **The Economist**, *23 February–1 March 1991, pp. 72–73. © 1991 The Economist Newspaper Group, Inc. Reprinted with permission.*

The individual driving an automobile is subjected to only a fraction of the air and noise pollution that individual causes; other people, too, must breathe the bad air and suffer the extra traffic noise. Because of extra emissions and noise suffered by others, the marginal social cost of driving another mile exceeds the marginal private cost the driver bears. Another reason why the marginal social cost of driving exceeds the marginal private cost is the traffic congestion this causes. When a person drives an extra mile, she or he adds to the amount of traffic and thereby increases the time other drivers must spend to complete their journeys. The value of time other drivers lose is part of the social cost of a person driving an extra mile. Therefore, as a result of pollution and congestion,

$$\text{Marginal social cost} > \text{marginal private cost} \qquad (11.17)$$

320 CHAPTER 11 ACHIEVEMENTS AND FAILURES OF MARKETS

A person adds to the distance driven as long as the expected marginal private utility exceeds the marginal private cost the person must pay. Since some trips are more important than others, the marginal private utility a person enjoys declines as more miles are driven during a given time interval. Getting to work or college may be the highest-priority journeys; then might come shopping trips; and so on. People choose to drive more miles until the extra driving has reduced the marginal private utility to the marginal private cost, where the marginal private cost consists of gas, wear and tear, and the value of the person's own time. That is, people drive until

$$\textit{Marginal private cost} = \textit{marginal private utility} \qquad (11.18)$$

Combining Equations 11.17 and 11.18, we find that when there are externalities from driving, at the number of miles individuals choose to drive,

$$\textit{Marginal social cost} > \textit{marginal private utility} \qquad (11.19)$$

If the only benefit of driving is that enjoyed by the person driving,

$$\textit{Marginal private utility} = \textit{marginal social utility} \qquad (11.20)$$

By combining Equations 11.19 and 11.20, we find that at the number of miles people privately choose to drive,

$$\textit{Marginal social cost} > \textit{marginal social utility} \qquad (11.21)$$

Because of pollution and traffic congestion, people drive more than the socially optimal amount.

Equation 11.21 involves an inefficient allocation of resources. If people drove fewer miles than is in their private interest, the savings in costs from society's point of view, including cleaner air and less traffic congestion, exceeds the loss of social utility. Therefore, if there are external costs involved in driving, leaving individuals to decide privately how much to drive is not in the best interest of society.

Figure 11.6 graphically illustrates the case of external costs of consumption, as there are from driving. The curve MPU gives the marginal private utility from each mile driven per week. We assume that the driver is the only person benefiting from driving, so the marginal social utility MSU equals the marginal private utility MPU. The height of the $MPU = MSU$ curve at each number of miles, which is the marginal private utility, is the amount the driver would pay to drive the last mile. The curve slopes downward because different journeys are of different importance, with each extra mile driven providing less marginal utility than the previous mile.

The marginal private cost MPC is the cost of gas wear and tear, and the value of time spent driving each mile. This is assumed to be the same amount per mile, however many miles are driven. The marginal social cost consists of the sum of the marginal private cost plus the costs imposed on others from extra air pollution and traffic congestion. If the externalities suffered by others are valued at $\$t$ per mile driven, the marginal social cost curve MSC is $\$t$ above the marginal private cost curve MPC.

The optimal amount of driving from the driver's private perspective is the number of miles at which $MPU = MPC$, that is, q_p miles per week. This is too many miles from society's point of view because it is socially optimal to drive q_s miles

FIGURE 11.6   When the marginal social cost of driving exceeds the
marginal private cost because of increased traffic congestion
or pollution, people drive too many miles unless the
externality is internalized.

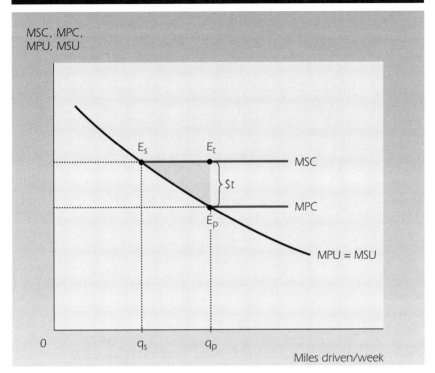

Because different journeys are of different importance, as more miles are driven per
week, the marginal private utility **MPU** of an extra mile declines. This is shown by the
downward-sloping curve **MPU**. If the driver is the only person enjoying utility from
driving, the marginal social utility **MSU** equals the private utility, that is, **MSU = MPU**.
The marginal private cost **MPC** consists of the cost of gas, wear and tear, and the value
of the driver's time. This is constant per mile driven, as shown by the horizontal **MPC**.
The marginal social cost **MSC** is the sum of **MPC** and the cost imposed on others from
increased pollution and congestion. People drive until **MPU = MPC** and therefore drive
q$_p$ miles per week. The socially optimal amount of driving is where **MSU = MSC**, that is,
q$_s$ miles per week. A tax equal to the value of the externalities, **$t**, will induce people to
drive the socially optimal amount.

per week. This is where the marginal social utility *MSU* equals the marginal social
cost *MSC*. We find that the unregulated solution involves too much driving for an
efficient allocation of resources; too many resources are devoted to driving.

If each individual driver were taxed an amount equal to the costs others bear,
that is, $t per mile, each individual would see the marginal private cost per mile as
MPC + $t, which equals *MSC*. Therefore, the tax would make it optimal for each
individual to drive the socially optimal number of miles; with *MSC* the cost the

individual pays per mile, consisting of $MPC + \$t$, it pays to drive the number of miles such that $MSC = MPU$, that is, q_s. The tax of $\$t$ per mile might be levied via a gasoline tax.[8] A better alternative would be for the government to record drivers' mileages when and where traffic congestion and pollution are caused and tax drivers accordingly. Efforts to do this have gone beyond the realm of science fiction, with cities such as Hong Kong and Singapore having already implemented such schemes. (See Example 11.3.)

If a tax of $\$t$ per mile were imposed and, as a result, the number of miles driven per week declined from q_p to q_s, the reduction in social utility from driving would be given by the area under the MSU curve between q_s and q_p. This is area $q_s E_s E_p q_p$ in Figure 11.6. However, the reduction in social cost is given by the area under the MSC line between q_s and q_p. This is area $q_s E_s E_t q_p$. The net social gain from the tax and consequent reduction in driving is the extent to which the savings in social costs exceeds the reduction in social utility. This is, the shaded triangle $E_s E_t E_p$.

An alternative to a tax would be to issue driving permits which limit the total number of miles people can drive to the socially optimal amount. For example, each driver might be given a book of permits allowing 10,000 miles per year. In effect, driving permits give drivers property rights to drive a particular distance. In principle, the permits could be traded between drivers so that those wanting to drive the most could acquire them from others. Indeed, a permit market might be established in which permits are bought and sold. Such a permit scheme would involve an efficient allocation of resources if the total number of miles was kept at the socially optimal amount.

Bee Keeping: An External Benefit of Production

With so much attention being paid to environmental damage from production, it might seem unlikely that production could bring benefits for others. However, beneficial externalities of production do occur from, for example, bee keeping.

Honey producers' bees pollinate fruit trees in nearby orchards. Therefore, by producing more honey, fruit output is also increased. The extra fruit provides utility in addition to the utility of the honey. That is, at the profit-maximizing output of honey where *marginal private cost = price*,

$$\text{Marginal social utility} > \text{marginal private cost} \qquad (11.22)$$

If the prices of factors of production used in producing honey reflect the social cost so that

$$\text{Marginal private cost} = \text{marginal social cost} \qquad (11.23)$$

it follows from Equations 11.22 and 11.23 that

$$\text{Marginal social utility} > \text{marginal social cost} \qquad (11.24)$$

---

[8] See Example 11.2 for a discussion of taxes on gasoline and other carbon fuels and the possible side benefits of such taxes.

Example 11.2

EFFICIENT TAXES

Using taxes to increase marginal private costs so that they reflect external costs adds to economic efficiency by bringing private actions closer to their socially optimal level. As the following article explains, depending on what is done with the revenue collected via a tax on carbon-based fuels, there also could be numerous other benefits, including a higher gross national product (GNP) and reduced fiscal deficits.

Most taxes discourage people from doing things that are good for the economy, like working hard and saving. Only a few taxes, dubbed "sin" taxes by economists, discourage people from doing things that are undesirable, like smoking and drinking alcohol. Now, some environmental economists have become proponents of a new kind of sin tax: taxes on pollution. Why not, they argue, raise more revenue from dirt taxes and recycle it to reduce the burden of taxes that impoverish the economy? That way, an economy could become cleaner and richer at the same time.

Favorite in most lists of possible dirt taxes is usually a carbon tax. This would be levied on the carbon content of fossil fuels in order to reduce the rate at which carbon dioxide, the main gas thought to cause global warming, is building up in the atmosphere. To tax fossil fuels in proportion to their carbon content would be simple, at least compared with most other environmental taxes: it could be imposed at the mine gate or oil-well head. The tax would fall most heavily on coal, least heavily on natural gas.

How would such a tax affect the economy at large? The answer depends partly on what taxes (if any) a carbon tax replaced. In Europe, where five countries have already introduced carbon taxes, one—Sweden—has used the tax as a partial replacement for other energy taxes. . . .

Last year the Environmental Protection Agency (EPA) . . . looked at the effect of taking a $15-a-tonne carbon tax and increasing it by a real 5% a year until 2010. The money might be used in half-a-dozen ways: to cut the federal deficit; to cut direct taxes, such as personal-income taxes or employees' payroll taxes; to cut the employers' part of payroll taxes; to offer tax credits for investment; or to reduce corporate-income taxes. The study found that the effects on GNP over 1991–2010 ranged from cumulative losses of $870 billion if the money went to cut personal-income tax, to gains of $2.6 trillion if it financed investment tax credits. . . .

To the extent that a government used carbon-tax revenues to boost investment credits, the money would not be available to help poor families with higher energy costs. Would they be hurt more than rich families? Studies by Dale Jorgenson, of Harvard University, and by Bruce Schillo, an EPA economist, suggest not, if carbon taxes are recycled in ways that make the economy work more efficiently. One reason is that the difference in spending on energy between the richest and poorest 20% of Americans is not huge: the richest spend 4.7% of their budgets on energy, the poorest, 7.5%. . . .

But while environmental taxes may not be the best cure for the inefficiencies of national tax systems, they are certainly the best alternative to the inefficiencies of environmental regulation. The sensible starting point is not to compare carbon taxes with other energy taxes, but to compare them with the packages of regulation and exhortation that governments are now designing to meet the goals they set themselves at the Earth Summit at Rio de Janeiro in June (1992). On that basis, carbon taxes win hands down.

Source: "Carbonated Growth," **The Economist,** August 8, 1992, p.59. © 1992 The Economist Newspaper Group, Inc. Reprinted with permission.

Example 11.3

THE PRICE OF CONGESTION

Traffic planners are in a jam. Gridlock, with bumper-to-bumper traffic just not able to move, is an increasingly commonplace problem in the world's major, and even a few minor, cities. Some freeways have become giant parking lots. The main problem is that each extra car on the road slows many others. Yet, when deciding whether to journey by car, each individual driver ignores his or her effect on the length of other drivers' journeys. And so the traffic planners are stuck. The problem has become so bad that in France and Germany in 1992, some traffic jams lasted almost 24 hours!

Fortunately, there may be an economic solution to the problem, although it comes at a price to drivers. The following excerpt from an article in **The Economist** *explains how it would work.*

There are two ways to tackle the [traffic] problem. Traditionally, governments have worked on the supply side, building better roads and improving public transport.

Small things can make a big difference, like eliminating street parking and improving the timing of traffic lights. But in the future there will have to be more influencing of demand. By pricing congestion, travel on roads at peak times would cost more. That would encourage motorists to make better use of roads by spreading their journeys throughout the day or using public transport. It would also raise money that could be invested in infrastructure.

New technology will make it easier for improvements on both the supply and demand sides, says William Spreitzer, GM's technical director of intelligent-vehicle highway systems. By linking electronics in the road and in the car, all sorts of new services will become possible. . . .

As cars get computerized navigation systems, the information can be used to pick the fastest route. Such systems could also pre-book parking spaces and even hotels. Eventually, with radar guidance and other tricks, automated highways could take over some of the driving. Cars would zoom along under computer control in a convoy. They

would be deposited at the driver's chosen exit—at which point he would be expected to put his hands back on to the steering wheel.

Computerized cars will also make it easier to charge for using roads at different times. Electronic tolls would monitor a vehicle's use of the road and automatically send bills to the owner or deduct prepaid units from a car's computer. "Drivers would gain a much better appreciation of the cost of their individual trip on society and expect to pay more if they want to travel at the most congested times," says Mr. Spreitzer.

Pricing pollution could prove just as effective. Americans pay little more than $1 for an American gallon of petrol (3.75 liters). European and Japanese motorists pay around three times as much. There is much less incentive for American drivers to reduce fuel consumption or even buy thrifty cars. And the more fuel cars burn, the more they pollute. . . .

Source: "Jam Tomorrow," **The Economist, The Car Industry: Survey,** October 17, 1992, p. 16. © 1992 The Economist Newspaper Group, Inc. Reprinted with permission.

Production of goods that provide benefits to others is less than socially optimal.

Equation 11.24 tells us that if honey producers increased production beyond the privately optimal amount, the additional utility for society would exceed the additional cost. That is, too few resources are devoted to producing honey when honey producers are not compensated for the help bees provide to neighboring fruit farmers.

Another example of beneficial production externalities is flood control, when downstream farmers benefit from the protection provided by an upstream neighbor. Since extra output of downstream farms is attributable to the effort of the upstream farmer who builds ditches or dams, the marginal social utility of drainage exceeds the marginal private cost. If the marginal private cost of resources used in drainage equals their marginal social cost, we again have the situation in Equation 11.24; there will be socially insufficient provision of drainage. A similar situation occurs with research and development, when discoveries are available for other producers to imitate, thereby making the marginal social utility of research exceed the marginal private cost.

The examples of honey production, drainage provision, transferable research and development, and so on involve cost reductions for other *producers,* but there are examples of external benefits of production enjoyed by *consumers.* Break-waters built to protect commercial vessels provide sheltered water for the enjoyment of pleasure craft; attractive lakes can result from dams built for hydroelectric generation; farms often offer pleasant vistas for travelers; stores allow passers-by to window-shop without charge; and so on. In all these cases, as with benefits enjoyed by other producers, privately determined outputs are smaller than is socially optimal.

When there are beneficial externalities of production enjoyed by consumers, production is less than socially optimal.

Home Improvement: An External Benefit of Consumption

Consumption as well as production can provide external benefits. For example, when a homeowner plants flowers, all those who can see or smell them enjoy utility. Similarly, when a homeowner upgrades his or her house, nearby houses may increase in value because people see what is possible and realize that the neighborhood is improving in status. When there are external benefits of consumption,

$$\textit{Marginal social utility} > \textit{marginal private utility} \qquad (11.25)$$

Therefore, if individuals consume until

$$\textit{Marginal private utility} = \textit{price} \qquad (11.26)$$

then, from Equations 11.25 and 11.26,

$$\textit{Marginal social utility} > \textit{price} \qquad (11.27)$$

If the price of what is consumed reflects the social cost of producing the good, that is,

$$\textit{Marginal social cost} = \textit{price} \qquad (11.28)$$

then, from Equations 11.27 and 11.28,

$$\textit{Marginal social utility} > \textit{marginal social cost}$$

Therefore, when there are external benefits of consumption, too little is consumed for an efficient allocation of resources; the social utility from additional consumption exceeds the social cost.

Too little is consumed of goods that provide benefits to others.

Positive versus Negative Externalities

In the event that the activities of producers or consumers hurt others, by increasing their costs or reducing their benefits, the externalities are called **negative externalities.** When the activities of producers or consumers help others, by reducing their costs or providing benefits, the externalities are called **positive**

When the activities of producers or consumers impose costs on others or reduce the utility enjoyed by others, the activities involve *negative* externalities, and when the activities of producers or consumers reduce others' costs or provide them with utility, the activities involve *positive* externalities.

A public good is a good or service that people cannot be excluded from enjoying whether they pay for it or not.

Free riders enjoy the benefits of goods and services provided by others without contributing to their cost. The incentive to free ride explains why public goods are not provided without government intervention.

externalities. Industrial air pollution, traffic congestion, landscape destruction by strip mining, air pollution caused by urban driving, and so on are all examples of negative externalities. Flower planting, home improvements, bee keeping, fruit farming, upstream drainage, artificial lakes created by dams, and so on are all examples of positive externalities.

PUBLIC GOODS

A **public good** is a good or service that people cannot be prevented from enjoying whether they pay for it or not. For example, a flood-control device such as a dam is a public good because all downstream farmers enjoy it whether they pay for it or not. The situation is similar for national defense; people are defended whether or not they pay toward it. Similarly, people can watch public television, listen to public radio, visit public parks, use public roads and sidewalks, benefit from street cleaning, and so on.

The problem posed by public goods is that because people can benefit without paying, they have little or no incentive to contribute voluntarily toward the cost. Therefore, people will not provide public goods on their own initiative even if the goods have a social benefit far in excess of their cost. This explains why such public goods as parks, roads and sidewalks, and defense are provided by the government. Let us explore this matter a little further by considering the example of a dam that benefits dozens of downstream farmers. Let us suppose that a farmer who is contemplating building the dam asks each downstream farmer how much he or she is likely to benefit, telling the farmers that their individual contributions to the dam's cost will be based on their declared benefits.

Because there are many farmers who benefit, it makes little or no difference to whether the dam is built if an individual farmer is honest and admits the true size of his or her benefits. Therefore, each farmer will say he or she receives little or no benefit. Thus the total amount of benefits declared and the contributions to the cost will be far short of the true value and cost of the dam. Consequently, the dam will not be built even if it is socially worthwhile.

If there were only one downstream farmer, there would be a much closer link between contributing to the cost of the dam and the likelihood that it is built. However, even in this case, if the downstream farmer believed that the dam would be built without his or her contributing to the cost, the downstream farmer would say that he or she would not benefit. On the other hand, if there was a chance that without a contribution the dam would not be built, the downstream farmer might contribute an amount up to the benefit enjoyed. More generally, the declared benefit would be just sufficient to ensure that the dam is built, provided this is smaller than the benefit the downstream farmer enjoys.

When there is more than one downstream farmer who benefits, the chance that any individual farmer's declared benefit and consequent contribution would tip the scales is smaller. Consequently, it pays each farmer to declare that he or she receives no benefit.

The reason the socially efficient action is not taken in the case of the dam is that when exclusion from benefits is not possible, each tries to be a **free rider.** A free rider knows that she or he can enjoy a public good whether or not she or he contributes to the cost. If an extra contribution to the cost would not be pivotal and cause the dam to be built, the expected private utility from making a contribution is zero, and no contribution is made. The more beneficiaries there are, the smaller is the chance the scales will be tipped by contributing and the greater is the incentive to free ride.

Because of the free rider problem, public goods are not generally provided, at least in the socially correct amount, without the intervention of government. But how is a government to decide when to intervene and, in particular, which public goods to provide?

Suppose that a government is considering whether to build a dam that farmers are unable to agree to build on their own because of the free rider problem. Suppose that the government has decided against charging individual farmers according to declared benefits because it knows this leads to understatement of benefits. Instead, the government tells the farmers that the dam is to be financed out of general revenues, but only if the sum of farmers' declared benefits exceeds the cost. Unfortunately, this approach will cause an overstatement of benefits; farmers have nothing to lose but could gain a dam. Therefore, a dam could be built even if it is not warranted.[9]

It is difficult to determine the correct amount to provide of a public good.

When it is only a country's own residents who enjoy a public good, that country's government can decide whether to provide the good itself. The situation is different for public goods that exist on a global scale.

Examples of Global Public Goods

Action to Combat Global Warming.   The Earth's atmosphere is shared. No one country can be excluded from any benefit that might come from an action taken to combat the so-called greenhouse effect. This means that action taken to reduce greenhouse gas emissions is a public good.[10] Let us consider a numerical example to show how this situation can frustrate actions to deal with global warming, a problem that could, according to some projections, be our most serious environmental problem.

Suppose that for each $1 spent to reduce carbon dioxide emissions, the most important greenhouse gas, all countries collectively benefit by $5. The benefits might accrue from reduced crop damage via reductions in drought and disease, from reduced energy requirements to power air conditioning, and so on.

From the global perspective, with a 5 to 1 benefit-to-cost ratio, the payoff of taking action clearly makes it worthwhile incurring the cost. However, action will not be taken if no individual country enjoys more than one-fifth the global benefit. For example, if the country gaining the most enjoys one-tenth the global benefit, this country's utility from each dollar it spends is one-tenth of $5, that is, $0.50. Why should the country spend $1 for 50 cents of utility? Other countries have even less reason to spend if they enjoy a smaller fraction of the global benefit.

[9] Schemes have been devised to extract the correct answers to government enquiries about benefits. These schemes involve penalties and rewards to encourage socially optimal declarations.

[10] From a strictly economic perspective, the greenhouse effect results from a negative externality because individual countries do not recognize the costs of gas emissions that are felt outside their borders. In general, when an action is taken to reduce a negative externality, the action is a public good.

Therefore, no country is willing to take action, even though the Earth would bene-fit by $5 for each $1 spent. The problem is that no country can be excluded from the benefits that derive from the spending of others, and therefore, all countries want action to be taken, but for the action to be paid for by other countries. Of course, with each country thinking this way, nothing is done despite the global gain if something were done.

The market failure with a global public good, such as taking action to combat the greenhouse effect, cannot be overcome by the usual mechanisms to handle public goods within a country. In the case of domestic public goods, such as roads, parks, national defense, education, and so on, the government can provide them out of general tax revenue; if the action is considered to be in the public's best interest, action can be taken. In the absence of global government, such an approach cannot be followed with global public goods.[11] This does not mean that action will never be taken, since international organizations such as the United Nations are charged with recognizing and dealing with global public goods prob-lems. However, coordinating action is difficult when each country would like to free ride.[12]

Conservation of Ocean Fish Stocks.   Fish stocks in the open oceans are shared. Overfishing can threaten these stocks and even cause extinction of some species; the cod stocks on the Grand Banks, for example, are such a threatened species. However, if any one country reduces its catch to preserve fish stocks, the benefit is shared with other countries; the conservation-minded country receives only a small part of the global benefit of its action. Indeed, other countries might simply catch what the conserving country does not take, leaving no benefit what-soever for the country trying to conserve stocks. The incentive is clearly for each country to catch more fish than is optimal from the global perspective. Fish con-servation in the open oceans is clearly a public good and will be underprovided via uncoordinated actions.

Property Rights over Global Public Goods

If there were private property rights over fish, countries would have an incentive to consider the long-run implications of overfishing and reduce catches when the future benefits make conservation worthwhile. Therefore, the problem of insuffi-cient conservation can be thought of as resulting from the absence of property rights or, alternatively, from the common ownership of fish in international waters.[13] Similarly, the problem of inadequate action to reduce greenhouse gas emissions can be attributed to the common ownership of the atmosphere. In the case of fish, the Law of the Sea, an international treaty negotiated in the 1970s,

---

[11] See Example 11.4 for a discussion of the particularly serious difficulty of dealing with global public goods problems.

[12] In the case of acid rain, where perhaps only two or, at most, a few countries are involved, as with the transborder emission of sulfer dioxide between the United States and Canada, the free rider problem is less serious because the mutual benefit can be perceived. Each country knows that action by the other is contingent on its own action, so the only major hurdle is deciding on the allocation of efforts or costs.

[13] There are also costs of negotiation and enforcement, as mentioned earlier.

Example   11.4

UNNATURAL SOLUTIONS

More and more environmental problems are taking on global proportions. Unfortunately, the use of traditional, market-based solutions to tackle global issues runs smack into the free rider problem. As the following excerpt from an article in **The Economist** *explains, the alternatives to market solutions have their own difficulties. In the absence of any method of dealing with externalities, we may ultimately have to depend on goodwill.*

Nature is no respecter of national boundaries. Across those dotted lines on the globe, winds blow, rivers flow and migrating species walk or fly. The dotted lines may carve up the earth, but the sea and the atmosphere remain open to all, to cherish or plunder. When people in one country harm that bit of the environment they assume to be theirs, many others may suffer, too. But how, and how much, can countries make their neighbors change their ways? . . .

Such problems pose new issues for diplomats and economists. Reaching agreement often means resolving conflicting goals and priorities. Even among countries of similar wealth, environmental goals may differ: think of the rows with Iceland and Japan over whaling, or the reluctance of Britain to curb sulphur dioxide from power stations. But cross-border arguments are harder to resolve when many countries are involved, and especially when those countries have widely differing living standards and environmental

priorities. Particularly intractable are . . . biological diversity and climate change. . . .

The market is unlikely to help. Even in an individual country it will rarely deliver what is best for the environment. The costs to individuals and companies of polluting or pillaging the environment will be lower than the costs their activities impose on the rest of society. National environmental policies therefore need government to step in and ensure that polluters carry the costs they would otherwise dump on their fellow citizens.

Without a world government, no institution can compel international polluters to pay. True, there has been a rapid growth of institutions that aim to set international environmental priorities or persuade governments to reach (and abide by) agreements on environmental goals. But such institutions are no stronger than the governments that set them up. Agreement can therefore be based only on the belief that acting together brings more benefits than acting alone.

That belief will frequently be true. If one of the countries living round a polluted lake tries to clean the water by acting alone, it may make heroic efforts but achieve little . . . If all act together, modest steps may achieve much. If, say, Norway stopped all output of carbon dioxide next week, it would take only 46m tonnes out of the atmosphere. The same amount could equally be saved if every country in the world cut its output of carbon dioxide by 0.22%.

Conversely, if all but one of those lakeside countries reduces the muck

it discharges into the water, that one country will still enjoy the improvement in water quality that the actions of its neighbours deliver. An individual country can generally do best of all by dropping out of a pact, as long as it cannot be excluded from the resulting gains. It can thus enjoy the rewards of travelling on the global bus without paying its fare, as a "free rider." This is the central paradox of international environmental agreements. All countries do better by co-operating than by acting alone; but individual countries often have a powerful incentive not to co-operate.

Countries are more likely to succumb to the temptation to hitch a free ride the more the costs of belonging to an international agreement diverge from the benefits it brings; or the longer the gap between the pain and the gain. The balance of costs and benefits will usually vary from one country to another. It will be partly a function of the number of countries involved. If only three countries live around that dirty lake, the gains that each enjoys from ending pollution will be much larger than if only two clean up. A completely clean lake is much nicer than a two-thirds clean lake. But if a dozen countries are involved, the difference made by the participation of one extra country will be small. The costs of participation to each country are the same, but the gains from co-operating are lower. . . .

Source: Frances Cairncross, "The Environment: Whose World Is It, Anyway?" **The Economist, The Environment: Survey,** May 30, 1992, pp. 5–6. © 1992 The Economist Newspaper Group, Inc. Reprinted with permission.

established ownership rights over the fish within 200 miles of a country's coastline to overcome the overexploitation problem. The Law of the Sea also provided ownership rights over fish found in international waters but which return to a country's rivers to spawn.[14] Furthermore, at the "Earth Summit" in Rio de Janeiro in June of 1992, delegates agreed to a conference to consider extending these ownership rights further.

The problem of overexploitation of commonly owned resources has been recognized for some time, having been seen as the cause of the observed overgrazing of village "commons" in both British and New England villages. (The commons were undivided fields dedicated to local people for grazing their animals.) Each individual owner of sheep or cattle with access to the commons had little incentive to reduce grazing when it was the other farmers who gained from their conservation by exploiting the grasses that the conserving farmer had left. Because the problem was recognized in this context, it has become known as the **tragedy of the commons.**[15] This is the same tragedy faced today with the Earth's atmosphere. The challenge with all public goods is to find ways to allocate property rights, a formidable problem in the case of globally commonly owned "goods" such as the atmosphere.

---

[14] Another example of where the allocation of rights has resulted in an improved outcome is described in Example 11.5.

[15] Example 11.6 explains that the tragedy of the commons comes in a variety of forms.

Example   11.5

GAME PLAN

The authorities in Zimbabwe had a big problem: how do you protect freely roaming endangered wildlife from bands of well-armed and ruthless poachers pursuing ivory and exotic skins? Military-style campaigns against the illicit hunters had not proven effective, so the wildlife-protection authorities adopted a novel approach involving the appropriation of wildlife property rights.

The game plan adopted by the government of Zimbabwe gives the rights to wildlife to the local tribesmen. They can do as they wish within their own territories. Skeptics argued the plan would mean slaughter of helpless animals. The reality was the very opposite.

Local leaders know that their property rights over animals in their territories are extremely valuable. The highest value, which can be collected only if local people keep the animals alive, is what hunters are prepared to pay to purchase the right to shoot them. There are intermediaries in this process

of selling "shooting rights," specifically, local guides who organize hunts for wealthy tourists who pay thousands of dollars, via payment to the guides, for the right to shoot a wild animal. "Campfire" meetings are held in the tribal areas to decide on how many lions, elephants, and so on can be culled without threatening survival. Leaders know how important it is to maximize long-run survivability, which is the way to maximize the long-run income from their "resource." Indeed, wildlife officials are invited to meetings to help determine the safe number of each species that can be culled.

Allocations of selected quotas are made after interviews with guides who provide descriptions of their hunting plans and how much they are willing to pay for the right to shoot. Guides meet different local groups, local groups interview different guides, and a process of bidding takes place. The amounts of money involved are so large that local tribesmen

who share in the proceeds go to great lengths to protect their animals. Using a combination of policing and informers, tribal leaders have embarked on a serious assault on roving poachers. The net result appears to be that by giving tribesmen the right to kill animals or to assign that right to others, fewer animals are being killed.

The success of the Zimbabwe game plan makes it clear that the allocation of property rights helps overcome the problem of overexploitation of public goods. By allocating property rights at the appropriate level, in this case that of the tribal community, the incentives become closer in line with the objective of long-term survival of the animal kingdom

---

Sources: "Wildlife Management in Omay 'Campfire' Project," **Zimbabwe Wildlife,** December 1990, pp. 21–25; and "People and Wildlife Are Campfire's Most Vital Resources," **Zimbabwe Wildlife,** March 1991, pp. 17–19.

 **E**xample 11.6

SOME TRAGEDIES OF THE COMMONS

In his narration to the British Broadcasting Corporation's documentary, "The Evolution of Cooperation," Richard Dawkins gave the following account of the tragedy of the commons. He explains that it can appear in many different forms.

If you go to a restaurant on your own then you have exactly what you want and you pay exactly what you want. But we have all had the experience of going to a restaurant in a gang of ten, say, and agreeing in advance that we are going to split the bill. You know what happens then: there's always somebody who has the most expensive dish on the menu, or who has an extra pint of lager, and the reason he does it is that he knows that the extra expense is going to be shared among the ten of them; he gets the benefit, we all pay the costs.

Now, this does not sound like a very serious example, but it does have its serious side in the real world, and it has been given the name, "the tragedy of the commons."

Now it so happens that in Oxford we have got a real tragedy of the commons on our own doorstep in the well known meadow called Port Meadow. . . .

I can assure you that ecologically speaking we really do have the makings of a tragedy here. When you get ragwort and thistles it tends to mean overgrazing, and for the past 15 years the ragwort and thistles have been steadily taking over this meadow. . . .

The problem is of the City Government's own making. Fifteen years ago, they asked each commoner how many animals he would like legal rights to graze on the common land. Naturally each of them, being human, submitted his own selfish estimate of the most he could possibly want. All those bids got accepted. So even if each farmer is only grazing what he is legally entitled to, there is a huge overcrowding problem, because when you add all those figures up, it is enormous. Some 1000 horses, 60 donkeys, over 1000 geese and 2000 cattle—far more than the Commons can support.

If one farmer owned all this land what would happen? He would make a rational decision so he would not under-use it, and he would not overgraze it either. But as it is common land, it is beyond individual restraint, because whatever everyone else does, each individual is better off being selfish. If everyone else keeps overgrazing,

what is the point in me reducing my herd? And, if everyone else cuts back their animals, my continuing to be selfish will not ruin the Commons. Everyone reasons selfishly and the Commons ends up ruined. The American biologist, Garrett Hardin uses this idea of the tragedy of the commons as a microcosm of how we humans, from wealthy Oxford to struggling Ethiopia, are gradually ruining our biggest resource, the Earth.

Earlier this century the British herring fishery in the North Sea was in its heyday. Harbors at Yarmouth and Lowestoft were bustling with herring drifters. Over 1800 boats fished the North Sea alone. It seemed as if this enormous resource was inexhaustible; the herring could never run out. But today, all that is left are . . . rotten reminders. The fishery is extinct and the fishermen gone. It is a tragedy.

Individual rationality has won again.

Source: Richard Dawkins, "The Evolution of Cooperation," **Horizon** (London: B.B.C. Television, 1986).

"I would suggest that you have two means of ridding yourself of that guilt. One, stop watching Channel 13. Two, send them some money."

Drawing by Modell; © 1967 The New Yorker Magazine, Inc.

UNLIMITED IMPLICATIONS OF MARKET LIMITATIONS

So much of what we do has effects on others that the list of externalities is almost endless. We have considered a number of production- and consumption-related externalities in this chapter and have shown that taxes can induce optimal behavior in the presence of negative externalities. We also have shown that property rights overcome the externality problem when these rights can be negotiated and enforced inexpensively. The relevance of property rights closely links economics and law. Indeed, the very existence of externalities and the need to deal with them means that law and economics are closely interconnected. For example, the body of criminal law can be thought of as applying when others are hurt by somebody's actions; in robbery, assault, libel, rape, homicide, and so on, the victims' losses are externalities from the perspective of the criminal.

While not all crimes have an economic motive, the legal and justice system can be viewed as a way of imposing an expected cost on criminals to deter them. Punishment is a deterrent if criminals weigh the expected utility against the expected cost of their actions and commit crime when the expected utility exceeds the expected cost, ignoring the cost to the victim. It is, of course, recognized that not all crimes are motivated by economic considerations and that, therefore, the crime rate also depends on numerous noneconomic factors. However, economists have argued that if the expected cost of crime is increased by increasing the probability of being caught or the length of imprisonment if caught, then the number of situations where expected utility exceeds the expected cost is reduced, and so is the crime rate.

Typically, in situations where the externalities of "criminal" activities are small, the penalties are also small, perhaps consisting of a citation and fine. This is the case with most by-laws relating to nuisances such as noise, allowing pets to foul public places, littering, and blocking traffic by illegal parking. The expected costs of such minor infractions can be kept low by keeping penalties low for those who are caught or by spending relatively little effort to catch perpetrators, that is, by keeping the probability of being caught low. Larger externalities such as burglary and murder are met with larger punishment and greater effort to catch the perpetrators, both of which increase the criminal's expected cost of crime. The academic discipline of criminology considers such matters as how expected costs can be varied according to the crime and what effects, if any, changes in expected costs—via changes in penalties or in the probability of being caught—have on the incidence of crime.

As well as with law and criminology, there is traffic across the bridge between political science and economics revolving around the existence of externalities. Not only are externalities often dealt with by public policy that is part of a political process, but also we can think of the behavior of politicians and voters in terms that involve externalities.

When an individual politician is implicated in, for example, a scandal, the cost is borne not only by that politician but also by other party members; the social cost exceeds the private cost. That is, there is a negative externality. Therefore, from the perspective of a political party as a whole, the care exercised by individual politicians to avoid questionable behavior is suboptimal. Similarly, because the benefit of distinguished work by a politician may be enjoyed by other party members—that is, there are positive externalities—the incentive to do distinguished public work is also inadequate from the party's perspective. We see that without some way to internalize externalities

> *It is very easy to be a free rider and enjoy public television without subscribing. Subscription to public television involves positive externalities. . . .*

involved in political behavior, the incentive to work for the public good or to avoid abusing the power of political office is too low.

Economic theory cannot easily explain why some people vote. The expected benefit of voting is the probability that the vote makes a difference multiplied by the incremental benefit to the voter if the selected party is elected. Since the probability of being the pivotal voter is extremely small and the incremental expected benefit to an individual of one party versus another is also small, the expected benefit is minuscule. The cost of voting involves the value of lost time in the course of voting and of traveling to the polls. Because this cost is likely to exceed the expected benefit, economic theory suggests that people should not vote.

The benefit of electing qualified, honest politicians with well-designed policy platforms is enjoyed not just by an individual who votes for these politicians but also by society as a whole. That is, voting involves positive externalities, with the social benefit of making a good choice exceeding the private benefit. The private cost to an individual of making a careful choice and of exercising this choice includes the cost of gathering information, as well as the time spent going to the polls. Even if the private cost of information gathering and of voting exceeds the expected **private** benefit, the **social** benefit, which involves the remainder of society, is very likely to exceed the private (and social) cost. For example, if everybody in the country benefits as much as the voter himself or herself and there are 250 million people in the country, the social benefit is 250 million times larger than the private benefit.

It may well be that individual voters do not consider only their expected private benefit of electing good politicians but rather consider some of the benefits they expect to accrue to other citizens. That is, the fact that people often do vote despite their minuscule private benefit may be because they bear in mind some of the social benefit. This socially responsible behavior requires that people be altruistic. Attention to the superego may be responsible for such socially responsible behavior, just as in buying decisions. There are other examples of altruism where individuals internalize social costs and benefits without any tax, subsidy, punishment, or reward that contradict the selfishness assumptions of traditional economics, and these are well worth discussing.

It is very easy to be a free rider and enjoy public television without subscribing. Subscription to public television involves positive externalities in that the money an individual contributes goes to improve the quality of programming for all who watch, not just the individual himself or herself. Indeed, the private utility from an individual's subscription is essentially zero; a $50 or $100 subscription makes no difference to what an individual sees on television. However, people do subscribe to public television, and some people are very generous. This suggests that some individuals do look further than their private costs and utilities, exhibiting altruistic behavior.

Sociobiologists have recognized that in particular circumstances there are reasons for altruism to result from natural selection. Consider, for example, seagulls. You may have noticed that when you throw a seagull food, it has an irresistible urge to squawk. This attracts other seagulls, and before you know it, the seagulls are scrapping with each other. From the perspective of an individual seagull, it would be better to keep quiet and not have to compete with others. However, from the perspective of seagulls as a species, squawking when finding food allows them to exploit food sources better, subject to limitations on the extent squawking attracts other types of birds that compete with seagulls; seagulls hap-

> *Sociobiologists have recognized that in particular circumstances there are reasons for altruism to result from natural selection.*

pen to be tough, so competition from other birds is usually not a problem. We can see that altruism is a trait that is favored in seagulls as a species.

The issue arises as to why individual seagulls do not free ride, letting others squawk but keeping the food they find for themselves. The free riders would gain by spending less energy per unit of food they eat. The "free rider gene" would then be passed on to future generations, and with free riders doing better than those who are altruistic, more and more seagulls would become free riders. This would reduce the success of seagulls and could even threaten the species. However, seagulls have been successful, so it would seem that free riding is somehow controlled, perhaps because the basis of natural selection is **group selection** rather than **individual selection**. Free riding among humans may similarly have been reduced by group selection in our own evolutionary history.

While nature may have its way of reducing free riding, and while many public television viewers refuse to free ride, there are instances where the law or carefully enforced institutional arrangements are needed to deal with free riding. For example, some parents are tempted to have their children protected against contagious diseases by allowing all **other** children to be vaccinated; if all others are protected, their own children gain protection and can avoid the (small) risk associated with being vaccinated. Of course, if everybody behaved this way, attempting to let everyone else provide them with positive externalities, nobody would be protected. For this reason vaccination in some countries is required by law. It is more difficult to use the law in situations where enforcement is difficult, such as in having school children use shampoo to rid themselves of head lice; all that is necessary is that there be one untreated child for the other children to be reinfested. We can see that even public health is related to economics via the existence of externalities. Other examples of temptations to free ride against the public good include allowing the United States to defend the free world—a temptation dealt with by pressure on the U.S. allies to join NATO—to cheat on exams—a temptation dealt with by expulsion or suspension—and so on.

Much of the joy artists and writers give to humanity cannot be captured by the artists or writers themselves. Similarly, scientific and medical researchers bring benefits to humanity from which they themselves do not profit. The economic analysis in this chapter suggests that such situations may result in too little art, music, writing, or research from the social perspective unless the artists and researchers are subsidized. Scholarships and fellowships for artists and scientists may be rationalized along such lines. Indeed, we may attempt to explain the fact that more financial assistance is offered to very clever students than to average or below-average students via graduate fellowships and so on by arguing that such students eventually create positive externalities; arguments of equity or airness may favor putting more resources into helping those in school who are having difficulties, not the very clever ones. We see that economics has close connections with the field of education as well as with all the other fields we have mentioned.

SUMMARY

1. In perfectly competitive markets, price equals marginal cost, whereas in imperfectly competitive markets, price exceeds marginal cost.

2. There is a net benefit from shifting factors of production from producing a perfectly competitive product to producing an imperfectly competitive product. With perfect competition in *all* markets, there is no net benefit from shifting factors of production.

3. An economy is allocationally inefficient if by using its resources differently it is possible to increase total utility without making anybody worse off. Imperfect competition is allocationally inefficient, whereas perfect competition is allocationally efficient.

4. Expected total utility can be measured from the area below the demand curve. Similarly, total cost can be measured from the area below the marginal cost curve. The net benefit from producing more of a product is the area between the demand curve and the marginal cost curve. The sum of net benefits from all products is at its maximum when markets are perfectly competitive.

5. The social cost of production is the private cost incurred by a firm plus the costs paid by other members of society without their consent.

6. Externalities are costs or benefits that are incurred or enjoyed by others. Externalities cause a socially inefficient allocation of resources.

7. External costs, like those arising from industrial air pollution, mean that when a perfectly competitive firm equates marginal private cost with the market price, the marginal social cost exceeds the market price. Since the price equals the marginal utility of the last unit purchased, the marginal social cost exceeds the marginal social utility the good provides; too much is produced.

8. A tax on a polluting manufacturer equal to the value of externalities internalizes social costs and makes private decisions socially efficient.

9. The Coase theorem states that economic consequences are the same whether property rights are owned by those suffering from or those imposing externalities. In either case there is an incentive to make payments that induce a socially optimal allocation of resources, provided the compensation agreements can be negotiated and enforced inexpensively.

10. Consumption can impose costs on others, such as when an individual drives a car. Consumption is then too high.

11. Production externalities can be beneficial, such as when a honey producer's bees pollinate nearby trees, when a farmer improves drainage, and so on. Privately determined output in these cases is less than socially optimal.

12. Consumption can result in beneficial externalities, such as when homeowners improve their houses or maintain attractive gardens. Consumption is then too small.

13. Externalities of production or consumption that provide benefits for others are called positive externalities, and externalities that impose costs on others are called negative externalities.

14. Public goods are those from which people cannot be excluded, so they can enjoy them whether or not they pay. Public goods include streets, parks, public television, and defense.

15. Free riders are those who enjoy public goods without paying for them.

16. Public goods are overexploited if property rights cannot be allocated. This is called the tragedy of the commons. When a public good is enjoyed by people in many different countries, it is difficult to allocate property rights, and individual counties may all be free riders. The atmosphere and the oceans are such global public goods.

QUESTIONS AND PROBLEMS

1. In what way might the inefficiency of resource allocation be larger in an imperfectly competitive market if demand is very inelastic?

2. Show graphically the effect of a beneficial production externality such as that from keeping honey bees. How may government payments to apiarists help achieve an efficient allocation of resources?

3. If honey production helps fruit farmers and fruit farming helps honey production, do you think there would be cooperation, or do you think one producer would buy the other?

4. Show graphically the effect of a beneficial consumption externality such as that from planting flowers that others can enjoy. Could a subsidy increase the number of flowers planted to the socially correct amount?

5. With positive production externalities and negative consumption externalities, could perfect competition result in an efficient allocation of resources?

6. In what way is litter an externality, and what method would you propose for reducing it?

7. Use Figure 11.6 to show that the number of miles driven could be correct from society's point of view if there are passengers, even when there are externalities from air pollution and traffic congestion. Might this provide a rationale for "subsidizing" car pools by providing express lanes or toll-free travel for cars with three or more passengers?

8. Might a case be made for government regulation of banks and other financial institutions based on the spillovers or externalities of failures of deposit-taking financial institutions?

9. Does vaccination against disease constitute a public good, and how could the widespread use of antibiotics constitute a negative externality?

10. How do negotiation and enforcement costs of reaching a compensation agreement vary with the number of people affected by externalities? Does your answer explain why the Coase theorem is likely to apply only when very few parties are affected?

11. How might a tax on driving affect peoples' choices of where they live vis-à-vis their place of employment and thereby affect traffic congestion and pollution?

12. Are there externalities from research and development?

PART IV

Macroeconomics

. . . [C]auses affecting price levels are as distinct from those affecting an individual price as the causes affecting the tides are distinct from those affecting an individual wave.

Irving Fisher (1912)

339

CHAPTER 12

. . . .
. . . .
. . . .
. . . . . . : National Income and
. . . . . . :
. . . . . . : Product Accounts
. . . .
. . . .
. . . .

Every short statement about economics is misleading (with the possible exception of my present one).

Alfred Marshall

Key Concepts

Microeconomics versus macroeconomics; different measures of national income and national product; difficulties in estimating national income and product; real versus nominal gross domestic product; economic growth; comparing economic performance over time and between countries; consumption, investment and other components of GDP

INTRODUCING MACROECONOMICS

All the preceding chapters have been devoted to that branch of economics called **microeconomics.** This is one of the two major divisions of the subject, the other being **macroeconomics,** which occupies the remainder of this book.

As we have seen, microeconomics is concerned with the prices and outputs of individual products and the prices of individual factors of production. On the other hand, macroeconomics is concerned with the condition of the economy taken as a whole. In particular, macroeconomics is concerned with the price level and output of the entire economy and with the total income of all the factors of production in the economy. Of course, the entire economy consists of the aggregate of all the individual markets which are dealt with in microeconomics, and therefore, there are close connections between macroeconomics and micro-economics. However, the principles that we have explored in previous chapters do not extend simply to the economy at large. Instead, somewhat different perspectives are required to view matters at the level of the entire economy than we have taken so far in this book.

Microeconomics is concerned with prices and outputs of individual products and factors of production. Macro-economics is concerned with the price level and output of the entire economy.

In what follows we take a phenomenological approach, discussing matters around the main issues of interest, specifically, inflation, unemployment, output, interest rates, and exchange rates. However, this and the next chapter introduce the necessary background for dealing with these important matters. This involves explaining the nature and measurement of output and income at the level of the entire economy, the meaning and importance of the national debt, the economically important characteristics of money, including the role commercial and central banks play in the creation and management of the nation's supply of money, and other such matters.

In each of the chapters devoted to the principal macroeconomic phenomena—inflation, unemployment, and so on—our purpose is to explain their relevance, as well as what causes these important variables to change over time and to differ between countries. For example, we consider who is hurt—and helped—by inflation. We also explain what makes inflation increase and why some countries have had runaway inflation in the thousands of percent while others have had stable prices. Where there are differences of opinion between economists, we present the main schools of thought not to show which school is correct but rather to indicate that different opinions exist and may not be mutually exclusive. Indeed, it is my opinion that, depending on the circumstances, each of the major schools of macroeconomic thought has something to offer. Indeed, a better understanding of the central macroeconomic issues comes from selectively applying different theories rather than by insisting that all answers come from the perspective of an individual camp.

This chapter begins our exploration of macroeconomics by explaining the way that the output of the economy is measured, namely, via the **gross domestic product (GDP).** The chapter demonstrates how the GDP can be adapted for evaluating the economic performance of a nation over time and for comparing the economic well-being of people in different nations. The chapter explains that the GDP is only one of a number of important statistics given in the national income and product accounts. Among the other important statistics are those involving the main components of a nation's output, specifically, consumption, investment, government spending, and exports. The chapter ends with a discussion of a matter that can affect future economic well-being, namely, the national debt. We explain that the national debt is increased when the government spends more money than it collects in taxes and that the impact of the debt on future economic well-being depends on why the debt is incurred, the fraction of the debt that is held by foreigners, and the effect that taxes have on the willingness of people to work, save, and invest.

MEASURES OF INCOME AND PRODUCTION

Defining Gross Domestic Product (GDP)

The gross domestic product (GDP) is an estimate of the combined value of all the final goods and services produced within a country during an interval of time, such as a calendar quarter or year. The gross domestic product includes the total value of loaves of bread, shoes, airplane journeys, haircuts, new homes, and everything else produced in the economy. For example, if domestic production involves $25 billion of bread, $50 billion of shoes, $75 billion of airplane travel, $10 billion of haircuts, and so on, we say the GDP is $(25 + 50 + 75 + 10 + \cdots)$ billion. Only **final goods and services** are included in the GDP. These are the end result of the production process and exclude items used in the course of production. For example, we include the value of bread, but not the flour and labor used in baking the bread.

As stated, the GDP is an *estimate* of the value of goods and services produced within a country, and as an estimate, it is subject to possible errors. Fortunately, estimation of the GDP is in some ways made easier by the close connection that exists between the value of goods and services produced—the GDP—and the value of incomes received or earned—the **national income.** The national income, as you might expect, is the total value of all the incomes earned in a country during an interval of time. The national income is roughly equivalent to the GDP. We should examine the reason for the rough equivalence of national income and gross domestic product before turning to the problems of measuring and interpreting these important macroeconomic magnitudes.

> The gross domestic product (GDP) is an estimate of the total value of all final goods and services produced *within* a country during an interval of time.

> National income is roughly equivalent to gross domestic product.

Equivalence of National Income and Gross Domestic Product

We can illustrate the rough equivalence of national income and the GDP, along with some other features of national income and product accounting, by referring to this economics book you are currently reading.

The copy of the book in front of you is part of the GDP of the year or calendar quarter in which it was manufactured. It enters the GDP statistics at a value equal to what you paid to purchase it—assuming you bought it new.[1] But why is this value also equal to the income derived from producing the book? This can be explained by looking at what goes into making a book. In producing this book, it was first necessary for loggers to fell trees used for paper production. The trees were sold to a paper manufacturer, whose output was sold to the printer, who, for simplicity, we assume is also the publisher. The publisher printed and bound the book and sold it to the bookstore. From there it was sold to you.

The various stages of production of an economics book with a selling price of $40 are shown in Table 12.1. We show logging as the first stage of production,

---

[1] As we saw in the preceding chapter, the expected marginal utility to the buyer must be at least as high as the price paid. Otherwise, it would not have been purchased.

TABLE 12.1

National income and gross domestic product are roughly equivalent.

	LOGGING OPERATION	PAPER PRODUCTION	PRINTING/ PUBLISHING	BOOKSTORE SALES
Payment to previous stage	$0	$ 4	$12	$28
Wages/salaries	$2	$3	$8	$5
Rent/interest	$1	$2	$4	$3
Profits	$1	$3	$4	$4
Income generated at each production stage	$4	$ 8	$16	$12
Value of sales	$4	$12	$28	$40

The total amount of income generated by all stages of book production is given by adding the $4 earned in logging, the $8 earned in paper production, the $16 earned in printing/publishing, and the $12 earned in retailing by the bookstore. The total of these is $40, which is the total income earned by people involved in producing the book. This is equal to the selling price of the book. The sum of incomes generated equals the amount paid for the book because somebody earns every dollar received. The value of income therefore equals the value of production.

with no payments being made to any previous stage of production. The amount of wood required to make the paper for the book is $4, with this wood being sold to the paper producer. This $4 appears as the bottom line of the logging operation and as the top line of paper production. In the table we assume that the logging company pays $2 of wages and salaries and $1 of rent and interest payments, so the $4 it receives from the paper producer leaves $1 of (accounting) profit.[2]

The $3 that the logging company pays as wages, salaries, rent, and interest is income for the people who receive it, while the $1 that remains as profit is income for the logging company. Therefore, the total income generated by the first stage of production is $4.

The paper producer pays the logging company $4. It then hires workers for $3, this amount being income for those receiving it in their wages or salaries. The paper producer also pays $2 of rent and interest, which is income for those who receive it. After meeting all these costs, which add up to $9, the paper producer sells the paper for $12. Therefore, it has $3 (or $12 − $9) of profit remaining, which is income for the paper producer. We find that the total income resulting from paper production is $8. This consists of $3 paid as wages and salaries, $2 paid as rent and interest, and $3 remaining as the paper producer's profit.

[2] The value of profit shown in the national income and product accounts is the total profit earned, whether this be a normal, required return on investment or profit in excess of this, the economic profit. In other words, profit in the national accounts is accounting profit.

We do not include the $4 paid for wood as part of income generated by the paper producer because this is not income due to paper production. Rather, this $4 is paid out by or earned as profit by the logging company, and to include the cost of wood in the paper producer's product would constitute **double counting;** we would be counting the wood twice, as part of the income generated in paper production and also as income from logging, when it really belongs only in the latter.

We see from Table 12.1 that the printer/publisher pays $12 for paper and sells the book to the bookstore for $28. The printer/publisher is therefore responsible for $16 of income, including profit. This $16 consists of $8 paid as wages and salaries, $4 paid as rent or interest, and $4 remaining as profit. The bookstore buys the book for $28 and sells it for $40, therefore generating $12 of income. The composition of income generated at these last two stages of production in terms of wages, interest, rent, and profit is shown in the table.

The sum of all the incomes generated by all stages of production combined is the sum of the amounts in the second-from-bottom row, namely, $40 [or $(4 + 8 + 16 + 12)]. This is equal to the amount paid for the book. The sum of all incomes earned in producing and selling the book equals the price of the book because somebody gets paid for every activity going into producing and selling it, and if the payment is not made outside the firm, it remains as profit which is income for the owners of the firm. The price paid for the book is the **value of final production.**[3] We discover that the total value of incomes earned equals the value of final production.

The income generated at each stage of production is called the **value added** by that stage of production. It follows that if we add up the values added by all stages of production, we have a total that is the same as the value of final production and which is also equal to the total of incomes earned.

Because the value added at each stage of production equals the amount earned as wages and salaries, rent, interest, and profits, we can calculate national income from the sum of these different types of incomes. Specifically, by adding across the rows in Table 12.1 for wages/salaries, rent/interest, and profits, we find

$$\text{Wages/salaries} = \$(2 + 3 + 8 + 5) = \$18$$

$$\text{Rent/interest} = \$(1 + 2 + 4 + 3) = \$10$$

$$\text{Profits} = \$(1 + 3 + 4 + 4) = \$12$$

The sum of these amounts earned, $40 [or $(18 + 10 + 12)], is the national income—and GDP.

In the example of the book we have ignored the possibility that some foreign-owned factors of production could be used in producing the book. Indeed, the author of this book lives in Canada, and some (very small) part of the income derived from producing the book—the author's royalty—is not part of the U.S. national income. Of course, at the same time that nonresidents of the United States earn income in the United States, residents of the United States are earning incomes in other countries. The presence of **factor incomes** paid to foreigners or

---

[3] The book is a final product, while the wood, paper, and so on are **intermediate products.**

> If the cost of inputs were included along with the value of outputs of goods and services produced, there would be double counting.

> The GDP and national income consist of the values added at all stages of production of all the goods and services produced within a country during an interval of time.

received from foreigners is one of the reasons we said there is only a *rough* equivalence between GDP and national income. Let us consider the effect of such factor income payments abroad and receipts from abroad before turning to the other reasons why GDP and national income are not exactly equal.

Gross Domestic Product versus Gross National Product

As we have explained, the gross domestic product (GDP) measures the value of goods and services produced *within* a country during an interval of time. For example, the GDP of the United States is the value of goods and services produced at locations in the United States during a calendar year or quarter.

Some of the goods and services produced within the United States are not made using factors of production provided by residents of the United States. For example, as we have said, the author's labor in writing this book was provided by a nonresident. More important in terms of magnitudes, some of the automobiles produced in the United States are made in factories owned by Japanese companies such as Honda and Toyota and some financial services within the United States are provided by foreign-owned companies such as Barclays Bank of Britain, Normura securities of Japan, and so on. Furthermore, to the extent that nonresidents own property in the United States, have made loans to U.S. businesses or to the federal or state governments, and have invested in shares of U.S. businesses, some of the rent, interest, and dividends earned in connection with goods and services produced in the United States are earned by nonresidents.

Just as nonresidents provide some of the labor and capital and own some of the land used in producing goods and services within a country, so residents provide labor and capital and own some of the land used in producing goods and services outside the country. For example, Americans have built factories and acquired property abroad, work in other countries, and have made investments and provided loans to foreign-based businesses and foreign governments.

> Gross *national* product (GNP) is the value of goods and services produced with factors of production provided by a country's residents. On the other hand, gross *domestic* product (GDP) is the value of goods and services produced within a country.

With foreign-provided factors of production contributing to the output within a country and some of a country's factors of production contributing to output in other countries, there is a difference between the value of goods and services *produced within a country* and the value of goods and services produced with factors of production *provided by the residents of a country*. The former, as we have seen, is called gross domestic product (GDP). The latter, that is, the value of goods and services produced with factors of production provided by the residents of a country, is called the **gross national product (GNP).**

Until 1991, the United States emphasized the GNP as its principal measure in the **national income and product accounts,** but in that year, the United States switched to emphasizing the gross domestic product. This switch brought the United States in line with other countries which shifted from GNP to GDP somewhat earlier.

The different bases of measurement of GDP and GNP concern incomes earned by foreign factors of production in a country and incomes earned by resident-owned factors from other countries. Table 12.2 shows the connection between GDP and GNP in the United States. The table shows that in order to calculate the U.S. GNP from the U.S. GDP, it is necessary to add to GDP the amount Americans earned from supplying factors of production to other countries and to subtract the

TABLE 12.2

The GNP equals GDP plus net factor income from abroad.

	Billions $
GDP	6,000
+ Factor income receipts from foreigners	110
− Factor income payments to foreigners	100
= GNP	6,010

The GDP is the value of goods and services produced **within** a nation, whereas the GNP is the value of goods and services produced by factors of production **provided by a nation.** Therefore, to obtain the GNP from the GDP, we need to add factor incomes received by residents from foreigners and subtract factor incomes paid by residents to foreigners.

amount earned by factors of production supplied by foreigners in the United States. This means adding the **net foreign factor income.** In terms of an equation,

$$\text{GDP} + \text{net foreign income} = \text{GNP} \qquad (12.1)$$

where

$$\text{Net foreign factor income} = \text{factor income receipts from foreigners}$$
$$- \text{factor income payments to foreigners}$$

Net foreign factor income is factor receipts from foreigners minus factor payments to foreigners. The GNP is the GDP plus net foreign factor income.

The difference between production in the United States, the U.S. GDP, and the income earned by Americans, the U.S. GNP, is small. However, for a country such as Canada, where a large number of businesses are owned by foreigners, and for countries such as India and Pakistan, where many citizens work as nonresidents abroad, the differences between GDP and GNP amount to several percent. Furthermore, the *rates of change* of GNP and GDP can differ substantially even in countries such as the United States where the *levels* of the two magnitude are similar. The possible differences are illustrated in Example 12.1.

Gross National Product versus National Income

Factor incomes received from foreigners and paid to foreigners are only one of the reasons for the difference between the value of production in a country and the income earned by people in that country. Two other causes of the difference between the value of production and income are **depreciation** and **indirect taxes.**

In our example involving the production of this book, we defined profit as the difference between the value of sales at a stage of production and the amounts paid as wages, salaries, interest, rent, and to the previous stage of production. For example, the profit from printing/publishing is the $28 received for the book from

Example 12.1

ALPHABET SOUP

In their invariably magnificent style, **The Economist***, a weekly magazine, set out to explain the significance of the shift from GNP to GDP. The following excerpt should help to reinforce the distinction described in this text.*

Did the American economy start to recover in the second quarter of this year [1991], or was it stuck in recession? America's real gross national product (GNP), the measure that is watched by the government and Wall Street and splashed across newspaper headlines, fell by 0.1% at an annual rate in the second quarter. However, gross domestic product (GDP) rose by 0.8% at an annual rate. By coincidence, the Department of Commerce has just decided that from November [1991] . . . it will concentrate more on GDP than on GNP.

GDP measures the value of all goods and services produced in America. GNP measures the total income of American residents, regardless of where it comes

from; profits from a firm's overseas subsidiary as well as its earnings in America are included. This means that GNP is equal to GDP plus net income from abroad: profits, dividends and interest earned overseas minus income payable to foreigners (the profits of a Japanese car factory in America, for instance).

Cynics might claim that the switch to GDP is a bid to fiddle the figures. In fact it is America's first step to bring its national accounts into line with most of the rest of the world. Nearly all other industrial economies now favor GDP—although the two other big ones, Japan and Germany, are sticking with GNP for the moment.

In most countries it makes little difference, as net income from abroad tends to be small compared with the rest of the economy. America's GNP is only about 1% bigger than its GDP. But in some countries the gap is huge. Kuwait's GNP is a third bigger than its GDP, thanks to its large overseas investments; Ireland's is 13% smaller than its GDP.

GNP is probably more useful in comparing the relative levels of income per head in different countries, but GDP provides a better guide to changes in domestic production—and hence is the better tool for steering economic policy. Because net income from abroad tends to be volatile, the two measures can often move in completely different directions from one quarter to another. Swings in America's GNP sometimes give a misleading picture of domestic economic activity. Over longer periods, however, the two measures usually fall into step. Indeed, since the third quarter of last year [1990], America's GDP and GNP have both fallen by exactly the same amount. The government cannot boost its flagging growth rate simply by revising its figures; that requires a revision of its policies.

Source: *"Alphabet Soup,"* **The Economist***, September 21, 1991, p. 33.* © 1991 The Economist Newspaper Group, Inc. Reprinted with permission.

Depreciation, which is also called capital consumption, is the value of capital that wears out during an interval of time.

the bookstore less the $8 for wages/salaries, the $4 for rent/interest, and the $12 for paper. This leaves a profit, an accounting profit, of $4 [or $(28 − 8 − 4 − 12)]. In reality, some of what we call profit in the example is not available for the owners of the publishing company to take as their income because printing machines and other capital wear out and need to be replaced. The extent to which capital wears out is called **capital consumption** or, more briefly, **depreciation,** and this part of what companies earn is not really part of income. On a national scale, too, it is necessary to subtract depreciation from the value of goods and services produced by factors supplied by a country, that is, the GNP, in the course of calculating national income.

The connection between GNP and national income is also affected by indirect taxes, specifically, sales taxes and tariffs (taxes) on imports. These taxes are called indirect because even if they are paid by the producer, the consumer pays indirectly via higher product prices. Indirect taxes are part of the value of goods and services entering into the gross national product but are not part of the national income; they are included in the value of what people produce and sell but are not part of people's incomes. In the context of our example summarized in Table 12.1, if \$2 of the \$40 received for the book is sales tax, then the income of the bookstore is not \$4 as shown and labeled "profit," but only \$2. That is, in calculating national income, it is necessary to deduct the amount of sales tax from the value of final production.

The fact that national income excludes depreciation and indirect taxes, both of which are contained in the GNP, is summarized by

$$\text{National income} = \text{GNP} - \text{depreciation} - \text{indirect taxes} \qquad (12.2)$$

Both depreciation and indirect taxes are small relative to GNP, but nevertheless, they are the reason why national income and GNP are only *roughly* equivalent.

If we wish to compare national income to GDP rather than to GNP, we can use Equation 12.1 in Equation 12.2. This gives

$$\begin{aligned} \text{National income} = \text{GDP} &+ \text{net foreign factor income} \\ &- \text{depreciation} - \text{indirect taxes} \end{aligned} \qquad (12.3)$$

Indirect taxes consist of sales taxes plus import duties. These are paid indirectly by consumers via higher prices.

National income is gross national product minus depreciation and indirect taxes.

PROBLEMS IN CALCULATING GDP AND NATIONAL INCOME

Measurement Difficulties

The national income accountant must consider a number of potential problems when calculating GDP, GNP, and national income. Among the more important measurement problems are the following.

Double Counting. As noted in our example, we have identified the value of the book as \$40, the amount paid at the bookstore for the final product. We would not want to add to this \$40 the \$28 that the bookstore paid the publisher, since this \$28 is already included in the \$40. If we added the \$28 paid to the publisher, we would be double counting that amount. In the same way, we would not want to include the \$12 the publisher paid the paper producer or the \$4 the paper producer paid the logging company for trees. These other payments are for intermediate transactions, and we must be careful to include only payments for final products when calculating the GDP.

When we avoid double counting by including only the value of final production, our measure of national income or product is not influenced by the level of **vertical integration**. The degree of vertical integration concerns the extent to which the various stages of production are combined. For example, if the logging and paper production for this book were done by the same, integrated firm, we would have to combine the first two stages as in Table 12.3. We find in Table 12.3 that since we do not include the payments to previous stages of production within national income or GDP, vertical integration does not affect these magnitudes.

The level of vertical integration concerns the extent to which different stages of production are handled by separate firms or by the same firm. The degree of vertical integration does not affect the GDP or national income.

....
TABLE 12.3

The amount of vertical integration does not affect the GDP or national income because we avoid double counting.

	LOGGING/PAPER PRODUCTION		PRINTING/ PUBLISHING		BOOKSTORE SALES
Payment to previous stage		$0		$12	$28
Wages/salaries	$5		$8		$5
Rent/interest	$3		$4		$3
Profits	$4		$4		$4
Value added		$12		$16	$12
Value of sales		$12		$28	$40

This table is obtained from Table 12.1 by adding the wages/salaries, rent/interest, and profits of the first two stages of production. We find by comparing the top row of this table with that of Table 12.1 that when logging and paper production are done by the same firm, we have fewer intermediate transactions. However, the sum of values added—the GDP or national income—is still $40, the same as the amount paid for the final product. The GDP is not affected because intermediate transactions are not included in the GDP.

Used Goods.   If you purchased this book used, then your purchase is not part of GDP. Only newly manufactured goods enter the GDP, and this is true for such items as houses and cars as well as books. We include only new goods because we want to measure production during the specified period of time, and used goods have already been measured. They were included when they were originally produced.

While the amount paid for used goods is not included in the GDP, the profit or income made on the sale of used goods *is* included. If a bookstore that sells used books buys a text for $20 and sells it for $30, they have presumably provided a recycling service worth $10. This amount would be contained in the income generated by the bookstore in wages and salaries, rent, interest, and profits. Similarly, the services of real estate agents and used-car salespeople in selling older homes or used cars are included in the current GDP, even though the used homes and cars are themselves not a part of the GDP.

Used goods are **not** *included in the GDP. However, the incomes earned in recycling used goods* **are** *included.*

Exports and Imports.   In practice, the GDP is obtained by measuring the value of *expenditures* on final goods and services rather than by measuring the value of *production*. The value of expenditures on final goods and services, excluding all intermediate sales, is called **final sales**. The value of final sales includes the amount spent on goods produced abroad, that is, **imports**, as well as the amount spent on goods produced at home. Imports include such items as cars from Japan, wines from France, teas from India, coffees from Brazil, and woolen sweaters from Great Britain. However, the GDP measures the value of only those goods produced *within* the nation. We must therefore be careful to deduct the value of imports from final sales to obtain the GDP and national income estimates. However, value added in marketing and retailing imports *is* part of the GDP. For example, if this economics book had been produced and published abroad and purchased by the local bookstore for $28, the value added by the bookstore is part of GDP or national income. If the book sells for $40, the $12 markup is included in the national income and GDP. The remaining $28 belongs to the GDP and income of the country in which the book was produced.

A similar problem arises with **exports.** Exports are items produced domestically but sold abroad and therefore do not appear in a nation's statistics on final sales. However, since exports are produced within the country, they generate income and are part of the GDP and national income. For example, if this economics book which was produced in the United States was sold to a foreign bookstore for $28, the U.S. GDP and national income would include this amount. Since this $28 is not part of the final sales statistics of the United States, the value of exports must be added to the final sales to obtain the U.S. GDP and national income statistics.

Imports are part of final sales in a country but are not *included in GDP or national income. On the other hand, exports, which are not part of final sales,* are *included.*

Change in Inventory Stocks. Another problem that derives from the way GDP is measured concerns changes in stocks of **inventories**, which are items that have been produced but not yet sold. As we have said, the national income accountant measures the value of the nation's final *sales* rather than the value of *production.* As with imports and exports, the existence of inventories means that adjustments have to be made to final sales to calculate the value of production, that is, the GDP. For example, if the GDP is being measured over a calendar year and some books produced and sold to a bookstore in that year remain on the shelves of the bookstore on December 31, the value of these books does not show up in final sales during that year. In order to remedy this problem, the national income accountant adds the change in inventories to final sales to obtain the GDP.

Inventories are goods produced but not yet sold. The change in inventories is included in the GDP and national income.

The inventory problem can work in either direction. Some goods sold in a given interval may not have been produced during that interval but instead have been carried forward as inventory from an earlier period. For example, if 6000 books had been sold but 1000 came from inventory stocks, only 5000 were produced in that year. In this case, the change in inventory stocks is negative. Whether inventories increase or decrease, we *add* the change in inventories to final sales. This means that if inventories increase so that the change in inventories is positive, the GDP is larger than final sales, and if inventories decrease so that the change in inventories is negative, final sales exceed the GDP.

Government Spending. Even in basically free enterprise economies like those of the United States, Canada, western Europe, and Japan, a large fraction of economic activity, measured, for example, by the number of people employed, involves "production" by some level of government. Government production includes, for example, national defense, public law and order, public education, public health, and so on.

Government spending is included in GDP and national income, valued at cost.

Little of what the government produces is sold in the market. Because most of what is produced by government does not appear in final sales, we calculate the value of the government's *production* from the amount the government *spends* via payments of incomes to bureaucrats, soldiers, teachers, and social workers and include this in the GDP and national income. That is, government production is valued at its cost. However, Social Security, welfare, and similar payments are *not* included in government spending when calculating GDP. These are considered as **transfers** from some individuals, the taxpayers, to others, the recipients, and are therefore not part of national output or income.

Goods versus "Bads." All traded items are valued at market prices and are included in the final sales, whether they be pornographic videos or new economics textbooks.[4] This is done so as to avoid making subjective judgments, but it does cause problems in interpreting GDP as a measure of well-being. For example, the GDP will be increased if a massive oil spill sweeps onto our beaches. The payments made to emergency workers who toil around the clock to contain the oil and the payments for vessels moving floating booms will all be included in the GDP. Since these people and the equipment would not be called into service without the spill there is no offset from income or production lost elsewhere. As a result, a higher GDP will occur because of an oil spill. Similarly, if a major earthquake were to cause damage in California, the lost property would lower the GDP only to the extent that it lowers some people's incomes and disrupts output.[5] However, all the extra building activity in replacing housing, roads, schools, and hospitals that were destroyed would be included in the GDP. Therefore, the gross domestic product might be increased from a natural disaster such as an earthquake.[6]

It is not possible for the national income accountant to select only some incomes or some products and value them as "goods" and to exclude or even subtract others that she or he considers "bads." Workers who are paid to produce wheat or to clean up after oil spills have both earned incomes and been involved in "production." Therefore, their incomes, and the value of what they produce, are included in the national income and product accounts. However, this does mean that the GDP is at best only a general guide to the quality of life and that increases in the measure do not necessarily mean improvements. There is another factor, however, that must be taken into account, and this is the rate of inflation.

Correcting GDP for Inflation

Inflation, which means a general increase in prices, will raise the GDP and national income; we will be adding higher values of goods or incomes because the prices of the goods and levels of incomes are higher. However, we do not wish to say a country is better off just because dollar values of production and incomes are higher. People are better off only if there is a larger output of goods and services for people to enjoy. Similarly, people are better off only if their incomes will purchase more.

In order to obtain a measure of national performance that does not show an improvement merely because prices have risen, we need to measure the change in the physical output of goods and services. This involves calculation of the change in GDP that would have occurred if all prices had remained at initial levels.

> The value of all production is included in the GDP and national income whether or not some of what is produced may be considered harmful.

[4] This assumes that the pornographic videos are not sold in the **underground** or **informal economy,** which is not observable to the law or the national income accountant. Of course, this points to yet another problem, that of illicit or tax-evasive activity, which may well represent an important component of overall economic activity but not be recorded.

[5] The rental on the property *would* be lost from GDP, but the market value of existing property itself does not enter the account. Net national product (NNP), which is discussed later, could be used to take account of destruction.

[6] Those natural disasters affecting the *flow* of output rather than the *stock* of capital have a negative effect on GDP. For example, the U.S. GDP, after adjusting for prices, was reduced by the severe drought during 1988 and flooding during 1993 because of their effects on farm income and output.

To obtain the change in physical output of goods and services, the national income accountant

1. Measures physical outputs of everything each year.

2. Values all outputs each year at the prices in a common, **base year.**

The physical outputs of all items each year are valued at the common base-year prices before they are added up to obtain the GDP. By valuing the output of each year at the same base-year prices, the national income accountant derives the value of output at unchanged prices. The relevance of this measure and the way it is calculated can be seen by an example.

Adjusting GDP for Inflation: An Example.   Imagine a very small and simple economy that produces only six items. Table 12.4 summarizes the amounts produced and the prices during 2 years that are a decade apart.

The ordinary dollar value of GDP, where the value is assessed at prices prevailing at the time the goods and services were produced, is called the **nominal GDP** or **current-price GDP**. Sometimes the label **current-dollar GDP** is used. The nominal GDPs for 1984 and 1994 in our example are simply calculated as

$$\begin{aligned} \text{Nominal GDP (1984)} &= (10,000 \times \$0.80) + (50 \times \$4800) + (1000 \times \$8) \\ &\quad + (50 \times \$100) + (20 \times \$5000) + (8 \times \$16,000) \\ &= \$489,000 \end{aligned}$$

$$\begin{aligned} \text{Nominal GDP (1994)} &= (15,000 \times \$1.50) + (60 \times \$8400) + (2000 \times \$10) \\ &\quad + (60 \times \$120) + (22 \times \$5600) + (8 \times \$26,000) \\ &= \$884,900 \end{aligned}$$

We find an increase in the nominal GDP of $395,900 (or $884,900 – $489,000), which is an increase of 80% over the 10 years 1984 to 1994. However, how much better off are people in this economy?

Table 12.4 shows that as well as there being more production of everything other than social work in 1994 than in 1984, there is also an increase in the price of everything. In order to discover how much of a real improvement has occurred in the economy when price increases are not included as part of the measured improvement, we value the 1994 outputs not at the prices in 1994 but instead at the prices prevailing in 1984. When this is done, GDP can increase only if more goods and services are available and not because of higher prices. Computing this from Table 12.4, we have

Nominal GDP is the value of goods and services produced within a country assessed at prices prevailing at the time the goods and services were produced.

$$\begin{aligned} \text{GDP (for 1994 at 1984 prices)} &= (15,000 \times \$0.80) + (60 \times \$4800) \\ &\quad + (2000 \times \$8) + (60 \times \$100) \\ &\quad + (22 \times \$5000) + (8 \times \$16,000) \\ &= \$560,000 \end{aligned}$$

This is less than 15% larger than the 1984 GDP, also measured in 1984 prices ($560,000 versus $489,000).

TABLE 12.4

Real GDP can be compared between years without the distortion of inflation.

	1984 OUTPUT	1984 PRICE	1994 OUTPUT	1994 PRICE
Bread	10,000 loaves	$0.80 each	15,000 loaves	$1.50 each
Rent	50 homes	$4,800/year	60 homes	$8,400/year
Utilities	1,000 units	$8/unit	2,000 units	$10/unit
Suits	50 suits	$100 each	60 suits	$120 each
Investment	20 machines	$5,000 each	22 machines	$5,600 each
Social services	8 workers	$16,000/year	8 workers	$26,000/year
Nominal GDP (current prices)	$489,000		$884,900	
Real GDP	$489,000		$560,000	

Nominal or current-price GDP is the value of output each year at current prices. Real or constant-priced GDP is the value of output during each year at base-year prices. Changes in real GDP occur only from changes in the volumes of outputs, not from changes in prices. During periods of inflation, real GDP increases less than nominal GDP.

Our example shows that during times of inflation, the growth in GDP calculated in each year at base-year prices is smaller than the growth in GDP measured in current prices. When there is **deflation**—which means prices in general are falling—the nominal or current-price GDP could conceivably fall even if the GDP measured with base-year prices is rising. This would mean that the output of goods and services increased while their prices were falling faster.

The name given to GDP that is measured in the prices of a base year is **real GDP.** The terms **constant-price GDP** and **constant-dollar GDP** are also sometimes used. The label **real** indicates that this measure of GDP is affected only by what *really* determines our standard of living, namely, the amount of goods and services produced, rather than the dollar value of goods and services. Real GDP is the value of production in a nation during an interval of time measured in constant, base-year prices.

An increase in real GDP is roughly equivalent to the extent national income increases faster than prices. The equivalence occurs because higher output of goods and services means that more output is available to be bought, and for people to be able to buy the extra output, their incomes must increase more than prices. (Example 12.2 illustrates how some people just cannot grasp this important fact—at least in the fiction of Mark Twain.)

Real GDP is the value of production of goods and services produced within a nation during an interval of time measured in base-year prices. Real GDP is also called the constant price or constant-dollar GDP.

Example 12.2

AN ARGUMENT OF REAL SIGNIFICANCE

Mark Twain understood very well how the real value of a given nominal income depends on the price level. What the following excerpt shows, however, is that he, or at least his literary embodiment as the Connecticut Yankee, overestimated the comprehension of others about this matter.

Dowley warmed to his work, snuffed an advantage in the air, and began to put questions which he considered pretty awkward ones for me, and they did have something of that look:

"In your country, brother, what is the wage of a master bailiff, master hind, carter, shepherd, swineherd?"

"Twenty-five milrays a day; that is to say, a quarter of a cent."

The smith's face beamed with joy. He said:

"With us they are allowed the double of it! And what may a mechanic get—carpenter, dauber, mason, painter, blacksmith, wheelwright, and the like?"

"On the average, fifty milrays; half a cent a day."

"Ho-Ho! With us they are allowed a hundred! . . . 'Rah for protection—to Sheol with free-trade!"

And his face shone upon the company like a sunburst. But I didn't scare at all. I rigged up my pile-driver, and allowed myself fifteen minutes to drive him into the earth—drive him *all* in—drive him in till not even the curve of his skull should show above ground. Here is the way I started in on him. I asked:

"What do you pay a pound for salt?"

"A hundred milrays."

"We pay forty. What do you pay for beef and mutton—when you buy it?" That was a neat hit; it made the color come.

"It varieth somewhat, but not much; one may say 75 milrays the pound."

"*We* pay 33. What do you pay for eggs?"

"Fifty milrays the dozen."

"We pay 20."

. . .

I prepared now to sock it to him. I said: "Look here, dear friend, *what's become of your high wages you were bragging so about a few*

minutes ago?"—and I looked around on the company with placid satisfaction, for I had slipped up on him gradually and tied him hand and foot, you see, without his ever noticing that he was being tied at all. . . .

But if you will believe me, he merely looked surprised, that is all! He didn't grasp the situation at all. . . . I could have shot him, from sheer vexation. With cloudy eye and a struggling intellect he fetched this out:

"Marry, I seem not to understand. It is *proved* that our wages be double thine. . . ."

Well, I was stunned; partly from this unlooked-for stupidity on his part, and partly because his fellows so manifestly sided with him and were on his mind—if you might call it mind.

Source: Mark Twain, **A Connecticut Yankee in King Arthur's Court** (New York: Harper & Row, 1889), pp.295–297 (emphasis in original).

Measurement of Economic Growth

Economic growth, which involves an expansion in the national income and product, provides the basis of improvements in the standard of living. However, we must be careful when measuring living standards from the national income and product accounts to employ the correct measure.

In measuring the rate at which the standard of living is advancing, we would not want to use the rate of improvement in a nominal magnitude such as the nominal GNP, since this would show improvements even when the increases stem from inflation. Instead, we must use something based on real magnitude that shows gains only from higher output of the overall economy, which is the basis of gains in the standard of living.

Net national product (NNP) is **gross** national product (GNP) minus depreciation.

The standard of living in a country is more closely related to GNP than to GDP. This is so because the incomes accruing to factors of production provided by residents of a country include net factor earnings from abroad, and these are part of GNP but not GDP. However, as we have seen, GNP includes income that must be set aside to cover depreciation of capital. When depreciation is deducted from GNP, the result is the net national product (NNP), that is:

$$NNP = GNP - depreciation \qquad (12.4)$$

By excluding the amount directed to replacing the capital that wears out, NNP gives a more accurate picture of economic performance or well-being than does GNP. Of course, NNP must be put in real or constant-price form so as to exclude the effect of inflation. This is achieved by computing real GNP and then subtracting the real or constant-price depreciation. The calculation of real depreciation requires valuation of the physical amount of wear and tear at the base-year prices of capital equipment.[7]

Real per capita NNP measures the amount of product available for an average citizen to enjoy. This is a commonly used measure for comparing standards of living from year to year or from country to country.

Further adjustment is necessary before obtaining a useful measure of the standard of living of an average individual. NNP, like GNP, will grow merely because there are more people engaged in production. However, what determines the amount of product available for an average citizen to enjoy is the amount of product per person, or per capita. Consequently, real NNP must be divided by the number of people in the country who share it in order to derive **real per capita NNP.** This is a commonly used measure for comparing economic performance from year to year or from country to country, although other measures which allow for distortions introduced by taxes are also used.

DIFFICULTIES WHEN COMPARING REAL NNPS

Comparing NNP Between Years

We have already indicated that measures of national income and product such as NNP count bombs and hospitals equivalently and can perversely show an improvement after human-caused or natural disasters. NNP can be increased by many other factors that we would consider undesirable. For example, if more is spent each year on health care and cleaning bills because of higher levels of air pollution, the real per capita NNP will increase even though we would not consider people to be better off. In a similar way, higher crime rates, which require that we incur higher expenditures each year to protect ourselves, to enforce the law, and to replace stolen or damaged property, also increase real NNP.[8]

---

[7] In deducting only capital that is used up there is presumed inexhaustability of other factors of production. A case can be made for making an allowance for the depletion in reserves of exhaustible resources in computing NNP from GNP. However, the national income and product accounts do not yet make this adjustment, despite suggestions that it be made. See Robert Eisner, *The Total Incomes System of Accounts* (Chicago: University of Chicago Press, 1989).

[8] Expenditures on crime protection made by individuals or government *are* part of GDP and NNP, but expenditures on crime protection by businesses are *not* included in NNP and GDP. Crime protection by business is considered to be an intermediate product and is therefore left out in calculating NNP and GDP.

Just as some undesirable developments are excluded from NNP, some desirable developments involving improvements in the quality of life are also left out of NNP. For example, restrictions on the cutting of trees in the wilderness reduce real NNP by lowering the number of trees available for building houses and furniture. Similarly, shorter work weeks reduce national output and hence real NNP. Changes in the quality of the environment and the amount of leisure are not likely to be dramatic enough to make comparisons completely meaningless when the years are close together, but they make for questionable comparisons over longer spans of time.

It is not only changes in the quality of the environment that may be missed when comparing real NNPs over time. Changes in the quality of goods and services also may not be captured. For example, newer motor vehicles provide a smoother ride and safer handling than earlier models. Electrical sound and viewing systems have improved greatly. On the other hand, construction standards in some furniture and homes and the quality of service at gas stations and some stores have declined. Despite the development of statistical methods for handling changes in quality for measuring real NNP, many of the measures used by national income accountants do not take quality changes fully into consideration. These and some other problems in comparisons between years (and countries) are discussed in Example 12.3.

Real per capita NNP is an imperfect measure of changes in the quality of life. It can be increased by pollution and crime and reduced by environmental improvements and increased leisure.

Comparing NNPs Between Countries

If anything, a comparison of standards of living based on real per capita NNPs is more difficult between countries than between years within a country. For one thing, when we compare per capita NNPs between, for example, Great Britain, Canada, Germany, and the United States, we cannot compare pounds sterling in Great Britain with Canadian dollars, with Deutschemarks, and with U.S. dollars. In order to make comparisons, we must express all NNPs in a common currency by, for example, multiplying NNPs in the foreign countries by the number of U.S. dollars trading in the foreign exchange markets for each other currency. Then, for example, a £5000 income in Great Britain when the exchange rate is $2 per pound, will be $10,000. It is only after this has been done that we can compare per capita NNP or income in Great Britain with that in the United States.

A potential problem arises when exchange rates do not reflect costs of living in the different countries. Exchange rates reflect a variety of factors, not just the prices of goods and services in the various countries. As a result, after putting all NNPs in terms of the same currency, it is necessary to make further adjustments for the cost of a typical consumer's "basket" of goods in different countries. (A typical consumer's basket is what an average or representative consumer purchases. The determination of a typical basket is discussed more fully in Chapter 14.) "Typical baskets," however, are different. This is so partly because people in different countries have different needs, tastes, and customs.

Comparisons of real NNPs per capita between countries are distorted by different costs of living in different countries.

Nature is kinder in some geographic locations than others. Those enjoying a temperate climate do not need to spend great sums heating their houses, and therefore, home heating expenditures are not a large part of a typical consumer's basket. Less lucky people who experience severe cold—as in northern parts of the United States and Canada—need more income just to pay the bills for keeping warm. Similarly, in countries where communities are highly dispersed—as in Australia and Canada—large amounts are needed for travel. In more compact

Example 12.3

THINGS DON'T ALWAYS ADD UP

Many of the points that we have made concerning the inadequacies of the national income and product accounts are dealt with in the following article by David Francis that appeared in **The Christian Science Monitor**.

Housewives don't count!

At least not in the national-income accounts. Because they are not paid in money, all the cooking, cleaning, and child-care hours of housewives (or, for that matter, house husbands) don't add one dime to the nation's gross national product (GNP).

If a working couple hires a maid service to help in the home or pays for child care, the charges are added to the national output of goods and services. But the same activities, done unpaid at home, are ignored by the statisticians in Washington.

The value of these activities is not questioned from a social standpoint. But they are considered too hard to measure accurately in dollars and cents. For example, could you determine by how much the multiplication of two-job families has reduced the time spent on household chores and child care? Should you subtract that amount from GNP?

Robert Repetto has a different complaint about national income accounts. He says they fail to encompass the concept of substainability.

"A country could exhaust its mineral resources, cut down its forests, erode its soils, pollute its aquifers, and hunt its wildlife and fisheries to extinction, but measured income would not be affected as these assets disappeared," he states in a study for the World Resources Institute in Washington.

In keeping the national books, the statisticians subtract depreciation of manmade assets, including plant and equipment, from the value of national production. They don't subtract the depletion of natural resources.

"It should be considered," says an official in the United Nations Statistical Office. "We are all advocating that."

The UN system of national accounts provides a statistical standard and model that in its basic elements is closely followed by most countries. A UN Statistical Commission is expected to recommend by 1991 that nations turn out a "satellite" account, separate from the current GNP standard account, that takes into consideration depletion (or restoration) of natural resources.

That commission is also reviewing, among other statistical controversies, the question of what to do about the unpaid production of

places, people can make visits and do business with less spent on travel. Generally, equal incomes do not mean equal standards of living when there are diverse physical conditions.

Another problem in comparing average per capita real NNPs concerns the distribution of incomes around the average. For example, in some of the richer countries measured solely by real per capita NNP or national income, there are a handful of fabulously rich families and the majority of families live barely above the property level. Average incomes in such countries may be quite high because of the massive incomes of the very few, but we would not view such countries as providing a good standard of living for the average citizen. In comparing countries, the equality of the distribution of income should somehow be taken into account. The Appendix following this chapter considers some of the problems related to the distribution of income.

Quality of the environment and conditions in the workplace are at least as much a problem when comparing living standards between countries as they are in comparing them over time. High per capita incomes that are earned at the

goods and services by households.

In the U.S., the Bureau of Economic Analysis in the Department of Commerce plans to reevaluate its count of national output in light of what the UN Commission recommends.

"We are watching closely what the UN experts are doing," says Carol Carson, a Bureau deputy director. She is actually one of the six "core" experts consulted by the UN commission.

Because such a huge proportion of the United States gross national product derives from services or industrial production, a full accounting of developments in natural resources might not make much difference in the GNP accounts. Though Americans think of their nation as being resource-rich, natural resources aren't so important to total output as in some other countries.

Further, there are offsets in the book-keeping. Depletion of some mineral resources (say, crude oil) might be offset by new discoveries of other minerals or natural gas. Or forests being cut down in the West might be replaced by new forest growth in New England.

But in some developing countries, the failure to extend the concept of depreciation to natural resources can be important. Mr. Repetto says this lack can give "misleading signals about the status of the economy."

With a group of graduate students, he did a calculation for Indonesia of "net" domestic product (NDP) [calculated as NNP minus resource depletion]—taking account of resource depletion. The annual growth rate of NDP from 1971 to 1984 on average came to 4 percent, way down from the 7.1 percent average annual growth calculated by the usual method of national accounting.

Moreover, their study only looked at the depletion of petroleum, timber, and soil resources. It ignored many other resources.

This study implies that Indonesia's natural resources are being depleted to finance current consumption.

"Such an evaluation should flash an unmistakable warning signal to economic policy makers that they were on an unsustainable course," holds Repetto. "An economic accounting system that does not generate and highlight such evaluations is deficient as a tool for analysis and policy in resource-based economies and should be amended."

Source: David R. Francis, "Should GNP Include Housewives and Resources," Reprinted by permission from **The Christian Science Monitor,** May 31, 1989, p.9. © 1989 The Christian Science Publishing Society. All Rights Reserved.

expense of polluted air, dirty streams and lakes, the risk of technologically induced nightmares, and vicious working conditions hardly qualify a country to head the league of the quality of life.

There are further problems related both to the "value" of what is produced and the nature of what it takes to generate different NNPs. For example, direct real per capita NNP comparisons do not distinguish between countries producing vast mountains of armaments and other countries in which a similar fraction of NNP is spent on medical research for the benefit of humanity.[9]

A related problem concerns the composition of different countries' national outputs between goods and services for immediate or current enjoyment versus goods and services to enhance future potential output. While countries putting aside for

---

[9] To the extent that government expenditures can be broken into defense versus nondefense categories, some allowances can be made. However, some budget items, such as research and development, are difficult to disentangle.

the future by devoting resources to improving the stock of machines and to educating people do not experience any immediate benefit in their NNPs, the opportunities for future economic growth in these countries are greater.

Since outputs and not inputs are measured in the accounts—except in the case of the contribution of government—problems in comparison occur when the same outputs take very different inputs. For example, as in the case of comparing real NNPs between years, a country in which the public enjoys a lot of leisure appears no wealthier than another country in which the same per capita real NNP is achieved by people typically working 60 hours a week. The country with the long work week and very little leisure may even appear to have a higher NNP, some of which goes to doctors or for medications aimed at helping workers cope with work-related stress. Similarly, a country in which a parent remains at home to raise the children will show a lower domestic product than an otherwise similar country in which both parents must work; work in the home is not counted in the GDP. Even the procedure for providing goods and services has an impact on real per capita NNP and is a potential source of error when comparing NNP between countries. For example, commercial television, which is supported by payments from advertisers, is considered an intermediate product and is *not* part of final output. This is despite the fact that the programming provides viewers with pleasure. On the other hand, publically funded television *is* part of NNP. This means that the measured NNP is influenced by the way television programming is provided.

There have been efforts to form intertemporal and intercountry comparisons from criteria other than real per capita NNP. Measures used include the number of automobiles and televisions per capita; the amount of open park space; the fraction of self-owned homes; the percentage of homes with refrigerators, telephones, or inside plumbing; and the number of different newspapers from which to choose. Other measures have included the incidence of mental illness and crime. These different measures are, however, difficult to combine. An attempt to combine different measures in an index is described in Example 12.4.

CATEGORIES OF GDP

Lumping all the different goods and services together in the GDP is useful for judging overall production but hides variations in some important categories of output. Therefore, as well as reporting total GDP, the national income and product accounts also show GDP in terms of its major components, as in Table 12.5. The component of national output that is for current or "immediate" use is given under the heading **personal consumption.** This includes such items as food and beverages, clothing, household appliances, entertainment, and so on. The amount of consumption is determined primarily by the incomes consumers have available to spend. Consumption itself is divided into durable goods, nondurable goods, and services. The sales and production of durable goods are affected not only by consumers' incomes but also by the interest rate on consumer debt.

The value of output produced to assist future production and sales rather than for current enjoyment, such as the output of buildings and equipment, is listed under the heading **investment.** The investment category also includes changes in

*Real per capita NNP comparisons between countries may not reflect relative standards of living because they may **not** reflect the quality of the environment, working conditions, the types of goods and services produced, and the distribution of income.*

*Consumption goods and services are for **immediate** use. Consumption depends primarily on consumers' incomes.*

Example 12.4

PERFORMANCE IN THE QUALITY-OF-LIFE RACE

A widening recognition that the quality of life depends on far more than real national income per capita has spawned a number of efforts to come up with a better index than is implied in the national income and product accounts. One of these, the Human Development Index, is described below.

Which nation on Earth has achieved the greatest good for the greatest number? And which lingers at the bottom of the pile when prizes for the successful pursuit of happiness are handed out? The United Nations Development Program has just produced a new index which sets out to provide answers to these questions. The Human Development Index—which we must doubtless learn to call the HDI—sets out to measure success not using the crude gauge of national wealth, but based on life span, literacy and basic purchasing power.

The results contain some surprises. The United States is the world's richest nation measured by gross national product per capita, but it rates only 19th on the HDI. Canada ranks fifth, Britain, 18th in wealth, ranks a full eight positions higher than the United States. The United Arab Emirates enjoys enormous wealth, with a GDP per capita among the highest in the world. But its adult literacy rate is low, so it falls below Sri Lanka, which is one-sixth as wealthy.

Japan comes out on top—GDP per capita $13,135, life expectancy 78, adult literacy 99 percent—while at the bottom is Niger. There, GDP per capita is a mere $452, life expectancy 45 and adult literacy a miserable 14 percent.

The index is calculated by working out the degree of deprivation suffered by each country in terms of the three variables chosen. The deprivation indicators are then averaged, and subtracted from the theoretical maximum of 1 to produce the HDI. Japan emerges with 0.996; the tiny deviation from a perfect score of 1 arises from the fact that is has yet to achieve 100 percent literacy. (Like all developed countries, it claims 99 percent.) Niger, at the other end of the scale, scores just 0.116.

The top 10 in this novel new game of one-upmanship runs as follows: Japan, Sweden, Switzerland, Netherlands, Canada, Norway, Australia, France, Denmark and Britain. The bottom ten, in order of increasing rank, are Niger, Mali, Burkina Faso, Sierra Leone, Chad, Guinea, Somalia, Mauritania, Afghanistan and Benin.

The study, published . . . by Oxford University Press for the UNDP, was carried out by a team lead by Mahbub ul Haq, a former minister of finance and planning of Pakistan (which is ranked 36th from bottom, incidentally). The object, an admirable one, was to try to build into the discussion of development the less tangible indices of a decent life that are sometimes forgotten.

By doing so, the team members were able to come to some interesting conclusions that do not always match the public perception of the development process. For example, they conclude that the developing countries have made significant progress towards human development in the past 30 years, and that North-South gaps have narrowed considerably, even while income gaps have widened. Further, they conclude that fairly respectable levels of human development are possible even at modest levels of income.

Sri Lanka, Chile, Costa Rica, Jamaica, Tanzania and Thailand, among others, do far better in human development than in income—while Oman, Gabon, Saudi Arabia, Algeria, Mauritania, Senegal, Cameroon and the United Arab Emirates do much worse.

Of course, a different index could have been constructed if different variables had been chosen. For example, the present one makes no distinction between democratic or authoritarian systems.

Conceding this, the team declares that over time the many different aspects of human freedom—such as free elections, a multi-party system, an uncensored press, the rule of law, free speech and so on—will be incorporated into HDI.

———
Source: *Nigel Hawkes,* **The Observer,** *1991.*

TABLE 12.5

The gross domestic product can be divided usefully into a number of components.

U.S. GROSS DOMESTIC PRODUCT (Billions $), 1992		
Personal consumption (C)		4,100
Durable goods	500	
Nondurable goods	1,250	
Services	2,350	
Investment (I)		800
Government (G)		1,150
Exports*(Ex)		650
Imports*(Im)		−700
		‾‾‾‾
Gross domestic product (Y)		6000
		‾‾‾‾

*Exports exclude factor income receipts from foreigners, and imports
   exclude factor income payments to foreigners.

Source: **National Income and Product Accounts, U.S.
Survey of Current Business** (Washington, D.C.: U.S.
Department of Commerce, 1993).

Investment is output produced to enhance future *output. Investment depends on interest rates.*

inventory stocks, which, as we have already explained, are goods that have been produced but not yet sold. Business investment in new buildings and equipment, as well as in inventories, is frequently financed through debt or via the sale of shares and is therefore influenced by the interest rate on borrowing and the expected return that must be offered to shareholders.

After showing consumption and investment, the GDP account gives the "output" of the government. However, as we have observed, instead of measuring government production, the account measures the amount the government spends on labor and other goods and services. Government spending is normally assumed to be a matter of economic policy that is determined in the political arena. However, there is also pressure to reduce spending when the government has a huge **national debt.** Wars also affect the size of government spending.

The GDP account includes the value of goods and services produced for export. A country's exports depend on prices in the exporting country compared with prices elsewhere, with lower relative export prices increasing the quantity sold. Exports also depend on the foreign exchange value of a country's currency and on incomes in foreign countries. Other factors affecting exports include import tariffs and quotas in potential markets.

While exports must be added to final sales, imports must be subtracted to obtain GDP. Like exports, imports depend on relative prices, exchange rates, incomes in the importing country, tariffs and quotas, and so on.

Table 12.5 summarizes our discussion of the components of GDP. We have written a symbol next to the various categories of the gross domestic product using the following notation:

$$\text{Consumption} = C$$

$$\text{Investment} = I$$

$$\text{Government} = G$$

$$\text{Exports} = Ex$$

$$\text{Imports} = Im$$

$$\text{GDP} = Y$$

We observe from the table that GDP consists of the sum of the various categories of production, specifically:

$$Y \equiv C + I + G + (Ex - Im) \tag{12.5}$$

We have used an identity sign in Equation 12.5 because it is a **tautology;** that is, it is always true. We see that GDP is the sum of the outputs of consumption goods and services *C*, investment goods *I*, government goods and services *G,* and exports minus imports (*Ex − Im*). The relationship (12.5) is known as the **national income accounting identity.**

The relative importance of the components of GDP differs substantially between countries. As Figure 12.1 shows, poorer countries such as Guatemala and Nigeria consume virtually all their GDPs; these countries need just about all their incomes just to keep people alive. In richer countries such as the United States, consumption is still the largest category of GDP, but it represents a smaller proportion than in the poor nations.

There is also substantial variation between countries in the amount of GDP going into investment. In general, those countries which consume a small part of GDP invest a relatively large amount. For example, both Singapore and Japan have high rates of investment and low rates of consumption.[10] Figure 12.1 also shows how the other two components of GDP, government spending and net exports, vary between countries. The importance of governments within GDPs depends on the amounts spent on defense, public health, education, and welfare. Net exports are seen in the figure to be positive contributions to GDP in Japan but a negative part in the United States; the United States has a **trade deficit,** with imports exceeding exports.

Figure 12.2 shows the relative importance of the different components of GDP for a larger range of countries than Figure 12.1. It confirms that the composition of GDP is a matter of substantial variation between countries.

The national income accounting identity shows GDP as the sum of consumption, investment, government spending, and exports minus imports.

The composition of GDP between consumption, investment, government spending, and exports minus imports varies substantially between countries.

---

[10] As we shall explain in Chapter 16, countries that invest relatively more of their GDPs also have relatively rapid economic growth.

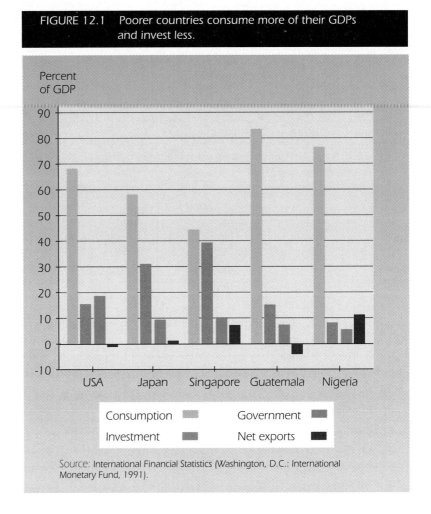

FIGURE 12.1 Poorer countries consume more of their GDPs and invest less.

Source: International Financial Statistics (Washington, D.C.: International Monetary Fund, 1991).

NATIONAL DEBT

An economic magnitude that has attracted increasing attention in recent years is the national debt, which is also sometimes referred to as the **public debt.** Figure 12.3 shows vividly why the national debt has become a focus of concern; between 1980 and 1992, the U.S. national debt increased a phenomenal 400%, from approximately $1 trillion to over $4 trillion. Other countries face a similar problem. For example, Figure 12.4 shows the explosive growth of Canada's national debt since 1970.

A commonly expressed concern is that national debt represents a burden on future generations and, indeed, that at the extremely rapid rate at which the debt has been growing, it represents a burden on people working today. Already, as Figure 12.5 on page 368 shows, interest payments on the U.S. national debt amount to approximately 20% of government outlays, and the fraction of government spending that is being devoted to interest has been growing in recent years. The need to find the money to make interest payments is forcing the U.S. govern-

FIGURE 12.2   There is substantial variation in the composition of GDPs across countries.

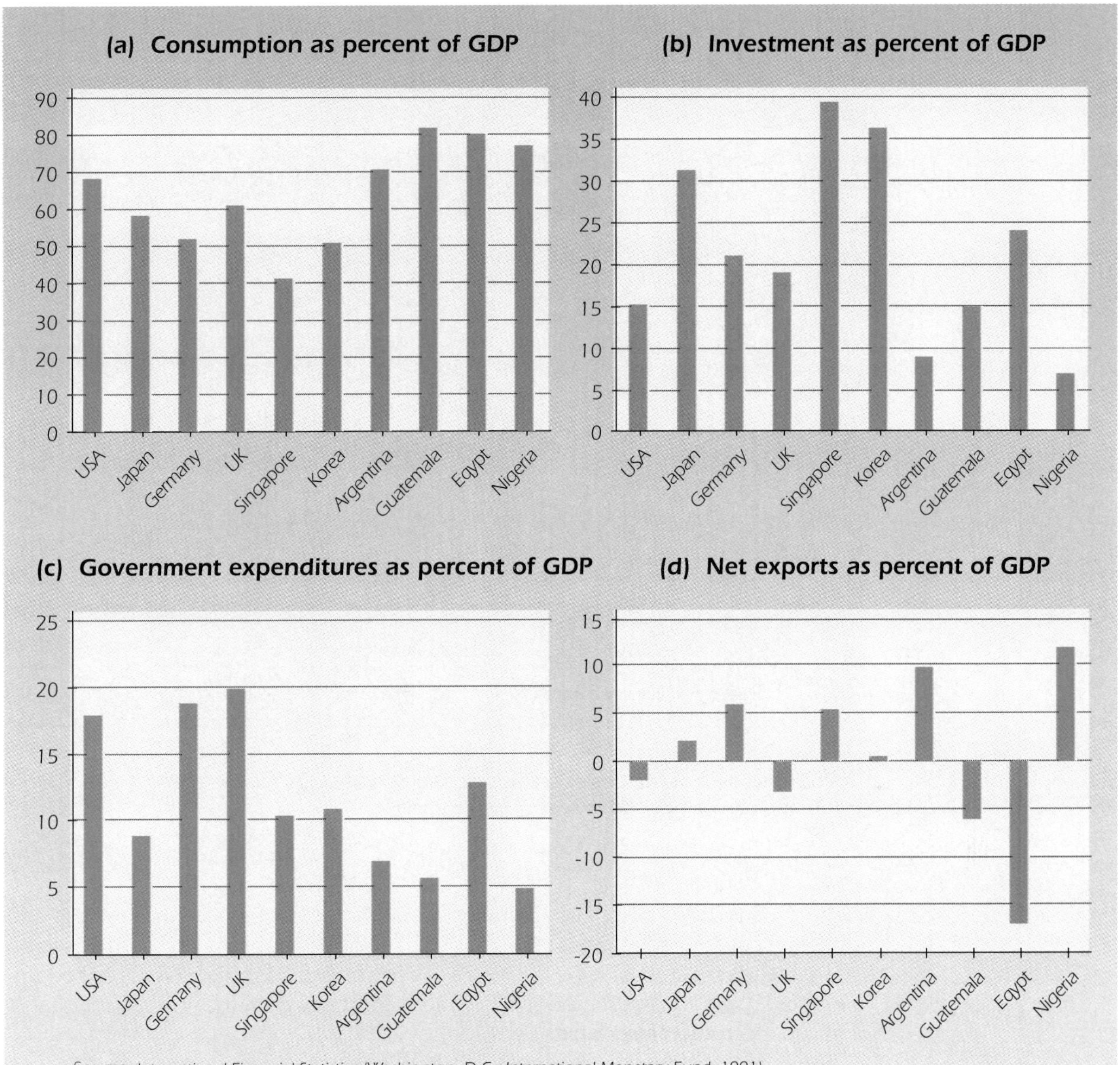

(a) Consumption as percent of GDP

(b) Investment as percent of GDP

(c) Government expenditures as percent of GDP

(d) Net exports as percent of GDP

Source: International Financial Statistics (Washington, D.C.: International Monetary Fund, 1991).

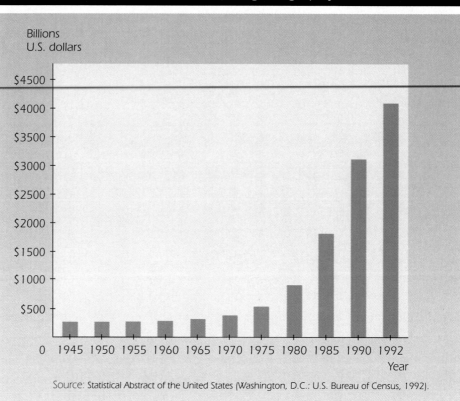

FIGURE 12.3   The national debt has been growing rapidly since the 1970s.

Source: Statistical Abstract of the United States (Washington, D.C.: U.S. Bureau of Census, 1992).

The national debt of the United States was relatively steady until the 1970s. During the 1980s and early 1990s, it grew extremely rapidly.

ment to consider carefully its spending on public health, education, research and development, transportation systems, and other programs which contribute to future well-being; a healthy, educated work force with sophisticated capital equipment and rapid transportation links is more productive than a work force that is denied crucial **infrastructure.**

The extent to which the national debt burdens future generations depends on a number of factors, including

1. Growth of national debt relative to the size of the national economy

2. The effect of higher taxes caused by growing interest payments on the willingness to work, save, and invest

3. The amount of debt owed to domestic residents versus foreigners

4. The amount of government spending directed toward improvement of the infrastructure essential for future economic development

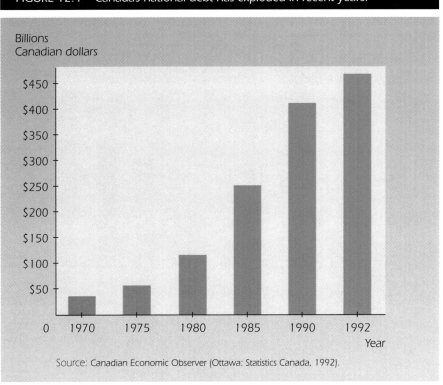

FIGURE 12.4   Canada's national debt has exploded in recent years.

Billions
Canadian dollars

Source: Canadian Economic Observer (Ottawa: Statistics Canada, 1992).

The national debt of Canada has increased at approximately 12.5% per annum compounded since 1970, far faster than the growth of the economy.

Let us review each of these four factors in turn.

National Debt Relative to the Size of the National Economy.   When a company's debt grows, there is not necessarily widespread concern among shareholders; money borrowed for new plant and equipment could mean a very healthy future. What matters is whether the company's income is growing sufficiently for it to meet all interest payments and scheduled repayments of principal. Similarly, in the case of national debt, what matters is whether the government's income is growing sufficiently for it to meet all its debt obligations. The base on which the government collects taxes which can be used to meet debt obligations is the national product; *ceteris paribus,* the higher the national product, the higher is the government's tax revenue. Therefore, the level of concern about the national debt depends on how rapidly the debt is growing relative to national product, as reflected in the GNP or GDP. This can be judged by looking at the ratio of debt to GNP or GDP. Figure 12.6 indicates that the U.S. national debt grew more slowly than the U.S. GNP from the end of World War II until the mid-1970s. However, since that time, the national debt has grown faster than the GNP, making it more difficult for the U.S. government to meet scheduled debt repayments.

The seriousness of the national debt depends on how rapidly it is growing relative to the size of the national economy.

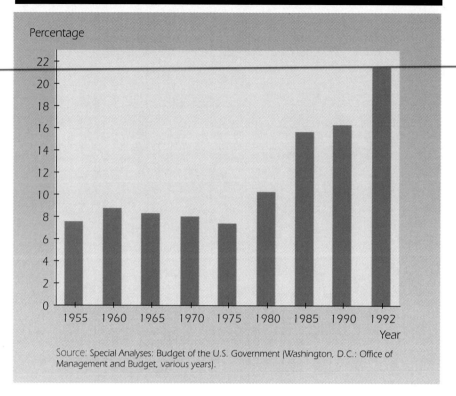

FIGURE 12.5   Interest payments constitute a growing proportion of U.S. government outlays.

Source: Special Analyses: Budget of the U.S. Government (Washington, D.C.: Office of Management and Budget, various years).

Since 1975, the fraction of U.S. government outlays going toward interest payments on the national debt has more than doubled.

Taxes and the Willingness to Work, Save, and Invest.   Most of the national debt consists of Treasury bills and Treasury bonds. These are sold by the government to allow it to run fiscal deficits, that is, to spend more than it collects in taxes. To the extent that the Treasury bills and bonds are owned by citizens, payments on the debt are transfers from one group to another within the same country. For example, if all U.S. Treasury bills and bonds were owned by Americans, payments on the U.S. national debt would simply be transfers from U.S. taxpayers to U.S Treasury bill and Treasury bond holders. Therefore, it might seem that the national debt imposes no cost to the nation considered as a whole; money is just paid by some people to others. However, even when all the national debt is held by citizens, there may still be a cost to the nation from the effect of taxes on incentives to work, save, and invest.

Those who pay the taxes to make interest payments on the national debt find their after-tax earnings reduced. If the taxes are on wages, workers may reduce their effort; the willingness to work overtime might, for example, be reduced because there is less reward. If the taxes are on interest received on savings, people may reduce the amount saved. Finally, if the taxes are on income from investment, for example, on profits earned from new plant and equipment, companies

Even when payments on the national debt are transfers within the country, there may still be a cost to the nation from higher taxes which can reduce currect and future national income.

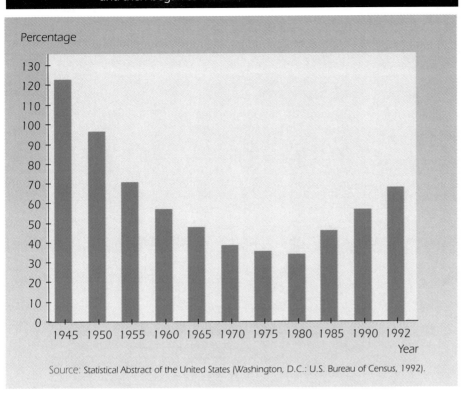

FIGURE 12.6   The national debt as a percentage of GNP fell until the mid 1970s and then began to increase.

Source: Statistical Abstract of the United States (Washington, D.C.: U.S. Bureau of Census, 1992).

As a fraction of GNP, the national debt fell from 1945 until the mid-1970s. During the early 1980s, the fraction began to grow rapidly.

may reduce investment. These disincentive effects of higher taxes represent a burden on current and future generations.

External Debt and Future Income.   In fact, contrary to our foregoing assumption, payments on the national debt are not merely transfers from some citizens, the taxpayers, to others, the Treasury bill and bond holders. Rather, as Figure 12.7 shows, part of the national debt is held by foreigners. Interest payments to foreigners are a drain on the income from the economy. Therefore, to the extent that a growing debt means that more money is collected from taxpayers and sent abroad, a growing national debt represents a growing burden, one that could leave future generations working in order to meet obligations incurred on their behalf, but without their consent.

Foreign-held debt is a burden on a country's taxpayers.

The Form of Government Expenditures.   To the extent that a government borrows money to increase the productive capacity of its economy, the debt that is incurred does not represent a burden; payments on the debt can be paid out of the additional income generated in the economy. For example, if much of what is done with borrowed money involves improvements in transportation systems, education, research and development, telecommunications systems, and so on, the

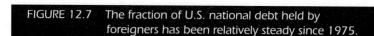

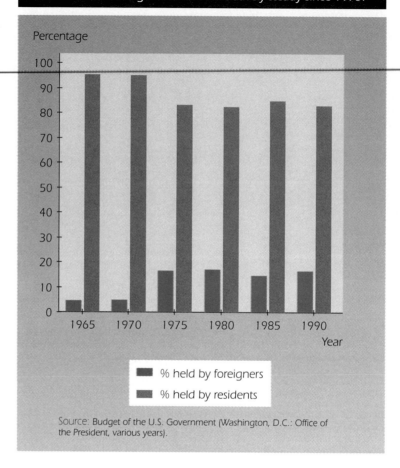

FIGURE 12.7 The fraction of U.S. national debt held by foreigners has been relatively steady since 1975.

Source: Budget of the U.S. Government (Washington, D.C.: Office of the President, various years).

The burden of debt faced by future generations depends on whether or not borrowed money is used to enhance the future productive capacity of an economy.

payoff from the better national infrastructure could make people much better off, even though there is a need to make payments on the debt which financed the infrastructure. On the other hand, if borrowed money is used in ways that do not enhance future productive capacity, going, for example, for higher civil service salaries, then the debt represents a burden.

CROSSING **BRIDGES**

ACCOUNTING FOR NATIONAL ECONOMIC PERFORMANCE

Humanity's interest in "keeping score" has a long history. Of course, keeping score requires a consistent numerical system and a framework for keeping records, and it can be argued that it was the needs of business and commerce for a numerical recording system that led to the early development of mathematics. Certainly, the commercial uses of mathematics arose early on for quoting prices, calculating revenues and costs, and recording debts. Accounting principles had emerged for reporting the performance and financial status of commercial enterprises well before they were written down by the Italian mathematician Luca Paciolo, whose **Summa de Arithemetica, Geometria, Proportioni et Proportionalita** was published in 1494. While Paciolo wrote about accounting for commercial enterprises, it was only a natural and short step before Sir William Petty and Gregory King in

Great Britain were formulating rules on the recording of national economic performance in national income and product accounts. The principal purpose of the national accounts was to keep score on how well a nation was doing in providing for the economic well-being of its citizens.

The national accounts have been refined and elaborated to a point where they do far more than just record overall national economic performance. The national income and product accounts today provide data of interest to political scientists, geographers, and public policymakers, as well as to economists, historians, and others.

The national income estimates show the division of income between wages, salaries, profits, interest, and rent. These data provide evidence on the behavior of the functional distribution of income over time, as well as during the ups and downs of the business cycle. The functional distribution of income is of interest to social scientists who are concerned with the division of income among owners of labor, land, and capital. Statistics on the income on capital, that is, profits, are also of interest to financial analysts.

The GDP estimates in the national accounts are not only divided into consumption, investment, government expenditures, and exports minus imports, as explained in this chapter, but also according to the industries responsible for the product and the regions of the country generating the product. These data are of interest to business economists trying to forecast changes in industrial structure over time, to geographers interested in shifts between rural and urban areas and between different parts of the country, and especially to economic historians.

Sociologists have an interest in the national income and product accounts not only because many social problems vary with the state of the economy—family violence, child abuse, depression, alienation, and so on increasing during economic downturns—but also because the accounts are affected by and reflect social trends. For example, the national income has been increased in recent decades by the movement of women into the labor force. Sociologists and economists have recognized that this social change has moved many previously nonmarket activities such as child care and home care into the market; homemakers, whose work in the home is not included in the GDP, are today paying others for what they used to do, without payment, themselves. For this reason, economists have realized that the growth of GDP has been exaggerated; earlier GDP statistics understated the value of work done to the extent that more unrecorded work was performed in the home.

Other social trends have affected the amounts recorded in the national accounts. For example, increases in the proportion of a cohort attending college temporarily reduce income and production because there are fewer people working, although **future** income and production are higher. At the other end of the age distribution, changes in retirement age also affect production; in a fully employed economy, the earlier people retire, the lower is the national income and product, because there are fewer people producing goods and services and earning incomes. Again, we see a link between social trends and economics via the national accounts.

Some social trends affect national income and product indirectly. For example, while trade in illicit drugs is not part of GDP even though it involves market transactions, the consumption of drugs does influence GDP. In particular, lost work time from drug addiction reduces output, although extra policing because of drug-related crimes may ironically increase "output." (As mentioned earlier in the chapter, police costs paid by government or consumers are a final output and part of GDP. However, police costs paid by business are an intermediate product and not part of GDP.) Other examples where GDP is affected by social trends include attitudes toward work-related stress—more time off reduces GDP—willingness to perform volunteer public service—more volunteer versus paid work reduces recorded GDP—and so on.

As well as **affecting** GDP, social trends are themselves sometimes the **result** of changes in GDP. For example, the need for two incomes to pay for housing may be due at least in part to average incomes advancing more slowly than people expected. Crime rates and mental illness also may be affected by GDP, both increasing as economic conditions fall behind what people expected. Again, we see that interests of psychologists as well as sociologists overlap with those of economists.

We mentioned in this chapter that there are many dimensions to human well-being other than the size of the average per capita real NNP, the way economic well-being is measured. As we

> "... for what is man advantaged if he gain the whole world, and lose himself, or be cast away?" (Luke 9:25).

372

explained, broader indexes have been constructed which factor in the amount of park space, the number of social problems, and so on to judge whether progress is being made and which countries offer their citizens the best living conditions. But what of such immeasurables as freedom, security, compassion, respect, leisure, and so on? When it comes to such matters and the role they play vis-à-vis economic performance as measured by GDP, theologists have more to say than economists.

All religions have warned against excessive emphasis on economic measures of reward. For example, Psalm 62:10 advises, "If riches increase, set not your heart upon them." Similarly, the New Testament teaches, "Man shall not live by bread alone" (Mathew 4:4), and warns, "for what is man advantaged if he gain the whole world, and lose himself, or be cast away?" (Luke 9:25). The Hindu "Bhagavad-Gita" in the **Mahabharata** warns, "Pondering on objects of the senses gives rise to attraction . . . till purpose, mind and man are all undone." The Buddhist **Dhamapada** likewise warns, "Cut down the whole forest of desire, not just one tree only." Similarly, in the "Chapter of the Night," the **Koran** cautions, "his wealth shall not avail

Attitudes toward materialism . . . differ fundamentally between cultures as well as religions and have undergone major transformations over the centuries.

him when he falls down [into hell]!"

Attitudes toward materialism, which manifest themselves in national consumption and product statistics, differ fundamentally between cultures as well as religions and have undergone major transformations over the centuries. As we mentioned in Crossing Bridges in Chapter 10, Max Weber has attributed much of what occurred in the Industrial Revolution to the sanctification of industriousness in the teachings of John Calvin and his followers. The changes in attitudes that have occurred are, however, due to more than shifts in the views of religious leaders. Attitudes toward hard work, investment, and the enjoyment of the economic fruits of these have been part of the evolving cultural picture of modern-day Japan, other rapidly growing newly industrialized countries (NICs), the United States, and more recently, eastern Europe and the independent states of the former Soviet Union. Economics is inextricably tied to many aspects of culture and to secular attitudes, with the culture and attitudes having important long-run implications for the national accounts and the satisfaction taken from progress reflected in these accounts.

SUMMARY

1. Gross domestic product (GDP) is the total value of goods and services produced within a nation during an interval of time such as a calendar year or quarter.

2. National income and GDP are roughly equivalent. This is true because the GDP and the sum of values added at all stages of production are equal; values added are received as incomes.

3. Gross national product (GNP) is the value of production by factors provided by residents of a country. GNP is GDP plus net foreign factor income.

4. National income is GNP minus depreciation and indirect taxes.

5. The national income accountant must avoid double counting and not include the sales of used goods. The accountant must include exports, exclude imports, and add in government spending and any change in inventories. The total, nevertheless, includes "outputs" that are undesirable.

6. Real GDP and real GNP value the national output at a constant set of prices. Real GDP and real GNP are not, therefore, distorted by inflation and deflation.

7. Net national product (NNP) is the gross national product (GNP) minus depreciation.

8. Economic growth can be measured from the growth rate in real per capita NNP.

9. National income and product comparisons between years can be misleading because of changes in outputs of undesirable products and changes in the quality of goods and services.

10. Income comparisons between countries can be misleading because exchange rates may not reflect differences in costs of living and because there are different requirements for a comfortable life, different degrees of equality of income distributions, different allocations between consumption and investment, different levels of inputs for the same national outputs, and different volumes of production of undesirables.

11. GDP is frequently categorized into the type of output—consumption, investment, government expenditures, and exports. Because each of these categories contains an imported component, imports must be subtracted in order to obtain the nation's output.

12. The composition of GDP among its various components differs substantially between nations.

13. The burden of the national debt depends on the extent it is growing relative to the economy; the effect higher taxes have on the incentives to work, save, and invest; the amount of debt held abroad; and the use to which borrowed money is put.

QUESTIONS AND PROBLEMS

1. Where is my royalty in Table 12.1?

2. What would happen to GDP if a book were stolen from the bookstore? What would happen if it were destroyed in a fire?

3. If foreign investment in the United States increased faster than U.S. investment abroad, what would happen to U.S. GDP versus U.S. GNP?

4. What ways exist for correcting GDP for inflation? Do we have to value current outputs at base-year prices, or might we adjust for inflation faced by the typical consumer?

5. What happens to the changes in real GDP versus nominal GDP when there is deflation?

6. When inventories increase, do you think this occurs because firms are unable to sell as much as they would like, or because they have a higher desired stock of inventories. Might it not be either?

7. What other factors, such as political freedom, do you think are a part of the quality of life but are not reflected in real per capita NNP?

8. During the 1970s, the per capita NNP of Bahrain was higher than that of the United States. Do you think that the United States had a lower standard of living than Bahrain for a typical person?

9. How might a growing national debt increase the future economic well-being of citizens? How does your answer depend on the rate of return on government versus private investment and on the extent to which government-borrowed money would otherwise have been privately invested?

10. When the national debt is growing faster than the economy, the debt can get out of control as a result of interest payments. Explain how this can happen.

. . . .
. . . .
. . . .

The Distribution of
National Income

. . . .
. . . .
. . . .

*And the moral of that is—"The more there is of mine, the less there
is of yours."*

Lewis Carroll, **Alice's Adventures In Wonderland**

The data on income distribution show large disparities between the rich and poor, whether the distribution is that of per capita incomes in different countries or of average incomes of different people in a single country. Let us quickly review what is revealed by the data.

THE GLOBAL
DISTRIBUTION OF INCOME

If we were to represent an average American's income by a person of average height, say, 6 feet, and we represented the incomes of the rest of humanity on this same scale, the very poorest would be shorter than mice. Indeed, we would find the vast majority of the Earth's population below the knees of the average American. Yet on this same scale we would find some industrial tycoons taller than New York's World Trade Center. The vast disparities of income for a number of countries are matter-of-factly and unemotionally revealed by data such as those in Figure 12A.1. These data, which give per capita GNP, are adjusted for purchasing power and yet still show absolutely massive disparities.

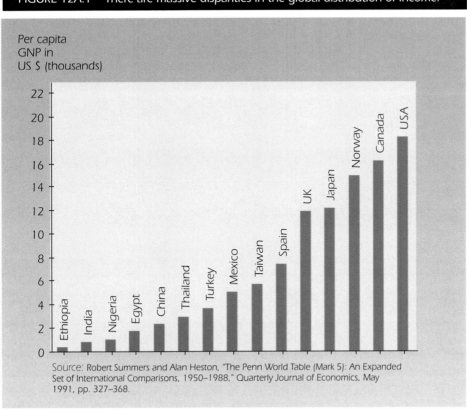

FIGURE 12A.1   There are massive disparities in the global distribution of income.

Per capita GNP in US $ (thousands)

Source: Robert Summers and Alan Heston, "The Penn World Table (Mark 5): An Expanded Set of International Comparisons, 1950–1988," Quarterly Journal of Economics, May 1991, pp. 327–368.

INCOME DISTRIBUTION AMONG AMERICAN FAMILIES

The shares of the U.S. national income going to the poorest 20% of families up to the most affluent 20% are shown in Table 12A.1. The table shows that the poorest 20% of U.S. families receive less than 5% of the total U.S. family income, whereas the most affluent 20% receive not much less than half the total family income. The inequality of income is substantially less between U.S. families than it is between countries, but there are still large disparities. In particular, while poverty is far less prevalent than in the global income distribution, there are many poor people in the United States. However, what ways are there of defining poverty?

POVERTY DEFINITIONS

Relative Deprivation

If poverty is viewed in terms of having a distinctly lower standard of living than is enjoyed by the average person, then the poor might be considered to be those people who, for example, are at the bottom 10% or 20% of the income distribution. This definition could be applied across the globe, just as it can to any individual

TABLE 12A.1

The poorest 20% of Americans have approximately one-tenth the share of income enjoyed by the most affluent 20%.

FAMILY INCOME RANK	PERCENT SHARE OF TOTAL INCOME
Lowest fifth	4.6
Second fifth	10.6
Third fifth	16.9
Fourth fifth	24.1
Highest fifth	43.7
Top 5%	16.9

Source: **Current Population Reports** (Washington, D.C.: U.S. Bureau of the Census, 1990).

country, but the definition has the distinct disadvantage of offering no measure of progress in the alleviation of poverty. Indeed, a relative deprivation measure suggests that poverty cannot be eliminated as long as any inequality remains. This does not mean that measures of relative deprivation have no value. In part, this is so because it may well be the case that people are dissatisfied by seeing others enjoying substantially more affluence. For example, a very low income American may indeed feel poor because she or he sees so much affluence close by, even though on an international scale she or he is relatively well off. In addition, defining poverty as the "tail" of the income distribution can be useful if we are interested in the types of people who are poor or in how much "turnover" occurs from year to year in the families turning up in the tail of the income distribution.

Absolute Deprivation

It is possible to define the poor as those who lack the basic necessities such as adequate food, clothing, shelter, health care, and education. Of course, this does beg the questions of what constitutes the basic necessities and what level of each is considered adequate. However, once these standards have been set, the proportion falling below the agreed poverty line can be used to judge, for example, if progress has been made in fighting poverty and how many families need welfare assistance.

Unfortunately, while absolute standards of poverty are of some use in a domestic context, it is difficult or even impossible to define useful standards when making comparisons on an international scale. This is true because the basic necessities of life differ markedly between nations. For example, housing, clothing, and nutritional needs differ greatly with climate; energy needs differ greatly with norms of travel and home comforts; and so on. What might leave an American barely able to subsist might provide a princely lifestyle on a South Sea island where heating is unnecessary and some food, such as fish and coconuts, may be available just for the taking.

THE CAUSES OF POVERTY

While it is difficult, for the reasons we have cited, such as the great variations in needs for a comfortable life, to decide categorically on which countries are poor, there is little doubt that the richer countries include those in Europe, North America, Japan, and Australia, and the poor countries are in Africa, the Asian sub-continent, and Central and South America. What is it, however, that has given rise to this distribution, that, to an extent, constitutes a "North-South" division, with the North generally being richer?[1]

An obvious candidate for an explanation of poverty versus affluence is **factor endowments,** by which we mean the good fortune or bad fortune that countries have enjoyed or suffered in the global distribution of natural resources, including good soil and water. (Example 12A.1 provides an interesting perspective on the role of good fortune concerning individuals' endowments.) While this might explain the high living standards in North America and perhaps parts of Europe, it cannot, however, explain why, for example, Japan which lacks energy and other natural resources, nevertheless has a high standard of living and why such city-states as Hong Kong and Singapore have done so well. The attribution of living standards to factor endowments also does not explain why parts of Africa which have large resource endowments remain desperately poor. Clearly, as reflection about Africa reveals, political stability, education, motivation, and the willingness to save and invest as well as to embrace the market mechanism must all play a role. Development economists who specialize in the study of the sources of economic progress have indeed identified such characteristics as influencing the level and pace of development, although there is no consensus on the *relative* importance of different factors.

The importance of investment, including investment in human capital that comes from allocating resources to education, helps point to the viciousness of the cycle of poverty in which so many desperately poor nations seem to be trapped. The very poor need all the income they can earn in order to subsist and can afford little or nothing to save and invest for the future by building infrastructure, capital equipment, institutions of higher and vocational learning, and spreading literacy. And because these countries cannot invest, they remain poor. It is little surprise that those countries which have managed to break themselves out of the vicious poverty cycle, such as India, Brazil, South Korea, and Thailand, have progressed rapidly after they have broken out of the poverty trap.[2]

---

[1] More specifically, the richer countries tend to be in the temperate regions, while the poorer ones are closer to the Equator.

[2] It is worth mentioning that the poverty trap is not limited to poverty on a global scale. It has been noted by anthropologist Oscar Lewis that a "culture of poverty" exists among the poor in capitalist countries amid their overall opulence. That is, some people seem to accept poverty as inevitable, thereby trapping themselves in continued poverty. See Oscar Lewis, "The Culture of Poverty," *Scientific American,* October 1966, Vol. 215, No. 4, pp. 19–25.

Example   **12A.1**   **A MONOPOLY ON BEING RICH**

As much as we like to believe that free enterprise gives everybody an equal chance, and as numerous as are the examples of poor people who have "made good," there are still advantages to starting the "game of life" with a head start. The following article explains how one social science instructor demonstrates this point to his students.

A sociology instructor found an effective way to teach his students that they cannot live a Park Place lifestyle on a Baltic Avenue salary.

Thomas Hewitt had 50 students at Pennsylvania State University's DuBois campus play Monopoly, but instead of starting out even, one-fifth were given the handicap of being poor and another fifth the benefits of being rich.

"We found out what we already suspected—the rich get richer and the poor get poorer," said Douglas Sversko, a freshman.

"I was trying to make it somewhat more realistic," said Mr. Hewitt, who has used the game in class for three years. "I was thinking there ought to be something to illustrate that we don't start life even." . . .

Mr. Hewitt gave one player in each game $5,100, three players $2,500 and one player $150. In a regular Monopoly game, players start with $1,500 each.

Also, instead of rolling dice to determine the first player, the rich people went first. All players could buy property immediately and begin building houses without first establishing a monopoly.

It did not take long for some to go broke. Some lasted only one roll.

"We didn't have any safety nets—no public assistance and no welfare," Mr. Hewitt said, although participants in one game established a relief program for its poor player,

who more than tripled her net worth.

"When I saw this, I asked who did this. That was kind of remarkable." Mr. Hewitt said. "The player answered, 'They took pity on me and gave me money.' They built a welfare system into their game."

The games also reached the point where crime did pay. Mr. Sversko, who started out poor, tried to snag a $100 bill from a neighbor when he ran out of money.

"Going to jail works," said Marcie Ott, a freshman. At least there, players did not have to pay exorbitant rents, she said.

The rich people won all five classroom games, more than doubling their opening worth of $5,100. The others were in the red.

Source: Kelley Kissel, "Roll of the Dice Makes Rich Richer," **The Globe and Mail,** Toronto, Canada, February 19, 1992, p. A7. Reprinted by permission of the Associated Press.

THE POOR IN AMERICA

Whether poverty in America is defined in relative or absolute terms, the same characteristics show up in who is likely to be poor. According to the U.S. Bureau of the Census, in the United States, families headed by a female without a husband present constitute more than half the families facing poverty. Partly because of this, children make up a large proportion of the poor, with well over a third of the poor in the United States being children under 18 years of age. A large proportion of the poor also come from the other end of the age distribution; the elderly constitute over 10% of the poor. There are also disproportionate numbers of visible minorities, largely blacks and hispanics, among the poor, even though in terms of absolute numbers, whites constitute approximately two-thirds of America's poor (see Figure 12A.2). Finally, it can be noted that particular regions, especially those suffering from chronic shortages of jobs, are disproportionately represented among the poor, and while there are many rural poor, a vast number of the poor are found in urban areas, even in the wealthiest states (see Table 12A.2 on page 382).

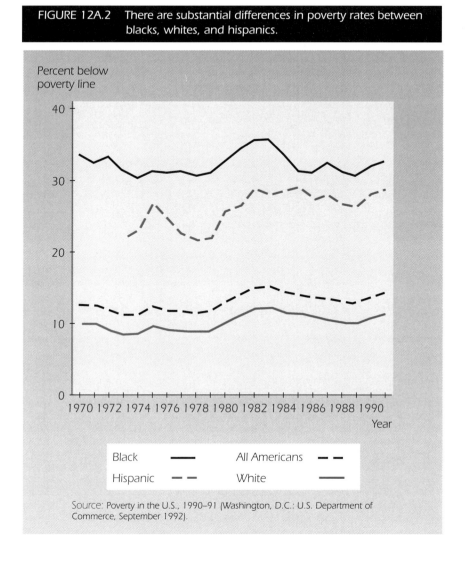

FIGURE 12A.2   There are substantial differences in poverty rates between blacks, whites, and hispanics.

Source: Poverty in the U.S., 1990–91 (Washington, D.C.: U.S. Department of Commerce, September 1992).

POVERTY VERSUS POPULATION: THE MALTHUSIAN TRAP

The vicious cycle of poverty in the desperately poor countries where meager incomes preclude surpluses for investing in the future is not helped by the tendency for the poorest of the poor to have many children. With odds heavily stacked against children surviving, and with no social assistance from the government for the aged, the desperately poor see their only hope for survival into old age in having a large family. This may indeed improve the prospects for those having the children, but it paradoxically puts an increasing strain on the already meager resources available to the nation. That is, there is a conflict between what makes sense for individual families and what makes sense for nations.

TABLE 12A.2

Poverty varies substantially across the United States.

STATE	POVERTY RATE*	INCOME†	STATE	POVERTY RATE*	INCOME†
United States	14.2	30,126	Mo.	14.8	27,926
Ala.	18.8	24,346	Mont.	15.4	24,827
Alaska	11.8	40,612	Neb.	9.5	29,549
Ariz.	14.8	30,737	Nev.	11.4	32,937
Ark.	17.3	23,435	N.H.	7.3	36,032
Calif.	15.7	33,664	N.J.	9.7	40,049
Colo.	10.4	31,499	N.M	22.4	26,540
Conn.	8.6	42,154	N.Y	15.3	31,794
Del.	7.5	32,585	N.C.	14.5	26,853
D.C.	18.6	29,885	N.D.	14.5	25,892
Fla.	15.4	27,252	Ohio	13.4	29,790
Ga.	17.2	27,212	Okla.	17	25,462
Hawaii	7.7	37,246	Ore.	13.5	30,190
Idaho	13.9	26,116	Pa.	11	30,367
Ill.	13.5	31,884	R.I.	10.4	30,836
Ind.	15.7	27,089	S.C.	16.4	27,463
Iowa	9.6	28,553	S.D.	14	24,639
Kan.	12.3	29,295	Tenn.	15.5	24,453
Ky.	18.8	23,764	Tex.	17.5	27,733
La.	19	25,299	Utah	12.9	28,016
Maine	14.1	27,868	Vt.	12.6	29,155
Md.	9.1	36,952	Va.	9.9	36,137
Mass.	11	35,714	Wash.	9.5	33,970
Mich.	14.1	32,117	W.Va.	17.9	23,147
Minn.	12.9	29,479	Wisc.	9.9	31,133
Miss.	23.7	19,475	Wyo.	9.9	29,050

*The poverty level in 1991 for one person was $6932; for a family of four, $13,924.
†Median (or middle) household income, 1991.

Source: **Poverty in the U.S., 1990-91** (Washington, D.C.: U.S. Department of Commerce, September 1992).

The tendency for the poor to have large families even though this pushes nations beyond their ability to feed their populations is well documented and accepted by demographers and economists specializing in economic development. Recognition of the virtual inevitability of the problem also has revived interest in the argument advanced in the early nineteenth century by Thomas Malthus. Taking note of the natural tendency for populations of plants, insects, and animals to expand to the limits of subsistence, Malthus was led to the conclusion that the fecundity of humans would push their numbers to the same subsistence limit. That is, given time, human populations would expand until competition for the Earth's limited resources pushed humanity to the level of subsistence, a conclusion that led Thomas Carlyle to dub economics the "dismal science." Counterarguments can be made against Malthus' reasoning, including the criticism that it overlooks the conscious choice toward smaller families that typically accompanies economic progress. Furthermore, the evidence on per capita food output, especially in the richer nations, so far casts doubt on Malthus' projections. Nevertheless, in the poorest parts of the globe, the occurrence of famine and the persistence of conditions bordering on subsistence have given neo-Malthusians reinforcement for their views.

GUNS VERSUS BUTTER AND THE POVERTY PROBLEM

It has been observed that if military budgets that exceed a trillion dollars globally were turned toward fighting poverty instead of preparing for war, we could overcome the poverty problem and still have plenty left over. For example, $500 billion from the U.S. defense budget would translate into approximately $10,000 per year for the poorest 20% of Americans. With the ending of the Cold War in the 1990s, conditions seem right for dealing with the poverty problem, which, if the translation from "guns" to "butter" using the type of calculation just made were correct, would be solved in the United States and greatly reduced worldwide. Unfortunately, the answer is not that simple.

The problem is that most of the *resources* used to produce military hardware cannot produce food or other basic necessities. Saying that each $1 billion transferred from military to welfare budgets will buy, for example, 250 million bushels of wheat at $4 per bushel overlooks this fact. It is not money transfers that produce wheat instead of rockets, but transfers of resources. The curvature of the production possibilities curve tells us that we gain less and less food for each unit of reduced output of military hardware. Unfortunately for solving the poverty problem, different resources are employed in producing armaments than food. This is not to say that we cannot go some way toward correcting the poverty problem, especially in the long run when we can shift research and development efforts away from military to civilian objectives. Rather, we are cautioning against the view that transfers of money are equivalent to transfers of resources, which in the aggregate is incorrect.

SUMMARY

1. There are massive disparities of per capita incomes among countries. U.S. family incomes vary less than do incomes between countries, but there are nevertheless very large differences.

2. Poverty can be defined relatively as being at the bottom end of the distribution of income, but while this does allow an analysis of who is likely to be poor and how long people remain poor, it does not permit the measurement of progress. The alternative of defining poverty absolutely in terms of being able to afford the necessities of life while allowing a measure of progress begs the question of what are the basic necessities.

3. Internationally, the poor countries do not necessarily suffer from low factor endowments. Other factors, such as the levels of political stability, education, motivation, savings and investment, and willingness to accept the market mechanism, appear to play a role.

4. In the United States, the poor tend to be in families headed by a female without a husband present, under age 18, or elderly, and from regions of chronic unemployment.

Most of the poor are white, but blacks and hispanics are disproportionately numerous among the poor.

5. The need to save and invest in order to enjoy economic progress means that those who are so close to subsistence that they have no surplus to save or invest are trapped in the poverty cycle.

6. The poorest of poor countries often have a population problem because parents choose large families to compensate for the low survival rates of children and the absence of government help for the aged.

7. There is revived interest in Malthus's view that population expands to the point of subsistence, at least in poor countries.

8. While it is possible to increase food production and provide other peacetime necessities when military budgets are trimmed, it is not money that needs to be transferred, but resources. The shifting of resources provides a transformation of outputs between "guns" and "butter," but this transformation is subject to the limitations of the production possibilities curve.

QUESTIONS AND PROBLEMS

1. Why is most of Africa so poor when the African continent is relatively rich in resources?

2. Graphically describe the trade-off between "guns" and "butter" with a production possibilities curve. Explain why poverty alleviation is not simply a matter of shifting dollars between priorities.

. . . .
. . . .
. . . .
. . . . Money, Banking, and Financial
. . . . Intermediation
. . . .
. . . .
. . . .

It would be too ridiculous to go about seriously to prove that wealth does not consist in money, or in gold and silver; but in what money purchases, and is valuable only for purchasing.

Adam Smith

Key Concepts

Advantages of money versus barter; value of money to an individual versus society; money defined; *M1, M2, M3;* money versus liquidity; money versus credit; money versus income; history of fractional reserve banking; money and the central bank; money multiplier; open market operations; discount rate; economic role of financial intermediaries; stocks and bonds; credit cards; debit cards

WHAT MONEY IS AND DOES

Confusions Surrounding Money

As simple as it may seem, there is probably more confusion about money than about any other topic in economics. For example, while many people believe that everybody would be better off if they were all given more money, in fact, it is only if *some* people were given more money that they would be better off—and others would be correspondingly worse off! In this and the next chapter we consider such issues and many other matters surrounding money. However, before we turn to these interesting issues, we should explain what money is and the role it plays in an economy.

The Nature and Role of Money

Money is the medium we receive for what we sell and pay for what we buy. What is bought and sold with the use of money includes final products, intermediate products, capital, land, raw materials, and the services of labor. For example, workers sell their labor for wages which are paid in money and then use the money to pay rent and buy groceries. People are willing to accept money because they know others, in turn, are willing to accept it from them. It is only because there is a generally acceptable medium for use in trade that we can avoid **barter,** which is the exchange of one good or service directly for another good or service.

Money is not something with value in and of itself; we cannot eat money, wear it, and so on. However, while money does not have intrinsic value, by allowing us to avoid the use of barter, money performs a fundamental and unparalleled role in an economy. Without something serving as money, we would be much poorer because the alternative of barter has a number of serious disadvantages. Let us consider some of these.

*Money allows us to avoid barter, which is the **direct** exchange of one good or service for another.*

The Disadvantages of Barter Exchange

Having all grown up using money, it is difficult to imagine ourselves functioning without it. However, let us put the power of our imaginations to the test and think of some of the difficult problems we would face if there were no money.

Finding Others with Coincident or Mutually Compatible Wants. Suppose you had a used car to sell and needed to pay your college tuition. It would be unlikely that a college would accept your car to cover your tuition. People often do not want what others are supplying in a barter exchange. However, if you could sell your car for money to somebody who likes the car, you could then pay your tuition with the money you received. Therefore, money avoids the need to find a party with coincident or mutually compatible wants. It does this by serving as a **medium of indirect exchange;** you exchange something for money and then exchange the money for something else.

Supplying and Buying Indivisible Products. Even when wants are coincident, there is a problem if the mutually desired items are of unequal value. In the context of the example of a car being used to pay for tuition, the car could be worth more than the tuition. Therefore, even if the college could find a use for your car, it would be unlikely that the college would accept only part of it. However, if you could sell the car for money, you could use part of the money for tuition and the remainder to cover living expenses. Money can be divided up or gathered into larger amounts, thereby making exchange much easier.

Supplying and Buying Perishable Products. Barter requires that the coincidence of wants occurs at the same moment in time. However, it might be, for example, that a farmer has crops available only at harvest time but needs to make purchases all year long. If the crops are perishable and therefore cannot be stored, it is not possible for the farmer to use barter. However, if the crops can be sold for money at the time of harvest, the money can be used subsequently as it is required. Therefore, money serves as a **standard of deferred payment** between the time of sales and the time of subsequent purchases.

Saving.   Even setting aside the problem of perishability, under a barter system it is difficult to save for the future. Holding every product that might be needed, or holding products to exchange for what might be needed, represents a major storage problem. Money serves the role of a **store of value**. In the absence of inflation, money saved today has a known buying power in the future.

Transporting Bulky or Heavy Products.   Even if we could overcome the problems of coincidence of wants and of dealing in perishable products, we would still face the problem of transporting items used in barter. Most monies offer the advantage of being compact and easy to move around. Indeed, it can take no more than the pressing of a few buttons or the stroke of a pen to make a payment with money held in a bank account.[1]

Measuring Prices and Keeping Records.   If money did not exist, just imagine all the different prices that would be faced. For example, there would be a price of economics books in terms of everything that might be traded for the books, such as political science books, hours of help in the college library, and so on. Each item would have a price in terms of every item for which it might be exchanged. Money allows us to state all prices in terms of a common unit, as so many dollars, francs, or whatever. It is a **numeraire**, allowing us to avoid the need to state the price of everything against the price of everything else. Money also allows us to add up values for accounting purposes because all prices and values are measured in the same unit. That is, money is also a **unit of account.**

> *Money serves as a medium of exchange, a standard of deferred payment, a store of value, and a unit of account. Most important, money frees up time and resources otherwise devoted to barter, and facilitates the division of labor.*

Enjoying Gains from the Division of Labor.   Because barter is so inconvenient and inefficient, if we did not have money as a medium of exchange, people would have to be more self-sufficient; the cost in terms of time and effort of finding others with whom to make direct exchanges would be so high, people would concentrate on supplying their needs themselves. While this may sound romantic, we would lose the advantages of the division of labor on which much of prosperity is based.[2] The gains from the division of labor are the gains from specialization described in Chapter 3. As we have explained, these gains come from a number of sources. They come from the ability to acquire expertise in the specific task each worker performs, from not having to continually change tools with consequent loss of time as each task is finished, from making it worthwhile to develop new machines which help in just one task, and from making it easier to innovate because a specialized task can be replicated more easily by a machine.

> *Money plays an important role in keeping the economy moving.*

The role of money in allowing a division of labor is similar to the role played by a network of roads. Without roads, we would be forced to become more self-

---

[1] In fact, while money is typically easy to move around, as Example 13.1 explains, there are some extremely bulky monies.

[2] Many movies project an appealing image of pioneers who are able to supply their many needs independently and ignore the hardships. In reality, the lives of the early pioneers were tough, and they were rarely entirely self-sufficient.

Example   13.1

ALL YOU NEED IS TRUST

Perhaps one of the strangest monies described by anthropologists is the stone money of Uap Island, also commonly written as Yap. The following account of Uap money explains how important faith is to the functioning of any medium of exchange.

On the island of Uap (one of the Caroline Islands), the medium of exchange is called *fei*. This currency consists of large, solid, thick stone wheels ranging in diameter from a foot to twelve feet, and in the center a hole varying in size with the diameter of the stone, so that the stones may be slung on poles and carried. They are not found on Uap itself, but are quarried in Babelthuap, some four hundred miles away to the south. Size is the most important factor, but also the *fei* must be of a certain fine, white, close-grained limestone. A traveler on Uap described the *fei* as follows:

"A feature of this stone currency, which is also an equally noteworthy tribute to Uap honesty, is that it is not necessary for its owner to reduce it to possession. After concluding a bargain which involves the price of a *fei* too large to be conveniently moved, its new owner is quite content to accept the bare acknowledgement of ownership; and without so much as a mark to indicate the exchange, the coin remains undisturbed on the former owner's premises.

"My faithful old friend Fatumak assured me that there was in a village near by a family whose wealth was unquestioned—acknowledged by every one, and yet no one, not even the family itself, had ever laid eye or hand on this wealth; it consisted of an enormous *fei,* whereof the size is known only by tradition: for the past two or three generations it had been, and at that very time it was lying at the bottom of the sea! Many years ago an ancestor of this family, on an expedition after *fei,* secured this remarkably valuable stone, which was placed on a raft to be towed homeward. A violent storm arose and the party, to save their lives, were obliged to cut the raft adrift, and the stone sank out of sight. When they reached home, they all testified that the *fei* was of magnificent proportions and of extraordinary quality, and that it was lost through no fault of the owners. Thereupon it was universally considered in their simple faith that the mere accident of its loss overboard was too trifling to mention, and that a few hundred feet of water off shore ought not to affect its marketable value, since it was all chipped out in proper form. The purchasing power of that stone remained, therefore, as valid as if it were leaning visibly against the side of its owner's house."

When the German Government purchased the Caroline Islands from Spain in 1898, there were no wheeled vehicles on Uap, and hence no roads. The paths, too, were in poor shape, and the Government ordered the natives to put them into better condition. Somehow or other the natives were quite happy with the paths as they were; the job did not get done. The Government was in a dilemma. It would be rather difficult to fine the natives and carry off the *fei* to Germany. In the first place, German shopkeepers might have been a little doubtful about exchanging their wares for *fei,* and then in the second place, it would have taken the labors of every available native to get the *fei* off the island, and the repairing of the paths would have had to wait while the natives paid up. Finally the Government hit on a sound scheme. They simply sent a man round to mark some of the most valuable stones with a cross in black paint to show the Government claim. The impoverished natives immediately fell to work, and the paths were soon in good order. Then a second man went round for the Government to remove the crosses; and there was great rejoicing on the island of Uap.

Source: Norman Angell, **The Story of Money** (New York: Garden City Publishing Co., 1929), pp. 88–89.

sufficient and to make do with a reduced standard of living. Like money, roads are useful for what they allow us to do, not because they have intrinsic value. Both money and roads keep the economy moving by serving as an important lubricant of the economic system. Of course, money also confers the benefits of offering a unit of account and store of value, in addition to the medium of exchange role by which it facilitates the division of labor.

The Value of Money: The Individual versus Society

To an individual who is holding money, the value of that money is equal to the value of the goods and services it can buy. For example, if a dollar bill will buy a hamburger or a newspaper, the dollar is worth a hamburger or a newspaper. It follows that if an individual has twice as much money, he or she can enjoy twice as many goods and services. However, society as a whole cannot enjoy more goods and services just by having more money. For example, if a helicopter were to drop money so that everybody had twice as much as before, there would still be the same output of goods and services for people to share. It is this output, measured as we have seen by the real per capita NNP, that is the basis of peoples' well-being, not the number of pieces of paper in their wallets or pocketbooks. The value of money to society derives not from what it will buy, but from the avoidance of the inconveniences and inefficiencies of barter that would be faced in a world without money. This distinction between the value of money to an individual versus society is the subject of Example 13.2.

> To an *individual*, the value of money is what it will purchase. However, to *society* as a whole, the value of money derives from its role in avoiding the inconveniences and inefficiencies of barter.

Defining Money

One way of determining what to consider as money is to identify what simultaneously serves as a medium of exchange, standard of deferred payments, unit of account, and store of value. However, it is simpler to ask what is a generally acceptable medium of exchange and then to check afterwards whether what serves as a medium of exchange also serves the other functions.

Because we know that others will accept coins and paper currency—the bills with pictures of former heads of state—from us, we are, in turn, willing to accept them from others. Therefore, coins and paper currency are a generally acceptable means of payment. Coins and paper currency also serve as a standard of deferred payment; they can be accepted today and spent later. They also serve as a unit of account and a store of value. Therefore, coins and currency are quite obviously money.

Relatively few payments are made with coins and paper currency. Far more payments are made by using checks. A check is an authorization for the transfer of funds from the payer to the payee. Checks do the same job as coins and paper currency, and indeed, checks are sometimes more convenient. Paper currency might be stolen and not easily retraced, whereas checks require a signature and can be canceled if they are stolen. Because of the close similarity of the functions of checks and paper currency, money consists at least of coins and paper currency plus checkable deposits. These checkable deposits are held at **financial institutions** such as commercial banks, savings banks, and credit unions.

The money supply, called M1, consists of currency, checkable deposits at financial institutions, travelers checks, and deposits that can be transferred at short notice into checkable accounts.

The sum of coin and currency held by the public plus checkable deposits at financial institutions constitutes the major share of the money supply referred to as **M1.** This particular monetary aggregate also includes travelers checks, such as those issued by American Express, which also can be used when making payments. *M1* also includes deposits at financial institutions, which, while not checkable, can be moved readily into a checkable deposit. For example, deposits that can be withdrawn or transferred at short notice or which are automatically transferred into accounts which are checkable are included in *M1*. This money supply aggregate is the most restrictive or narrow definition of money which is commonly used.

The broader money supply aggregates M2 and M3 consist of M1 plus a variety of other deposits at financial institutions.

Banks and other financial institutions have been innovative in offering different types of deposits. For example, there are numerous varieties of savings accounts and **time deposits**—deposits made for an agreed period of time—which offer a higher interest rate than checkable and easily transferable deposits. However, there are penalties if the funds are withdrawn without sufficient notice in the case of savings accounts or before the maturity date in the case of time deposits. Therefore, savings accounts and time deposits are not as useful as currency or checkable deposits as a medium of exchange. Nevertheless, savings and time deposits are sufficiently similar to some of the deposits included in *M1* that they cannot be ignored when calculating the money supply. The same is true of funds held in banks' **money market funds.** A money market fund is a pool of interest-bearing securities such as Treasury bills held by a bank against which the bank's customers hold claims. Because the savings accounts, time deposits, money market funds, and even some U.S. dollar deposits held abroad can quickly become a medium of exchange, two broader money supply aggregates are computed and published, called **M2** and **M3.** These differ according to the specific items included, with *M3* being even broader than *M2*. The relative sizes of these different monetary aggregates are shown in Table 13.1.

TABLE 13.1

Currency represents only part of the money supply.

	(Billions $, November 1992)
M1	$1,022
Currency $290	
Travelers checks 8	
Demand deposits 343	
Other checkable deposits 381	
M2	$3,511
M3	$4,192

The majority of the money supply consists of deposits in financial institutions. Currency is relatively small, even vis-à-vis the narrowest definition of money, **M1**.

Source: **Bulletin**, Board of Governors of the Federal Reserve System, Washington, D.C., December 1992.

Example 13.2

LOSING MONEY

The value of money to a nation is very different from the value of what the nation's money will buy. One of the clearest statements that this is so is the following paragraph by Sir Denis H. Robertson.

If one unit of money were suddenly abolished, the possessor of the particular unit selected for abolition would clearly be the poorer. Nobody who has ever lost a sixpence through a crack in the floor will dispute this. But it is by no means obvious that

the world as a whole would be impoverished in the same degree: for the command over real things surrendered by the loser of the sixpence is not abolished, but passes automatically to the rest of the community whose sixpences will now buy more. If indeed there were a large and simultaneous loss or destruction of money, society might easily find itself hampered in the conduct of its business, and the consequent check to exchange and production might lead to a serious decrease in its real economic welfare. But the fact remains that

the value of money is (within limits) a measure of the usefulness of any one unit of money to its possessor, but not to society as a whole: while the value of bread is also a measure (within limits) of the *social* usefulness of any one loaf of bread. And the reason for this peculiarity about money is the fact that nobody generally speaking wants it except for the sake of the control which it gives over other things.

Source: Sir Denis H. Robertson, **Money** (Chicago: University of Chicago Press, 1959),pp. 25–26.

The Money Supply versus Liquidity

You might be thinking, "Why stop our definition of money after including coin, currency, checking and savings accounts, time deposits, money market funds, and the other items in *M2* and *M3*? If people want to make payments, they can sell off short-term securities such as Treasury bills. Indeed, they can sell off stocks, bonds, or even their cars or houses. Why, then, are not all these other parts of wealth considered to be money?[3]

One way to answer this question is that while people can sell off these other assets, they do not know precisely how much they will receive. If somebody has a one-dollar bill, it can be used to settle one dollar in payments. So can a one-dollar check, even if a dollar of funds must first be transferred from a savings account. However, assets such as stocks and bonds have uncertain value, changing in price from day to day or even from minute to minute, and involve a brokerage cost to convert into money; stockbrokers have to be paid. Furthermore, many assets, such as automobiles and houses, are not readily marketable; it might be necessary to considerably lower the price on an automobile to sell it quickly enough to pay the rent. We therefore say that stocks and automobiles and other such assets are not money because they are not significantly **liquid.** Liquidity refers to the costs and uncertainties that exist when one converts assets into other goods and services.

Money is the most liquid asset, where liquidity refers to the uncertainties and costs of converting an asset into other goods and services.

---

[3] In fact, there is an aggregate that is calculated to include Treasury bills and privately issued short-term securities, called L. However, this stops short of including stocks, bonds, and so on and is not as closely followed as M1, M2, or M3.

Money, as we have defined it, consists of the most liquid of assets, those which can be converted into goods or services without uncertainty of value and without incurring any cost; "a dollar is a dollar" in the case of money, but not for other assets. Indeed, it is because money is liquid that it has emerged as the medium of exchange.

The Money Supply versus Credit

A considerable number of payments are made with credit cards. We might well ask how these credit cards should be treated in our definition of money, since many of the cards are quite generally acceptable as a means of making payments.

Credit cards allow people to spend now and pay later, with money. Therefore, credit cards are not money.

Credit cards give their holders the right to what their name suggests, specifically preapproved **credit.** This means that cardholders can make purchases up to some preapproved limit, making no payment until the settlement date on the next billing statement. The credit is usually provided with zero interest up to the settlement date, with interest applying after that point. However, even if cardholders do not settle immediately, and therefore use their credit, they must eventually pay with money. In other words, they must use money in their checking accounts to pay the amounts on their billing statements. In this sense, credit cards are not money, and so the credit limits on them should not be included in addition to bank accounts and other items that are included in the definition of the money supply. (This does not mean that credit cards are irrelevant. They can affect spending by providing preapproved credit and can allow the public to economize on holding money.)

The Money Supply versus Income

Income, as we observed in our discussion of national income in the preceding chapter, is a flow. It is so much *per period of time.* Money, on the other hand, is a **stock.** Money is so many dollars *at a point in time.* This is true whether we are speaking about a nation's or an individual's money supply. The currency and bank deposits you hold on a particular date do not sum to $1000 per month. They sum to $1000, period. This is a stock, not a flow. Your income may be $2000 per month while your money holdings are $1000, $100, or any other amount.

Money is a stock, while income is a flow.

With the distinction between money and income being so important, it is remarkable how common it is to hear sloppy use of these terms. For example, the question, "How much money do you earn?" is poorly expressed. It would be better to ask, "What is your income?" We can correctly ask, "How much money do you *have*?" It is true that we generally receive our income in the form of money, but holdings of money are different from income because money is a stock and income is a flow. To make our distinction between money and income even clearer, we can observe that some people may easily consider themselves to have too much money but are never likely to consider their incomes to be too high. Let us explain this further.

The Limited Demand for Money

As we have indicated, the amount we hold in coins, currency, or bank deposits is only part of our wealth. We also hold wealth as stocks and bonds, automobiles, houses, furniture, and university degrees. (A university degree is human capital and therefore a component of wealth, and like other components such as stocks and bonds, it provides income in the future.)

When we hold a dollar in the form of currency or in a non-interest-bearing bank deposit—both components of *M1*—we give up the interest we could otherwise have earned if instead the funds had been put in a bond. Because money is convenient for buying our lunch, paying the rent, and so on—that is, it is liquid— we hold some money despite the interest we might otherwise have received. Suppose, however, that we had decided on holding a given amount of money for its convenience when bonds offered 8% interest and the bond interest rate then rose to 15%. How would we feel about the amount of money we are holding?

As the convenience of money costs us more in forgone interest on bonds, we generally want to hold less money. That is, the amount of money demanded decreases when there is an increase in the opportunity cost of holding money. For example, what was considered as the correct amount of money vis-à-vis other assets at an interest rate of 8% is too much when the interest rate increases to 15%. We find that we can have too much money vis-à-vis the other components of our wealth. However, very few people would ever consider themselves to earn too much income. Money and income are clearly completely different.

The amount of money demanded decreases with an increase in the opportunity cost of holding money.

THE HISTORY AND CREATION OF MONEY

Banks as Creators of Money: An Historical Perspective

As we can see from Table 13.1 on page 390, currency makes up only part of even the narrow definition of the money supply called *M1* and is only a few percent of the broader monetary aggregates *M2* and *M3*. The major part of the money supply is "created" by commercial banks and other financial institutions. The process of creating money dates back at least to the time of the goldsmiths of Europe. The way the goldsmiths became creators of money serves as an excellent background to a discussion of the **fractional reserve banking system** of today.

Before the advent of paper money as we know it today, many payments were made using gold and silver. However, with the values of these metals being high, and with insurance and police protection poorly developed, there were risks involved in using precious metals as money.

In prebanking times, the people who owned the strongest safes in town were the goldsmiths whose work required that they keep a supply of gold and silver on hand. The goldsmiths' safes were known to others who would sometimes ask the goldsmiths if they would take gold in for safekeeping. The goldsmiths might oblige and charge a small fee. They would issue "depositors" receipts which simply stated that the persons named had deposited so many ounces of gold or silver.

Rather than go to the goldsmith to redeem gold as needs arose, some depositors asked if they could sign over their receipts to whomever they owed money. This helped avoid the risk of theft of the gold in between taking it out and making delivery. The receipts would simply be transferred over from the payer to the payee. Indeed, to facilitate this transfer of title to gold, the goldsmiths often issued a number of receipts, each representing a claim to a small fixed weight of gold. These could easily be made out to "pay the bearer on demand" so as to avoid the need for the receipts to be signed each time they were transferred to new owners.

With paper "claims" such a convenient means of making payment, they circulated freely without people demanding their gold from the goldsmiths.

It was not uncommon for governments and businesses to ask goldsmiths for loans. The goldsmiths could oblige because they knew that most of the gold they had on deposit sat idly in their vaults, with the holders of the deposit receipts rarely coming in to redeem their bullion. A trustworthy borrower could be loaned a number of paper receipts with the knowledge that they would circulate just like the rest and only a small fraction would be redeemed at any particular time. Consequently, goldsmiths moved more and more into the lending business, issuing more receipts than they had gold in their vaults. Since they could charge borrowers interest and would usually be repaid eventually, the more loans the goldsmiths made, the richer they became.

Now, of course, there were limits on the volume of paper gold receipts each goldsmith could issue. Even though they would eventually be repaid on their loans, they had less gold on hand than there were paper receipts in circulation. This did not necessarily cause problems, since only a fraction of receipt holders would arrive at any one time to demand gold. Furthermore, the loans would be repaid eventually, with interest. However, the amount of gold each goldsmith kept back had to be sufficient to reimburse whatever number of receipt holders might reasonably be expected to turn up. Any fear that the goldsmith had run out of gold might cause a "run on the bank" that the vaults might not bear. To avoid this, each goldsmith had to ensure that he or she had a prudent volume of bullion in his or her **gold reserve.** Each knew that the more gold that was held on reserve, the more loans could be safely granted. And the more loans that were granted, the higher were the profits.

Goldsmiths issued more paper receipts than they had gold in reserve. A prudent amount of gold had to be held to ensure that they could deliver on their obligations.

In order to attract more gold into a goldsmith's vaults, where it could serve to back up a larger volume of receipts issued, the storage fees on depositors' gold were reduced. Eventually, the goldsmiths paid money to depositors to "interest" them in depositing gold. The value of these "interest" payments on deposits was determined by a competitive process. Each goldsmith wanted more gold reserves so that he or she could grant additional loans. In an effort to attract depositors' gold away from other goldsmiths, each goldsmith raised the rate of interest paid on gold deposits until the profit that remained from interest earned on loans was not out of line with profits in other endeavors.

The goldsmiths are the ancestors of the banks we know today. In particular, like our modern commercial banks, they held a fractional reserve of deposits. The remainder of their assets were interest-earning loans. They paid interest on deposits and, in return, earned interest on their loans. There was a sufficient difference—or **spread**—between the interest paid on deposits and the interest charged on loans for a profit to remain. This profit was the return to their enterprise and risk.

Governments today issue legal tender money. This is money because of a fiat, or declaration, backed by the law.

The profitability of issuing paper money attracted the attention of governments, who decided to go into the business themselves. At first, the governments issued paper money that could be converted into gold on demand, just as were goldsmiths' receipts. The convertibility of money for gold was the **gold standard** system that existed in many parts of the world until the early part of the twentieth century. After a while, however, the new issuers of currency, the governments, learned that they could ensure that the public held their paper currency even if they did not offer to convert it into gold. By making currency **legal tender** by an appropriate fiat, or order, the government could make it illegal not to accept its

fiat money—so named because of the order, or fiat, to accept the currency—in payment for any private or public obligation. This is clearly stated on the top left-hand side of U.S. currency and on currencies of other countries too.

With paper and ink relatively cheap, governments found the money-making business to be very profitable indeed. How profitable we will discover in the next chapter when we turn to the topic of inflation. Before doing that, we should observe that in the United States, the creator of bank notes is the Federal Reserve System. That is why your dollar bills are headed "Federal Reserve Note." The Federal Reserve is also responsible for controlling other components of the money supply and as such plays an important role in government economic policy.

The U.S. Federal Reserve System

The **Federal Reserve System,** or **Fed,** functions as the central bank of the United States. As such, the Fed plays the central role in setting and administering U.S. **monetary policy.** By monetary policy, we mean the availability of money, either in terms of the supply of money such as *M1* or *M2* or in terms of the price of borrowing money, which is the interest rate.

The Federal Reserve System was established in the Federal Reserve Act of 1913. The Fed consists of a Board of Governors in Washington, D.C., that is headed by a chairman, and twelve regional Federal Reserve banks. The regional banks are located in New York, Boston, Chicago, Cleveland, Philadelphia, Richmond, St. Louis, Atlanta, Kansas City, Dallas, Minneapolis, and San Francisco. The circle to the left of center on each Federal Reserve Note in your wallet or pocketbook reveals the Federal Reserve bank that issued it.

Commercial banks that are members of the Federal Reserve System keep their reserves either as cash, that is, Federal Reserve Notes, or as deposits with their regional Federal Reserve bank. If a customer of one commercial bank writes a check in favor of a customer of a different commercial bank, the banks must settle up between themselves. What happens is that the receiver of the check places it in her or his bank account. The bank **credits** the check receiver's account and presents the check to the bank against which it was drawn.[4] The latter bank **debits,** that is, reduces, the deposit of the person who wrote the check. The banks then settle between themselves, with the bank against which the check was drawn paying the bank in which the check was deposited. By the member banks keeping deposits with the Fed, the settlement between commercial banks involves the simple transfer of these deposits from one member bank to another. This is part of the **check-clearing function** of the Federal Reserve System.

The Fed serves as the U.S. government's bank, handling a considerable volume of government business. This includes the sale and redemption of Treasury bills and bonds—which are issued by the U.S. Treasury but handled by the Federal Reserve Bank of New York—as well as much of the day-to-day banking business of government.

The Federal Reserve System sets U.S. monetary policy which concerns the availability of money, either in terms of the supply of money or the interest rate. The interest rate is the price of borrowing money.

Regional Federal Reserve banks clear checks between member commercial banks. This is done by crediting and debiting accounts member banks have at the Fed.

[4] The term credit is used in two ways. As in our discussion of credit cards, the word refers to lending, where a buyer does not have to pay until later. In the context here, the word refers to an addition made to an account. The context determines the meaning of the word.

Many smaller banks are not members of the Federal Reserve System. However, many of the smaller banks keep accounts at larger banks that are members, and therefore, directly or indirectly, most banking business takes place through the Fed. There are also institutions which offer many of the services of banks but are actually savings and loan associations (S&Ls) or credit unions. The role of these so-called **near banks** is an issue of controversy, and their importance and relationship to the banking system are frequently under review.

The deposits of most banks in the United States, whether they are members of the Federal Reserve System or not, are insured by the **Federal Deposit Insurance Corporation (FDIC).** This institution was established in 1933 after the failure of many thousands of U.S. banks in the **Great Depression** (1929–1933). The FDIC provides insurance to depositors on their deposits of up to $100,000 against the risk of failure of the bank. The purpose of the FDIC is to reduce the risk of "runs" on banks—where people rush to take their money out—due to depositors suspecting poor management. Because the deposits are insured, there is less need for depositors to withdraw their funds because of rumors.

The existence of deposit insurance became extremely important in the **savings and loan crisis** of 1989–1992, where the public's losses on deposits would otherwise have run into many hundreds of billions of dollars and where the FDIC helped prevent financial panic. We shall say more about the savings and loan crisis later in this chapter.

The Federal Deposit Insurance Corporation insures deposits in banks which are members of the FDIC.

The Reserve Ratio and Money Multiplier

We have mentioned that commercial banks that are members of the Federal Reserve System keep reserves either as currency in their vaults or as deposits in their regional Federal Reserve bank.[5] The commercial banks must maintain a minimum fraction of the value of their deposits in the form of reserves. This fraction is called the **minimum reserve ratio** and is determined by the Board of Governors of the Fed. The commercial banks prefer not to hold more reserves than they are required to hold because there is no interest earned on reserves. However, the banks cannot plan on holding less than the minimum required reserve. The effect of this is that there is a relatively predictable change in the money supply from a given change in banks' reserves. Let us see why this is so by assuming that $100 of currency is deposited by an individual into the First National Bank. Let us assume that the minimum required reserve ratio on deposits is 5%.

After the deposit of $100 of currency, the bank owes this amount to the depositor. This is the "original deposit" entry of $100 in Table 13.2 that appears as a liability of the bank in the bank's **balance sheet.** (The balance sheet records assets and liabilities at a given point in time.) The currency itself appears on the asset side of the balance sheet. The currency held is divided into $5 of additional required reserves to meet the 5% minimum required reserve ratio on the $100 deposit and $95 of **excess reserves.** (Recall that reserves consist of bank-held currency plus deposits at the Federal Reserve.)

Banks must hold a minimum ratio of reserves versus deposits.

---

[5] While only approximately half the banks in the United States are members of the Fed, these banks are generally large and therefore account for the majority of deposits. This is why we concentrate on member banks.

....
TABLE 13.2

After a deposit of currency, a bank has excess reserves.

BALANCE SHEET: FIRST NATIONAL BANK			
Assets		Liabilities	
Required reserve	$ 5	Original deposit	$100
Excess reserve	95		
	–		–
TOTAL	$100	TOTAL	$100

Of the $100 of deposit, which is a liability of the bank, $5 is required as reserves, and the remaining $95 is excess reserves, which can be loaned out at interest.

After setting aside the required reserve of $5, the excess reserves can be put into use by granting a loan and charging interest. Let us suppose that someone wishes to borrow $95 to buy a bicycle. The borrower would be required to sign an IOU promising to repay the $95 plus interest, and the borrowed funds would be credited, that is, added, to the borrower's account. This is shown in Table 13.3.

Individual banks loan funds they are not required to hold as reserves against deposits.

After granting a loan of $95 by crediting the borrower's account, the First National Bank has a total of $195 of deposits. With a 5% minimum reserve ratio, $9.75 (or 0.05 × $195) is required as a reserve against the deposits of $195. The remaining $90.25 (or $100 − $9.75) of the original deposit of $100 of currency is an excess reserve. The IOU against the $95 loan is an asset of the bank. However, this situation, shown in Table 13.3, is temporary, because people do not generally borrow unless they have some purpose for the loan—like our borrower's desire to purchase a bicycle. Consequently, the borrowed funds are unlikely to remain in the borrower's bank account.[6] In our example, the payment for the bicycle could be made either by withdrawing the funds in currency or by writing a check. As we shall show, in either case the First National Bank loses its excess reserves.

If the bicycle is paid for with currency, the loss of the First National Bank's excess reserves will occur as the $95 of currency is withdrawn. However, the receiver of the funds from the sale of the bicycle may then deposit the $95 in his or her own bank account. With approximately 10,000 banks in the United States, there is a good chance that this is not the original borrower's bank. Let us assume that the bicycle seller uses the Second National Bank. The balance sheets for both the First National Bank and the Second National Bank are given in Table 13.4.

The payment to the bicycle seller results in his or her account being credited with $95, while the buyer's account is debited. The $95 of deposits by the bicycle seller requires the holding of $4.75 (or 0.05 × $95) of reserves, leaving the remaining $90.25 (or $95 − $4.75) as excess reserves at the Second National Bank.

[6] Indeed, because the bank can anticipate the borrowed funds being spent and coming out of the borrower's account, it may not keep reserves against the temporary deposit.

TABLE 13.3

Banks grant loans by crediting borrowers' bank accounts in return for borrowers signing IOUs.

BALANCE SHEET: FIRST NATIONAL BANK			
Assets		**Liabilities**	
Required reserve	$ 9.75	Original deposit	$100
Excess reserve	90.25	Borrower's deposit	95
Loan (IOU)	95		
TOTAL	$195	TOTAL	$195

After granting a loan and before the borrowed funds are spent, the bank's liabilities include the original deposit and, **temporarily,** the funds placed into the borrower's account. The loan is an asset of the bank.

TABLE 13.4

One bank's loan becomes another bank's deposit.

FIRST NATIONAL BANK			
Assets		**Liabilities**	
Required reserve	$ 5	Deposit (original)	$100
Loan (IOU)	95		
TOTAL	$100	TOTAL	$100

SECOND NATIONAL BANK			
Assets		**Liabilities**	
Required reserve	$ 4.75	Deposit	$95
Excess reserve	90.25		
TOTAL	$95	TOTAL	$95

When funds borrowed from the First National Bank are spent and become a deposit at the Second National Bank, a new bank deposit is created, along with excess reserves for making further loans.

If payment is made with a check instead of cash, the settlement still follows the lines we have indicated. The bicycle seller deposits the check in his or her bank, the Second National. This bank credits the bicycle seller's account with $95 and then presents the check to the First National Bank for collection. If both banks are members of the Federal Reserve System, this is done through the regional Federal Reserve banks. The Federal Reserve credits the **reserve account** of the Second National Bank and debits the reserve account of the First National Bank. The check is then returned to the First National Bank, which debits $95 from the account of the original borrower. What was an excess reserve for the First National Bank becomes the reserve of the Second National Bank.

Unlike the First National Bank, with its actual reserves equal to required reserves, the Second National Bank is holding excess reserves. With only $4.75 required against the $95 of deposits, it can loan out the remaining $90.25 at interest. Suppose that it finds a willing borrower who wants $90.25 to buy a pair of skis. The bank will credit the account of the borrower, which becomes a deposit liability of the bank. The bank will have an offsetting asset of the borrower's IOU. When the borrower pays for his or her skis, the $90.25 of excess reserves is removed from the asset side of the Second National Bank's balance sheet. The payment from the ski-buyer's account also reduces the bank's liabilities.

If the seller of the skis deposits the $90.25 in the Third National Bank, this bank needs to keep $4.51 (or $0.05 \times \$90.25$) to satisfy the 5% minimum reserve ratio. It can create an interest-earning loan for the remaining $85.74 (or $\$90.25 - \$4.51$). This might be spent on something sold by a person banking with the Fourth National Bank, which keeps $4.29 (or $0.05 \times \$85.74$) and loans the remaining amount, and so on. Four stages of this sequence, which could continue indefinitely, are shown in Table 13.5.

One bank's loan is likely to become another bank's deposit.

Since we have agreed that the supply of money consists of coin, currency, and some or all of private bank deposits, the money supply has been increased by the initial deposit of $100 of currency. If our process continues indefinitely, the total value of created bank deposits is

$$\Delta D = \$100 + \$95 + \$90.25 + \$85.74 + \cdots \qquad (13.1)$$

where ΔD stands for the change in bank deposits. The original deposit of $100 of currency moves through the banking system, creating additional deposits at every step. Since these bank deposits are money, the multiple increase in the money supply from extra reserves is the result of the banks creating money. The sum of numbers in Equation 13.1 has a finite value even if we take it an infinite number of steps. Let us calculate this value.

We begin by multiplying both the left- and right-hand sides of Equation 13.1 by 0.95, giving

$$0.95\Delta D = \$95 + \$90.25 + \$85.74 + \$81.45 + \cdots \qquad (13.2)$$

Equation 13.2 can be subtracted from Equation 13.1 by subtracting the left-hand sides and the right-hand sides, giving

$$\Delta D - 0.95\Delta D = 0.05\Delta D = \$100 + (\$95 - \$95) + (\$90.25 - \$90.25)$$
$$+ (\$85.74 - \$85.74) + \cdots$$

TABLE 13.5

The sequence of bank deposit creation can continue indefinitely in diminishing amounts.

FIRST NATIONAL BANK			
Assets		**Liabilities**	
Required reserve	$ 5	Deposit	$100
Loan	95		
	———		———
TOTAL	$100	TOTAL	$100

SECOND NATIONAL BANK			
Assets		**Liabilities**	
Required reserve	$ 4.75	Deposit	$90
Loan	90.25		
	———		———
TOTAL	$95	TOTAL	$95

THIRD NATIONAL BANK			
Assets		**Liabilities**	
Required reserve	$ 4.51	Deposit	$90.25
Loan	85.74		
	———		———
TOTAL	$90.25	TOTAL	$90.25

FOURTH NATIONAL BANK			
Assets		**Liabilities**	
Required reserve	$ 4.29	Deposit	$85.74
Loan	81.45		
	———		———
TOTAL	$85.74	TOTAL	$85.74

We see that all but the $100 on the right-hand side disappears; after an infinite number of steps, the "last" number is so small that it can be ignored. Therefore,

$$0.05\,\Delta D = \$100$$

or
$$\Delta D = \$2000$$

We find that the deposit of $100 of additional reserves into the banking system has raised bank deposits by a total of $2000—a multiple of 20 times the original increase in reserves.[7] This multiple, obtained by dividing the change in the money supply by the change in reserves, is called the **money multiplier.** In our example, the money multiplier is 20.[8]

The money multiplier is the ratio of new deposits to the original increase in bank reserves.

Our example shows that banks do indeed create money. Without the example, one might have believed that since currency and bank deposits are just two different forms of money, taking currency from your pocket and depositing it in the bank would leave the total money supply unchanged. Yet with fractional reserve banking we find that the money supply is increased. Whichever way new bank reserves are created, the supply of money is increased by a multiple of the reserve increase. Let us consider other ways in which the supply of money can be increased and focus on the role of the central bank.

With fractional reserve banking, commercial banks create money.

THE CENTRAL BANK AND THE MONEY SUPPLY

There are several ways in which a central bank such as the Fed can change the money supply. The procedure used most commonly in countries where money and capital markets are well developed, as they are in the United States, western Europe, and Canada, is **open market operations.**

Open Market Operations

In the United States, open market operations involve the purchase and sale of securities by the Federal Reserve Bank of New York, which acts as agent for the Federal Reserve System. The securities that are bought and sold are generally those issued by the government—Treasury bills and Treasury bonds.

Open market operations involve central bank purchases and sales of securities.

We have seen that an increase in the money supply will occur if there is an increase in bank reserves and that the money supply increases by a multiple of the reserve increase. The reserves of the banking system are increased when the Federal Reserve *buys* securities in the open market. The converse is true when the Fed *sells* securities. The securities are purchased from or sold to dealers who act on their own behalf or on behalf of their clients.

---

[7] When, as in our example, the extra bank reserves come out of currency, the currency is no longer held by the public. The currency has therefore disappeared from the money supply, which includes only publically held currency plus deposits. Therefore, the precise increase in the money supply is $2000 of extra deposits minus the $100 reduction in circulating currency. That is, the money supply grows by $1900, slightly less than the increase in bank deposits.

[8] The value of 20 is 1/0.05. More generally, the multiplier is 1 divided by the required reserve ratio.

Purchases of securities by the central bank *increase* commercial bank reserves and thereby allow an increase in the money supply. *Sales* of securities *reduce* commercial bank reserves and thereby reduce the money supply.

When the Federal Reserve buys a Treasury bill from a securities dealer, it pays by check. This check is drawn against funds in an account at the Fed. The dealer deposits the check in its account at a commercial bank, and, in turn, the commercial bank presents the check to the Fed. When the Fed credits the bank for the value of the check, the bank's reserves are increased.[9] The extra reserves the commercial bank then holds allow it to increase its deposits by offering loans. The proceeds of the loans, when spent, cause the extra reserves to move through the banking system, resulting in an overall multiple expansion in bank deposits and the money supply. The reverse pattern occurs from an open market sale of securities by the Fed. In particular, when the Fed sells securities to a dealer, the dealer pays with a check drawn on an account at a commercial bank. When the Fed receives the check, it debits the bank's reserve account. In this way the sale of securities in the open market results in a shrinking of the commercial bank's reserve account. The bank is then forced to reduce its deposits or try to regain its reserves in order to maintain the required reserve ratio. While an individual commercial bank may be able to increase its reserves—banks can borrow reserves from each other—the commercial banking system in general cannot itself create reserves. The only way reserve ratios can be met collectively after a decrease in reserves is via a decrease in deposits and hence in bank loans. The effect on the banking system is like that shown earlier and summarized in Table 13.5, only working in reverse.

Discount Rate

The discount rate is the interest rate commercial banks pay to borrow reserves from the Federal Reserve.

Another way the Fed can influence the money supply is by changes in the **discount rate.** This is the interest rate at which commercial banks can borrow reserves from the Fed if they are short of reserves.

Each bank must satisfy the minimum reserve requirement by having average holdings of reserves over a 2-week period that are sufficient, given the bank's average deposits over the 2-week period. If there are sufficient reserves in the banking system as a whole, then even if some banks have insufficient reserves, they can borrow from other banks with excess reserves. This exchange of reserves takes place in the **federal funds market** at the **federal funds interest rate.** When the banking system as a whole has insufficient reserves, it is not possible for all reserve-deficient banks to satisfy their minimum reserve requirements by borrowing from other commercial banks. Then commercial banks must borrow reserves from the Fed.

Commercial banks borrow reserves from each other in the federal funds market at the federal funds rate.

Today, getting extra reserves involves the commercial banks taking **advances** from the Fed, called **repurchase agreements.** The commercial banks are required to hold government securities to guarantee their obligations to repay the advances.

The discount rate determines the risk commercial banks take in having deficient reserves. Specifically, if the discount rate is considered high, banks create fewer deposits for a given amount of reserves in order to reduce the chance of having to borrow in the federal funds market or from the Fed because of deficient reserves.

---

[9] We assume that the commercial bank is a Federal Reserve member. If not, the nonmember bank deposits the check with a member bank, and the member bank's reserves are increased.

When the discount rate is low, banks worry less about being forced to borrow and therefore create more deposits by offering more loans. Therefore, *ceteris paribus,* the lower the discount rate, the larger is the money supply, and vice versa.

Changes in Reserve Requirements

A highly effective, albeit blunt, instrument for changing the money supply is by changes in the required reserve ratio, that is, the fraction of deposits that must be held in reserves. If the required reserve ratio is increased, the same bank reserves can support fewer deposits, that is, a smaller money supply, while a lower reserve ratio means a larger money supply.[10]

Even a small change in the required reserve ratio can cause an extremely large change in the money supply. This is so because a change of only $\frac{1}{2}$% or 1% in the required reserve ratio is large vis-à-vis the base of the typical required reserve ratio. As a result, in countries with well-developed markets for buying and selling securities, open market operations are a more commonly employed means of changing the money supply than the relatively crude instrument of changes in reserve requirements. For example, in the United States, reserve requirements are often unchanged for several years, with virtually all monetary policy instead being performed via open market operations. In economies with less well developed security markets, open market operations may not be feasible. In such economies, changes in reserve requirements can be relatively frequent.

FINANCIAL INTERMEDIATION

Commercial Banks as Financial Intermediaries

As well as being the most important providers of the means of payments, banks serve the crucial role of bringing savers and investors together. The banks gather funds that savers—those spending less than they earn—are not yet ready to spend and make them available to borrowers who wish to invest in new factories, machines, automobiles, houses, and so on. In their performance of this role, banks are serving as **financial intermediaries.** It is well worth pausing to consider what would happen if there were no institutions to bring savers and investors together.

If there were no banks or other financial intermediaries, it would be difficult for those wishing to borrow to locate others wishing to lend. Borrowers would have to incur **search costs,** such as payments for advertising and so on, in order to locate lenders. At the same time, lenders would have to incur search costs to locate borrowers to whom they are prepared to lend. Banks serve to reduce the costs of borrowers locating lenders and of lenders locating borrowers. Borrowers

Ceteris paribus, the lower the central bank's discount rate, the larger is the money supply, and vice versa.

The *lower* the required reserve ratio, the *higher* is the money supply, and vice versa.

Banks serve as financial intermediaries between savers who deposit funds and borrowers who invest funds.

---

[10] In fact, there are different reserve requirements on different types of bank deposits. Smaller reserves are required against time (or savings) deposits than against demand (or checkable) deposits. Also, the calculation of required reserves depends on the size of banks. Smaller banks have a different reserve maintenance cycle than larger banks.

and lenders can both go to banks and, in effect, pay for the banks' services in bringing them together and serving as the intermediary. In serving as financial intermediaries, banks make profits by charging borrowers higher interest rates than they pay to lenders, that is, depositors.

Even if lenders and borrowers could locate each other directly without the intermediation of banks, there would still be problems to overcome. Savers would have to determine the credit worthiness of borrowers, with this involving the evaluation of information that requires accounting and other skills. Furthermore, even after lenders had found creditworthy borrowers, it would still be necessary to know how to draft loan agreements according to correct legal principles. It is a lot easier to take savings to a bank and let the bank's experts determine which borrowers are creditworthy and take care of drawing up documents.

A further problem we would have in the absence of banks and other financial intermediaries is that the amounts lenders typically have available are smaller than the amounts borrowers need to pay for their house, automobile, factory expansion, and so on. Banks serve the function of gathering up lots of small deposits to make large loans. Of course, sometimes there are deposits that are larger than small loans. However, typically, the amounts people put in their banks at any time are small relative to the size of bank loans.

An additional problem that stems from the small size of what savers have available to lend is that if there were no financial intermediaries, savers would be poorly **diversified,** perhaps with their only asset being a loan to one person or company. Because banks have numerous loans which are unlikely to all turn bad at the same time, banks have diversified portfolios of assets, and therefore, banks' depositors indirectly acquire the protection of these diversified portfolios.

The added costs of savers locating investors, preparing documents, and so on would mean that without financial intermediaries, savers would be tempted to spend more of their earnings or to invest their savings in their own projects. In general, the savers' own projects would not be as profitable as the projects that would otherwise have been pursued. This is so because those with large savings are not necessarily those with the best opportunities for investment. Therefore, if we did not have banks and other intermediaries, we would have less investment or else investment that offered a lower rate of return. Whether it would be lower investment or investment with a lower rate of return, we would have slower economic growth without financial intermediation; economic growth depends on investment and the rate of return on investment.

Financial intermediaries such as banks reduce the cost of savers locating investors, and vice versa. They also provide accounting and legal expertise and allow savers to enjoy indirectly the benefits of diversification of risky assets.

Financial intermediaries mean either more investment or investment with higher returns, either of which increases economic growth.

Other Institutions Bringing Savers and Investors Together

Being on so many Main Streets and in so many downtown plazas, banks are the most visible of the financial intermediaries that bring savers and investors together, but they are by no means unique in serving this role. Other links between savers and investors are provided by

1. Nonbank deposit-taking institutions, "thrifts"
2. Non-deposit-taking institutions such as pension funds
3. The money and bond markets
4. The stock market

Thrift Institutions.   The work of commercial banks in gathering deposits and extending loans is parallel to the work of the **thrift institutions.** These "thrifts" are also known as near banks. The thrifts consist of **mutual savings banks,** which are largely located on the Eastern seaboard of the United States, and savings and loan associations (S&Ls) and credit unions, both of which are located all over the United States. While the thrifts serve the function of bringing savers and borrowers together in the same way as do commercial banks, the nature of the savers and borrowers is a little different.

The thrifts specialize in real estate lending and consumer loans. Of course, the commercial banks also provide loans to home and automobile buyers. However, commercial banks allocate most of their funds to business and government lending, the latter involving the purchase of Treasury bills and bonds. For deposits, the thrifts depend almost exclusively on **retail deposits,** which are funds gathered in street-level offices. While commercial banks also depend heavily on retail deposits as a source of funds, large commercial banks also raise funds via the sale of **certificates of deposit,** which are interest-bearing negotiable instruments, and via money market funds, mutual funds, and other means.

Prior to the 1980s, real estate lending typically was limited to home buyers, but liberalization of lending rules led many savings and loans to move into commercial real estate. It has been argued that this was one of the principal factors leading to the **S&L crisis** of the late 1980s and early 1990s. An alternative explanation is the deregulation of the financial industry that began in the 1980s and allowed the S&Ls to expand without close supervision.[11] Whatever the cause, which was almost certainly a combination of these and yet other factors, the S&L crisis had a profound impact on the relative importance of S&Ls within the financial industry and on the attention paid to regulating financial institutions including banks.

Nondeposit Institutions.   Large amounts of savings are gathered in and invested by **pension funds.** Pension funds do not take in deposits as do banks and thrifts but rather, as their name suggests, collect and invest peoples' savings for retirement. Contributions to the funds may be made monthly from salaries or perhaps once each year. Pension funds invest in stocks, mortgages, and corporate and government bonds. In this way, pension funds bring savers and borrowers together. Pension funds also invest in real estate.

Money and Bond Markets.   Large corporate and government borrowers can circumvent banks and other financial institutions and borrow directly from those with savings via the money and bond markets. For example, well-recognized companies with a good track record for repaying debt can borrow by selling **commercial paper,** which is purchased by those with surplus funds. Commercial paper is an obligation of a company—a **promissory note**—to pay the holder a certain sum at a particular future date, with the repayment date commonly 30 or 90 days after the paper is sold. Commercial paper is sold in the **money market,** which is where negotiable interest-bearing securities with maturities of up to 1 year are bought and sold.

---

[11] The role of real estate lending and poor supervision is illustrated by the story of Community Savings and Loan of Bethesda, Maryland, in Example 13.3. Problems in Maryland in the mid-1980s quickly fanned out across the United States, revealing large-scale corruption and officials who failed to act even when aware of the seriousness of the problem.

Example 13.3

A RUN FROM THE BANK

The S&L crisis in the United States, which reached its peak in terms of public attention during the period 1989–1991, can be attributed to poor regulation and no shortage of people willing to pocket depositors' money when they could get away with it. The following article from the **Washington Post** explains how one S&L official is reputed to have siphoned off vast amounts of money to dubious schemes and, ultimately, to have run away with the depositors' money.

Tom J. Billman, mastermind of a disastrous real estate venture that destroyed his Community Savings and Loan in Bethesda, received about $50 million from Community and related companies, and hid at least $8 million in Swiss banks before apparently fleeing to Europe to avoid prosecution, according to court documents and sources.

Billman, of McLean, who founded a nationwide real estate tax-shelter scheme known as EPIC, is the target of a federal criminal investigation into Community's collapse during Maryland's 1985 savings and loan crisis, U.S. Attorney Breckingridge L. Willcox announced . . . in Baltimore. He said Billman apparently disappeared. . . .

A private lawyer who helped represent the state in a civil case against Billman . . . said . . . that much of the $50 million that Billman received while heading Community in the early 1980s remains unaccounted for.

"He hid everything," said the lawyer, who asked not to be identified.

In addition to his use of Swiss bank accounts, Billman had several million dollars in a London bank account, but emptied it some time in 1988, the lawyer said. . . .

Billman received the estimated $50 million—much of it in cash, stocks and bonds—during a 33-month period beginning in late 1982.

The rest of the $50 million included interest in oil wells in Ohio and West Virginia, a 180-acre estate called Batt's Neck on Maryland's Eastern Shore, at least one airplane and several boats. Billman eventually sold the plane and the boats, the lawyer said. . . .

According to an affidavit in support of the arrest warrant, federal authorities said they had traced $8,075,000 in transfers by Billman from the United States to two Swiss banks, The Union Bank of Switzerland and Banque Scandinave Geneva.

Billman had traveled to Bermuda and London, according to the

Companies that are not well known to potential lenders can pay for commercial banks to guarantee their obligations to repay the holders of their commercial paper. The guarantee takes the form of a bank stamping on a company's paper that the bank is prepared to repay the holder the promised amount on the company's commercial paper, whatever the financial status of the company when payment is due. A company's commercial paper guaranteed in this way is called a **banker's acceptance,** and by having its paper accepted, a company can borrow at an interest rate that reflects only the riskiness of the bank offering the guarantee. Banks are prepared to offer their guarantee because they can collect a fee for the service without themselves having to raise the funds required by the borrower. A large number of banker's acceptances arise from credits granted in international trade; the checks for payment for exports at a future date, called **bills of exchange,** are accepted by banks and then sold in the money market.

Those who wish to borrow directly from savers but who wish to repay after more than 1 year can use the **bond market** rather than the money market. **Bonds** are obligations of a company or a government to pay a sequence of interest payments known as **coupons** and repay the **principal** that was borrowed at an agreed future date or according to an agreed schedule over a period of more than

A banker's acceptance is commercial paper on which payment is guaranteed by a bank.

affidavit, "and would have had the opportunity to go to Switzerland" to make the initial deposits. He returned some of the money to the United States.

"These transfers all represent wire transfers of proceeds of the fraud on Community," the affidavit said. . . .

[At] the Billman home in the 7700 block of Georgetown Pike, a Mercedes, a BMW and a Mazda were parked in the garage, and a young woman emerging from the house would not comment on Billman's whereabouts.

Billman, a former FBI fingerprint clerk from rural southern Ohio, worked for real estate firms until he founded EPIC—Equity Programs Investment Corp.—in 1974. The brainchild of Billman and a former college roommate, Clayton McCuistion of McLean, EPIC acquired 20,000 single-family houses across the country and packaged them into

sophisticated tax shelters for investors.

In the civil case, the state alleged that Billman and his associates acquired Community in 1982 "to feed the EPIC machine."

The jury found that the defendants' mismanagement of Community left it ripe for collapse when depositors lost confidence in Maryland's S&L industry in the spring of 1985 and began frantic withdrawals.

EPIC planned eventually to sell the houses for substantial profits. In the meantime, EPIC offered the houses for rent. But because maintenance costs, mortgage payments and other expenses exceeded rental incomes, the investors were able to claim losses on their tax forms. EPIC made up for the operating deficits with millions of dollars in unsecured loans from Community.

The EPIC partnerships were

deprived of their main cash source during the 1985 S&L crisis, when depositors began making large withdrawals from Community and new deposits ceased. As a result, the partnerships defaulted on $1.4 billion in mortgages from institutions across the country, sending a tremor through the nation's home-financing industry.

Because EPIC was Community's largest single borrower, the failure of the partnerships left Community in collapse.

Source: Paul Duggan and Paul W. Valentine, with contributions by Susan Schmidt, "S&L Chief Said to Take $50 Million," **Washington Post,** June 28, 1989, pp. B1 and B7. © 1989, The Washington Post. Reprinted with permission.

1 year.[12] The bond market where bonds are bought by savers and sold by borrowers is not housed in any specific location. Instead, it consists of an informal linkage of traders who contact each other by telephone. Most large **brokerage houses** have special bond departments that, for a fee, arrange for the issue of bonds (or stocks) for their corporate clients, an activity known as **underwriting.**[13] The informal nature of the bond market contrasts with the **stock market,** which is the other component of the **capital market,** the capital market consisting of the stock plus bond markets.

Bonds are obligations to pay interest and repay the principal amount over a period of more than 1 year. Bonds, along with stocks, are sold in the capital market.

[12] Not all bonds pay coupons. Some bonds are sold at a price below what is eventually to be paid to the holder, with the appreciation from the issue price to the value at maturity being the way the holder earns "interest." Such bonds are discount bonds and are so-called because they are sold at a discount from their maturity value. However, most bonds pay coupons and are not discount bonds.

[13] The issue of bonds or stocks for a corporate client is called underwriting because the brokerage house arranging for the issue of the bonds or stocks gives an assurance, setting a floor or minimum selling price. This means that if the brokerage house cannot sell the bonds or stocks, it purchases them itself.

The Stock Market. Stocks are exchanged on the trading floor of a **stock exchange** such as the New York Stock Exchange or the exchanges in Chicago, Los Angeles, San Francisco, Philadelphia, London, Paris, Tokyo, Toronto, and so on. The traders on the floors of the stock exchanges are linked to brokerage houses that are, in turn, in contact with clients. The stock exchanges are, therefore, only the focal points of an informal linkage between savers and those requiring funds. (Most trades in the stock market are exchanges of previously issued stocks rather than new issues. It is only at the time of issue that savers and investors are brought together.)

Stocks are subordinate to bonds as a financial obligation of a company.

Unlike bonds, stocks represent claims to the ownership of a company, and any payment to the owners of stocks, the **shareholders,** can be made only after scheduled payments to all bondholders have been made. The amount left over to pay shareholders after meeting all prior claims to bondholders and other creditors of a company is uncertain and depends on the company's profitability. In contrast, bondholders receive the agreed amount of interest or principal repayment, provided a company is solvent. Stated somewhat differently, stocks are subordinate to bonds as claims against a company. However, despite this important difference, we should not lose sight of the fact that the stock and bond markets share the role of bringing savers and investors together.

The sale of stocks, like the sale of bonds, is handled by brokerage houses. Whereas banks earn their incomes from the spread between borrowing and lending interest rates, brokerage houses earn their incomes from **brokerage charges** paid by the companies issuing the stocks and bonds and by the public buying stocks and bonds.

Because the payment to shareholders in the form of **dividends** is uncertain, as is the market value of stocks, savers who place their funds in stocks require a return that compensates them for the risk. Since the return is not known in advance, what is required is that their **expected return** compensates for the risk shareholders take.

Interest rates and expected returns depend on the associated risks.

Risk is greater on stocks than on bonds. Since it is generally assumed that people are **risk averse**—that is, they do not like risk—expected returns on stocks must be higher than returns on bonds. The expected return on stocks consists of expected dividends and changes in the stocks' prices. The extent to which the expected return on a particular stock must exceed the return on bonds depends on the perceived riskiness of the stock.[14] However, while it is not obvious, the riskiness of a stock does not depend only on the amount of possible variation in its market value and variation in its dividends. A stock's riskiness depends on how much more variable it makes the wealth of a person who holds the stock in a portfolio of many stocks and other assets. This is so because an individual stock is rarely, if ever, held on its own. Therefore, the stock market determines an expected return based on the fact that shareholders hold diversified portfolios. In fact, since all stocks trading in the market must be held by somebody, the return on any individual stock depends on how much risk the stock adds to a portfolio of all stocks and other assets.

---

[14] In fact, it is only if bonds are held to maturity that the return on them is known, and furthermore, there may be a default risk on corporate bonds; default risk is the risk that a company goes bankrupt and cannot pay its bondholders. Bonds are normally less risky, however, than stocks.

Computers, Debit Cards, and Money

The nature of money and the nature of financial intermediation have changed over the years, and we should not expect them to remain indefinitely as they are. Therefore, it is worthwhile looking at current trends in the nature of money and the nature of financial intermediation to see in which direction they are heading.

Changes in the nature of money are already occurring as a result of computers. In France, Japan, and, to a limited extent, Canada and the United States, people are using magnetic cards not unlike credit cards but which are **debit cards.** Debit cards can be used to make payments instantaneously, rather than to accumulate totals over a month as with credit cards. The computer determines whether the buyer can pay for the purchase and transfers money from the payer's to the payee's account immediately if the funds are available. Card users have personal ID numbers like those in use today with automatic cash machines.

Debit cards look like credit cards, but payments via debit cards are immediate.

A system of **electronic funds transfer (EFT)** using debit cards may one day replace the use of checks and credit cards. However, there are still some problems to overcome, which include

1. Who is to own the required computers? If there are numerous banks offering the service of electronic funds transfer, immediate debiting and crediting must involve a link between the banks; the buyers of products do not necessarily have accounts at the same banks as sellers. There is a tendency toward monopoly in such a situation because the first bank to become large attracts a large number of extra customers. In this sense, the EFT system has characteristics of a public utility, being a potential natural monopoly. Therefore, it may be necessary to run the system with similar regulations as currently govern other public utilities.

2. How would an individual's privacy be protected? If payment via an EFT system became commonplace and replaced currency, a person's activities could be traced by recording the pattern of purchases.

3. How does somebody prove that a mistake has been made without keeping records on paper? If we have to record everything on paper, we cannot enjoy all the benefits of an automated payments system.

4. What is the money supply, and how can a central bank control it? The amount each person has available to spend may well be measurable from bank accounts, but money could change hands at a faster rate, and as we shall see in the next chapter, this would be inflationary.

5. Could computers eventually directly match potential buyers with potential sellers, allowing barter to overcome the drawback of a need for a coincidence of wants? By feeding into the computer what a person has to sell and wants to buy, the computer might not only facilitate the payment but also match the parties of the transaction. The nature of money is changed with such a system of barter exchange, requiring us to redefine money and our views on how money contributes toward inflation. However, despite some localized arrangements, computer exchange is not yet a reality. Therefore, we can still use our definition of money given earlier in this chapter.

Numerous problems must be overcome before an electronic funds transfer system can replace the current system of payments.

MONEY: A MATTER OF CONSIDERABLE INTEREST

Economists are not the only people who are interested in money. However, economists are more or less alone in viewing money so favorably, with their emphasis on money as a means of avoiding the inefficiencies of barter.

Money is a prize sought by archaeologists. This is so not because ancient money necessarily has a market value to collectors, but because it tells so much about the lives of its users. For example, discoveries of money provide information on the patterns of international trade and influence two millennia ago when Greek and then Roman coins were used widely in commerce from the Mediterranean to the Baltic. Spanish "pieces of eight"—8-reales coins—paint a picture of conquest and trade in the sixteenth century. The imprints on monies provide archaeologists and historians with other information, including who held power at a particular time; coins were fre- quently issued to commemorate the coronations of rulers and their successes on the battlefield. Mesopotamian coins, which consist of inscribed tablets, even provide information on prices of im- portant items of trade, such as wool and barley.

An amazing array of objects has served as money: bark cloth in Samoa, huge round stones in the Yap Islands, beads in Pelew, feathers in Santa Cruz, fur in Alaska, and shells in the Soloman Islands. Rice, tea, salt, cattle, slaves, silk, cigarettes, wine, and of course, bronze, copper, gold, and silver have all served as money.[15] Demands for convenience have resulted recently in the almost universal use of paper currency and magnetic records in bank computers.

---

[15] A fascinating account of different monies and the roles they played is provided by Paul Einzig's penetrating study, **Primitive Money** (London: Eyre and Spottiswoode, 1948).

Money has long had a ritual significance and has been the object of numerous superstitions. Anthropologists note how in many societies money has been used to drive off demons, provide cures for illness, protect soldiers in battle, fend off plagues, and bring fertility to newly married couples. Numerous rituals involve the exchange of coins as an appeal to some external power or "spirit." Even today we talk of the "high priests of finance" and of people being "obsessed" by money, with misers being obsessed by their own money and thieves by other peoples' money. Money is both revered and feared, viewed as good—when it involves charity—and as evil—when it involves acquisitiveness and single-minded desire. To some, money is viewed as having transformative power, able to turn Cinderella into a princess or a lottery winner's miserable existence into a life of joy.

The ritual significance of money probably predates its use as a medium of exchange, and money still retains a ritual significance. William Desmonde and, more recently, Russel Belk and Melanie Wallendorf have claimed that money originated as a ritual symbol, citing the fact that money played a role in societies in which exchange of goods and services outside the family was very limited.[16] Just as the acquisition of food signified special hunting and gathering skills such as endurance, daring, and intelligence, so today the acquisition of money signifies possession of necessary life skills. Certainly, we still see extremely rich people working feverishly to add further to their wealth, perhaps more out of a desire to increase their power, stature, control, and prestige than to exchange their money for items to consume. While we must distinguish desires for money from desires for wealth—money is but a narrow component of wealth, being just liquid wealth—it does appear that "money" is linked to status, serving as a medal of achievement and perhaps giving its owner a sense of immortality and durability.

Money is surrounded by emotions and taboos, the emotions reflected in use of such terms as **bond** and **security**. While bonds and securities are not themselves money, these terms reflect the feelings attached to the ties of indebtedness and the comfort of having money. Reference is also made to **trust** companies, **confidence** crises, bank **panics**, market **optimism**, and so on, imbuing institutions and circumstances relating to money with human emotions.

The taboos associated with money are many. They include the social rules governing money as a gift. For example, it is usually unacceptable to give money as a gift to nonfamily members. Money can be given within the family and, indeed, is a sign of devotion, but traditionally, money is given down the age ladder from older to younger family members, not the reverse. In addition, when giving money, new, crisp notes are better than old, limp ones, and it is better to give a $100 bill than a bundle of $5 or $10 bills. There are also taboos when making payments with money. For example, payment for the services of a doctor or dentist are made to a receptionist or via a check in the mail rather than directly. Similarly, it is not acceptable to give money to a neighbor for a friendly gesture such as a gift of produce from their garden. However, a return in kind is considered appropriate—if separated sufficiently in time so as not to seem as a payment. So strong are the taboos surrounding money, and particularly the discussion of money, that David Krueger in his **Last Taboo** notes that some people are more open discussing sex than money.[17]

Marxists have noted that the use of money detaches workers from the objects they make and puts worker-employer relations on an impersonal footing. On the other hand, it also has been noted how much human interaction revolves around the exchange of money, making

[16] William Desmonde, **Magic, Myth and Money: The Origins of Money in Religious Ritual** (Glencoe, N.Y.: Free Press, 1962); and Russel W. Belk and Melanie Wallendorf, "The Sacred Meanings of Money," **Journal of Economic Psychology** 2:35–67, 1990.

[17] David W. Krueger, **Last Taboo: Money as Symbol and Reality in Psychotherapy and Psychoanalysis** (New York: Brunner-Mazel, 1986).

money a focus of interpersonal relations; the exchange at the supermarket checkout, with the bus driver, or at the gas station or newsstand is a human interaction involving money.

Money relates to the law. In particular, typically a currency is declared to be **legal tender**, meaning that it must be accepted by vendors if they agree to the terms of a sale. (Vendors are not required to sell their goods or services, but once they have agreed to a sale, they are required to accept the country's legal tender in exchange.) As well as applying to the acceptability of currency, the law also applies to the establishment and management of the banks and other financial institutions whose liabilities represent the major component of the money supply. Federal and state law is rich in legislative enactments and case precedents relating to banking and financial intermediation. Indeed, **liability** is a term spanning law and finance.

The emergence, spread, and occasional collapse of banks weave threads in the fabric of history, from the influence and power of the Flemish and Lombardian banks to the turmoil surrounding the collapse of thousands of U.S. banks

> *Money is surrounded by emotions and taboos. . . .*

in the Great Depression. Because of its ramifications for social and political developments, monetary history is an integral part not only of economic history but also of general history.

As we saw in the preceding chapter, many religions view money—or more generally, wealth—as corrupting the soul if it becomes regarded with reverence. The need to prevent the desire for money from obfuscating more important "otherworldly" objectives is at the core of a large body of liturgical writings. Readers of books in that other "otherworldly" discipline, astronomy, might be forgiven for thinking that money is also at the core of a large body of their literature, that relating to the more easily identifiable nebulae and galaxies. This is so because according to the classification system of the French astronomer Messier, the most visible blurry patches in the sky are labeled **M1**, **M2**, . . . , **M31** (Andromeda), **M32**, and so on. With the numerous innovations in different kinds of deposits and financial institutions, the pressure is on for more definitions of money than the current **M1**, **M2**, and **M3**, although it is hoped that the listing of monies falls short of cosmic proportions.

SUMMARY

1. Money is the medium we accept for what we have to sell and then use to make purchases and thereby allows exchange to be indirect.

2. Money offers a number of advantages over barter. Money overcomes the need for a coincidence of wants and the problems of exchanging indivisible products, perishable products, and products that are difficult to carry around. Money also offers a common

   unit of measurement of prices and incomes. Because money has these advantages, we are able to specialize and thereby enjoy the gains from the division of labor.

3. Money can be defined as whatever is acceptable as a medium of exchange and which also serves as a standard of deferred payment, a store of value, and a unit of account.

4. *M1* consists of coin, currency, and checkable deposits at financial institutions and deposits which can be quickly shifted into checkable deposits.

5. While savings accounts, time deposits, money market funds, mutual funds, and so on cannot themselves be used to make payments, they can be converted quickly into checkable accounts and are therefore included in the broader definitions of the money supply called *M2* and *M3*. These broader monetary aggregates differ according to the particular savings categories they contain.

6. Money is the most liquid asset. Every asset has some degree of liquidity, but only money avoids all uncertainty and costs when making purchases.

7. Holding money because of its convenience in making purchases involves forgoing interest that could be earned otherwise. The higher the interest rate forgone by holding money, the lower is the quantity of money demanded.

8. Paper money arose from the deposit-taking activity of goldsmiths who issued paper claims against the gold held in their vaults.

9. The Federal Reserve System is the central bank of the United States. It has a chairman and Board of Governors in Washington, D.C., and twelve regional banks. The Federal Reserve holds commercial member banks' reserves, clears checks between member banks, serves as the government's bank, and manages the supply of money. Runs on banks are effectively prevented by the Federal Deposit Insurance Corporation, which insures deposits at member banks.

10. The fractional reserve system enables commercial banks to create money. Through the money supply creation process via redepositing and the granting of loans, the supply of money increases by a multiple of any increase in bank reserves.

11. The Federal Reserve can affect the money supply by open market operations, by changing the discount rate, and by changing reserve requirements.

12. Commercial banks gather up funds from those earning more than they spend and make these funds available to those wishing to spend more than they earn. The former group consists of savers, and the latter group consists of investors, and consumers who wish to consume today and pay later.

13. Financial intermediaries reduce the cost of channeling savings to investors and thereby increase investment and economic growth.

14. Savers and investors are also brought together by thrifts, which consist of mutual savings banks, credit unions, and savings and loan associations, as well as by pension funds, money and bond markets, and the stock market.

15. Stocks represent a claim to the ownership of a company. Stocks are subordinate to bonds in that bondholders must be paid before a firm can pay anything to shareholders.

16. Stocks are riskier than bonds, and because people are risk averse, the expected return on stocks must exceed the return on bonds. The degree of riskiness of a stock does not depend only on how volatile its value is, but rather on how much volatility it contributes to a diversified portfolio of stocks and other assets, specifically the portfolio of all stocks, bonds, and other assets.

17. Electronic funds transfers based on debit cards may change the character of the financial system, but there are still many problems to overcome.

QUESTIONS AND PROBLEMS

1. What features of gold have given it such an important historical role as a medium of exchange, unit of account, and store of value? How liquid are gold and silver?

2. Should balances on department store–issued credit cards be considered part of the money supply?

3. What variables are relevant to an individual's decision about how much money to hold?

4. Do you think the demand for money would vary more closely with wealth than income?

5. If many of the customers of a bank gave lengthy advance notice to withdraw their deposits, would the bank be able to meet their demands? What would it sell to obtain currency for its customers?

6. Why doesn't the government leave insurance of bank deposits to private insurance companies, as it does with most other types of insurance?

7. An individual bank merely lends money that people deposit and therefore does not add to the money supply. How, then, does the banking *system* add to the money supply?

8. How does the interest rate on bank loans versus the central bank discount rate influence commercial bank decisions on how much to lend?

9. How do financial intermediaries increase economic growth?

10. Most sales of stocks are "secondary sales," that is, the resale of stocks, rather than the original sale of new issues. Why are secondary sales important in assisting the sale of new issues?

11. What are the differences between the money, bond, and stock markets, and how do these differences affect the nature of the people who raise funds in these different markets?

12. What is the difference between a credit card and a debit card?

. . . .
. . . .
. . . .
. . . .
. . . .
. . . . . . Inflation
. . . .
. . . .

The government is the only organization that can operate with a deficit and still make money.

Anonymous

Key Concepts

Consumer price index; GDP deflator; difficulties measuring inflation; quantity theory of money; money demand versus money supply; cost-push versus demand-pull inflation; hyperinflation; inflation as a hidden tax; gains and losses from inflation; importance of inflationary anticipations

UPS AND DOWNS IN INFLATION

At different times and in different countries, inflation has been a matter of major concern, of little or no concern, and of just about every level of concern in between. That is, inflation has varied greatly over time within countries and also differs substantially among countries. For example, as Figure 14.1 shows, in the decades of the 1970s and 1980s, inflation in Brazil and Argentina went from relatively modest levels in the "double digits" to approximately 3000% per annum, and then dropped substantially. Figure 14.2 shows that during the same period, inflation in Japan and the United States, while low by Brazilian and Argentinean standards, still varied significantly over time, being much higher in the 1970s than in the 1980s. Figures 14.3 and 14.4 on pages 418 and 419 show that inflation has occurred at all sorts of rates, rising and declining in Israel, staying relatively stable in Germany, and being a repeated problem in Great Britain and Mexico.

Inflation rates differ greatly between countries and within countries over time.

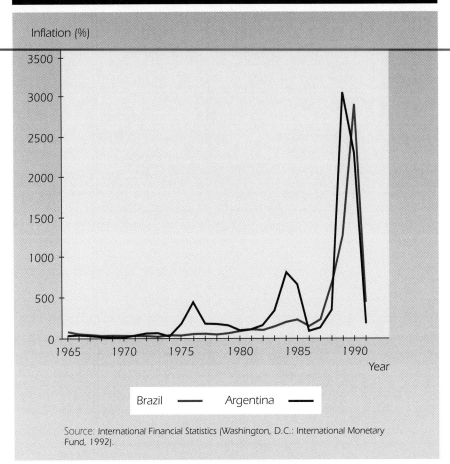

FIGURE 14.1   Inflation in Brazil and Argentina increased substantially from double digits to thousands of percent and then dropped dramatically.

Source: International Financial Statistics (Washington, D.C.: International Monetary Fund, 1992).

This chapter explains what is behind the variations in inflation that are so apparent in Figures 14.1 to 14.4. The chapter also discusses the effects of inflation and the importance of how accurately inflation is forecasted by savers, workers, and others. As we shall see in later chapters, inflation has an important bearing on other macroeconomic phenomena, including unemployment, GDP, interest rates, and exchange rates. This is why we set out to deal with as many aspects of inflation as we can here, all in one chapter; later chapters can then build on these important foundations. However, before dealing with the causes and effects of inflation, it is useful to consider how inflation is measured and the accuracy of the alternative measures used. We shall see that as with most important macroeconomic variables, published inflation statistics are estimates that require some care in interpretation.[1]

[1] Recall that in Chapter 12 we spoke of *estimates* of GDP, national income, and so on. Even money supply statistics are estimates, being based on sampling procedures, just as are unemployment estimates and so on.

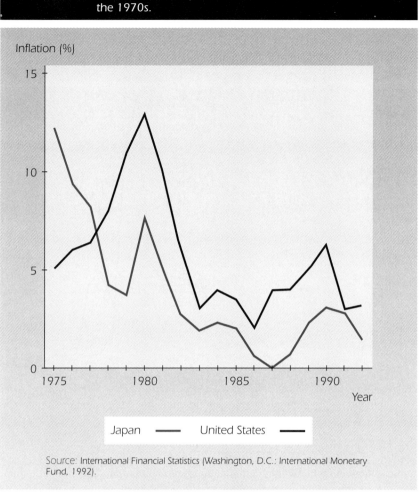

FIGURE 14.2   Inflation in the United States and Japan has declined since the 1970s.

Source: International Financial Statistics (Washington, D.C.: International Monetary Fund, 1992).

MEASURING INFLATION

As we are all too aware, inflation reduces the buying power of any given dollar amount of income or savings. The rate of inflation is measured by the rate at which an index of prices goes up (or goes down in the case of deflation). The **price index** is designed to measure "prices in general," which requires that it provides a way of combining the prices of different items. Several price indexes are calculated, but two are particularly important. These are the consumer price index (CPI) and the GDP implicit deflator.

The Consumer Price Index

The **consumer price index (CPI)** combines the prices of items purchased by an "average" or "representative" consumer. However, the representative consumer must be defined. This is difficult because each person has his or her own preferences which affect what he or she buys. For example, while some people like to

The rate of inflation is the rate at which prices in general are increasing. It is computed from changes in an index which measures the level of prices in general.

FIGURE 14.3 Inflation in Mexico and Israel has gone above 100 percent but has subsequently been reduced.

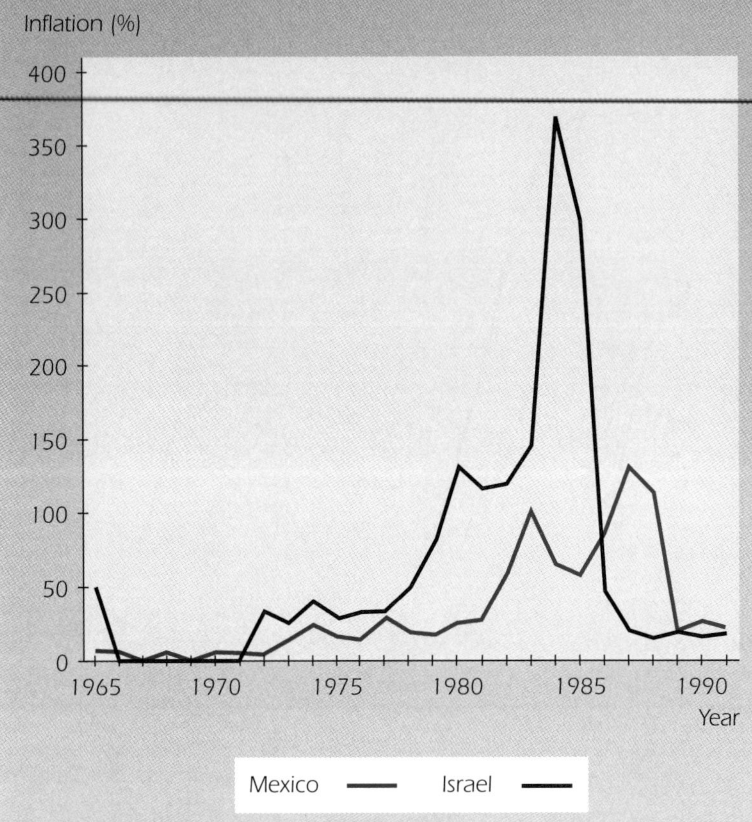

Source: International Financial Statistics (Washington, D.C.: International Monetary Fund, 1992).

precede their evening meal with such delights as caviar and expensive paté, others are content to forgo appetizers and settle for bologna and fried eggs. Similarly, while patrons of the arts might feel dissatisfied without tickets to the symphony and a visit to the opera, others get their pleasure from the cheaper activities of a hike in the country or an evening watching television.

To define the representative consumer, a survey is made of the spending of a sample of consumers during a month-long period in a particular year, called the base year. The survey focuses on urban households and records everything the sampled households purchase. An average is taken of what the households spend to determine the relative importance of different products. In this way the representative consumer's **market basket** is defined.

A highly simplified market basket is given in the first column of Table 14.1. This basket is computed from purchases during the base year 1984. Table 14.1 also gives the prices of the items in the market basket in 1984. The cost of the 1984 basket in 1984 can therefore be calculated and is

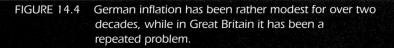

FIGURE 14.4   German inflation has been rather modest for over two decades, while in Great Britain it has been a repeated problem.

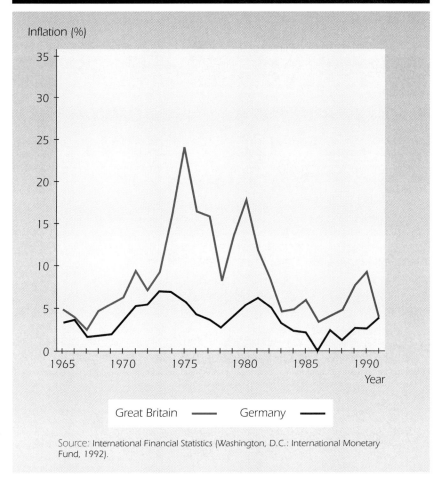

Source: International Financial Statistics (Washington, D.C.: International Monetary Fund, 1992).

$$\text{Cost of 1984 market basket in 1984} = (20 \times \$1.80 + 15 \times \$0.80$$
$$+ 12 \times \$0.50 + 1 \times \$400$$
$$+ 2000 \times \$0.05 + 1 \times \$100)$$
$$= \$654$$

Table 14.1 shows that by 1994 the price of every item has risen. The cost of the 1984 market basket valued at 1994 prices is

$$\text{Cost of 1984 market basket in 1994} = (20 \times \$2.94 + 15 \times \$1.56$$
$$+ 12 \times \$0.65 + 1 \times \$700$$
$$+ 2000 \times \$0.075 + 1 \times \$120)$$
$$= \$1060$$

········
TABLE 14.1

The consumer price index values a base-year market basket in successive months or years.

CONSUMPTION ITEM	UNITS PURCHASED IN BASE YEAR, 1984	PRICE PER UNIT IN 1984	PRICE PER UNIT IN 1994
Beef	20 pounds	$1.80	$2.94
Bread	15 loaves	$0.80	$1.56
Potatoes	12 pounds	$0.50	$0.65
Rent	1 month	$400	$700
Electricity	2,000 kilowatt-hours	$0.05	$0.075
Suits	1 suit	$100	$120

The consumer price index values a base-year market basket at base-year prices and at later prices. The ratio of these two values gives the CPI for the later period. The rate of inflation is computed from the rate at which the cost of the basket changes over time. That is, the rate of inflation is the rate of change of the CPI.

The CPI for 1994 compared with 1984 is derived by taking the ratio of the two sums we have calculated and multiplying by 100. Therefore, the CPI for 1994 compared with 1984 is

$$\text{CPI (1994 versus 1984)} = \frac{\text{cost of 1984 market basket in 1994}}{\text{cost of 1984 market basket in 1984}} \times 100$$

$$= \frac{\$1060}{\$654} \times 100 = 162$$

More generally, the CPI for the current year is

$$\text{CPI} = \frac{\text{cost of base-year basket using current prices}}{\text{cost of base-year basket using base-year prices}} \times 100 \qquad (14.1)$$

The consumer price index (CPI) measures the cost of a representative consumer's market basket vis-à-vis a base year.

We see from the definition in Equation 14.1 that the CPI compares the cost of the market basket in an earlier period with what it costs later. We find that in 1994, prices are 162% of what they were in 1984—a 62% increase over the ten-year period.

By looking at the CPI from year to year, the annual rate of inflation can be calculated. For example, if in 1995 the CPI has a value of 169 vis-à-vis the value of 162 in 1994, the annual percentage rate of inflation between 1994 and 1995 is

$$\text{CPI inflation 1994 to 1995} = \frac{169 - 162}{162} \times 100 = 4.3\%$$

More generally,

$$\text{CPI inflation } t-1 \text{ to } t = \frac{\text{CPI year } t - \text{CPI year } t-1}{\text{CPI year } t-1} \times 100 \qquad (14.2)$$

It is important to observe that

1. The CPI includes only consumption goods and services.

2. The CPI is based on purchases of a representative consumer and therefore may not reflect the price level facing many actual consumers.

3. The CPI is based on an infrequently revised market basket.

4. The CPI is based on past, not present, consumption patterns.

5. The CPI is based on goods and services available in the base year and consequently omits newer products.

6. The CPI may be distorted by quality changes.

Each of these observations implies that the CPI is an *estimate* of the price level and that, therefore, inflation computed from the rate of change of the CPI is an *estimate* of inflation.

> *Inflation can be estimated from the rate of change of the CPI.*

There is an alternative price index that can be used to calculate the rate of inflation which avoids the approximations and limitations we have listed, although it has limitations of its own. This alternative price index is based on the national income and product accounts and is called the **GDP deflator** or, more fully, the **GDP implicit deflator.**

The GDP (Implicit) Deflator

The **GDP deflator** is implicit in the measures of nominal GDP and real GDP. Specifically, the GDP (implicit) deflator is the GDP in the current year at current prices—the nominal GDP—divided by the GDP in the current year assessed at base-year prices—the real GDP. That is,

$$\text{GDP deflator} = \frac{\text{GDP in current year at current prices}}{\text{GDP in current year at base-year prices}} \qquad (14.3)$$

For example, the GDP deflator for 1994 compared with 1984 is defined by

$$\text{GDP deflator} = \frac{1994 \text{ GDP valued in } 1994 \text{ prices}}{1994 \text{ GDP valued in } 1984 \text{ prices}}$$

Symbolically, the GDP deflator can be written as

$$P = \frac{\text{nominal GDP}}{\text{real GDP}} = \frac{Y}{Q} \qquad (14.4)$$

> *The GDP (implicit) deflator is the GDP in the current year—the nominal GDP—divided by the GDP in a base year—the real GDP.*

where P is the GDP deflator, Y is nominal GDP, and Q is real GDP. If we refer back to Table 12.4 on page 354, which was used to illustrate real versus nominal GDP, we have

$$\text{GDP deflator} = \frac{\$884,900}{\$560,000} = 1.58$$

If the price level had not increased, the GDP deflator would have had a value of unity; it is conventional to present the CPI with a base of 100 and the GDP deflator with a base of 1. Instead, we find from our example that inflation has occurred and that prices in general have risen from 1984 to 1994 by 58%.

As with the CPI, the rate of inflation is calculated from the GDP deflator by taking the change in the deflator from one year to the next and multiplying by 100. For example, if the GDP deflator for 1995 is 164 and the GDP deflator for 1994 is 158, inflation between 1994 and 1995 is given by

$$\text{GDP deflator inflation 1994 to 1995} = \frac{164 - 158}{158} \times 100 = 3.8\%$$

More generally,

$$\text{GDP deflator inflation } t{-}1 \text{ to } t = \frac{\text{GDP deflator year } t - \text{GDP deflator year } t{-}1}{\text{GDP deflator year } t{-}1} \times 100$$

The price level and rate of inflation calculated from the GDP deflator are generally different from those calculated from the CPI because

1. The GDP deflator includes not only consumer goods and services prices but also the prices of goods and services that are exported, invested, and produced by the government.

2. Since all goods and services are included, there is no need to define a representative consumer and, therefore, no need to take surveys to determine the market basket. Rather, the weights of different items are based on relative outputs in the GDP.

3. The GDP deflator considers prices only of goods and services currently being produced and therefore excludes prices of used cars, existing houses, and so on, prices that *are* included in the CPI.

4. The GDP deflator uses *current* period weights, those in the current GDP. The CPI, on the other hand, uses *previous* period weights, those in the base-year market basket.

While the first three of these differences between the CPI and GDP deflator could cause either of the indexes to increase by more, the fourth difference works toward a higher inflation measure with the CPI than with the GDP deflator. Let us explain why.

The Distortions in Inflation Estimates.   Within any given overall rate of inflation, some prices are always changing at a rate different from other prices. For example, during the several years for which the same base-year basket of consumption is used, heating oil prices may go up by 25%, while natural gas prices may increase by only 10%. Beef prices may increase by 40%, while chicken prices may increase by only 5%. Consumers adjust to these changes in relative prices by using more of the items that have become relatively cheaper. For example, there would be a shift toward greater use of natural gas vis-à-vis oil if the relative price of natural gas declines. More chicken and less beef would be eaten if the relative price of chicken falls.

In construction of the consumer price index, we persist in using the base-year consumption basket for several years. If, as in our example, the relative prices of oil and beef increase and people economize on these items vis-à-vis natural gas and chicken, the consumption adjustments are not reflected in the CPI until the next revision of the market basket of the representative consumer. This requires another household survey. While the older weights are still being used, a larger volume of oil and beef are included in the market basket than is currently being purchased. By using a larger volume than we really should of items whose prices have risen relatively quickly, we attach too much importance to the higher-inflation items. As a result, inflation estimates based on the CPI tend to overstate inflation because the index "overincludes" the faster-increasing prices. Furthermore, the CPI underincludes the items with relatively slower moving prices, since more of these will be bought currently than is shown in the (past) market basket. With the faster-increasing prices given too much weight and the slower-moving prices too little weight, the measure of inflation given from the CPI will exceed the "true" rate of inflation.

Inflation calculated from the CPI tends to overstate the true rate of inflation.

The GDP (implicit) deflator suffers from the reverse problem. As can be seen by looking at the definition of the GDP deflator in Equation 14.3, it is computed using *current* quantities, those that are in the current GDP. The use of current quantities means that goods and services that have risen rapidly in price and which are therefore used sparingly are given relatively little weight. In a similar manner, items that have faced more modest inflation and are therefore purchased extensively receive relatively heavy weight. With faster-increasing prices underrepresented and slower-moving prices overrepresented, the GDP deflator understates the true rate of inflation.

Inflation calculated from the GDP deflator tends to understate the true rate of inflation.

Since the CPI overestimates inflation, if wages are revised according to the CPI, they will overcompensate for increases in the cost of living. However, compensation according to the GDP deflator, or at least the component deflator for consumption, will do the reverse and be insufficient compensation for inflation.

The Producer Price Index

Another frequently quoted index is the **producer price index,** which used to be called the **wholesale price index.** This index calculates the prices of materials at the wholesale level. While not directly relevant for consumers, the producer price index gives an idea of what might happen later to the CPI when the wholesale goods reach the retail level. For this reason, inflation in the producer price index is often taken as an indicator of future inflation in the CPI. The method of calculating the producer price index is like that for the CPI, except that the importance

The producer price index measures prices at the wholesale level.

attached to different items is based on volumes sold at the wholesale level rather than the typical basket bought by a consumer.

THE CAUSES OF INFLATION

Having shown how to measure inflation from the rate of change of any of several price indexes, we can turn to the question of what causes inflation. This is easier said than done because different theories of inflation have been in vogue at different times and there has never been consensus on the cause of the problem. We shall look at two theories that have been the most prominent and have vied with each other for general acceptance. These two theories are the Monetarists' theory and the Keynesians' theory, with the latter taking its name from British economist Lord John Maynard Keynes. However, since the Keynesian theory was devised as a theory of GDP and national income rather than of inflation, we shall leave the Keynesian explanation of inflation until we deal with the determination of GDP and national income in Chapter 16.

The two main theories of inflation are the Monetarists' theory and the Keynesians' theory.

Before beginning here with the Monetarists' inflation theory, we can note that the division of opinion over the two competing hypotheses has been so sharp that it has split many of the leading economists into two distinct camps. It is the rare individual who can venture into either camp and embrace aspects of both schools of thought, despite the fact that the truth almost certainly involves judicious selection of parts of each of the two theories.

The Quantity Theory of Money

The Monetarist's theory of inflation enjoys a long history and is known as the **quantity theory of money.** Initially developed and advanced in the eighteenth century by the **classical school,** most particularly by David Hume and John Stuart Mill, and developed further in the early twentieth century by U.S. economist Irving Fisher, the quantity theory fell out of favor during the revolution of macroeconomics that followed publication of the *General Theory* by Lord John Maynard Keynes.[2]

According to the quantity theory of money, inflation is caused by too much money chasing too few goods.

Revised by Milton Friedman at the University of Chicago and his **Chicago school,** the quantity theory has gained support from numerous economists, politicians, central bankers, and businesspeople. Briefly stated, the quantity theory of money says that inflation is caused by "too much money chasing too few goods."

Intuitive View of the Quantity Theory

Imagine a small island with a miraculous tree. Upon this tree each and every year grow 1000 highly unusual and useful fruits. These fruits constitute the national output of the island and can be eaten, burned as fuel, made into clothes and paper products, and so on. Let us imagine that on this island with its annual crop of 1000

---

[2]The *General Theory* is an abbreviation of the title of Keynes' book. The full title is *The General Theory of Employment, Interest and Money* (London: Macmillan, 1936).

fruits there are 1000 bills saying, "This is one dollar." Let us assume also that for some reason or other the one-dollar bills are used, on average, once each year.

If 1000 fruits are sold each year and the 1000 one-dollar bills are used, on average, once each year for making payments, then, by definition, the fruits must cost an average of one dollar each: how else can $1000 be handed to the fruit growers and 1000 fruits handed back! If the number of fruits produced and sold each year were to remain at 1000, while the number of one-dollar bills doubled to 2000, with the dollar bills still changing hands, on average, once a year, the average price of a fruit would rise to two dollars each. This must be so because $2000 is changing hands in one direction while 1000 fruits change hands in the other direction. We find that, in this case, when the money supply is doubled, the price level also doubles. Of course, it is crucial in this example both that the number of fruits remain at 1000 and that the average turnover rate of the one-dollar bills remains at once each year whatever the money supply.

In our example it seems reasonable to think of the national product being determined by the physical constraint of the number and fertility of trees so that the most questionable part of our example involves not the constancy of output but the assumption that money continues to be used once each year, even when the supply of money is doubled. The number of times money is used each year is called the **velocity of circulation of money,** and the nature of this velocity has become a focal point in the study of the validity of the quantity theory of money.

The critics of the quantity theory say that when, for example, the money supply is doubled, the velocity could halve. Then, for example, our 1000 fruits would still sell for one dollar each even if 2000 one-dollar bills exist, because only half the dollars would be used each year. On the other hand, proponents of the quantity theory argue that the velocity of circulation of money is determined by the nature of the financial system in which payments are made and that the nature of the financial system changes only slowly. This, claim advocates of the quantity theory, causes the velocity of circulation to be reasonably predictable rather than a will-o'-the-wisp, moving this way and that to offset changes in the money supply.

> The velocity of circulation of money is the average number of times money is used each year. Monetarists believe that this velocity is reasonably predictable.

In order to decide on the validity of the quantity theory, we need to judge the extent to which the velocity of circulation of money offsets changes in the money supply. From the persistence of strong divisions of opinion on the cause of inflation, it is clear that the evidence is open to interpretation, being viewed differently by the Monetarists and their critics.

The Quantity Theory Derived

The quantity theory can be derived from the **quantity equation of exchange.** The quantity equation of exchange relates the money supply to the value of transactions according to

$$M \cdot V_{\mathrm{T}} \equiv T \tag{14.5}$$

where

M = money supply

T = total value of transactions

V_{T} = transactions velocity of circulation of money

Equation 14.5 says that the amount of money multiplied by the number of times it is used during any period is the value of transactions occurring in that period. This is true as a matter of definition, which is why we used the identity sign ($\equiv$) in Equation 14.5; transactions velocity is defined as the value of transactions divided by the amount of money (that is, $V_T \equiv T/M$), which is just a rearrangement of Equation 14.5.

In reality, statistics on the value of transactions are not collected. The transactions occurring in an economy include payments to factors of production, payments for final goods and services (thereby double counting the payments to factors of production), payments for financial assets such as stocks and bonds, payments for used cars and houses, and so on. The measure that corresponds most closely to total transactions is the GDP, which records final output, or value added. If we replace the term T with the nominal GDP Y, then we have from Equation 14.5

$$M \cdot V \equiv Y \tag{14.6}$$

where V is a different velocity than before and is the **income velocity of circulation of money** rather than the **transactions velocity of circulation of money.** The income velocity is the average number of times money is used in the course of generating the gross domestic product.

Using GDP in place of transactions does not make the quantity equation into a theory as long as we continue to define the velocity—in this case, the income velocity—in terms of the other variables in the equation. In order to move to a theory, we must determine V from outside the quantity equation, and the most straightforward way of doing this, among the many ways it can be done, is to assume that V is constant.[3] If we denote the assumed constant value by $\bar{V}$, we then have a theory, the quantity theory of money, which we can write as

$$M \cdot \bar{V} = Y \tag{14.7}$$

If we refer back to the definition of the GDP deflator in Equation 14.4, we find that

$$P \equiv \frac{Y}{Q}$$

which can be rearranged into

$$Y \equiv P \cdot Q$$

The quantity theory of money can be written as $M \bar{V} = P \cdot Q$.

This states that the nominal GDP is the price index P, in the form of the GDP deflator, multiplied by the real GDP Q. If we use this in Equation 14.7, we have another popular form of the quantity theory:

$$M \cdot \bar{V} = P \cdot Q \tag{14.8}$$

---

[3] An amusing view of velocity is described in Example 14.1. This indicates that even noneconomic variables outside the quantity equation may affect velocity—such as the weather!

Example 14.1

A FAST LESSON IN VELOCITY

The quantity equation makes it clear that a doubling of the money supply has the same effect on nominal GDP **Y** as does a doubling of the velocity of circulation of money. This follows because nominal GDP is the product of **M** and **V** that appears in the quantity equation, and so either has the same effect on the other side of the equation, that is, **Y**. Sir Denis H. Robertson has offered a delightful demonstration of this symmetry between money supply and velocity. His story was adapted from an earlier and lengthier account by F. Y. Edgeworth.*

Here is a little story to illustrate this conception of the velocity of circulation of money. On Derby Day two men, Bob and Joe, invested in a

* F. Y. Edgeworth, review of R.A. Lehfeldt, **Gold Prices and the Witwatersrand** (London: King, 1919), **Economic Journal,** 1919), Vol. 29, No. 115, pp. 327–330.

barrel of beer, and set off to Epsom with the intention of selling it retail on the racecourse at sixpence a pint, the proceeds to be shared equally between them. On the way Bob, who had one threepenny-bit left in the world, began to feel a great thirst, and drank a pint of beer, paying Joe threepence as his share of the market price. A little later Joe yielded to the same desire, and drank a pint of beer, returning the threepence to Bob. The day was hot, and before long Bob was thirsty again, and so, a little later, was Joe. When they arrived at Epsom, the threepence was back in Bob's pocket, and each had discharged in full his debts to the other: but the beer was all gone. One single threepenny-bit had performed a volume of transactions which would have required many shillings if the beer had been sold to the public in accordance with the original intention.

The threepence in this story is sufficient for all the transactions

that occur in the minieconomy consisting of trade between Bob and Joe. It makes it clear that it is not just the quantity of money in existence that matters but also the velocity at which it circulates. In turn, the velocity of circulation is affected by the willingness to demand money to hold versus the desire to spend it. The burning thirsts of Bob and Joe led to a burning desire to spend the threepence, therefore making the threepence a sufficient supply of liquidity for the trade between them. If just one of them had pocketed the money and not put it back into circulation, the transactions would immediately have stopped—at least until they had reached their destination.

———

Source: Sir Denis H. Robertson, **Money** (Chicago: University of Chicago Press, 1959), p. 27.

In this form, the quantity theory can be turned into a theory of inflation.

Since inflation is the rate at which the price level P is changing, to turn Equation 14.8 into a theory of inflation, we must examine how P is changing. Writing $\%\Delta M$, $\%\Delta Q$, and $\%\Delta P$ as the percentage changes, respectively, in M, Q, and P, and assuming V is constant, we can state Equation 14.8 in percentage terms[4] as

$$\%\Delta M = \%\Delta P + \%\Delta Q$$

That is

$$\%\Delta P = \%\Delta M - \%\Delta Q \qquad (14.9)$$

---

[4]The percentage changes in P and Q are *added* because when the changes are small, the percentage change in the product $P \cdot Q$ is the sum of percentage changes of the variables. It is worth noting that if velocity is not assumed to be constant, then instead of Equation 14.9, inflation is given by $\%\Delta P = \%\Delta M + \%\Delta V - \%\Delta Q$, where $\%\Delta V$ is the rate of change in the income velocity of circulation of money.

Equation 14.9 tells us that %ΔP, the rate of inflation, equals the rate of change of the money supply %ΔM minus the rate of change of real GDP %ΔQ. According to Equation 14.9, inflation occurs if the money supply is growing more rapidly than real output, and this explains why inflation has been attributed to "too much money chasing too few goods."

If we assume that output growth is determined by the rate of change of technology and the supply of factors of production, we can take %ΔQ as given.[5] We can then conclude from the quantity theory in Equation 14.9 that variations in inflation %ΔP result from variations in the growth rate of the money supply %ΔM. Since the amount of money in circulation can be influenced by the Federal Reserve System, according to the Monetarists, it is the Fed which determines the rate of inflation. For this reason, the best known Monetarist, Milton Friedman, has argued that the Fed should be instructed to keep the rate of growth of the money supply at a steady and limited amount, for example, %$\Delta M = 4\%$ per annum. [With %ΔQ also equal to 4%, which is what we might reasonably expect, we would enjoy stable prices, since from Equation 14.9 we would then have %$\Delta P = 0.04 - 0.04 = 0.0$.]

According to the quantity theory of money, inflation is caused by the Federal Reserve allowing the money supply to grow more rapidly than real output, or GDP.

Evidence on Money Supply Growth and Inflation

Not surprisingly, factors other than the growth rate of the money supply affect inflation. Therefore, in a comparison of inflation and money supply growth, the correspondence is not perfect. Nevertheless, the evidence for the relationship between the rate of growth of the money supply and inflation is quite close, especially in situations of rapid inflation. For example, Figure 14.5 shows the relationship between the growth rate of money, measured by *M1*, and inflation, measured from the CPI, for Bolivia for the period 1975–1990. The two series are seen to move in tandem, both jumping in the mid-1980s. Similarly, Figure 14.6 shows the case of Mexico over the same period, with money growth and inflation following each other through the major ups and downs.

Rates of inflation tend to move in line with rates of growth in money supplies, especially when inflation is very rapid.

Figures 14.7 and 14.8 on pages 431 and 432 show the correspondence between inflation and the growth of the money supply in the United States and Japan, respectively. While the ups and downs on the series do not track each other very closely, the rates of inflation in these countries are similar to the average rates of growth of their money supplies. Example 14.2 on page 433 provides more evidence of the link, albeit an imperfect one, between money and inflation in Great Britain, a country in which the Monetarists' ideas have been applied in setting economic policy.

Before we leave the Monetarists' theory of inflation, we should say a little more about how the quantity theory of money has been developed into a theory of the demand for money. This is important because it is in the form of a demand for money function that the quantity theory has been subjected most intensively to empirical examination.

[5] Recall from Chapter 2 that it is technology and the supply of factors of production that shift the production possibilities curve. Since neither technology nor factor supplies are affected by %ΔM, we can assume %ΔQ is given when considering the effects of variations in %ΔM.

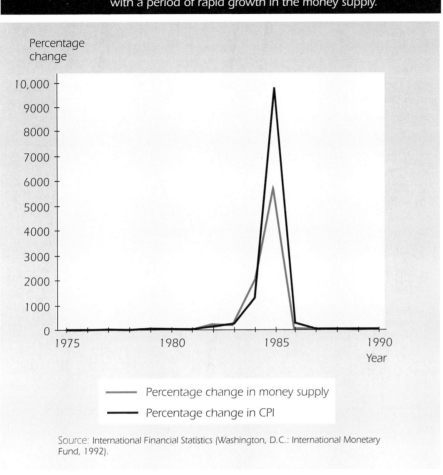

FIGURE 14.5   The period of extremely rapid inflation in Bolivia is associated with a period of rapid growth in the money supply.

Source: International Financial Statistics (Washington, D.C.: International Monetary Fund, 1992).

The Quantity Theory as a Demand for Money

We can rewrite the quantity theory in Equation 14.8 as

$$\frac{M}{P} = \frac{1}{\overline{V}} \cdot Q \qquad (14.10)$$

The M in Equation 14.10 can be interpreted as the amount of money people *want* to hold. That is, we can interpret M as the quantity of money *demanded* in an economy. Since P "deflates" M for the price level of what people buy, M/P can be interpreted as the *real* demand for money. [The conversion of nominal magnitudes to real magnitudes is always achieved by dividing nominal magnitudes by P. For example, Equation 14.4 can be rearranged into $Q = Y/P$. That is, *real* GDP Q is found by dividing *nominal* GDP Y by the price level P.] Therefore, Equation 14.10 states that the real buying power people want to hold as money is a constant proportion of real national income, or real GDP. (Recall that $\overline{V}$ is constant, so M/P

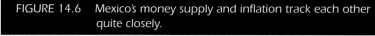

FIGURE 14.6 Mexico's money supply and inflation track each other quite closely.

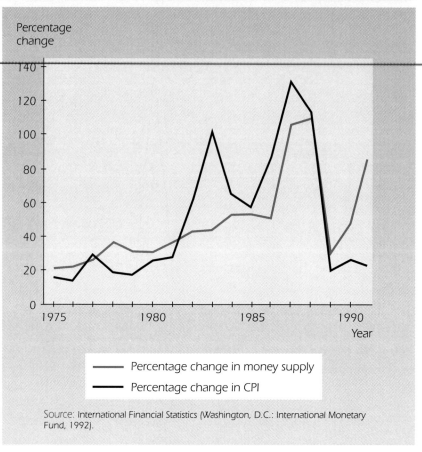

Source: International Financial Statistics (Washington, D.C.: International Monetary Fund, 1992).

Ceteris paribus, the demand for nominal money holdings varies in proportion to the price level.

varies only with *Q*.) An important implication of Equation 14.10 is that if real GDP were to remain constant while the price level *P* doubled, people would demand twice the nominal money holdings *M*. If we give this conclusion a moment of thought, we will see that it makes good sense for the nominal demand for money to vary in proportion to the price level.

We hold money to make payments as needed. Money gives us the liquidity that allows us to avoid having to sell assets such as bonds or stocks in order to make purchases. If the newspaper costs 50 cents, lunch costs $5, and so on, we might leave home in the morning with (say) $20 of money in our pocketbooks to meet both predictable and unpredictable needs. However, if newspapers suddenly increase in price to $1, lunches to $10, and so on, that is, prices double, we would want to leave home in the morning with twice as much nominal money; it would take twice as much nominal money to have the same real buying power.

Equation 14.10 makes the extreme assumption that the real demand for money, *M/P*, is a constant fraction, $1/\overline{V}$, of real GDP, Q. The quantity theory as refined in the twentieth century by Milton Friedman takes a more moderate form in which velocity is not assumed constant. Rather, money demand is assumed to depend on

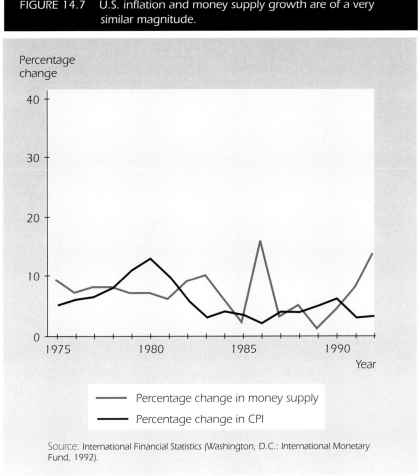

FIGURE 14.7   U.S. inflation and money supply growth are of a very similar magnitude.

Percentage change in money supply

Percentage change in CPI

Source: International Financial Statistics (Washington, D.C.: International Monetary Fund, 1992).

interest rates and other factors that affect the opportunity cost of holding money (that is, what is given up by holding money). As interest rates rise, the real demand for money is assumed to decline. However, as we shall see, if we can predict by how much interest rates affect money demand we can still use the quantity theory to explain the rate of inflation. Let us do this by considering the quantity theory in terms of money supply versus money demand.

Money Supply versus Money Demand*

The quantity of money supplied and the quantity of money demanded must be equal for equilibrium to hold; as with everything else, equilibrium requires that quantity supplied equals quantity demanded. Let us consider how equilibrium is achieved by assuming that the supply of and demand for money are initially equal and then there is a sudden 10% increase in the money supply.

---

* Sections or numbered items marked by an asterisk may be omitted without a loss of continuity.

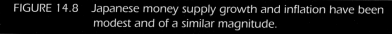

FIGURE 14.8   Japanese money supply growth and inflation have been modest and of a similar magnitude.

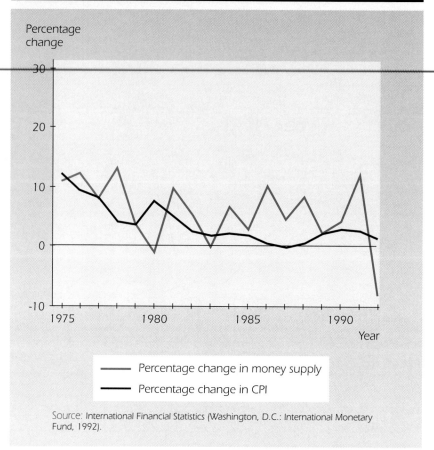

Source: International Financial Statistics (Washington, D.C.: International Monetary Fund, 1992).

If the quantity of money supplied and demanded were equal before the supply of money was increased, the supply of money will exceed the demand for money after the increase in the money supply. An excess supply of money means the public is holding money it does not want to hold; for the current rate of spending, the public would prefer to hold less than it finds itself holding. Two ways by which the public can attempt to get rid of the excess supply of money are to buy more goods and services, and to invest in bonds.[6] To the extent that the money is used to buy more goods and services, it will push up prices of goods and services via the increased demand. To the extent that the money is used to buy bonds, it will increase bond prices and lower their **yields.** [Yield is the percentage return earned by holding a bond, and the reason increased bond prices reduce yields can be seen by an example. Suppose that an investor can buy a bond that offers $10

---

[6] We say that the public can "attempt" to get rid of the unwanted money because each individual can reduce money holdings only by transferring money to somebody else. In this sense, money is like the "hot potato" in the game of that name; somebody ends up holding it.

xample   14.2

FROM IDEOLOGICAL MONETARISM TO MUDDLED PRAGMATISM

The link between money supply growth and inflation is far from perfect. However, as the following article suggests, some connection between money and inflation is usually present.

British monetary policy makers have had a strange record in the 1980s. At the beginning of the decade no government in the industrial world was more articulate about the need to curb money growth to reduce inflation than Mrs. Thatcher's. From 1979 to 1985 it adhered to monetary control with such self-consciousness, determination and success as to astonish the British people and international opinion-makers. Then, having established its credibility, it proceeded to abandon a policy of sound money. Four years later its inflation rate of nearly 8% is higher than in all other major industrial countries, including Italy. . . .

In the six years to late 1985, the Thatcher government had made reductions in the growth rate of broad money (as measured by *M*3, which includes currency in circulation and bank deposits) the centerpiece of its campaign to lower inflation. The ideological purity was compromised in light of experience, but in general terms the approach had worked. The average annual rate of broad money growth had been held down to about 10% in the four years to mid-1985, consistent with inflation of about 5% a year, steady real growth of 3%, and a small fall in velocity, or the turnover rate of money in the economy.

But, after the abandonment of broad money targets, the monetary arithmetic changed abruptly. In the $3\frac{1}{2}$ years from mid-1985 to end-1988, the average annual rate of broad money growth doubled to 20%. Although inflation stayed under control for a surprisingly long time and velocity fell even more sharply than before, domestic demand received a powerful stimulus. . . .

Recent economic policy in Britain has only one simple message for other countries. It is that sustained monetary control is an essential condition for a sustained reduction in inflation. This message is hardly new and, after the flood of monetarist propaganda at the start of the 1980s, it should not need to be repeated. Since 1979 the British government has gradually slipped from ideological monetarism to pragmatic monetarism to muddled pragmatism. In the process its inflation performance has steadily worsened relative to the rest of the world. . . .

Source: Tim Congdon, "Why Inflation Under Thatcher?" **The Wall Street Journal,** March 30, 1989, p. A14.

per year of interest on each $100 face value of bond, a yield of 10%. Suppose that suddenly, because of extra purchases of bonds, bond prices increase from $100 to $110. Then the $10 of interest each year on the original investment is received on a bond with a market value of $110, a yield of only 9%. We find that bond yields decline as bond prices increase.]

If prices of goods and services were to increase 10% from the assumed 10% increase in the money supply, the quantity of money demanded would again equal the quantity supplied. This occurs because, as we have said, the demand for money varies in proportion to the price level. Therefore, *if* prices increased 10% from a 10% increase in the money supply, the quantity of money demanded would again equal the quantity supplied, and we have the quantity theory prediction of prices increasing by the rate of change in money supply. Indeed, we have provided a mechanism for the quantity theory to work, namely, via the actions of the public spending the excess supply of money on goods and services. But what of the effect of the excess supply of money working via buying more bonds and thereby reducing bond yields?

Equilibrium between the quantity of money supplied and demanded can be restored by changes in the price level and by changes in bond yields.

Lower bond yields following an increase in the money supply mean that the opportunity cost of holding money is reduced; the opportunity cost of holding money is what could have been earned by holding bonds. This increases the quantity of money demanded toward the increased supply. The greater the influence of lower bond yields on money demand, the greater the extent to which restoration of money demand with the increased money supply will occur via the effect of the lower bond yields rather than higher prices. Only if the demand for money does not increase at all as the opportunity cost of holding money declines do we need prices to increase by the full percentage increase in the money supply.

Cost-Push versus Demand-Pull Inflation*

Accommodation of Higher Wages.   When we view the quantity theory from the perspective of money holders responding to changes in the money supply, we see that inflation is the result of extra *demand* for goods and services. For this reason, the quantity theory is a **demand-pull explanation of inflation.** However, can the quantity theory also explain what is referred to as **cost-push inflation**? This is inflation that is caused by increases in wages and other costs of production which force up final product prices. Does the quantity theory's demand-pull flavor mean that the Monetarists reject the view that inflation is sometimes caused by cost increases?

The quantity theory of money is a *demand-pull* explanation of inflation.

Cost-push inflation is often attributed to the effect of trade unions on wages. It is argued that increases in wages increase production costs and causes firms to increase prices. It is sometimes further argued that inflation can become self-perpetuating if the increase in prices causes trade unions to again demand higher wages to compensate for the increase in the cost of living. If wages again rise, so do prices, then wages, and so on, and we have the roots of sustained inflation. How does a Monetarist respond to this reasoning that, at least on the surface, would appear to make sense?

Cost-push inflation is caused by increases in production costs that are passed on in higher product prices.

According to Monetarists, the problem with our foregoing description of sustained cost-push inflation is that it does not tell us how the higher and higher wages and prices can be paid. If the money supply is constant and the velocity of circulation of money is not expanding without limit, it is not possible to pay ever-higher prices and wages. Only if the cost-push inflation induces the central bank to allow the money supply to expand, or if velocity continues to increase, can the cost-push explanation be valid for *sustained* inflation. However, many Monetarists believe that the central bank might allow the money supply to be expanded if wage increases lead to unemployment. The unemployment could occur because if unions succeed in raising wages, a number of trade union members may lose their jobs; as we saw in Chapter 10, at higher wages but with the same prices of products, the quantity of labor demanded declines. The increase in unemployment may induce the central bank to expand the money supply to improve employment. If this happens, the central bank has allowed itself to **accommodate** the original cause of inflation.

Accommodation of Higher Energy Prices.   When energy prices go up, the immediate effect is inflationary, since it means increased prices for gasoline, heating oil, and so on; these higher prices appear in indices used to measure inflation.

However, if there is no more money in circulation and peoples' incomes remain unchanged, the need to pay more for energy reduces the ability to buy other products. For example, if gasoline and heating bills increase from $200 to $250 a month, there is a reduction of $50 in income available for eating out, paying the rent, and so on. This will lower demand outside the energy sector and reduce prices there. This will offset the inflation in energy prices with no *long-term* effect on the overall price level. However, if the inability to buy other products causes job losses in the nonenergy sector, the central bank might increase the money supply to help maintain demand and prevent layoffs. Unemployment from an energy price increase may be avoided in this way, but at the expense of accommodating the inflation triggered by the higher energy prices.

Sustained cost-push inflation requires accommodation of the central bank.

How Bad Can Inflation Become?

The situation where inflation is completely out of hand is called **hyperinflation** or, sometimes, **galloping inflation.** Unlike the cause of small or moderate inflation, about which there are at least two schools of thought (the Monetarists, whose views we have given, and the Keynesians, whose views await our account of GDP and national income), when it comes to hyperinflation, virtually all economists are Monetarists in that they agree that hyperinflation is the result of printing more and more money.

Extremely rapid inflation in the hundreds or thousands of percent per annum is called hyperinflation.

Statistics on hyperinflation are stunning. For example, in Germany in November 1923, prices were 755,700 *million* times higher than in 1913. It cost many million Reichsbank marks merely to send a letter in the mail, and many postage stamp collectors have the evidence in their stamp albums. Inflation in Hungary reached the point where it took approximately 40 million paper pengos to buy a U.S. cent. Indeed, the 1931 Hungarian gold pengo, which was at that time worth one paper pengo, had by June 1946 become worth 13,000,000,000,000,000,000 paper pengos. Notes circulated with a face value of 100,000,000,000,000,000,000 pengos. Larger and larger denominations merely required a different arrangement of ink. Unfortunately for those who suffered these hyperinflations, there was no shortage of ink for printing the many zeros on the notes.

Hyperinflation was so bad at certain times in Hungary and Germany that people were paid at lunch time so they could shop before evening. Some people even joked that they would buy two beers each time they went to the bar because the beer deteriorated more slowly than did the money!

Hyperinflation has not been limited to short periods in certain Europe countries. For example, Bolivia, Brazil, and other South American countries have experienced inflation of over a thousand percent per annum, with some very costly consequences, as Example 14.3 dramatically illustrates.

During hyperinflation, use of the country's paper money tends to be abandoned as people demand other items for settling financial obligations. The alternative media of exchange have included relatively stable external currencies such as the U.S. dollar in Latin America and in Israel, commodity monies such as gold and silver, and valued items such as cognac, wine, and flour. Barter also becomes common. As we have seen in the preceding chapter, barter is very inefficient. The beauty of paper money is that it is cheap to produce and yet can serve to avoid the double coincidence of wants, serve as a unit of account, and so on—provided

Hyperinflation can cause an abandonment of money and a return to barter.

Example 14.3

GALLOPING TO STAY EVEN

The real cost of inflation comes in the form of wasted resources which go into dealing with the inflation. The following account of the daily struggle with inflation in Brazil explains how much human time and effort can be lost to runaway inflation.

It was a balmy evening in Rio, the sort of weather that invites one to relax at an outdoor café in Copacabana or Ipanema and take in the beachfront action.

But on this particular recent evening the hottest spot in town wasn't one of the cafés, bars or restaurants that line the city coast. The place to be was the gas station.

"The price of gas is going up 60% at midnight, so I want to fill up my tank before that happens," explained a taxi driver as he pulled into the line at the Petrobras gas station on Copacabana's Avenida Atlantica. It was close to 11:30 P.M. and there were a good 30 cars ahead of him. "I hope I reach the pump before midnight," he said. "Otherwise, my money will buy only 20 liters instead of 34.". . .

In 1987, inflation was 365%. In 1988, it was 934% and pundits started to say that the country was on the verge of collapse. But in 1989, inflation reached 1765% and the country has held together. Some wonder how long this can go on. For the month of January, inflation is expected to reach about 55%—an annual rate of about 19,000%.

By some measures that puts Brazil in the unenviable club of countries suffering from hyperinflation. Some economists say hyperinflation is when the monthly rate exceeds 50%. Other economists say hyperinflation can't be defined by a number, but occurs when the economy is in a state of total disorganization, which isn't yet the case. Brazilian economist Carlos Langoni has a more vivid definition: "Hyperinflation," he says, "is when you discover that it's a better deal to pay for lunch before the first course than after dessert."

Things aren't quite that bad here, but they're getting there. Vacationers returning from their Christmas break were in for a shock: The taxi that charged them 127 cruzados novos to take them to the airport in late December charged them 290 cruzados novos to take them back into the city two weeks later. That is if they only took two weeks off. If they went away for three weeks, the taxi back cost them 435 cruzados novos. If they bought the *Veja* newsweekly to read on the plane when they left, they paid 40 cruzados novos in late December. If they wanted to catch up on the news upon their return, the new issue of *Veja* cost 60 cruzados novos.

Every day, the newspapers are full of articles announcing new price rises. Newspapers also offer advice on such matters as whether it's better to stock up on food and consumer products to anticipate price increases, or invest one's money. (The answer: go shopping. Since mid-November, supermarket prices have risen an average of 218%, while the stock market and gold rose by 175%, the dollar by 163% and the overnight [deposit]—a one-day savings account that most Brazilians place their money in as a hedge against inflation—by 137%.)

With prices going up every time they blink, some Brazilians are confused. The other day, Jorio Dauster, the president of the Brazilian Coffee Institute, was asked by the daily *Folha de São Paulo* how much a cup of coffee cost. "It's two cruzados novos," he answered. "Or is it five? To tell you the truth, I don't know," he said.

---

it is generally accepted. When we resort to barter, we give up the gains from having a generally accepted money.

Hyperinflation cannot continue without vast quantities of money being added to the money supply; it cannot take a barrel of money to buy a loaf of bread without there being barrels and truckloads of money in circulation. It is therefore difficult not to agree with the Monetarists that hyperinflation is the result of an extremely rapid expansion of the money supply.

Prices vary. Going to supermarkets to compare prices has become a favorite recreational activity. Noemia Souza Pauferro, a 45-year-old book distributor in São Paulo, says inflation has forced her to cut back on traveling. And what does she do instead? "We go to the supermarket to see the prices," she says.

Inflation has spawned an inflation of work, ideas and even jobs designed to deal with inflation. Isak Marcel Aizim Diamante, the 29-year-old general manager of a São Paulo company that makes blinds, says he spends about two hours a day reading business newspapers to decide what to do with his money.

Some don't have the time to do this themselves, so they leave it to their secretaries.

"That's all I do in the morning," says 25-year-old Maria Claudia Gebaili, a secretary at a São Paulo newspaper. "When I come in, the first thing I do is call the bank. Usually it's busy because everybody else is trying to do the same thing. So I have to go over to the bank and wait in line to talk to the manager and ask him to take money out of my boss's short-term funds and put some in the checking account to cover the checks he wrote overnight. On Fridays, I always have to make sure that my boss's checking account is emptied because the money left there would get devalued over the weekend. But on Monday morning, some of the checks he wrote over the weekend have already appeared at the bank. So I have to race over to make sure he doesn't get an overdraft. It wears you down."

Brazilians are also constantly trying to devise the best way of paying for goods. Daniel Cherman, a 24-year-old employee in a real estate promotion company, has four different credit cards that fall due at different dates. He always tries to use the one payable at the latest date so that by the time his account is debited, the cost of the purchase has been cut in half.

Businesses are wising up however. Most restaurants no longer accept credit cards. And most stores now have price tags with two different prices: one if you pay cash, and one, much higher, if you pay with a credit card. At the Mesbia department store in São Paulo, for instance, a pair of Levi's jeans sells for 859 cruzados novos in cash and 1561 cruzados novos with a credit card.

For a long time, despite the difficulties involved, Brazilians took all this in stride. They were helped, in large part, by what economist Edmar Bacha calls Brazil's "diabolical indexation system" that protects regular wage-earners from the worst ravages of inflation but creates a lot of inflation by obliging the government to print money to pay the ever-rising wages.

Now, however, there are growing signs that Brazilians are getting fed up. More and more unions are asking that salaries be paid bi-monthly, or even weekly, rather than monthly and that salaries be indexed on a projection of the current month's inflation rather than the previous month's inflation.

Businesses are also frustrated by the near-impossibility of making any long-term plans and keeping accounts current. The Pao de Acucar supermarket group keeps its accounts in its own invented currency unit, the real.

Source: Thomas Kamm, "Daily Inflation Struggle Obsesses Brazil," **The Wall Street Journal,** January 29, 1990, p. A10. Reprinted by permission of The Wall Street Journal, © 1990 Dow Jones & Company, Inc. All Rights Reserved Worldwide.

INFLATION AS A HIDDEN TAX

Taxing by "Printing" Money

If hyperinflation means resort to the inefficiencies of commodity monies and barter, why has any country allowed it to occur? The answer is that inflation is a tax that can be applied when other taxes cannot be collected, such as, for example, during or just after a war. In order to see why inflation is as a tax, we can consider two examples. While the examples do not involve governments, they immediately suggest why governments use the inflation tax.

An Englishman on Vacation.   Suppose that an honest and upright Englishman has for decades vacationed on the same Aegean island, paying for most of what he buys with checks. Suppose that the islanders have become so confident in the soundness of the checks that they accept them from each other. Indeed, suppose that the checks circulate on the island alongside the island's own money and are never returned to England for payment. Under such circumstances, who pays for the Englishman's vacation?

Some people are tempted to answer that those who pay are the last ones holding the checks. This is incorrect because they too can spend the checks as long as the checks remain generally acceptable. The answer is that all the islanders pay. Clearly, this is so because the Englishman does not pay, and the goods and services he consumes come from somewhere.[7] The islanders pay by giving the Englishman the implicit power to "print" money. The extra "money" increases the price level, thereby reducing the buying power of the island's own money. (The higher prices can be rationalized via the quantity theory of money.) The holders of the island's own money therefore pay for the Englishman's vacation via a hidden "inflation tax." That is, the inflation applies a tax on the island's own money.

Counterfeit Notes.   Another amusing and revealing application of inflation as a tax concerns the effect of counterfeit bills. Suppose that someone has cleverly but deviously found a means to manufacture $20 bills. Suppose that this person enjoys a fine time with the phony bills, eating great meals and enjoying an indefinite vacation, fine clothes, good wine, unlimited travel, and expensive entertainment. Who is paying for the counterfeiter's pleasure? Furthermore, how are they paying?

It should be obvious that somebody pays for what the counterfeiter enjoys because if there is full employment, more goods and services consumed by the counterfeiter means fewer goods and services for others to enjoy.[8] The people who pay the tax from counterfeit money are those holding the preexisting legal money. They pay because the addition to the supply of money from the counterfeit notes raises prices (for example, as in the quantity theory of money) and thereby reduces the purchasing power of the genuine money. The extent to which the illegal money will buy fewer goods is the extent to which the inflation tax is paid. The amount of tax equals the amount of goods and services consumed by the counterfeiter because in real terms this is what is given up by others. We should note that those who pay the inflation tax are not only those who accept the phony money, because they in turn may use it in making purchases. It is everybody who holds genuine money who pays.

Those holding money are taxed by inflation, the proceeds going to those who print the money which causes the inflation.

What is illegal for counterfeiters in terms of collecting "taxes" via printing money is legal for central banks. The difference is that when a central bank prints

---

[7] As will become clear in the next chapter, if there is unemployment, the Englishman's checks could stimulate a larger output. The Englishman would then get pleasure without correspondingly reducing the amount others have to enjoy, although it would be at the expense of others working harder.

[8] As we mentioned in the preceding footnote, if there is unemployment and an increase in output, then in a sense nobody pays other than by means of extra work.

money, taxpayers benefit in that tax rates on income, sales, and so on do not need to be as high as they otherwise would have been for the same level of provision of government goods and services.

The Inflation Tax in Reverse

During the nineteenth century, America's industrial barons became outrageously wealthy and showed off their affluence by lighting cigars with $20 bills at extravagant, ostentatious dinner parties. Were these so-called robber barons destroying anything of value? The answer is clearly "no." All they burned were pieces of paper and nothing more; they were not destroying bread or clothes or anything of value in and of itself. In fact, when the robber barons set fire to money, they were being generous. We should explain this rather surprising statement because it helps make clear the nature of money as having no value in and of itself.

When robber barons lit cigars with $20 bills, they reduced the money supply. They also reduced their own ability to buy bread, clothes, more cigars, comfortable dinner parties, and so on. But what happened to the $20 of bread, clothes, and so on that the robber barons denied themselves by their demonstration of affluence? To the extent these items were already produced, they were made available for others to purchase, where these others were in general poorer. Prices were therefore reduced until the "liberated" items were sold. The lower prices follow from the quantity theory of money; the reduced money supply reduced the price level. In other words, by lighting cigars with $20 bills the robber barons were making $20 worth of goods available to poorer people via a reduced price level resulting from a reduced money supply.[9] Money lost or destroyed by any means makes others richer and those no longer with the money correspondingly poorer.

When people stuff dollar bills into their mattresses and leave them there, others make gains at the money hoarders' expense. Similarly, when foreigners use U.S. dollars for day-to-day purposes rather than use their own local monies, the American public gains by enjoying the products foreigners sold to acquire dollars, paying only with paper which does not return to the United States.

*While **inflation** taxes holders of money, **deflation** rewards holders of money.*

GAINERS AND LOSERS FROM INFLATION

People often talk as if everybody loses from inflation. A common view is that if somehow prices did not increase, wages and salaries would still increase at their old rate, and people's incomes would buy more. This view is clearly false. If prices were not increasing, wages would not increase rapidly. Wages might well go up because of increases in real incomes facilitated by advances in productivity and real GDP, but with stable prices, wage increases are limited to the real growth rate of national income and output.

A more accurate view of inflation suggests that there are many who make substantial gains as well as many who lose. Indeed, the gains of some people are the

[9] When money is given away rather than burnt, the gainers are the recipients rather than all holders of money. Therefore, it is the distribution of gains rather than the size of gains that differs.

losses of others. It is instructive to examine the major categories of gainers and losers. We begin by making an important distinction between anticipated and unanticipated inflation because the effects of inflation depend on the extent to which it was previously expected.

Anticipated versus Unanticipated Inflation

Unanticipated inflation is the difference between expected and realized inflation. This difference can be positive or negative.

At any particular time, people hold a view about what the rate of inflation will be for the next year, or perhaps the next decade. While different people hold different anticipations, we can usefully assume that there is some rate we can call the public's average anticipated rate of inflation.

The realized rate of inflation, that is, the rate that actually occurs, could well be higher or lower than what the public had anticipated. The difference between the realized inflation and the anticipated inflation is **unanticipated inflation,** and this could equally be positive or negative as anticipations turn out to have been too low or too high.

Effects of Anticipated Inflation

In order to see the effects of anticipated inflation, let us suppose that by careful economic policies inflation has been 0% and that suddenly, because of external factors, the public begins to expect inflation of 6%. Let us consider what this would do to wages and interest rates and hence to those earning or paying wages or earning or paying interest.

Wages and Anticipated Inflation. When inflation is anticipated, workers demand higher wages to compensate for higher prices, and if they succeed, they are not hurt by anticipated inflation. However, would we expect workers to succeed in receiving wages that increase at the anticipated rate of inflation?

There should be no real effects on wage earners or employers if realized inflation is as anticipated.

Employers should realize that paying wages that increase by the anticipated rate of inflation does not reduce expected profits if the prices of what they are producing are expected to increase at the same rate. Therefore, we would expect employers to allow wages to increase at the anticipated rate of inflation; they won't be thrilled by this, but competition for labor will force it. Then, if actual inflation is the same as was anticipated, wage earners do not gain or lose in real, buying-power terms. Similarly, employers do not gain or lose in real, buying-power terms. There is, therefore, no real effect on wage earners or employers if actual inflation is equal to anticipated inflation.

Many labor contracts contain a **cost-of-living adjustment (COLA)** clause which automatically results in higher wage rates when prices go up, whether the inflation was anticipated or not. In the presence of COLA clauses, workers do not lose and employers do not gain even from unanticipated inflation.

The nominal or market interest rate is the rate observed in the market. The real interest rate is the nominal interest rate minus anticipated inflation.

Interest Rates and Anticipated Inflation. Anticipated inflation should not affect lenders or borrowers. In order to explain this, let us assume that lenders had earned 4% interest when anticipated inflation was zero. A jump in anticipated inflation to 6% would reduce lending unless interest rates increased to 10%. This is so because with 6% inflation, lenders need $106 after 1 year to buy what $100 would buy today, and only if they received back $110 on each $100 would they earn 4% after adjusting for inflation. The 4% lenders earn after inflation is called the **real interest rate.** If the **nominal** or **market interest rate**—the actual rate that lenders receive—does compensate them for anticipated inflation, then we can write

$$\text{Nominal rate} = \text{real rate} + \text{anticipated inflation} \qquad (14.11)$$

That is, the nominal interest rate observed in the market is the real interest rate plus anticipated inflation. Alternatively, we can think of the real interest rate as the nominal interest rate minus anticipated inflation.

The connection between nominal interest rates and anticipated inflation in Equation 14.11 seems well founded when we consider the interest rate that would be demanded by lenders in the face of anticipated inflation. However, in order to argue that nominal interest rates fully compensate for anticipated inflation, we also must ask if borrowers would be willing to pay the higher interest rates.

What is purchased with borrowed funds, such as houses, new capital equipment, and so on, should produce benefits in the form of increased expected future profits or market values that reflect anticipated inflation. In our example, if borrowers pay a 10% interest rate when houses or machines purchased with borrowed funds are expected to increase in market value by 6% per year or to produce higher future profits worth 6% more per year, the *real* borrowing cost is only 4% (or 10% − 6%). This is the same real borrowing cost we assumed with 0% inflation. Therefore, borrowers should be prepared to pay nominal interest rates that reflect anticipated inflation. With borrowers willing to pay what lenders demand, nominal interest rates should reflect anticipated inflation. Consequently, there are no gains or losses if actual inflation is as anticipated.

Market interest rates compensate for anticipated inflation. Consequently, there should be no gains or losses of lenders versus borrowers from correctly anticipated inflation.

Effects of Unanticipated Inflation

Unanticipated Inflation and Wages versus Profits.   Wage contracts that do not have automatic inflation adjustments allow only for inflation workers anticipate over the period for which the contracts apply. (Wage contracts are formed for a future period of time, for example, for the next year or two. This is why it is *anticipated* inflation for this period and not *actual* inflation up to this period that must be considered in contract negotiations.) If inflation turns out to exceed what had been anticipated, the buying power of wages will be smaller than expected. The loss for workers is a gain for the owners of firms, who find themselves selling their products for more than expected while paying only contracted wages. Therefore, *ceteris paribus*, unanticipated inflation shifts real buying power from workers to firms; that is, it increases profits at the expense of wage earners.

Unanticipated disinflation, which means inflation that is lower than expected, causes the reverse shift of buying power, namely, from owners of firms to workers. This occurs because wages which were negotiated to compensate for anticipated inflation turn out to have been overly generous given what subsequently happened to prices while these wages were being paid. According to economists who believe people's expectations are "rational," unanticipated disinflation is as likely as unanticipated inflation. As we shall see in the next chapter, by definition, **rational expectations** are those which consider all the relevant facts. People who consider all relevant facts are unlikely to consistently overestimate or to consistently underestimate inflation. This is not to say that they make no mistakes.

Unanticipated infla-tion, where inflation is higher than expected, shifts buying power from those earning wages to those earning profits. Unanticipated disinflation, where inflation is lower than expected, causes the reverse shift in buying power.

Rather, it says that the errors in forecasts by rational people are random, with an average forecasting error of zero.

Unanticipated Inflation and Lenders versus Borrowers.   When inflation is faster than anticipated, interest rates undercompensate lenders for the actual increase in prices that occurs. This happens because, as seen from Equation 14.11, only anticipated inflation is reflected in interest rates received by lenders and paid by borrowers. Consequently, unanticipated inflation makes lenders worse off than they expected and makes borrowers better off than they expected. The lenders lose because what they receive back buys fewer goods and services than they expected. The borrowers gain because they find themselves owning assets or earning profits with a larger dollar value than they had expected; prices and therefore asset values and profits end up higher than they had thought. We find that unanticipated inflation rewards borrowers at the expense of lenders.

Unanticipated inflation *benefits debtors and penalizes creditors, while unanticipated* disinflation *benefits creditors and penalizes debtors*

Since borrowers are **debtors** and lenders are **creditors,** the conclusion is sometimes alternatively stated that unanticipated inflation rewards debtors and penalizes creditors (see Example 14.4). Similarly, unanticipated disinflation, that is, inflation that is smaller than expected and which means interest rates overcompensate lenders, rewards creditors and penalizes debtors.

The biggest debtor in most countries is the government, which owes the national debt—the outstanding value of government borrowing from the public. It is therefore the government that gains most from inflation being faster than anticipated. The government gains because inflation reduces the real value of the debt. If the government gains, so do taxpayers taken as a whole. This is so because it is they who, in general, have to pay taxes to cover interest on outstanding debt. Therefore, we reach the conclusion that unanticipated inflation that hurts the holders of government debt, that is, government bondholders, helps taxpayers. This fits the general conclusion reached above in that bondholders are creditors and taxpayers are, indirectly, debtors. That is, we again find unanticipated inflation redistributing wealth from creditors to debtors.

Unanticipated inflation hurts holders of government bonds and helps taxpayers. It also hurts holders of corporate bonds and helps shareholders, hurts issuers of mortgages and helps homeowners, and more generally redistributes wealth from creditors to debtors.

After the government, the next most important group of debtors is composed of corporations. Corporations are debtors to the extent that they have sold bonds or borrowed from banks. When corporations gain from unanticipated inflation, the gains are really those of the shareholders, who are the owners of corporations. Therefore, with corporate debt, the redistribution is between shareholders and bondholders, with unanticipated inflation favoring shareholders at the expense of bondholders and banks.

It isn't only the big institutions, the government and corporations, which gain when inflation is faster than expected. Any debtor gains, including the many homeowners who have incurred mortgages. During the term of mortgages while interest rates are fixed, unanticipated inflation makes the value of houses increase more than was expected but leaves mortgage payments unchanged. Homeowners therefore gain from unanticipated inflation. The sizes of homeowners' gains are larger the longer the period of mortgage over which interest rates are fixed. It is only with mortgages on which interest rates are continuously revised—called **flexible-** or **adjustable-rate mortgages**—that homeowners do not gain. Of course, what homeowners gain, the providers of the mortgage funds lose, because the interest they receive does not compensate for the declining buying power of the amount advanced. The creditors in the case of mortgages include banks, savings and loan associations, pension funds, and insurance companies.

Example 14.4

INFLATION AND THE BALANCE SHEET

Inflation redistributes income and wealth. The following excerpt explains how this is related to the extent to which nominal interest rates reflect inflation.

Inflation has many effects, but most discussed are its effects on the distribution of income and wealth. If inflation were fully and correctly anticipated, nominal interest rates on fixed claim assets would adjust to compensate for the declining purchasing power of the principal. Generally, however, interest rates have not completely compensated for inflation. As a result, periods of inflation have been accompanied by arbitrary transfers of real net worth from net monetary creditors to net monetary debtors when inflation is accelerating, or vice versa when it is decelerating.

The key factors in determining whether economic units will benefit from, or be harmed by, inflation are (1) whether the inflation is anticipated and (2) whether the economic units are net monetary creditors. Net monetary creditors are harmed by unanticipated inflation because the purchasing power of their monetary assets declines more than the real value of their monetary liabilities. Similarly, net monetary debtors benefit from unanticipated inflation.

These effects take place without any action on the part of the economic unit and represent a passive redistribution of wealth.

Even if inflation is anticipated and reflected in nominal interest rates, added uncertainty about future prices can affect economic decisions. As a result, economic units will attempt to redistribute their assets for protection from inflation.

Source: Keith Carlson, "The U.S. Balance Sheet: What Is It and What Does It Tell Us?" **Review,** Federal Reserve Bank of St. Louis, September-October 1991, p. 15.

Inflation Anticipations, Fixed Incomes, and Uncertainty

The people most frequently identified in popular discussions as losing from inflation are those on **fixed incomes,** such as pensioners who depend on private savings and Social Security. It should be clear from what we have said that to the extent that anticipated inflation is compensated for in interest rates on retirement savings, it is only unanticipated inflation which reduces pensioners' real incomes. Furthermore, even unanticipated inflation should not lower the buying power of Social Security receipts, if these are **indexed** to inflation. (Inflation indexing means that Social Security checks are increased in line with increases in the price level.) We therefore find that it is only unanticipated inflation that is likely to hurt those on fixed incomes, and their losses are likely to be made primarily on interest income on private savings, not on Social Security.

There is, however, a sense in which we are all hurt by inflation. This is so because *uncertainty* about the rate of inflation can dampen confidence and thereby reduce investment and the rate of economic growth. Uncertainty results from not knowing whether inflation will be faster or slower than is currently expected. Some of the cost of uncertainty about inflation comes in the form of higher unemployment, which we turn to next.

ECONOMICS DOESN'T EXIST IN A VACUUM

Mention the word **inflation** to most people and they are likely to think about the matter we have dealt with in this book, namely, rising prices. However, if the person hearing the word is a physicist, it may bring something different to mind. To a physicist, inflation is what occurs when, for example, air is blown into a balloon or an automobile tire. More generally, in physics, **inflation** refers to the phenomenon involving the expansion of volume, such as the volume of a contained gas. Surprisingly perhaps, while the physicist and economist have different phenomena in mind when considering inflation, the principles behind the phenomena are similar.

Contained gas atoms or molecules move in all directions at a variety of velocities. Let us consider a container in which there are **N** atoms or molecules each with mass of **m**, so their total mass is **M** = **N** · **m**. Let us assume that the average velocity of the atoms or molecules is $\bar{\mathbf{v}}$ and that in collisions of atoms or molecules with themselves or the walls of a container, **momentum** and **energy** are conserved. Using these terms and assumptions, the **kinetic theory of gases**[10] can be stated as

$$M \cdot \tfrac{1}{3} \, \bar{v}^2 = P \cdot Q \qquad (14.12)$$

---

[10] The derivation of the kinetic theory can be found in most introductory physics textbooks. See, for example, Joseph F. Mulligan, **Introductory College Physics** (New York: McGraw-Hill, 1985), pp. 228–231. For purposes of comparison of the kinetic theory and the quantity theory, we use **M** instead of **N** · **m** in the kinetic theory. We also use **P** for "volume" and **Q** for "pressure," whereas in physics books volume is usually written as **V** and pressure as **P**. Of course, these changes are just matters of notation and are made so the connection between the two theories is as clear as possible.

In Equation 14.12, M and $\bar{v}$ are as we have just defined them, namely, the total mass of atoms or molecules and average velocity. In addition, P is the volume of the container and Q is the pressure on the container's surface. Alternatively, if we write $\bar{V} = \frac{1}{3}\bar{v}^2$, then we can write the kinetic theory of gases as

$$M \cdot \bar{V} = P \cdot Q \qquad (14.13)$$

Let us compare the implications of Equation 14.13 with those of the quantity theory of money, which from Equation 14.8 also can be written:

$$M \cdot \bar{V} = P \cdot Q \qquad (14.8)$$

As we have explained, the variable $M = N \cdot m$ in Equation 14.13 is the number of atoms or molecules N moving around in a container multiplied by their individual mass m. We can think of N as being parallel to the number of checks or bills moving around an economy and m as their average face value so that $M = N \cdot m$ is parallel to the money supply circulating in an economy. That is, we can draw a parallel between $M = N \cdot m$ in Equation 14.13—the aggregate mass of atoms or molecules moving within a container of gas— and M in Equation 14.8—the aggregate money supply moving within an economy.

Let us consider a container such as a balloon that expands such that the pressure Q on its surface is constant. In such a case the volume P inflates when there is an increase in the variables on the left-hand-side of Equation 14.13. Specifically, with Q constant, by increasing $M = N \cdot m$, we increase P in the same proportion as M. This is similar to what happens when we increase the money supply M in the quantity theory of money, holding real GDP constant. In particular, the price level P inflates in the same proportion as M.

The parallel between the effect of $N \cdot m$ on P in the kinetic theory of gases and of M on P in the quantity theory of money should come as little surprise to those knowing both theories. As we have seen in this chapter, "pumping" more money into circulation with the same volume of goods and the same velocity of circulation causes inflation in proportion to the money supply. Similarly, pumping more atoms or molecules of gas into a container with the same surface pressure and velocity of atoms or molecules causes inflation in proportion to the supply of atoms or molecules. This occurs because if the surface pressure is constant and velocity is constant, the number of atoms or molecules striking a given surface area in a given time also must be constant, and this requires expanding the volume of the container in proportion to the number of atoms or molecules. (Pressure is constant if collisions per unit area and time are constant and the velocity and mass of atoms or molecules are also constant.)

The effect of changing the velocity of gas atoms or molecules on the volume of a contained gas is similar, although not precisely the same, to the effect of changing the velocity of circulation of money on prices. In particular, increasing the square of the velocity of gas atoms or molecules $\bar{v}^2$ with their total mass and pressure constant increases the volume of the gas proportionately; in Equation 14.12, if $M = N \cdot m$ and Q are constant, P increases in proportion to $\bar{v}^2$. Similarly, increasing the velocity of circulation of money $\bar{V}$ in Equation 14.8 with money supply M and real output Q constant increases the price level. Both the **ceteris paribus** effects $\bar{v}^2$ on P in Equation 14.12 and of $\bar{V}$ on P in Equation 14.8 are proportional effects.

The parallels between the kinetic theory of gases and the quantity theory of money follow because atoms and molecules impact when they collide with a container's surface, while money "impacts" when offered in exchange for goods and services. Atoms and molecules of gas charging around a container and applying pressure when brought into contact with its surface behave very much like money moving around an economy and applying pressure when brought into contact with the economy's output.

We know that in a gas container such as a balloon, reducing pressure in one area increases the pressure somewhere else. The same is true in an economy. In particular, holding some prices down by, for example, price controls increases inflationary pressures on uncontrolled products. This occurs because money saved on controlled products is freed up for buying the uncontrolled products.

Turning from the physics of inflation to other dimensions of the subject, we can note that inflation has been considered as a weapon for war and as such is of interest to political scientists and historians. For example, both sides of the conflict in World War II considered dropping vast quantities of superb-quality counterfeit notes on the enemy. Forged Bank of England notes found in Germany after the war were of such high quality they would have been virtually impossible to distinguish from genuine money. The idea was to cause economic havoc and to deny the legitimate money-making authorities the power to use the inflation tax. Interestingly, despite going to the trouble of forging the monies, the counterfeit notes were not deployed by dropping them **en masse** from aircraft. Some historians have argued that this was not attempted because the inflation weapon is so powerful that neither side was willing to risk retaliation from the other.

While fear of retaliation has discouraged countries from using inflation as a weapon of war, inflation has nevertheless frequently resulted from war. This is so because wars are extremely expensive and difficult to finance via explicit taxes. Governments have therefore resorted to "printing" money, that is, using the inflation tax. The need to print money rather than use taxes on incomes, profits, or sales is particularly strong in the aftermath of war when governments face huge expenditures shifting their economies from military to civilian activities, finding jobs for returning soldiers, restructuring factories, and so on. As well as requirements for vast amounts of funds after war, the tax-collection infrastructure may have been disrupted by war. Resort to the printing press is therefore common at such times, as in Europe after World War I.

Atoms and molecules of gas charging around a container and applying pressure when brought into contact with its surface behave very much like money moving around an economy and applying pressure when brought into contact with the economy's output.

Inflation has been often the cause of civil disorder. Historians trace the rise of Nazism in Germany in the 1920s and 1930s in part to the turmoil caused by the hyperinflation which ravaged the country. Recently, price increases of food in Poland in the mid-1980s and of staples in Brazil in the late-1980s led to street riots. Political scientists study both the overt consequences of very rapid inflation and the more subtle consequences of moderate inflation that show up in opinion polls. For example, they have shown that increased uncertainty about inflation typically reduces political support for the U.S. president.

Countries that have experienced hyperinflation, such as interwar Germany and Hungary, appear to continue functioning more or less normally until a level of inflation is reached where money ceases to be used; people switch to using barter or commodity mediums of exchange such as brandy and cigarettes. At the point of abandoning money, the economy grinds to a virtual standstill. The process is not unlike the **denaturing** of living cells that occurs at a high temperature. At low and moderate temperatures, cells continue to function more or less normally, with little more than minor discomfort and some slowing of processes. However, there comes a point where the cell denatures, shuts down completely, and cannot be revived. This process is most familiar from what happens to an egg when the temperature reaches approximately 50°C; the egg cell changes form, and no subsequent cooling can make the egg return to its "precooked" state. While there are a few examples of reversal of hyperinflation, usually the problem becomes so severe that it is necessary to scrap the old money and start again.

As well as being of interest to historians, political scientists, and physicists, inflation is studied by psychologists, cosmologists, and other researchers. Psychologists are concerned with the formation of inflationary anticipations, which, as we have shown, are important for the consequences of inflation. They are interested in the way inflationary anticipations are formed—whether expectations are rational, unbiased, and so on—and people's attitudes toward uncertainty about inflation. Cosmologists have a theory of expansion of the universe, the **new inflationary theory of the universe,** which describes transition from extremely dense matter to the matter currently occupying the universe. Economists have a parallel concern, the theory of the evolution of money. Unfortunately, the theory of the evolution of money is no more easily resolved from the left-over evidence than the theory of expansion of the universe.

SUMMARY

1. Inflation is the rate at which prices in general are increasing.

2. The consumer price index (CPI) measures prices in general from the market basket bought by a typical or representative urban household. This basket is determined by surveys of consumers and is done for a base year.

3. The GDP (implicit) deflator measures prices in general by including items according to their importance in the current gross domestic product. The GDP deflator is derived by taking the ratio of the gross domestic product valued at current prices—the nominal GDP— to the gross domestic product valued at earlier prices—the real GDP.

4. The CPI tends to overstate inflation because it does not allow for substitutions consumers make toward products that have become relatively cheaper than when the basket was determined. Therefore, the CPI attaches too much weight to items which have increased relatively rapidly in price and too little weight to items which have increased relatively slowly in price.

5. The GDP deflator tends to understate inflation.

6. The quantity theory of money attributes inflation to too much money chasing too few goods.

7.* The quantity theory of money can be recast as a theory of the demand for money. In this form, it relates the real buying power people want to hold as money to the real level of their purchases.

8.* The quantity theory is a demand-pull explanation of inflation. Cost-push inflation, which is inflation due to increases in wages, can be sustained only if it is accommodated by monetary authorities.

9. Hyperinflation can occur only from printing money and is likely to be observed when other means of collecting taxes have become infeasible. This is so because inflation is a hidden tax, enabling those with the power to "print" money to enjoy goods and services at the expense of others.

10. Anticipated inflation is built into interest rates and wages. It therefore causes little redistribution of buying power.

11. Unanticipated inflation favors debtors at the expense of creditors and employers at the expense of workers.

12. The major debtor gaining from unanticipated inflation is the government. Other debtors who gain from unanticipated inflation include corporations with debt and homeowners who have fixed-interest mortgages.

13. People on fixed incomes are not hurt by inflation that was anticipated at the time they provided their fixed incomes. When Social Security is indexed to the price level, recipients are not generally hurt, even by unanticipated inflation.

QUESTIONS AND PROBLEMS

1. What substitutions have consumers made since 1984 that would bias the CPI based on a typical 1984 market basket toward overstating inflation?

2. Do you think that producer prices influence the CPI, or do you think the direction of influence is the reverse, with consumers' demands working back to influence prices of wholesale commodities?

3. How would a Monetarist think about the effect of a government program which stimulates the economy by employing people to dig up boxes of money?

4. Why, during wartime, have counterfeit monies been manufactured to drop on an enemy?

5. Why should unanticipated inflation over a long time period average zero?

6. What type of information would enter into inflation forecasts?

7. What happens to homeowners when there is an unanticipated disinflation, that is, inflation that was slower than expected?

8. What happens to mortgage issuers when there is unanticipated disinflation?

9. Why do flexible interest rates overcome the redistribution otherwise resulting from unanticipated inflation?

10. Assuming that

   Rate of growth of money supply $= 6\%$

   Rate of growth of real GDP $= 4\%$

   Anticipated inflation $= 3\%$

   Real interest rate $= 2\%$

   a. What is the rate of inflation implied by the quantity theory of money?

   b. What would be the nominal interest rate?

   c. If actual inflation turned out to be 4%, would creditors or debtors gain?

   d. How might an anticipated change in velocity of circulation of money explain a higher anticipated rate of inflation than is implied by the quantity theory?

. . . .
. . . .
. . . .
. . . .
. . . .
. . . . . . Unemployment
. . . .
. . . .

It's not what you pay a man, but what he costs you that counts.

Will Rogers

Key Concepts

Measuring unemployment; different causes of unemployment; the meaning of full employment; the aggregate supply of and the demand for labor; unemployment and wage inflexibility; inflation versus unemployment; the natural rate of unemployment

Each month, government officials, business analysts, and others await the release of the unemployment statistics, hoping to obtain a picture of the general direction of the economy. Behind the cold, harsh facts of the unemployment figures lies the hardships and dejection of those unable to find work. This chapter examines a number of aspects of unemployment, including the way it is measured, what is meant by full employment, whether full employment is necessarily accompanied by inflation, and why full employment rarely prevails. We shall see that, to a large extent, unemployment is caused by inflexibility in the wage rate and that, contrary to common opinion, there is no permanent solution to unemployment from adopting inflationary macroeconomic policies.

MEASURING AND CATEGORIZING UNEMPLOYMENT

Measuring Unemployment

Unemployment is not as clear-cut a concept as would appear from the confident way the term is used in everyday language. While many people know that it is the percentage of the work force without employment, what is not so well known is what exactly constitutes the work force and who in particular is counted as being unemployed. In the United States, the size of the work force and the number who are considered unemployed are determined via monthly household surveys by the U.S. Bureau of the Census of the Department of Labor. In these surveys and similar ones in other countries, the relevant magnitudes are determined as follows:

1. The number of people counted as **full-time unemployed** is the number who are not working full time during the week prior to the survey and who were actively looking for full-time work.

2. The number of people in the **work force** is the number who were fully employed during the week prior to the survey plus the number who were not working but were actively looking for full-time work.

The monthly surveys are made representative of regional, racial, and other characteristics of the population so that although only a minute proportion of households is included each month, the estimates are reasonably accurate. Of course, the surveyors must be armed with definitions of "actively looking for employment" and "full time", and they must determine whether the job search was indeed active and employment was full time by asking further questions.

The data from the surveys are used to calculate the full-time unemployment rate as the ratio of the number unemployed vis-à-vis the size of the work force. This is put on a percentage basis by multiplication by 100. Symbolically,

$$\text{Unemployment rate} = \frac{U}{E+U} \times 100 \qquad (15.1)$$

where

U = number without full-time employment but actively looking for full-time work

E = number employed full time

The denominator in Equation 15.1, $E+U$, is the work force, which consists of those working and those looking for work.

In the United States, in addition to calculating the full-time unemployment rate for the entire nation, the data are analyzed to compute rates of unemployment for different geographic locations, for blacks versus whites, for males versus females, and for heads of families versus others. As with the national income and product account statistics, further adjustments are made for the season, with these adjustments based on an examination of average month-to-month variations in unemployment over a number of earlier years.

> The full-time unemployment rate is the number of people without full-time work and actively seeking work divided by the work force. The work force consists of those *with* full-time work plus those *seeking* full-time work.

Clearly, there are some difficulties with using the unemployment statistics as a precise measure of the unemployment problem. For example, people laid off without any planned recall are not considered unemployed if they are waiting in hope of being taken back in their old job; they are not counted as unemployed because they are not actively looking for work. In a similar way, people who have been unemployed so long that they have given up looking are not counted as being unemployed, although they are included separately in a **discouraged worker** category. There are also difficulties introduced by part-time work that is being done because full-time jobs are not available; part-time workers are not counted in the full-time unemployment statistics, although statistics on part-time work are separately reported.

Structural and Frictional Unemployment

Even at the best of times, unemployment is not zero. This occurs because in a dynamic economy, several forces are at work, including the following.

Changing Demands.   People are constantly changing buying patterns. Consider, for example, how fashions change in footwear, from Oxfords to loafers to runners to lightweight walkers, the different styles generally being supplied by different companies. The wearing of hats rises and declines, with different styles from different suppliers having their day and then vanishing, along with their producers. Patterns of entertainment shift, from live theater to movies to home videos, each requiring different skills to provide. Preferences change in the home, with different wall coverings, one year paper, then paint, then paper again, and with different floors, from wood to linoleum to carpet to tile. In the face of these constantly changing buying patterns, workers are displaced in the companies facing declining demands. At the same time, new jobs are offered in the companies enjoying growing demand. However, even if displaced workers have the requisite skills, it takes time to locate new openings. The new opportunities may be in different cities, and unemployed workers may want to look locally before digging up roots. While still looking, the displaced workers are counted as unemployed.

Changing Technologies.   While new technologies generally result in new jobs in producing the new products and capital equipment, they also make old skills obsolete. For example, the development of microcomputers for word processing has created new jobs in hardware production, software development, manual preparation, and computer literacy training. The skills needed in the new, expanding roles are different from those needed in the typewriter industry, which was largely replaced by microprocessors, just as the skills needed for making typewriters were different from those needed for making the fountain pens that typewriters replaced. Old-fashioned watch and clock makers and repairers faced rapidly shrinking demands for their skillful hands as accurate electric and then quartz clocks and watches created new jobs for technologists and microelectronic engineers. In the face of these changing technologies, there may be many openings without the skilled workers to fill them, while at the same time there are many who are unemployed because their old skills are no longer in demand.[1]

---

[1] Example 15.1 explains that the 24-member government-sponsored economic research organization, the Organization for Economic Cooperation and Development, has strongly advocated job retraining to deal with such unemployment that occurs alongside shortages of skilled workers.

Example 15.1

TRAINING TO AVOID STRUCTURAL UNEMPLOYMENT

*The aggregate unemployment statistics hide pockets of shortages of labor with special skills. The following article from **The Wall Street Journal** shows how unemployment would be reduced from job-training programs that expand the work force in particular areas rather than by stimulating demand.*

France officially has 2.3 million people, equal to 9.3% of the work force, seeking jobs. French employers, meanwhile, say they're having more trouble finding enough people to hire than at any time since 1979. West German employers, despite an unemployment rate of about 6% . . . have absorbed hundreds of thousands of East German refugees this year, and still say they're short of skilled help. . . .

Paradoxes like these have led the Organization for Economic Cooperation and Development to shift the emphasis on its advice to its 24 industrialized members on how to cut unemployment. The OECD for the past decade has urged policies that stimulated macroeconomic growth, coupled with the removal of regulations or other internal impediments to creating jobs, all softened by generous unemployment benefits to tide people over until the jobs were created.

Now, though, the government-sponsored research body is suggesting that governments worry more about ensuring a continuing supply of future workers.

Governments currently spend about 2% of their gross national product on job programs, the OECD says, with two-thirds of the money going to benefit payments, and one-third to training. The OECD's annual Employment Outlook suggests that governments would do better shifting direct payments to programs to train workers or expand the work force. More women should be tempted back into the workplace by offering better child care. Unemployment payments should be increasingly tied to training programs. The efficiency of public and private job-search and job-matching agencies should be increased. . . .

Both anecdotal and statistical evidence suggests that, particularly in Europe, the people who've been out of work the longest either don't have the skills employers are looking for; or won't trade unemployment benefits for low-paying manual jobs; or won't move to where the jobs are, even within their own countries. This lack of labor mobility—mobility that is one of the great strengths of the U.S.—isn't expected to improve much in Europe even after the 1992 program removes most barriers to the movement of people across European borders.

Meanwhile, necessary jobs are being filled from outside, even as national unemployment rolls remain long. Paris's street cleaners are nearly all immigrants. West Germany's vast, usually family-owned machine tool industry desperately seeks tool-and-die makers, thin on the ground in Duesseldorf, but plentiful in Dresden and elsewhere in East Germany. The long-term unemployed in Europe don't all have to become street sweepers, but thousands could be retrained as technical workers. Unemployed Germans can't all set dies, but they could be drawn back into the work force through subsidized on-the-job training programs, the OECD says.

Source: Philip Revzi, "Fearing Wage Inflation, OECD Urges Member Nations to Expand Work Force," **The Wall Street Journal,** July 13, 1990, p. A5. Reprinted by permission of The Wall Street Journal, © 1990 Dow Jones & Company, Inc. All Rights Reserved Worldwide.

Changing Patterns of International Trade.   Jobs are created and lost by changing patterns of international trade. For example, as Japan has improved automobile design, quality, and performance and attracted a growing share of the U.S. market, U.S. workers have been displaced. At the same time, Japanese success in automobiles and other products has meant rising incomes and Japanese demand for American products, such as beef, fruit, wide-bodied jet aircraft, fast food, movies, and television shows. Even if the number of jobs created by international trade were the same as the number lost, unemployment would temporarily rise; without training automobile workers cannot move to new opportunities demanding different skills. With the signing of the North American Free Trade Agreement in 1992, which removes or reduces trade barriers on a substantial part of cross-border U.S., Canadian, and Mexican trade, effects on jobs could be substantial. An effort was made to smooth the transition by reducing tariffs gradually over 15 years. This lengthy phase-in, like that accompanying the U.S.–Canadian Free Trade Agreement of 1989, was motivated by the recognition that it takes time for employment to adjust following a shift in the pattern of international trade. However, with the difficulty of retraining older workers and the regional shifts in opportunities that occur, it can take a generation before the transition has fully occurred; old workers must retire and new workers must choose areas where job opportunities expand.

Job Shifting.   In order to move ahead professionally, it is not uncommon to have to change jobs. It is also not uncommon for people to leave one job for another to try something new. Frequently, the search for better job opportunities requires people to leave their old jobs; employers are often unwilling to let employees travel on company time for job interviews, especially when it is the employee's choice to leave. In the time between leaving an old job and locating a new one, a person is counted as being unemployed.

New Entrants to the Work Force.   Not every high school or college graduate finds a job before graduation, and therefore, the unemployment statistics include graduates who are looking for their first job.[2] Those actively looking for employment also include women returning to the labor market after an absence working at home raising their families.

Changing technologies, changing trade patterns, and changing demands are often referred to as causes of **structural unemployment;** they contribute to unemployment as they change the industrial structure of an economy. Job shifting and new entrants to the work force are causes of **frictional unemployment;** both contribute to unemployment because it takes time for people to move from one endeavor to another.

Some countries handle their structural and frictional unemployment better than others. For example, Figure 15.1 shows that even at the best of times, unemployment rates in the United States and Great Britain are much higher than in Japan. By retraining and career planning, Japanese firms manage to keep people working in the face of structural change. Furthermore, frictional unemployment is low in Japan because workers do not shift jobs as frequently as in other countries and because job placement of students generally occurs well before graduation.

Cyclical Unemployment

Figure 15.1 shows that unemployment rates in the United States and Great Britain have varied substantially over time. The variability in unemployment comes through even more clearly in the century-long plot of the U.S. unemployment rate in Figure 15.2. The pace of structural change does not vary sufficiently over time

Structural unemployment is caused by changing demands for different products, changing patterns of international trade, and changing technologies of production. *Frictional* unemployment is caused by people shifting between jobs and new workers joining the work force.

Full employment occurs when the number of job *vacancies* equals the number of people *looking* for work.

[2] To some extent, unemployment of new entrants to the work force is a seasonal phenomenon. As such, it is taken care of in the seasonally adjusted unemployment statistics.

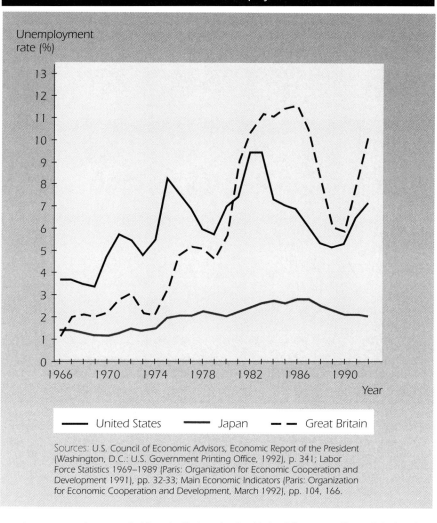

FIGURE 15.1   Countries differ substantially in average unemployment rates and in the variations in unemployment over time.

Sources: U.S. Council of Economic Advisors, *Economic Report of the President* (Washington, D.C.: U.S. Government Printing Office, 1992), p. 341; *Labor Force Statistics 1969–1989* (Paris: Organization for Economic Cooperation and Development 1991), pp. 32-33; *Main Economic Indicators* (Paris: Organization for Economic Cooperation and Development, March 1992), pp. 104, 166.

Even when unemployment is historically low in the United States or Great Britain, the unemployment rate is higher than in Japan. Japan manages to deal with structural change without much unemployment, and frictional unemployment is low in Japan because workers change jobs relatively infrequently.

to explain the observed ups and downs in the proportion of people without jobs. Similarly, shifting between jobs and new entrants into the work force, the causes of frictional unemployment, cannot explain such large volatility. Rather, what the data on unemployment suggest is a cyclical element to unemployment. Indeed, it has been suggested that there are different cycles of different lengths overlying the pattern of unemployment. Specifically, it has been argued that there may be cycles of a few years duration, of 8 to 10 years duration, and of about 50 years, all simultaneously driving the unemployment rate over time. Unfortunately, there is no consensus on the length of the unemployment cycle, or cycles, or on the theory behind cycles.

FIGURE 15.2   The path of unemployment rates over a long period of time suggests a cyclical component.

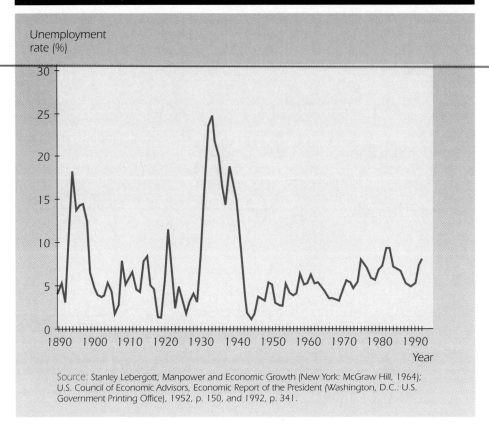

Source: Stanley Lebergott, Manpower and Economic Growth (New York: McGraw Hill, 1964); U.S. Council of Economic Advisors, Economic Report of the President (Washington, D.C.: U.S. Government Printing Office), 1952, p. 150, and 1992, p. 341.

The U.S. unemployment rate for the last century shows both small and large variations. In particular, we see the high unemployment in the depression of the mid-1890s and in the Great Depression of 1929–1933, as well as smaller variations at other times. It has been suggested that there are cycles of different lengths which are occurring simultaneously, one on top of the other. However, there is not sufficient regularity in the cyclical pattern of unemployment for consensus on the nature of the cycle or of its cause.

Full Employment

Since World War II, governments have striven for full employment, although different governments have held different views on how full employment should be defined. Because people remain without jobs even at the best of times, it is clearly inappropriate to define **full employment** as everybody who wants a job having one. A more useful and frequently adopted definition is where there are as many people looking for work as there are job openings. Specifically, full employment can be defined as the situation where there are as many people out of work and actively looking for employment as there are openings. With this particular definition of full employment, everybody could, in principle, have a job. The problem is aligning those who are looking for work with the appropriate vacancies.

The definition of full employment in terms of equality of the number looking for work and the number of unfilled positions is equivalent to defining full employment in terms of equality of the quantity of labor supplied and demanded. Specifically, if we think of the quantity of labor supplied as those people already working plus those looking for work and of the quantity of labor demanded as those people already working plus the number of job vacancies, then the quantity supplied equals the quantity demanded if the number looking for jobs equals the number of vacancies; the quantity of labor supplied and demanded both contain the number already working, and therefore, equality depends only on the number looking for jobs versus the number of vacancies. It follows that unemployment in excess of full employment occurs when the quantity of labor supplied exceeds the quantity of labor demanded. But why should such a disequilibrium between supply and demand occur? As we shall show below, the answer has to do with the inflexibility of wages.

> *Full employment occurs when the quantity of labor supplied equals the quantity of labor demanded. Unemployment in excess of full employment occurs when the quantity of labor supplied exceeds the quantity of labor demanded.*

UNEMPLOYMENT AND THE LABOR MARKET

When we discussed supply and demand in Chapter 6, we distinguished between equilibrium prices, which are the prices at which quantity supplied equals quantity demanded, and market prices, which are the prices we actually observe. However, we explained that there are forces moving market prices toward equilibrium prices, so the practice of comparing equilibria, called comparative statics, gives useful predictions.

As we have just explained, unemployment occurs when there is an excess of the quantity of labor supplied over the quantity demanded. It follows that if the forces of supply and demand invoked in Chapter 6 are free to work speedily in labor markets, unemployment above the full-employment level is merely fleeting. That is, if the price of labor, the wage, moves quickly toward the equilibrium level, we will not observe unemployment rates above full employment, other than during the brief moments that wages are changing. However, the reality is that unemployment persists. This suggests that wages do not adjust quickly to equilibrium levels. Let us explain the role of slow wage adjustments within the framework of the labor market developed in Chapter 10.

> *Unemployment is caused by wages adjusting too slowly for the labor market to remain in equilibrium.*

The Aggregate Demand for Labor

In Chapter 10 we explained that the demand for labor is derived from the demand for the final goods and services labor produces. This is true whether we are considering the demand for labor by an individual industry, which was the focus of attention in Chapter 10, or the demand for labor in the economy as a whole.

The demand for labor in the economy as a whole is the **aggregate demand for labor.** As with the demand for labor by an individual industry, the quantity of labor demanded is such that for the last worker, the value of the marginal product *VMP* equals the wage; that is,

$$VMP = wage \qquad (15.2)$$

If we assume all firms sell in perfectly competitive markets so that product prices are given, the value of the marginal product of labor is the marginal physical product *MPP* times the price of output; that is, $VMP = MPP \times price$. In the case of the aggregate demand for labor, *MPP* refers to the marginal physical product of labor in general, and the *price* refers to the price level in the economy. With these interpretations of *MPP* and *price* we can, as in Chapter 10, say that the aggregate quantity of labor demanded is that at which

$$MPP \times price = wage \tag{15.3}$$

The *MPP* of labor declines as more labor is employed. This is the consequence of the law of diminishing marginal product, which applies to labor in the economy as a whole just as it does to any particular category of labor. This means that as in the case of the demand for labor in an individual industry, the aggregate demand for labor slopes downward with respect to wages. That is, the lower the wage, the greater is the quantity of labor demanded; the lower the wage, the more workers can be employed before the *VMP* of the last worker equals the wage. Similarly, as with an individual industry, the demand curve for labor shifts upward with increases in the *MPP* of labor and the price of output and in proportion to the increases in the *MPP* and the price of output.

> The *aggregate* demand curve for labor shows the quantity of labor demanded in an *economy* at different possible wages.

Figure 15.3 shows downward-sloping aggregate demand curves for labor, where, as we have stated, the downward slope is the result of the law of diminishing marginal product. The figure also shows what happens to the labor demand curve after an increase in the price level. Curve D_1 is the demand curve for labor before an increase in the price level, while curve D_2 is the demand curve after the price level has increased. As in the case of labor demand curves for individual industries, D_2 is above D_1 in proportion to the extent the price level has increased. For example, if the price level increases 25%, demand curve D_2 is 25% higher than curve D_1 at every quantity of labor employed. Similarly, if the price level were to decrease, the demand curve for labor would shift downward in proportion to the decline in prices.

> The aggregate demand curve for labor is downward-sloping vis-à-vis the wage and shifts up and down in proportion to changes in the price level of output.

The Aggregate Supply of Labor

In Chapter 10 we saw that the supply of labor to an individual industry depends on the opportunity cost of labor in terms of what each successive worker could have earned in their next best alternative employment opportunity. The aggregate supply of labor also depends on the opportunity cost, but not in terms of alternative *employment* opportunities. This is so because when considering the aggregate supply of labor, there is no alternative employment opportunity; if we are considering the *total* number of people willing to work in some job or other, then, by definition, the others are not working. In the case of the aggregate supply of labor, the opportunity cost of working is what is given up by *not* working. The opportunity cost might therefore involve the chance to otherwise spend more time being educated, taking care of the family or house, going skiing or hiking, and so on.

For a given price level, that is, for a given cost of what workers buy, the higher the wage, the more people will find the benefit of working to exceed their opportunity cost. For example, at higher wages more women will enter the work force, more older people will decide to delay retirement, more students will decide not

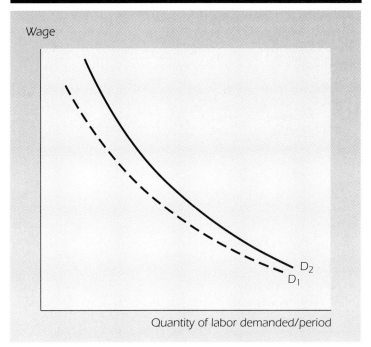

FIGURE 15.3   The aggregate demand curve for labor is downward-sloping with respect to wages and shifts up and down in proportion to the price level.

The quantity of labor demanded is such that for the last worker employed, the value of the marginal product of that worker equals the wage paid. With **VMP = MPP** × **price,** and with **MPP** diminishing as more labor is employed as a result of the law of diminishing marginal product, the demand curve for labor slopes downward. That is, the lower the wage, the greater is the quantity of labor demanded. This is so because the lower the wage, the more workers can be employed before the last worker's **VMP** equals that wage. The height of the demand curve for labor depends on the price level because the quantity of labor demanded is such that the wage rate equals the **VMP** of the last worker hired and the **VMP** increases with the price level. That is, **D**₂ is above **D**₁ in proportion to the increase in the price level.

to attend school or college, more members of the "leisure set" will decide work is not as terrible as was previously considered, and so on. In addition, at higher wages those already working might opt to work more hours. However, it is also possible that at very high wages some people will opt for more leisure and therefore work fewer hours. This can occur when wages and incomes are so high that working for more income to buy yet more goods and services is not as desirable as enjoying more leisure. Nevertheless, despite this possibility, it is usually assumed that the quantity of labor supplied increases with the wage, as shown in Figure 15.4.

The two upward-sloping labor supply curves in Figure 15.4 are drawn for different price levels. Curve S_1 is the supply curve before prices increase, and curve S_2

Each individual balances the benefit of working with the opportunity cost of forgone leisure, education, and so on. For a given price level, the higher the wage, the more people are likely to consider the wage to exceed the opportunity cost, so the quantity of labor supplied is higher.

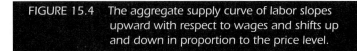

FIGURE 15.4   The aggregate supply curve of labor slopes upward with respect to wages and shifts up and down in proportion to the price level.

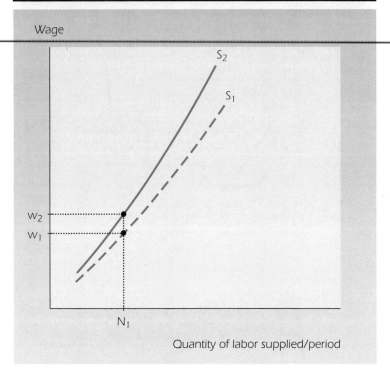

The aggregate quantity of labor supplied depends on wages versus the opportunity cost of working in terms of leisure, further education, and so on. For a given price level, the higher the wage, the more people will find that it exceeds their opportunity cost and therefore will be willing to work. That is, the higher the wage, the higher is the quantity of labor supplied. This is shown by the upward slopes on **S**$_1$ and **S**$_2$. An increase in the price level means nominal wages have to increase in the same proportion as prices for the quantity of labor supplied to remain unchanged. For example, if the price level increases 25%, the wage at which **N**$_1$ workers is supplied also increases 25%. That is, **w**$_2$ is 25% higher than **w**$_1$, where **S**$_2$ is the supply curve of labor after a 25% increase in the price level.

The *real* wage is the wage after allowance for the price level of what workers buy. Because the quantity of labor supplied depends on the real wage, the supply curve of labor shifts up and down in proportion to the price level.

is the supply curve after a 25% increase in prices. Taking any given quantity of labor supplied, for example, N_1 people per month, we find by drawing a vertical line at that quantity that it occurs with wages of w_1 per month at the original price level. After an increase in the price level of, for example, 25%, the same quantity of labor supplied, that is, N_1 people per month, occurs at a wage of w_2 per month, where w_2 is 25% higher than w_1. This occurs because when prices increase by 25%, it is necessary to have a 25% increase in the **nominal wage,** that is, the dollar amount received, for the **real wage** to remain unchanged; the real wage is the wage after allowance for the price level of what workers buy. Indeed, at each quantity of labor supplied it is necessary for the nominal wage to increase in proportion to the price level for the quantity of labor supplied to remain unchanged. This is so because the quantity of labor supplied depends on the real wage, and the real wage is unchanged only if nominal wages and prices change by the same percentage.

Unemployment and Equilibrium versus Actual Wages

In the preceding discussion we have explained that the demand curve for labor shifts up and down in proportion to the price level and that the same is true for the supply curve of labor. Therefore, the equilibrium wage moves up and down in proportion to the price level. For example, if the supply and demand curves for labor both shift up 25% from a 25% increase in prices, as in Figure 15.5, the equilibrium nominal wage also increases 25%; S_2 and D_2 are, respectively, 25% above S_1 and D_1, and so w_2 is 25% above w_1. If the actual wage is always equal to the equilibrium wage, the quantity of labor supplied remains equal to the quantity demanded, at N_F, and full employment is maintained. How then can unemployment occur, where unemployment means an excess of the quantity of labor supplied over the quantity demanded? For unemployment, the actual wage must exceed the equilibrium wage. For example, if the actual wage increases to w_3 when the labor supply and demand curves are S_2 and D_2, the quantity of labor supplied exceeds the quantity demanded by $N_S - N_d$.

Let us illustrate how actual wages can differ from equilibrium wages by considering the supply and demand curves for labor more carefully, making a distinction between the *actual* curves and *anticipated* curves. We shall use this illustration not only to show how unemployment can occur but also to show the relationship between inflation and unemployment.

> If *actual* wages always equal *equilibrium* wages, the quantity of labor demanded equals the quantity supplied, and there is full employment. Unemployment occurs when actual wages *exceed* equilibrium wages.

Wage Rigidity, Inflation, and Unemployment

Peoples' wages are not changed from day to day or even month to month as labor market conditions vary. Rather, wages are typically negotiated and set for an upcoming period of time, such as for the next year or two. This is true whether wages are negotiated between employers and a trade union or between workers and firms in personal wage contracts. For example, it might be agreed that the wage is to be $10.95 per hour for the next year and $11.25 per hour for the following year in a 2-year contract.

In reaching agreement on a wage that will apply for the next year or two, it is necessary for employers and employees to judge what labor market conditions *will be* during that future time period. This means that both employers and employees have to anticipate what the price level is likely to be. Only by forming an expectation of what the price level will be can employers and employees reach a view of what would be an appropriate wage to agree on for the future.[3] In effect, what workers and firms have to do is estimate what the future equilibrium wage will be, knowing that this depends on the future price level.

> Workers and firms must *anticipate* future equilibrium wages when setting wage contracts that will apply into the future. Anticipated future equilibrium wages depend on the anticipated future price level.

---

[3] The future equilibrium wage also depends on the future *MPP* of labor. We focus on the price level here because this enables us to also illustrate the relationship between unemployment and inflation.

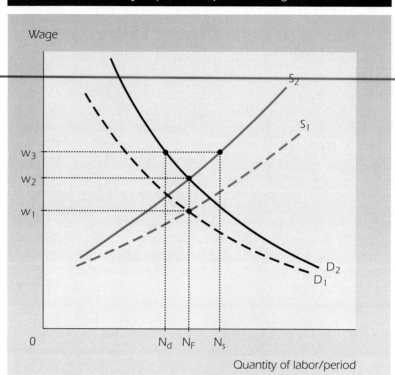

FIGURE 15.5   Unemployment does not occur if the actual wage always equals the equilibrium wage.

At the original price level, the labor market is in equilibrium at a wage w_1, where the quantity of labor supplied, given by S_1, equals the quantity of labor demanded, given by D_1. After a 25% increase in the price level, equilibrium occurs at a wage w_2, where the new labor supply curve S_2 intersects the new labor demand curve D_2. The new equilibrium wage w_2 is 25% higher than w_1 because S_2 is 25% above S_1 and because D_2 is 25% above D_1. If actual wages increase to w_2, the quantity of labor supplied stays equal to the quantity demanded, both equal to N_F, and full employment is maintained. However, if the actual wage exceeds the equilibrium wage and is, for example, w_3 when labor demand and supply curves are D_2 and S_2, there is a larger quantity of labor supplied than is demanded. Than is, there is unemployment of $N_s - N_d$.

While workers and firms will do their best to anticipate the price level that will prevail during the wage contract period correctly, the actual price level that materializes typically will not be exactly as expected. That is, actual inflation in general differs from anticipated inflation. To see the consequence of actual inflation differing from anticipated inflation, let us suppose in parts (a) and (b) of Figure 15.6 that at the price level anticipated by both workers and firms, the demand and supply curves of labor are, respectively, D^* and S^*, where the asterisk signifies that these curves are based on the anticipated price level. Let us also suppose that wages have been agreed on and contracted at their anticipated market equilibrium level w, given by the intersection of the curves D^* and S^*. Suppose further, for the

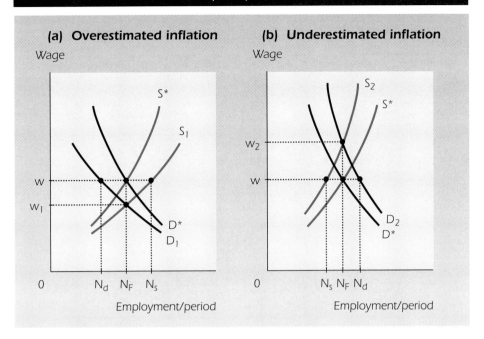

FIGURE 15.6   Labor supplies and demands which determine contracted wages are based on anticipated prices.

(a) Overestimated inflation

Wage

(b) Underestimated inflation

Wage

When inflation is as anticipated, full employment will prevail during the contract period because at the contracted wage **w**, the supply and demand curves for labor intersect; **D*** intersects **S*** in parts (a) and (b) at the wage **w**. However, if inflation is overestimated as in part (a), unemployment will exceed the full-employment level. This occurs because the relevant demand and supply curves for labor will be **D**₁ and **S**₁, and at the contracted wage **w**, **S**₁ > **D**₁; that is, there is unemployment. Only if the wage is flexible and falls to **w**₁ would unemployment be avoided. Similarly, if inflation is underestimated as in part (b), unemployment declines below the full-employment level. This occurs because the relevant demand and supply curves for labor will be **D**₂ and **S**₂, and at the contracted wage **w**, **D**₂ > **S**₂, thereby reducing unemployment. Only if the wage is flexible and increases to **w**₂ is unemployment unaffected.

sake of argument, that the anticipated price level incorporated in D^* and S^* is based on anticipation of 8% inflation.

If inflation is as anticipated, the contracted wage rate w will be correct, and the economy will be fully employed with $D^* = S^*$. This situation is described in Figure 15.7, which relates inflation and unemployment, by point R, which is at full employment U_F and an actual rate of inflation of 8%.

Let us next suppose that after wages have been contracted and set equal to w, based on inflationary anticipations of 8%, inflation turns out to be less than had been expected, say, only 5%. With the lower inflation, the future price level ends up below what had been anticipated. After the lower than anticipated price level become recognized by workers and firms, the relevant, actual supply and demand for labor curves become S_1 and D_1 in part (a) of Figure 15.6. (See also Example 15.2.) If wages could fall to the new equilibrium w_1, where $S_1 = D_1$, unemployment

When the equilibrium wage is lower than the actual contracted wage, it is difficult to renegotiate lower wages. Wages are therefore said to be "rigid" or "sticky" in a downward direction.

FIGURE 15.7   Incorrectly anticipated inflation can cause disequilibrium wages only temporarily, and therefore, any trade-off between inflation and unemployment occurs only in the short run.

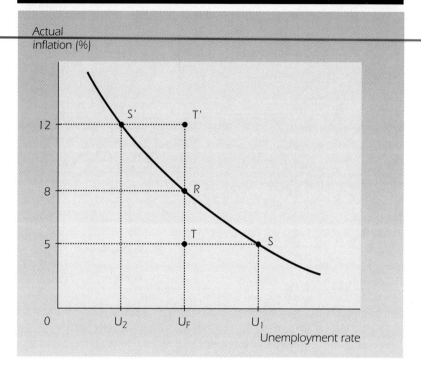

If inflation is lower than had been anticipated when reaching wage agreements, unemployment increases if wages are inflexible downward; we move from point **R** to point **S**. However, when wage adjustments eventually occur and move wages to the equilibrium level, unemployment returns to its "natural" level **U**F; we move from point **S** to point **T**. If inflation is greater than anticipated, we have a temporary decline in unemployment, moving from point **R** to point **S'**. However, eventually, as prices are correctly anticipated, we return to full employment at **T'**.

would remain at U_F. That is, if wages could be instantaneously revised to reflect actual inflation, there would be no unemployment, at least above the level at full employment. However, in reality, wages cannot be renegotiated to reflect actual inflation easily, especially when this means a wage reduction. Even though such a renegotiation of wages would mean jobs instead of unemployment for some workers, cuts in wages are usually resisted, especially if renegotiation could be seen as a sign of weakness in future wage negotiations. This is especially so when wages are negotiated by trade unions.[4] The difficulty of reducing wages to a new,

---

[4] Despite the resistance to wage cuts, there certainly are precedents. For example, U.S. automobile workers accepted wage rollbacks in the early 1980s, and in Japan, numerous rollbacks of previously negotiated wages have occurred.

lower equilibrium level than was anticipated is generally stated in terms of wages being "rigid" or "sticky" in a downward direction.

If wages are rigid downward, unemployment increases when actual inflation is lower than had been anticipated. This is shown in part (a) of Figure 15.6. Specifically, with wages stuck at w when inflation is 5% instead of the expected 8%, and with the relevant supply and demand curves for labor becoming S_1 and D_1, unemployment increases by the distance between S_1 and D_1 at wage w. That is, unemployment increases by $N_s - N_d$ in part (a) of Figure 15.6.

If wages are rigid downward, unemployment increases when inflation is less than anticipated.

The increase in unemployment in part (a) of Figure 15.6 occurs along with 5% actual inflation. We show this with point S in Figure 15.7, which is drawn with unemployment of U_1 and inflation of 5%.[5] That is, we move from point R to point S as a result of inflation being less than anticipated. However, wages would eventually move toward equilibrium. That is, in subsequent wage agreements, any previous overestimation of inflation would be allowed for, and wages would move toward the level where the quantity of labor supplied and demanded are equal. For example, if after unexpectedly dropping to 5%, inflation remained at 5%, unemployment would return to the full-employment level U_F along with the 5% inflation; with correctly anticipated inflation, wages would move to where the quantity of labor supplied and demanded are equal. In terms of Figure 15.7, this would mean a movement from point S to point T, where T shows 5% inflation and full employment.

Let us next consider what would happen if, after again anticipating inflation of 8%, inflation turns out to be 12%. That is, in this case actual inflation exceeds expectations. The higher than anticipated inflation means a higher than anticipated future price level. The new supply and demand curves for labor are vertically above the original curves and are shown in part (b) of Figure 15.6 as S_2 and D_2. If wages are contracted and stuck at w because employers refuse to increase them, unemployment declines below U_F by the distance between S_2 and D_2 at w, that is, $N_d - N_s$ in part (b) of Figure 15.6. With the 12% inflation and lower unemployment than U_F, we move from point R to point S' in Figure 15.7, where S' denotes 12% inflation and reduced unemployment U_2. (If it seems odd that unemployment can fall below the full-employment level, recall that even at full employment there are unemployed workers. Furthermore, as we shall see, the situation is temporary.)

Changes in unemployment from incorrectly anticipated inflation are temporary.

If inflation remained at the higher rate of 12%, eventually it would be anticipated correctly by both workers and firms, and wages would consequently move toward their equilibrium level. Therefore, unemployment eventually would increase from the abnormally low rate U_2 back to the full-employment level U_F in Figure 15.7. We would move from point S' to point T'. There is therefore no permanent decline in unemployment from higher than anticipated inflation.

If we review what we have said, we find that when inflation is lower than had been anticipated, there is a temporary increase in unemployment. Similarly, when inflation is greater than had been anticipated, there is a temporary decrease in unemployment. These outcomes occur because mistakes in forecasting inflation

The *natural* rate of unemployment is the rate of unemployment which prevails in the long run when inflation has been anticipated *correctly*. Underestimation of inflation causes unemployment to decline temporarily below the natural rate, while overestimation of inflation causes unemployment to increase temporarily above the natural rate.

[5] The distance $N_s - N_d$ between S_1 and D_1 at wage w in part (a) of Figure 15.6 is the number of unemployed, not an unemployment rate. It must be converted into an unemployment rate before adding it to U_F to reach a value such as U_1.

 **15.2**

NOT SIMPLY THE INFLATION RATE

The overall price index hides variations in inflation between different categories of products. Two categories of products with particularly different inflation at certain times are, first, products with prices set freely by supply and demand and, second, products with regulated prices, such as utilities, college tuition, public transport, and property taxes. Specifically, inflation of products with freely determined prices typically falls more quickly than inflation of products with prices that are subject to approval and control. This, as the following excerpt from a **New York Times** article explains, can cause unemployment during economic downturns. The article also points to the importance of inflation being steady, a matter to which we have paid repeated attention; with steady inflation, wages do not depart from the equilibrium because of errors in prediction.

Among the numerous diagnoses [of the severe recession of 1990–1992] a

new one is appearing that goes a long way toward explaining the national hardship. It is the falling inflation rate.

Not since the mid-1960s has the Consumer Price Index hovered for so long a period—18 months now—at an annual rate of 3% or less. But while low inflation was a boon in the 1960s, suitable to the times, it is a heavy burden today, helping to explain why the economy fails to revive.

"The downward trend causes the trouble," said Albert Sommers, a senior economist at the Conference Board, a business organization. Going from a 5% inflation rate in 1990 to 3% today, he said, "is much more disruptive than having had low but steady inflation for a considerable period, as was the case in the 1960s."

The problem today is different for individuals than for companies. Average wages for individuals have virtually stagnated, the Labor Department reports, but some major household expenses have sharply risen: health care, college tuition, home repair, utilities and property taxes. That plus heavy consumer debt loads, a burden absent in the

1960s, squeezes Americans, making them reluctant to buy, a prerequisite for an economic revival.

American corporations, on the other hand, suffer from almost no inflation at all in product prices. Unable to get price increases for a great variety of goods, they have preserved profits by cutting costs, especially labor costs. The results are wage and hiring freezes or outright layoffs, that have prolonged the hard times for workers. What's more, wholesalers and retailers decline to stockpile goods, depressing production. Why stockpile shoes at $50 a pair if the price three months from now won't change, or might even drop?

Source: Louis Uchitelle, "Low Inflation: Is It the Culprit?" **The New York Times,** October 20, 1992, p. C2; see also, Albert S. Dexter, Maurice D. Levi, and Barrie R. Nault, "Regulated versus Freely-Determined Prices: Implications for the Link Between Money and Inflation," **Journal of Money, Credit and Banking,** Vol. 25, no. 2, May 1993, pp. 222–230.

cause contracted wages to differ from their equilibrium level. If we plot the higher unemployment with the lower than anticipated inflation and the lower unemployment with the higher than anticipated inflation, as in Figure 15.7, the points trace out a downward-sloping curve *S'RS*. However, movements along the curve *S'RS* due to inflation forecasting errors occur only in the short run. In the long run, that is, after wages have been recontracted, we return to the same rate of unemployment, whatever the rate of inflation. This rate of unemployment, which we have related to the full-employment level, is called the **natural rate of unemployment** because it is where the economy is naturally tending.

The Phillips Curve: A Short-Run Phenomenon

An empirical relationship between inflation and unemployment looking like curve $S'RS$ in Figure 15.7 was found in a study by A. W. Phillips, and the curve with this shape has become known as the **Phillips curve.**[6] Phillips examined data for Great Britain for the period 1861–1957 and found a general tendency toward higher inflation with lower unemployment, and vice versa.

The validity of the Phillips curve has been challenged both empirically and theoretically. Empirically, it turns out that other than for some weak evidence for short periods of time, there is little or no support for a trade-off between inflation and unemployment. Indeed, the empirical evidence shows that higher inflation occurs as often with higher unemployment as with lower unemployment. Theoretically, the Phillips curve has been challenged as being only a short-run phenomenon, as we have explained. The theoretical challenge explains why it has been so difficult to find Phillips curves empirically when examining data drawn from over a long period of time.

> The Phillips curve shows a trade-off between inflation and unemployment. However, any such trade-off is at most only a short-run phenomenon.

ALTERNATIVE THEORIES OF UNEMPLOYMENT*

Rational Expectations and Macroeconomic Policy

The most important implication of the relation between inflation and unemployment that we have derived is that there is no sustained benefit in terms of reduced unemployment from increased inflation. There is a short-run decrease in unemployment from an unanticipated increase in inflation as the economy moves along a short-run Phillips curve, but as the increased inflation becomes correctly anticipated so that wages return to equilibrium, unemployment returns to the natural rate. This has important consequences for the conduct of government policy. It suggests that trying to reduce unemployment by, for example, increasing the rate of growth of the money supply can achieve only temporary relief. Indeed, in the long run, such a policy merely causes higher inflation.

Some economists, led by University of Chicago economist Robert Lucus, Jr., have argued that it is not even possible to reduce unemployment *temporarily* by, for example, increasing the rate of growth of the money supply. The reason for this agnostic view about the benefits of monetary policy is that these economists assume that inflationary expectations are rational. By **rational expectations**, they mean that all relevant information is reflected in peoples' anticipations of inflation, so they are as likely to underestimate as to overestimate inflation; rational people do not ignore relevant information. This means that workers cannot be fooled by, for example, an increase in the rate of inflation to accept a reduced real wage. Instead, workers will take account of, for example, more rapid money supply

> Rational expectations are based on all relevant information. If people's expectations are rational, there is not even a temporary trade-off between unemployment and inflation.

---

[6] A. W. Phillips, "The Relation Between Unemployment and the Rate of Change of Money Wages in the United Kingdom," *Econometrica,* November 1958, pp. 283–299.

*Sections or numbered items marked with an asterisk may be omitted without a loss of continuity.

growth and build this into wage agreements. Indeed, if expectations are rational, errors in forecasting inflation during one period of time are unlikely to be repeated in the next period of time, so unemployment is likely to vary randomly around the natural rate.[7]

Those who believe that inflationary expectations are rational have argued that governments should avoid **discretionary stabilization policy**—policy consciously used to stabilize unemployment and real economic growth. Instead, they believe that governments should just try to reduce uncertainties by not changing policies too often. Policy changes, they argue, increase uncertainty and in this way reduce the amount of investment in new capital. In turn, this causes slower economic growth. We consider this possibility in the next chapter.

Efficiency Wages and Persistent Unemployment

According to the efficiency wage theory, wages may exceed the equilibrium level as a result of firms paying workers higher wages to increase worker productivity.

Those basing their views on the rationality of workers' expectations have difficulty explaining persistent unemployment above the full-employment level, and yet at times such unemployment persists. This situation has given rise to a search for an alternative theory of unemployment which can explain why unemployment sometimes lasts for many years.[8] One alternative theory is based on the gains that employers derive from paying employees more than is necessary. This alternative theory is known as the **efficiency wage theory** because it associates the efficiency or productivity of workers with the wages they are paid. Specifically, according to the efficiency wage theory, *MPPs* at each level of employment are larger at higher wages. The efficiency wage theory uses a variety of arguments to reach a positive association between wages and worker productivity. The essential idea of these arguments is that firms pay above-equilibrium wages to induce workers to be more productive, but at the above-equilibrium wages, the quantity of labor supplied exceeds the quantity demanded; that is, there is unemployment. Furthermore, there is no force to reduce this unemployment because firms *want* to keep wages high.

One line of argument that has been advanced is that higher wages prevent workers from slacking or shirking on the job. According to this argument, it may be cheaper for firms to pay higher wages rather than to try to identify slackers by hiring inspectors, which adds to costs and also may reduce morale.

An alternative explanation for paying above-equilibrium wages is based on the sociologic role of gifts, which tend to be reciprocal and create a bond. If we think of extra wages as a gift from firms to workers, it makes sense to think that firms can expect a gift in return in terms of increased worker loyalty. Other factors which might induce firms to pay above-equilibrium wages are efforts to reduce costly turnover and retraining and to increase the quality of the work force. Another factor, which works during downturns, is the reluctance to cut wages and

---

[7] By "random" variation in the unemployment rate, we mean that the rate of unemployment is not predictable from one wage-contract period to the next. Nevertheless, unemployment could stay high or low for a long period of time if the length of wage contracts is long.

[8] As Example 15.3 explains, the search for a theory of persistent unemployment has captured the interest of a large number of America's leading economists.

Example   15.3

ECONOMISTS FULLY EMPLOYED EXPLAINING UNEMPLOYMENT

*Unemployment extracts a high price. Of course, the highest price is borne by those desperately trying to find a job, but others pay too in taxes to provide assistance and, more generally, in lost potential output in the economy as a whole. Therefore, it is little surprise that the unemployment problem has attracted some of the best economic minds of all time, tempted by the challenge of reducing this social ill. The following article from **The Wall Street Journal** takes a long view of the path that economists have traveled in their search for **the** ultimate answer. The article takes us through the theories discussed in this chapter and touches on insights dealt with in Chapter 16.*

When George Akerlof was 11 years old, he worried about this: If his father lost his job, he would stop spending, causing someone else to lose a job, who would also stop spending, and so on until the economy crashed to a halt.

Fortunately, young George's theory was flawed. His father periodically did lose his job, but the economy survived.

That early intellectual misfire didn't discourage Mr. Akerlof, now an economist at the University of California at Berkeley, from continuing to think about unemployment. He and his wife, Janet Yellen, are members of a small band of maverick economists exploring new theories of joblessness. The group, which includes Joseph Stiglitz at Princeton and

Lawrence Summers at Harvard, is pursuing ideas that eventually could help explain why unemployment stays high despite relatively healthy economic growth.

"It's one of the first theories to offer an intellectually coherent explanation of normal unemployment," says Kenneth Arrow, a Nobel-laureate economist at Stanford. "I think that's a very important development."

Unemployment has always puzzled economists. Classical theorists assumed that if the demand for goods fell, wages and prices would fall as well, restoring the balance in the economy and keeping everyone employed. Confronted with high unemployment during the depression, British economist John Maynard Keynes tried to modify classical theory. He and his followers argued in part that wages are "sticky" and slow to fall, causing at times a market imbalance that results in joblessness. But even the Keynesians couldn't explain adequately why joblessness would persist for long periods.

The new theories expand on Keynesian ideas. They say businesses may find it in their long-term interest to pay workers more than the market requires. By paying higher wages, they can increase worker productivity and their profits, these economists contend. As a result, wages stay too high, and the workings of the market can't assure everyone a job. Businesses stay competitive, but unemployment persists.

The path from abstract theory to practical economic policy is long

and rugged. For example, many dismissed out of hand Mr. Keynes's unemployment theories when they were first published in 1936; a couple of decades later, his theories set the assumptions underlying government policies around the globe. As Mr. Keynes himself wrote, practical men may disdain academic theory but nonetheless "are usually the slaves of some defunct economist."

Whether the new theories will guide future policy makers is far from clear. The theories are young, and skeptics abound. "It's hard to say what their ultimate significance will be," says Robert Solow, a professor of economics at the Massachusetts Institute of Technology.

But the ideas are attracting some bright minds and seem to signal an important change in the direction of macroeconomics, the study of the economy's overall performance. After a decade of disillusionment, macroeconomists are focusing with renewed vigor on unemployment and other important problems. "I think we're in a very exciting period for macroeconomics," says MIT's Paul Samuelson, another Nobel laureate.

In the late 1970s and early 1980s, some academic macroeconomists began to doubt whether they had a role to play in public policy. Inflation and its effects seemed to shoot down many traditional Keynesian theories, and "supply-side" politicians and journalists dominated economic debates with their proposals to spur growth by cutting taxes. Many economists thought that "supply-side economics was silly from an academic point of

Example 15.3 (continued)

view," contends John Taylor, a Stanford professor, and "serious macroeconomists felt blown out of the water."

Many academics turned away from policy problems and concentrated on sharpening their technical skills. "Rational expectations" theory became the rage. The theory emerges from the idea that individuals and businesses act rationally based on their expectations of the economy's future course. Based on this notion, young academics constructed complex mathematical models of economic activity.

However, these models rarely bore much resemblance to reality. Among other things, they reverted to the classical idea that Adam Smith's "invisible hand" would guarantee all willing workers a job. Unemployment was assumed to be "voluntary." The government's jobless figures, many of these economists say, measure only "the demand for leisure." . . .

Classical economists, trained in free-market theory, have always found it difficult to understand why, in the words of economist Robert Hall at the Hoover Institution, "the labor market doesn't behave like the onion market." When the sup-ply of onions exceeds the demand for onions, prices fall. But when the supply of labor exceeds the demand for labor—that is, when there is unemployment—wages don't always fall.

In a free market, classical economists argue, a company shouldn't be able to pay workers more than the going wage for a prolonged period. If Ace Widget Co. offers its workers $5 an hour when workers who seem equally qualified are willing to work for $3 an hour, another widget entrepreneur will seize the bargain and drive Ace out of business.

But the new theory—known as "efficiency wage theory"—provides a possible answer as to why a company may pay more than the market requires. If Ace Widget employees work harder because they are paid more, then low-wage companies may not be able to compete with Ace. Wages remain higher than necessary, and the result is persistent unemployment. The traditional free-market story breaks down. "Adam Smith's invisible hand turns out to be a little bit palsied," Mr. Stiglitz says.

Harvard's Prof. Summers is one of the newer converts to the efficiency-wage theory. Though only 30 years old, he is already considered one of the bright new lights in economics. He introduces the theory to a group of New York University graduate students with this story:

"In 1914, in the midst of a recession, Ford Motor Co. made a startling decision to raise its wage for industrial workers to $5 a day. At the time, prevailing daily wages at other companies ranged from $2 to $3. Ford's announcement lured to its gates thousands of people hoping for a job.

"Conventional economic theory suggested that the move would prove disastrous. But Henry Ford insisted that it was good business. In a history of Ford Motor, Alan Nevins writes that the dramatic move had 'improved the discipline of the workers, given them a more loyal interest in the institution and raised their personal efficiency.'"

Scribbling a mathematical model on the blackboard to explain this change in attitude, Mr. Summers says companies pay above-market wages to keep employees from neglecting their work. Unable to monitor workers closely, a company can catch only a fraction of those who shirk. If the company pays the "market-clearing" wage that

then let workers make their own decisions about who leaves; those leaving are likely to be the best workers because they have the best opportunities. Firms may prefer to maintain wages at above the equilibrium level and then decide themselves whom to lay off. Whatever the explanation of above-equilibrium wages, the result is a persistent excess supply of labor. What the efficiency wage theory suggests is that this can result from profit-maximizing behavior of firms.

traditional theory suggests, a worker risks little by shirking: if caught, he faces only temporary discomfort before finding another job at the going wage.

But if the company pays higher wages, the shirker's risks rise; if caught, he may face a long bout of unemployment while seeking an equivalent job or he may end up in a lower-paying job.

At Berkeley, Mr. Akerlof and Ms. Yellen have developed a somewhat different brand of the efficiency-wage theory based in part on insights that Mr. Akerlof gathered from sociological studies.

For an economist to use sociology in his work, Ms. Yellen says, is a bit like "wearing a loud shirt." Economists view people as motivated by rational, economic concerns; sociologists are more likely to delve into the irrational. Hoover's Mr. Hall reflects the attitude of most of his colleagues in saying he stops reading whenever he sees the word "sociological" in an economics paper.

Mr. Akerlof defends his efficiency-wage work. "With a little sociology, it's very easy to show how unemployment occurs," he says. In recent years, he has been reading sociological studies of "gift exchange," and he believes that in them he has found a convincing explanation of why companies pay higher wages than the market requires.

Mr. Akerlof argues that an employee's effort depends partially on the "norms" of the group in which he works. By paying workers a "gift" wage in excess of the minimum required, a company can raise group norms and get back a "gift" of extra effort. The theory also helps explain why companies may not fire or pay lower wages to less productive workers. Such moves would undermine the morale of all of a company's workers and reduce productivity.

In many ways, Princeton's Prof. Stiglitz is the father of efficiency-wage theories. A classmate of Mr. Akerlof's at MIT, Mr. Stiglitz began thinking about such theories during a visit to Kenya in 1969. Economists studying underdeveloped countries had for some time realized that higher wages could make workers more productive by improving their nutrition. But Mr. Stiglitz suspected that a related phenomenon might explain unemployment in the developed world.

By paying above-market wages, he reasons, a company might be able to reduce turnover and cut training costs. And he has studied the possibility that companies may pay higher wages to improve the quality of their employees. Unable to assess fully the skills of each potential employee, a company may improve the odds that it will get and retain good workers by paying more money.

"Any of these explanations by themselves may seem a little shaky," he says. "But I think the truth may be a complicated interaction of all of them." . . .

Source: Alan Murray, "Jobless Puzzle: Why Unemployment Lingers on Stirs Renewed Interest," **The Wall Street Journal,** December 26, 1985, pp. 1 and 4. Reprinted by permission of The Wall Street Journal, © 1985 Dow Jones & Company, Inc. All Rights Reserved Worldwide.

THE COST OF INFLATION VERSUS UNEMPLOYMENT

There is a high social cost to unemployment. The most obvious cost is borne by the unemployed themselves, who suffer the hardship of financial deprivation and the psychological impact of not feeling they have a place in society. If the psychological suffering is particularly severe, it can be felt within families, where children may experience damage in terms of their own motivation and chance to receive further education and where spouses and children may even suffer physical abuse. These severe costs contrast with those of inflation, which, as we saw in the preceding chapter, are faced primarily in terms of wealth redistribution and result more from errors in inflationary anticipations than from the inflation itself. Most of the costs of inflation, therefore, are canceled by the gains, while the lost incomes of the unemployed and the lost output of the nation are truly lost and can never be recovered.

Because of the relatively large social costs of unemployment, various groups have urged economic policymakers to lower unemployment, even if taking this step means a chance of higher inflation. However, as we have seen, any gain in reduced unemployment via government policy which increases inflation is only temporary. For this reason, those supporting government restraint have argued that attempts to reduce unemployment give short-term gain but long-term pain. On the other hand, people supporting a more active role of government argue that there are other ways of getting people back to work, including, as we shall see in the next chapter, government-funded projects and general increases in government spending. Furthermore, these people argue that because there is no opportunity cost when an unemployed person is given work—there is no forgone alternative output—it is worthwhile taking steps to help maintain full employment. For example, when the government pays unemployed people to plant trees, clean up inner-city streets and parks, repair worn-out roads, or provide assistance to the elderly, if these jobs would not have been done otherwise and if those employed would have been idle, the benefits of the government projects come at zero opportunity cost.

Without attaching values to the costs of inflation and unemployment, we cannot make proper public trade-offs between them. It is unlikely that we will ever be able to attach such costs. Not least of the problems in attaching costs is that the same rate of inflation carries a different cost according to how predictable it is and the same rate of unemployment carries a different cost according to whether it is due to the same people remaining unemployed for lengthy periods or to a large number suffering short-term unemployment.[9] The latter type of unemployment can be argued to involve a lower cost than the former, since short absences from the job market may be more affordable through the use of savings and may offer people an opportunity to paint their houses or finish certain chores.[10] There is the further difficulty of placing a social value on what the unemployed would have produced—nuclear weapons versus bread, for example—but this is a general problem in valuing national income, as we saw in Chapter 12.

[9] We could have 1 million people unemployed, for example, as a result of 1 million people being out of work all year or 1 million people losing their jobs and 1 million people finding jobs each month. For this reason, the unemployment surveys ask about the duration of unemployment.

[10] Example 15.4 points out that there are other "silver linings" to the unemployment problem.

Example   15.4   DOING WELL IN BAD TIMES

Just as umbrella sales increase when it rains, there are even silver linings to high unemployment. Consider, for example, the following excerpt from a **Business Week** article:

Denis duNann will be sorry to see the recession end. Although his company, Seattle-based Electronic Transaction Corp., is small, some of the nation's top retail executives have made room for him on their schedules. Why? They're worried about check fraud, and ETC has a low-cost solution: a check-verification data base. "They prevent rather than cure a problem for us," says Mike Meiberg, a business-systems buyer a J.C. Penney Co. "We know whether a check is good or bad before we take it."*

The check-verification business is not the only one that prospers when the economy declines. Lawyers and accountants who specialize in handling bankruptcy find their workloads running counter to the economy at large. Indeed, law and accounting firms can smooth the ups and downs in their own performance by focusing some of their services on the "bankruptcy business": when new incorporations are declining during economic slowdowns, bankruptcy-related business takes up the slack. Others who gain from the misfortune of others

include debt collectors, liquidators, and those who seize automobiles and other property when buyers are unable to make their installment payments.

The moral and legal obligations employers have assumed for their employees are creating new opportunities in career counselling and retraining programs, with many companies and government agencies paying substantial sums to help fired workers find alternative employment. While "restructuring" and "downsizing" are going on all the time, the outplacement counselors and retraining agencies enjoy their briskest business when unemployment is rising.

While the bankruptcy lawyers, debt collectors, and outplacement counsellors have been around for a while, new niches are appearing in the tough-times business that have offered a boom for those who have seized the chance. Again, consider the following excerpt from the previously cited **Business Week** article:

Ever heard of "sales testing"? Not many companies are hiring sales representatives these days, but when they do, they can't afford to make a mistake. Hiring one wrong person for a technical job can cost $7000 for the first three months in wasted salary and training, according to Gregory Lousig-Nont. His Las Vegas-based company markets honesty

tests and drug tests. In June, 1990, he introduced a new test, screening skills rather than personality, for companies hiring salespeople. His revenues last year [1991] jumped 60%, and his client list more than doubled."[†]

One of the consequences of a recession can be an acceleration in the rate at which work is contracted out, as companies look for ways to cut costs and increase efficiency. A large range of activities have been shifted in this way, providing extra business for those taking on what other firms no longer handle. For example, while many department stores once offered their own credit cards, many have transferred this activity to banks and credit collection agencies. Data processing, wage-bill handling, office cleaning, ground maintenance, and numerous other activities have similarly been shifted to outside firms, with the push to make the change often coming during rising unemployment and tough economic times. Consulting firms have seen the market for advice on cost-cutting surging with the unemployment rate, making their own employment prospects the mirror image of the employment situation in the economy at large.

*"Where Gloom and Doom Equal Boom," **Business Week,** January 13, 1992, p. 28.

[†]ibid.

PHYSICAL AND HUMAN DIMENSIONS
OF REDUNDANCY

Not everybody thinks of work as being synonymous with employment or of redundancy as being synonymous with unemployment. For example, to physicists, **work** is not what people do for wages or what students do when studying. Rather, physicists define **work** as the force applied to an object multiplied by the distance the object moves in the direction of the force. This means that while some of what is done in the course of employment is work, specifically that of a physical kind, such as pushing a plough or pulling a load, most of what people do on the job or while studying is not **work** as understood in physics. However, despite the different meanings of **work,** when it comes to the amount of work that is done versus the amount of work that might have been done, physicists and economists think in similar ways.

In judging different kinds of machines, physicists and engineers use a concept to which econ-

omists can relate easily, namely, **efficiency**. A standard physics textbook[11] definition of efficiency **e** is

$$e = \frac{\text{work output}}{\text{work input}} \times 100\%$$

The purpose of this measure is to describe numerically how well a machine is operating relative to other machines and relative to the "perfect" machine, which cannot exist in practice but for which **e** = 100%.

To measure how well the economy operates relative to other economies and to the "perfect" economy, which also cannot exist in practice, economists use measures like the physicists' effi-

---

[11]Joseph F. Mulligan, **Introductory College Physics** (New York: McGraw-Hill, 1985), p. 156.

ciency. An economy may not function "perfectly" because not all of each factor of production is working. The percentage of labor not working is measured by the unemployment rate, which can be converted easily into an employment rate; the employment rate is simply 100 minus the unemployment rate. While based on only one input, labor, the employment rate, like the physicists' **e,** describes how well the economy is doing relative to an ideal state. Similarly, economists employ a measure, the **capital utilization rate,** to describe how close the economy is to using all of its capital stock. Again, like **e,** this measure describes how well the economy is doing relative to an ideal state.[12]

Machines have efficiencies below 100% because of such factors as **friction,** which, as we have seen, is also a reason for unemployment, that is, frictional unemployment. Both machines and economies also can suffer from structural problems.

Engineers have learned that in designing a machine for a task, it is generally desirable to build in slack. This can reduce downtime and provide room for handling heavier loadings when absolutely necessary. The human body also has some built-in slack. For example, the heart can handle heavier loads than normal for short periods of time, and this has helped in survival. The economy is very similar to machines and living organisms in benefiting from having some slack in employment of capital, and labor. The slack reduces wear and tear on machines and people and is a necessary part of a dynamic, evolving economy.

Biologists have found an interesting example of "unemployment" in the case of the DNA molecule in human cells. It would appear that more than 95% of the information in the molecule is redundant, going unused.[13] While slack or flexibility is of value when conditions are changing, this amount of redundancy is difficult to explain. It can be argued that it is the low cost of carrying the redundant information that allows it to be carried from generation to generation. Furthermore, the "redundant" information could have value later when the environment has changed, making retained, previously unfavored variations useful in the new environment.

Unemployment can have devastating psychological and social consequences, adding noticeably to case loads of social and public health workers. The unemployed suffer from increased anxiety, decreased life satisfaction, difficulty concentrating, and listlessness.[14] The consequences can spill over to those keeping their jobs but fearing the fate of their redundant colleagues. With the unemployed also suffering from boredom and anger, family members may be affected, especially when distress leads to alcoholism and depression.

The depth of despair that can fall on those who are displaced is often the result of being cut off from the social contact that goes with working. Moreover, there is a commonly felt duty to work, to maintain dependents, and to be "doing something." The first question asked when meeting someone is often "And what do you do?" The work ethic runs deep, leaving a gaping hole for the unemployed.

The duty to work and the indignity associated with not working are made especially clear in W. R. Greg's summary of what the philosopher Thomas Carlyle had done for his age: "He has

---

[12] Economists also employ a measure of **potential GDP,** which is what the gross domestic product would be if **all** factors of production were fully employed, and then compute

$$\frac{\text{Actual GDP}}{\text{Potential GDP}} \times 100\%$$

Because potential GDP is based on their being some unemployment, that occurring at "full employment," the ratio of actual to potential GDP can be 100% when the employment rate and capacity utilization rate are below 100%. The ratio of actual to potential GDP is similar to what physicists call **Carnot efficiency.** This is the efficiency of a machine relative to the best **technically possible** machine.

---

[13] Richard Dawkins, **The Blind Watchmaker** (Harlow, England: Longmans, 1986), p. 116.

[14] See Stephen E. G. Lea, Robert M. Tarpy, and Paul Webley, **The Individual in the Economy: A Survey of Economic Psychology** (Cambridge, England: Cambridge University Press, 1987), especially p. 157 and the references contained therein.

preached . . . the duty and the dignity of work, with an eloquence which has often made the idle shake off their idleness, and the frivolous feel ashamed of their frivolity."[15]

The sociologic aspects of unemployment go beyond the human consequences suffered by those taken away from their work and work-related social contact. Statistics show decisively that those likely to suffer unemployment are in the same sociologic categories as those suffering from other forms of discrimination. In particular, unemployment is more likely to affect blacks than whites, women than men, blue-collar than white-collar workers, lower-class than upper-class people, and young versus middle-aged people.

The perceived imperative to work and its human consequences for the unemployed have prompted religious leaders to question fighting inflation with high unemployment, a fight that we have shown in this chapter to offer no more than a temporary victory. For example, in their pastoral letter, **Catholic Social Teaching and the American Economy,** the bishops of the U.S. Roman Catholic church have made it clear that their sympathies are with those suffering from unemployment, not those affected by inflation.

When it has been particularly severe, unemployment has become part of history. Grim images of soup lines of despondent people during the Great Depression and of men and women fighting for the occasional job offered at the factory gate fill history-book accounts of the "dirty thirties." The statistics of up to 25% without jobs hide the human tragedies behind the statistics, the men and women desperately fighting to keep themselves and their families from starvation. Also, earlier, in Victorian times, the squalid conditions of the "poor houses," full of diseased and downtrodden orphans and hopeless individuals, are part of the history of unemployment.

Urbanization and unemployment together meant that for many the gutter or the "poor house" was their home and the soup kitchen their only hope of staving off starvation and disease.

The tragedies of the unemployed inspired such novelists as Charles Dickens and John Steinbeck. In novels from **Oliver Twist** to **Hard Times** Dickens depicts, with passionate concern for their unrelieved misery, the depravity that fell on the unemployed of Victorian England. In Depression-era America, the tragic experiences of Dust Bowl Okies inspired John Steinbeck in his masterpiece, **The Grapes of Wrath.** Steinbeck employs tropes such as "tractored out" and speaks of "The tractors which threw men out of work, the belt lines which carry loads, the machines which produce . . . ," linking the plight of the heroic Joad family with the mechanization he believed to be the cause of unemployment.[16] Nevertheless, Steinbeck grapples with the tension between unemployment due to mechanization and the higher standard of living he recognized as flowing from mechanization.[17]

Today the safety net has been lifted to prevent some of the worst physical consequences of unemployment, but the matter remains one of public concern. This concern can translate into the opinion polls and government job-creation programs, just as in the past the New Deal, which gave Americans the Tennessee Valley Authority, the Bonneville and Hoover dams, and rural electrification, came about as a result of public concern over the unemployment of the Great Depression.

> *Unemployment can have devastating psychological and social consequences. . . .*

---

[15]W. R. Greg, "Kingsley and Carlyle," in **Literary and Social Judgements,** 4th ed., Vol. 1 (London: Trübaer & Co., 1877), p. 171.

[16]John Steinbeck, **The Grapes of Wrath** (New York: Viking Press, 1939), p. 325.

[17]**Ibid.,** Chapter 25.

Geographers, too, have found it necessary to consider the consequences of chronic unemployment. For example, the immigration to the Americas sprang from a lack of jobs in Ireland, Russia, Italy, Greece, and China, among other countries. The search for jobs sparked the migration of Americans within the United States from the Appalachians to the Northeast and Midwest and, more recently, from the Rust Belt to the Sun Belt.

The ways different cultures deal with shifts in labor supplies and demands vary; for example, Japanese workers accept wage cuts to avoid unemployment more readily than do Americans or Europeans. The social and historical factors behind these cultural differences, as well as behind the "gift exchange" mentioned in this chapter in the context of efficiency wage theory, interest sociologists and anthropologists. They are, of course, also of interest to researchers in the business/economics areas of labor relations and organizational behavior.

In novels from Oliver Twist *to* Hard Times *Dickens depicts . . . the depravity that fell on the unemployed of Victorian England. In Depression-era America, the tragic experiences of Dust Bowl Okies inspired John Steinbeck in his masterpiece,* The Grapes of Wrath.

Thomas Malthus, the philosopher and member of the English clergy mentioned in Crossing Bridges in Chapter 2, had a particularly pessimistic view about the labor market which determines unemployment. Malthus argued that in the long run, the supply of labor would expand until it had driven the wage rate to the subsistence level—the real wage at which people could just survive. Malthus based his dismal view of the labor market on his observation of nature, where populations of species expand until the limits of available resources, and where large numbers perish at the maximum feasible populations; high birth rates just balance the death rates. Experience in the richer countries has shown that economic prosperity invalidates Malthus' dismal predictions. However, with so many dying from hunger and disease, the parallels between nature and the labor market remain disturbingly evident in many parts of the third world.

SUMMARY

1. The work force is determined by a monthly household survey and consists of the number of people working full time the week before the survey plus the number not working but actively looking for full-time work. The number without a full-time job and seeking employment is written as a fraction of the work force to compute the rate of full-time unemployment.

2. Full employment can be defined as the situation where there are as many people looking for jobs as there are jobs available. There are always people looking because of changes in demands and methods of production, shifting patterns of international trade, new people joining the work force, and people leaving jobs to search for better opportunities.

3. Full employment also can be defined in terms of equality between the supply of and demand for labor. The latter view lends itself to an explanation of unemployment in terms of supply and demand analysis and suggests that unemployment above the full-employment level is due to actual wages being higher than equilibrium wages.

4. The equilibrium wage occurs where the quantity of labor supplied is equal to the quantity of labor demanded. The actual wage can differ from the equilibrium wage if wages are inflexible.

5. If wages are flexible, an economy always has full employment. *Ceteris paribus*, wages then move in proportion to the price level.

6. Actual inflation may differ from the anticipated rate built into contracted wages, making contracted wages different from equilibrium wages. If wages are rigid downward, unemployment increases when inflation is lower than was anticipated. However, eventually an economy returns to the natural rate of unemployment as anticipations become correct and wages are recontracted.

7. The Phillips curve is a downward-sloping relation between inflation and unemployment, suggesting a trade-off between the two problems. However, since Phillips' original study, there has been little empirical support for a long-run trade-off between inflation and unemployment.

8.* If workers' expectations are rational, being based on all relevant factors that could affect future equilibrium wages, there is not even a short-run inflation-unemployment trade-off.

9.* Unemployment may persist if wages are kept high in order to increase productivity of workers. Above-equilibrium wages may increase productivity if they reduce slacking on the job or result in worker loyalty.

10. The cost of unemployment is higher than that of inflation. However, it is difficult to quantify either of these costs, so a social choice between them cannot be made easily.

QUESTIONS AND PROBLEMS

1. In some European countries, unemployment is measured from the number registering as being unemployed at government offices, with registration often being necessary for the unemployed to collect benefits. How do you think this method of estimating unemployment compares with the survey method used in the United States, and which do you think, on average, produces the higher unemployment estimates from the same "true" unemployment rate?

2. It has been said that free trade with a low-wage country such as Mexico causes the permanent loss of American jobs. Do you think this claim is valid?

3. How might retraining programs reduce unemployment?

4. How might an improvement in unemployment benefits affect the supply curve of labor and hence the equilibrium wage?

5. What determines how quickly equilibrium wages are reached?

6. How might computer technology be used to help reduce the rate of unemployment?

7. How can an unexpected decline in *MPP* of labor cause unemployment by making negotiated wages too high?

8. Might longer-term wage contracts make the Phillips curve valid for longer periods?

9.* Why might firms who pay above the going market wage be able to survive in a competitive industry?

10.* Why is the marginal physical product of labor dependent on the wage rate, whereas the marginal physical products of other factors of production are unrelated to the amount paid to use them?

. . . .
. . . .
. . . .
. . . .
. . . . . . National Output
. . . .
. . . .
. . . .

I don't think the president understands why there's high inflation and high unemployment at the same time. But then neither does anybody else.

United States Treasury Official

Key Concepts

Long-term growth versus short-run output fluctuations; macro-economic equilibrium; multiplier effects of changes in spending; price versus output responses to changes in aggregate demand; supply shocks; role of fiscal policy; the circular flow of income; business cycles; influences on long-term growth; forecasting short-term output fluctuations and long-term growth

TRENDS VERSUS FLUCTUATIONS IN REAL GDP

We explained in Chapter 12 that it is real rather than nominal domestic product that matters for our standard of living, because it is the real domestic product that measures the output of goods and services which forms the basis of our national and individual material satisfaction. As the upper parts of Figures 16.1 through 16.4 (pages 481–484) show, for the United States, Canada, France, and Spain, as for most other countries, the trends of real gross domestic products (GDPs) have been distinctly upward, but with some pauses and even some brief declines. Fluctuations around the trends of real GDPs show up especially clearly when we examine the rates of change of real GDPs in the bottom parts of the figures. This chapter considers the reasons for fluctuations in real GDP and also explains the

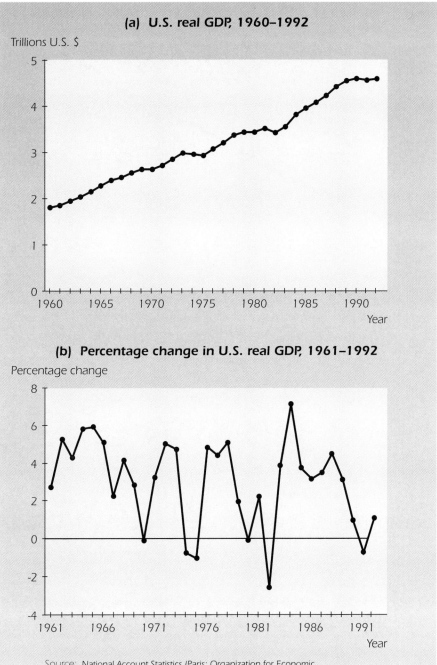

FIGURE 16.1   U.S. real GDP has more than doubled since 1960, with substantial variations around the trend growth rate of approximately 3%.

(a) U.S. real GDP, 1960–1992

Trillions U.S. $

(b) Percentage change in U.S. real GDP, 1961–1992

Percentage change

Source: National Account Statistics (Paris: Organization for Economic Cooperation and Development, 1993). 1985 prices.

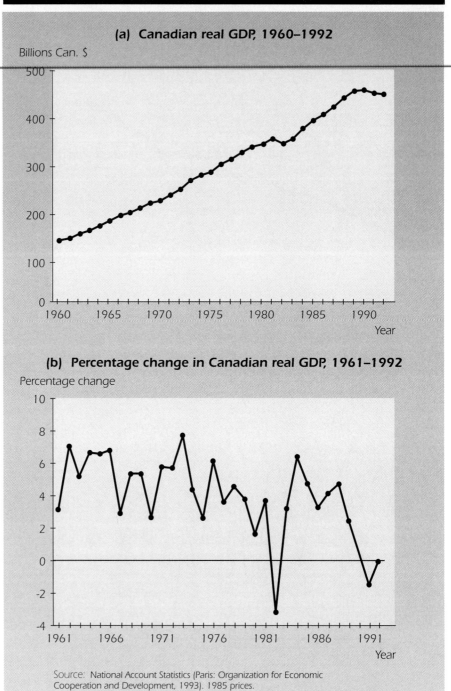

FIGURE 16.2   Canada's real GDP more than tripled since 1960, with two major setbacks.

(a) Canadian real GDP, 1960–1992

Billions Can. $

(b) Percentage change in Canadian real GDP, 1961–1992

Percentage change

Source: National Account Statistics (Paris: Organization for Economic Cooperation and Development, 1993). 1985 prices.

FIGURE 16.3   France's GDP has grown substantially since 1960, but the rate of growth has declined.

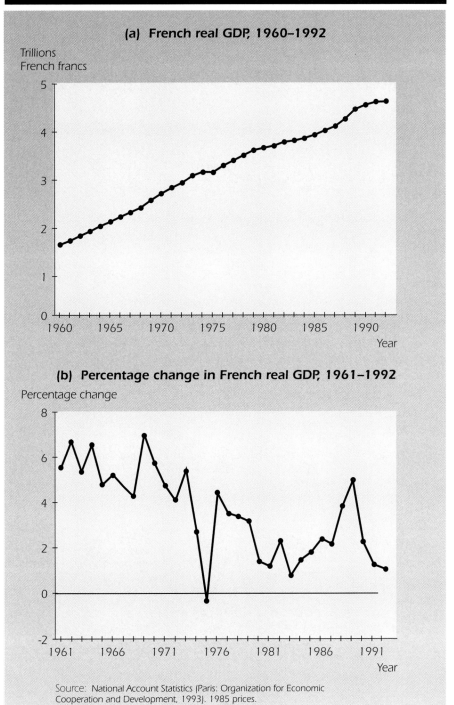

(a) French real GDP, 1960–1992

(b) Percentage change in French real GDP, 1961–1992

Source: National Account Statistics (Paris: Organization for Economic Cooperation and Development, 1993). 1985 prices.

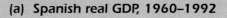

FIGURE 16.4 Spain's GDP has quadrupled since 1960, but the rate of growth has been erratic and declining.

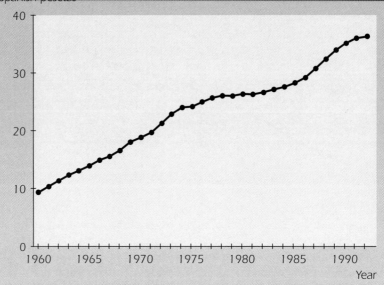

(a) Spanish real GDP, 1960–1992

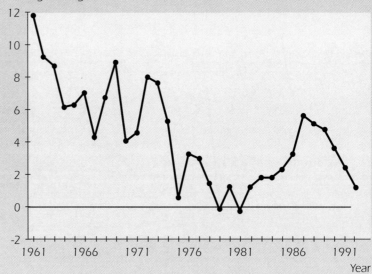

(b) Percentage change in Spanish real GDP, 1961–1992

Source: National Account Statistics (Paris: Organization for Economic Cooperation and Development, 1993). 1985 prices.

principal factors affecting the rate of economic progress reflected in the trend of the real GDP. We shall see that different factors affect fluctuations than affect trends and also that economists differ in the emphasis they place on different factors. Let us begin by considering the case of fluctuations in real GDP and examine first the perspective taken by the Keynesians, who, as we mentioned in Chapter 13, are those adhering to the ideas of the influential British economist John Maynard Keynes, whose book, *The General Theory of Employment, Interest and Money,* sparked a revolution in macroeconomic thinking.

Different factors cause short-run fluctuations in real GDP than influence the long-run growth in real GDP.

THE KEYNESIAN THEORY OF FLUCTUATIONS IN GDP

The Keynesian theory of fluctuations in the GDP is based on the relationship between desired expenditure and the actual output of goods and services. In particular, Keynesians argue that GDP grows more rapidly than usual when people collectively want to buy more goods and services than are being produced. If there is unused productive capacity when desired expenditure exceeds output, the increase in GDP is in the real GDP Q, and if the economy is fully employed, the increase is in prices P. The traditional Keynesian arguments were invoked when the world's economies had substantial unused productive capacity. Therefore, it was the real GDP, or Q, that was assumed to increase, not prices P.[1] However, since an increase in Q with P constant still means an increase in nominal GDP Y, we can think of the increase as being in nominal GDP Y. (Recall from Chapter 12 that $Y = P \cdot Q$, so a higher Q or a higher P means a higher Y.) Similarly, Keynesians argue that when desired expenditure is less than output so that some output is unsold, firms react by reducing output, thereby lowering real GDP, or by reducing prices. In either case, nominal GDP declines. Only when desired expenditure is equal to output is there no tendency for GDP to change. Therefore, the Keynesian theory of GDP involves an examination of the factors which determine desired expenditure.

Nominal GDP increases when desired expenditure exceeds output and declines when desired expenditure is less than output.

We can think of desired expenditure E as being made up of the same components itemized in our discussion of the national income and product accounts in Chapter 12. In particular, we can write

$$E = C + I + G + (Ex - Im) \qquad (16.1)$$

where

C = desired consumption

I = desired investment

G = desired expenditure by government

Ex = desired expenditure by foreigners, i.e., exports

Im = desired imports

[1] Later we deal in more detail with the circumstances under which real GDP or prices respond to differences between desired expenditure and output.

Equation 16.1 categorizes desired expenditure E in the same way we categorized the GDP Y in Equation 12.5. However, we should note that although we use the same symbols here as before, the C, I, G, Ex, and Im in Equation 16.1 are all *desired amounts that people want to buy*, whereas in Equation 12.5 they refer to *actual amounts produced.*

Desired expenditures change when there is a change in desired consumption, investment, government spending, exports, or imports.

Desired consumption C is the value of goods and services households want to purchase. Desired investment I is the amount firms would like to spend on new plant, equipment, and increased inventory holdings to aid in future production and sales. Desired government expenditure G is government spending on education, health, defense, infrastructure, administration, and so on. Desired expenditure by foreigners on a nation's goods and services is, of course, the nation's exports, while desired imports are what households, firms, and the government would like to purchase from abroad. Equation 16.1 therefore breaks up desired total spending into that of households, firms, the government, and the foreign sector.

We can find out what causes variations in E, and thereby causes fluctuations in GDP, by considering the factors behind each of the components of desired expenditure. We can then show why it is actual investment that differs from the desired level until desired expenditure equals GDP.

Desired Consumption.   Common sense and a vast accumulation of empirical evidence suggest that the amounts people want to spend depend primarily on their after-tax incomes: the higher a person's income after taxes, the higher is that person's consumption. Because a higher income after taxes, for given tax rates, means a higher before-tax income, we also can say that desired consumption varies with before-tax income. For example, if before-tax income increases by $1, after-tax income might increase by 75 cents, and desired consumption might, in turn, increase by 60 cents. We could then say that desired consumption increases by 60 percent of the increase in before-tax income.

The consumption function shows the change in desired consumption associated with a change in national income or GDP.

Since each individual is likely to want to increase consumption as their before-tax income increases, it is also the case that aggregate desired consumption in an economy rises as aggregate before-tax income rises. The income for the economy as a whole is the national income, which is approximately the same as the GDP, or Y. Therefore, aggregate consumption varies in the same direction as GDP, as shown geometrically by the line labeled C in Figure 16.5. This line is called the **consumption function.** The slope of the consumption function shows the change in C that results from a change in Y.[2] The slope of the consumption function is less than 1, for example, 0.6, because the change in desired consumption is smaller than the change in GDP. This occurs both because after-tax income does not increase as much as before-tax income and because some after-tax income is saved. For example, if the slope of the consumption function is 0.6, then for every $1 increase in Y there is a 60-cent increase in desired consumption, with the remaining 40 cents consisting of taxes and savings.

The extent to which desired consumption changes with income is very important in Keynesian economics. It is called the **marginal propensity to consume (*MPC*).** Specifically, the marginal propensity to consume is the value of the

---

[2]The slope of a line is the change in height divided by the change along the horizontal axis. For example, the 45-degree line from the origin in Figure 16.5 has a slope of 1.0.

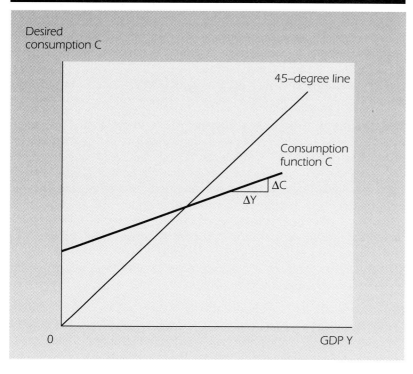

FIGURE 16.5   The consumption function describes the way desired consumption varies with changes in GDP.

The consumption function shows the extent to which desired consumption changes as national income or GDP changes. The slope of the consumption function is less than one because of income taxes and because people save part of after-tax incomes.

change in desired consumption per dollar change in nominal GDP. That is, the marginal propensity to consume *MPC* can be written as

$$MPC = \frac{\Delta C}{\Delta Y} \qquad (16.2)$$

where

ΔC = change in desired consumption

ΔY = change in nominal GDP

In our example of each extra dollar of *Y* resulting in extra desired consumption of 60 cents, the *MPC* is

$$MPC = \frac{0.60}{1.00} = 0.6$$

When consumption changes because GDP is changing, the change in consumption is called **induced consumption;** it is induced by the change in GDP and national income. This means a movement *along* the consumption function in Figure 16.5. The consumption function itself *shifts* up and down as a result of changes in such factors as consumer confidence and interest rates charged on

The marginal propensity to consume (*MPC*) is the value of the change in desired consumption per dollar of change in the nominal GDP.

Induced consumption is the part of consumption that depends on GDP. *Autonomous* consumption is the part that does *not* depend on GDP.

loans for new automobiles, houses, and major appliances. These shifts affect the level of the intercept of the consumption function, that is, where the consumption function touches the vertical axis. Numerous studies of the relationship between consumption and income have shown that the slope of the consumption function, the *MPC,* is relatively constant, while the level of the function, as given by the intercept, fluctuates. As we shall see, it is these fluctuations in the intercept that cause fluctuations in GDP. The value of the intercept of the consumption function, that is, what consumption would be at a zero GDP, is called **autonomous consumption.** This part of consumption does not depend on income.

Desired Investment.   As shown in Figure 16.6, investment is assumed to be unrelated to the GDP *Y.* This is reflected in the drawing of the **investment function** as a horizontal line. The lower the interest rate, the more investment will occur at all values of *Y* and the higher up the vertical axis in Figure 16.6 will be the investment function.[3] Similarly, the higher the interest rate, the lower is the height of the investment function. Other relevant factors that determine the height of the investment function are expectations for sales of extra output produced with the help of newly acquired capital, prospects for economic and political stability, corporate taxes, and even what Keynes referred to as "animal spirits"—the result of psychological factors. As we shall see, by affecting the height of the investment function *I,* all these factors can cause fluctuations in GDP.

The investment function shows desired investment at different values of GDP. The height of the investment function depends on interest rates, business confidence, and corporate taxes.

Desired Expenditure by Government.   In Figure 16.6 we treat desired government spending *G* as being unrelated to GDP. Alternatively, we could have drawn a downward slope on *G* if we felt that higher income and output reduce the amount the government wants to spend; the government might feel less obligated to spend in a stronger economy. However, the effect of GDP on government spending is likely to be small, and allowing for such an effect would have little impact on the overall picture. Therefore, we show *G* as horizontal and argue that shifts of this line up and down the vertical axis are the result of political decisions. It is the effect of these political decisions on the volatility of GDP that interests us.

Government spending depends largely on political decisions.

Desired Expenditure by Foreigners: Exports.   Desired spending by foreigners, that is, exports *Ex,* depends on foreign incomes, not domestic incomes. Therefore, if we were to draw *Ex* on its own against *Y,* we would draw a horizontal line. However, we do not show *Ex* on its own. Rather, we show desired exports minus desired imports. The difference between exports and imports (*Ex − Im*) is called the **balance of trade surplus** when positive and the **balance of trade deficit** when negative.

Desired Imports.   The amount of goods and services people buy from abroad increases with national income. That is, *Im* increases with *Y.* With *Im* subtracted from *Ex* in constructing the line (*Ex − Im*) in Figure 16.6, (*Ex − Im*) slopes downward as we move toward higher *Y.* However, for simplicity, we assume that imports depend so little on *Y* that (*Ex − Im*) is horizontal. But what is it that makes (*Ex − Im*) shift up and down?

----

[3] The effect of interest rates on investment is covered in the next chapter. For the time being, the reader is asked to accept this.

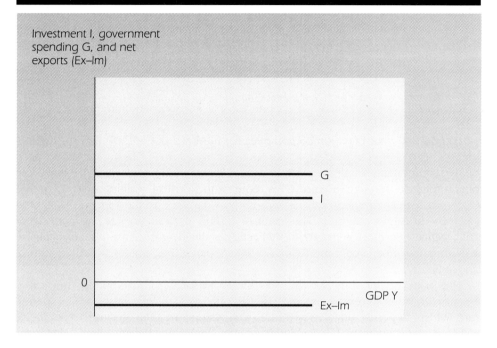

FIGURE 16.6   If desired investment, government spending, and exports minus imports are assumed to be unaffected by GDP, they can be represented as horizontal lines.

The investment function shows desired investment at different values of GDP. Here we assume that **I** does not depend on GDP. The level of the investment function depends on interest rates, business confidence, corporate taxes, and so on. Similarly, we show government spending **G** and exports minus imports (**Ex − Im**) as being unaffected by **Y**. The height of **G** depends largely on political decisions of how much to spend, while the height of (**Ex − Im**) depends on exchange rates, prices, foreign incomes, and trade barriers.

Ceteris paribus, the higher domestic prices are versus foreign prices, the smaller are exports and the larger are imports. Therefore, *ceteris paribus*, the higher domestic prices are versus foreign prices, the smaller is ($Ex - Im$). Similarly, the lower foreign incomes are, the smaller are exports and the lower is ($Ex - Im$). The height of ($Ex - Im$) is also affected by exchange rates and import tariffs and quotas. We draw ($Ex - Im$) below the horizontal axis, which is the situation if imports exceed exports. As with I and G, variations in the height of ($Ex - Im$) can cause fluctuations in GDP.

The balance of trade depends on domestic versus foreign prices, exchange rates, tariffs, and quotas.

Finding the Equilibrium GDP

We have noted that when desired expenditure E is not equal to GDP Y, GDP tends to be changing, and only when E equals Y does GDP remain steady. Using the categorization of E in Equation 16.1 on page 485, this means that GDP is steady only when

$$E = Y$$

that is,

$$C + I + G + (Ex - Im) = Y \qquad (16.3)$$

where C, I, G, Ex, and Im are components of desired expenditure and Y is actual GDP.

To find out what Equation 16.3 implies for the level of the GDP and for the factors that can change this level, let us consider Figure 16.7. The figure shows each of the components of desired expenditure. These components can be added to obtain total desired expenditure. This requires the vertical addition of C, I, G, and $(Ex - Im)$. Vertical addition means adding the value of C to the values of I, G, and $(Ex - Im)$ at each value of Y. The result of adding all these lines is line E in Figure 16.7. [Since $(Ex - Im)$ is negative, this reduces the height of the line E in Figure 16.7, but the other components of desired expenditures put the resulting line E above line C.]

The slope of line E is the same as the slope of the consumption function C because consumption is assumed to be the only element of total desired expenditure which depends on Y. Therefore, the change in total desired expenditure induced by a change in Y is the result only of the induced change in C. However, the intercept of line E on the vertical axis is the result of all the components of desired expenditure. *Ceteris paribus,* the larger the intercept of any component of expenditure, the higher up the vertical axis is the intercept of the total expenditure line E.

The 45-degree line shown in Figure 16.7 gives those points in the diagram where the value on the vertical axis equals the value on the horizontal axis. Therefore, points on the 45-degree line are points where desired expenditure, as measured along the vertical axis, equals GDP, as measured along the horizontal axis. This enables us to locate the level of GDP where $E = Y$. This is found by determining where the desired expenditure line $E = C + I + G + (Ex - Im)$ intersects the 45-degree line.

The GDP where the desired expenditure line E cuts the 45-degree line is Y_e. At a GDP below Y_e, such as at GDP $(Y_e - \epsilon)$, the height of the desired expenditure line E is above the 45-degree line, so E exceeds Y. (The height of the 45-degree line equals Y because along the line, $E = Y$.) At a level of GDP above Y_e, such as at GDP $(Y_e + \epsilon)$, we have the reverse situation. Here line E is below the 45-degree line, and hence E is less than Y. Only at Y_e is $E = Y$.

The *equilibrium* GDP is that level at which desired expenditure is equal to actual output.

The level of income where $E = Y$, that is, Y_e, is called the **equilibrium GDP.** It is called the equilibrium GDP because only at Y_e does the amount of goods and services people *want* to buy E, equal the amount of goods and services *actually* produced Y, so there is no reason for GDP to change.

The GDP Y_e is a **stable equilibrium** in that if GDP is disturbed from this level while line E remains unchanged, forces will return GDP to this level. To see this, suppose that after initially being Y_e in Figure 16.7, there is a sudden increase in

FIGURE 16.7   The equilibrium GDP is where desired expenditure equals GDP.

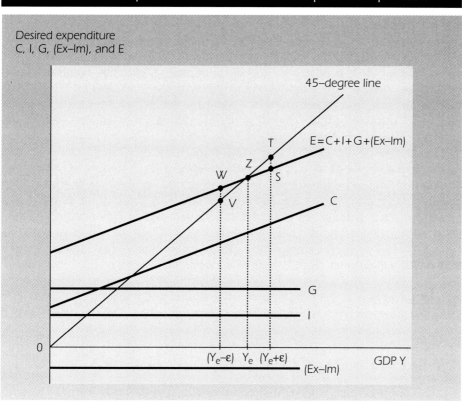

The 45-degree line represents potential equilibria where desired expenditure **E**, given on the vertical axis, equals GDP **Y**, given on the horizontal axis. The line labeled **C** is the consumption function. The consumption function slopes upward. All other components of desired expenditure—investment **I**, government spending **G**, exports **Ex**, and imports **Im**—are assumed to be unrelated to GDP. The sum of the desired expenditure line is **E**=**C**+**I**+**G**+(**Ex** − **Im**). This cuts the 45-degree line at **Z**, which gives the equilibrium GDP at **Y**$_e$. At (**Y**$_e$ − ϵ), desired expenditure exceeds GDP, so GDP increases. At (**Y**$_e$ + ϵ), desired expenditure is less than GDP, so GDP decreases. Therefore, forces push the GDP toward **Y**$_e$.

GDP to $(Y_e+\epsilon)$. We can see by drawing a line from the horizontal axis up to line E at GDP of $(Y_e+\epsilon)$ that E is less than Y by the distance between T and S. That is, the public wants to buy TS less than is being produced. This would result in lower production or lower prices, either of which would cause a decline in nominal GDP Y. Keynesians argue that if prices are "sticky" in a downward direction, then it is a decline in real GDP Q that is the basis of the decline in Y.

If, instead of increasing above Y_e, GDP declined to $(Y_e-\epsilon)$, E would be greater than Y by the distance between V and W. That is, people would want to buy VW more than is being produced, causing firms to increase production or prices. Either

When *desired* expenditure exceeds *actual* output, GDP expands, and when *desired* expenditure is smaller than *actual* output, GDP contracts.

would cause an increase in GDP Y. However, Keynesians traditionally argue that if there is a lot of underutilized capacity in the economy, it is real GDP Q and not prices P that increases.

The actual signal as to whether desired expenditure E is larger or smaller than production Y comes in the form of an unplanned change in inventory stocks. This is so because when people want to buy more than is currently being produced, firms meet the extra demand by running down their inventories. This signals firms to increase production or prices. Similarly, when people want to buy less than is being produced, the unsold goods are added to inventories. This signals firms to reduce production or prices.

The changes in inventories that signal firms whether to increase or decrease production are counted as part of *actual* investment. For example, when production exceeds desired expenditure, causing inventories to increase, the increase in inventory is included in actual investment and is hence a part of the actual expenditure of firms. Therefore, by definition, the actual value of expenditure, including changes in inventory stocks, must equal the value of output. However, while the national income accounts always show *actual* expenditure equal to actual output, only at the equilibrium GDP is *desired* expenditure equal to actual expenditure, with both equal to GDP. As we have seen, when GDP is not in equilibrium so that actual expenditure differs from desired expenditure, it is actual investment, not the other categories of GDP, which is different from the desired amount.

Keynesian Factors Causing Fluctuations in the GDP

Suppose that we begin with desired consumption, investment, government spending, and exports minus imports such that the total desired expenditure line is E_1 in Figure 16.8 and equilibrium GDP is therefore Y_1. Then, suppose that there is an increase in desired investment at all levels of GDP from I_1 to I_2. Since the total desired expenditure line is obtained by adding C, I, G, and $(Ex-Im)$, the effect of an increase in investment from I_1 to I_2 is to shift the aggregate desired expenditure line upward from E_1 to E_2, where E_2 contains the higher desired investment I_2. The new E_2 differs from E_1 at each GDP only because E_2 contains the higher desired investment I_2. With the new desired expenditure line we obtain a new equilibrium GDP Y_2, which is higher than the original equilibrium GDP Y_1. The new equilibrium GDP would be achieved via desired expenditures exceeding output at the original equilibrium Y_1, causing an unplanned reduction in inventories and a consequent increase in output or prices.

An increase in government spending G, net exports $(Ex-Im)$, or the autonomous component of consumption C—that part reflected in the intercept of the consumption function—will all have the same effect as an increase in investment; all shift the expenditure line upward, causing an increase in the equilibrium GDP. Similarly, decreases in government spending, net exports, or autonomous consumption reduce the equilibrium GDP.

Some of the factors which could cause an increase in desired expenditure, and hence in equilibrium GDP, are listed in Table 16.1, along with the components of

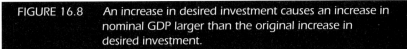

FIGURE 16.8   An increase in desired investment causes an increase in nominal GDP larger than the original increase in desired investment.

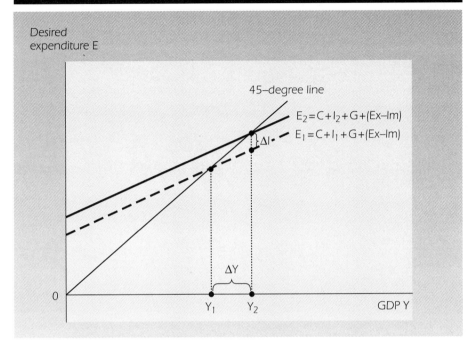

When investment increases from I_1 to I_2, the desired total expenditure line **E** shifts upward from E_1 to E_2. This increases the equilibrium GDP, that is, the GDP at which **E=Y**. The increase in investment is Δ**I**. The increase in income Δ**Y** is larger than the increase in investment Δ**I** because of the multiplier. The multiplier results from the successive spending of an original injection of funds.

desired expenditure they affect. These are the factors which a Keynesian would list if asked for the causes of fluctuations in GDP.

The fact that increases in desired investment, government spending, and so on cause increases in GDP should come as little or no surprise. What might come as a surprise is the *extent* to which income is increased by an increase in desired investment, government spending, and so on. As an examination of Figure 16.8 indicates, the change in income shown by ΔY (or $Y_2 - Y_1$) is larger than the change in investment ΔI (or $I_2 - I_1$) that brought it about. That is, the change in investment from I_1 to I_2, which equals the vertical distance between E_1 and E_2, is smaller than ΔY, the change in GDP. Similarly, changes in the other categories of desired expenditure cause a larger change in GDP than the change in desired expenditure. Let us consider why GDP can increase a multiple of the increase in investment or other component of desired expenditure.

Equilibrium GDP is changed by a change in investment, government spending, net exports, or autonomous consumption. Equilibrium GDP changes by a *multiple* of the change in desired expenditure.

....

TABLE 16.1

Keynesian factors which could cause an increase in GDP.

INCREASED I	INCREASED G	INCREASED (Ex − Im)	INCREASED C
Lower interest rates	Politically determined	Lower domestic prices relative to foreign prices	Lower taxes
Higher expected sales or future profitability			Improved confidence
		Depreciation in country's exchange rate	Lower interest rates on consumer debt
Wearing out of existing capital			
Reduced corporate income taxes		Higher incomes in foreign countries	
"Animal spirits"		Higher tariffs on imports	

The Multiplier

The multiplier is equal to the multiple by which the change in equilibrium GDP exceeds the change in autonomous expenditure that caused the change in GDP.

The relationship between the original change in desired expenditure and the change in GDP is called the **multiplier.** The multiplier is defined as

$$\text{Multiplier} = \frac{\text{change in equilibrium GDP}}{\text{change in autonomous expenditure}} \qquad (16.4)$$

where by **autonomous expenditure** we mean expenditure that is not induced by the GDP itself.

The denominator of the multiplier, which we have called the "change in autonomous expenditure," is the original change in desired expenditure that brings about the change in equilibrium GDP and which is not itself caused by the change in GDP. The GDP can change by more than the change in desired expenditure because of what is popularly referred to as "trickle down." For example, suppose the government spends $1 billion to hire labor during a time of heavy unemployment. Table 16.2 shows this as the "original injection" of spending. Table 16.2 shows that when the marginal propensity to consume is 0.8, the recipients of the initial $1 billion of wages spend an extra $0.8 billion on food, housing, travel, and so on. This is shown as the "second stage." The recipients of the extra $0.8 billion, for whom this is income, spend 0.8 of what they receive, which is $0.64 billion (or $0.8 \times \$0.8$ billion). This is shown in Table 16.2 as the "third stage." At each successive stage, 0.8 of receipts from the previous stage is spent. By adding up the extra incomes from all stages, we find that from an initial $1 billion increase in spending when $MPC = 0.8$, GDP is increased by $5 billion.

TABLE 16.2

The multiplier is higher if the marginal propensity to consume **MPC** is higher.

	MPC = 0.8		MPC = 0.9	
	RECIPIENT'S INCOME ($ billion)	ACCUMULATED INCOME ($ billion)	RECIPIENT'S INCOME ($ billion)	ACCUMULATED INCOME ($ billion)
Original injection	1.00	1.00	1.00	1.00
Second stage	0.80	1.80	0.90	1.90
Third stage	0.64	2.44	0.81	2.71
Fourth stage	0.51	2.95	0.73	3.44
Fifth stage	0.41	3.36	0.66	4.10
Sixth stage	0.33	3.69	0.59	4.69
Seventh stage	0.26	3.95	0.53	5.22
Eighth stage	0.21	4.15	0.48	5.70
Ninth stage	0.17	4.32	0.43	6.13
Tenth stage	0.13	4.45	0.39	6.52
•	•	•	•	•
•	•	•	•	•
•	•	•	•	•
TOTAL		5.00		10.00

We assume an initial increase in autonomous spending of $1 billion and show the effects when the **MPC** takes two values, 0.8 and 0.9. The recipients of the original injection of spending treat the $1 billion as income. With the **MPC**s of 0.8 and 0.9, the original recipients increase their consumption by $0.80 billion and $0.90 billion, respectively. These amounts become increased incomes of others, who in turn spend 0.8 and 0.9 of **their** income increases, meaning consumption increases of $0.64 billion (or 0.8 × $0.80 billion) and $0.81 billion (or 0.9 × $0.90 billion). These amounts are in turn increased incomes of others, and in this way the original injection trickles down. The "accumulated income" from the original spending is the total increase in income up to and including each stage. The total accumulated increase in income is $5 billion when **MPC**= 0.8 and $10 billion when **MPC**= 0.9. Therefore, the multiplier when **MPC**= 0.8 is 5. When **MPC**= 0.9, the multiplier is 10.

With the multiplier defined as in Equation 16.4, we find for an $MPC=0.8$,

$$\text{Multiplier} = \frac{\$5 \text{ billion}}{\$1 \text{ billion}} = 5$$

If we calculate the multiplier when $MPC=0.9$ in Table 16.2, we discover it has doubled to

$$\text{Multiplier} = \frac{\$10 \text{ billion}}{\$1 \text{ billion}} = 10$$

The larger the marginal propensity to consume, the larger is the multiplier.

We can calculate the multiplier without having to calculate the extra spending at each stage by noting that

$$\text{Multiplier} = \frac{1}{1 - MPC} \qquad (16.5)$$

In particular, we see that when $MPC = 0.8$, the multiplier is 5 [or $1/(1-0.8)$], and when $MPC = 0.9$, the multiplier is 10 [or $1/(1-0.9)$].

Real GDP versus Price Fluctuations

As we have mentioned, the traditional Keynesian view is that fluctuations in desired expenditure translate into fluctuations in real GDP rather than into fluctuations in prices. In the case of increases in GDP due to desired expenditure exceeding output, we attributed the traditional Keynesian view to a presumption about slack in the productive capacity of an economy; with slack such as with the high unemployment Keynes saw in the Great Depression of 1929–1933, extra demand would translate into more being produced, not higher prices. In the case of decreases in GDP due to desired expenditure being less than output, we attributed the traditional Keynesian view of a decline in real GDP rather than prices to a presumption about prices being "sticky" in a downward direction. So far we have not carefully described what we mean by slack and sticky prices. Let us remedy this situation and do so by considering Figure 16.9.

Figure 16.9 shows **aggregate demand curves** and an **aggregate supply curve** for an economy. These curves should not be confused with those used in the microeconomic theory of supply and demand in Chapters 6 to 11 because here we are referring to total or aggregate demand and supply in an economy, not supply and demand in individual markets.

The aggregate demand curve shows how much demand there is for an economy's total output at different price levels. It does not slope downward because lower prices make one good cheaper than another good, which is the reason for downward-sloping demand in Chapter 6; here there are no other goods, since we are considering the economy in general. Rather, the aggregate demand curve slopes downward because

The aggregate demand curve slopes downward with respect to the price level because lower prices increase real wealth and thereby increase consumption. A lower price level also causes an excess supply of money, and thereby increases investment, and makes exports cheaper, thereby increasing exports.

1. A lower price level makes peoples' assets with a given face value, such as currency, worth more in real terms. This is called a **wealth effect** and leads to increased consumption C.

2. A lower price level reduces the demand for money. (This was explained in Chapter 14.) For a given money supply, the lower demand for money means an excess supply of money. This causes extra expenditure on goods and bonds as people try to reduce their money holdings. The buying of goods directly affects total expenditure E by affecting C. The buying of bonds causes higher bond prices. This means lower interest rates and more investment I.[4]

---

[4] The connection between interest rates and investment is discussed more fully in the next chapter.

FIGURE 16.9 Fluctuations in aggregate demand translate into fluctuations in real GDP when a country is producing below capacity and into changes in the price level when a country is producing at or above capacity.

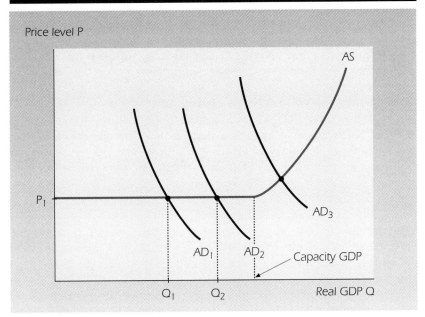

The aggregate demand curve shows how the aggregate quantity of goods and services demanded depends on the price level. A lower price level means that fixed-face-value assets such as currency are worth more. This wealth effect increases consumption. In addition, a lower price level causes an excess supply of money, which increases the amount spent. A lower price level also increases exports. Therefore, the aggregate demand curve is downward sloping. The aggregate supply curve shows how the price level varies with real GDP. If prices remain steady when production is below capacity, the aggregate supply curve is horizontal. In the horizontal range of the aggregate supply curve, fluctuations in aggregate demand translate into fluctuations in real GDP. However, when the aggregate demand curve cuts the aggregate supply curve above capacity output, the price level changes with fluctuations in aggregate demand.

3. A lower price level makes a country's exports cheaper vis-à-vis those of other countries, thereby increasing exports *Ex*.

We see that a lower price level can cause an increase in the aggregate quantity of goods and services demanded. Therefore, the aggregate demand curve slopes downward in Figure 16.9.

The reason the aggregate supply curve slopes upward, as in Figure 16.9, depends on whether we are considering the short run or the long run. In the short run, as the economy expands, the quality of inputs drawn into production diminishes; the best inputs are used first, then the next best, and so on. Therefore, as the economy expands, costs increase, and these costs are eventually passed on in

The *aggregate* supply curve slopes upward with respect to the price level in the *short run* because lower-quality inputs are drawn into production as real GDP expands, and this increases costs and prices. The aggregate supply curve slopes upward in the *long run* because input prices increase as real GDP expands, and higher input prices eventually cause higher output prices.

higher prices. That is, in the short run P increases as real GDP expands because of diminishing input quality. In the long run, expansion of the real GDP increases input prices. These eventually translate into higher product prices.

We have drawn the aggregate supply curve AS in Figure 16.9 as horizontal until the economy reaches its **capacity GDP,** which is the output that can be produced with all factors fully employed. After this level of GDP, the AS curve slopes upward.[5] The short-run aggregate supply curve takes this shape if input quality remains constant until the economy reaches capacity, and then input quality suddenly diminishes. The long-run aggregate supply curve takes this shape if input prices are constant when factors are not fully employed, and then factor prices increase when the economy reaches its capacity GDP.

Figure 16.9 shows that fluctuations in aggregate demand result in fluctuations in real GDP but not in prices if aggregate demand is below the capacity GDP. For example, if aggregate demand shifts from AD_1 to AD_2, real GDP increases from Q_1 to Q_2, in line with the horizontal shift in the aggregate demand curve. The price level remains unchanged at P_1. This happens because there is slack in the economy, with production below capacity. However, if aggregate demand increases as high as AD_3, this translates into higher prices.

We can use an aggregate supply–aggregate demand figure to consider not only shifts in demand, such as those from AD_1 to AD_2 to AD_3 in Figure 16.9, but also to consider **supply shocks;** supply shocks are sudden upward shifts in the aggregate supply curve. This is done in Figure 16.10.

An example of a supply shock is a jump in the price of imported oil. Such a jump, as occurred in 1973 and again in 1979, means higher production costs at all outputs of the economy. That is, the aggregate supply curve AS suddenly shifts upward. The height of the aggregate supply curve gives the price level at which each level of real GDP is supplied, and this price level increases with increases in the cost of production. Figure 16.10 shows that an upward shift in the aggregate supply curve results in a *higher* price level and a *lower* real GDP. That is, unlike demand fluctuations such as those beyond capacity GDP in Figure 16.9, where the price level and real GDP move in the same direction, in the case of supply shocks, the price level and real GDP move in opposite directions.

Supply Shocks and Stagflation

The shape of the short-run Phillips curve discussed in the preceding chapter suggests that higher inflation, or at least unanticipated inflation, is (temporarily) associated with lower unemployment. Since real GDP is higher when unemployment is lower—more people working means more output—it follows from a short-run Phillips curve that higher (unanticipated) inflation would be associated with higher real GDP. This was the view of most economists until the economic experience of the period of the 1970s, during which time inflation was rapid even when the real GDP was growing slowly or even declining. Economists coined a new term for this condition, **stagflation,** a hybrid of **stagnation,** meaning "a slowly growing or shrinking real GDP," and inflation.

Capacity real GDP is the economy's output when all factors of production are fully employed.

A supply shock is a sudden upward shift in the aggregate supply curve.

Changes in aggregate demand change real GDP and the price level in the same direction. Changes in aggregate supply change real GDP and the price level in opposite directions.

Stagflation is the combination of a stagnating real GDP and high inflation.

[5] As we explained in Chapter 15, even at full employment not all factors of production are working. Therefore, it is possible for output to increase above the full-employment level, at least temporarily.

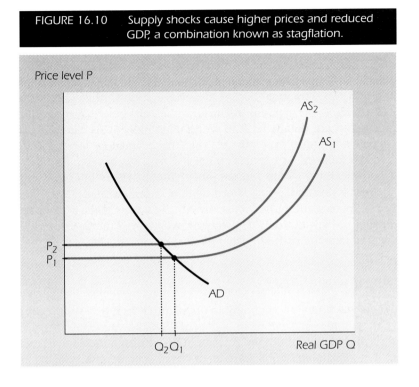

FIGURE 16.10   Supply shocks cause higher prices and reduced GDP, a combination known as stagflation.

The entire aggregate supply curve shifts upward if production costs increase at each level of real GDP, and this increases the price level. Such shifts in aggregate supply cause increasing prices at the same time as they cause a declining real GDP, a situation called stagflation.

Examination of Figure 16.10 shows that stagflation is what we would expect after supply shocks, such as after a jump in the price of oil. Consideration of the implications of Figure 16.10 shows that any presumption that high inflation would be associated with a rapidly increasing real GDP is based on an assumption that demand shifts, not supply shifts, are the cause of fluctuations in real GDP. Keynesian economists tended to think in such demand-shift terms until the stagflation following the first oil price shock. Today, it is recognized that either aggregate demand or supply can shift, although demand is more likely to fluctuate than supply.

The Paradox of Thrift

The traditional Keynesian view that fluctuations in real GDP are due to fluctuations in aggregate demand led naturally to a view that governments should intervene to keep aggregate demand steady, thereby reducing the fluctuations in real GDP, unemployment, and so on. The belief that such intervention is necessary was reinforced not only by the chronic unemployment that existed just prior to the publication of Keynes' *General Theory* but also by Keynes' recognition of how aggregate spending responds to increasing unemployment.

When an economy becomes weaker and people lose their jobs, it is natural for those still working to prepare for tougher times ahead by increasing savings. After all, if others are losing their jobs, it also could happen to them, and it is better to be prepared. Therefore, as unemployment grows, those with jobs tend to increase savings, which, in turn, means spending less of their incomes. That is, as unemployment grows, consumption declines. Keynes dubbed this phenomenon the **paradox of thrift.** It is a paradox because at the very time that increased expenditure is needed to put people back to work, what individuals naturally do to protect themselves is reduce expenditure. This makes matters worse. Keynes and those who have adhered to his ideas were led to advocate steps by the government to counteract what would happen quite naturally to the other private components of aggregate demand as conditions in an economy worsened.

The paradox of thrift is that as the economy slows, people reduce expenditure even though the economy needs increased expenditure.

The idea of intervening in the economy revolves around the role of fiscal policy. Keynesians see this not only as a way of overcoming the paradox of thrift but also as a way of keeping real GDP from fluctuating.

The Role of Fiscal Policy

We have seen that when an economy is operating at below capacity, an increase in desired expenditure and hence in aggregate demand causes an increase in real GDP, and a reduction in desired expenditure causes a decline in real GDP. However, if a decline in, for example, investment I is matched by an equal increase in government spending G, total desired expenditure can be prevented from changing. This is clear from Figure 16.8, where the value of G can be varied in the opposite direction to variations in I to keep the height of line E, and hence equilibrium GDP, unchanged. We also can see this from the definition of desired expenditure as

$$E = C + I + G + (Ex - Im) \qquad (16.1)$$

where G can be varied to offset variations in I to keep E constant. According to traditional Keynesians, the task of government is to keep track of C, I, and $(Ex-Im)$ and to change government expenditure (or taxes which can affect the height of C) to maintain a constant aggregate demand and maintain full employment.

A difficulty that the government has in implementing **discretionary fiscal policy**—the conscious manipulation of government spending and taxes—is taking action sufficiently early. The ability to act early is affected by the need to

1. Recognize the problem
2. Select the solution
3. Implement the solution
4. Allow for delay before the policy works

That is, there are a number of lags in recognizing the problem, taking action, and so on. The recognition lag is reduced by maintaining the regular collection of data on the factors influencing the gross domestic product and on the behavior of GDP itself. However, data tend to reveal a problem only after it has begun, and even if the problem were recognized early on, there is still the policy selection lag, the implementation lag, and the lag in the policy working.

It has been argued by some Monetarists that the lags in recognition, policy selection, implementation, and response are so long that by the time the policy is working the economy is likely to be rebounding on its own steam. Fiscal policy may then make fluctuations in GDP even larger than they would have been without fiscal interference.

Whether or not active discretionary fiscal policy can keep an economy on an even keel is, of course, at the center of debate over the role of government in the economy.[6] Not surprisingly, the data have been scrutinized for evidence on lags and policy effectiveness, but the very fact that both supporters and opponents of active intervention can still be found is evidence that no conclusive answer has been reached.

Discretionary fiscal policy is the conscious *variation of government spending and taxes to maintain a steady GDP and full employment.*

AN ALTERNATIVE VIEW OF EQUILIBRIUM: LEAKAGES VERSUS INJECTIONS

Finding the equilibrium GDP by looking for the GDP at which desired expenditure equals actual output, as we have in Figure 16.8, is not the only way to locate the equilibrium GDP. An alternative and equivalent method is based on the flows between different sectors of an economy.

Figure 16.11 shows the **circular flow of income** between firms and households. If households receive all the incomes paid by firms and then households spend all these incomes on products made by the firms, the flow of income can circulate indefinitely without changing. For example, if firms produce $1 trillion of final goods and services and pay $1 trillion to households in wages, rents, interest, and profits and then households spend this $1 trillion on the products sold by firms, the firms can then produce another $1 trillion of final goods and services, pay the households, who then buy the firms' products, and so on. This circular flow is characterized by the arrows on the outside of Figure 16.11 going from firms to households and from households to firms. However, in reality, the flow of funds between households and firms is subject to leakages. There are also injections into the flow from outside. The leakages from the circular flow of income result from funds received by households that are not subsequently spent on firms within the economy because of imports, savings, and taxes. The injections into the circular flow of income result from exports, business investment, and government spending. Let us begin by considering the effects on the circular flow of income of imports and exports.

If households spend all *they receive from firms and firms pay* all *they receive to households, the circular flow of income continues unabated.*

Imports constitute a leakage from the circular flow because they mean that some of what households receive as income from firms is not spent on goods and services produced by domestic firms. Instead, it leaks abroad, being spent on imported products. This is shown in Figure 16.11 by $Im(-)$, that is, imports of households from the rest of the world.[7] The negative sign next to $Im(-)$ shows

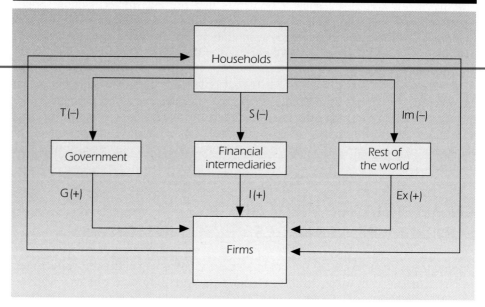

FIGURE 16.11   The circular flow of income continues at an unchanged rate if the leakages from the circular flow equal the injections into the flow.

In this figure, **Im** is desired imports by households, **Ex** is desired exports, **S** is desired savings, **I** is desired investment, **T** is taxes paid by households, and **G** is desired government spending. Only when the sum of all the desired injections, shown by (+), into the circular flow of income equals the sum of all the desired leakages, shown by (−), can the circular flow of income, and hence GDP, remain stable. (For simplicity, we ignore firms' savings and taxes, transfers from government to households, and imports by firms and the government.)

that this is a leakage from the circular flow of income between domestic firms and domestic households. Another reason households do not spend all they earn on firms is because some income is paid to the government as taxes. This is shown in Figure 16.11 by $T(-)$, households' taxes. An additional leakage between households and firms occurs because some household after-tax income is saved and placed in financial markets and institutions. This is shown by $S(-)$.

Offsetting the leakages from the circular flow of income are a number of injections. These are shown by plus signs in Figure 16.11. Injections result from exports $Ex(+)$, which are part of spending on the output of domestic firms but are not due to the spending of domestic households. Injections also result from business investment $I(+)$, which is financed by financial markets and institutions rather than from the revenue of firms. Finally, injections come from government expenditure $G(+)$. We assume that government buys only from firms.

The circular flow of income cannot remain stable if more flows out than in or if more flows in than out. If injections exceed withdrawals, the circular flow of income will expand. A useful analogy to the circular flow of income with its leakages versus injections is a bathtub or sink. If more flows into a bathtub (the injections) than goes down the drain (the leakages), the bathtub will overflow. This is like the situation of expansion in an economy. If, on the other hand, more flows down the drain than flows in from the tap, the bath or sink will empty. In an economy, withdrawals exceeding injections means a decline in GDP. The only way that the level of water or the level of GDP is maintained is for injections to equal withdrawals. That is, for GDP to be in equilibrium, injections must equal withdrawals.

If injections equal withdrawals, then the items with plus signs in Figure 16.11 have a total value equal to the total value of the items with minus signs. This means that for a stable circular flow of income, we need

$$I + G + Ex = S + T + Im \qquad (16.6)$$

A stable circular flow of income requires that injections into the circular flow of income—investment plus government spending plus exports—equal withdrawals from the circular flow of income—savings plus taxes plus imports.

The left-hand side is the sum of injections, and the right-hand side is the sum of withdrawals.

The condition for a stable income in Equation 16.6 is equivalent to the condition we described earlier, namely, $E = Y$. This can be seen by adding C to both sides of Equation 16.6 and moving Im to the left-hand side, giving

$$C + I + G + (Ex - Im) = C + S + T \qquad (16.7)$$

The left-hand side is E, as it was defined and used in Equation 16.1. The right-hand side of Equation 16.7 is Y, because, by definition, before-tax household income Y is either taken as taxes, consumed, or saved; that is,

$$Y \equiv C + S + T$$

Hence Equation 16.7 equates E on the left-hand side with Y on the right-hand side, and Equation 16.6 is equivalent to $E = Y$.

Equation 16.6, while equivalent to the equality of E and Y, puts different emphasis on the factors affecting the equilibrium GDP than does a consideration of E versus Y. In particular, Equation 16.6 makes clear that GDP is in equilibrium when, at the same time,

$$I = S \qquad (16.8)$$

$$G = T \qquad (16.9)$$

and $$Ex = Im \qquad (16.10)$$

Equation 16.8 points to the importance of the withdrawal of funds by savers being matched by the amount being reinjected by borrowers who are investing. The recycling that is needed is done by banks and other financial institutions and by the stock and bond markets.

Equation 16.9 points to the relevance of the government running a balanced budget, a situation which is determined in the political arena. When a government runs a **fiscal deficit,** which is the situation in which government spending exceeds tax receipts, Keynesians view this as expansionary unless the fiscal deficit offsets a lack of private demand.

A fiscal deficit occurs when government spending exceeds tax receipts. Ceteris paribus, fiscal deficits are expansionary.

Example   16.1

THE CYCLE OF ECONOMIC IDEAS

The best evidence that no school of macroeconomic thought has a monopoly on the truth is the continual swing of ideas between Monetarists, Keynesians, and others. Consider, for example, the following article from **The New York Times.** It describes a renewed interest in Keynesian activist policy at the depth of the stubborn 1990–1992 recession. The article discusses the relevance of lags in the effect of fiscal policy and of the effect government borrowing has on private spending. The cycle of ideas suggests that all major schools of macroeconomic thought have something to offer and that the one providing the most useful solution depends largely on circumstances at any particular time.

John Kennedy's 1962 tax cut was widely celebrated as the dawn of the millennium of can-do economics. But by . . . 1990, the notion of adding to the budget deficit for any reason seemed folly.

Now the pendulum is swinging back. How could anyone believe that policies so long discredited would do more good than harm?

The answer offered cautiously—very cautiously—by economists is that much has been learned in the last few decades. And in any case, they argue, the brief against an active fiscal policy has never been as clear-cut as it appeared.

Today it seems almost self-evident that tax cuts and government spending can influence output and jobs by putting more money in people's pockets. But contrary to myth, the ideas of John Maynard Keynes, the great British theorist who changed the face of economics

in the 1930s, were not explicitly tested in the United States until the 1960s.

Walter Heller of the University of Minnesota and James Tobin of Yale, then members of the President's Council of Economic Advisers, persuaded a reluctant John Kennedy to support tax cuts for business, even at the risk of increasing the budget deficit. The apparent success of the Kennedy initiative in setting off a vigorous expansion that did not end until 1970 ushered in a golden era of interventionist economics. In fact, it was widely assumed that economics would soon tame natural swings in employment and output, much the way medical science was taming bacterial diseases.

But something—well, lots of things—happened to shatter confidence in the "science" of fine-tuning. Sharp increases in the price

Equation 16.10 shows that the state of a nation's balance of trade—its exports minus imports—can be important for a steady national product. If a country is buying far more from abroad than it sells, this can cause a declining GDP.

Equation 16.6 makes it clear that for a steady circular flow of income, each individual equality, shown by Equations 16.8, 16.9, and 16.10, does not have to hold as long as any differences between the two sides of any equation balance differences in the other equations. The factors that could result in an overall difference between injections and withdrawals are the same as those we listed in the context of discussing E versus Y and are shown in Table 16.1 on page 494.

INFLATIONARY EXPECTATIONS AND GDP FLUCTUATIONS

The arguments in the preceding chapter about how differences between actual, realized inflation and anticipated inflation cause variations in unemployment also can be used to explain fluctuations in real GDP. In order to extend the arguments of the preceding chapter to fluctuations in real GDP, we must first describe the of imported oil in 1974 and again in 1979 worked like tax increases, depressing demand for goods and services made in America. At the same time, the higher energy prices raised the cost of producing virtually everything. . . . And while economists were eventually able to make some sense of what had happened within the Keynesian framework, their inability to cope with stagflation in the 1970s opened the door to revisionism.

Indeed, research in the 1970s and 1980s had the effect of breaking the faith in fine-tuning and redirecting economists' efforts toward the more modest goal of smoothing the path toward long-term economic growth. One reason for the new skepticism was the problem of lags—the time it took to translate the need for stimulus into more concrete poured and more autos sold.

Government spending is particularly problematic because it takes months to plan new public works on top of the months it takes to pass the enabling legislation. "We have a history of adopting fiscal stimulus when it is no longer needed," concluded Robert Reischauer, the director of the Congressional Budget Office.

Tax cuts, especially across-the-board cuts that show up in reduced withholding from paychecks, work faster. But there is evidence that people are reluctant to spend increases in income that they do not expect to be permanent. Thus, additions to the deficit in the form of temporary tax cuts do not seem to add much to demand.

This frustrating complication in manipulating private spending became part of a much broader critique of activist economic policy. Once people and corporations get wind of what the Government is trying to do, the argument goes, they will change behavior in ways that offset the impact in unpredictable fashion or even cancel it entirely.

In the purist's scenario, offered by Robert Barro of Harvard, adding an extra dollar to the deficit would add nothing to overall demand because people would prudently set aside a dollar to cover the expected increase in their future taxes. . . .

Source: Peter Passell, "Taste for Fiscal Stimulus Returns," **The New York Times,** October 10, 1992, pp. 1 and 21. Copyright © 1992 by The New York Times Company. Reprinted by permission.

connection between employment and output. This connection is provided by the **production function,** which is a relationship showing how much output is obtained from various quantities of inputs of factors of production. There are production functions for individual products, as well as a production function for the nation as a whole. The production function for the nation as a whole is called the **aggregate production function.**

> The *aggregate* production function is the relationship that shows how much output a *nation* gets from various levels of inputs.

The Aggregate Production Function: Real GDP versus Employment

The aggregate production function tells us what size of real GDP will result from different inputs of capital, labor, and other inputs. The volume of real GDP clearly depends on the quality as well as the quantity of capital and labor and on the efficiency with which the inputs are used, with efficiency of input use determined in part by the quality of management.

The quality of labor depends on the level of education, and the quality of capital depends on the state of knowledge and available technology. These can be assumed to be fixed in the short run. Also, the effectiveness of management can be assumed fixed in the short run. These assumptions are based on the view that the level of education of workers, available technology, and the ability of management are the result of the accumulation of knowledge, which, while constantly improving, advances relatively little in a short period; even when rapid learning is taking place, the flow of new knowledge during any given year is small relative to the stock of knowledge inherited from the past. The *quantity* of capital also can be assumed fixed in the short run for a similar reason that the *quality* of labor, capital, and management is assumed to be fixed; it takes many years to build up the stock of factories, production equipment, roads, bridges, and so on.

The assumptions of a fixed quality of capital, labor and managerial ability and a fixed quantity of capital allow us to concentrate on the only remaining variable, the quantity of labor. That is, given our assumptions, we can explain short-run changes in real GDP in terms of the quantity of labor employed. The connection between real GDP and employment is described diagrammatically in Figure 16.12. The figure shows that the higher the employment level, the higher is real GDP. Because factors of production other than labor are fixed, the added real GDP for given increases in employment becomes smaller as employment expands. This is the result of the law of diminishing marginal product discussed in Chapter 10. We have marked the level of employment at which full employment occurs as N_F, and the level of real GDP associated with this level of employment, the full-employment GDP, as Q_F.

With the quality of labor, capital, and management and the quantity of capital all fixed in the short run, variations in real GDP result from variations in the quantity of labor employed.

Unanticipated Inflation and Real GDP

When describing the Phillips curve, we saw that because of inflexible wages, employment increases when inflation exceeds what had been anticipated; this is when contracted wages are too low. Consequently, increases in real GDP occur when there is unanticipated inflation. Similarly, reductions in employment and real GDP occur when inflation is smaller than had been anticipated; this is when contracted wages are too high. This is summarized in Figure 16.13, which shows unanticipated inflation on the vertical axis and changes in real GDP on the horizontal axis. When inflation is correctly anticipated, we show real GDP growing at the trend rate, which is that due to the normal advance in productivity and so on. Faster growth in real GDP than the trend rate occurs when realized inflation exceeds expectations, that is, when there is unanticipated inflation. Slower growth than the trend rate occurs when realized inflation is below expectations, that is, when there is unanticipated disinflation. A substantial amount of unanticipated disinflation can even cause the growth in real GDP to be negative. In Figure 16.13, this occurs if unanticipated disinflation exceeds $0A$.

Ceteris paribus, real GDP will grow above its trend when there is unanticipated inflation and below its trend when there is unanticipated disinflation.

Rational Expectations and Real GDP Fluctuations*

In Chapter 15 we explained that if inflationary expectations are rational, then inflation is just as likely to be overestimated as underestimated. This is so because by rational expectations we mean that all relevant information about what could

---

*Sections or numbered items marked with an asterisk may be omitted without a loss of continuity.

FIGURE 16.12   With technology, the stock of capital, and the quality of management and labor all constant in the short run, changes in real output depend on changes in employment.

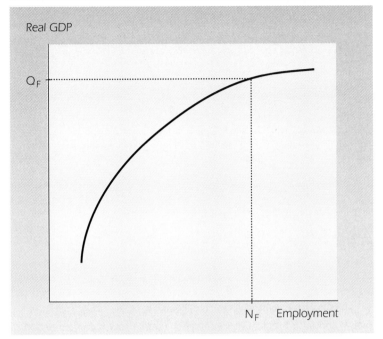

Full employment, with **N_F** people working, results in the full-employment real GDP **Q_F**. Variations in real GDP around this full-employment level are caused by variations in employment and hence by variations in unemployment.

affect future inflation is taken into account in inflation forecasts. Under such conditions, inflation is as likely to be overestimated as underestimated. If inflation expectations are indeed rational, then in terms of Figure 16.13 the economy is just as likely to have unanticipated inflation—that is, be above zero on the vertical axis—as have unanticipated disinflation—that is, be below zero on the vertical axis. The growth rate of real GDP would then fluctuate around its trend, being as often above the trend as below.

The length of time the growth rate of real GDP is above or below the trend depends on the lengths of wage contracts. This is so because if, for example, there is unanticipated disinflation and wages are therefore too high, the longer wage contracts are, the longer are wages above equilibrium.[8] This means that even

---

[8] At any time there are newly agreed wage contracts, expiring contracts, and contracts with various lengths of continuing validity. Our comments therefore relate to the *average* length of wage contracts in the economy.

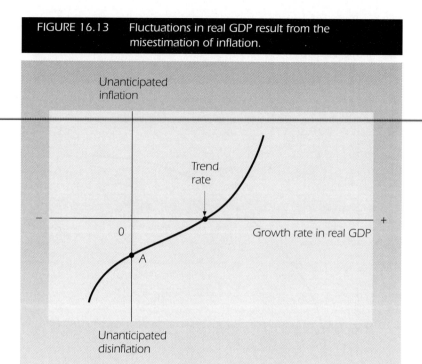

FIGURE 16.13   Fluctuations in real GDP result from the misestimation of inflation.

If inflation is anticipated correctly, we are at zero on the vertical axis and have the long-run trend rate of growth of real GDP. In any year actual growth can exceed this if actual inflation exceeds what had been expected, that is, if there is unanticipated inflation. Actual growth can be below the trend rate if actual inflation is below expectations, that is, if there is unanticipated disinflation. Sufficiently large unanticipated disinflation, exceeding **0A**, can cause real GDP to decline.

though expectations may be rational, unemployment could be high or low for months or even years on end. For example, if inflation unexpectedly declines but many wage contracts have 2 or even 3 years before expiration, unemployment could persist for 2 or 3 years. Therefore, instead of having just short-term, random fluctuations of unemployment and hence of real GDP growth around the trend, the economy could exhibit variations that take the longer up and down sweeps characteristic of a business cycle.

PHASES OF THE BUSINESS CYCLE

The **business cycle,** or **trade cycle** as it used to be called, refers to a recurring pattern of variations in GDP growth rates around the trend and the associated variations in unemployment around the natural rate of unemployment. There are four phases to a business cycle: the **trough,** which is when unemployment is highest and growth of real GDP is lowest; the **recovery,** when unemployment declines and real GDP growth increases; the **peak,** when unemployment is lowest and real GDP growth highest; and the **contraction,** when unemployment is increasing and

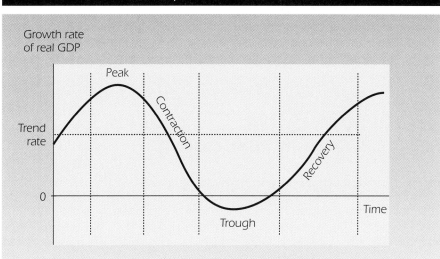

FIGURE 16.14   A business cycle involves a recurring pattern of troughs, recoveries, peaks, and contractions.

A business cycle can be divided into four phases: the peak, when the economy is growing at the maximum; the contraction, as the economy slows; the trough, when the economy has low growth and is perhaps even contracting; and the recovery, when the economy picks up again. The term boom is sometimes used instead of peak and recession instead of trough. The length of a business cycle is measured from peak to peak or trough to trough. Actual data in an economy do not exhibit regular patterns, making it a complex matter to determine the length of a business cycle and where in the cycle an economy is at any moment.

real GDP growth is decreasing. These phases of the cycle are illustrated in Figure 16.14. Other terms used in the context of the business cycle are **boom,** when the economy is at a peak, and **recession,** when the economy is at a trough. The term recession is usually used to describe the situation of two successive calendar quarters of a declining real GDP, although official declarations of recessions are made by the National Bureau of Economic Research (NBER). The NBER considers real GDP as well as other factors such as unemployment in its determination of when recessions begin and end.

The length of one complete business cycle is the time from one peak to the next peak or from one trough to the next trough. A glance back at Figures 16.1 to 16.4 shows that it is not a simple matter to identify a regular, recurring pattern with a constant length when faced with actual growth rate data. In the United States, the NBER has developed a complex procedure for identifying all phases of its **reference cycle,** with this being used widely in government policy.[9] The most common length of NBER cycles is in the range of about 8 to 10 years.

---

[9] Some U.S. government programs depend on whether there is a recession, making the NBER reference cycle an important factor in government policy.

In all our discussion about rational expectations and the business cycle, we have spoken in terms of fluctuations of the GDP growth rate about its trend rather than of fluctuations around zero. We do this because an economy typically grows, with recessions being only temporary and relatively short pauses in that growth. Let us consider the factors affecting the trend rate of growth in real GDP. As we shall see, the trend rate itself can take on different values at different times and in different countries.

DETERMINANTS OF THE TREND GROWTH IN REAL GDP

Labor, Capital, and Managerial Inputs

As the upper parts of Figures 16.1 to 16.4 show very clearly, the trend in real GDP has been upward. Indeed, average growth rates of real GDPs have exceeded population growth rates by several percent in most countries, meaning improved living standards.[10] Not surprisingly, since economic growth is the result of developments in the overall economy, many factors are responsible for the trend in real GDP. In particular, the real GDP has expanded over time as a result of

1. Growth in the quantity of capital

2. Growth in the quantity of labor

3. Growth in the quality of capital

4. Growth in the quality of labor

5. Growth in the efficiency of production due to technological advances and improvements in management

Our account of fluctuations in real GDP concentrated on the second factor, the quantity of labor, and assumed everything else to be constant. While this is a reasonable assumption when considering fluctuations in real GDP from quarter to quarter or even from year to year, it will not do for explaining the trend rate of growth of real GDP over a number of years. For this we must study all the influences on growth of real GDP listed above. Let us consider each in turn.

The capital stock grows when there is net investment. Net investment is the total investment, called gross investment, minus depreciation.

Growth in the Quantity of Capital. Growth in the quantity of capital is the immediate consequence of **net investment**. Net investment is defined as **gross investment**, which is the total value of investment, minus **depreciation.**

---

[10] Nevertheless, there is a general perception, especially in recent years in the United States, that people are worse off. Examples 16.2 and 16.3 present opposing views of what has happened. However, despite their contradictory tone, the two examples show agreement on the importance of peoples' expectations; they suggest a frustration in not moving ahead as fast as expected and as fast as people in some other countries.

Depreciation is the value of capital which wears out during an interval of time. As we said in Chapter 12, depreciation is also referred to as **capital consumption.**

As we shall see in the next chapter, net investment depends on the profitability and risk associated with new plant and equipment. When investors have the funds to invest, profitability is judged relative to the opportunity cost of investment in terms of returns available on bonds and other alternatives. When investors do not have the funds, profitability depends on the cost of raising them. The cost of raising capital and the opportunity cost of investor-owned capital both increase with increases in interest rates. That is, *ceteris paribus*, the higher the interest rates, the lower is net investment. Investment is also affected by the tax rate on income from investment—higher taxes reduce investment—and uncertainty about the business environment—increased uncertainty reduces investment.

Ceteris paribus, the lower the interest rates, taxes, and uncertainty, the higher is net investment.

Growth in the Quantity of Labor.   While the trend growth rate in the number of people is largely determined by demographic factors such as birth rates, migration rates, and death rates, the size of the work force is also related to economic factors. We have already seen when discussing the labor market in Chapter 15 that the quantity of labor supplied, in terms of hours worked or the number of people working, depends on real wages. This is so because real wages affect the choice between working and alternative activities, such as additional education, retirement, leisure, or work at home. However, there are also other relevant factors, some of which are economic and others of which are legal or sociological.

The quantity of labor depends on demographic, economic, sociological, and legal factors.

There has been a substantial increase in the percentage of the work force made up of women. This has contributed significantly to the growth of real GDP in the aggregate and, of course, the incomes of those families with the extra source of income. The basis of the increase in the female work force participation rate is related in part to the sociological and political liberation women have experienced but also may be due to labor-saving technological changes in the home such as

Example   16.2

GETTING WORSE

There has been growing frustration with the pace of economic improvement and an increased perception that things have actually deteriorated. Indeed, as the following excerpt from a **New York Times** article suggests, data can be found that show people falling behind. Nevertheless, as Example 16.3 shows, there is another side to what is happening. However,

even though the tone of this example and Example 16.3 are very different, there is agreement that people are not doing as well as they had expected and that this is the major cause of spreading pessimism.

Several new economic reports demonstrate starkly the extent to which Americans' incomes have

stalled, painting a depressing picture of workers struggling to crawl up a down escalator. . . .

As President Ronald Reagan once did, the Democrats are asking, often, whether Americans are better off than they were four years ago. The Economic Policy Institute, a Washington research center with close ties to the Democrats, released a study . . . showing that high school graduates now earn 26.5% less in entry-level jobs than similar

Example 16.2 (continued)

graduates did in 1979. That study also found that after-inflation wages for workers with college degrees fell 3.1% between 1987 and 1991.

In another study, Congress's Joint Economic Committee said . . . that a 30-year-old male with a high school education earned $3500 less than a comparable 30-year-old did in 1979. The committee, dominated by Democrats, said most young men entering the work force should expect lower lifetime earnings than the previous generation of men. Too few women were in the work force a generation ago to make an equivalent comparison.

The Republicans have responded by berating Democratic "declinists" who assert that the next generation of Americans will be poorer than the current generation. The Republicans blame the Democratic Congress for the economy's poor performance and assert that the economy performed far worse under President Jimmy Carter than it has under President Bush.

But Republicans could find little comfort in [the] economic news. A Census Bureau report . . . for example, found that median household income had fallen 5.1% since 1989, after inflation was factored in. That report also found that the number of Americans living in poverty rose last year [1991] by 2.1 million, to 35.7 million. . . .

"Contrary to the past, when people could anticipate that they would do better over their lifetime and their children would do better than they have done, now they face stagnation and even decline in their income," said Senator Paul S. Sarbanes, the Maryland Democrat who is the chairman of the committee. "The American dream of improving yourself and moving forward has not been realized over the last decade and a half." . . .

William A. Niskanen Jr., a member of President Reagan's Council on Economic Advisers and chairman of the Cato Institute, a conservative research center, saw several reasons for the wage stagnation. He cited low growth in worker productivity since 1973 and the internationalization of the American economy, two trends that have increased wage pressures on American workers. "It's put our low-skilled workers more in competition with low-skilled workers in other countries."

Wages have also been held down, he said, by the rapid increase in non-wage costs paid by employers, most notably those for health care.

Liberal economists say slow growth in the minimum wage and the weakening of unions have also contributed to low wage growth. . . . Conservatives usually propose cutting taxes, especially those on capital gains; Democrats generally favor increased public investment on highways, railroads and tele-communications, which they say will spur growth and efficiency.

The one area that Republicans and Democrats agree on for raising growth and incomes is improving education, but they disagree on how.

Michael J. Boskin, chairman of the President's Council of Economic Advisers, said the slowdown in wage growth and productivity growth dated from well before President Bush's election (1988). He attributes the slowdown in productivity in large part to the reduced rate of capital investment per worker, and "the enormous growth and changing composition of the labor force."

Many economists say the flood of the baby boomers and women into the labor force has helped push down productivity growth and wages since 1973. People in these groups were new to the labor force and thus relatively inexperienced.

"To get wage growth up over the long haul, we need to get productivity growth up," Mr. Boskin said. "And to do that, we need tax incentives to spur investment and entrepreneurship as well as enormous improvement in elementary and secondary-school performance."

Source: Steven Greenhouse, "Income Data Show Years of Erosion for U.S. Workers," **The New York Times,** September 7, 1992, pp. 1 and 20. Copyright © 1992 by The New York Times Company. Reprinted by permission.

Example   16.3

GETTING BETTER

Example 16.2 explains how economic conditions have become worse, while the article here, written less than 1 month earlier, says the opposite. What the opposing viewpoints suggest is that income performance depends on the precise data that are considered and on the standards against which income statistics are compared. However, there is no disagreement that people are frustrated at not getting ahead as fast as they had hoped and that expectations are based on progress made in earlier decades. One line in the example captures this better than any other: "[T]he good news isn't as good as it used to be."

As pessimistic as many of its people seem to be, by many measures America remains a land of prosperity and opportunity.

Consider this:

—The poor aren't necessarily poorer. As a group, the poorest 20% of households saw their mean household income—adjusted for inflation—increase 5% from 1980 to 1990. A smaller study tracking individuals showed a more dramatic gain among the poor: In the past two decades, their average family income increased 77%, while the richest gained 5%.

—Whatever they might think, many of today's middle-aged adults are better off than their parents. Today, one in four women has a college degree, compared with one in 10 of their mothers. The average income of a young family of 25- to 35-year-olds, adjusted for inflation, is 40% higher than 30 years ago, when their parents were their age.

—The U.S. retains the highest standard of living in the world. Per capita income is still 17% higher than in Japan. The Japanese, who work an average 6% more hours each year than Americans, pay twice as much rent as residents of New York City and 28% more for basic staples from apples to appliances.

—Many Americans can and do improve their lot. One study by the Urban Institute found that nearly half the people in the lowest income level moved up in each of the past two decades. In fact, in all but the highest income level, more people stayed the same or moved up than fell behind.

Of course, studies can be drummed up to support almost any proposition. Lately those getting the most attention suggest that things have been getting worse.

Fabian Linden, an economist with the Conference Board, says the general malaise is so great that if you dare suggest things aren't terrible, "people become enraged. . . ."

[A] broadly held notion is that the real weekly income of the average American is down 19.1% since 1973, a figure widely reported and attributed to economist Wallace Peterson of the University of Nebraska. As it turns out, the average American isn't average at all. Dr. Peterson's data don't include self-employed professionals, anyone who supervises another worker, pensioners or anyone employed in the public sector, including teachers or government employees. A better measure of income, he concedes, is inflation-adjusted family income, which according to his calculations has risen 0.57% annually on average since 1973. That's a total real gain for the period of 5.4%.

Still, the good news isn't as good as it used to be. Productivity gains have slowed to 1% from 3% in the 1940s through the 1970s. And while the U.S. is still ahead of Japan, that country has closed ranks since 1960, when America's standard of living was 70% higher. Wages in the U.S. are rising, but not as fast as they once did. And today's adults can't expect the same leaps as their grandparents, who worked themselves into the middle class on the backs of grade-school education and sometimes saw their children earn six-figure incomes by the time they reached 30.

microwaves, dishwashers, and so on. Whatever the cause, the increase in the number of women in the work force has been an important source of growth in real GDP. The size of the work force is also affected by legal factors such as the minimum age at which people can enter the work force and the presence or absence of mandatory retirement laws.

A further factor that can influence the supply of labor is the income tax rate. The reward for selecting work rather than an alternative activity, such as retirement or school, is the *after-tax* wage rate.

Growth in Quality of Capital. While it is difficult in practice to distinguish between the quantity and quality of capital, there is strong evidence that real GDP has grown as a result of improvements in the technology incorporated into machines as a result of research and development (R&D). This is especially true in manufacturing, but is also true in areas other than manufacturing. Today, microcomputers are causing a revolution in the service sector that could even overshadow the Industrial Revolution in manufacturing of the eighteenth century. With robotics and ever-better computer software and hardware, the quality of machinery is not only advancing but might even be accelerating.

Technological advance does not just result from major scientific breakthroughs by researchers in government institutes, huge corporations, and large research-oriented universities. Rather, many of the improvements in production methods that have been incorporated in capital equipment have occurred in small or medium-sized firms and have resulted from innovative solutions to very specific, isolated problems. Ingenuity is not the sole domain of scientists with years of expensive and formal education but is a quality that surfaces in small workshops, offices, and similar places of employment. However, the chance that ingenious solutions will be found, whether in large or small settings, depends on there being a well-educated work force.

Growth in Quality of Labor. Education represents an investment in human capital that, as with investment in physical capital, has allowed increased output to come from the same number of hours of labor input. The benefit has been enjoyed both directly from a better-educated work force and indirectly via the contribution that educated people have made to the quality of physical capital.

Growth in Effectiveness of Management. Not all the increases in real GDP can be attributed to growth in the quantity and quality of capital and labor. Production requires that labor and capital are used effectively, and this requires effective business management.

Improvements in management have taken a variety of forms, some of which have had pervasive effects on the economy. Perhaps one of the most important of these managerial improvements is the widespread application of **just-in-time inventory-control systems.** Aided by parallel developments in computer technology and communication systems, companies have installed mechanisms for ordering just what they need as it is needed and for suppliers to deliver according to precise schedules. This cuts down on losses from waiting for crucial parts to arrive and on storage costs from the need to hold inventory in case of unexpected delays. Other managerial improvements have occurred in quality control, financial management, cost-accounting methods, and organizational efficiencies. These improvements in management have been a result of better education in general and perhaps business education in particular; courses are now common in production control, financial management, organizational design, cost accounting, and the other managerial areas in which advances have been made.

Other Influences on the Trend Growth Rate of Real GDP

Factor Supplies.   The availability of factors of production can affect the trend rate of growth of real GDP as well as fluctuations of real GDP around the trend. In our discussion of *fluctuations* of real GDP, we called a sudden disruption in the availability of an input such as imported oil a supply shock. If the availability of an input diminishes gradually over the long run rather than suddenly, this can affect the *trend* rate of growth. For example, if Canada were to run out of untapped sources of hydro-electric power, the ability to continue to grow by producing and selling electric power would diminish, reducing the growth rate of Canada's real GDP.

Better Allocation of Resources and Economies of Scale.   With a vast pool of talented people distributed over all sociological and ethnic groups, as barriers have slowly been removed, more women, blacks, and so on have been better able to develop their potential. This is an improvement in the allocation and utilization of resources and has benefited society in general as well as those with expanded opportunities. The allocation of resources also has been improved between nations by international trade. This has allowed nations to exploit their advantages to everybody's benefit, as well as to exploit economies of scale. All these allocational gains translate into long-term gains in real GDP.

The Importance of Different Factors

Table 16.3 shows the estimates of the contribution of different factors responsible for economic growth according to the work of Edward Denison. We can see that all the factors we have listed are part of the explanation of growing real GDP. No individual factor appears to dominate the others. Therefore, it is unlikely that any individual policy that the government might adopt could have a dominant effect. Indeed, it is remarkable how evenly divided are the different contributing factors to overall economic growth. While there is the potential for errors in the estimates and for the potential importance of different factors to change over time, it would appear that we must look to every factor we have listed in order to fully explain economic growth.

No individual factor influencing long-term or trend economic growth has a dominant effect.

Taxes and Long-Term Economic Growth

We mentioned earlier that net investment and hence growth in the quantity of capital depends on tax rates on income from investment. This is so because the tax on income from investment affects the profitability of investment. We also mentioned that the quantity of labor supplied depends on tax rates because the decision to work depends on after-tax real wages. If higher tax rates do indeed reduce growth in the quantity of capital and labor, then higher tax rates can reduce the growth rate of the economy. Indeed, some economists have blamed

TABLE 16.3

Real GDP has grown as a result of numerous factors.

PERCENT RATE OF U.S. ANNUAL GROWTH, 1929–1982, ATTRIBUTABLE TO:	
Quantity of capital	0.56
Quantity of labor	0.77
Quality of capital	0.66
Quality of Labor	0.57
Better allocation of resources and economies of scale	0.36
	⎯⎯
TOTAL	2.92

The quality of capital involves primarily the effects of new inventions, better machines, improved production methods, and so on but also includes other factors not listed elsewhere. The quality of labor involves only the direct benefit of better education. The estimates suggest that no individual cause of economic growth is dominant. This, in turn, suggests that no individual policy that the government might impose could have a dominant impact.

Source: Edward F. Denison, **Trends in American Economic Growth, 1929–1982** (Washington, DC: Brookings Institution, 1985).

increasing effective rates of tax on investment and labor income during the 1960s and 1970s for the relatively low real output growth that occurred during those decades. This view, that increasing tax rates reduce the rate of growth of real GDP, is a major component of **supply-side economics.** Supply-side economics emphasizes the supply of inputs in the determination of economic growth and is an economic philosophy that shaped economic policy in the 1980s, including general reductions in tax rates.

A leading advocate of the position that tax reductions stimulate investment and hard work and thereby add to economic growth is Arthur Laffer, who argues that the effect of taxes on labor supply, capital investment, and the willingness to report income to the tax authorities is so substantial that lower tax *rates* could actually result in higher tax *revenues;* the lower rates on their own would mean fewer taxes collected, but the extra employment, investment, and willingness to report income could more than offset this.[11] Laffer's claim is illustrated by the

---

[11] The avoidance of reporting income to tax authorities is the principal motivation for the underground economy.

Laffer curve in Figure 16.15. We draw two curves and note that both curves show total tax revenues of zero at a 0% tax rate and at a 100% tax rate. The zero tax revenue at a 0% tax rate occurs because no taxes are collected at such a rate. The zero tax revenue at a 100% tax rate occurs because there would be no incentive to work, invest, or report any income if all income was taken in taxes. The important question is how the Laffer curve is shaped between the extremes. If it is believed that the Laffer curve is shaped like the solid line shown in Figure 16.15, then reducing tax rates from τ_2 to τ_1 would increase total tax receipts. However, if the correct curve is really the dotted line, a policy of lower tax rates would reduce total taxes collected.[12]

The Laffer curve relates tax revenues to the tax rate.

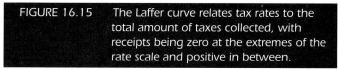

FIGURE 16.15   The Laffer curve relates tax rates to the total amount of taxes collected, with receipts being zero at the extremes of the rate scale and positive in between.

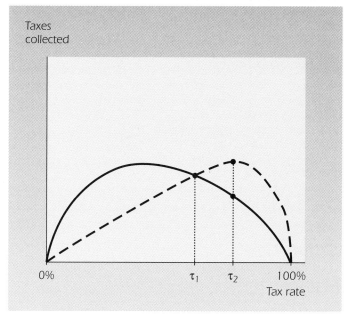

Total tax revenues are zero at a 0% tax rate but are also zero at a 100% tax rate because it would not pay to work, invest, or report any income. In between these extremes there are positive total tax revenues. If the tax rate is reduced when it is above the rate for maximum revenues, the lower rate increases total revenues. For example, with the solid-line Laffer curve, reducing rates from τ_2 to τ_1 will increase total taxes. However, if the true Laffer curve is the dashed line, the policy of reducing the tax rate from τ_2 to τ_1 will reduce total tax revenues.

[12] As Example 16.4 shows, the Laffer curve may have been discovered in the fourteenth century.

Example   16.4   **THE LAFFER OR KHALDUN CURVE?**

Not much is new, as the following excerpt clearly shows.

It should be shown that at the beginning of a dynasty, taxation yields a large revenue from small assessments. At the end of the dynasty, taxation yields a small revenue from large assessments.

The reason for this is that when the dynasty follows the ways of Islam, it imposes only such taxes as are stipulated by the religious law, such as charity taxes, the land tax, and the poll tax. These have fixed limits that cannot be exceeded. . . .

Therefore, the individual imposts and assessments, which together constitute the tax revenue, are low. When tax assessments and imposts upon the subjects are low, the latter have the energy and desire to do things. Cultural enterprises grow and increase, because the low taxes bring satisfaction. When cultural enterprises grow, the number of

individuals imposts and assessments mounts. In consequence, the tax revenue, which is the sum total of . . . [the individual assessments], increases.

When the dynasty continues in power and their rulers follow each other in succession, they become sophisticated. The Bedouin attitude and simplicity lose their significance, and the Bedouin qualities of moderation and restraint disappear. . . . As a result, the individual imposts and assessments upon the subjects, agricultural laborers, farmers, and all the other taxpayers, increase. Every individual impost and assessment is greatly increased, in order to obtain a higher tax revenue. . . . Eventually, the taxes will weigh heavily upon the subjects and overburden them. . . .

. . . The result is that the interest of subjects in cultural enterprises disappears, since when they compare expenditures and taxes with their income and gain and see

the little profit they make, they lose all hope. Therefore, many of them refrain from all cultural activity. The result is that the total tax revenue goes down, as individual assessments go down. Often, when the decrease is noticed, the amounts of individual imposts are increased. This is considered a means of compensating for the decrease. Finally, individual imposts and assessments reach their limit. It would be of no avail to increase them further. The costs of all cultural enterprise are now too high, the taxes are too heavy, and the profits anticipated fail to materialize. Finally, civilization is destroyed, because the incentive for cultural activity is gone.

Source: Ibn Khaldûn, **The Muqaddimah,** 1377. Translated by Franz Rosenthal, edited and abridged by N. J. Dawood. (Princeton, N.J.: Princeton University Press, 1967), pp. 230–231.

FORECASTING GDP

Short-Term Forecasts

With different factors being responsible for short-term fluctuations in real GDP than are responsible for longer-term trends, when making forecasts of GDP we must consider different things. In the case of short-term forecasts, say, for up to 1 year, real GDP should grow relatively rapidly when realized inflation exceeds anticipated inflation. Similarly, real GDP should decline, at least below its trend, when realized inflation is less than anticipated inflation. However, we have seen that these effects on real GDP are short term. This is so because if workers' expectations are rational, the same errors in anticipations are not repeated. That is, people should not underestimate or overestimate inflation for long periods.

Actual inflation is likely to exceed what had been anticipated when inflation is increasing, so we expect increasing real GDP to occur, albeit temporarily, with increasing inflation. But how can we predict when inflation is likely to increase? Monetarists look at statistics on the money supply. However, the weekly or monthly data which are available are very volatile, fluctuating a great deal from week to week or month to month. Therefore, it is difficult to clearly identify lasting changes in the growth rate of the money supply which, according to the quantity theory, should precede increases or decreases of inflation.

Keynesians recognize, as do Monetarists, that employment is determined in the labor market and that, therefore, it is the actual wage versus the equilibrium wage that matters. They are therefore also concerned with errors in inflationary anticipations which can cause wages to differ from their equilibrium level, but they also consider other factors. In particular, Keynesians believe that declines in autonomous consumption, investment, government spending, or exports could cause a decline in the demand for labor, making contracted wages too high and thereby causing unemployment and a slowdown or decline in real GDP. They also believe that this can happen as a result of increased savings, taxes, or imports. These are the same factors they believe can reduce aggregate demand. Therefore, when trying to forecast short-run changes in GDP, Keynesians consider the factors listed in Table 16.1 on page 494, which are the factors affecting the components of desired expenditure.[13]

Long-Term Forecasts

As we have seen, economists from both major schools of thought recognize that long-term growth in real GDP occurs as a result of changes in the quantity and quality of factors of production. They both look at net investment, which determines the future quantity of capital; current spending on R&D, which determines the future quality of capital; the growth rate and age composition of the population, which determine the future quantity of labor; and current spending on education, which determines the future quality of labor, capital, and management. (These matters are discussed in Example 16.2 on pages 511 and 512.)

Monetarists and Keynesians disagree about the policies that will best achieve a rapid growth of the quantity and quality of capital and hence of future GDP. As we shall see in the next chapter, Monetarists think that fiscal deficits, where government spending exceeds taxes, crowd out private spending on investment via the effect of fiscal deficits on interest rates. In particular, they believe that interest rates ration the available supply of funds for borrowing such that if more funds are being siphoned off to cover fiscal deficits, interest rates increase to limit investment to the value of remaining funds. In this way, Monetarists believe that fiscal deficits reduce the growth of real GDP. Keynesians argue that to the extent that fiscal deficits are used only to make up for deficient demand in the private sector, they help keep resources active which would otherwise have been idle. Furthermore, if these resources are used to build roads, airports, communication satellites, knowledge, and so on, they add to the stock of capital, in particular, **public capital** in the form of **infrastructure,** and therefore add to future real GDP. Further differences between Monetarists and Keynesians are indicated in Example 16.1 on pages 504 and 505.

In deciding whether a fiscal deficit is merely compensating for deficient demand in the private sector or the cause of too much total demand, we can use

The full-employment deficit is the fiscal deficit that would occur if the economy had full employment.

---

[13] Example 16.5 discusses the accuracy of short-term economic forecasts.

Example 16.5

SEEING FURTHER AND BETTER

Advances in macroeconomic theory and forecasting techniques appear to be paying off, with the accuracy of predictions of economic conditions generally improving. As the following excerpt from **The Economist** *explains, the improvement in the record of forecasters comes despite additional uncertainties.*

While Albert Einstein is queuing to enter heaven, he meets three men. He asks about their IQs. The first replies 190. "Wonderful," exclaims Einstein. "We can discuss my theory of relativity." The second answers 150. "Good," says Einstein. "I look forward to discussing the prospects for world peace." The third mumbles 50. Einstein pauses. "So what is your forecast for GDP growth next year."

This old joke sums up most people's view of economic

forecasters. Their reputation has been severely dented of late, not least because they failed to predict the strength of the world economic boom in the late 1980s and then, worse still, failed to warn of the consequent recession.

Are forecasts becoming less accurate? Financial deregulation and globalisation have made it harder to track the economy, so you might expect the answer to be yes. The facts, however, suggest otherwise.

. . . [T]he forecasting record of Britain's Treasury over the past 13 years . . . shows . . . [d]uring 1985–91 the average error for growth was 0.7 of a percentage point, compared with 1.2 points in the previous six years. The Treasury's forecasts of inflation and the current account also seem to have improved.

But such tests depend upon the time horizon. Looking at the forecasts which the Treasury made

in the previous November of each year, its GDP forecasts for the period since 1985 seem to be more off beam than before, though it has got better at predicting inflation.

Victor Zarnowitz,* an economist at the University of Chicago, has studied a large number of American forecasts over the past 30 years. . . . [H]e finds that the accuracy of growth forecasts has hardly changed. . . . Inflation forecasts have become less accurate since the 1960s—but that is not surprising, given the surge in inflation in the 1970s.

Mr. Zarnowitz also compared the average error of these forecasts with the error from forecasts using a crude extrapolation of four year

*Victor Zarnowitz, "Has Macro-Forecasting Failed?" National Bureau of Economic Research, Cambridge, Mass., Working Paper No. 3867, 1992.

When unemployment exceeds the full-employment level, the actual *deficit exceeds the* full-employment *deficit. The increased actual deficit during increased unemployment serves as a built-in stabilizer of the economy.*

the **full-employment deficit,** which is sometimes also referred to as the **high-employment deficit** or the **cyclically adjusted deficit.** By definition, the full-employment deficit is what the fiscal deficit would be if the economy were fully employed.

When there is heavy unemployment during a recession, government tax revenues are low because peoples' and firms' incomes on which taxes are collected are low. The low tax revenues contribute toward a larger fiscal deficit, but the extra deficit should not be reduced. Cutting the deficit would mean higher taxes or lower government spending at a time of heavy unemployment, making things worse. Indeed, it is fortunate that the structure of taxes brings about a larger fiscal deficit during a recession. The automatically caused fiscal deficit serves as a **built-in stabilizer,** helping to keep the economy on a relatively even keel.

To judge whether an actual fiscal deficit is the result of a built-in stabilizer or the result of a **structural deficit**—a deficit that would have occurred even if there moving averages of output and inflation. Professional forecasters will be relieved to know that the extrapolations proved much less accurate.

Further evidence that American forecasters have improved their aim comes from *Blue Chip,* an American newsletter, which polls about 50 economists each month. The mean absolute error of October forecasters for GDP growth in the following year fell from 1.1 percentage points in 1977–83 to 0.9 of a point in 1984–91.

Forecasters may be no worse than they used to be, but that is still not good enough. In particular, their biggest blunders tend to be at turning-points, when the economy dips into recession—the very time when forecasts are most needed.

Conventional forecasting relies upon a computer model built from the economist's favourite theory about how the economy works. Using past data, he tries to get the best fit for hundreds of equations

that attempt to explain the relationships between economic variables. Assumptions about such things as tax rates, which cannot be forecast because they are decided by governments, are then plugged in and the computer cranks out an economic forecast.

Disappointment with the results of such models has encouraged some economists to test different kinds of crystal balls. Two developments pursued in America over the past decade have attracted growing interest.

- The first is vector auto-regressive models (VARs). These are much simpler, with far fewer variables than standard macro-economic models. The process makes virtually no use of economic theory to establish causal links. Each variable is "explained" largely by detecting patterns in its own statistical history; to make a

prediction, the forecaster extrapolates this history into the future. Experience in America suggests that VAR models may be helpful in predicting turning points.

- A second development is the use of financial-spread variables (eg, the gap between short- and long-term interest rates) and business-confidence surveys as leading indicators of activity. Past experience suggests that financial indicators are also good at spotting turning-points. For example, if short-term interest rates rise relative to long-term rates, this typically heralds an economic slowdown. . . .

Source: "The Future Is Not What It Used to Be," **The Economist,** June 13, 1992, p. 75. © 1992 The Economist Newspaper Group, Inc. Reprinted with permission.

had been full employment—it is necessary to compute what the fiscal deficit would have been if there had been full employment. In turn, this means calculating what taxes and government spending would have been at full employment.

Figure 16.16 illustrates the principles involved. It shows higher actual tax receipts at higher real GDPs as a result of higher collection of income taxes and sales taxes; more tax revenue is collected when income and sales are high, that is, when GDP is high. Figure 16.16 also shows government spending, assumed to be the same at all levels of GDP. The result of the behavior of taxes is a larger fiscal deficit as GDP goes lower. The figure also shows the level of real GDP at full employment Q_F on the horizontal axis. The actual deficit or surplus at Q_F is the same as the full-employment deficit or surplus. In the figure there is a deficit. At levels of real GDP lower than the full-employment level, the actual deficit exceeds the full-employment deficit. If the fiscal deficit is zero at full employment, any actual deficit is the result of slack in the economy and is not a structural deficit.

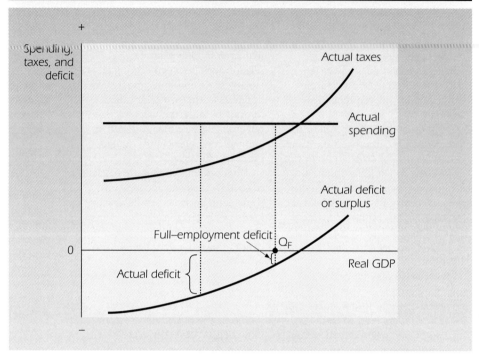

FIGURE 16.16   The full-employment deficit is what the actual deficit would be at full employment.

The full-employment deficit is what the actual deficit would be at Q_F, the full-employment GDP. Because tax receipts by government are lower the lower is real GDP, the actual deficit exceeds the full-employment deficit at real GDPs below Q_F.

Leading Indicators

There are numerous statistical measures that indicate whether economic conditions are likely to improve or worsen. These measures are referred to as **leading indicators** and include

1. Average work week

2. Average weekly initial claims for unemployment

3. New orders for consumer goods and materials, adjusted for inflation

4. Net business formation

5. Stock prices

6. Contracts and orders for plant and equipment, adjusted for inflation

7. New building permits for private housing

The index of leading economic indicators combines 12 factors each of which relates to the direction of the economy.

8. Retail sales

9. Change in inventories, adjusted for inflation

10. Change in sensitive materials prices

11. Money supply (*M2*), adjusted for inflation

12. Change in credit outstanding

The twelve measures are combined into a monthly **index of leading economic indicators** which is closely watched by government and business economists. The use of an index rather than any individual factor tends to smooth out erroneous signals that might be given from individual component measures. The reason for the inclusion of many of the series in the index of leading economic indicators is self-evident, but it is still illustrative to look at the rationale going into their selection.

Before employers begin to hire extra labor, they frequently expand the amount of overtime available to their existing employees. This offers more flexibility if an increase in demand turns out to be temporary and is also a useful stopgap while the selection of new workers is being made. The average number of hours worked is thus a measure that increases before the number of people employed increases. The same is true of the number of initial claims for unemployment compensation. However, because claims for unemployment tend to decline only as the economy expands and increase as the economy contracts, statistics on initial claims for unemployment compensation have a short **lead time.**

New orders for consumer goods, measured in real terms to reflect the quantity of goods being ordered, not only precede production and hence employment—orders being placed before the goods are produced—but are also related to consumer confidence. While not itself an index of consumer confidence, orders for large appliances and so on tend to be related to confidence about the future.

Net business formation, which measures the difference between the number of new incorporations and the number of failures, reflects both the employment opportunities of the future and the confidence businesspeople have about future earnings potential. The inclusion of stock prices is also based on confidence about the future, since stock prices are a barometer of investors' expectations about expected earnings of companies.

Contracts and orders for plant and equipment are the initial step in business investment, and we have already seen how investment can affect GDP. The value of contracts and orders for plant and equipment is an indicator of future job opportunities in making plant and equipment, including the multiplier effects this has on the economy, and of the confidence of business decision makers about future demand.

Increases in building permits serve as a measure of confidence of those deciding to build. In addition, peak employment in house construction occurs some time after building has begun, which itself occurs after permits have been granted. For example, tradespeople doing plumbing, wiring, carpeting, roofing, and so on are active several months after foundations are put in place. Furthermore, people with new houses tend to buy new furniture, appliances, and so on. This makes statistics on housing permits an important signal of future economic activity.

The level of retail sales is both a measure of confidence and a signal about how much to produce. The change in inventory stock is also a measure of confidence. However, inventory changes could work in either direction as a forecasting tool. Firms build up inventories of finished goods in anticipation of strong sales. A *planned* increase in inventories can therefore be viewed as a sign that business-people are confident that sales will increase. On the other hand, when sales are unexpectedly low, there is an *unplanned* increase in inventory. Therefore, rising *actual* inventory stocks could signal strong business confidence or unexpectedly poor economic conditions. Generally it is believed that in the initial stages of recovery the planned inventory buildup in anticipation of sales is the dominant effect. Consequently, inventory accumulation is viewed as a positive sign.

The prices of basic materials such as metals and lumber move up and down more than the prices of most consumer goods, and indeed, prices move in anticipation of final demand, since basic materials must be bought before final goods are manufactured. Therefore, materials prices serve as an indicator of future demand.

It might be thought that the money supply is included in the index of leading indicators because of the arguments we have given about the possible effects of money on future real GDP, but the inclusion of money also can be rationalized differently. Some economists argue that as businesses borrow for plant and equipment, and consumers take on loans to buy durable goods, there is an expansion of both sides of banks' balance sheets—larger assets in the form of loans and larger liabilities as consumer deposits expand. In this way, the confidence and actions of businesses and consumers translate into an increase in the money supply. The same rationale is behind the inclusion of credit outstanding in the index of leading indicators; more credit is granted when both lenders and borrowers have confidence in the future.

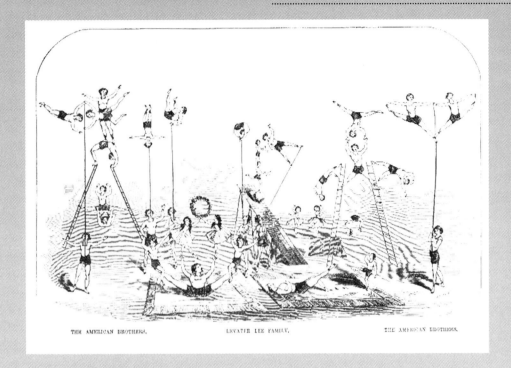

THE AMERICAN BROTHERS.   LEVATER LEE FAMILY.   THE AMERICAN BROTHERS.

BALANCING ACTS AND PERPETUAL MOTION

The process of production can be thought of as the creation of "order" from "disorderly" natural resources. That is, we can think of appetizing food on supermarket shelves and shining automobiles in their showrooms as being the result of creating the desired order of matter from the "chaotic" distribution of resources from which the products are made. In other words, the process of converting nutrients into food or iron ore into automobiles can be considered as a process of adding value by giving resources a higher desired form of organization. Viewed in this way, the gross domestic product appears in sharp contrast to that essential principle of physics, the **second law of thermodynamics.** According to this law, the universe exhibits increasing disorder, or increasing **entropy.** For example, if different parts of a body of matter have varying amounts of heat, the warmer parts lose heat to the cooler parts until the heat is evenly distributed. The heat is then at a greater level of disorder or, alternatively, at a higher entropy. Everything from the motion of heavenly bodies to the behavior of atoms is subject to the second law of thermodynamics, making it clear that there must be a level at which order is sacrificed in the productive activity of an economy; in economics as in physics, "there is no such thing as a free lunch."[14]

If the domain of measurement is expanded from the calculation of GDP to one that includes the exploitation of order held inside natural resources going into the GDP, such as the breaking down of long hydrocarbon chains in fuel used as energy or of molecules that make up the

---

[14] This expression simply means that everything has an opportunity cost. There are direct parallels to the **first law of thermodynamics.**

nutrients and other resources of nature, we find that we are still subject to the second law of thermodynamics. Any appearance of a violation of this law is only because we employ partial measurement when computing the sum of values added in the economy that constitutes real GDP. But how much disorder, or entropy, is caused by our efforts to satisfy our desires for material satisfaction? We can cast the tension between the environment and economy in such terms. The side one takes depends essentially on one's view of how long the planet's finite stock of ordered matter can last at the existing rate of depletion; we empty nature's bank account when we use energy at a faster rate than it is created by the Sun.

The circular flow of income between firms and households resembles recycling principles known as the carbon and nitrogen cycles.

The circular flow of income between firms and households resembles recycling principles known as the carbon and nitrogen cycles. As we saw in this chapter, if injections balance leakages in the circular flow of income between households and firms, the circular flow is in equilibrium, without tendency to run down or expand. If leakages from the flow of income in the form of taxes, savings, and exports are exactly balanced by injections from government spending, investment, and exports, the circular flow can continue indefinitely. Similar principles apply to the balancing acts of the carbon and nitrogen cycles. For example, the carbon cycle involves a balance between carbon dioxide emissions from the respiration of animals and decay of plants and the absorption of carbon dioxide by green plants, with the energy driving all this coming from the Sun. The nitrogen cycle involves similar balancing of flows among plants, animals, and bacteria, with the ability of the soil to support living matter being dependent on maintenance of the circular flow of nitrogen; any difference between leakages and injections would rapidly destroy the balance on which life depends.

As well as distinct parallels involving the application of thermodynamic and recycling principles that unite the natural sciences with economics in the context of the gross domestic product, there are additional connections through the application of **simple nonlinear dynamic systems,** which are processes that result in **chaos**. A number of scientific phenomena, from the weather, to the flow of a stream, to smoke from a fire, to evolution of a species, to the stock market, have been found to follow potentially simple nonlinear dynamic processes, where just the tiniest change in specification completely changes behavior. The characteristic of such chaotic processes is that while motion from one point to the next or even over a small number of points is reasonably predictable, it is not possible to tell what will happen over longer horizons. For example, weather predictions for the next day are generally quite accurate, for the next few days weather predictions are useful, but beyond that, weather forecasts have little validity; the tiniest change in starting conditions can mean a totally different outcome in the long run.[15] The same is true for the smoke rising from a fire. The motion at the source is predictable, but little can be said of where any particular particle of smoke will be when it is a couple of yards from the source; the most minuscule draft could cause the smoke to follow a totally different path. Just as with the weather, smoke, and so many other physical phenomena, so it is with the national income and product. From quarter to quarter it is possible to predict, for example, the growth rate of real GDP with a reasonable degree of accuracy. It is also possible to make forecasts with some limited validity for growth rates in about 1 year. However, beyond this, forecasts of the

---

[15] As it has been put, a butterfly flapping its wings could set off a violent hurricane in a distant place. This and other remarkable claims for the ubiquitous principle of chaos are contained in James Gleick's very readable book, **Chaos** (New York: Viking Press, 1987).

growth rate of GDP are no more accurate than the long-range weather forecasts that so often miss the mark.

Turning from the physical to the social sciences, we can note that just as inflation and unemployment have impacts on the political stage, so too does the behavior of the real GDP. The expectation of advances in the standard of living is so built into the psyche of voters that they vent their frustrations at the polls when they are dissatisfied with the pace of progress. This pace of progress is most clearly visible from GDP statistics. That is, even though each voter is likely to consider her or his own economic achievements vis-à-vis what she or he had anticipated, it is in the aggregate statistics showing real GDP that the typical voter's progress is most evident. Secret ballots may ensure that politicians no longer buy votes, but it is still pocketbook issues that matter at election time.

Progress, as reflected in real GDP, and **consumerism,** which has become the driving force even of formerly socialistic economies, are intimately related. Dreams are based on progress, on having more, on doing better, on being transformed by a higher income and a greater buying power. Human wants appear insatiable, and advances in real GDP are the route to the greater luxury and comfort that people demand and expect. This appetite for perpetual progress has been so built into societal norms that it is a basic axiom, rarely questioned except by the odd philosopher who reevaluates the dominant currents that have been set in motion by **"Homo economicus,"** that is, by modern economic human beings. However, it would be an injustice not to mention the detractors who have noted that economic progress does not necessarily go hand in hand with spiritual values, with a deeper human condition, and today more than anything else, with preservation of the environment. Such a critic of the "controlling ideology" of progress is modern American philosopher Christopher Lasch.[16] While a great deal can be said in favor of targeting for an ever-growing real GDP, the critics of progress such as Lasch and the philosophers he cites make it clear that there is more to achievement than is reflected in the national income and product accounts.

> *[The] appetite for perpetual progress has been so built into societal norms that it is a basic axiom, rarely questioned except by the odd philosopher who reevaluates the dominant currents. . . .*

---

[16] See Christopher Lasch, **The True and Only Heaven: Progress and Its Critics** (New York: Norton, 1991).

SUMMARY

1. Different factors cause short-run fluctuations in real GDP than affect the trend rate of growth of real GDP.

2. Traditional Keynesian arguments apply to an economy with substantial unused capacity, so expansions take the form of increasing real GDP rather than increasing prices. Similarly, by assuming downwardly sticky prices, contractions take the form of decreasing real GDP rather than declining prices.

3. The equilibrium real GDP is where desired expenditure equals actual output. When desired expenditure exceeds output, there is an increase in the equilibrium GDP, and when desired expenditure is smaller than output, there is a reduction in the equilibrium GDP.

4. The marginal propensity to consume is the fraction of an increase in GDP spent on consumption. The marginal propensity to consume is smaller than unity because some GDP is collected in taxes and because some of increased income is saved.

5. Keynesians believe that the factors which cause fluctuations in GDP are those which affect desired investment, consumption, government spending, and the balance of international trade.

6. Increased spending causes increases in the equilibrium GDP by a multiple of the original spending increase. The multiple by which the equilibrium GDP increases vis-à-vis spending is called the multiplier.

7. The multiplier is the result of trickling down, as successive people spend extra income, and is larger the more that trickles down. Therefore, the larger the marginal propensity to consume, the larger is the multiplier.

8. The Keynesian view that expansions and contractions in desired expenditure result in fluctuating real GDP rather than prices can be explained in terms of an aggregate supply curve that is horizontal below capacity output. Then variations in aggregate demand translate into variations in real GDP.

9. Aggregate supply shocks, such as those caused by rapidly increasing imported oil prices, cause an increase in the price level at the same time as real GDP is decreasing. Such a situation is called stagflation.

10. When real GDP is declining and unemployment is increasing, individuals who still have jobs reduce consumption in case they lose their jobs. This behavior makes matters worse and is called the paradox of thrift.

11. Equilibrium income is where desired expenditure equals GDP or where withdrawals from the circular flow of income equal injections. The withdrawals are taxes, savings, and imports, and the injections are investment, government spending, and exports.

12. Real GDP increases when there is unanticipated inflation and decreases when there is unanticipated disinflation.

13. A recurring pattern of variations in real GDP is called a business or trade cycle. A business cycle involves moving from peak, to contraction, to trough, to expansion, and back to a peak again.

14. The long-run trend in real GDP depends on growth in the quantity and quality of factors of production.

15. Growth in the capital stock requires net investment. Net investment is gross investment minus depreciation.

16. The number of hours of labor supplied depends on income tax rates. Therefore, lower tax rates can increase the quantity of labor supplied and thereby increase real GDP.

17. The quality of capital is improved by improvements in technology which themselves come from research and development.

18. Education improves the quality of labor and also helps to improve the quality of capital because it trains people who do research and development.

19. The empirical evidence suggests that growth in the quantity and quality of all factors of production has contributed to economic growth.

20. In making short-term forecasts of real GDP, Monetarists examine money supply statistics, while Keynesians look at the factors influencing desired consumption, investment, government spending, and net exports. In making longer-term forecasts of the real GDP, all economists look at the size of net investment, R&D expenditure, demographic trends, education, and so on.

21. Because income and sales tax receipts decline as GDP declines, there is an automatic, built-in stabilizer in an economy; deficit spending occurs during recessions. The full-employment deficit or surplus is what the deficit or surplus would be at full employment.

22. The index of leading economic indicators is formed from 12 measures reflecting future economic activity.

QUESTIONS AND PROBLEMS

1. Assume the following values of desired expenditure:

   Autonomous consumption = $100 billion

   Investment = $20 billion

   Government spending = $30 billion

   Net exports = − $10 billion

   a. Assuming that the marginal propensity to consume is 0.6, what is the value of the equilibrium GDP?

   b. What would happen to unplanned changes in inventories if actual GDP were $340 billion? What would happen if the actual GDP were $360 billion?

   c. Assume that investment increases to $25 billion. What is the new equilibrium GDP, and what is the size of the multiplier?

2. How do you think the multiplier is affected by the income tax rate?

3. In what ways is the downward slope on the aggregate demand curve different from the downward slope on demand curves for individual goods and services?

4. Add arrows to Figure 16.11 representing firms' taxes, firms' savings, government transfers to households, household borrowing, firms' imports, and government imports. Use the extended figure to show that Equation 16.6 holds in equilibrium, where S is all savings, T is all taxes, and so on.

5.* Why could an increase in the growth rate of the money supply increase real GDP?

6. How might education improve economic growth both directly and indirectly? Why don't very poor nations devote more resources to education to improve their future standards of living?

7. Is the full-employment fiscal deficit or surplus a more meaningful way of comparing the intended fiscal stimulus than the actual fiscal deficit or surplus?

8. Do you think a policy of making people retire early would help unemployment and living standards in the long run?

9. Why is productivity so important to economic progress?

10. In what ways can the government help or hinder long-term economic performance?

· · · · · · · · · · ·
· · · · · · · · · · ·
· · · · · · · · · · ·
· · · · · · · · · · · ·
· · · · · · · · · · · ·
· · · · · · · · Interest Rates*
· · · · · · · _____
· · · · · · · · · · · ·

Gentlemen prefer bonds.

Andrew Mellon

Key Concepts

Interest rates and the supply of loanable funds; interest rates and the demand for loanable funds; the market versus the equilibrium interest rate; monetary policy and interest rates; real growth and interest rates; real versus nominal interest rates; anticipated inflation and interest rates; fiscal deficits, crowding out, and interest rates; international capital flows and interest rates

THE INTEREST IN INTEREST RATES

Interest rates have a substantial effect on borrowing and spending decisions of businesses and consumers and thereby on employment, gross domestic product (GDP), and other measures of macroeconomic activity. For example, as we shall see, interest rates influence the willingness of businesses to invest in new plant and equipment and thus have an effect on the size of the GDP.

....
* This entire chapter may be omitted without loss of continuity.

At the same time that interest rates affect the economy, the economy affects interest rates. This occurs as a result of the effects that national income, inflation, and confidence about the future have on the willingness of consumers and businesses to borrow and invest and hence on the "price" of borrowing, which is the interest rate. With the direction of flow being in both directions, from interest rates to the economy and from the economy to interest rates, in order to explain interest rates, we need a theory that captures this two-way flow of influence. Such a theory is the **loanable funds theory.** While there are numerous other theories of interest rates, the loanable funds theory embraces many aspects of these other theories and therefore serves as an ideal window onto the world of interest rates.

LOANABLE FUNDS THEORY OF INTEREST

According to the loanable funds theory, interest rates are determined by the supply of and demand for loanable funds. Therefore, in order to explain this theory, we must begin by considering loanable funds supply and demand.

The Supply of Loanable Funds

The supply of loanable funds consists of changes in the money supply and current savings.

There are two components to the supply of loanable funds:

1. Changes in the money supply

2. Savings out of current income

Let us consider these two components in turn.

The change in the money supply is determined primarily by the central bank.

Changes in the Money Supply.   As we saw in Chapter 13, the money supply consists of coin and currency plus deposits at financial institutions. We also saw that a nation's money supply is determined primarily by its central bank, which influences both the availability of reserves and the required reserve ratio. If we assume that the size of reserves and the required reserve ratio are not affected by interest rates, then the money supply is not affected by interest rates. This allows us to represent the change in money supply by a vertical line such as ΔM^s in Figure 17.1. This line is vertical because the change in the money supply is assumed to be the same whatever the interest rate. The more expansive the central bank's policy, the further to the right is the vertical line ΔM^s.

If, rather than assuming that the money supply is not influenced by interest rates, we assume instead that the central bank determines the money supply *according* to interest rates, the line ΔM^s in Figure 17.1 is no longer vertical. For example, if we assume that the central bank reduces the growth of the money supply when interest rates are low and increases the growth of the money supply when interest rates are high, ΔM^s is an upward-sloping line; the higher interest rates are, the larger is ΔM^s. For simplicity, we shall assume that ΔM^s is vertical as in Figure 17.1, although the way we draw ΔM^s can be altered to accommodate different central bank objectives, if necessary. We also shall assume that the position of ΔM^s along the horizontal axis depends on decisions of the central bank and that these decisions can be taken as given, or exogenous.

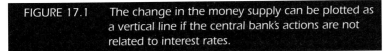

FIGURE 17.1   The change in the money supply can be plotted as a vertical line if the central bank's actions are not related to interest rates.

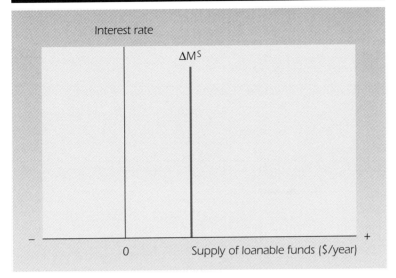

The change in the money supply is determined primarily by the central bank. If the central bank's actions are unrelated to interest rates, we can plot the actual change in money supply as a vertical line vis-à-vis the interest rate.

Savings Out of Current Income.   The part of income which is not spent or paid as taxes is saved and placed in financial institutions and stock and bond markets. In turn, the financial institutions and financial markets make the saved funds available to borrowers. Savings are in this way a component of the supply of loanable funds. Furthermore, the financial institutions and markets provide the service of channeling, or intermediating, the funds between savers and borrowers.

The proportion of national income that is saved depends on interest rates. We must consider in what way interest rates affect savings before we can determine how the total supply of loanable funds varies with interest rates.

When a person decides to spend his or her income rather than save, the cost is the forgone interest income that person would have earned.[1] The higher the interest rate, the more interest income is lost from a given amount spent today. In other words, the higher the interest rate, the higher is the opportunity cost of spending rather than saving. For example, if the interest rate is 5%, every dollar spent today means forgoing $1.05 of spending next year, but if the interest rate is 10%, the cost of spending each dollar today is $1.10 of forgone spending next year. It follows that as interest rates increase, the opportunity cost of spending

The higher the interest rate, the higher is the quantity of savings.

_____

[1] For the time being, we ignore inflation. Later, we shall see that it is the *real* interest rate, which was met in Equation 14.11, that determines savings.

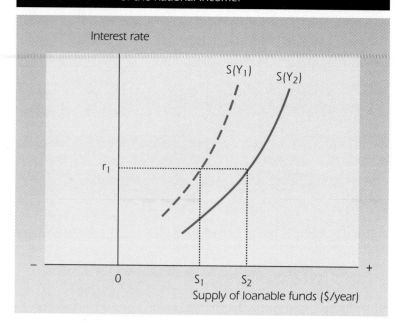

FIGURE 17.2   The savings curve slopes upward with respect to interest rates and shifts with changes in the size of the national income.

The higher the interest rate, the more interest income is forgone by spending rather than saving. It follows that people spend less and save more of a given income at higher interest rates. Therefore, the savings curve slopes upward. The savings curve shifts with income. For example, if national income increases from Y_1 to Y_2, the savings curve shifts from $S(Y_1)$ to $S(Y_2)$, so at a given interest rate r_1, savings increase from S_1 to S_2.

today increases, so a larger proportion of the national income is saved. This is shown in Figure 17.2 by the curve $S(Y)$, which has an upward slope, showing higher savings at higher interest rates.

Savings increase with increases in the national income.

    The position of curve $S(Y)$ depends on national income Y; this is why we put Y in parentheses. The larger the national income, the more is saved at every interest rate, and therefore, the further to the right is curve $S(Y)$. For example, if national income increases from Y_1 to Y_2, the savings curve shifts from $S(Y_1)$ to $S(Y_2)$ in Figure 17.2. This means that at a given interest rate r_1, savings increase from S_1 to S_2 as income increases from Y_1 to Y_2.

    The total supply of loanable funds consists of savings plus the change in the money supply. Therefore, to obtain the curve representing the total supply of loanable funds, we take the horizontal sum of $S(Y)$ and ΔM^s. [The horizontal sum of $S(Y)$ and ΔM^s is the sum of savings and the change in money supply at each interest rate.] This is labeled L_s in Figure 17.3. Since savings increase as interest rates increase, the supply curve of loanable funds slopes upward vis-à-vis interest rates. This upward-sloping supply curve of loanable funds must be combined with the demand curve to determine the interest rate at which the supply of and demand for funds are equal.

QUESTIONS AND PROBLEMS

1. Assume the following values of desired expenditure:

   Autonomous consumption = $100 billion

   Investment = $20 billion

   Government spending = $30 billion

   Net exports = − $10 billion

   a. Assuming that the marginal propensity to consume is 0.6, what is the value of the equilibrium GDP?

   b. What would happen to unplanned changes in inventories if actual GDP were $340 billion? What would happen if the actual GDP were $360 billion?

   c. Assume that investment increases to $25 billion. What is the new equilibrium GDP, and what is the size of the multiplier?

2. How do you think the multiplier is affected by the income tax rate?

3. In what ways is the downward slope on the aggregate demand curve different from the downward slope on demand curves for individual goods and services?

4. Add arrows to Figure 16.11 representing firms' taxes, firms' savings, government transfers to households, household borrowing, firms' imports, and government imports. Use the extended figure to show that Equation 16.6 holds in equilibrium, where S is all savings, T is all taxes, and so on.

5.* Why could an increase in the growth rate of the money supply increase real GDP?

6. How might education improve economic growth both directly and indirectly? Why don't very poor nations devote more resources to education to improve their future standards of living?

7. Is the full-employment fiscal deficit or surplus a more meaningful way of comparing the intended fiscal stimulus than the actual fiscal deficit or surplus?

8. Do you think a policy of making people retire early would help unemployment and living standards in the long run?

9. Why is productivity so important to economic progress?

10. In what ways can the government help or hinder long-term economic performance?

13. A recurring pattern of variations in real GDP is called a business or trade cycle. A business cycle involves moving from peak, to contraction, to trough, to expansion, and back to a peak again.

14. The long-run trend in real GDP depends on growth in the quantity and quality of factors of production.

15. Growth in the capital stock requires net investment. Net investment is gross investment minus depreciation.

16. The number of hours of labor supplied depends on income tax rates. Therefore, lower tax rates can increase the quantity of labor supplied and thereby increase real GDP.

17. The quality of capital is improved by improvements in technology which themselves come from research and development.

18. Education improves the quality of labor and also helps to improve the quality of capital because it trains people who do research and development.

19. The empirical evidence suggests that growth in the quantity and quality of all factors of production has contributed to economic growth.

20. In making short-term forecasts of real GDP, Monetarists examine money supply statistics, while Keynesians look at the factors influencing desired consumption, investment, government spending, and net exports. In making longer-term forecasts of the real GDP, all economists look at the size of net investment, R&D expenditure, demographic trends, education, and so on.

21. Because income and sales tax receipts decline as GDP declines, there is an automatic, built-in stabilizer in an economy; deficit spending occurs during recessions. The full-employment deficit or surplus is what the deficit or surplus would be at full employment.

22. The index of leading economic indicators is formed from 12 measures reflecting future economic activity.

The Demand for Loanable Funds

There are two components of the demand[2] for loanable funds:

1. Changes in the demand for money

2. The demand for funds to finance capital investments

Let us consider these two components in turn.

Changes in the Demand for Money. If people want to hold more money than they are already holding, the extra amount of money demanded is part of the demand for loanable funds. The demand for money was discussed in Chapter 14, where we interpreted the quantity theory as a theory of demand for money.

When we discussed the demand for money in Chapter 14, we mentioned that the quantity of money demanded depends on interest rates. Specifically, *ceteris paribus,* the quantity of money demanded decreases as the interest rate goes up; the interest rate is the opportunity cost of holding money, so less money is held at higher interest rates.[3] This means that when we plot the change in demand for money curve ΔM^D as in Figure 17.4, it has a downward slope. However, another factor affecting the demand for money is the GDP or national income. This occurs because the more people earn and spend, the larger the money holdings they need to facilitate their transactions. *Ceteris paribus,* the greater the *change* in GDP and national income, the larger is the *change* in the demand for money ΔM^D. This is true whether the GDP and national income change as a result of an increase in the price level or from a change in real GDP. For example, if the price level doubles, people need twice as much money to make their payments, just as if the quantity of goods and services purchased doubles.

The demand for money curve $\Delta M^D(\Delta Y_1)$ in Figure 17.4 shows that with real GDP changing by ΔY_1 and the interest rate r_1, there is no demand for additional money. However, the curve $\Delta M^D(\Delta Y_2)$ shows that if GDP is increasing by ΔY_2, which is larger than ΔY_1, there is a demand for more money equal to $0M$ at r_1.

Capital Investment. In Chapter 10 we explained that the higher the interest rate, the lower is the rate of capital investment. This is so because higher interest rates mean that the present values of incomes generated by investments are lower. In other words, if there are many potential investments with different possible pay-offs, at higher interest rates fewer investments will have present values of incomes that exceed the costs of the investments. That is, the higher the interest rate, the smaller is investment.

The demand for loanable funds consists of the change in demand for money and the demand for funds to finance investment.

The lower the interest rate, the higher is the quantity of money demanded. At any interest rate, the change in demand for money is larger the more GDP increases.

[2] A further demand for funds occurs when governments raise funds because of fiscal deficits. We consider this later.

[3] In fact, the opportunity cost of holding money is the interest rate that could be earned on some other asset such as a bond minus any interest earned on money. Some forms of bank deposits included in the money supply earn interest, and therefore, the opportunity cost is less than the interest rate on bonds and other such nonmoney assets. For our purposes here, we can ignore interest earned on money. We can do this either by assuming that we are dealing with a narrow definition of money which excludes interest-earning deposits or by assuming that any interest earned on money changes little relative to interest rates on bonds or other such assets.

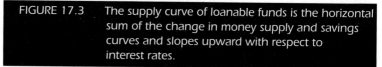

FIGURE 17.3   The supply curve of loanable funds is the horizontal sum of the change in money supply and savings curves and slopes upward with respect to interest rates.

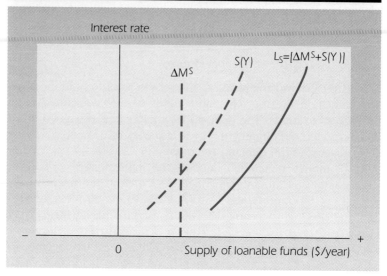

The supply of loanable funds is the sum of the change in the money supply ΔM^s and savings $S(Y)$. This is the curve $L_s = [\Delta M^s + S(Y)]$.

The effect of interest rates on investment is shown by the curves $I(\Delta Y_1)$ and $I(\Delta Y_2)$ in Figure 17.5. These curves show that the lower the interest rate, the higher is the rate of investment, and hence the larger is the quantity of loanable funds demanded to finance investment. The investment curves have ΔY in parentheses because, as in the case of the change in demand for money, changes in GDP affect investment and hence the position of the investment curve. In the case of investment, it is changes in *real* GDP that have an effect. Real GDP affects investment because the number of machines and size of plant that firms want to have depend on the outputs of goods and services they want to produce, and in aggregate, the output firms produce is the real GDP. The greater the increase in real GDP, the larger is the desired increase in the number of machines and size of plant and the greater is investment. That is, the larger the increase in *real* GDP, the higher is investment at any interest rate and, therefore, the further to the right is curve I.[4] For a given change in price level, the more real GDP increases, the more nominal GDP increases. Therefore, for simplicity, we show the position of the investment curve in Figure 17.5 depending on ΔY, the change in the *nominal* GDP. The larger ΔY is, the further to the right is the investment curve. For example, $I(\Delta Y_2)$ is to the right of $I(\Delta Y_1)$ if ΔY_2 is greater than ΔY_1.

The lower the interest rate, the higher is the quantity of funds demanded for investment. At any interest rate, investment is higher the larger is the increase in GDP.

[4] The link between real GDP and investment is explained more precisely in the Appendix to this chapter.

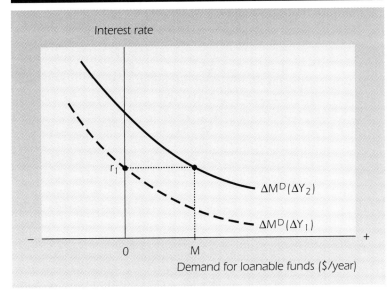

FIGURE 17.4   The change in demand for money curve is downward sloping vis-à-vis the interest rate and is further to the right the larger is the increase in GDP during any period.

The opportunity cost of holding money is the interest earnings that are forgone. The higher the interest rates, the lower is the quantity of money demanded. Therefore, the demand for money curve slopes downward vis-à-vis the interest rate. At a given interest rate, the position of the curve depends on the change in GDP. The more GDP increases, the larger is the increase in money demand. This means that the downward-sloping demand for money curve is further to the right the larger is the increase in GDP during any period of time; $\Delta Y_2 > \Delta Y_1$ in the figure.

The total demand for loanable funds is the sum of the change in demand for money and investment at each interest rate. This is shown in Figure 17.6, where the curve labeled L_D is the horizontal sum of curves $\Delta M^D(\Delta Y)$ and $I(\Delta Y)$. L_D slopes downward because curve $\Delta M^D(\Delta Y)$ and curve $I(\Delta Y)$ both slope downward. Furthermore, L_D moves further to the right the more GDP increases.

We should note carefully that it is ΔY, the *change* in GDP, that shifts the demand curve for loanable funds L_D, whereas it is the *level* of GDP that shifts the supply curve of loanable funds L_S. This is why we have Y in parentheses in Figure 17.3, which shows L_S, and ΔY in parentheses in Figure 17.6, which shows L_D. The reason L_D shifts with the change in GDP is that funds are demanded if there is a demand for *extra* money holdings and if firms need *extra* capital, and both these situations occur when GDP is *increasing*. On the other hand, the supply of loanable funds is influenced by the level of GDP because the amount saved during any period depends on peoples' incomes and hence on the level of GDP. The importance of distinguishing between the level of GDP Y and the change in GDP ΔY is that *while GDP is increasing,* $\Delta Y > 0$ and the demand for funds is high, but once GDP ceases to increase and just *stays at the higher level,* $\Delta Y = 0$, and the demand for funds declines.

The demand for loanable funds depends on the *change* in GDP, whereas the supply of loanable funds depends on the *level* of GDP.

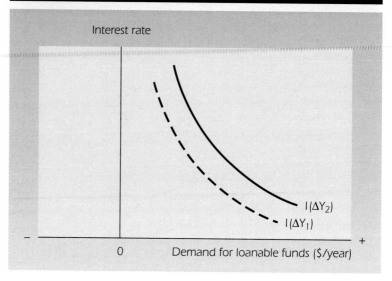

FIGURE 17.5 The higher the interest rate, the lower is investment. At any interest rate, investment is higher the larger the increase in GDP.

The higher the interest rate, the lower are the present values of future incomes from investments. As a consequence, fewer investments are worthwhile at a higher interest rate. Therefore, if there are many potential investments with different degrees of profitability, at higher interest rates, investment is smaller. Therefore, the investment curve slopes downward vis-à-vis the interest rate. The position of the investment curve depends on the change in real GDP. The more real GDP increases, the larger is investment at any interest rate. For a given change in the price level, the more real GDP increases, the more nominal GDP increases. Therefore, for simplicity, we put ΔY in parentheses in the investment curve; $\Delta Y_2 > \Delta Y_1$ in the figure.

Market and Equilibrium Interest Rates

The market interest rate equates the supply of and demand for loanable funds.

According to the loanable funds theory, the interest rate observed in the market-place, called the **market interest rate,** is the rate equating the supply of and demand for loanable funds. We can find this rate by plotting the supply curve of loanable funds L_S from Figure 17.3 and the demand curve for loanable funds L_D from Figure 17.6 in the same figure. This is done in Figure 17.7. We see that L_S and L_D intersect at the market interest rate r_m.

As well as showing L_S and L_D, Figure 17.7 also shows the curves behind the supply of and demand for loanable funds. Because L_S is the horizontal sum of ΔM^S and S, and L_D is the horizontal sum of ΔM^D and I, that is, $L_S = \Delta M^S + S$ and $L_D = \Delta M^D + I$, at the market interest rate,

$$\Delta M^s + S = \Delta M^D + I \tag{17.1}$$

We see that there is no requirement that at the market interest rate savings be equal to investment, since the change in the supply of and demand for money

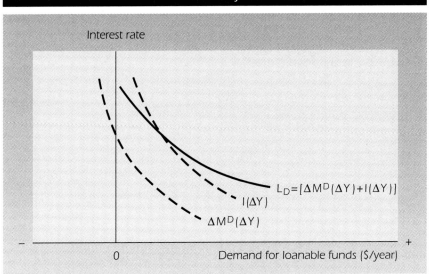

FIGURE 17.6   The demand for loanable funds curve is the horizontal sum of the demand for money and investment curves.

The demand for loanable funds is the sum of $\Delta \mathbf{M}^D$ and $\mathbf{I}$ at each interest rate and is plotted as curve $\mathbf{L}_D$. Since both $\Delta \mathbf{M}^D$ and $\mathbf{I}$ slope downward, so does $\mathbf{L}_D$. Both $\Delta \mathbf{M}^D$ and $\mathbf{I}$ are further to the right the larger is $\Delta \mathbf{Y}$. Therefore, $\mathbf{L}_D$ is further to the right the larger is $\Delta \mathbf{Y}$.

may not be equal. For example, if ΔM^s is larger than ΔM^D, then Equation 17.1 tells us that at the market interest rate, I exceeds S. This situation is shown in Figure 17.7. We see from the figure that the excess of ΔM^s over ΔM^D is equal to the excess of I over S.

With it being possible for S to differ from I at r_m, the market interest rate is not in general an equilibrium rate. This is so because if, for example, I exceeds S at r_m so that injections into the circular flow of incomes exceed withdrawals, then, *ceteris paribus*, GDP will increase to a higher level. The increase in GDP will shift the savings curve to the right until $S=I$.[5] With $S=I$, and also with the market interest rate such that $L_s=L_D$, that is,

$$\Delta M^s + S = \Delta M^D + I$$

it also must be the case that $\Delta M^s = \Delta M^D$. This rate of interest at which $S=I$ and $\Delta M^s = \Delta M^D$ is called the **equilibrium interest rate.**

The changes in national income that move the market interest rate to the equilibrium interest rate are likely to occur only gradually, allowing the market rate to

The *equilibrium* interest rate equates savings and investment. Over time, the *market* interest rate moves toward the equilibrium interest rate.

[5] *While* GDP is increasing, ΔM^D and I are also shifting because ΔM^D and I depend on ΔY. However, the shifts in ΔM^D and I cease after the level of Y, that is, GDP, has increased sufficiently that S has risen to equal I; after $S=I$, ΔY returns to zero.

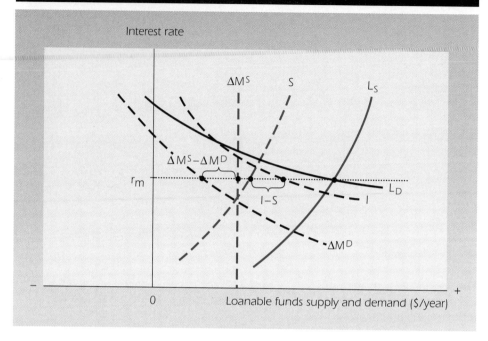

FIGURE 17.7   According to the loanable funds theory, the market interest rate equates the supply of and demand for loanable funds. This rate is not, in general, an equilibrium rate.

The market interest rate is **r$_m$**. This is the rate that equates the supply of and demand for loanable funds. At the market interest rate, savings and investment are not generally equal. The imbalance between savings and investment is offset by an imbalance between the change in supply of and demand for money. According to Keynesian thinking, the effect of savings being different from investment is to change national income so that **r$_m$** is not an equilibrium interest rate.

differ from the equilibrium rate for some time. During that time, the market rate moves up and down with the factors affecting L_s and L_D; that is, market interest rate changes with variations in ΔM^s, S, ΔM^D, and I in Figure 17.7

FACTORS AFFECTING INTEREST RATES

Monetary Policy

Monetary policy is reflected in the *growth rate* of the money supply rather than the *level* of the money supply. This is so because the demand for money grows along with GDP, and it is normal for central banks to allow the money supply to grow along with money demand. Monetary policy is more **expansionary**—designed to allow the economy to expand—or more **contractionary**—designed to slow the economy down—according to how rapidly the central bank allows the money supply to grow.[6] The more expansionary is monetary policy the higher is the rate of growth of the money supply. The loanable funds theory is well suited to showing the effects of changes in the growth rate of the money supply because it is cast in terms of changes in the money supply ΔM^s. A faster rate of growth of the money supply simply means that the vertical line ΔM^s in Figure 17.7 is further to the right.[7]

Figure 17.8 shows the effect of an increase in the growth rate of the money supply and the consequent rightward shift of ΔM^s from ΔM_1^s to ΔM_2^s. Since ΔM^s is part of the supply of loanable funds, the rightward shift in ΔM^s also causes L_s to shift to the right. (Recall that L_s is the horizontal sum of ΔM^s and S.) We find that an increase in the rate of growth of the money supply reduces the market interest rate from r_m^1 to r_m^2, given the positions of all other curves. However, this so-called **liquidity effect** is only temporary if at the market interest rate savings are not equal to investment so that GDP changes. These changes in GDP have further effects on interest rates. Let us therefore consider the effect of changes in GDP.

An increase in the rate of growth of the money supply reduces the market interest rate via the liquidity effect. However, this effect is only temporary.

Growth in GDP

The faster the growth in GDP, that is, the greater is ΔY, the greater is the demand for loanable funds via both the demand for money and investment. Therefore, the larger the increase in GDP, the further to the right is the demand curve for loanable funds L_D. This is illustrated in Figure 17.9, where ΔY_2 is larger than ΔY_1. The figure shows that the larger the growth in real GDP, the higher is the market interest rate.

The conclusion that equilibrium interest rates are higher when economic growth is faster means, *ceteris paribus,* that more income is available to pay the higher interest rates. This provides some theoretical support for the way "interest rates" are determined in Islamic tradition, as described in Example 17.1.

More rapid growth in the GDP increases the demand for loanable funds via increasing the demand for money and investment and thereby increases market interest rates.

Changes in Anticipated Inflation

In Chapter 14 we introduced a link between anticipated inflation and interest rates, namely,

$$\text{Nominal rate} = \text{real rate} + \text{anticipated inflation} \qquad (14.11)$$

We pointed out that if the real interest rate is unaffected by anticipated inflation, increases in anticipated inflation cause equal increases in the nominal interest rate. Let us now consider how Equation 14.11 relates to the loanable funds theory by showing how anticipated inflation affects the positions of the demand for loanable funds curve L_D and the supply of loanable funds curve L_s. We shall concentrate on

---

[6] Frequently, interest rates are viewed as a *measure* of monetary policy. However, as we shall show, interest rates are the *result* of monetary policy.

[7] Strictly speaking, in Figure 17.7 we plot the change in money supply rather than the *rate* of change. To calculate the *rate* of change, we need to calculate the change as a percentage of the initial stock of money. However, given the initial stock, the larger the change ΔM^s, the larger is the rate of change. Therefore, we can think of variations in ΔM^s as implying variations in the rate of change.

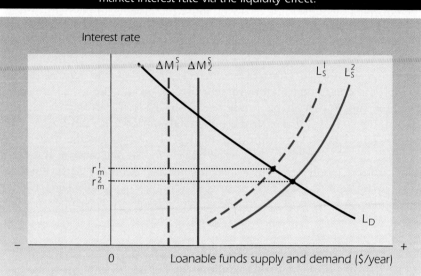

FIGURE 17.8   A faster rate of growth of the money supply reduces the market interest rate via the liquidity effect.

A faster growth rate in the money supply means a rightward shift in $\Delta \mathbf{M}^s$ from $\Delta \mathbf{M}_1^s$ to $\Delta \mathbf{M}_2^s$. Since curve $\mathbf{L}_s$ includes $\Delta \mathbf{M}^s$, $\mathbf{L}_s$ shifts to the right by an equal amount, from $\mathbf{L}_s^1$ to $\mathbf{L}_s^2$. For a given demand for loanable funds, $\mathbf{L}_D$, the market interest rate declines from $\mathbf{r}_m^1$ to $\mathbf{r}_m^2$. This decline in the interest rate is only temporary because savings would not equal investment after the interest rate change if they were equal before the change.

the effects of anticipated inflation only on the savings and investment curves behind L_s and L_D. That is, we ignore ΔM^D and ΔM^s. We do this because to deal with ΔM^D and ΔM^s as well as S and I makes the analysis substantially more complex without affecting the *qualitative* conclusions. (Question 10 deals with the more complex situation.)

Anticipated Inflation and Savings S.   The curve labeled S_1 in Figure 17.10 on page 546 shows the amount saved at different nominal interest rates when anticipated inflation is zero. For example, at an interest rate of 2%, savings are $120 billion—point A_1—while at 6%, savings are $180 billion—point B_1.

Let us suppose that there is a sudden increase in anticipated inflation from 0% to 4%. This means that savers anticipate needing 4 cents of interest on each dollar saved for 1 year to maintain their real buying power.[8] If with zero anticipated inflation savers were prepared to save $120 billion at a 2% interest rate, then with 4% anticipated inflation they would require 6% to continue saving $120 billion; a 6% nominal interest rate with 4% anticipated inflation preserves the 2% real interest rate. In terms of Figure 17.10, this means that we have a new point A_2 on a new savings curve S_2 which shows savings of $120 billion at a 6% interest rate. Similarly, if with 0% anticipated inflation savings are $180 billion at a 6% interest

---

[8] We ignore income taxes on interest earnings.

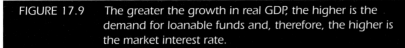

FIGURE 17.9   The greater the growth in real GDP, the higher is the demand for loanable funds and, therefore, the higher is the market interest rate.

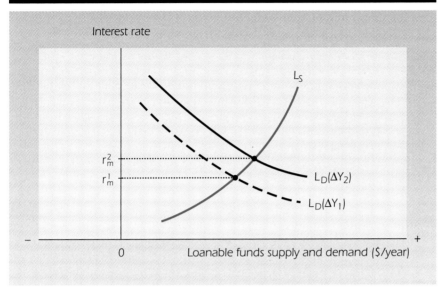

A larger growth in GDP ΔY means an increase in demand for money and an increase in investment, both of which shift the demand curve for loanable funds L_D to the right. Therefore, market interest rates increase with more rapid growth in GDP.

rate—point B_1—then when anticipated inflation jumps to 4%, savings are $180 billion at a 10% nominal interest rate; a 10% interest rate with 4% anticipated inflation is a real interest rate of 6% (or 10% − 4%). This defines point B_2 directly above point B_1 on S_2. Indeed, for any given quantity of savings, the required nominal interest rate is 4% higher with 4% anticipated inflation than with 0% anticipated inflation. This means that the entire savings curve is shifted upward by the antici- pated rate of inflation; S_2, the savings curve with 4% anticipated inflation, is 4% higher than S_1, the savings curve with 0% anticipated inflation.

The savings curve shifts vertically upward by the anticipated rate of inflation.

Anticipated Inflation and Investment *I*.   As we explained in Chapter 10, capi- tal investment is made in order to increase future profits. When there is anticipated inflation, the nominal values of profits anticipated from investments grow along with the anticipated inflation. However, the higher anticipated *nominal* profits with inflation do not make investments more profitable. Indeed, if calculated at a nominal interest rate that incorporates anticipated inflation, anticipated future prof- its have the same present values with anticipated inflation as without anticipated inflation. Let us show this by using our example from Chapter 10 involving a farmer who is considering buying a combine harvester that is expected to increase future profits by $10,000 per year for the next 10 years.

The situation facing the farmer without and with inflation is summarized in Table 17.1 on page 547. In constructing the table, we have assumed that the con- stant $10,000 per year of expected profit in the absence of inflation is the result of expected total revenue of $100,000 per year and total cost of $90,000 per year.

Example   17.1

RISK SHARING, ISLAMIC STYLE

In Western countries, firms can finance their expansion by selling shares, called equity financing, and by borrowing, called debt financing. The interest payments on debt are fixed and are paid as long as companies remain solvent, whereas dividend payments on shares vary with the profitability of firms and can be terminated if poor profits do not provide a surplus to distribute. The way "interest rates" are determined in the Islamic tradition makes debt rather like what Western economies would call equity. The following article from **The Economist** considers the benefits and drawbacks of the Islamic system. Other religious views on paying interest are explained in the Crossing Bridges section in this chapter.

. . . [E]ven among those westerners who know what "Islamic banking" really means—a system of finance based on the sharing of risk and profit, rather than on the payment of interest—few take it seriously as a way for a modern economy to do business. In some ways, this . . . is a mistake.

Earlier this year [1992] Pakistan's Federal Shariat Court ruled that all forms of interest paid or charged by banks and other financial institutions were un-Islamic. The government has until the summer to amend its financial laws accordingly; otherwise, the religious court ruled, the existing laws "will cease to have effect." Foreign and domestic bankers predicted financial disaster. The tenor of their comments was that the court had given the government six months to abolish capitalism and design a replacement—which does seem rather ambitious. But is that a fair interpretation?

Islamic banking is not merely consistent with capitalism (i.e., with a market-driven allocation of capital, labour and other resources), but in certain respects may be better suited to it than western banking. On one view, the mistakes that have led western banks and economies into their present financial troubles are precisely the errors that Islamic banking is at pains to avoid.

Islam considers the charging of interest an injustice. Western economists talk of an interest rate that reflects, among other things, "pure time-preference"—i.e., the notion that consumption today is worth more than consumption tomorrow. Islamic scholars point out that mere hoarding of cash ought, on that view, to warrant an economic reward. But an economic reward becomes available for distribution only if consumption forgone is translated into investment that yields a real economic return. Lenders are entitled to part of any such return, according to Islam, but only to the extent that they help to create wealth.

That, in turn, means that they must accept a share of the risk. In Islam, this idea is not confined to banking. In general, Islamic laws of contract insist that risks should be shared: wherever there is uncertainty, contracts that assure one party of a fixed return come what may are discouraged.

Many Muslim countries have banking systems that follow, at least in part, Islamic principles. A variety of partnership agreements has

---

The present values of the profits attributable to the machine when there is 0% inflation are calculated at an interest rate of 4%. For example, $10,000 in year 1 is worth $9615 (or $10,000 ÷ 1.04), while $10,000 in year 2 is worth $9246 [or $10,000 ÷ (1.04 × 1.04)], and so on.

When inflation is 4%, we assume expected total revenues and total costs both grow at 4%. The expected total revenues and costs with 4% anticipated inflation are shown in the bottom part of the table, along with expected profits. We can see that expected profits also grow at the anticipated inflation rate. For example, in the first year, expected total revenue and expected total cost grow by 4% to $104,000 and $93,600, respectively, and expected profit therefore grows to $10,400 (or developed to allow lending without interest. Under schemes such as *mudarabah* (often an equivalent of short-term commercial credit) and *musharakah* (long-term equity-like arrangements), banks receive a contractual share of the profits generated by borrowing firms. Depending on the contract, this may be a share of all profits, or a share in the profits created by a particular investment project. The banks' depositors, in turn, receive a share of the banks' profits.

This approach to finance, on the face of it, has many advantages. It encourages equity (or similar forms of investment) and discourages debt. A common criticism of Anglo-American capitalism is that it is inefficiently biased in the other direction. Moreover, Islamic principles oblige lenders to worry about the profitability, as opposed to the creditworthiness, of the firms they are lending to. This leads them to be more conservative in their decision-making, and to undertake more careful monitoring of borrowers. Under this model, you might also argue, "popular capitalism" is a reality. Because

financial intermediaries are not allowed to shoulder all the risks of lending, bank depositors have a direct stake in industrial profitability.

Some of the supposed disadvantages of Islamic banking can be overcome. One is that without interest rates the monetary authorities have no control over monetary policy. This need not be so: control can still be exercised through limits on the cash base of the economy, or through reserve requirements for the banks. Another difficulty is government borrowing, especially from abroad: how is a government to finance its deficit if it cannot pay a fixed rate of interest on its bonds? One answer would be to pay a rate that varied according to the economy's growth and inflation rates.

Other disadvantages are harder to get around. The western model relieves depositors of the need to appraise their banks. By and large, a deposit at one bank is as good as a deposit at any other. Islamic banking places on depositors the burden of gathering information about the past performance and future prospects of banks. In practice, many Islamic systems meet

the demand of lazy depositors for a guaranteed return by fudging the issue: they allow a range of transactions that are orthodox western deposits by another name. If the Islamic goal of risk-sharing were pursued uncompromisingly, the danger would be that the extra burden on depositors would simply lead people to save less, thereby reducing the supply of funds for investment.

Pakistan's reforms may yet prove to be the disaster that some have predicted—not because Islamic banking makes no sense, but because the Shariat court appeared to call for the sudden conversion of all existing financial contracts. That seems an impossible task. But Pakistan's more gradual moves towards Islamic banking since the mid-1980s seem to have worked quite well—as, in principle, you would expect.

Source: *"Banking Behind the Veil," **The Economist**, April 4, 1992, p. 49.* © 1992 The Economist Newspaper Group, Inc. Reprinted with permission.

$104,000 - \$93,600$). This is an expected 4% increase in profit. We see that when total revenues and total costs grow at 4%, profits also grow at 4%.

Because expected future nominal profits are higher with anticipated inflation than without, if we computed the present values of profits using the same interest rate in both cases, we would find that the present values would be higher when there is anticipated inflation. However, if we computed the present values of anticipated profits that are growing with inflation using an interest rate that is increased by the anticipated rate of inflation, the present values of profits would be the same with and without inflation. This is seen by comparing the two present-value columns in Table 17.1. For example, the first year's profits of $10,000 with 0%

The present values of future profits are unchanged by inflation if *computed at an interest rate that is increased by the rate of inflation.*

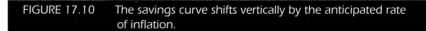

FIGURE 17.10   The savings curve shifts vertically by the anticipated rate of inflation.

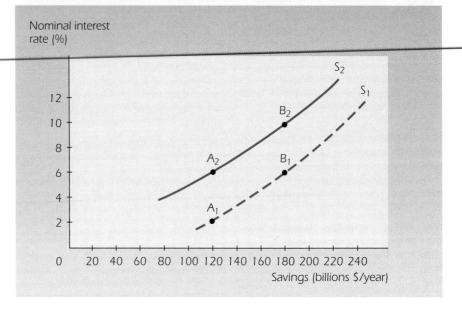

With 0% anticipated inflation, the amount saved at different interest rates is given by curve **S₁**. This curve shows that at a 2% interest rate, savings are $120 billion—point **A₁**—while at a 6% interest rate, savings are $180 billion—point **B₁**. If anticipated inflation increases from 0% to 4%, savings of $120 billion per year occur if the real interest rate remains at 2%, and this requires a 6% nominal interest rate. Therefore, with 4% anticipated inflation, the interest rate at which savings are $120 billion is 6%, as shown by point **A₂**. Similarly, with 4% anticipated inflation, the interest rate at which savings are $180 billion is 10%, as shown by point **B₂**. Joining points **A₂** and **B₂** gives **S₂**, the savings curve when anticipated inflation is 4%. We see that the savings curve shifts upward by the anticipated rate of inflation.

anticipated inflation has a present value at 4% of $9615 (or $10,000 ÷ 1.04). Similarly, the $10,400 first year's profit with 4% inflation has a present value at 8% of $9615 (or $10,400 ÷ 1.08).[9] The same is found for the profits in subsequent years. This is important for the effect anticipated inflation has on the investment curve. To see what the conclusion drawn from Table 17.1 implies for the position of the investment curve, we must return to the criterion for evaluating an investment.

In Chapter 10 we argued that an investment is worthwhile if the total present value of expected future profits attributable to the investment exceeds the cost of

[9] In fact, the present values in the bottom part of Table 17.1 are calculated at 8.16% rather than 8%. The reason is that Equation 14.11 is an approximation of the effect of anticipated inflation on interest rates. The buying power of both principal and interest, not just the principal, is reduced by inflation. For example, if a person received $1.04 after 1 year with 0% inflation, he or she would need $1.0816 (or $1.04 × 1.04) after 1 year with 4% inflation; with goods costing 1.04 times what they used to cost, $1.0816 has a real value of $1.04 (or $1.0816 ÷ 1.04).

....
TABLE 17.1

Anticipated inflation leaves the present values of expected future profits generated by investment unchanged if the interest rate used for computing present values is increased by the anticipated rate of inflation.

	ANTICIPATED INFLATION (0%)			
YEAR	EXPECTED REVENUE	EXPECTED COST	EXPECTED PROFIT	PRESENT VALUE OF EXPECTED PROFIT AT 4%
1	$100,000	$90,000	$10,000	$9,615
2	100,000	90,000	10,000	9,246
3	100,000	90,000	10,000	8,891
4	100,000	90,000	10,000	8,548
5	100,000	90,000	10,000	8,219
6	100,000	90,000	10,000	7,903
7	100,000	90,000	10,000	7,599
8	100,000	90,000	10,000	7,307
9	100,000	90,000	10,000	7,026
10	100,000	90,000	10,000	6,756

	ANTICIPATED INFLATION (4%)			
YEAR	EXPECTED REVENUE	EXPECTED COST	EXPECTED PROFIT	VALUE OF EXPECTED PROFIT AT 8%*
1	$104,000	$ 93,600	$10,400	$9,615
2	108,160	97,344	10,816	9,246
3	112,486	101,238	11,248	8,891
4	116,986	105,287	11,699	8,548
5	121,665	109,499	12,166	8,219
6	126,532	113,879	12,653	7,903
7	131,593	118,434	13,159	7,599
8	136,857	123,171	13,686	7,307
9	142,331	128,098	14,233	7,026
10	148,024	133,222	14,802	6,756

*In fact, present values are calculated at 8.16% not 8%. See footnote 9 in text.

The top part of the table shows revenues, costs, and profits with 0% inflation. The bottom part of the table shows anticipated revenues, costs, and profits with 4% anticipated inflation. We see that if revenues and costs grow at the inflation rate, so does the difference, profits. The table also shows the present values of profits. When there is 0% inflation, the present values are calculated at a 4% interest rate, and when there is 4% inflation, present values are calculated at an 8% interest rate (see footnote 9 in text). We see that present values are the same in the two cases.

the investment. For example, a new harvester is worthwhile if the total present value of profits generated by the harvest exceeds the price of the harvester. The cost of an investment, such as the price of a harvester, is not affected by anticipated *future* inflation if this cost is incurred immediately; inflation affects only *future* costs, so today's price of a harvester is the same whether or not there is anticipated future inflation. Furthermore, as we have just shown, the present value of expected future profits is also unchanged by anticipated inflation *if computed at an interest rate that is increased by the anticipated rate of inflation.* This means that if interest rates increase by anticipated inflation, the same rate of investment would occur with inflation as would have occurred without inflation at the correspondingly lower interest rate; neither today's cost of investment nor the present value of profits is changed. The implication of this for the investment curve I is to move the curve vertically upward by the anticipated rate of inflation, as shown in Figure 17.11. That is, investment is unchanged provided interest rates increase by anticipated inflation.

In Figure 17.11, I_1 is the investment curve with 0% anticipated inflation. The curve shows that at point A_1 there is $100 billion of investment at an interest rate of 8%. From what we have said, with 4% anticipated inflation, there is still $100 billion of investment if the interest rate becomes 12% (or 8%+4%). This gives point A_2 on a new investment curve I_2, the investment curve with 4% anticipated inflation. Similarly, at B_1 on I_1, $180 billion of investment occurs at a 2% interest rate. There is still $180 billion of investment when anticipated inflation increases to 4% if interest rates increase to 6% (or 2%+4%), giving point B_2 on the new investment curve I_2. Therefore, as with savings, the investment curve shifts up by the increase in anticipated inflation.

Figure 17.12 puts together the upward shifts in the savings and investment curves from Figures 17.10 and 17.11. Figure 17.12 shows that the nominal interest rate at which savings equals investment increases with anticipated inflation and by the amount of anticipated inflation. That is, with 0% inflation and relevant savings and investment curves S_1 and I_1, the nominal interest rate is approximately 4%, while with 4% inflation and relevant savings and investment curves S_2 and I_2, the nominal interest rate is approximately 8%. That is, the nominal interest rate is increased by the anticipated rate of inflation. This provides the rationale for Equation 14.11. As we can see from Figures 17.13 and 17.14, which show *actual* inflation and interest rates in the United States and Japan—*anticipated* inflation is not known—the correspondence between the variables is not perfect, but interest rates do move roughly in line with inflation, as predicted by Equation 14.11.[10]

Other Influences on Interest Rates

The loanable funds theory can be extended to explain additional influences on interest rates, such as the effects of fiscal deficits and foreign borrowing. The extensions illustrate the flexibility of the loanable funds theory for describing the wide range of factors that can influence interest rates.

[10] The fact that nominal interest rates increase by anticipated inflation has important implications for judging monetary policy. See Examples 17.2 and 17.3.

The investment curve shifts vertically upward or downward by the rate of anticipated inflation.

The shifts in savings and investment curves caused by anticipated inflation cause the nominal interest rate to increase by anticipated inflation.

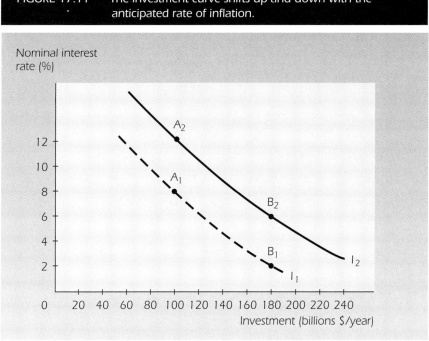

FIGURE 17.11   The investment curve shifts up and down with the anticipated rate of inflation.

The present value of future profits from investment is unchanged by anticipated inflation if we compute the present value using an interest rate that is increased by the anticipated rate of inflation. The same amount of investment therefore occurs at interest rates that increase with the anticipated rate of inflation. For example, if investment is $100 billion at an 8% interest rate when inflation is 0%, point A_1 on I_1, then investment is $100 billion at a 12% interest rate when inflation is 4%, point A_2 on I_2. Similarly, if investment is $180 billion at a 2% interest rate and 0% inflation, point B_1 on I_1, it is $180 billion at a 6% interest rate and 4% inflation, point B_2 on I_2. More generally, the investment curve with 4% anticipated inflation is 4% higher than that for 0% anticipated inflation.

The Effect of Fiscal Deficits.   When explaining the loanable funds theory, we considered only two sources of demand for loanable funds: people wanting to hold more money and investors buying new plant and equipment. However, when a government spends more than it receives in taxes, that is, when a government has a fiscal deficit, the government also demands loanable funds. This adds to the other two demands for funds and shifts the total demand for funds curve L_D to the right.[11] The larger the fiscal deficit, the greater is the shift in L_D. This is illustrated in Figure 17.15 on page 554.

[11] When the government finances its deficit by selling Treasury bills or bonds to the central bank rather than to commercial banks or the public, there is both a demand for and a supply of loanable funds; the demand for funds is that of the government, and the supply of funds is facilitated by the central bank. In such a situation, the loanable funds demand and supply curves *both* shift to the right.

Anticipated inflation shifts the savings and investment curves upward by the anticipated rate of inflation, as shown in Figures 17.10 and 17.11. When these curves are drawn in the same figure as we do here, we see that the nominal interest rate at which **S** = **I** increases by the anticipated inflation rate. That is, when there is 0% inflation so that the relevant savings and investment curves are **S**₁ and **I**₁, the nominal interest rate is 4%. When there is 4% inflation so that the relevant savings and investment curves are **S**₂ and **I**₂, the nominal interest rate is 8%. At the old and new "equilibria" **E**₁ and **E**₂, the quantities of savings and investment are unchanged.

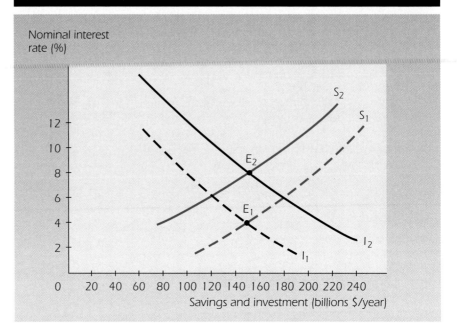

FIGURE 17.12   The nominal interest rate increases by the anticipated rate of inflation.

The ups and downs of inflation correspond quite closely to variations in nominal interest rates. If anticipated inflation were known, it would probably be even more closely related to interest rates than is actual inflation in the figure.

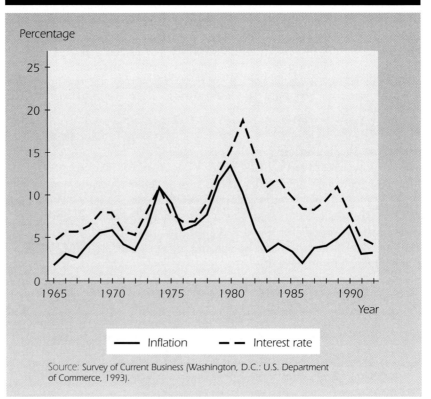

FIGURE 17.13   Inflation and interest rates in the United States.

Source: Survey of Current Business (Washington, D.C.: U.S. Department of Commerce, 1993).

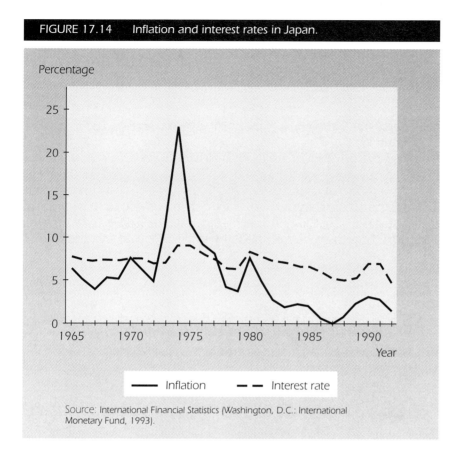

FIGURE 17.14   Inflation and interest rates in Japan.

Source: International Financial Statistics (Washington, D.C.: International Monetary Fund, 1993).

In the mid-1970s, inflation was rapid in Japan as a result of a major increase in oil prices. At that time, actual inflation exceeded interest rates, but it is possible that anticipated inflation was lower than actual inflation. The figure also shows the effect of another oil price shock in 1979. Other than for those periods, inflation and interest rates have followed similar paths.

In Figure 17.15 we assume that the government borrows the amount given by the distance $(Q_2 - Q_3)$, whatever the interest rate. Therefore, the effect of government borrowing is to shift the total demand curve for funds to the right by $(Q_2 - Q_3)$, from L_D^1 to L_D^2. This increases the market interest rate from r_1 to r_2.[12] The quantity of loanable funds supplied (and demanded) increases by $(Q_2 - Q_1)$ as a result of the government borrowing. However, the extra quantity of funds supplied is less than the amount the government borrows, which is distance $(Q_3 - Q_2)$. Therefore, when the government borrows, the quantity of loanable funds that remains available to private investors and money holders is reduced by distance

Fiscal deficits crowd out private demanders of loanable funds and force market interest rates up.

---

[12] When we allow for fiscal deficits, the definition of equilibrium is no longer where savings equal investment. Rather, it is where withdrawals from the circular flow of income, which consist of savings plus taxes, equal injections into the circular flow of income, which consist of government spending plus investment.

Example   17.2

TIGHT VERSUS EASY MONEY

In the traditional interest rate jargon, "tight money" means high interest rates and "easy money" means low rates. Of course, tight and easy refer to a central bank's willingness to expand the money supply, with, for example, tight money occurring when the central bank is holding a tight reign. The translation from money supply to interest rates then follows from the influence that restrictive growth of the money supply has on interest rates. When the change in money supply is small, **ceteris paribus,** borrowing costs are high, and vice versa.

Milton Friedman has argued that high interest rates do not mean that monetary policy is tight. Rather, he says, high rates mean that monetary policy **has been** easy. Similarly, he says that low interest rates do not mean that monetary policy is easy, but that it **has been** tight. The logic behind this concerns inflation. More precisely, it concerns **anticipated** inflation and the connection this has to past growth in the money supply.

The really big swings in interest rates and really big disparities between interest rates in different countries are due to inflation. For example, it was primarily the rapid inflation of the early 1980s that led to the "prime interest rate"—the rate banks charge their most creditworthy customers such as large, secure corporations—leaping to over 20%. Similarly, it has been the very rapid inflation in Mexico and Brazil that has forced interest rates to the hundreds and even thousands of percent per annum. And where does the inflation come from that causes these astronomical interest rates? This is where past monetary policy enters the picture.

High anticipated inflation for the future typically follows when there is high actual inflation today, and high inflation today comes from rapid money supply growth in the past. This is so because it takes time for money supply growth to show up as inflation, perhaps a year or two. This is why Friedman says that high interest rates mean that monetary policy has been easy and low rates mean that monetary policy has been tight. High interest rates mean high anticipated inflation, which follows high actual inflation, which in turn follows rapid earlier growth in the money supply. Needless to say, today's monetary policy also plays a role, but that role has at least two parts.

On the one hand, slower money supply growth means a smaller supply of loanable funds and a consequently higher interest rate. This is an increase in the real rate of interest, that part of the interest rate not due to anticipated inflation. However, working in the other direction is the effect slower money supply growth has on anticipated inflation itself. With slower money growth working to lower inflationary expectations, it also works to lower interest rates. This offsets the effect of higher real rates from the monetary tightness. The net effect depends on the length of time over which the interest rates apply, that is, on "maturity." (This matter is taken up in Example 17.3.) However, whatever the outcome, it is tightness of monetary policy in the recent past, not just the monetary policy of today, that lies behind the bigger swings of interest rates we have seen.

Source: Milton Friedman, "Money—Tight or Easy?" **Newsweek,** March 1, 1971, p. 80.

Example 17.3

THE LONG AND SHORT OF IT

The response to monetary policy of short-term interest rates—those on Treasury bills and other such securities with a maturity of less than 1 year—can be strikingly different from the response of long-term rates. Indeed, the very ability of a central bank to influence short-term versus long-term rates is noticeably different. Consider, for example, the following commentary on interest rates in the **Washington Post.**

The Federal Reserve can push short-term interest rates down quite a lot by pouring money into the banking system. But it has little direct control over the long-term rates—and it's the long-term rates that finance industrial expansion, home building and economic growth in general. The long-term rates are strongly influenced by investors' judgments about future inflation. That creates a trap for the Federal Reserve. If it turns on the spigot and floods the markets with money to reduce interest rates, that signals higher inflation ahead and the interest on the longer loans will rise. That's the monetary paradox: too much political pressure for lower interest rates will result in higher interest rates.*

Long-term interest rates reflect both current and expected future short-term interest rates. For example, if rates on 1-year securities are currently 8% and

1-year rates are widely expected to be 10% next year, today's rate on 2-year securities would have to be approximately 9%. If 2-year rates were less than this, people would invest today for 1 year, receiving $1.08 on each invested dollar. They would then invest this amount for a further 1 year next year, expecting to earn 10% on $1.08, thereby receiving $1.1880 (or $1.08 × 1.10) from their 2 years of investment. This is approximately 9% per annum. If interest rates on 2-year securities were less than 9%, say, 8.5%, investing in a 2-year security would provide only $1.177 (or $1.085 × 1.085) after 2 years. This is less than two successive 1-year securities would be expected to provide. Similarly, if rates on 2-year securities were higher than 9%, say, 10%, investors would not buy 1-year securities. Instead, they would buy 2-year securities.

For a 2-year security to compete with reinvesting in two successive 1-year securities, the 2-year security would have to offer at least as much as the 1-year securities. Indeed, a 2-year security would have to offer a little more to make up for the illiquidity; 2-year securities are less liquid than 1-year securities, having less certain value at any moment. For 1-year and 2-year securities to be competitive with each other, the 2-year security would have to offer the "average" of the current and

expected future 1-year interest rates plus a little extra as a "liquidity premium."[†] More generally, longer-term rates are an average of current and all future short-term rates during the maturity of the longer-term security.

This explains the paradox facing a central bank when it "turns on the spigot and floods the markets with money." Doing this causes fears of inflation in the future, and this raises expected future short-term interest rates. With these expected short-term interest rates figuring into current longer-term interest rates, a monetary flood flows over into higher longer-term interest rates right away. Even if the flood dampens rates in the immediate short term before the inflationary consequences have worked themselves through, the anticipations about higher interest rates in the future will swamp the immediate effects and result in higher longer-term interest rates immediately. And as the **Washington Post** quotation makes clear, it is these longer-term rates that are so important for industrial expansion, home construction, and economic growth in general.

---

* "The Future of Interest Rates," **Washington Post,** October 18, 1990, p. A22.

[†] The average is not the usual "arithmetic average," where the two interest rates are added and divided by 2, but is a "geometric average." This involves taking products of one plus each year's interest rate, taking the square root, and then subtracting 1.

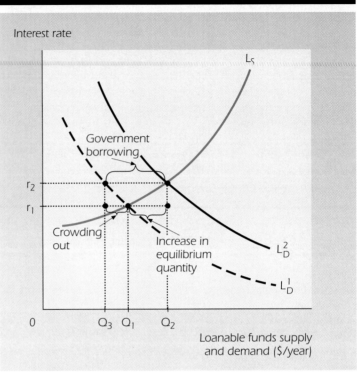

FIGURE 17.15   Fiscal deficits increase interest rates and crowd out private demanders of funds.

If a fiscal deficit is financed by borrowing $(Q_2 - Q_3)$, the demand for loanable funds curve shifts to the right by this amount, that is, from L_D^1 to L_D^2. The effect of the extra demand for funds is to increase the interest rate where the supply of and demand for funds are equal from r_1 to r_2 and the quantity of funds demanded and supplied from Q_1 to Q_2. However, the amount borrowed by the government is $(Q_2 - Q_3)$, which is larger than the increase in the quantity of funds supplied. Therefore, the quantity of funds available to investors and money demanders is reduced from Q_1 to Q_3, that is, by the distance $(Q_1 - Q_3)$. Thus, fiscal deficits crowd out private demanders of funds.

$(Q_1 - Q_3)$; this is the difference between what the government borrows $(Q_2 - Q_3)$ and the increased quantity of loanable funds supplied resulting from the government borrowing $(Q_2 - Q_1)$. That is, government borrowing to finance fiscal deficits **crowds out** private demanders of funds and increases their borrowing costs.

The Effect of Foreign Lenders.   With the increasing globalization of financial markets that has occurred in recent years, loanable funds are now generally available from foreign suppliers of funds, as well as being demanded by foreign users of funds. It might be thought that the presence of foreign suppliers of and demanders for loanable funds simply means rightward shifts of the L_S and L_D curves in, for example, Figure 17.7, with the effect on interest rates depending on foreign demand for funds versus foreign supply. However, since most individual countries' financial markets are small relative to the global financial market, the effect of for-

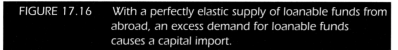

FIGURE 17.16   With a perfectly elastic supply of loanable funds from abroad, an excess demand for loanable funds causes a capital import.

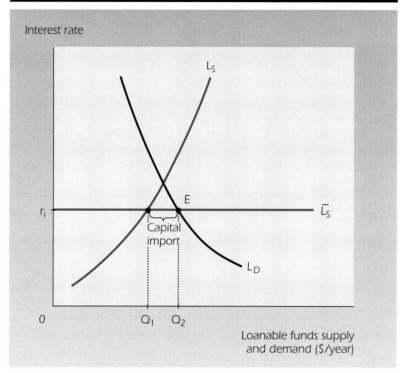

The country's demand curve for loanable funds is **L$_D$**, and the country's own supply curve of loanable funds is **L$_S$**. The country is assumed to be able to borrow from other countries at **r$_i$**, whatever the amount borrowed. This makes the supply curve of foreign funds the perfectly elastic curve **$\bar{L}_S$**. The total supply of and demand for funds are equal at **E**, with an interest rate equal to that of other countries, the international interest rate. At this interest rate, the quantity of loanable funds demanded is **Q$_2$**, and the quantity supplied by the country itself is **Q$_1$**. The difference between the quantity of funds demanded and the quantity supplied by the country itself is (**Q$_2$**−**Q$_1$**). This is borrowed from other countries and constitutes a capital import.

eign suppliers of and demanders for funds can be characterized more appropriately as in Figure 17.16. The figure shows an individual country's supply of and demand for loanable funds curves L_S and L_D, respectively. We assume that the individual country's borrowing represents a small amount relative to the supply of funds from all other countries combined, so the country can borrow more from offshore without raising the international interest rate. Therefore, the supply curve of funds from the rest of the world is perfectly elastic at the international interest rate r_i. That is, the supply curve of funds facing the individual country is $\bar{L}_S$.

At the international interest rate r_i, the quantity of funds demanded by the individual country is Q_2, given off the L_D curve, and the quantity of funds supplied by

If the supply of funds to a country is perfectly elastic at the international interest rate, shifts in the local demand for and supply of loanable funds do not change the equilibrium interest rate. Rather, they cause variations in the size of capital imports.

the country itself is Q_1, given off the L_s curve. (Recall that L_s is the country's own supply of loanable funds.) The excess of the quantity of funds demanded over the quantity supplied by the country itself is the distance $(Q_2 - Q_1)$. This amount is borrowed from the other countries and constitutes a **capital import.** That is, the total supply of and demand for funds are equal at point E in Figure 17.16, with the country facing an interest rate of r_i and quantity of loanable funds demanded of Q_2. Of the total quantity of funds demanded, Q_1 is supplied by the country itself—from its savers and via increased money supply—and the remainder $(Q_2 - Q_1)$ is supplied from other countries.

Consideration of Figure 17.16 shows that shifts in the country's own loanable funds demand and supply curves do not affect the country's interest rate. Rather, shifts in L_s and L_D in Figure 17.16 affect only the quantity of capital imports. For example, if the L_D curve shifted to the right, capital imports would increase, but the interest rate would not change. However, there would be implications of the capital import for further flows of funds out of the country as interest is paid on foreign debt. Issues such as these are discussed in the next chapter, which considers the balance of payments and exchange rates.

A LONG HISTORY OF INTEREST

While the term **usury** originally referred merely to the charging of interest, today it usually connotes **exorbitant** interest, as in the expression **"usurious interest."** This change in the meaning of usury reflects a general shift in attitudes toward an acceptance of the charging of interest, with only excessive, or gouging, rates of interest being viewed as unethical.

The potential oppression of interest payments and of debt permeates language. For example, an instrument of debt is the **bond,** with its meaning of "binding" and consequent denial of the borrower's freedom. A bond is to give **security** to the lender, where the securing of, for example, something loose means tying it down so that it cannot move. The **collateral** on loans comes from the word meaning "subordinately connected," the subordination of the borrower to the lender being in the same vein as being bound and secured.

Lending against real property on a **chattel** mortgage again connotes being tied or enslaved.

Repayment of a bond involves **redemption,** a freeing from the oppression of being in debt. A feature of a bond is a **covenant,** a term reflecting a solemn and binding agreement, as, for example, was made with the Jewish people. The obvious parallel between religious values and matters related to interest rates extends even to the factors which are behind the determination of interest rates as described in this chapter. For example, the piety associated with the act of **saving** is evident in the common root of this word and that of **salvation.** And on the other side of interest rate determination is the act of **investment,** a word which according to **Webster's** means to "clothe; array; adorn . . . to furnish with power, privilege, or authority," as when a priest is installed in office.

Investment, specifically investment in inventory stocks, is a feature of the biblical account of the ascent of Joseph, son of the Patriarch, Jacob, to the Court of the Pharaoh. After earning a reputation for interpreting dreams, the Israelite Joseph is brought to the mighty Pharaoh to be told of his troubling dream of seven fat cows and seven thin cows, and of seven fat ears of corn, and of seven withered, thin ears (Genesis 41:17–24). Joseph explains that this foretells of 7 years of bountiful harvests to be followed by 7 years of famine. He advises that one-fifth of the product of the good years be stored away as inventory for feeding people in the bad years. The stockpile is indeed sold in the ensuing famine (Genesis 41:25–57), providing great relief for Egypt and for its neighbors and an early example of the socially productive role of successful inventory speculation. (In this case of inventory speculation, the amount invested is equal to the amount saved, so the storage of corn is both investment and saving.)

Investments provide a **yield,** as does the planting of crops. Indeed, the sowing of seed, which could itself provide sustenance if eaten right away, occurs because when "invested" in the ground, the seed yields increased future amounts of food, the essence of successful investment. As with investments in stocks and bonds, higher crop yields may come only at the price of higher risk. For example, the planting of strains of wheat developed during the "Green Revolution" has sacrificed diversity for the sake of higher expected yields. This has increased the risk of total crop failure; today's vast, continuous fields planted with a common strain of wheat allow insects and diseases to spread more easily than they did in the past, when between fields with a particular crop or strain of wheat were other crops or strains. We see that in agriculture as in finance there is a trade-off between maximizing expected yield and the risk this incurs.

The biblical admonition on the charging of interest is based on three Old Testament commands. The first, in Exodus 22:25–26, states: "If you lend to one of my people among you who is needy, do not be like a money lender; charge him not interest. If you take your neighbor's cloak as a pledge, return it to him by sunset, because his cloak is the only covering he has. . . ." This command makes it clear that the prohibition is on charging interest to those with whom a lender resides, such as a family or clan member, or a resident alien. The reference to the pledge, which is what occurs today with mortgages where buildings are pledged, has implications for both borrowers and lenders. For the borrower, the loss of a cloak was an annoying reminder that it is necessary to repay all debts. For the lender, the inconvenience of having to go to the debtor's house every evening to return the cloak and every morning to collect it again served to discourage the taking of pledges.

The second biblical admonition on charging of interest, in Leviticus 25:35–37, extends the restriction from money to food, for which the need to return more food than was borrowed constituted the charging of interest: "If one of your countrymen becomes poor and is unable to support himself among you, help him as you would an alien or a temporary resident. . . . Do not take interest of any kind from him. . . . You must not lend him money at interest or sell him food at a profit." This makes explicit the restrictions on collecting interest from a resident alien, who was likely to be a sojourner, without land and probably poor. As in the case of the first mention of interest, the guiding principle is to provide help to the needy and not to profit from their misfortune; in the largely agricultural society of the time and place, drought, locusts, and other natural events could rapidly turn a person's fate.

> "If you lend to one of my people among you who is needy, do not be like a money lender; charge him not interest." (Exodus 22:25–26)

The third biblical reference to interest, in Deuteronomy 23:19–20, while reinforcing the restrictions on charging interest on food and loans to countrymen, removes the ban on interest when lending to "foreigners," who from the context are probably traveling merchants: "Do not charge your brother interest, whether on money or food or anything else that may earn interest. You may charge a foreigner interest, but not a brother Israelite. . . ." It is likely that the permission to charge interest to a foreigner was designed to make a distinction between **commercial** lending which constitutes an investment, as when lending to a (foreign) merchant, and **personal** lending which went toward consumption, as when lending to a poor countryman. Further consideration of this final Old Testament reference to interest led to the acceptance of what is, in effect, the practice of financial intermediation when rabbinical interpretation suggested that a third party, the intermediary, could charge interest to the borrower and compensate the provider of credit. Whatever the detailed interpretation, it is clear that in certain circumstances the charging of interest is acceptable.

Christian and Islamic scriptures echo the concern over usurious interest. For example: "And if you lend to those from whom you expect repayment, what credit is that to you? . . . But love your enemies, do good to them, and lend to them without expecting to get anything back" (Luke 6:34–35). Again, lenders are commanded to be charitable, even to the point of forgiving repayment. Nevertheless, the commercial needs

> *"And if you lend to those from whom you expect repayment, what credit is that to you? . . . But love your enemies, do good to them, and lend to them without expecting to get anything back."*
> *(Luke 6:34:35)*

for credit stretched the interpretation of legitimate circumstances for the charging of interest, although the term **interest** has sometimes been replaced with **dividend, service charge, credit fee,** and other such euphemisms for interest payments.[13]

The Hebrew word for interest, **neshech,** has the same root as the word **bite.** This common meaning has not been lost by those who know how interest can grow to the point of total ruin. For example, the great biblical interpreter Rabbi Shemuel ben Meir (1085–1174), also known as Rashbam, when commenting on the common root of **neshech** as "interest" and "bite," points out that as with the bite of a snake, there is no pain at the time it is incurred, but it spreads to affect the entire body, just as interest can become a crushing sum. This power of interest, with its deceptively innocent beginnings, is behind the Old Testament institution of the sabbatical, whereby debts were to be canceled after 7 years, although all ties and bonds, including debts and relationships between slaves and their masters, could be renewed by mutual consent. However, in the Jubilee Year, which occurred in the fiftieth year after seven sabbaticals, forgiveness of all debts and other contracts was unequivocally required, even if there was mutual consent to continue. Indeed, the word **finance** has its roots in the latin **finis,** "to end."

---

[13] See Example 17.1 on page 544 for the way interest is determined in the Islamic tradition.

SUMMARY

1. Interest rates can have important effects on spending by consumers and businesses and thereby an important impact on an economy.

2. The loanable funds theory explains how interest rates are determined by the supply of and demand for loanable funds.

3. The supply of loanable funds consists of additions to the money supply and savings out of current income.

4. The money supply is controlled by the central bank and may or may not depend on interest rates. Savings are determined by the public and increase with increasing interest rates.

5. The demand for loanable funds consists of additions to the demand for money and the demand for financing capital investment.

6. The larger is the increase in GDP, the larger is the increase in quantity of money demanded. Because interest earnings are forgone when holding money rather than bonds, the higher the interest rate, the smaller is the quantity of money demanded.

7. Fewer investments are profitable as the interest rate rises, and therefore, investment decreases as the interest rate rises. Investment increases with increases in GDP because higher output requires more plant and equipment.

8. The market interest rate is the interest rate at which the supply of and demand for loanable funds are equal. In general, savings do not equal investment at the market interest rate.

9. The equilibrium interest rate is the rate at which savings equals investment. The market interest rate moves toward the equilibrium rate.

10. An increase in the rate of change of the money supply causes a rightward shift in the supply of loanable funds curve, lowering market interest rates. However, because savings and investment are not affected, the equilibrium interest rate is not affected.

11. Increases in economic activity as measured by the change in GDP increase the demand for money and investment. Therefore, increases in the change in GDP cause increases in market and equilibrium interest rates.

12. The savings curve shifts upward by the increase in anticipated inflation because only at a nominal interest rate that reflects anticipated inflation is the real interest rate earned by savers unchanged. The investment curve also shifts upward by anticipated inflation because only at a nominal interest rate that reflects anticipated inflation is the profitability of investment unchanged. As a result of the shifts in the savings and investment curves, nominal interest rates increase by the change in anticipated inflation.

13. A fiscal deficit represents a demand for loanable funds and causes an increase in market and equilibrium interest rates.

14. When loanable funds are available from other countries at the international interest rate, variations in a country's supply of and demand for loanable funds cause variations in capital imports but do not change the interest rate.

QUESTIONS AND PROBLEMS

1. Why would a central bank policy of maintaining a given, targeted interest rate make the curve showing the change in money supply a horizontal line? How would such a horizontal money supply curve affect the conclusions reached using the loanable funds theory concerning, for example, the effects of a more rapidly growing GDP and larger fiscal deficits.

2. Do you think a central bank could maintain an artificially low nominal interest rate for very long?

3. What could make ΔM^s slope upward? Would an upward slope to ΔM^s make much difference to the supply curve for loanable funds?

4. Can you redraw Figure 17.7 so that the market interest rate is also the equilibrium interest rate?

5. Why is it that changes in real GDP affect investment, while changes in nominal GDP affect the demand for money?

6. What determines the amount of crowding out from fiscal deficits? Think in terms of slopes of curves in Figure 17.15 and the underlying savings and investment curves.

7. Why might the supply curve of funds from abroad to a large economy such as the United States have an upward slope? How would this influence the conclusion concerning the effect of government borrowing on interest rates, savings, and capital imports?

8. Is the increase in interest rates in Figure 17.15 an increase in the market rate, the equilibrium rate, or both?

9. Redraw Figure 17.16 to describe the situation of a country that exports capital.

10. The demand for money depends on the nominal, not the real, interest rate. Therefore, the ΔM^D curve does not shift with anticipated inflation. Similarly, ΔM^s does not shift with anticipated inflation. Therefore, L_s and L_D do not shift upward by the full extent of anticipated inflation; only the S and I components of L_s and L_D shift by anticipated inflation. Show what this implies for market versus equilibrium interest rates when there is anticipated inflation.

APPENDIX TO CHAPTER 17

. . . .
. . . .
. . . .
. . . .
. . . .
. . . . Investment and Real GDP
. . . .
. . . .

To determine the link between investment and real GDP, assume that the number of machines and size of plant that firms want is proportional to their output. Because the national output is the real GDP, this allows us to write

$$K^d = \alpha Q \qquad (17A.1)$$

where K^d is the aggregate desired real capital stock, Q is real GDP, and α is a constant showing by how much K^d changes with Q. The equation tells us that the desired *stock* of capital moves up and down with real GDP. However, the equation does not yet tell us how capital *investment* varies with real GDP.

Investment is, by definition, the *change* in the capital stock. What this means is that if firms achieve their desired stock of capital by the end of each period of time, we can write investment[1] as

$$I_t = K^d_t - K^d_{t-1} \qquad (17A.2)$$

where I_t refers to investment during time period t, and K^d_t refers to the desired stock of capital for the end of period t. Equation 17A.2 says that if firms always have the stock of capital they want, then investment during period t is the difference between the stock of capital they want to have by the end of t, that is, K^d_t, and the stock they began with at the beginning of t, that is, K^d_{t-1}.

---

[1] In fact, it is *net* investment that is equal to the change in the capital stock. However, the demand for loanable funds comes from all investment, that is, *gross* investment. By definition, gross investment is the sum of net investment and depreciation. Therefore, Equation 17A.2 gives only part of investment but is sufficiently accurate for our purposes.

If we put time subscripts on the K^d and Q in Equation 17A.1 in order to show the desired stock of capital for the end of each period to be proportional to real GDP during that period, we have

$$K^d_t = \alpha Q_t \qquad\qquad (17A.3)$$

Similarly, since we assume the link between K^d and Q also occurs in other time periods, such as in period $t-1$, we can also write

$$K^d_{t-1} = \alpha Q_{t-1} \qquad\qquad (17A.4)$$

Substituting Equations 17A.3 and 17A.4 into Equation 17A.2 gives

$$I_t = K^d_t - K^d_{t-1} = \alpha Q_t - \alpha Q_{t-1} = \alpha (Q_t - Q_{t-1})$$

This can be abbreviated to

$$I_t = \alpha \Delta Q_t \qquad\qquad (17A.5)$$

where $\Delta Q_t \equiv Q_t - Q_{t-1}$. This tells us that there is a relationship between investment and the *change* in real GDP. The faster real GDP grows, the higher is investment and hence the larger is the demand for loanable funds.

. . . .
. . . .
. . . .
. . . .
. . . .
. . . . . . Exchange Rates
. . . . . .
. . . .

*As for foreign exchange, it is almost as romantic as young love,
and quite as resistant to formulae.*

H. L. Mencken

Key Concepts

Interpreting exchange rates; balance of payments account; the
balance of trade; exchange rate effects on exports and imports;
J-curve; effects of inflation on exchange rates; exchange rates
and living standards; gold standard; Bretton Woods system of
fixed exchange rates

THE RELEVANCE OF EXCHANGE RATES

Few people have anything to do with exchanging currencies, and it might therefore seem that exchange rates have limited relevance for most of us. Such a conclusion is totally unwarranted. For one thing, exchange rates have important
effects on a country's competitiveness. Not only are exports affected, but competition at home between domestic goods and imports depends on exchange rates.
For example, the ability of U.S. automobile makers to sell automobiles abroad *and*
in the United States is affected by the foreign exchange value of the dollar; competition from Japan, Germany, and elsewhere is more severe when the U.S. dollar is
high versus the Japanese yen and German mark. Another important effect of
exchange rates is on international borrowing and investment. *Ceteris paribus,*
countries with "weak" currencies have trouble attracting foreign capital to finance

business investment and fiscal deficits. These and other effects of exchange rates eventually translate into effects on jobs and the standard of living. This chapter deals with such consequences of exchange rates and at the same time explains the factors that can cause exchange rates to change.

THE NATURE OF EXCHANGE RATES

Most people use only their own nation's currency in everyday domestic commerce.[1] This means that when they buy goods, services, stocks, bonds, real estate, and so on from a resident of a foreign country, they must first exchange their domestic currency for foreign currency. The rate at which domestic currency exchanges for foreign currency is the **exchange rate.** Specifically, the exchange rate is the number of units of one country's currency, for example, German marks, required to purchase one unit of another country's currency, for example, the U.S. dollar.

The exchange rate is the amount of one country's currency it takes to purchase one unit of another country's currency.

Table 18.1 shows the exchange rates of a number of currencies vis-à-vis the U.S. dollar on December 14, 1992. For each currency, the exchange rate is quoted in two ways: in terms of the amount of foreign currency to buy one U.S. dollar—in the first column—and in terms of the number of U.S. dollars needed to buy one unit of the foreign currency—in the second column. The amount of foreign currency needed to buy one U.S. dollar is simply the inverse, or reciprocal, of the number of U.S. dollars needed to buy the foreign currency. For example, it takes 1.45 Australian dollars to buy 1 U.S. dollar, and it therefore takes 0.69 (or $1 \div 1.45$) U.S. dollars to buy 1 Australian dollar. Similarly, it takes 123 Japanese yen to buy 1 U.S. dollar, or 0.0081 (or $1 \div 123$) U.S. dollars to buy 1 Japanese yen.

It is possible to determine the exchange rate between any two currencies from their exchange rates vis-à-vis the U.S. dollar. For example, it is possible to find the exchange rate between the German mark, written as DM for Deutschemark, and the British pound, written as £, from the exchange rates of the mark versus the dollar and the pound versus the dollar. For example, as shown in Table 18.2, with DM/$ = 1.56, and $/£ = 1.57, the number of marks per British pound is DM/£ = (DM/$) × ($/£) = 1.56 × 1.57 = 2.45, where DM/£ is the number of German marks per British pound, DM/$ is the number of marks per U.S. dollar, and $/£ the number of dollars per pound. Similarly, the number of Canadian dollars per pound is simply C$/£ = (C$/$) × ($/£) = 1.28 × 1.57 = 2.01. More generally, we can find the amount of currency i for one unit of currency of j from

The exchange rate between any pair of currencies can be obtained from the exchange rate of each of the currencies against the U.S. dollar.

$$i/j = (i/\$) \cdot (\$/j) \qquad (18.1)$$

While the dollar has become the conventional **reference currency** for quoting exchange rates, in theory, any currency would do. Indeed, a commodity such as gold also can be used. In fact, as explained later in this chapter and in the Crossing Bridges section, gold was used until the early part of this century. The

---

[1] There are places where foreign currencies are used side by side with domestic currency, but these are typically localized tourist centers or countries suffering from very rapid inflation.

·············
TABLE 18.1

Exchange rates are most frequently quoted in terms of the U.S. dollar.

	FOREIGN CURRENCY PER U.S. DOLLAR	U.S. DOLLARS PER FOREIGN CURRENCY
Australia (dollar)	1.45	0.69
Brazil (cruzeiro)	11,111	0.00009
Britain (pound)	0.64	1.57
Canada (dollar)	1.28	0.78
France (franc)	5.26	0.19
Germany (mark)	1.56	0.64
Hong Kong (dollar)	7.69	0.13
Israel (shekel)	2.70	0.37
Italy (lira)	1429	0.0007
Japan (yen)	123	0.0081
Mexico (peso)	3125	0.00032
Netherlands (guilder)	1.75	0.57
Singapore (dollar)	1.64	0.61
Switzerland (franc)	1.41	0.71

Source: Based on various bank quotations, December 14, 1992.

TABLE 18.2

All possible exchange rates can be obtained from the exchange rate of each currency versus the U.S. dollar.

	$	£	C$	DM
$	1	1.57	0.78	0.64
£	0.64	1	0.50	0.41
C$	1.28	2.01	1	10.82
DM	1.56	2.45	1.22	1

All possible exchange rates can be obtained from the rates versus the U.S. dollar. For example, the number of British pounds (£) per German mark (DM) is the number of pounds per dollar (£/$ = 0.64) multiplied by the number of dollars per German mark ($/DM = 0.64). This gives £/DM = (£/$) × ($/DM) = 0.64 × 0.64 = 0.41. Similarly, the number of German marks per Canadian dollar (DM/C$ = 1.22) is equal to the number of German marks per U.S. dollar (DM/$ = 1.56) multiplied by the number of U.S. dollars per Canadian dollar ($/C$ = 0.78), which gives DM/C$ = 1.56 × 0.78 = 1.22. The convention of quoting against the U.S. dollar evolved from the important role the U.S. dollar has played in international trade and finance.

U.S. dollar offers advantages over gold and other currencies because there are numerous international commercial transactions involving dollars and therefore very frequent exchange rate quotations vis-à-vis the dollar.

When there is an increase in the amount of foreign currency per U.S. dollar, the U.S. dollar is said to have **appreciated** and the foreign currency is said to have **depreciated.** For example, when the number of German marks per U.S. dollar goes from 1.56 to 1.60, the U.S. dollar has appreciated—it is worth more—and the German mark has depreciated—it is worth less.

The terms appreciation and depreciation are used with **flexible exchange rates,** which occur when exchange rates are determined by market forces. With **fixed exchange rates,** which occur when exchange rates are set by central banks, instead of appreciating a currency is said to have been **revalued,** and instead of depreciating it is said to have been **devalued.** (See Example 18.1 for more on variations in exchange rates.)

When the number of units of foreign currency per U.S. dollar increases, the U.S. dollar has appreciated and the foreign currency has depreciated.

THE BALANCE OF PAYMENTS ACCOUNT

The numerous different factors that can cause an appreciation or depreciation of a country's currency are summarized in the **balance of payments account.** The balance of payments account provides a tabulation of the amounts of a country's currency that are demanded and supplied for various purposes during an interval of time. The factors giving rise to a demand for a country's currency are listed as **credits** and are preceded by a plus sign in the balance of payments account. The factors giving rise to a supply of a country's currency are listed as **debits** and are preceded by a minus sign. In this chapter we shall show how the various factors behind the supply of and demand for a currency influence the equilibrium exchange rate.

Table 18.3 is a summary of the U.S. balance of payments account for 1992. We see that the largest item giving rise to a demand for U.S. dollars is exports, consisting of merchandise and of services. (U.S. exports are, of course, U.S. goods and services sold abroad.) The largest item giving rise to a supply of U.S. dollars is imports, which also consist of merchandise and of services. (U.S. imports are, of course, foreign goods and services purchased by U.S. residents.) U.S. exports represent a demand for U.S. dollars because foreigners must buy dollars to pay Americans for the goods and services Americans sell, and U.S. imports represent a supply of U.S. dollars because Americans supply dollars to the foreign exchange market in exchange for the currencies they need to pay for foreign goods and services.

Because exports and imports constitute such important components of the total supply of and demand for a currency, they have major effects on exchange rates. In turn, exchange rates have major effects on exports and imports. We shall describe both the effects of exports and imports on exchange rates and the effects of exchange rates on exports and imports. Let us begin by considering the effects of exchange rates on exports and imports, focusing on how exports and imports represent a demand for and supply of a nation's currency. Later we shall consider the effects of exports and imports on exchange rates, as well as how other items listed in the balance of payments account affect exchange rates.

The balance of payments account lists the reasons why a currency is demanded and why it is supplied and shows the amounts demanded and supplied for various purposes during an interval of time.

Exports cause a demand *for the exporter's currency. Imports cause a* supply *of the importer's currency.*

Example 18.1

FOREIGN EXCHANGE: THE BIGGEST MARKET ON EARTH

Most people have little or nothing to do with foreign exchange, and so it may come as quite a surprise to learn that the foreign exchange market is the largest market on Earth. The following excerpt answers some questions that are commonly asked about this fascinating and volatile market.

Here are answers to some commonly asked questions about exchange rates and the dollar.

How big are the world's currency markets?

Huge. According to a 1990 survey by the Bank for International Settlements, $650 billion a day of foreign exchange is traded round the globe. That's more volume than the New York Stock Exchange rings up in two months.

Who does all this trading?

A wide range of players. Major banks are most active, accounting for nearly 80% of trading, according to the New York Federal Reserve Bank. But multinational companies account for billions of dollars of trading as well. Global money managers, individual speculators and tourists also are active.

Where does trading occur?

Most trading is done electronically, via bank-to-bank phone links. There isn't any dominant exchange that handles spot trading—the trading of currency for immediate delivery. Instead, activity during any 24-hour period migrates from one time zone to another, moving from Europe to the U.S., Australia, Japan and then back to Europe.

But about $14 billion a day of currency futures are traded at the Chicago Mercantile Exchange. And the Philadelphia Stock Exchange does a sizable business in currency options.

Can countries control their exchange rates?

Not very well. World exchange rates have been left to float since 1971, though members of the European Economic Community have tried to loosely link their currencies for most of the past two decades. But as certain European currencies become unusually strong or weak, authorities repeatedly have been forced to change the targeted values of those currencies in what is known as a currency realignment.

Does anyone regulate currency trades?

Central banks such as the Fed provide some degree of oversight. And futures trading, in particular, is watched by the Commodities Futures Trading Commission. But in general, the currency markets are much more lightly regulated than stock or bond trading.

Aside from revaluations, can countries do anything to control their exchange rates?

Each year, countries' central banks make billions of dollars in currency trades designed to stabilize exchange rates. But such central-bank intervention often proves futile, as even the trading might of the U.S. Federal Reserve, the Bank of England or the German Bundesbank proves insufficient to overcome market forces.

Which of the world's currencies are the most important ones in traders' eyes?

At the top of the list, alongside the dollar, are the mark and the yen. A survey of 300 major traders last year by Greenwich Associates found that 28% of the dollar trading in North America is in the mark, 23% in the yen, 13% in the British pound and 9% in the Swiss franc. Rounding out the list of major trading currencies, at 3% to 7% each, are the Canadian dollar, Australian dollar and French franc.

Why are there no old currency traders?

It's an intensely stressful job. "The roller coasters at an amusement park are very tame compared to what happens in the foreign exchange market," says James Oliff, a Chicago futures trader specializing in the pound. After a day of what he termed "very expensive" trading, the 44-year-old Mr. Oliff declared: "Today, I feel like I'm 82."

Source: George Anders, "Answers to Commonly Asked Questions About Currency Trading in a Wild Week," **The Wall Street Journal,** September 17, 1992, p. A6. Reprinted by permission of The Wall Street Journal, © 1992 Dow Jones & Company, Inc. All Rights Reserved Worldwide.

TABLE 18.3

The U.S. balance of payments account is a summary of the number of U.S. dollars demanded for each of many purposes and supplied for each of many purposes in a given time interval.

LINE		(CREDITS +, DEBITS −, Billions $)	
1	Exports		+725
2	Merchandise	+440	
3	Services	+285	
4	Imports		−755
5	Merchandise	−535	
6	Services	−220	
7	Unilateral transfers (net)		−28
8	U.S. private holdings of foreign assets (net change)		−37
9	Direct investment abroad	−39	
10	Foreign securities and claims	+2	
11	Foreign private holdings of assets in the United States (net change)		+73
12	Direct investment in the United States	+5	
13	U.S. securities and claims	+68	
14	U.S. government holdings of foreign assets (net change)		−2
15	Foreign official holdings of U.S. assets (net change)		+42
16	Change in U.S. official reserves		+2
17	Statistical discrepancy		−20
			0

Memoranda

1. Balance on merchandise trade (lines 2 and 5)	−95
2. Balance on goods and services (lines 1 and 4)	−30
3. Balance on current account (lines 1, 4, and 7)	−58
4. Increase (+) in foreign official reserves (line 15)	+42
5. Increase (−) in U.S. official reserves (line 16)	+2

Factors giving rise to a demand for U.S. dollars are listed as credits and marked (+), while those giving rise to a supply of U.S. dollars are listed as debts and marked (−). Note that the sum of the principal items is zero.

Source: Extrapolations from **Survey of Current Business** (Washington, D.C.: U.S. Department of Commerce, December 1992).

EXPORTS, IMPORTS, AND EXCHANGE RATES

The Effect of Exchange Rates on Exports and the Demand for U.S. Dollars

The effect of exchange rates on U.S. exports is shown in part (a) of Figure 18.1. The consequent effect of exchange rates on the demand for U.S. dollars is shown in part (b) of Figure 18.1. The curve labeled D in part (a) of Figure 18.1 shows the quantity of wheat demanded by American consumers at each price of wheat. D is nothing other than the American demand curve for wheat. The curve labeled S shows the quantity of wheat supplied by American farmers at each price. Therefore, S is nothing other than the U.S. supply curve of wheat. (For simplicity, we assume that wheat is the only export.)

The price of wheat is not in general where U.S. supply and demand curves intersect. This is so because the market for wheat is international, and the equilibrium price is where the *global* quantity supplied equals the *global* quantity demanded. Let us assume that the global equilibrium occurs at DM10 per bushel and that the going exchange rate is DM2.5 per dollar. This means that American producers and consumers can take the dollar price of wheat as $4 (or DM10 ÷ DM2.5/$) per bushel.[2]

At a price of $4 per bushel, Americans demand 4 billion bushels of wheat per year but produce 9 billion bushels. The excess of the quantity supplied over the quantity demanded, that is, 5 billion bushels, is the quantity of wheat exported.

It is the *value* of exports, not the *quantity,* that gives the number of dollars foreigners need in order to pay for U.S. exports; the value of exports is the price of exports multiplied by the quantity of exports. Assuming that wheat is the only export, we can find the number of dollars foreigners must buy, and therefore the number of U.S. dollars foreigners demand, by multiplying the price of wheat by the quantity of wheat exported. Since 5 billion bushels of wheat are exported when the price is $4 per bushel, the number of U.S. dollars demanded is $20 billion (or $4 × 5 billion). This is represented in part (a) of Figure 18.1 by the area of the shaded rectangle, which has a height of $4 and a base of 5 billion bushels. (This shaded area is equal to the dollar value of U.S. wheat exports because it is equal to the price of exports in U.S. dollars multiplied by the quantity sold.)

The exchange rate at which the price of wheat is $4 per bushel and at which $20 billion of U.S. dollars per year is demanded is DM2.5 per U.S. dollar. Therefore, we can plot point A on the demand curve for dollars in part (b) of Figure 18.1, showing $20 billion of U.S. dollars demanded to pay for U.S. wheat at the exchange rate DM/$ = 2.5.

In order to find other points on the demand curve for dollars, we take different exchange rates and calculate the number of U.S. dollars spent on U.S. wheat exports at each exchange rate. For example, let us suppose that the U.S. dollar depreciates against the German mark from DM2.5/$ to DM2/$. Let us also assume

---

[2] International commodity prices are traditionally *quoted* in U.S. dollars. However, if the United States represents only part of the worldwide market for a commodity, the fact that prices are quoted in dollars does not prevent the U.S. dollar price of the commodity from being affected by exchange rates.

FIGURE 18.1   The lower the foreign exchange value of the U.S. dollar, the larger is the quantity of U.S. exports and the larger is the quantity of U.S. dollars demanded.

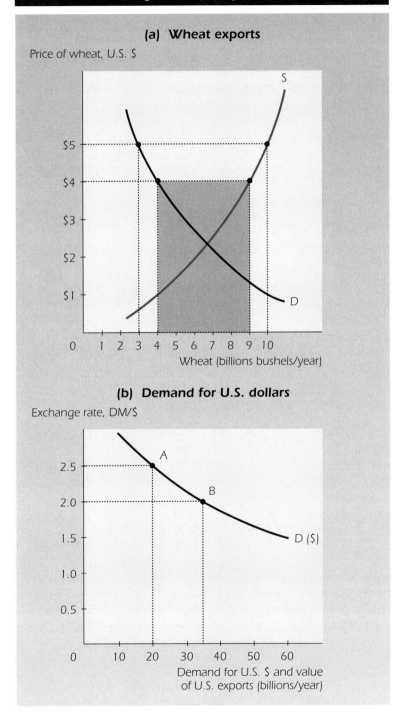

(a) Wheat exports

Price of wheat, U.S. $

Wheat (billions bushels/year)

(b) Demand for U.S. dollars

Exchange rate, DM/$

Demand for U.S. $ and value of U.S. exports (billions/year)

Suppose that the price of wheat in the international wheat market is DM10 per bushel, whatever the exchange rate. When the exchange rate is DM2.5/$, this means that the price of wheat in U.S. dollars is $4 per bushel. At this price, U.S. wheat production exceeds U.S. wheat demand by 5 (or 9 − 4) billion bushels. With this quantity exported, the value of wheat exports is $20 billion (or $4 × 5 billion) per year. This is plotted in part (b) at the exchange rate DM2.5/$. At the exchange rate DM2/$, the price of wheat is $5 per bushel and the quantity of wheat exported is 7 (or 10 − 3) billion bushels per year. The **value** of exports at DM2/$ is therefore $35 billion (or $5 × 7 billion). This is plotted in part (b) at the exchange rate DM2/$. We find that the demand curve for U.S. dollars vis-à-vis the exchange rate **D**($) is downward sloping.

that the price of wheat in terms of German marks in the international market is not affected by the change in the exchange rate, remaining at DM10 per bushel. This means that the price of wheat in terms of U.S. dollars increases from $4 per bushel to $5 (or DM10 ÷ DM2/$) per bushel.

At $5 per bushel, Americans demand 3 billion bushels of wheat per year, a smaller amount than before, and supply 10 billion bushels, a larger amount than before. Therefore, exports increase as a result of the depreciation of the dollar, from 5 billion bushels to 7 (or 10−3) billion bushels per year. The *value* of U.S. exports is also increased by the depreciation of the U.S. dollar. With the new price of wheat of $5 per bushel, the value of wheat exports is $35 billion (or $5×7 billion). This is larger than the previous amount, which was $20 billion, both because the U.S. dollar price of wheat is higher and because the quantity of wheat exported is larger. We plot the new value of exports against the new exchange rate in part (b) of Figure 18.1 as point *B*. This shows the number of U.S. dollars demanded, $35 billion per year, at the exchange rate of DM2/$ and is a point on the demand curve for dollars. By joining the points on the demand curve for dollars *D*($), we find that at a lower foreign exchange value of the dollar, a larger number of dollars is demanded. That is, the demand curve for dollars is downward sloping vis-à-vis the German mark price of the U.S. dollar.

A decrease in the foreign exchange value of a currency causes an increase in the quantity of that currency demanded.

The Effect of Exchange Rates on Imports and the Supply of U.S. Dollars

Dollars are supplied by U.S. residents when they pay for imports. Figure 18.2 shows how the exchange rate affects both the quantity of U.S. imports and the number of U.S. dollars supplied by U.S. residents when paying for these imports. Part (a) of Figure 18.2 shows the U.S. supply and demand curves for automobiles. For simplicity, we assume that automobiles are the only import and are all the same. Part (b) shows the consequent supply of U.S. dollars at each exchange rate. Let us show how this supply curve of U.S. dollars is obtained from the supply of and demand for automobiles.

We note first that the price of automobiles is determined from global supply and demand. Let us assume that the price is DM20,000 and that this amount is unaffected by the foreign exchange value of the dollar.

At the exchange rate of DM2.5 per U.S. dollar, the dollar price of an automobile is $8000 (or DM20,000 ÷ DM2.5/$). Part (a) of Figure 18.2 shows that at this price the quantity of automobiles demanded in the United States is 7.5 million, while the quantity supplied in the United States is only 2.5 million per year. Therefore, the United States is a net importer of automobiles, buying 5 million vehicles per year from abroad.[3] The amount spent on this number of imported automobiles is $40 billion (or $8000×5 million). This is the number of U.S. dollars Americans supply to the foreign exchange market to buy imported automobiles when the exchange rate is DM2.5/$ and is plotted as point *V* in part (b) of Figure 18.2.

[3]We can see from comparing Figures 18.1 and 18.2 what it is that determines whether a country is an importer or an exporter of a product. What matters is whether the price without trade would be higher or lower than the going international price.

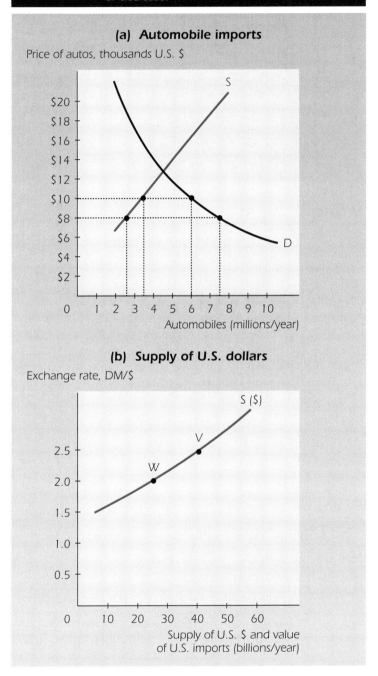

FIGURE 18.2   A decline in the foreign exchange value of the U.S. dollar reduces the quantity of imports, but the supply of U.S. dollars may increase or decrease.

(a) Automobile imports

Price of autos, thousands U.S. $

Automobiles (millions/year)

(b) Supply of U.S. dollars

Exchange rate, DM/$

Supply of U.S. $ and value of U.S. imports (billions/year)

If the internationally determined price of an automobile is DM20,000, at the exchange rate DM2.5/$, the U.S. dollar price is $8000. Part (a) shows that at this price 7.5 million automobiles are demanded, 2.5 million are produced domestically, and hence 5 million are imported. This involves an expenditure of $40 billion (or $8000 × 5 million), which is the number of U.S. dollars supplied at exchange rate DM2.5/$. This is plotted as point **V** in part (b). If the dollar depreciates to DM2/$, the price of an automobile increases to $10,000. Part (a) shows that at this price the quantity of automobiles demanded is reduced to 6 million, while the quantity produced domestically is increased to 3.5 million. Therefore, imports are reduced to 2.5 (or 6 − 3.5) million. This involves an expenditure on imports of $25 billion (or $10,000 × 2.5 million), which is the number of U.S. dollars supplied at DM2/$. This is plotted as point **W** in part (b). In this case the supply curve of U.S. dollars slopes upward.

To see how the supply of U.S. dollars varies with the exchange rate, let us consider the effect of a depreciation of the U.S. dollar from DM2.5/$ to DM2/$. At the new exchange rate, the U.S. price of a DM20,000 automobile increases from $8000 to $10,000. Part (a) of Figure 18.2 shows that at a price of $10,000, the quantity of automobiles demanded in the United States is 6 million, while the quantity supplied domestically is approximately 3.5 million per year. Therefore, imports decline as a result of the U.S. dollar depreciation from 5 million to 2.5 (or 6 2 3.5) million automobiles per year.

The value of imports at the exchange rate DM2/$ is $25 billion (or $10,000 3 2.5 million). This is the supply of U.S. dollars at DM2/$ and is plotted as point *W* in Figure 18.2. We find in this case that a depreciation of the U.S. dollar has reduced the quantity of U.S. dollars supplied. The supply curve of U.S. dollars is hence upward sloping with respect to the German mark price of U.S. dollars, as shown by *S*($) in part (b) of Figure 18.2. However, an upward-sloping currency supply curve is not the only possibility.

Figure 18.3 shows why the supply curve of U.S. dollars might not be upward sloping. The only difference between Figures 18.3 and 18.2 is that in Figure 18.3 the supply and demand curves for automobiles are more inelastic than in Figure 18.2. As before, we initially assume that the exchange rate is DM2.5/$ and the price of automobiles is DM20,000. This means an $8000 price in the United States; DM20,000 4 DM2.5/$ 5 $8000. Therefore, as before, imports are 5 (or 7.5 2 2.5) million automobiles per year. The supply of U.S. dollars is therefore $40 billion (or $8000 3 5 million) per year, which is shown as point *V* in part (b) of Figure 18.3, the same point *V* as in Figure 18.2. Next, as before, we assume that the dollar depreciates to DM2/$. This increases the automobile price to $10,000. In Figure 18.3 part (a), at a price of $10,000, U.S. automobile imports are 4.25 (or 7 2 2.75) million per year, and spending on imported automobiles is therefore $42.5 billion (or $10,000 3 4.25 million) per year. The exchange rate DM2/$ and supply of U.S. dollars of $42.5 billion is plotted as point *W'* in part (a) of Figure 18.3. When we join points *V* and *W'* in part (b) of Figure 18.3, we find that the supply curve of U.S. dollars slopes downward. That is, in this case more is spent on imports when the dollar depreciates.

The reason more may be spent on imported automobiles after a dollar depreciation and consequent increase in automobile prices is that the quantity of imports may decline proportionately less than prices increase; in Figure 18.3, automobile prices increase by 25%, from $8000 to $10,000, but the quantity imported decreases only 15%, from 5 million to 4.25 million automobiles. In other words, a downward-sloping supply curve of U.S. dollars occurs when the demand for imported automobiles is inelastic. (Inelastic demand is defined in Chapter 4.)

The J-Curve in the Balance of Merchandise Trade

The difference between the value of exports and the value of imports during a given time interval is called the **balance of merchandise trade** or, more briefly, the **balance of trade.** This is shown as the first memorandum item in the balance of payments account in Table 18.3. The balance of trade is in **surplus** if the value of merchandise exports exceeds the value of merchandise imports and is in **deficit** if the value of merchandise imports exceeds the value of merchandise exports. Table 18.3 shows that the United States has a large balance of trade deficit.

The supply curve of a currency slopes *downward* with respect to the foreign exchange value of that currency if the country's demand for imports is *inelastic.*

The balance of merchandise trade is the difference between the value of merchandise exports and merchandise imports in a given time interval.

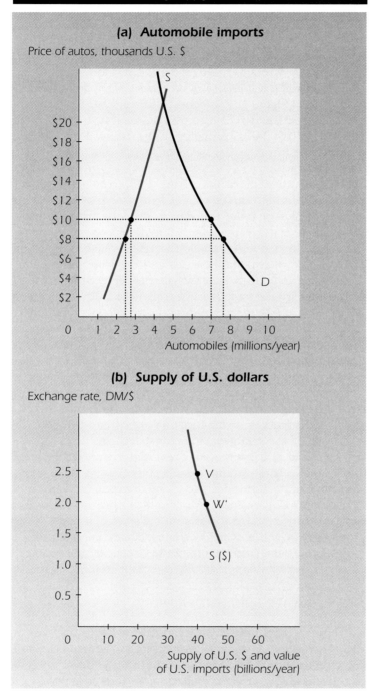

FIGURE 18.3 When the quantity of imports changes proportionately less than the exchange rate the currency supply curve slopes downward.

(a) Automobile imports

Price of autos, thousands U.S. $

(b) Supply of U.S. dollars

Exchange rate, DM/$

Supply of U.S. $ and value of U.S. imports (billions/year)

At exchange rate DM2.5/$, the U.S. dollar price of a DM20,000 automobile is $8000 (or DM20,000 ÷DM2.5/$). Part (a) shows that at this price automobile imports are 5 (or 7.5−2.5) million per year, so the supply of U.S. dollars is $40 billion (or $8000×5 million). At the depreciated value of the dollar of DM2/$, automobile prices are $10,000 and imports are 4.25 (or 7.0 −2.75) million per year. The supply of U.S. dollars at DM2/$ is therefore $42.5 billion (or $10,000×4.25 million). Plotting the exchange rate against the supply of U.S. dollars in part (b) gives point **W '**. By joining points **V** and **W '** we obtain a downward-sloping U.S. dollar supply curve. The supply curve of a currency slopes downward like this when the percentage change in the quantity of imports is smaller than the percentage change in local currency price of imports caused by a change in the exchange rate. That is, the supply curve of a currency slopes downward when the demand for imports is inelastic.

The effect of a change in the exchange rate on the balance of trade depends on the effects of exchange rates on the values of exports and imports. We have studied these effects in this chapter in our derivation of the currency demand and supply curves from exports and imports. Specifically, we have shown that the value of exports increases when a currency depreciates. (This follows from Figure 18.1, which shows that when the U.S. dollar depreciates—a movement down the vertical axis in part (b)—the value of exports, and hence the quantity of U.S. dollars demanded, increases.) We also have shown that the value of imports may decrease or increase when a currency depreciates. This follows from Figures 18.2 and 18.3. In the case of Figure 18.2, a depreciation of the U.S. dollar—a movement down the vertical axis in part (b) of Figure 18.2—reduces the value of imports and hence the quantity of U.S. dollars supplied. In the case of Figure 18.3, a depreciation of the U.S. dollar increases the value of imports and hence the quantity of U.S. dollars supplied.

The conclusion that a depreciation of the U.S. dollar increases the value of exports means that *from the export side of the balance of trade,* a depreciation increases a trade surplus or reduces a deficit. If, along with the increase in the value of exports, there is a decline in the value of imports, as in Figure 18.2, then we know unequivocally that a depreciation increases a trade surplus or reduces a trade deficit; the value of exports increases and the value of imports decreases. However, if the value of imports increases after a depreciation, as in Figure 18.3, then the consequence for the trade balance is less clear. The outcome depends on whether the increase in the value of exports from a depreciation is larger or smaller than the increase in the value of imports. If the value of exports increases more than imports, the trade balance improves, but if the value of exports increases less than imports, the trade balance worsens.

The possibility of the trade balance worsening after depreciation is generally thought to exist only in the short run. This is so because it is generally believed that the demand for imports is inelastic only in the short run. (Recall that if the demand for imports is inelastic, a depreciation causes an increase in the value of imports as a result of the quantity of imports declining less than the price of imports increases.) Import demand could be inelastic in the short run because it takes time after a depreciation before domestic firms can produce goods that were previously imported and for consumers to locate domestic products. In the interim, the quantity of imports may decrease less than their prices increase, increasing the value of imports. However, in the longer run, higher import prices should increase domestic production of goods which were previously imported and cause consumers to shift toward these **import substitutes,** reducing the quantity of imports by more than the increase in import prices. Therefore, in the long run, the value of imports should decline.

In the *short run,* a depreciation may increase the value of imports, but in the *long run,* a depreciation should reduce the value of imports.

If following a depreciation the value of imports increases in the short run but decreases in the long run, the balance of trade may follow a path like that in Figure 18.4. The figure shows the balance of trade on the vertical axis and time on the horizontal axis. At time zero on the horizontal axis, a depreciation is assumed to occur when the balance of trade is in deficit. In the short run, the depreciation is assumed to increase the value of imports more than it increases the value of exports. Therefore, following the depreciation, the balance of trade worsens. However, after a while, the value of imports begins to decline, exports increase, and therefore the balance of trade improves. This is shown by the change from a

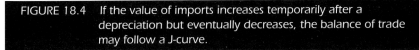

FIGURE 18.4   If the value of imports increases temporarily after a depreciation but eventually decreases, the balance of trade may follow a J-curve.

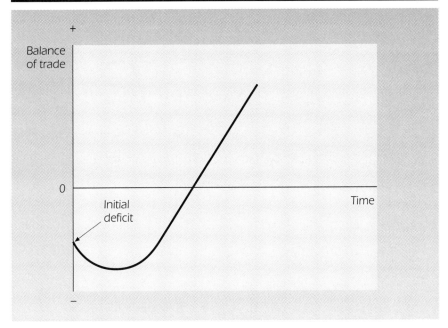

If the demand for imports is inelastic, a depreciation causes import prices to increase by more than the quantity of imports declines, so the value of imports increases. If the value of exports does not increase sufficiently to offset the higher value of imports, the balance of trade is worsened. Eventually, however, the **quantity** of inputs is likely to decline further as a result of import substitution, causing the **value** of imports to decline. In addition, the value of exports will expand further. With the value of imports declining and the value of exports expanding, in the long run the trade balance improves. The path of the trade balance is therefore shaped like a J.

downward slope to an upward slope of the curve in Figure 18.4. That is, even though a depreciation may have a negative effect on the balance of trade in the short run, in the long run the effect is likely to become positive. Because of the shape of the path in Figure 18.4, the phenomenon of a short-run worsening and long-run improvement in the balance of trade after a depreciation is called the **J-curve effect.**

The behavior of the U.S. and Japanese balances of trade after a rapid deprecia-tion of the U.S. dollar and appreciation of the yen in 1985 can be used to illustrate the J-curve. As Figure 18.5 shows, the U.S. balance of trade was already in deficit in 1985, and the Japanese balance of trade was in surplus. A substantial deprecia-tion of the U.S. dollar and appreciation of the yen that occurred at the end of 1985 were followed initially by even larger U.S. deficits and Japanese surpluses. What happened is that American consumers reduced the quantity of imports very little even though import prices increased with the dollar depreciation. Therefore, Americans spent more on imports, making their trade deficit worse. At the same

After a depreciation, the balance of trade may worsen in the short run but improve in the long run. This pattern of the trade balance is called the J-curve effect.

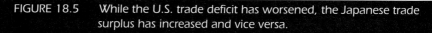

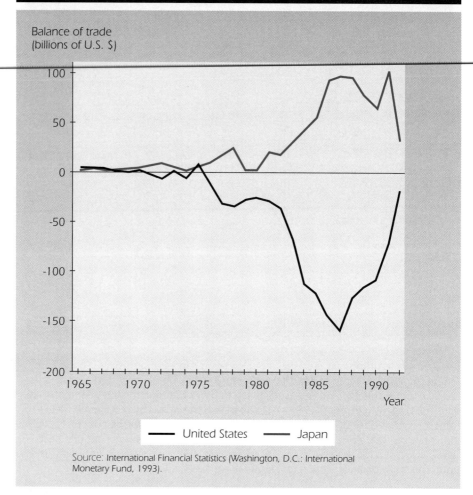

FIGURE 18.5   While the U.S. trade deficit has worsened, the Japanese trade surplus has increased and vice versa.

Source: International Financial Statistics (Washington, D.C.: International Monetary Fund, 1993).

The U. S. balance of trade moved into deficit after the mid-1970s, whereas Japan's balance of trade moved into surplus. The paths of the trade balances illustrate the J-curve. For example, the reduction in the U.S. deficit and Japanese surplus beginning in early 1987 followed the depreciation of the U.S. dollar and appreciation of the yen at the end of 1985. At first these exchange rate changes made matters worse; the U.S. deficit widened further and the Japanese surplus increased. However, eventually, the dollar depreciation reduced the U.S. trade deficit and the yen appreciation reduced the Japanese trade surplus.

time, Japanese consumers did not initially increase the quantity of imports as much as import prices declined from the yen appreciation. They therefore spent less on imports, increasing the Japanese trade surplus. In the long run, however, the dollar depreciation increased the value of U.S. exports, reduced the value of U.S. imports, and began to shrink the U.S. trade deficit. This began in early 1987.

Similarly, in Japan, exports were hurt by the appreciation, imports were encouraged, and the trade surplus shrank.

When deriving the currency supply and demand curves earlier in this chapter, we showed how the values of exports and imports change with changes in exchange rates. Specifically, we showed that the demand curve for the U.S. dollar is downward sloping with respect to the German mark price of the dollar; the cheaper the U.S. dollar in terms of German marks, the larger is the quantity of U.S. dollars demanded to pay for U.S. exports. We also showed that the supply curve of U.S. dollars may be upward sloping or downward sloping with respect to the German mark price of the dollar depending on the elasticity of demand for imports. It is time to switch our focus from movements *along* the currency supply and demand curves to *shifts* of the curves. That is, rather than focus on how changes in exchange rates cause changes in quantities of currency supplied and demanded along the demand and supply curves, our interest is now in how shifts in exports and imports brought about, for example, by inflation can cause changes in exchange rates.

EFFECT OF INFLATION ON EXCHANGE RATES*

Inflation and the Demand Curve for a Currency

Figure 18.6 illustrates how inflation affects U.S. exports and the demand curve for U.S. dollars. We assume that wheat is the only U.S. export and begin with the supply and demand curves for wheat from Figures 18.1. As before, we assume that the internationally determined price of wheat is DM10 per bushel. At an exchange rate of DM2.5/$, this translates into $4 (or DM10 ÷ DM2.5/$) per bushel. At this price, U.S. exports are 5 (or 9 − 4) billion bushels per year, and the demand for U.S. dollars to pay for wheat is $20 billion (or $4 × 5 billion) per year. This is plotted as the quantity of U.S. dollars demanded at DM2.5/$ in part (b) and is shown as point A on curve $D(\$)$.

Suppose that all U.S. prices and nominal incomes increase 20% but prices and incomes in other countries are constant. Since the prices of wheat and all other goods in the United States increase in the same proportion as nominal incomes, the quantity of wheat demanded by Americans will not change; if nominal incomes and all prices increase by the same proportion, real incomes and relative prices are unchanged, and so quantities demanded are unaffected. This means that the quantity of wheat demanded at, for example, $4.80 per bushel after the inflation is the same as at $4 per bushel before the inflation. Therefore, we can plot points on a new demand curve for wheat 20% above the points on the original demand curve for wheat; for example, point R' on curve D' is 20% above point R on curve D. That is, the demand curve for wheat shifts upward by the amount of inflation.

Inflation also affects the supply curve of wheat. With wages and other production costs 20% higher after inflation, the price of wheat at which any given output would be produced is 20% higher. For example, if 9 billion bushels are produced

---

*Sections and numbered items marked by an asterisk may be omitted without a loss of continuity.

FIGURE 18.6   Inflation only in the United States shifts up the demand and supply curves for wheat and shifts the demand curve for U.S. dollars to the left.

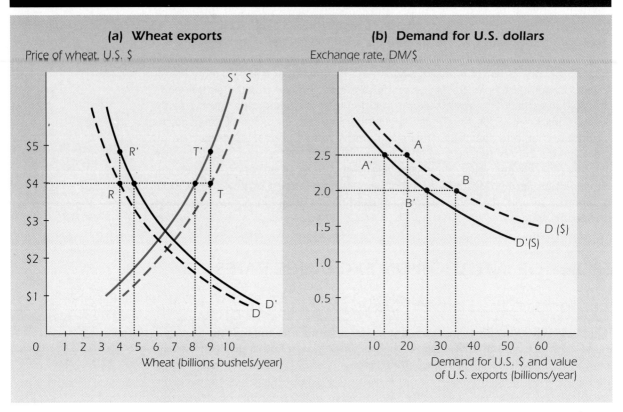

(a) Wheat exports

Price of wheat, U.S. $

(b) Demand for U.S. dollars

Exchange rate, DM/$

We assume that the internationally determined price of wheat is constant at DM10 per bushel and begin by assuming that the exchange rate is DM2.5/$. Therefore, the price of wheat is $4 per bushel, and at this price, the U.S. exports 5 (or 9−4) billion bushels per year. Therefore, the demand for U.S. dollars to pay for U.S. wheat is $20 billion (or $4×5 billion) per year. This occurs at the exchange rate of DM2.5/$ and is plotted as point **A** on **D**($). Suppose that 20% inflation occurs only in U.S. prices and nominal incomes. The increase in prices and nominal incomes shifts the U.S. demand curve for wheat vertically upward 20% from **D** to **D'**. The increase in wages shifts the U.S. supply curve of wheat upward 20% from **S** to **S'**. At the unchanged international price of wheat, exports are reduced to 3.4 billion bushels per year. Therefore, the demand for U.S. dollars is reduced to $13.6 billion (or $4×3.4 billion) per year. This is the quantity of U.S. dollars demanded on a new demand curve for dollars at exchange rate DM2.5/$ and is plotted as point **A'** on **D'**($). Similarly, at other exchange rates, inflation reduces the quantity exported and the demand for U.S. dollars. Therefore, the entire demand curve for U.S. dollars is shifted to the left.

at a price of $4 per bushel before inflation, it will take a price of $4.80 per bushel to induce farmers to produce this same output after the 20% inflation. Therefore, the point on the new supply curve for wheat in Figure 18.6 corresponding to point T on the original supply curve is above point T by 20%. This is point T' on the supply curve S'. The same is true for every quantity supplied. Therefore, the supply curve for wheat is shifted up by the amount of inflation, from S to S'.

With the new supply and demand curves for wheat as in Figure 18.6, there is a reduction in wheat exports at each price. For example, at $4 per bushel, which corresponds to DM10 per bushel and an exchange rate of DM2.5/$, U.S. wheat exports are reduced from 5 billion to approximately 3.4 billion bushels per year, which is the distance between S' and D' at $4 per bushel.[4]

The number of U.S. dollars needed to pay for 3.4 billion bushels of U.S. wheat exports at $4 per bushel is $13.6 billion (or $4 × 3.4 billion) per year. This is the new quantity of U.S. dollars demanded at the exchange rate DM2.5/$ and gives point A' on the new, after-inflation demand curve for U.S. dollars $D'(\$)$. Similarly, at an exchange rate of DM2/$, the U.S. dollar equivalent of the DM10 per bushel price of wheat is $5 (or DM10 ÷ DM2/$) per bushel. At this price U.S. wheat exports are approximately 5.4 billion bushels per year. (This is the gap between D' and S' at $5 per bushel.) The value of these exports and consequent demand for U.S. dollars is $27 billion (or $5 × 5.4 billion) per year. This gives point B' on the new demand curve for U.S. dollars $D'(\$)$ at exchange rate DM2/$. Point B' is to the left of point B on the before-inflation U.S. dollar demand curve. More generally, the effect of U.S. inflation is to shift the entire demand curve for U.S. dollars to the left, from $D(\$)$ to $D'(\$)$.

Inflation reduces the value of a country's exports at each exchange rate and shifts the demand curve for the country's currency to the left.

Inflation and the Supply Curve of a Currency

The effect of inflation on the supply curve of a currency is illustrated in Figure 18.7, where we assume for simplicity that the supply curve of the currency is upward sloping. We begin by noting that with 20% inflation in the United States, the supply and demand curves for automobiles shift upward 20%. These shifts occur for the same reasons the supply and demand curves for wheat shifted upward. At an exchange rate of DM2.5/$ and an internationally determined price of automobiles of DM20,000, the translated price in U.S. dollars is $8000. Before inflation, this resulted in imports of 5 (or 7.5 − 2.5) million automobiles per year and a consequent supply of U.S. dollars of $40 billion (or $8000 × 5 million) per year. This is plotted on the supply curve of U.S. dollars $S(\$)$ as point V. After inflation, imports increase to 6.65 (or 8.4 − 1.75) million per year—the distance between D' and S' at $8000 in part (a) of Figure 18.7—and the supply of U.S. dollars increases to $53.2 billion (or $8000 × 6.65 million) per year. This gives point V' on the new postinflation supply curve of U.S. dollars $S'(\$)$ at exchange rate DM2.5/$.

We can repeat our procedure to find the new supply of U.S. dollars after inflation at different selected exchange rates. For example, at DM2/$ and a consequent automobile price of $10,000 (or DM20,000 ÷ DM2/$), automobile imports are 4.25

[4] We leave the German mark price of wheat the same after U.S. inflation as before because we have assumed that the inflation occurs only in the United States.

FIGURE 18.7   Inflation only in the United States shifts the supply curve of U.S. dollars to the right.

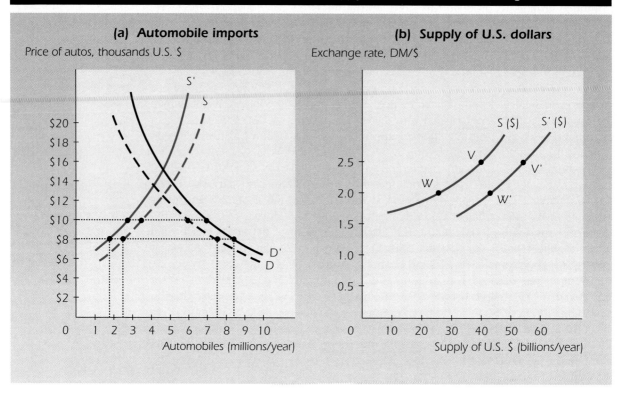

(a) Automobile imports

Price of autos, thousands U.S. $

(b) Supply of U.S. dollars

Exchange rate, DM/$

At the exchange rate DM2.5/$, a DM20,000 automobile costs $8000. From the before-inflation demand and supply curves for automobiles **D** and **S**, automobile imports into the United States at $8000 per automobile are 5 (or 7.5−2.5) million per year. Therefore, U.S. spending on imported automobiles and hence the supply of U.S. dollars at DM2.5/$ is $40 billion (or $8000×5 million) per year. After a 20% inflation, the supply and demand curves for automobiles shift upward 20% from **S** to **S'** and from **D** to **D'**. With the new supply and demand curves for automobiles, at the exchange rate DM2.5/$ and consequent U.S. dollar automobile price of $8000, imports increase to the difference between **D'** and **S'** at this price, or 6.65 (or 8.4−1.75) million per year. Therefore, spending on imported automobiles and the supply of U.S. dollars increase to $53.2 billion (or $8000×6.65 million) at DM2.5/$. This gives a point on the new supply curve of dollars **S'($)** to the right of the point on the preinflation curve. Similarly, at DM2/$ and a consequent U.S. dollar price of $10,000, U.S. automobile imports after inflation are 4.25 (or 7−2.75) million. Therefore, the supply of U.S. dollars is $42.5 billion (or $10,000×4.25)million per year. At each exchange rate we find a larger quantity of U.S. dollars supplied after inflation than before. Hence the U.S. dollar supply curve is shifted to the right by inflation.

(or 7−2.75) million per year; this is the distance between D' and S' at $10,000 in part (a) of Figure 18.7. Therefore, the supply of U.S. dollars is $42.5 billion (or $10,000 × 4.25 million) per year at DM2/$, as shown by point W' on curve $S'(\$)$. This is higher than the supply of U.S. dollars before inflation at DM2/$, which was only $25 billion (or $10,000 × 2.5 million), point W. Selecting further exchange rates shows the same pattern of a larger supply of U.S. dollars resulting from the U.S. inflation, that is, a rightward shift in the currency supply curve.

By drawing the supply and demand curves for U.S. dollars on the same figure, we can find the effect of U.S. inflation on the foreign exchange value of the U.S. dollar. This is done in Figure 18.8. Assuming as we have that inflation occurs only in the United States, the equilibrium German mark value of the U.S. dollar is reduced from DM2.15/$ to approximately DM1.75/$. This is a depreciation of approximately 20%. We discover that inflation causes a currency to depreciate. We also discover that, *ceteris paribus,* with inflation not occurring elsewhere, the extent of depreciation is equal to the country's rate of inflation.

The conclusion that depreciation equals a country's rate of inflation is due to the assumption that inflation elsewhere is zero. More generally, the amount of depreciation of one currency versus another equals the extent to which the first country's inflation exceeds inflation in the other country. This link between inflation and exchange rates is called the **purchasing power parity (PPP) principle.** Example 18.2 presents an alternative view of this principle based on the role of international **commodity arbitrage,** which is what happens when goods are moved from country to country to take advantage of differences in prices. Example 18.3 considers PPP from yet a further angle, one involving the price of a Big Mac.

The correspondence between inflation and exchange rates is illustrated in Figure 18.9. The figure shows the annual rate of change of the exchange rate between the U.S. dollar and Mexican peso and the **inflation differential** between these two countries. The inflation differential is measured as Mexican inflation minus U.S. inflation, and the change in the exchange rate is the annual percentage change in pesos per dollar. The figure shows that the higher the inflation differential, the bigger is the change in the exchange rate. That is, the two lines in the figure move up and down approximately together.

Actual movements in exchange rates are not only the result of inflation. Exchange rates are also influenced by the many other factors which affect exports and imports. For example, exports increase with increases in national incomes of countries which buy a country's exports. Therefore, *ceteris paribus,* the higher foreign incomes are, the greater is demand for the exporting country's currency and the higher is the value of its currency. Similarly, the higher a country's own national income, the higher are imports and the greater is the supply of its currency. Therefore, *ceteris paribus,* the higher a country's own national income, the lower is the value of its currency. Other factors affecting exports and imports and hence exchange rates include chance discovery of commodities such as oil, import tariffs, import quotas—which are limits on the numbers of imported goods allowed into a country—and so on.

Exchange rates are also heavily influenced by the factors affecting the many other items listed in the balance of payments account. Changes in these many other items make exchange rates change at different rates than indicated by the supply and demand curves for currencies derived solely from merchandise exports and imports. Therefore, let us consider these other factors by examining the

Inflation increases the value of a country's imports at each exchange rate and shifts the supply curve of the country's currency to the right.

Ceteris paribus, inflation causes a depreciation of a country's currency by that country's rate of inflation.

FIGURE 18.8   *Ceteris paribus,* inflation causes a depreciation of the equilibrium foreign exchange value of an inflating country's currency by the country's rate of inflation.

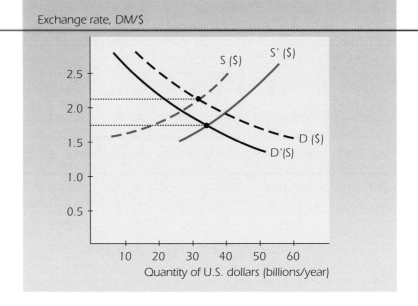

Exchange rate, DM/$

Inflation shifts the demand curve for a currency to the left from **D**($) to **D'**($) and the supply curve of a currency to the right from **S**($) to **S'**($). The new equilibrium where **D'**($) intersects **S'**($) is at a lower foreign exchange value of the inflating country's currency by an amount given by the country's rate of inflation.

FIGURE 18.9   The more Mexico's inflation has exceeded U.S. inflation, the larger has been the depreciation of the Mexican peso.

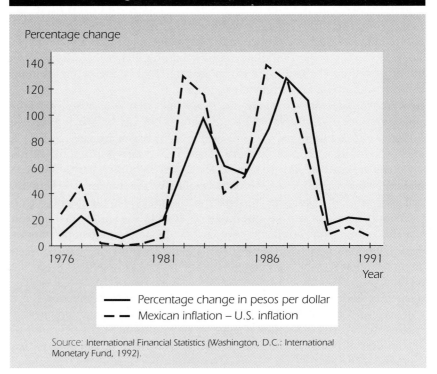

Percentage change

The dashed line shows Mexican inflation minus U.S. inflation, while the solid line shows the percentage change in the number of pesos per U.S. dollar. The figure shows that Mexican inflation has greatly exceeded U.S. inflation and that the peso has depreciated vis-à-vis the dollar by a similar amount. Indeed, the more Mexican inflation has exceeded U.S. inflation, the larger is the peso depreciation. The correspondence between the two lines suggests that inflation is a major influence on exchange rates when there is widely different inflation between countries.

Percentage change in pesos per dollar
Mexican inflation – U.S. inflation

Source: International Financial Statistics (Washington, D.C.: International Monetary Fund, 1992).

Example 18.2

THE PURCHASING POWER PARITY PRINCIPLE

If we could rule out "frictions" such as shipping costs, import tariffs, sales taxes, quotas, and the like, it would not be difficult to explain exchange rates. All we would need to know would be product prices in each country. For example, suppose we knew the prices of wheat in Great Britain and the United States, with these being £1 per bushel and $2 per bushel in the countries' monies. There could be no other exchange rate than $2 per £1. If the exchange rate were to differ from this, the opportunity to profit would soon be noticed. For example, if the exchange rate were $2.1 per £1, attentive arbitragers would sell their pounds for dollars. With £1 buying $2.1, each £1 would permit the purchase of more than 1 bushel of wheat in the U.S. Indeed, via purchasing $2.1, each £1 would buy 1.05 (or $2.1 ÷ 2) bushels of wheat in the United States. When this wheat was shipped to Great Britain in this frictionless world and sold for British pounds, the arbitrager would enjoy a profit; 1.05 bushels of wheat at £1 per bushel rewards the arbitrager with £1.05. Having started with £1, a profit has been made.

With opportunities for profitable arbitrage being evident to many,

and with all who arbitrage buying dollars with pounds, the value of the pound would soon fall below $2.1. Only at $2 per pound would the dollar buying cease and arbitrage end.*

Just as the exchange rate cannot exceed $2 per £1 when wheat is $2 and £1 per bushel, respectively, in the United States and Great Britain, so too the exchange rate cannot be less than $2 per £1. For example, at $1.9 per pound an arbitrager could take $1.9, buy £1, use this to buy a bushel of wheat in Great Britain, and ship the wheat to America for sale at $2. Having begun with $1.9, a profit is made. With others cashing in on the same opportunity, and buying pounds as part of this arbitrage process, it would not be long before the dollar price of the pound was $2. This is the only exchange rate at which arbitrage does not occur.

If what happens with wheat happens with every other product, and a price level is calculated for a "basket" of goods that can be shipped anywhere, the prices of this basket in different countries determines exchange rates. For example, if a £100

*This assumes that wheat prices are given, so the exchange rate adjusts rather than wheat prices.

basket of goods in Great Britain costs $200 in the United States, we can again conclude that the exchange rate is $2 per £1. Further, if the prices of the baskets change differently in the two countries, the exchange rate also changes. For example, if British prices are stable and U.S. prices increase by 10%, raising the dollar basket price to $220, the exchange rate becomes $2.2 per £1, a 10% depreciation of the dollar. This view of exchange rates from the perspective of prices of a basket of goods is the essence of the purchasing power parity principle.

In reality, of course, frictions abound. There are shipping costs, import tariffs, sales taxes, quotas, and other barriers to international trade. Some products such as housing and services are impossible to ship; they are non-traded products. Furthermore, it is no trivial matter to compute prices of the same basket in different countries; price indexes are based on local baskets and peoples' baskets differ. Nevertheless, equilibrium-based arguments, including the effect of exchange rates on inflation as described in the text, suggest that eventually exchange rates should reflect prices, even though "eventually" might be a very long time.

Example **18.3**

BIG MACURRENCIES

The purchasing power parity (PPP) principle relates overall price levels in different countries to exchange rates. It has been suggested by **The Economist** that rather than use price levels, we might view equilibrium exchange rates from prices of Big Macs.

The Economist's Big Mac index was first launched in 1986 as a ready reckoner to whether currencies are at their "correct" exchange rate. . . .

The case for munching our way around the globe on Big Macs is based on the theory of purchasing-power parity. This argues that the exchange rate between two currencies is in equilibrium when it equalises the prices of an identical basket of goods and services in both countries. Advocates of PPP argue that in the long run currencies tend to move towards their PPP.

Our basket is simply a Big Mac, one of the few products that is produced locally in a great many countries. Many of our readers ask why we do not simply derive our PPPs from different cover prices of *The Economist*. But because the magazine is not printed in every country, local prices would be distorted by transport and distribution costs.

The Big Mac PPP is the exchange rate that leaves hamburgers costing the same in each country. Comparing the current exchange rate with its PPP gives a measure of whether a currency is under- or overvalued.

For example, the average price of a Big Mac in four American cities is $2.19. In Japan our Big Mac watcher had to fork out ¥380 ($2.86) for the same gastronomic delight. Dividing the yen price by the dollar price gives a Big Mac PPP of $1=¥174.

On April 10th the actual dollar exchange rate was ¥133, which implies that on PPP grounds the

....

TABLE 18.A

The Hamburger Standard.

COUNTRY	BIG MAC PRICE* IN LOCAL CURRENCY	IMPLIED PPP† OF THE DOLLAR	ACTUAL EXCHANGE RATE 10 April 92	PERCENT OVER (+) OR UNDER (–) VALUATION OF DOLLAR
Argentina	Peso3.30	1.51	0.99	–34
Australia	A$2.54	1.16	1.31	+13
Belgium	BFr108	49.32	33.55	–32
Brazil	Cr3,800	1,735	2,153	+24
Britain	£1.74	0.79	0.57	–28
Canada	C$2.76	1.26	1.19	–6
China	Yuan6.30	2.88	5.44	+89
Denmark	DKr27.25	12.44	6.32	–49
France	FFr18.10	8.26	5.55	–33
Germany	DM4.50	2.05	1.64	–20
Holland	FL5.35	2.44	1.84	–24
Hong Kong	HK$8.90	4.06	7.73	+91
Hungary	Forint133	60.73	79.70	+31
Ireland	I£1.45	0.66	0.61	–8
Italy	Lire4,100	1,872	1,233	–34
Japan	¥380	174	133	–24
Russia	Rouble58	26.48	98.95‡	+273
Singapore	S$4.75	2.17	1.65	–24
S. Korea	Won2,300	1,050	778	–26
Spain	Pta315	144	102	–29
Sweden	SKr25.50	11.64	5.93	–49
United States§	$2.19	—	—	—
Venezuela	Bs 170	77.63	60.63	–22

*McDonald's prices may vary locally.
†Purchasing-power parity; local price divided by dollar price.
‡Market rate.
§New York, Chicago, San Francisco and Atlanta.

Source: "Big MacCurrencies," **The Economist**, April 18, 1992, p. 81.

dollar is 24% undervalued against the yen.

On similar sums, the dollar is 20% undervalued against the D-mark, with an estimated PPP of DM 2.05. The dollar has moved further away from its PPP over the past year: in April 1991 it was under-valued by only 13%. How can the dollar have become more undervalued when its actual exchange rate has barely budged? The answer lies in price movements. Big Mac prices have fallen by an average of 3% in America over the past 12 months; in Germany they have risen by 5%.

As Table 18.A shows, the dollar seems to be undervalued against most currencies. The exceptions are the currencies of countries where Big Macs cost less in dollars than in America: the Australian dollar, the Brazilian cruzeiro, the Chinese yuan, the Hong Kong dollar, the Hungarian forint and last, but by no means least, the rouble. Moscow is the best place for burger-bargain hunters: a Big Mac costs only 59 cents at the market exchange rate. In other words, the rouble is undervalued by 73% against the dollar.

Some readers find the Big Mac index hard to digest. To be sure, hamburgers are primitive predictors of exchange rates. Local price differences may be distorted by taxes, property costs or trade barriers. Nevertheless, the Big Mac can provide a rough and ready guide to how currencies might move over the long term. Experts who calculate PPPs by more sophisticated means come up with results that are not radically different. Indeed, many of them suggest that the dollar is even more undervalued than the hamburger standard indicates.

The message, therefore, is that the greenback should rise in the future. But when? Exchange rates can deviate significantly from PPPs for long periods. . . .

Source: "Big MacCurrencies," **The Economist,** April 18, 1992, p. 81. © 1992 The Economist Newspaper Group, Inc. Reprinted with permission.

remainder of the line items in the balance of payments account in Table 18.3 on page 569. As we do this, recall that the items preceded with a plus sign give rise to a demand for the currency, while those preceded by a minus sign give rise to a supply of the currency. Consequently, the larger any plus item is, the further to the right is the total currency demand curve and, *ceteris paribus,* the higher is the foreign exchange value of the country's currency. Similarly, the larger any minus item is, the further to the right is the currency supply curve and, *ceteris paribus,* the lower is the foreign exchange value of the country's currency. That is, we can think of these other items as shifting the currency demand and supply curves and thereby changing the equilibrium exchange rate.

OTHER FACTORS AFFECTING EXCHANGE RATES

Factors Affecting Service Exports and Imports

Service exports and imports are given on lines 3 and 6 in Table 18.3. Exports and imports of most services, such as travel, shipping, banking, consulting, and so on, respond to exchange rates and other economic factors in the same way as merchandise exports and imports. This means that what we have said about merchandise applies also to these service imports and exports.

While most services behave the same way as merchandise, one important service does not. This is **debt service,** which consists of interest and dividend payments made to foreigners and received from foreigners. Interest and dividends are considered debt service because they can be thought of as maintenance payments for funds provided by or to foreigners in the past. The amount of interest residents pay to foreigners is a service import, while interest received from foreigners is a service export. Interest payments are an import because they give rise to a supply

Debt service consists of interest and dividends paid to foreigners or received from foreigners. The size of debt service depends on past foreign investments and returns on investments.

of the payer's currency, and interest receipts are an export because they give rise to a demand for the recipient's currency.

Interest payments and receipts depend on the amount borrowed from or loaned to foreigners in the past and on the interest rate. Similarly, dividend payments made to foreigners or received from foreigners depend on previous investment by foreigners in the United States or previous investment by U.S. residents abroad, as well as on the profitability of these investments. *Ceteris paribus,* the larger the amount invested in a country in the past by foreigners, the greater is the current supply of the country's currency via interest payments to foreigners. This is so because the country's currency is sold either in order to make interest and dividend payments to foreigners or by the foreign recipients of these payments. Similarly, the larger the amount residents of a country have invested abroad in the past, the greater is the current demand for that country's currency from the receipts from foreigners of interest and dividends on those investments. In addition, the higher a country's interest rates or dividends, the greater is the supply of that country's currency arising from income on past investments in that country by foreigners and the greater is the demand for the currencies of those who made the past investments.

Countries whose residents have invested more abroad than has been invested at home by foreigners are called **net creditors.** The demand for the currencies of net creditor nations from interest and dividends paid to them exceeds the supply of these currencies from interest and dividend payments made to foreigners. Switzerland, Japan, Saudi Arabia, and Bahrain are net creditors, as was the United States until it became a **net debtor** in 1985. Net debtor nations include Brazil, Canada, Mexico, the Commonwealth of Independent States, and Venezuela. *Ceteris paribus,* the greater a country's net indebtedness and the higher the interest rates and dividend yields, the greater is the supply of the country's currency and the lower is the foreign exchange value of its currency.

The extent to which there is a difference between the supply of and demand for a currency as a result of merchandise and services combined is called the **balance on goods and services.** This is shown as the second memorandum item in the U.S. balance of payments account in Table 18.3.

The balance on goods and services is the difference between the supply of and demand for a country's currency from merchandise and service payments and receipts.

Factors Affecting Unilateral Transfers

Unilateral transfers shown on line 7 in Table 18.3 involve the receipt or payment of foreign aid and gifts. The size of foreign aid is determined more in the political than the economic arena, and the size of private gifts is more the result of perceived needs and the benevolence of providers than of inflation and the other economic factors affecting exports and imports.

Richer countries like the United States and Japan make far more unilateral transfers abroad than they receive from abroad. Therefore, there is a greater supply of a currency such as the U.S. dollar or the Japanese yen on account of unilateral transfers than there is a demand for such a currency. Poorer countries like Bangladesh, Egypt, Ethiopia, India, and Pakistan face the opposite situation for their currencies. Unilateral transfers represent a net demand for their currencies.[5] However, since a

---

[5] Private gifts received from abroad constitute a relatively large demand for a currency of a country such as Pakistan or India, where many nationals leave for jobs overseas but support family members at home by sending frequent gifts.

large part of aid is frequently tied to the recipients buying goods and services from the donor country, there is often an offsetting item in merchandise or service imports that cancels much of the effect of increased aid on a country's exchange rate.

When we add unilateral transfers to the balance on goods and services, we obtain the **balance of payments on current account.** This is shown as the third memorandum item in the balance of payments account in Table 18.3.

The current account of the balance of payments is the balance on goods and services plus unilateral transfers.

Factors Affecting Private Holdings of Foreign Assets

Net private investments are shown on lines 8 and 11 in Table 18.3. Net investments made by *residents* in foreign assets are preceded by a minus sign in the balance of payments account because they give rise to a supply of the investors' home currency. If and when foreign assets are sold so that there is a net **divestment** of foreign assets, there is a demand for the investors' home currency and a plus sign in front of the "change in private holdings of foreign assets" in the balance of payments account.

Similarly, an increase in the amount *foreigners* invest in a country gives rise to a demand for that country's currency and therefore is preceded by a plus sign in the balance of payments account. A divestment by foreigners gives rise to a supply of the country's currency and is therefore preceded by a minus sign. In terms of the U.S. balance of payments in Table 18.3, there is a large demand for U.S. dollars as a result of foreign private investment in the United States, amounting to more than the deficit in the U.S. current account.

The balance of payments account divides changes in residents' holdings of foreign assets and changes in foreigners' holdings of domestic assets into two components: the part that is in securities such as stocks and bonds, and the part that is in **direct investment.** A direct investment is one where the foreign investor controls the operation of the business, such as when a multinational corporation builds a new factory overseas.

Control is difficult to define. It certainly occurs when the investor owns more than 50% of the voting shares in a company. However, since there are often numerous shareholders each with only a few shares, a much smaller fraction of the shares than 50% can often give effective control. The division in the balance of payments account is made at 10%. When 10% or more of the voting shares is held by the investor, the investment is classified as a direct investment.

Direct investment is one in which the foreign investor holds 10% or more of voting shares.

Different factors affect direct investment than affect investment in securities. Therefore, it is worth discussing these investments separately.

Factors Affecting Direct Investment.   Direct investment is shown on lines 9 and 12 of Table 18.3. The most obvious factor determining how much direct investment takes place in a country is the expected rate of return in that country versus the expected rate of return elsewhere. In turn, expected rates of return depend on the strengths of the markets served by the businesses in which direct investment takes place. Rates of return also depend on wage rates, tax rates charged by host governments, and depending on the type of industry, the availability of raw materials and energy, the cost of satisfying environmental and safety regulations in the host country, and so on. For example, whether a U.S. computer manufacturer builds a plant in Korea depends on how many computers it can sell in Korea and in other countries from its Korean plant, the wage rate in Korea, and the tax rate on profits in Korea. Furthermore, since the rate of return in

Korea is compared with what it is in other countries, the ultimate determination of whether a plant is built in Korea depends on Korean wages *relative* to wages in other countries, *relative* tax rates, and so on. These days, with so much production being in the hands of giant multinational corporations which can examine the numerous possible locations for a plant with relative ease, direct investment in a country is sensitive to even small changes in wage rates, tax rates, and so on.

The relative expected rates of return from direct investments in different countries are compared with the associated risks. The relevant risks include not only the ordinary business risk that is present wherever an investment takes place but also the political risk which takes on prime importance for direct foreign investment. Political risk includes the possibility of **expropriation**—which is a takeover of foreign-owned investment by a government *with* compensation to owners—and **confiscation**—where the takeover is *without* compensation. Evaluation of political risk involves an examination of the strengths of different political parties and their attitudes toward a company and toward the company's home government. The latter attitude is relevant because action may be aimed not at a company itself but at its government, and yet the company may lose its assets.

The calculation of political risk is complicated by the fact that it can be influenced by how direct investment is financed. Specifically, participation by local investors can reduce the chance of expropriation or confiscation. Local participation can take the form of a **joint venture** with a local company or of borrowing from local banks. Political risk also can be reduced by producing different components of a product in different countries so that the facilities in any one country cannot profitably function alone. However, despite the various ways political risk can be reduced, it is clear that any event that affects the perceived political stability of a country can have a damaging effect on direct investment. For example, the election of a socialist government in place of a pro-business government may damage direct investment and hence reduce demand for a country's currency and its exchange rate. Even an increased possibility that an unfriendly government may eventually be elected can reduce direct investment. This means a decline in the demand for the currency and, *ceteris paribus,* a depreciation. That is, political events viewed as unfavorable by investors can cause a depreciation. Alternatively, favorable political events cause an increase in direct investment and hence in the demand for a country's currency and a consequent appreciation.

Factors Affecting Private Holdings of Domestic and Foreign Securities.
Changes in holdings of a country's securities such as bonds and stocks shown on lines 10 and 13 of Table 18.3 result from changes in the country's interest or expected dividend rates relative to interest or expected dividend rates in other countries. This is so because investors move funds internationally according to expected rates of return in different countries. However, exchange rates are also relevant. *Ceteris paribus,* the more a country's currency is expected to increase in value, the greater is foreign investment in that country's securities. This is so because part of the return earned by investing in foreign securities comes from changes in the value of the foreign currencies.[6]

Expropriation occurs when foreign-owned investments are taken over by a government with *compensation. Confiscation occurs when there is* no *compensation.*

Direct investment in a country depends on the expected rate of return from businesses in that country relative to elsewhere and on relative business and political risks. An increase in perceived risk reduces investment and, ceteris paribus, *causes depreciation.*

---

[6] Indirectly, by affecting interest rates, the borrowing requirements of government and business can affect foreign holdings of a country's securities (see Example 18.4).

The same factors increasing foreigners' holdings of a country's securities also result in residents holding relatively more of their own country's securities. For example, an increase in U.S. interest rates relative to rates elsewhere will cause U.S. investors to hold more U.S. assets relative to foreign assets at the same time as foreigners hold relatively more U.S. assets.

The impact of changes in foreigners' and residents' holdings of a country's assets on the foreign exchange value of its currency can be substantial. For example, a relatively small increase in interest rates in the United States can cause a large increase in demand for dollars—via Americans and foreigners moving funds into U.S. assets—and a large decrease in supply of dollars—via fewer Americans and foreigners moving funds abroad. In this way a small increase in U.S. interest rates can cause a substantial increase in the value of the dollar. The size of the effect of interest rates on exchange rates is large because the *stock* of assets is so large that minor shifts in the proportion of investment portfolios allocated to a particular country's assets constitute substantial changes in currency *flows.*[7]

Variations in investment flows have more effect on exchange rates in the short run than do variations in exports and imports or any of the other factors considered earlier. That is, when considering what it is that causes short-run variation in exchange rates, the principal factor at work is flows of investment into domestic and foreign securities. Particularly volatile are flows of funds into and out of short-term securities such as Treasury bills, bank deposits, and money market "paper," which consists of securities representing borrowing by governments, businesses, finance companies, investment dealers, and so on. While these securities may have maturities of several months, some of them have maturities of only a few days. Indeed, money moving into and out of bank deposits may be only "overnight." The funds invested for these short maturities are shuffled from country to country in search of the tiniest interest-rate advantage, moving so quickly that such funds are referred to as **hot money;** like a hot potato, nobody holds these funds for very long.

Increasing interest rates and expected dividend rates in a country relative to other countries increases investment in the country's securities.

*Day-to-day fluctuations in exchange rates are largely due to **short-term** investment flows which respond quickly to small changes in interest rates in one country versus another.*

Changes in Official Assets and Reserves

Changes in official assets and reserves occur when there is intervention by governments in the foreign exchange markets. Intervention involves central bank buying and selling of currencies to affect exchange rates. In the case of U.S. official intervention, this is seen in Table 18.3 on page 569 by the entry in line 16. This is also given as memorandum item number 5, "Increase (−) in U.S. official reserves." The +$2 billion in line 16 and memorandum item 5 means that U.S. official reserves decreased by $2 billion; as always, a plus sign means a demand for U.S. dollars, with these dollars being bought by the Fed using its foreign reserves. (The plus sign means that U.S. dollars were demanded, and hence foreign currency was supplied.) Similarly, the +$42 billion entry in line 15 and memorandum item number 4, "Increase (+) in foreign official reserves," means that foreign reserves (U.S. dollars) held by foreign central banks in the United States increased by $42 billion; again, the plus sign means a demand for U.S. dollars.

[7] The stock of assets is the amount held at a point in time. The stock of assets is the result of many years of investment and is large relative to the amount invested during a period of time and where the latter is a flow.

Example 18.4

FISCAL DEFICITS VERSUS TRADE DEFICITS

It is no mere coincidence that America's twin deficits have grown in tandem, with the fiscal and trade shortfalls both exploding into unchartered territory since the early 1980s. The two deficits are linked via the foreign exchange value of the dollar, and we can follow this connection most easily from the balance of payments account.

The U.S. fiscal deficit, which grew from approximately $20 billion in 1980 to almost $400 billion 12 years later, has to be financed. The Treasury bills and bonds that raise the funds for the federal deficiency of taxes versus spending could all be sold to Americans. That is, they could all be sold to Americans if Americans saved enough to buy them all. But with all the other demands on Americans' savings, such as the bills, stocks, bonds, and mortgages that finance business and household needs for capital, there are not enough savings left to finance the fiscal deficit.

Therefore, the U.S. government has to raise part of its borrowing requirement overseas, selling its bills and bonds to European and Asian investors.

Just as with other exports, when foreign buyers pay for U.S. government securities, they must first purchase dollars. The more securities foreign investors buy, the larger is the demand for dollars and the higher goes the foreign exchange value of the dollar. That is, the greater the extent that the fiscal deficit is financed by borrowing offshore, the higher is the foreign exchange value of the dollar. This means expensive U.S. exports and cheap imports. In turn, this hurts exports, increases imports, and puts the trade balance deeper in deficit. That's the consequence of a bigger fiscal deficit—a bigger trade deficit. And it works via the exchange rate.

The balance of payments account explains the linkage well. The sum of all the credits

and debits in the account is zero. If there is an inflow of funds from foreigners increasing their holdings of domestic securities—a positive entry in the account—there must be an offset via negative components somewhere else in the account. This comes in the form of the trade deficit. Indeed, the trade deficit arises from the higher-valued dollar caused by the inflow of funds that finance the fiscal deficit.

What does the double deficit linkage tell us? Since there are limits on the size of trade deficits that a country can sustain, it is not possible to indefinitely finance fiscal deficits offshore. Either the government borrowing must be reduced or more of the fiscal deficit must be financed at home. Domestic financing requires domestic saving. Only when savings increase or fiscal deficits decline will the trade deficit disappear.

U.S. official reserves increase when the Fed buys foreign currencies. Because foreign currencies are paid for with U.S. dollars, the Fed supplies U.S. dollars when it buys foreign currencies. Similarly, foreign official reserves in the United States increase when foreign central banks buy, that is, demand, U.S. dollars. *Ceteris paribus,* a demand for U.S. dollars by the Fed or by foreign central banks increases the foreign exchange value of the U.S. dollar. Official intervention occurs when central banks are trying to reduce or prevent changes in exchange rates. For example, if the Fed wants to prevent a decrease in the value of the U.S. dollar, it buys dollars and sells foreign currency. This helps keep up the value of the dollar because it represents an added (official) demand for dollars. This shows up in the balance of payments account as a decrease in U.S. reserves.

Statistical Discrepancy

The **statistical discrepancy,** which can be a very large amount, as line 17 of Table 18.3 shows, is the supply of or demand for a currency that has not been recorded in the other items listed in the balance of payments account. If all sources of supply of and demand for a currency are recorded in the account, the sum of all the pluses must equal the sum of all the minuses. If these sums are not equal, some items must have been recorded incorrectly. This is no surprise given the number of illegal transactions in drugs, the inaccuracy of knowledge of what is spent on travel, problems in matching payments with exports and imports when there is trade credit, and so on. The statistical discrepancy, while large, does not suggest any specific factors to add to our list of factors that can change exchange rates.

EXCHANGE RATES: CAUSES AND CONSEQUENCES

Exchange Rate Changes in the Short Run and Long Run

We have already indicated that in the short run—from minute to minute, day to day, or even month to month—changes in exchange rates are due primarily to changes in residents' holdings of foreign short-term securities and foreigners' holdings of domestic short-term securities. These changes in short-term security holdings are, in turn, largely due to changes in interest rates.

Changes in exchange rates in the long run—over years or decades—are determined primarily by inflation and not by interest rates. Countries with relatively rapid inflation experience depreciations of their currencies versus currencies of slower-inflating countries. It might be felt that by maintaining high interest rates a country could keep funds flowing in from abroad and thereby maintain a high exchange rate, even if the country were suffering from rapid inflation. However, high interest rates can only postpone eventual depreciation, because if a country's currency does not depreciate over the long run by as much as its inflation exceeds inflation elsewhere, that country will suffer from recurring current account deficits. This is the direct result of its products being uncompetitive in the international marketplace. If the country finances its current account deficits via increases in foreign debt, its interest payments to foreigners grow, and as we have seen, interest payments represent a supply of the country's currency. Therefore, the deficit in the current account, which is where interest payments appear, becomes larger. This necessitates further borrowing from abroad to maintain the exchange rate. This causes even larger deficits in subsequent years due to additional interest payments, eventually causing the currency to depreciate.

Effect of Depreciations and Appreciations

An increase in the value of a country's currency caused by higher interest rates makes the country's exports more expensive and thereby reduces employment both in export-oriented industries and in industries selling products domestically that compete with imports. Therefore, we might wonder why a country would ever force interest rates up to support or increase the foreign exchange value of its currency.

The benefit of a high value of a currency is that it makes imports cheaper. In this way, it can contribute toward lower inflation and a higher standard of living; cheaper imports mean that a country's income will purchase more. However, the improvement in the standard of living is brought about by importing more, thereby allowing the number of goods and services consumed, invested, or bought by the government to exceed the amount produced. This can be seen from the way GDP is defined in Equation 12.5 on page 363, namely,

$$Y \equiv C + I + G + (Ex - Im)$$

By rearrangement, this tells us that

$$(Ex - Im) \equiv Y - (C + I + G)$$

If we think of all items in real terms, we see that a goods and services deficit, that is, $(Ex - Im)$ being negative, means the country is producing less than its consumers, investors, and government are spending; that is, Y is less than $(C + I + G)$.

A country cannot indefinitely produce less than its consumers, investors, and government are spending. It can do so only as long as other countries provide credit. This is no different than in the case of an individual who can consume more than he or she earns only as long as he or she can borrow. Eventually credits must be repaid, whether they are incurred by an individual or by a country. Given that the real GDP is limited by a nation's resources, in the long run a country must accept the standard of living it can support by its own production.

Changes in exchange rates are a mechanism by which a country is forced to live within its means. What happens is that a country which finances current account deficits by borrowing faces a growing debt service.[8] This increasing supply of its currency eventually causes depreciation of its currency. The depreciation, in turn, reduces the country's standard of living. There are two ways to explain why a depreciation reduces a country's standard of living.

First, a depreciated currency does not buy as much in the international marketplace. For example, it takes more of the depreciated currency to buy wheat, oil, foreign cars, foreign travel, and other internationally traded items.[9] Second, when a country's currency depreciates, residents' average incomes, when translated into foreign currency for the purpose of comparing average incomes in different countries, translate into smaller amounts. That is, countries with depreciating currencies move down the "league table" of living standards. Of course, this drop in relative living standards is a manifestation of the fact that incomes in the country no longer buy as much internationally, making the second view of the effect of a depreciating currency just an alternative perspective to the first view. A country that is living beyond its means by borrowing from abroad eventually faces depreciation, and this results in a decline in the standard of living of its people.

> In the long run a country must live within its *own* ability to produce.

> A depreciation means a *reduction* in a country's standard of living, and an appreciation means an *increase* in a country's standard of living.

---

[8] If a current account deficit involves the import of capital goods that add to future output, the debt service could be provided via increased future exports. In what follows we assume that the current account deficit is not because of capital goods imports.

[9] Even the country's own products which are traded internationally will cost its residents more of their own currency after a depreciation. This is so because traded products have prices set in the international marketplace so that, for example, a barrel of oil costs more of the depreciated currency even if the oil is produced domestically.

Just as a depreciation means a decline in the living standards, an appreciation means an improvement. Again, this can be seen either in the additional buying power of the currency in the international marketplace or in the movement up the table of standards of living that a currency appreciation brings about.

A depreciation caused by having a current account deficit and living beyond a country's means not only forces a reduction in the country's standard of living but also tends to reduce the deficit. The depreciation does this via making exports cheaper and imports more expensive, causing exports to increase and imports to decline.[10]

EXCHANGE RATES AND THE INTERNATIONAL FINANCIAL SYSTEM

Until the beginning of the twentieth century, the international financial system was based on gold, a system known as the **gold standard.** The essential feature of the gold standard was that governments fixed the prices of their paper currencies to gold and thereby fixed the exchange rates between their paper currencies. In order to see why fixing currencies to gold fixes exchange rates between currencies, let us assume that the Federal Reserve sets the price of gold at $40 per ounce and the Bank of England sets the price of gold at £20 per ounce. This fixes the exchange rate between dollars and pounds at $2/£ because if the exchange rate were anything else there would be **arbitrage**, that is, buying and selling currencies and gold for profit. For example, suppose that the exchange rate was $2.1/£ and that the cost of shipping gold between the United States and Great Britain was so low it could be ignored. Then somebody could take $40, buy an ounce of gold from the U.S. Federal Reserve, send the gold to Britain, and sell it to the Bank of England for £20. With the exchange rate of $2.1/£, that person could sell the £20 for $42 (or $2.1/£ × £20). Since the person started with $40, he or she would make a $2 profit. With many people trying to make this **arbitrage profit,** there would be so many people going through this process, which at the end involves selling British pounds for U.S. dollars, that this would drive down the price of the pound. This pressure on the value of the pound would continue until the exchange rate was only $2/£.

Similarly, if the exchange rate were the other side of $2/£, for example, $1.9/£, arbitragers could take £20, buy an ounce of gold in Great Britain, send it to the United States, sell the gold for $40, and then sell the dollars for pounds. With $1.9/£, the number of pounds per dollar is £0.526/$ (or 1 ÷ $1.9/£), so the arbitragers would receive £21 (or £0.526/$ × $40). Since they began with £20, they would make an arbitrage profit. With many people seeking this profit, there would be many people going through the arbitrage process, which at the end involves buying pounds with U.S. dollars. This would push up the price of the pound, that is, the number of dollars to buy a pound, until it was $2/£. We see that the

---

[10] As we saw in discussing the J-curve, in the short run a depreciation could worsen the balance of trade and hence the balance on current account if import demand is inelastic. However, eventually a depreciation should reduce a current account deficit.

The exchange rate between currencies can be set by governments fixing the price of gold. This is known as a gold standard.

exchange rate between dollars and pounds if gold is \$40 per ounce in the United States and £20 per ounce in Great Britain would be \$2/£.[11]

The gold standard was in effect until the beginning of World War I and was again tried briefly in the interwar period. With World War II following closely on the heels of the Great Depression, exchange rates became highly regulated, with many nations suspending the conversion of their currencies into foreign exchange. As World War II drew to an end, the Western allies realized the need to have a new exchange rate system that would force countries to again make their currencies convertible and that also would prevent countries from trying to create employment by keeping their exchange rates artificially low, thereby making their exports cheap and keeping imports expensive.

The Bretton Woods Agreement fixed exchange rates within a permitted range.

The system which arranged for currency convertibility and limited the ability of nations to manipulate exchange rates for their own purposes was worked out in 1944 at a meeting of experts and officials from the United States and the allied powers. They met in the attractive surroundings of Bretton Woods, New Hampshire, and so the agreement they reached became known as the **Bretton Woods Agreement.** The same meeting at Bretton Woods resulted in the establishment of the **International Monetary Fund (IMF)** to help countries with temporary balance of payments problems and to monitor compliance with the Bretton Woods Agreement.

Under the Bretton Woods Agreement, each central bank maintained a fixed exchange rate, intervening in the foreign exchange markets to keep its exchange rate moving in a very narrow range. Each central bank would buy its own currency in the foreign exchange market when it fell to the lower end of its permitted range, thereby preventing it from falling further. Similarly, it would sell its currency when it approached the top end of its permitted range, thereby preventing it from increasing further. By standing ready to sell unlimited amounts of its currency at the top end of the permitted range, a central bank could ensure that the value of its currency never went above its **ceiling value.** Similarly, by standing ready to buy unlimited amounts of its currency at the lower end of its permitted range, a central bank could keep its currency above its **floor value.**[12]

The exchange rate each central bank set out to maintain was that of its own country's currency vis-à-vis the U.S. dollar. Therefore, each central bank bought its own currency with U.S. dollars when the value of its currency was falling against the dollar and sold its own currency for U.S. dollars when the value of its currency was increasing against the dollar.[13] The Bretton Woods system started to break down during the early 1970s and had been abandoned by 1973. Since the breakdown of the Bretton Woods system, the major international currencies have had flexible or floating exchange rates, whereby exchange rates adjust until the private

---

[11] Example 18.5 considers some wider questions concerning the gold standard.

[12] Being ready to buy its currency at its floor value necessitated the holding of foreign exchange reserves. These reserves could, and occasionally did, run out, forcing devaluation of the currency.

[13] Since the non-U.S. central banks were fixing exchange rates, the U.S. central bank, the Fed, did not have to intervene in the foreign exchange market; if the other central banks maintained the exchange rates of their currencies relative to the dollar, they also maintained the exchange rates of the dollar relative to their currencies. Instead of intervening in the foreign exchange markets, the United States agreed to buy gold from and sell gold to foreign central banks at a fixed dollar price.

Example 18.5

SPACED OUT

The gold standard is one way of fixing exchange rates. However, as these two short excerpts from one of my earlier books suggest, there are probably better things to fix currencies to than gold.

What is a star standard?

A number of years back, a magazine, which I've never heard anyone admit to reading and which you'll find on the racks at the checkout line in your supermarket, announced that Fort Knox—and the New York Fed—didn't have as much gold as they said they did. Perhaps it had been stolen. Well, that isn't the sort of story that you'd like to spread abroad, even if the magazine made a living on stories far more sensational than this. Some members of the U.S. Congress, who obviously peek at these magazines while standing in line at supermarkets, demanded a complete investigation. They were taken deep into the vaults for proof that indeed there were many shiny bars neatly stored away underground.

But does it really matter if the gold is there? Isn't what matters what people believe? Under the gold standard, central banks settled imbalances between themselves by moving gold, which each held at the New York Fed, between their different storage areas. They never actually checked their vaults to count their gold reserves. They took the word of the Fed that the gold was there.

But what would have happened if the gold had never existed? The financial system will work just fine as long as we believe that the gold exists. Financial systems, like banks, are based upon trust. If trust is present, you need no precious metal or anything else. But this gives us an interesting possibility.

Suppose we were to allocate ownership of a large number of the stars that we could never reach, at least not with existing technology. Suppose each country were told that it owned so many celestial bodies and that an account was being kept. These assets, if you like, were created from thin air, rather like SDRs are.* Countries could settle their debts by moving around ownership of the stars, rather like

*SDRs, or Special Drawing Rights, are balances held by countries at the International Monetary Fund (IMF). They are created simply by crediting countries' accounts at the IMF.

moving around gold. This could happen at the ISF—the International Star Fund. We could allocate extra stars every year to facilitate extra needs. Each currency would be worth so many stars, which would determine their exchange rates: £1 million sterling per star and $2 million per star means $2 per £1. What a lovely financial system. As long as countries accept stars as payment it would work. And, remember, there is a fixed supply, just like gold.

How about returning to gold as an international money standard?

Some people think we should return to a gold standard. But just think what that means. Poor people would work under very difficult conditions in South African and Russian mines to bring it out of the ground. It is then flown, under tight security, to Fort Knox and the New York Fed and places such as these, where it is again placed back in the ground. Surely we can think of better ways of spending our time.

Source: Maurice Levi, **Economics Deciphered: A Layman's Survival Guide** (New York: Basic Books, 1981), pp. 247–248 and 273.

demands for currencies equal the private supplies.[14]   With truly flexible exchange rates there are no changes in official foreign exchange reserves, and market forces are the only influence on exchange rates.[15] These are the forces we explained in our account of the balance of payments earlier in this chapter.

---

[14] As Example 18.6 vividly demonstrates, the forces of supply and demand evolve naturally, even where they have not existed before.

[15] Since 1985, central banks have again bought and sold currencies when they felt foreign exchange markets were "disorderly." This mixture of flexible exchange rates with periodic intervention is called a **managed float.**

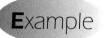 **E**xample   **18.6**

THE RAPID RATE OF [EX]CHANGE

The following article by Louis Uchitelle in **The New York Times** *explains how easily a new currency can catch on and how quickly exchange rates can be established. Indeed, even government officials can be surprised.*

Ahead of schedule and unannounced, the Ukrainian Government has in effect given birth to a new national currency that makes the growing separation of the Ukrainian and Russian economies seem impossible to reverse.

The new bills, which are the size of Monopoly money and called coupons, were originally issued as ration tickets that entitled Ukrainians, and not outsiders, to buy the republic's limited supplies of food and other essentials. Actual payment was in Russian rubles. But with Russia's reported failure ... to supply Ukraine with enough ruble notes, officials here hastily transformed the coupons into cash.

A month into this process, the Ukrainian Government just now is acknowledging that the coupons are in effect a national currency, created at least five months before the Government had intended to issue one.

"I suppose you have to call the coupons money, although they are not officially a currency," said Leonid G. Steshenko, the First Deputy Prime Minister for Foreign Economic Relations. The new currency, when it comes, will be the hryvnia (pronounced HRIV-nee-uh).

In Moscow, President Boris N. Yeltsin's Government raised no objections to the debut of the coupon as a national currency but Nikolai Domonov, a deputy at Russia's Central Bank, criticized Ukraine's ad hoc procedure.

"If the Ukrainians are going to operate as a separate unit," he said, "then their central bank should draw in the rubles, in exchange for coupons, and send the rubles back to our central bank."

The central bank could then withdraw them from circulation. Mr. Domonov said. Instead, as coupons became more widely used, the rubles they replace are already beginning to flow into Russia.

That happens as Russians sell merchandise in Ukraine for rubles and bring the cash home rather than converting rubles into coupons. One result is higher inflation in Russia as more rubles become available to buy the same quantity of goods, Mr. Domonov said.

Whatever the official status, this nation of 52 million people is now operating with two currencies: the Russian ruble, which is slowly disappearing, and the coupons. Having been printed as ration tickets, the coupon bears neither the national seal nor serial numbers. But half of each Ukrainian's wage is now being paid in coupons and a growing list of products are now priced in coupons.

"The conception of our Government is to use the coupon only as cash, and not for commercial payments through bank transfers, but that won't be possible," said Oleksander V. Savchenko, deputy governor of the Ukrainian National Bank. "A restaurant that collects in coupons from customers has to be able to deposit this money and pay bills. In one month, the coupon will be a complete currency." . . .

Now although no formal exchange system exists, the coupon is traded for dollars. In the Kiev black market this month, 16 coupons purchased a dollar, and each coupon was valued at between 2 and 7 rubles. Although the coupon is supposed to be used primarily to buy essentials in state stores, merchants appear willing to accept coupons for nearly any product and for various services.

The coupon might even overshadow the ruble soon. Mr. Savchenko, the National Bank official, said. Only 35 billion rubles are in circulation in the republic, he said, and by summer that many coupons may also be circulating.

CROSSING **BRIDGES**

PRECIOUS PARALLEL[16]

When L. Frank Baum penned his much-loved enchanted tale, **The Wonderful Wizard of Oz**, he was not only creating a treasure for generations of delighted children but also was making a sophisticated and penetrating commentary on one of the central economic issues of the day. That issue was whether the United States should remain on the gold standard or should instead add to the size of the money supply by the free, unrestricted mintage of silver coins at a fixed price vis-à-vis gold.

The Wonderful Wizard of Oz was published in 1900, so if we are to understand the contemporary influences that shaped Baum's characters and plot, we must describe the principal features shaping the economic landscape in the years leading up to its publication. Near the top of the list of high-profile issues stood the great monetary debate, sparked by secular deflation that had

gripped the United States for several decades. Specifically, from 1869 to the late 1890s, the price level in the United States had fallen more than 30%, and food prices had fallen even further, dropping over 50% during the same period.[17] Not surprisingly, with prices of what they had to sell declining so much faster than what they purchased, American farmers were greatly displeased. In the run-up to the presidential election of 1896, which was the low point of prices, the farmers' displeasure was channeled directly to President Cleveland in Washington,

---

[16] This section has been greatly influenced by Hugh Rockoff's insightful article, "The 'Wizard of Oz' as a Monetary Allegory," **Journal of Political Economy,** August 1990, pp. 739–760.

[17] See Rockoff, **ibid.**, p. 742.

the "Wicked Witch of the East" who had been instrumental in the repeal of the Sherman Silver Purchase Act that had kept the United States on a gold standard rather than the bimetallic standard—one based on gold and silver—favored by western farmers.[18]

The fight over the choice between a gold standard and a bimetallic standard reached its climax in the presidential nominations and campaign of 1896. Deflation, especially in food prices, was at its most rapid rate as the presidential nomination process gathered steam. The background to this deflation was monetary growth, so limited by the U.S. stock of gold that it was not sufficient to keep up with the growth in U.S. national output and the demand to hold U.S. dollars. (For example, the money supply grew at approximately 2.6% per annum from 1869 to 1879, while real output grew at approximately 5%. In addition, the demand for money holdings grew rapidly, reducing the ratio of income to money, that is, reducing the velocity of circulation of money.[19])

Stirred on by the pro-silver forces at the 1896 Democratic National Convention in Chicago, presidential candidate William Jennings Bryan gave his celebrated, rousing "Cross of Gold" speech, in which he brought the delegates to their feet by commanding the Republicans: "Thou shalt not crucify mankind upon a cross of gold." The enthusiastic outpouring from his inspirational oratory carried the nomination, and so Bryan

The Munchkins are unable to direct Dorothy to Kansas, so she is sent . . . to see the Wizard of Oz, who lives in the Emerald City . . . at the end of the Yellow Brick Road. . . .

began his campaign against Republican William McKinley. Bryan entered the election campaign carrying the silver banner, advocating adding to the U.S. supply of money to end the deflation that Bryan and his supporters had attributed firmly to the gold standard.

When writing **The Wonderful Wizard of Oz,** Baum would have witnessed all this and also the fiercely fought presidential battle that Bryan and the silver forces lost. Baum would also have seen the buildup to the repeat battle of 1900 in which the incumbent, William McKinley, was again to take on Bryan, whose commitment to bimetallism had begun to be doubted by the silver backers.

As the fanciful story goes, honest, compassionate, and principled Dorothy who lived with her hardworking and poor Aunt Em on an impoverished farm in Kansas, in the American West where the silver movement began, is swept up by a cyclone, a metaphor for the gathering mood of discontent. Alone with her dog Toto,[20] Dorothy lands square on top of the Wicked Witch of the East in the land of Oz—the standard abbreviation for ounce, as in, for example, $350/oz. for gold—a barely disguised reference to the land of the gold standard and its eastern base of support. To the delight of the residents of Oz, the Munchkins who had been subjected to the Wicked Witch of the East, Dorothy's landing disposes of the Witch, leaving only her silver slippers.[21]

---

[18] If not personalized in Cleveland, Baum's reference to the "Wicked Witch of the East" may have referred to eastern business and financial interests which largely supported keeping the United States on a gold-only standard.

[19] Recall from Chapter 14 that the income velocity of circulation of money is the national income divided by the money supply. **Ceteris paribus**, as with monetary growth less than output growth, a declining velocity means deflation.

[20] The bimetallic standard had received backing from the Prohibition Party. Therefore, Toto is a reference to the friendly "teetotalers," as the Prohibitionists were popularly called.

[21] In the movie the witch's slippers are ruby. This is Hollywood's adaptation of the silver slippers, a license also taken with numerous other shining metallic objects that Baum refers to at several other points in the book.

The Munchkins are unable to direct Dorothy to Kansas, so she is sent, along with the silver slippers, to see the Wizard of Oz, who lives in the Emerald City (Washington, D.C.) at the end of the Yellow Brick Road, where Dorothy, like others, will find that the answer is **not** to be found. The Yellow Brick Road is, of course, the path taken by the gold advocates, who, according to those promoting bimetallism, had caused the problems Dorothy and her hard-working relatives had suffered in Kansas.

On her way, Dorothy first encounters the scarecrow, a manifestation of the western farmer. She is told sadly that the scarecrow has no brains because his head is stuffed with straw, but she soon discovers the clear, latent ability the scarecrow possesses. Baum is telling the reader that even on complex issues like those involving the choice between gold and bimetallism, the farmer is most capable of reason. Dorothy then encounters the Tin Woodsman, the personification of America's industrial worker. The Tin Woodsman has lost his heart and been subdued by the Wicked Witch of the East, a characterization of the detachment and alienation of American industrial workers.

The fourth leg in the odd coalition is the Cowardly Lion. This is presidential hopeful Bryan himself. The bimetallic standard advocates had become troubled that Bryan was losing his dedication to their movement as he embraced other issues and as gold discoveries, good U.S. crops, and the inflow of gold from European purchases of U.S. wheat led to a sudden end to the deflationary period. Indeed, the Cowardly Lion falls asleep in a field of poppies, and it is the mice, representative of ordinary, little people, who pull him back to the cause.

When finally they arrive at the Emerald City, the Wizard has a pot of courage waiting for the Cowardly Lion (Bryan), capped by a golden plate to prevent it from overflowing, another reference to the containment of prosperity that the gold standard represented to its opponents. Before entering the city, all must wear green-tinted glasses or be locked up forever with a gold buckle; those financiers who direct policy in the city force everybody to see the world through money-colored glasses. Dorothy and her friends then pass through seven passages and up three flights of stairs, a reference to the so-called **Crime of 73**, the 1873 legislation that had ended the minting of silver dollars.

The Wicked Witch of the West, William McKinley, uses one of the wishes granted by the Gold Cap—again pointing to the powerful, oppressive gold standard—to enslave the Yellow Winkies, a thinly veiled reference to McKinley's decision not to grant independence to the Philippines. The Witch deviously seeks to seize Dorothy's silver slippers, which the Witch knows to be powerful, and is delighted to seize one, knowing that divided, the pro-silver forces would lose power. Dorothy pours water over the witch, and the witch simply disappears, demonstrating that all it would take for the farmers' plight to end was good rains on the western prairie that had suffered years of damaging drought.

With the Wicked Witch dissolved, Dorothy frees her friends. The Tin Woodsman is given a new axe with a gold handle and a blade that glistened like silver—a clear reference to bimetallism—but Dorothy is still unable to return to Kansas, getting only a ride in a hot air balloon; all the promises she receives are like hot air. So Dorothy tries to find Glinda, Good Witch of the South; the South was generally in favor of adding silver to the monetary system. With the help of the South in the person of Glinda, the problem is solved as Dorothy clicks her silver slippers three times and returns to Kansas.

When she wakes, her slippers are gone, just as by 1900 the silver issue had disappeared. The U.S. Congress passed the Gold Standard Act in that year, ending years of indecision and setting the United States firmly on the gold standard, an exchange rate system that was to last until World War I.

SUMMARY

1. The exchange rate is the amount of one currency it takes to buy one unit of another currency. Exchange rates are typically quoted in terms of the U.S. dollar.

2. The exchange rate between any two currencies can be determined from the exchange rates of each currency against the U.S. dollar.

3. An increase in the amount of foreign currency per dollar means an appreciation of the dollar and a depreciation of the foreign currency.

4. The balance of payments account is a tabulation of the amounts of a country's currency supplied and demanded for various purposes during a given time period. Items resulting in the supply of a country's currency are identified by minus signs, and items resulting in the demand for the country's currency are identified by plus signs.

5. A major reason for currency being supplied is imports, and a major reason for currency being demanded is exports.

6. A depreciation of a country's currency reduces the price of its exports to foreigners. This increases the quantity of the country's currency that is demanded and means a downward-sloping demand curve for the currency.

7. A depreciation of a country's currency increases the price of imports and thereby reduces the *quantity* of imports. The effect of the depreciation on the *value* of imports and hence on the supply of the currency depends on the quantity decrease versus the price increase. If the quantity of imports

decreases *more* than the price of imports increases, the value of imports declines after a depreciation of the country's currency. However, if the quantity of imports decreases *less* than the price increases, the value of imports increases after a depreciation.

8. The balance of merchandise trade is the value of exports minus the value of imports. The balance is in surplus if the value of exports exceeds the value of imports and is in deficit if imports exceed exports.

9. A depreciation of a currency can cause a temporary worsening of the balance of merchandise trade. This happens if the increase in prices of imports following depreciation causes more to be spent on imports—which requires inelastic import demand—and if the increase in the value of imports exceeds the increase in the value of exports.

10. When a depreciation causes a worsening of the balance of trade in the short run but an improvement in the long run, the path of the balance of trade follows a J-curve.

11.* *Ceteris paribus,* inflation causes a depreciation of the inflating country's currency by the country's rate of inflation.

12. Adding exports and imports of services to the balance of merchandise trade gives the balance on goods and services.

13. Unilateral transfers involve foreign aid and private gifts. When these are added to the balance on goods and services, the result is the balance of payments on current account.

14. Increases in residents' assets held abroad result in a supply of the country's currency, while increases in foreigners' holdings of domestic assets result in a demand for the country's currency.

15. Direct investment occurs when a foreign investor owns more than 10% of voting shares. Direct investment depends on the expected rate of return in a country versus expected rates of return in other countries and on business and political risks.

16. Investment in foreign securities depends on interest rates and expected returns in foreign countries versus interest rates and expected returns at home, and on expected changes in exchange rates.

17. The supply of or demand for a country's currency can be affected by the country's central bank if it attempts to fix the exchange rate. Central bank buying or selling of a country's currency results in changes in official reserves.

18. Over longer periods of time, inflation rates determine the paths of exchange rates. However, short run changes in exchange rates depend on interest rates more than other factors.

19. A country that produces less than its consumers, investors, and government spend has a goods and services deficit which must be financed by borrowing abroad. This eventually causes a depreciation which reduces the country's standard of living.

20. The gold standard involved central banks fixing the price of gold vis-à-vis their paper currencies. The Bretton Woods Agreement of 1944–1973 required each non-U.S. central bank to buy and sell its currency for U.S. dollars whenever the exchange rate reached either end of a narrow band.

QUESTIONS AND PROBLEMS

1. What would happen if, when DM/$ =1.6 and $/£ =1.5, banks are quoting DM/£ =2.5, and what would happen if banks are quoting DM/£ =2.3?

2. Assuming that the demand for imports in inelastic in the short run but not in the long run, what happens to the balance of trade over time after a currency *appreciation?*

3. Why is a sustained deficit in the balance of merchandise trade undesirable?

4. Why is a sustained surplus in the balance of merchandise trade undesirable?

5. How do you think changes in real GDP at home versus real GDP abroad are likely to affect currency supply and demand curves and hence exchange rates?

6. In what various ways can interest rates affect exchange rates?

7. Via what mechanism might an *expected* appreciation of a currency cause the currency to *actually* appreciate?

8. Why can we calculate the exact size of the statistical discrepancy in the balance of payments account if we know the change in official foreign exchange reserves?

9. In what sense does a country with a repeated balance of trade surplus, such as Japan, live below its means, and how might exchange rates correct the situation?

10. If a currency supply curve slopes downward, could the exchange rate at which the quantity of currency supplied and demanded are equal be unstable? (An unstable equilibrium is one where small deviations from equilibrium price set up forces which push the price even further away from equilibrium.)

Appendix:
Indifference Curves and Demand

People never buy what they need—they always buy what they want.

Charles F. Kettering

Key Concepts

Indifference curve; budget line

INDIFFERENCE CURVES

Assume that a consumer is allocating her or his entire income to housing and food. Let us measure the quantity of housing by square feet rented per month and the quantity of food by pounds consumed per month. The amounts of housing rented and food consumed per month are measured along the axes of Figure A.1. The vertical axis shows the amount of food, and the horizontal axis shows the amount of housing. Any combination of food and housing appears as a point in the figure.

The objective is to find out what makes consumers buy particular combinations of products and how these combinations are affected by changes in prices and incomes. This can be done by constructing **indifference curves.** Indifference curves show the amount of one product that must be offered to keep a consumer's total utility from changing as the amount of another product is reduced. Let us explain this by considering Table A.1 and Figure A.1.

Suppose that a consumer is currently renting 1000 square feet of housing and consuming 80 pounds of food per month. This is the combination at point *A* in Figure A.1 and in the middle row of Table A.1. Suppose that the consumer is

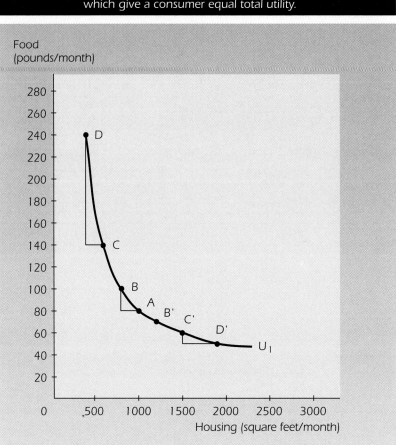

FIGURE A.1   Indifference curves show the combinations of products which give a consumer equal total utility.

As the amount of housing is reduced, it is necessary to compensate the consumer with extra food to keep total utility unchanged. The smaller the amount of housing from which reductions are made, the greater the required compensation with food. For example, in going from **D'** to **C'**, starting with 1900 square feet of housing, the consumer needs only 10 pounds of extra food per month to compensate for 400 square feet of housing, whereas going from **A** to **B** and starting with less housing, the required compensation is 20 pounds of extra food for 200 square feet of housing.

asked how much more food she or he would want in order to be willing to give up 200 square feet of housing. Suppose that she or he says that she or he would just, and only just, be willing to give up 200 square feet of housing if compensated with 20 extra pounds of food. This means that the consumer is indifferent between combinations A and B in Figure A.1 and Table A.1, where B involves 800 square feet of housing—200 square feet less than at A—and 100 pounds of food—20 pounds more than at A. Because the consumer is indifferent between A and B, they must offer the consumer equal total utility.

....
TABLE A.1

Combinations between which a consumer is indifferent are obtained by finding how much of one product the consumer requires to forgo a given amount of another product.

COMBINATION	HOUSING (square feet per month)	FOOD (pounds per month)
D	400	240
C	600	140
B	800	100
A	1,000	80
B'	1,200	70
C'	1,500	60
D'	1,900	50

Starting with combination **A,** the amount of housing is changed in steps, and the amount of food the consumer requires at each step to leave her or his total utility unchanged is recorded. This allows an indifference curve to be drawn, where this curve shows the combinations of housing and food which provide equal total utility.

Suppose that having agreed to move to combination B, the consumer is again asked how much food she or he wants in order to be willing to forgo a further 200 square feet of housing. Because the marginal utility of housing is higher the less housing a consumer has, and because the marginal utility of food decreases the greater the amount of food consumed, the consumer requires more compensation than before. Suppose that she or he wants 40 more pounds of food to give up an extra 200 square feet of housing. This gives point C in Figure A.1 and Table A.1. The table and figure also show that for the next 200 square feet, the required compensation increases to an additional 100 pounds of food to leave satisfaction unchanged; compare point C with point D. Points $A, B, C,$ and D are combinations offering equal total utility; the consumer is indifferent between them.

Let us return to A and ask how much extra housing is required to leave the consumer's total utility unchanged as her or his food consumption is successfully reduced. Figure A.1 and Table A.1 show that to go from 80 to 70 pounds of food the consumer requires 200 square feet of housing, to go from 70 to only 60 pounds of food requires 300 square feet of housing, and so on. More generally, as the consumer begins with less and less food, it takes a larger compensation of housing for food. This is the same as found when moving in the other direction from A.

The points plotted on Figure A.1 can be joined to show an indifference curve labeled U_1. The U_1 signifies that the combinations of the two items shown along the curve offer the consumer equal total utility.

An indifference curve traces out the combinations of goods and services offering a consumer equal total utility. A consumer is indifferent between any two points along an indifference curve.

CONSTRUCTING A HIGHER INDIFFERENCE CURVE

Suppose that instead of beginning on indifference curve U_1 the consumer had begun at a point with more housing and more food, such as R in Figure A.2 and Table A.2. Since R contains more of both items than A, R offers more total utility and will be preferred to A.

Table A.2 and Figure A.2 show that other combinations such as S, T, S', and T' offer the consumer equal total utility to R and are hence indifferent to point R. Because R offers higher total utility than A, all points on the indifference curve through point R, labeled U_2, must be preferred on all points on the indifference curve through A, labeled U_1. In general, entire "families" of indifference curves can be constructed, with those further away from the origin of the figure offering higher total utility than those closer to the origin. Figure A.2 shows such a family of indifference curves with total utility on U_4 being higher than on U_3, total utility on U_3 higher than on U_2, and so on. Indeed, there are an infinite number of possible indifference curves.

THE BUDGET LINE AND INCOME

The combinations of items that are attainable, and hence the highest indifference curve that is reachable, depend on the budget the consumer has available and on the prices of goods and services. Assume that the available budget is the same as a consumer's income for the month and that this is $1000. Also assume that the price of food is $4 per pound, and the (rental) price of housing is 40 cents per square foot per month. The left-hand side of Table A.3 shows how much food and housing the consumer can afford with the $1000 per month income.

Table A.3 shows that if the entire $1000 per month is allocated toward buying food, it provides 250 pounds per month. Therefore, an attainable combination of the two items is 250 pounds of food and zero square feet of housing. At the other extreme, an attainable combination is 2500 square feet of housing and no food. Intermediate combinations also are attainable, such as 200 pounds of food and 500 square feet of housing. The attainable combinations in Table A.3 are plotted in Figure A.3. All points are on a straight, downward-sloping line called the **budget line.** Points interior to the budget line such as A and B are also attainable, because they can be bought with the income of $1000. Indeed, any combination within the shaded area of Figure A.3 that is bounded by the $1000 budget line is an attainable combination.

If the consumer's income changes, the budget line shifts. The combinations on the right-hand side of Table A.3 corresponding to a budget of $1200 are plotted in Figure A.3. The combinations form another budget line parallel to the previous line, but further from the origin. Any point on this new line or interior to it represents an attainable combination with a budget and income of $1200 per month.

*The budget line shows the **maximum** attainable combination of products a consumer can buy.*

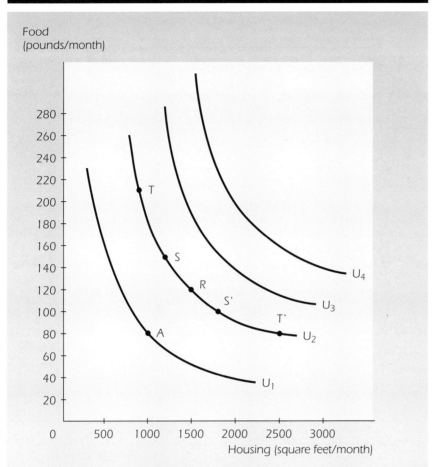

FIGURE A.2   Indifference curves can be drawn for different levels of total utility.

Since more is preferred to less, point **R** is preferred to point **A**. This means that all points on indifference curve U_2, which plots combinations of equal utility to **R**, are preferred to all points on indifference curve U_1. Similarly, all points on indifference curve U_3 are preferred to all points on U_2. That is, the further away the indifference curve is from the margin, the higher is the total utility it offers.

····················
TABLE A.2

An indifference curve with more of both items at some point than that on another curve offers higher total utility.

COMBINATION	HOUSING (square feet per month)	FOOD (pounds per month)
T	900	210
S	1,200	150
R	1,500	120
S'	1,800	100
T'	2,500	80

All combinations shown in this table are preferred to all combinations in Table A.1. This follows because combination **R** in this table is preferred to combination **A** in Table A.1, and therefore, all combinations offering equal total utility to combination **R** must be preferred to all combinations offering equal total utility to combination **A**.

····················
TABLE A.3

For a given set of prices, attainable combinations expand with the consumer's budget or income.

ATTAINABLE COMBINATIONS WITH $1,000 PER MONTH		ATTAINABLE COMBINATIONS WITH $1,200 PER MONTH	
FOOD (pounds per month)	HOUSING (square feet per month)	FOOD (pounds per month)	HOUSING (square feet per month)
250	0	300	0
200	500	240	600
150	1,000	180	1,200
100	1,500	120	1,800
50	2,000	60	2,400
0	2,500	0	3,000

All combinations of items in the table result in the consumer spending her or his entire income. The attainable combinations are shown for a price of food of $4 per pound and a price of housing of 40 cents per square foot per month. For example, $1000 buys the combination 200 pounds of food and 500 square feet of housing; $200 \times \$4 + 500 \times \$0.4 = \$1000$. Similarly $1200 buys 180 pounds of food and 1200 square feet of housing; $180 \times \$4 + 1200 \times \$0.4 = \$1200$.

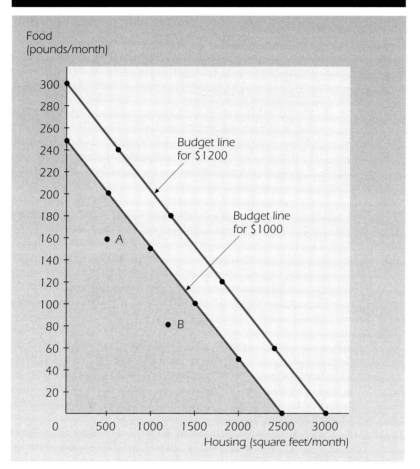

FIGURE A.3   The budget line shows the boundary to the combinations of items a consumer can afford with a given budget or income and moves outward as income is increased.

The budget line is obtained as follows: First, the amount of food the consumer could afford if only food were purchased is calculated. This gives the intercept on the vertical axis. For example, with an income of $1000 and food costing $4 per pound, the vertical intercept for the $1000 budget line is 250 pounds of food. Second, the amount of housing the consumer could afford if only housing were purchased is calculated. This gives the intercept on the horizontal axis. All points on the straight line joining these points also cost $1000 and are therefore also attainable combinations.

MAXIMIZING UTILITY

Consumers are assumed to allocate income between products to maximize the total utility they receive, given the limitations imposed by their budgets or incomes. The maximization of total utility is shown graphically in Figure A.4. The figure shows a family of indifference curves and the budget line for a consumer with an income of $1000. We use a price of food of $4 per pound and a price of housing of 40 cents per square foot. Maximum total utility is achieved by finding that combination of food and housing which is within the shaded region of Figure A.4 and that reaches the indifference curve with highest total utility. This combination is at point E on indifference curve U_4, with the consumer buying 1250 square feet of housing and 125 pounds of food. Any other allocation of the consumer's budget provides lower total utility. For example, while point A represents an attainable combination, it results in reaching only indifference curve U_3, as does the attainable combination at point B.

> Consumers choose the combination offering the *highest* possible utility.

Consumers are assumed to maximize total utility subject to the limitations of their incomes. This means choosing a combination of products to reach the highest indifference curve attainable with a given budget and product prices. This is the combination at point **E**. If the consumer selects a different combination, she or he is not achieving the maximum possible total utility. For example, the total utility with combination **A**—an attainable combination, since it is on the budget line—could be increased by moving toward **E**. The same is true of combination **B**.

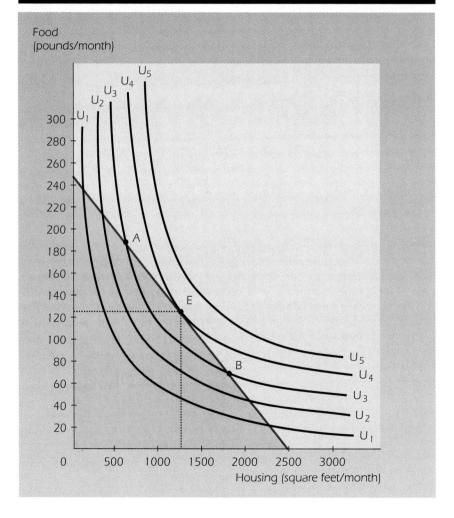

FIGURE A.4   Consumers allocate their budgets to reach the highest indifference curve they can.

EFFECT OF CHANGES IN INCOME

Changes in a consumer's income affect demand at any given price. For example, higher income generally means more housing being demanded at 40 cents per square foot, more at 50 cents per square foot, and so on.

Figure A.5 shows the effects of changes in income on the demand for food and housing. The price of food is held at $4 per pound and the price of housing at 40 cents per square foot. The figure shows the utility-maximizing allocations of income as income increases from $600, to $800, to $1000, and so on per month. These allocations are determined by locating where each budget line touches the

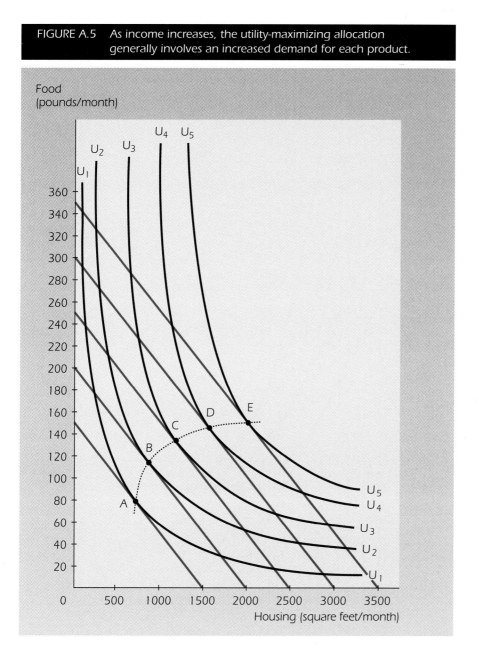

FIGURE A.5   As income increases, the utility-maximizing allocation generally involves an increased demand for each product.

The budget lines moving away from the origin are for incomes of $600, $800, $1000, $1200, and $1400 per month. The utility-maximizing allocations of income with each level of income are given, respectively, by the points **A, B, C, D,** and **E**. In this figure, as income increases, the demands for both products increase. This is the case for normal goods.

Increasing income may increase or decrease the amount purchased.

highest indifference curve. In Figure A.5, the demand for both products increases as income increases. This is the situation for normal goods.

Figure A.6 shows that demand may *decrease* after increases in consumers' incomes. The figure shows indifference curves between potatoes and "other food." The initial budget is assumed to be $200, with potatoes costing 20 cents per pound and other food $2 per pound. The total food budget is expanded to $250 and then to $300. The consumption of potatoes with a food budget of $300 is lower than with a budget of $250, and consumption with a budget of $250 is lower than with $200. That is, the demand for potatoes decreases with increases in the consumer's income. When consumption behaves as in Figure A.6, with the demand for potatoes declining with increases in income, potatoes are an inferior good.

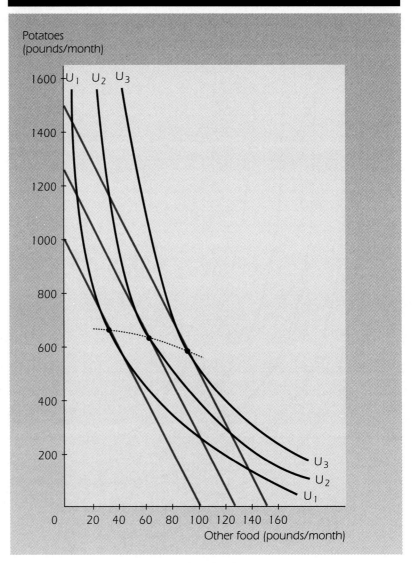

FIGURE A.6 For inferior goods, demand declines as the consumer's income increases.

The consumer's income is increased from $200 to $250 to $300, with potatoes costing 20 cents per pound and other food costing $2 per pound. The increased income causes a decrease in the demand for potatoes but an increase in the demand for other food. Since the demand for potatoes declines with income, potatoes are an inferior good. Other food is a normal good, with demand increasing with income.

EFFECT OF CHANGES IN PRICES

The effect of an increase in price on quantity demanded is shown in Figure A.7. We assume that the price of food increases from $4 to $6 per pound and the price of housing remains unchanged at 40 cents per square foot. We also assume that the consumer's income remains unchanged at $1000 and all income is spent on food and housing.

The original combination of food and housing is given by E_1. This involves 125 pounds of food and 1250 square feet of housing. After the increase in the price of food, the budget line changes from the solid line in Figure A.7 to the broken line. The new budget line has a smaller intercept on the food axis due to the higher price of food but the same intercept on the housing axis because the price of housing has not changed. (Recall that an intercept is calculated by finding

Increases in prices reduce the quantity demanded.

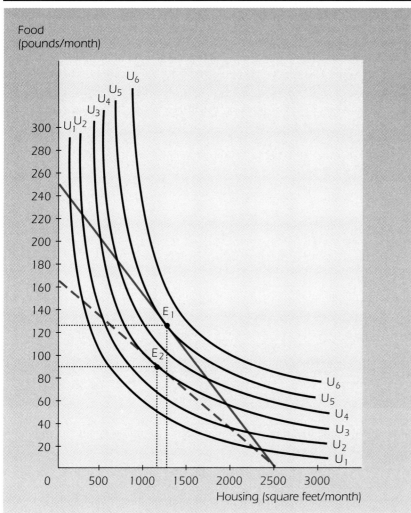

FIGURE A.7 An increase in the price of food reduces the quantity of food demanded.

A higher price of food means that if the consumer's entire income is allocated to food, it buys a smaller amount than before. Therefore, the intercept on the vertical axis, which is the amount attainable with the entire income, is reduced. An unchanged price of housing means that the maximum attainable quantity of housing is unchanged. The intercept on the horizontal axis is therefore the same as before. The new budget line, shown by the broken line, is flatter than before. The highest attainable total utility with this budget line involves consumption of food and housing at point E_2, with food consumption lower than at E_1, the utility-maximizing combination before the increase in the price of food.

how much of an item the consumer could afford if the entire income were allocated to that item.) The highest indifference curve the consumer can reach with the broken budget line is U_3. Reaching this highest utility requires that the consumer buys 90 pounds of food. This compares with the previous consumption of food of 125 pounds. Therefore, the increase in the price of food has reduced the quantity of food demanded.

The increase in the price of food assumed in constructing Figure A.7 can be considered as having two effects on the consumer via

1. Making food relatively more expensive than housing

2. Making the consumer worse off

For normal goods, these two effects imply a reduction in the consumption of food; the consumer buys less food because food is relatively more expensive and also less food because the consumer is worse off. However, for inferior goods, the effect of the consumer being worse off is to increase food demand. It is possible to determine the effect only of food being relatively more expensive by compensating the consumer for the loss in buying power due to the price increase. When this is done, consumers can be shown to reduce always the quantity demanded of goods which increase in price, and vice versa.[1]

[1] Question 2 on page 617 deals with this matter. The question provides guidance on how to compensate a consumer for loss of buying ability to find the effect solely of changes in relative prices.

SUMMARY

1. Indifference curves trace out combinations of goods and services which offer a consumer equal total utility.

2. There are "families" of indifference curves, with those further from the origin offering a consumer higher total utility.

3. The budget line is the boundary of combinations of items that are attainable, given a consumer's budget and product prices. Any point on the budget line or interior to it is attainable.

4. The budget line makes parallel moves away from the origin if the consumer's total budget expands and toward it if the budget shrinks.

5. For normal goods, an increase in the consumer's income increases demand, and vice versa. For inferior goods, an increase in the consumer's income reduces demand, and vice versa.

6. A reduction in price increases quantity demanded and vice versa.

QUESTIONS AND PROBLEMS

1. What do you think indifference curves look like for the following pairs of items:

   a. Time spent sleeping versus jogging

   b. Suit jackets versus suit pants

   c. Butter versus margarine

   d. Margarine versus fish

2. Trace out a figure such as Figure A.7 onto some graph paper. Then draw a line that is tangent to utility curve U_5—that is, a line that just touches U_5—and which has the same slope as the broken budget line. (That is, the new line is parallel to the broken line but is tangent to U_5.) The line you draw should be tangent to U_5 below and to the right of point E_1. Label this point of tangency E_3. Your constructed line restores the consumer's real income in the sense that after the price of food has increased, total utility is unchanged. Consider the decline in food consumption between point E_1 and point E_2. How much of this reduction do you think is the result of the higher price of food on the buying power of the consumer's income, and how much is due to the change in relative prices of food versus housing?

Crossing Bridges
Illustration Descriptions and Credits

Chapter 1, page 18. This German anatomical drawing illustrates the heart and kidney areas of the body. (The Bettman Archive)

Chapter 2, page 42. (*Left*) "Flowery Mede of the Garden of Eden," showing both the Temptation and the Expulsion in one picture, with flowers growing singly throughout the garden. This is a sixteenth-century Spanish woodcut. (North Wind Picture Archives) (*Right*) Thomas Robert Malthus (1766–1834), English economist, is shown in this engraving by J. Linnell. (The Bettman Archive)

Chapter 3, page 64. (Left) Leaf-cutting ants are photographed at work in the Panama rainforest. (© Mark Moffett/Minden Pictures) (Right) The French sociologist Emile Durkheim (1858–1917) is shown seated in this photo. (The Bettman Archive)

Chapter 4, page 99. (*Left*) A consumer browses in a German record store. (Photo Researchers, Inc., © Ulrike Welsch) (*Right*) Sigmund Freud (1856–1939), Viennese physician and founder of psychoanalysis, is shown in this photograph. (Mary Evans/Sigmund Freud Copyrights)

Chapter 5, page 136. (*Left*) The anabolic and catabolic reactions of a cell are shown in this illustration. (From *Biology: Discovering Life* © 1991 by D. C. Heath and Company) (*Right*) The English naturalist Charles Darwin (1809–1882) is shown seated in this engraving by Thomas Johnson. (North Wind Picture Archives)

Chapter 6, page 171. The carbon cycle is shown in this illustration. (From *Biology: Discovering Life* © 1991 by D. C. Heath and Company)

Chapter 7, page 204. (*Left*) Adam Smith (1723–1790), Scottish philosopher and economist, is shown in this 1802 profile engraving by Ridley. (The Bettman Archive) (*Right*) A running back is gang tackled during a football game. (© Sam C. Pierson, Jr./Photo Researchers, Inc.)

Chapter 8, page 234. Shah Allum, Mogul of Hindostan, is shown reviewing the British East India Company's troops. The engraving is based on a 1781 painting by Tilly Kettle. (North Wind Picture Archives)

Chapter 9, page 262. This group of musk-oxen inhabit Nunivak Island, Alaska. (© Michio Hoshino/Minden Pictures)

Chapter 10, page 299. The German sociologist and historian Max Weber (1864–1920) is shown in this photograph. (German Information Center)

Chapter 11, page 333. Cartoon. (Drawing by Modell; © 1967 The New Yorker Magazine, Inc.)

Chapter 12, page 371. The settlement of year-end accounts by a Rouen charity in 1466 is shown in this fifteenth-century French miniature. (The Mansell Collection Ltd., London)

Chapter 13, page 410. An assortment of U.S. currency is shown in this photograph. (© Day Williams 1990/Photo Researchers, Inc.)

Chapter 14, page 444. A week's payroll is drawn from a bank for a large firm in Germany during the historic inflation of August 1923. (Culver Pictures, Inc.)

Chapter 15, page 474. (*Left*) This scene from the movie *The Grapes of Wrath* (1940) shows Henry Fonda as Tom Joad. (Springer/Bettman Film Archives) (*Right*) "Oliver amazed at the Dodger's Mode of 'going to work,'" from Charles Dickens's *The Adventures of Oliver Twist*. The illustration is by George Cruikshank. (North Wind Picture Archives)

Chapter 16, page 525. The balancing act of an American circus troupe is shown in this woodcut signed by Peirce. It appeared in *Ballou's Pictorial*, Boston, December 6, 1856. (North Wind Picture Archives)

Chapter 17, page 557. Joseph, Overseer of Pharaoh's Granaries, is shown in this engraving by Lawrence Alma-Tadema (1836–1913). The engraving appeared in the *Illustrated London News*. (North Wind Picture Archives)

Chapter 18, page 599. Jack Haley as the Tinman, Judy Garland as Dorothy, and Ray Bolger as the Scarecrow are shown in this scene from the movie *The Wizard of Oz* (1939). (Springer/Bettmann Film Archive)

Index